T0122796

Spring Boot in Practice

SOMNATH MUSIB
Foreword by JOSH LONG

MANNING
SHELTER ISLAND

For online information and ordering of this and other Manning books, please visit www.manning.com. The publisher offers discounts on this book when ordered in quantity. For more information, please contact

Special Sales Department
Manning Publications Co.
20 Baldwin Road
PO Box 761
Shelter Island, NY 11964
Email: orders@manning.com

Manning Publications Co.
20 Baldwin Road
PO Box 761
Shelter Island, NY 11964

Development editor: Jennifer Stout
Technical development editor: Ubaldo Pescatore
Review editor: Mihaela Batinić
Production editor: Andy Marinkovich
Copy editor: Christian Berk
Proofreader: Jason Everett
Technical proofreader: Giampiero Granatella
Typesetter: Dennis Dalinnik
Cover designer: Marija Tudor

ISBN: 9781617298813
Printed in the United States of America

To my parents—for sacrificing everything to raise us

and

To my son, Abhirup—for adding new meaning and purpose to my life

brief contents

contents

foreword

We might be on to something

I remember sitting with cloud luminaries and colleagues, James Watters and Andrew Clay Shafer, in a café in Santa Monica, California in 2015. We were at a crossroads. The Spring team had launched Spring Boot in 2013, and it was generally available in 2014. And in 2015, it was taking off. We knew people were excited about the possibilities, and we knew people were embracing it, but we also knew we hadn't quite gotten *there*. It was too big to know when or where *there* was. I still don't know if we know. It is early 2022 as I write this, and the project is growing day by day. I still don't know if we know where *there* is.

"We might be on to something," we agreed. Indeed.

I still don't know if we're *there*, of course. But I *do* know that to get *there*, we need people to be on the same page and familiar with the landscape. You can't find your way around without proper orientation. This book, *Spring Boot in Practice*, gives me hope. It avoids the vertigo typical of most attempts to scale the rock face that is server-side application and service development by offering a steady hand.

The book almost immediately gets right into the business of building an application straight out of the gate. First, there's a quick primer on the fundamentals, and then *boom*, you're building something! I think that's the best way, too. With something this big, you just have to start exploring. It won't matter how much, or in what detail, I try to describe the place or even depict it cartographically; it's just not the same. You need to see it; you need to explore the space!

After the primer, it feels like we're working our way up the conceptual ladder, starting with the foundational stuff you will deal with when building any Spring Boot-based application. Then, we get into data access, the Spring Boot observability support through the Spring Boot Actuator support, securing your applications with Spring Security, and building HTTP services with Spring MVC and Spring Webflux. If you get this far, you won't know every nook and cranny, but you'll know where to go. You'll be correctly oriented.

Where you go next is anybody's guess, but author Somnath Musib does a good job here, as well, charting out some newer neighborhoods in the wide and wonderful world of Springdom, including Kotlin, GraphQL, and GraalVM. Kotlin is an ever-changing and vibrant language that maps nicely to the Spring ecosystem. Spring GraphQL is a brand-new project that brings the GraphQL Java project to the Spring developer. And Spring Native is a fantastic way to turn Spring Boot 2.x and Spring Framework 5.x code into GraalVM native images. Both Spring GraphQL and Spring Native are relatively new projects, so I am delighted to see them covered here in this book, your reliable guide to Spring.

Somnath Musib does a great job navigating the area, and his guidance no doubt makes it easier to focus on the journey that matters: the journey to production. When you enjoy success in production, when you're *there*, I hope you too can look at your friends and colleagues and say, smiling, "We might be on to something."

—Josh Long, Spring Developer Advocate,
Tanzu, a division of VMWare, @starbuxman

preface

As of the writing of this book, Spring Boot is the most popular Java framework, and it is way ahead in its usage and acceptance from its competitor frameworks, such as Dropwizard, Quarkus, and Micronaut. With the industry-wide adoption of microservice-based architecture, the popularity of Spring Boot is skyrocketing, and it has become the most preferred Java framework to learn amongst the developers.

Despite its popularity, the biggest challenge newcomers come across is knowing where to start. Both Spring and Spring Boot reference documentation is humongous and not beginner friendly. Spring Boot provides several guides on how to do certain things with Spring Boot. These guides are good for a quick start but fail to provide practical examples and a comprehensive understanding of the capabilities of Spring Boot. There are numerous tutorials, articles, and blog posts available across the internet. But again, those are scattered, incomplete, and far from providing a complete picture of Spring Boot.

Spring Boot in Practice attempts to address many of these issues. When we started working on the book, we had two major goals. The first was to provide our readers with a clear picture of Spring Boot and its many internal concepts, such as auto-configuration, actuator, and security. The second was to enrich the readers' learning journey with practical examples of Spring Boot, rather than traditional textbook-style, theory-oriented examples. We are confident that we have kept ourselves focused on these two goals.

Spring Boot in Practice covers a wide variety of Spring Boot materials. Primarily, the book is focused on beginner- to intermediate-level readers. The book aims to take the readers on a journey starting with basic Spring Boot concepts and how to use various Spring Boot features effectively, supported by ample real-world use cases that lead to more advanced topics. Although the book is primarily focused on entry-level to intermediate-level developers, it has materials for seasoned developers as well. Concepts such as Spring Boot with Kotlin, Spring Native Image with GraalVM, Spring Boot with GraphQL, Hashicorp Vault, and Multi-Factor Authentication (MFA) will all be useful for senior developers.

I sincerely hope that readers appreciate and benefit from the contents of this book and find it useful in their Spring Boot application development. Any remarks or suggestions for improving the content of the book are most welcome and eagerly awaited. You may reach the author on LinkedIn at https://www.linkedin.com/in/musibs/.

acknowledgments

While it is my name listed on the front cover, this book came about with the help of many people, and I would like to thank all of them for helping to make it one of the best Spring Boot books available.

First, I would like to express my heartfelt gratitude to my wife, Jhinuk. You've patiently waited and allowed me to spend hours writing this book. Thank you for all your support and encouragement throughout this journey. I love you.

Next, I would like to thank my newborn child, Abhirup, for giving me a new meaning and purpose in my life. My gratitude is also due to my parents and my brother, Sumanta, and sister, Supriya, who have always believed in me and motivated me to achieve new heights in my life.

I'd like to thank my mentors, colleagues, and friends who taught me many invaluable lessons in my career. This list is large, but I must mention the following people: Amit Chitnis, Ashwani Singh, Midhuna Babu, Kiran N. S., Sandeep Salian, Priya Ponnekanti, Minal Barve, Shravan Kumar Singh, Suhasini C. H., Ramya S., and Parijat Pathak.

I'd also like to acknowledge my development editor at Manning, Jennifer Stout, for working with me, making me believe I could write this book, and for making the journey easier. I'd also like to thank the book's acquisition editor, Mike Stephens; review editor, Mihaela Batinić; production editor, Andy Marinkovich; copy editor, Christian Berk; and proofreader, Jason Everett. Thank you for providing me with the opportunity to write a Manning book. Thanks as well to all other people at Manning who worked with me on the production and promotion of the book. It was truly a team effort.

Thank you to all the reviewers who took the time to read the manuscript at various stages during its development and provided their invaluable feedback. To Ajit Malleri, Al Pezewski, Alain Lompo, Alex Saez, Amrah Umudlu, Andres Sacco, Anindya Bandopadhyay, Ashley Eatly, Asif Iqbal, Becky Huett, Chad Johnston, Fernando Bernardino, Gabriele Bassi, Giampiero Granatella, Harinath Kuntamukkala, Ilya Sakayev, Javid Asgarov, Jean-François Morin, João Miguel Pires Dias, John Guthrie, Kent R. Spillner, Krzysztof Kamyczek, Lachman Dhalliwal, Maqbool Patel, Mladen Knežić, Mohamed Sanaulla, Najeeb Arif, Neil Croll, Rafał Gorzkowski, Raffaella Ventaglio, Raghunath Nedumpurath, Raymond Cheung, Richard Meinsen, Ruslan Vidzert, Sambaran Hazra, Satej Sahu, Sergio Britos Arevalo, Søren Dines Jensen, Tan Wee, Tiziano Bezzi, and William Fly, you all helped make this a better book.

Special thanks to the technical reviewer of the book, Ubaldo Pescatore, for all the reviews and feedback. And a big thank you to Giampiero Granatella, the technical proofreader, for his careful review of the code one last time, shortly before the book went into production.

Finally, thank you to the Spring and Spring Boot team. You've created something incredibly useful and made life easier for developers around the world.

about this book

Spring Boot in Practice is written for Java developers who would like to learn Spring Boot and how to use it in their application development. This book belongs with Manning's "In Practice" series and is focused on the practical use of Spring Boot with lots of real-world examples. The book is written in the problem, solution, discussion pattern, where we first introduce a problem and then provide a solution for it. Lastly, we provide an in-depth discussion of each feature in the discussion section.

Who should read this book?

Spring Boot in Practice is written for beginner- to intermediate-level application developers and provides plenty of real-life examples for using Spring Boot. This book attempts to emphasize various Spring Boot internal concepts as well as emerging features, such as Spring Boot with GraalVM Native Image, GraphQL, and reactive application development. Thus, this book has enough material for senior Spring Boot application developers to add to their existing knowledge. Anyone who wishes to learn Spring Boot, or brush up on their Spring Boot knowledge, will find the book useful.

How this book is organized: A roadmap

Spring Boot in Practice has 10 chapters and two appendixes, which span five parts.

Part 1 contains an introduction to Spring Boot and its various features:

- Chapter 1 provides a high-level discussion on Spring Boot, its characteristics, and the various features it offers.

Part 2 contains several concepts and techniques for Spring Boot application development:

- Chapter 2 discusses how you can perform several commonly used application tasks with Spring Boot. This includes various ways of managing configuration, using logging, data validation, and more.
- Chapter 3 discusses several techniques for accessing a database from a Spring Boot application.
- Chapter 4 provides an in-depth discussion on Spring Boot autoconfiguration and actuators. In this chapter, we discuss how autoconfiguration is designed and its internals. We also cover the Spring Boot actuator, creating custom endpoints, and Prometheus monitoring in considerable depth.
- Chapter 5 introduces Spring Security and several techniques for securing a Spring Boot application. We introduce how Spring Security works, various important filters, and how to customize various security parameters in your Spring Boot application.
- Chapter 6 takes the concepts introduced in chapter 5 to the next level by discussing several advanced production-grade security features that can be implemented in a Spring Boot application.
- Chapter 7 introduces how to develop RESTful APIs with Spring Boot. We discuss handling exceptions in RESTful API development, document APIs, version APIs, and, lastly, securing RESTful APIs

Part 3 discusses performing reactive application development with Spring Boot:

- Chapter 8 introduces how to develop reactive applications with Spring Boot. We also cover using WebSocket and RSocket with Spring Boot.

Part 4 highlights various techniques for deploying Spring Boot applications into various platforms:

- Chapter 9 discusses how to deploy Spring Boot applications on various platforms. We start with basic JAR and WAR deployment of Spring Boot applications. We then discuss deploying Spring Boot applications in Cloud Foundry and Heroku. Lastly, we demonstrate how to run Spring Boot applications as containers and deploy in Kubernetes Cluster and Red Hat OpenShift.

Part 5 discusses using Spring Boot with Kotlin, GraalVM, Native Image, and GraphQL:

- Chapter 10 talks about using Kotlin to develop Spring Boot applications. We also discuss generating native images of the Spring Boot application with Spring Native. Lastly, we introduce how you can use GraphQL in a Spring Boot application.

About the code

This book contains many examples of source code, both in numbered listings and in line with normal text. In both cases, source code is formatted in a `fixed-width font like this` to separate it from ordinary text. Sometimes code is also **`in bold`** to highlight code that has changed from previous steps in the chapter, such as when a new feature adds to an existing line of code.

In many cases, the original source code has been reformatted; we've added line breaks and reworked indentation to accommodate the available page space in the book. In rare cases, even this was not enough, and listings include line-continuation markers (➥). Additionally, comments in the source code have often been removed from the listings when the code is described in the text. Code annotations accompany many of the listings, highlighting important concepts.

You can get executable snippets of code from the liveBook (online) version of this book at https://livebook.manning.com/book/spring-boot-in-practice. The complete code for the examples in the book is available for download from the Manning website at www.manning.com/books/spring-boot-in-practice, and from GitHub at https://github.com/spring-boot-in-practice/repo.

liveBook discussion forum

Purchase of *Spring Boot in Practice* includes free access to liveBook, Manning's online reading platform. Using liveBook's exclusive discussion features, you can attach comments to the book globally or to specific sections or paragraphs. It's a snap to make notes for yourself, ask and answer technical questions, and receive help from the author and other users. To access the forum, go to https://livebook.manning.com/book/spring-boot-in-practice/discussion. You can also learn more about Manning's forums and the rules of conduct at https://livebook.manning.com/discussion.

Manning's commitment to our readers is to provide a venue where a meaningful dialogue between individual readers and between readers and the author can take place. It is not a commitment to any specific amount of participation on the part of the author, whose contribution to the forum remains voluntary (and unpaid). We suggest you try asking the author some challenging questions lest his interest stray! The forum and the archives of previous discussions will be accessible from the publisher's website for as long as the book is in print.

about the author

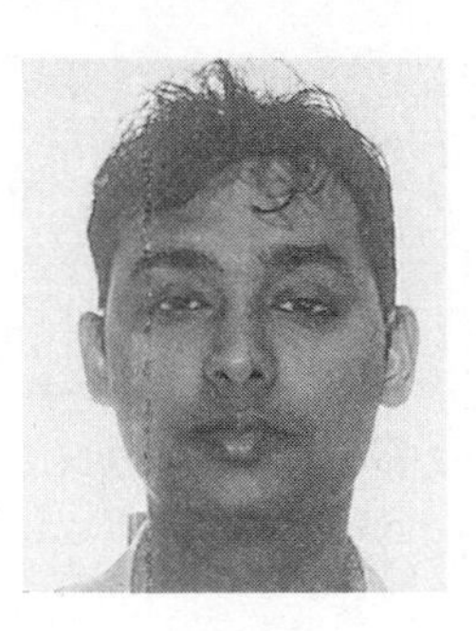

SOMNATH MUSIB is a polyglot developer with 10+ years of experience. He has been using Spring Boot since 2015 and is actively involved in Spring Boot application development. Somnath loves teaching and likes to explain complex topics to people in an easy-to-understand manner. In his spare time, he loves writing about technologies on his Medium blog at https://musibs.medium.com/.

about the cover illustration

The figure on the cover of *Spring Boot in Practice* is "Femme de Navarre" or "Woman from Navarre," taken from a collection by Jacques Grasset de Saint-Sauveur, published in 1797. Each illustration is finely drawn and colored by hand.

In those days, it was easy to identify where people lived and what their trade or station in life was just by their dress. Manning celebrates the inventiveness and initiative of the computer business with book covers based on the rich diversity of regional culture centuries ago, brought back to life by pictures from collections such as this one.

Part 1

Part 1 of this book consists of chapter 1, which introduces you to Spring Boot and some of its important characteristics. Chapter 1 covers the overview of Spring Boot, its various components, and some of its important features, such as Spring Boot starter, autoconfiguration, actuator, and failure analyzers. We also explore the project structure and various elements of a Spring Boot application. Chapter 1 also discusses creating an executable JAR file from a Spring Boot application and explores the JAR file components.

1 Booting Spring Boot

This chapter covers

- Introducing Spring Boot
- Project structure and various elements of a generated project
- Creating an executable JAR file and the generated JAR structure
- An overview of Spring Boot starter, autoconfiguration, failure analyzer, and actuator
- Introducing Spring Boot developer tools to increase developer productivity

Welcome to Spring Boot—the most popular Java framework out there! It has revolutionized the way Spring applications or, more specifically, Java applications are developed these days. Spring Boot is an open source extension of the Spring Framework designed to simplify the Spring application development. The popularity of Spring Boot is mostly attributed to its ability to create standalone, production-ready, Spring-based applications, in no time, that you can run without worrying much about the configuration hazards.

This chapter provides an overview of Spring Boot, discussing what Spring Boot is, its purpose, its project structure, and several key Spring Boot features. Are you ready? Let's *boot* our journey!

1.1 Introducing Spring Boot

In this section, we'll introduce you to the Spring Boot framework and briefly answer a few common questions about Spring Boot. We'll discuss why we need Spring Boot framework, introduce you to the framework, the various features it offers and various components of the framework.

1.1.1 Why Spring Boot?

As we venture out on this beautiful voyage of getting ourselves familiar with Spring Boot, the very first question that appears in mind is: why should we learn it in the first place? To find an answer to this question, let's understand what problem Spring Boot promises to solve.

The Spring Framework started its journey to simplify the Java Enterprise application development. It became immensely popular due to its simplified application development strategies and the heavy-lifting nature of the framework. Further, as the use of Spring as a framework increased, the need to further simplify the Spring application development process was also amplified.

Although Spring provides a great deal of support to the developers in focusing only on solving their business problems, before Spring Boot there is still a significant amount of work that needs to be done by the developer to make things work. For instance, the following are a few challenges you'll face once you start developing a Spring-based web application:

- Gain understanding of Servlet and the associated deployment descriptor web.xml concepts.
- Familiarize yourself with the `WAR` and `EAR` directory structures to package the application components.
- Understand application server-specific concepts, such as the domain, port, threads, and data sources while you deploy your application.
- Deal with complicated class loading strategies, application monitoring, management concepts, and logging facilities.

There are too many technical buzzwords out there. What if, instead, you could write the business logic for your application, build an executable file, and just run it in a command line? You wouldn't need to define complicated XML configurations or perform application server deployment or other technical juggleries. All these pieces of the puzzle would be mysteriously solved by some experienced magician, which would be impressive, right? Well, you'll soon discover that Spring Boot is this magician.

Spring Boot was introduced as a subproject under the Spring Framework to empower developers with a fast startup experience and exempt them from most of the configuration hazards. As you proceed with your Spring Boot journey, you'll notice how seamlessly Spring Boot addresses several configuration and integration issues. For instance, in your Spring Boot project, you'll not be forced to define a deployment descriptor web.xml file. You also won't be forced to use an application server to run your application unless you specifically decide to run on an application server. Most of the time, Spring Boot's default configuration can easily meet your needs.

1.1.2 What is Spring Boot?

Spring Boot was released in April 2014 to reduce some of the burdens of developing a Java web application. It allowed developers to focus more on the business logic rather than the boilerplate technical code and associated configurations. Spring Boot intends to create Spring-based, production-ready, standalone applications with little configuration changes on behalf of the application developer. It takes an opinionated view of the Spring Framework, so the application developers can quickly get started with what they need. It provides an additional layer between the Spring Framework for the user to simplify certain configuration aspects.

Figure 1.1 shows how Spring Boot sandwiches itself between you, as the application developer, and the Spring Framework. As an intermediate layer, Spring Boot performs

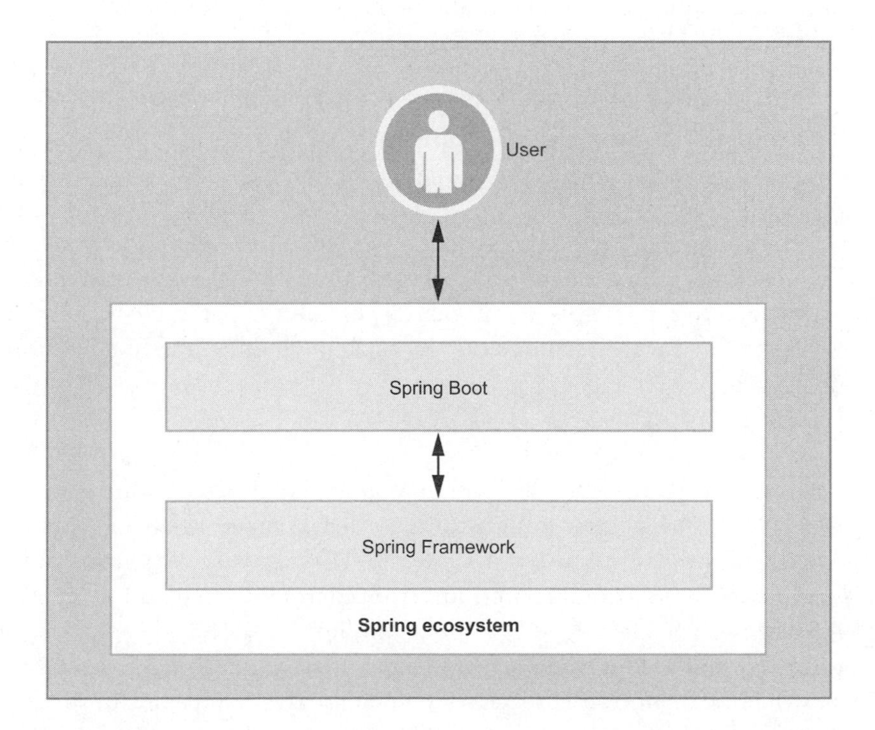

Figure 1.1 Developer view of Spring Boot. It sandwiches itself between the developer and the Spring Framework. Several Spring Framework components are automatically configured by Spring Boot based on the Spring components a developer uses.

many configurations, which you'll otherwise need to do yourself if you interact directly with the Spring Framework.

1.1.3 Spring Boot core features

Spring Boot has several notable features that make it stand out from the crowd of other frameworks:

- *Fast bootstrapping*—One of the primary goals of Spring Boot is to provide a fast startup experience in Spring application development. Let's say you want to build a web application using Spring in a traditional approach. You'll most likely follow the steps outlined below:
  1. Configure a Maven or Gradle project with Spring MVC dependencies.
  2. Configure the Spring MVC `DispatcherServlet`.
  3. Package the application components into a WAR file.
  4. Deploy the WAR file into a servlet container (e.g., Apache Tomcat).

  With Spring Boot, you can generate an application by specifying the dependencies you need in your application, and Spring Boot takes care of the rest.
- *Autoconfiguration*—Spring Boot automatically configures the bare minimum components of a Spring application. It does this based on the presence of the JAR files in the classpath or properties configured in the various property files. For instance, if Spring Boot detects the presence of a database driver JAR file (e.g., H2 in-memory database JAR) in the classpath, it automatically configures the corresponding data source to connect to the database.
- *Opinionated*—Spring Boot is opinionated. It automatically configures several components to start with a Spring application. Spring Boot does this with a set of starter dependencies. A starter dependency targets a specific area of application development and provides the related dependencies. For example, if you need to develop a web application, you can configure the `spring-boot-starter-web` dependency, which ensures that all related dependencies for developing a web application, such as `spring-web` and `spring-webmvc`, are available in the application classpath.
- *Standalone*—Spring Boot applications embed a web server, so they can run standalone and do not necessarily require an external web or application server. This enables Spring Boot applications to be packaged as an executable JAR file and run with the `java -jar` command. This also allows Spring Boot applications to be easily containerized and candidates for cloud-native application development.
- *Production-ready*—Spring Boot provides several useful production-ready features out of the box to monitor and manage the application once it is pushed to production, such as health checks, thread dumps, and other useful metrics.

1.1.4 Spring Boot components

Spring Boot consists of several components with each component focusing on a specific area of the application development. Some of these are core components, and you'll use them often with almost every Spring Boot project. For example, the `Spring Boot` is the primary component you'll use in almost every Spring Boot project. Figure 1.2 shows the Spring Boot components, and the following list briefly discusses these components:

- *spring-boot*—This is the primary Spring Boot component that provides support to other components. For example, it contains the `SpringApplication` class, which contains several static methods to create a standalone Spring Boot application. It also provides support for embedded web servers (e.g., Tomcat) and supports externalized application configurations (e.g., database details of your application), etc.
- *spring-boot-autoconfigure*—This component provides the necessary support for the automatic configuration of a Spring Boot application. Spring Boot autoconfiguration guesses and configures the spring beans based on the dependencies

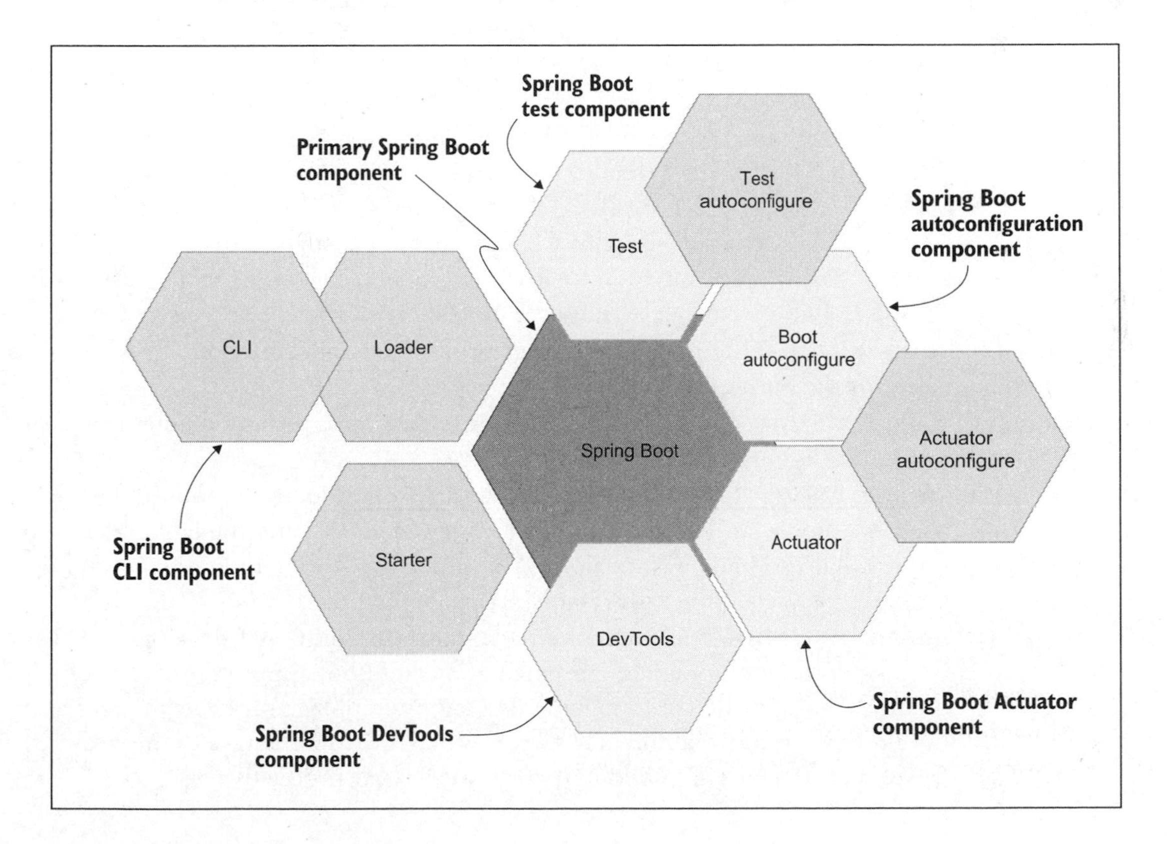

Figure 1.2 Spring Boot components

present in classpath and the properties configured. However, autoconfiguration backs away from the default configuration if it detects user-configured beans with custom configurations.

- *Spring-boot-starters*—Starters are a set of prepackaged dependency descriptors provided for developer convenience. A Spring Boot starter assists in providing a set of Spring and related technologies to the developer, which otherwise, the developer needs to manage themselves.
- *spring-boot-CLI*—This is a developer-friendly command-line utility that compiles and runs groovy codes. It can also watch files for changes, so you do not need to restart your application on modifications. This CLI tool exempts you from the need for dependency management tools, such as Maven or Gradle. Also, it lets you quickly prototype Spring applications without worrying much about dependency management and other builds-related issues. Refer to appendix A to learn how to use the Spring Boot CLI.
- *spring-boot-actuator*—This component provides the actuator endpoints to interact with, monitor, and audit a Spring Boot application. An actuator in Spring Boot can be managed through JMX or HTTP endpoints. Spring Boot provides a predefined list of actuator endpoints that cover a range of application aspects. If that does not satisfy your need, you can also create your custom actuator endpoints specific to your application. Spring Boot actuator also provides configurations to let you decide which actuator endpoints you want to enable and provides several means to secure them from unauthorized access.
- *spring-boot-actuator-autoconfigure*—This component provides support to autoconfigure the actuator endpoints based on the classpath. For instance, if the `Micrometer` (https://micrometer.io) dependency is present in the classpath, Spring Boot automatically configures the `MetricsEndpoint`.
- *spring-boot-test*—This module contains annotations and methods to write test cases for the Spring Boot application.
- *spring-boot-test-autoconfigure*—This component supports the autoconfiguration of the test cases of your application.
- *spring-boot-loader*—This component allows a Spring Boot application to be packaged as a single fat JAR file, including all dependencies and the embedded web servers that can be run standalone. You don't use this module independently; instead, it is used along with Maven or Gradle plugins.
- *spring-boot-devtools*—This component contains an additional developer toolkit for a smooth development experience of Spring Boot applications. The toolkit includes features such as automatic detection of application code changes and `LiveReload` server to automatically refresh any HTML changes to the browser. Developer tools are intended to increase developer productivity.

1.2 Code examples

In this section, we'll discuss the code examples and the technologies we'll use to develop the examples. We'll talk about the build system, programming language, and the database that we'll use in this book. We'll also introduce you to Lombok, which helps us to simplify the POJO class definitions with simple annotations.

1.2.1 Maven vs. Gradle

Spring Boot lets you create a Spring Boot project with either Apache Maven (https://maven.apache.org/) or Gradle (https://gradle.org/) build tools. In the Spring Initializr (https://start.spring.io/) tool, you can choose the build system of your choice and generate the project. In this book, we'll use Apache Maven as the preferred build system, as most readers are familiar with Apache Maven. However, if you are a Gradle user, you will find it is quite easy to port the code examples to Gradle seamlessly.

1.2.2 Java vs. Kotlin

You can use both Java and Kotlin (https://kotlinlang.org/) programming languages in your Spring Boot project. Spring Framework 5.0 has incorporated support for Kotlin, and since then there is a constant effort to provide better support for Kotlin in the Spring Framework. For instance, in Spring Security 5.3, the Spring team has introduced a Kotlin version of their domain-specific language (DSL) support to Spring Security. You can read more about Spring Framework's Kotlin support at http://mng.bz/Bxw8.

In this book, we'll primarily use Java as our preferred language in most of the code examples. We'll cover the major Kotlin features in Spring Framework (through Spring Boot) in chapter 10.

1.2.3 Database support

Several coding examples in this book require database access to demonstrate the concepts. Spring Boot extends support to an array of SQL and NoSQL databases. For the ease of testing of the coding examples, we'll use an H2 in-memory SQL database in all our code examples (with a few exceptions).

1.2.4 Lombok

Lombok (https://projectlombok.org/) is a Java library that automatically generates the constructors, getter, setter, toString, and others based on the presence of a few annotations in the plain old Java object (POJO) class. All you need to do is use the appropriate annotation in the POJO class. For instance, to generate a getter method for all member variables in the POJO class, you can specify `@Getter` annotation in the class. We'll use Lombok in this book in the code examples.

If you are not interested in using Lombok, you can simply provide the getter, setter, and constructors, as applicable to the code. The code examples should work as expected.

Record

Java 14 has introduced the concept of *records* in the Java language. Records are immutable data classes that require you to specify only the type and name of the fields. The Java compiler can then generate the `equals`, `hashCode`, and `toString` methods. It also generates the private final fields, getter methods, and public constructor. If you do not wish to use a third-party library, such as Lombok, you may consider using Java records.

A record can be defined as follows:

```
Public record Course(int id, String name, String description, int rating) {}
```

The compiler generates the public constructor with all the defined fields and provides getter methods with the same as the field names (e.g., `id()`, `name()` etc.) as well as `equals` and `hashCode` methods. You can find more information about Java records at http://mng.bz/donO.

1.3 Getting started with Spring Boot

You now have an overview of Spring Boot and know the purpose of the framework. In this section, you'll learn to generate a Spring Boot project and the various parts of the generated project.

1.3.1 Your first Spring Boot project

Spring Boot provides a tool called Spring Initializr that lets you generate a skeleton Spring Boot project. You can access the Spring Initializr tool at https://start.spring.io. Further, Spring Boot also provides APIs that allows the mainstream IDE vendors to integrate Spring Initializr and provide built-in support to generate a Spring Boot project in the IDE itself. If you are new to Spring Initializr, refer to appendix A to learn various ways to create a Spring Boot project. We've generated a Spring Boot project for your reference in the book's companion GitHub repository at http://mng.bz/razD.

1.3.2 Spring Boot project structure

A generated Spring Boot project structure is relatively simple and consists of only the components you need to proceed with Spring Boot application development. It contains the following components:

- A pom.xml file that contains the dependencies you've selected during project generation.
- A Maven wrapper file that lets you build the project without installing Maven in your local machine.
- A package structure that contains the source and tests Java files. The source package contains a Java class with the main method, and the test package has an empty test class.

- A resources folder to maintain additional project artifacts and an empty application.properties file.

Let's discuss the key components of the generated project in detail.

THE MAVEN POM.XML FILE

The pom.xml file of the generated project is shown in the following listing.

Listing 1.1 The pom.xml file of generated Spring Boot project

```
<?xml version="1.0" encoding="UTF-8"?>
<project xmlns="http://maven.apache.org/POM/4.0.0"
➥ xmlns:xsi="http://www.w3.org/2001/XMLSchema-instance"
      xsi:schemaLocation="http://maven.apache.org/POM/4.0.0
➥ https://maven.apache.org/xsd/maven-4.0.0.xsd">
    <modelVersion>4.0.0</modelVersion>
    <parent>
        <groupId>org.springframework.boot</groupId>
        <artifactId>spring-boot-starter-parent</artifactId>
        <version>2.6.3</version>
        <relativePath/> <!-- lookup parent from repository -->
    </parent>
    <groupId>com.manning.sbip.ch01</groupId>
    <artifactId>spring-boot-app-demo</artifactId>
    <version>1.0.0</version>
    <name>spring-boot-app-demo</name>
    <description>Spring Boot Demo Application</description>
    <properties>
        <java.version>17</java.version>
    </properties>

    <dependencies>
        <dependency>
            <groupId>org.springframework.boot</groupId>
            <artifactId>spring-boot-starter-web</artifactId>
        </dependency>
        <dependency>
            <groupId>org.springframework.boot</groupId>
            <artifactId>spring-boot-starter-test</artifactId>
            <scope>test</scope>
            <exclusions>
                <exclusion>
                    <groupId>org.junit.vintage</groupId>
                    <artifactId>junit-vintage-engine</artifactId>
                </exclusion>
            </exclusions>
        </dependency>
    </dependencies>
    <build>
        <plugins>
            <plugin>
```

Current project declares Spring Boot starter parent as its parent to indicate that this project is a child Spring Boot project. This ensures several features of the application, such as plugin and dependency management, can be managed by Spring Boot.

Current project's artifact details

List of declared Maven dependencies: Spring Boot starter web and Spring Boot starter test

Spring Boot starter test dependency provides necessary support to perform testing Spring Boot applications with popular testing libraries, such as Junit, Hamcrest, and Mockito. This dependency excludes junit-vintage-engine dependency to leverage Junit 5 features with junit-jupiter-engine.

Spring Boot Maven plugin is a Maven plugin that provides useful goals to perform several application management activities. For instance, you can quickly start the Spring Boot application with this plugin using mvn spring-boot:run command.

```
                <groupId>org.springframework.boot</groupId>
                <artifactId>spring-boot-maven-plugin</artifactId>
            </plugin>
        </plugins>
    </build>
</project>
```

There are three segments of the pom.xml you'll explore in this section:

1. The `parent` tag
2. The `dependencies` section
3. The Spring Boot Maven plugin

The `spring-boot-starter-parent` is the parent dependency for all Spring Boot starter dependencies. It also indicates that the current Spring Boot project is a child Spring Boot project and extends a few details from the parent project.

A `spring-boot-starter-parent` is a special type of starter dependency that provides several default configurations, such as the default java version and default configurations for several Maven plugins to a Spring Boot project. For example, the `maven-war-plugin` and `maven-surefire-plugin` are automatically included by the starter parent dependency.

Further, `spring-boot-starter-parent` also assists in dependency management. Notice that there is no dependency version specified for any of the declared dependencies. The appropriate version of these libraries is specified in the `spring-boot-starter-parent`.

Does your project already have a parent pom?

It is possible that you already have an existing Maven project set up with a parent pom, and you are upgrading this project to the Spring Boot. In this scenario, how can your child Spring Boot project extend the parent pom, since it is already extending a custom parent pom?

You can still leverage several benefits, such as the dependency management offered by Spring Boot parent pom, by adding the following dependency. You can specify `spring-boot-dependencies` in the `dependencyManagement` section of the pom.xml file:

```
<dependencyManagement>
    <dependencies>
        <dependency>
            <groupId>org.springframework.boot</groupId>
            <artifactId>spring-boot-dependencies</artifactId>
            <version>2.6.3</version>
            <type>pom</type>
            <scope>import</scope>
        </dependency>
    </dependencies>
</dependencyManagement>
```

In the second section of the pom.xml file, Spring Boot starter dependencies are declared. Spring Boot starter dependencies are one of the key features of the Spring Boot framework. Refer to the Spring Boot starter dependency sidebar for a quick overview.

Spring Boot starter dependency

A Spring Boot starter dependency is intended to make the Spring Boot application development easy, rapid, and effective. If you have previous experience developing Java applications with a build tool such as Apache Maven or Gradle, you can recall that managing dependencies is one of the key challenges for an application developer.

The first challenge is to identify the libraries (dependencies) you need to develop a specific component of your application. Once you identify them, you need to find the right versions of the libraries. Even if you find the right libraries and versions, in this fast-paced world of application development, it is relatively easy to become out of sync with the versions. To further increase your issues, the dependencies you choose have their own dependencies or, more precisely, transitive dependencies. In some cases, you even need to control those as well. Spring Boot starter dependency is a solution in Spring Boot to relieve you of all the above-mentioned issues.

A starter dependency groups together a set of dependencies you might need to develop a part of your application. If you choose to develop a web application with Spring Boot, you'll most likely choose the `spring-boot-starter-web` dependency. It ensures that all required dependencies to develop a web application are available in your application. Of course, this is opinionated, and you get the set of dependencies that the Spring team recommends you need to have to develop a web application. However, the key part here is that you are relieved from the dependency versioning, upgrades, and many other issues.

A starter dependency can also depend on another starter dependency. For instance, the `spring-boot-starter-web` needs a few common starter dependencies, such as the `spring-boot-starter`, `spring-boot-starter-tomcat`, and `spring-boot-starter-json` dependencies. These starters pull another set of dependencies related to Spring Boot, Tomcat, and JSON, respectively. You can refer to the Spring Boot documentation for a list of Spring Boot starters available at http://mng.bz/VlJO.

The concept of *starter dependency* is extendable. Spring Boot lets you build starters that you can use in your application. This is useful for large applications to modularize and manage dependencies in terms of custom starters. You'll learn how to create a custom starter later in the book.

In the generated project, we've included two starter dependencies: `spring-boot-starter-web` and `spring-boot-starter-test`. The web starter dependency includes required JARs to build a web application, whereas the test dependency lets you write test cases for your application.

In the final section of the pom.xml presented in listing 1.1, you can find the `spring-boot-maven-plugin`. This plugin is provided for developer convenience to simplify several application management activities. For instance, you'll often notice it is quite straightforward to build an executable JAR or WAR file of a Spring Boot application. This is because the repackage goal of the spring-boot-maven-plugin ensures that it takes the Maven-generated original JAR or WAR file (which is not an executable) and repackages it to make it executable. Table 1.1 shows the list of available goals of spring-boot-maven-plugin with syntax and a brief description:

Table 1.1 List of Spring Boot Maven plugin goals

Goal name	Maven command syntax	Description
Build an image	spring-boot:build-image	Packages the application into an open container initiative (OCI; see https://opencontainers.org/) image. You will learn more about images and their deployment into containers in chapter 9.
Generate build-info properties	spring-boot:build-info	Generates a build-info.properties file based on the current Maven project. You can find this file at ${project.build.outputDirectory}/META-INF/build-info.properties.
Display help information	spring-boot:help	Shows the help content of the spring-boot-maven-plugin. You can use mvn spring-boot:help -Ddetail=true -Dgoal=<goal-name> to view parameters allowed in a goal. For example, mvn spring-boot:help -Ddetail=true -Dstart shows detailed information about the start goal.
Repackage Spring Boot JAR or WAR archives	Spring-boot:repackage	This goal intends to repackage the existing JAR or WAR files to make them executable from the command line (e.g., java -jar somejar.jar). By default, this goal binds itself in the Maven lifecycle package phase and makes the generated JAR or WAR archive executable. You can use mvn clean install spring-boot:repackage to see how this goal works. Alternatively, you can also use mvn package to generate the same executable archive.
Run a Spring Boot application	spring-boot:run	Runs a Spring Boot application in place
Start a Spring Boot application	spring-boot:start	Starts a Spring Boot application
Stop a running Spring Boot application	spring-boot:stop	Stops an application that was started using the start goal

You can refer to table 1.1 to learn more about each of these goals. For instance, if you would like to run the current Spring Boot application, you can execute the following command in command-line or terminal from the same directory where `pom.xml` is located: `mvn spring-boot:run`. You'll see the application starts and runs on default HTTP port `8080`, as shown in figure 1.3:

```
C:\sbip\repo\ch01\spring-boot-app-demo>mvn spring-boot:run
[INFO] Scanning for projects...
[INFO]
[INFO] -------------< com.manning.sbip.ch01:spring-boot-app-demo >-------------
[INFO] Building spring-boot-app-demo 0.0.1-SNAPSHOT
[INFO] --------------------------------[ jar ]---------------------------------
[INFO]
[INFO] >>> spring-boot-maven-plugin:2.6.3:run (default-cli) > test-compile @ spring-boot-app-demo >>>
[INFO]
[INFO] --- maven-resources-plugin:3.2.0:resources (default-resources) @ spring-boot-app-demo ---
[INFO] Using 'UTF-8' encoding to copy filtered resources.
[INFO] Using 'UTF-8' encoding to copy filtered properties files.
[INFO] Copying 1 resource
[INFO] Copying 0 resource
[INFO]
[INFO] --- maven-compiler-plugin:3.8.1:compile (default-compile) @ spring-boot-app-demo ---
[INFO] Nothing to compile - all classes are up to date
[INFO]
[INFO] --- maven-resources-plugin:3.2.0:testResources (default-testResources) @ spring-boot-app-demo ---
[INFO] Using 'UTF-8' encoding to copy filtered resources.
[INFO] Using 'UTF-8' encoding to copy filtered properties files.
[INFO] skip non existing resourceDirectory C:\sbip\repo\ch01\spring-boot-app-demo\src\test\resources
[INFO]
[INFO] --- maven-compiler-plugin:3.8.1:testCompile (default-testCompile) @ spring-boot-app-demo ---
[INFO] Changes detected - recompiling the module!
[INFO] Compiling 1 source file to C:\sbip\repo\ch01\spring-boot-app-demo\target\test-classes
[INFO]
[INFO] <<< spring-boot-maven-plugin:2.6.3:run (default-cli) < test-compile @ spring-boot-app-demo <<<
[INFO]
[INFO]
[INFO] --- spring-boot-maven-plugin:2.6.3:run (default-cli) @ spring-boot-app-demo ---
[INFO] Attaching agents: []
```

Figure 1.3 Running a Spring Boot application using Spring Boot Maven plugin in command line

A careful observation of the command line output shows that this goal, indeed, invokes several other Maven plugins, such as `maven-resources-plugin` to copy resources (e.g., copying Java source files from src/main/java folder to the associated output directory) and `maven-compiler-plugin` to compile the source code before it starts the application. The `spring-boot-maven-plugin` abstracts all these low-level tasks from the developer.

The Spring Boot main class

In the generated project, you can find that Spring Initializr has generated a Java class with a Java `main()` method in it. The following listing shows this.

Listing 1.2 The Spring Boot main class

```java
package com.manning.sbip.ch01;

import org.springframework.boot.SpringApplication;
import org.springframework.boot.autoconfigure.SpringBootApplication;

@SpringBootApplication
public class SpringBootAppDemoApplication {
```

```
    public static void main(String[] args) {
        SpringApplication.run(SpringBootAppDemoApplication.class, args);
    }

}
```

Let's examine the following components of the generated Java file:

1. Using the `main()` method
2. Using the `@SpringBootApplication` annotation
3. The role of `SpringApplication` class

In general, to run a web application, you build and package the application components in a WAR or EAR archive file and deploy it into a web (e.g., Apache Tomcat) or application server (e.g., Red Hat JBoss). Spring Boot simplifies this process to a certain degree. It does not enforce you to build a WAR or EAR file of your application. Instead, it lets you run the Spring Boot application like a regular Java application using a conventional `main()` method.

Although Spring Boot follows a familiar approach to keep things simple for developers, it performs a decent amount of heavy lifting behind the scenes. For instance, a Servlet-based web application can run only in a Servlet Container, such as Apache Tomcat or Jetty. Spring Boot enables this support by using an embedded Apache Tomcat server in the application by default. Thus, when you start your Spring Boot application using the `main()` method, Spring Boot starts an embedded instance of the Apache Tomcat server and runs the web application inside it.

If you explore the `spring-boot-starter-web` dependency further, you can find it has a transitive dependency on the `spring-boot-starter-tomcat` module. You can execute the `mvn dependency:tree` command from the path where the pom.xml file is located to explore the dependency tree of the application.

You may notice that the class in the generated Java file is annotated with the `@SpringBootApplication` annotation. This is a convenient annotation that consists of three annotations: `@EnableAutoConfiguration`, `@ComponentScan`, and `@SpringBootConfiguration`, each of which is performing a specific task in the application.

Let's understand these annotations based on their actions:

- `@EnableAutoConfiguration`—Spring Boot provides several `@Enable*` annotations to enable specific features in your Spring Boot application. The `@EnableAutoConfiguration` annotation provides the necessary support for Spring Boot to autoconfigure your application based on the JAR dependencies present in the application classpath. You'll learn more about autoconfiguration in chapter 4.
- `@ComponentScan`—Provides support to scan the packages for Spring components in the application. A component in Spring is a Java bean that is managed by Spring and annotated with the `@Component`, `@Bean`, or specialized component annotations. With the presence of `@ComponentScan` annotation, the

Spring Boot application scans for all components present in the root package and subpackages under it to manage their lifecycle. The key point to remember with `ComponentScan` is that the scan starts from a root package and continues to all child packages. Thus, if you have packages that are not in the root or its subpackage, none of those components will be scanned by the component scan.

- `@SpringBootConfiguration`—This annotation indicates that the annotated class provides the Spring Boot application configuration. It is meta-annotated with Spring `@Configuration` annotation so that the configurations in the annotated class can be found automatically by Spring Boot. Thus, the beans defined in this main class can be autodetected and loaded by Spring.

Also, note that the Spring Boot application main class needs to be in your application root package, as the `@SpringBootApplication` annotation is configured in this class. `@SpringBootApplication` annotation uses the root package as the base package. This base package and all other subpackages are automatically scanned by Spring Boot to load Spring components (e.g., classes configured with `@Component`, `@Configuration`, and other Spring annotations) and other types. You can find more details at http://mng.bz/xv8e.

The next, and final, component is the use of the `SpringApplication` class in the generated Java file. This class is provided by Spring Boot to conveniently bootstrap a Spring Boot application. Most of the time, you'll use the static `run()` method of `SpringApplication` to bootstrap and launch your application. Spring Boot performs several activities while it executes the `run()` method:

1. Creates an instance of an `ApplicationContext` based on the libraries present in the classpath
2. Registers a `CommandLinePropertySource` to expose command line arguments as Spring properties
3. Refreshes the `ApplicationContext` created at step 1 to load all singleton beans
4. Triggers the `ApplicationRunners` and `CommandRunners` configured in the application

Revisiting ApplicationContext

Most Java applications you develop consist of objects. These objects interact with each other, and there are dependencies among them. To effectively manage object creation and interdependencies, Spring uses the principles of dependency injection (DI). This dependency injection or the inversion of control (IoC) approach lets Spring create the objects (or, more appropriately, the *beans* in Spring parlance) and inject the dependencies externally. The bean definitions are presented to Spring either through the XML bean definition files (e.g., applicationContext.xml) or through the annotation-based configurations (`@Configuration` annotation). Spring loads these bean definitions and keeps them available in the Spring IoC container.

> ***(continued)***
>
> The ApplicationContext interface acts as the Spring IoC Container. Spring provides a plethora of ApplicationContext implementations based on the application type (Servlet or Reactive application), the bean definition configurations (e.g., to load from classpath or annotation), and so on. You can refer to the Java documentation of the ApplicationContext interface (http://mng.bz/AxJK) to learn more about it and its available subtypes.

The SpringApplication class attempts to create an instance of ApplicationContext based on the JAR dependencies present in the classpath. A Spring Boot web application can be either Servlet-based or reactive type. Leveraging Spring's class loading techniques, and based on the availability of the classes in the classpath, Spring deduces the current application's type. Once the application type is known, Spring Boot applies the below strategy to load the application context:

1. If the application is identified as a Servlet-based web application, Spring Boot attempts to create an instance of AnnotationConfigServletWebServerApplicationContext class.
2. Alternatively, if the application is reactive type, Spring Boot creates an instance of the AnnotationConfigReactiveWebServerApplicationContext class.
3. If the application is neither a Servlet-based nor a reactive application, Spring Boot attempts to create an instance of AnnotationConfigApplicationContext class.

You start a Spring Boot application using the static run() method of SpringApplication class. Although using the static run() method is useful, Spring Boot additionally lets you create an instance of SpringApplication class to customize the application bootstrap mode. For instance, if you are aware of the application type, you can directly set it in the SpringApplication instance, as shown in the following listing.

Listing 1.3 Customizing SpringApplication to select the application type as reactive

```
package com.manning.sbip.ch01;

//imports

@SpringBootApplication
public class BootstrappingSpringBootAppApplication {

    public static void main(String[] args) {

        SpringApplication springApplication = new
➥ SpringApplication(BootstrappingSpringBootAppApplication.class);

        springApplication.setWebApplicationType(WebApplicationType.REACTIVE);
```

Customizing SpringApplication class to set the application type as Reactive

Create an instance of SpringApplication

```
        springApplication.run(args);
    }
}
```

`SpringApplication` also provides several setter methods, so you can control various Spring Boot features, such as setting additional Spring profiles or setting a resource loader to load application resources. You can refer to the latest version of the Spring Boot reference manual (http://mng.bz/ZzJO) to learn more about `SpringApplication`.

CONFIGURATION MANAGEMENT WITH THE APPLICATION PROPERTIES FILE

Spring Initializr generates an empty application.properties file in the src/main/resources folder. This property file allows you to externalize various application configurations (e.g., server details or database details) for your application. Although there are multiple ways to externalize application properties for a Spring Boot application, this is the most frequently used approach. This property file lets you specify the configurations in a `key-value` pair format, where a key is separated from the associated value by a = character. The following listing shows a sample configuration in the application.properties file for configuring the server address and port of a Spring Boot application.

Listing 1.4 The application.properties contents to configure the application address and port

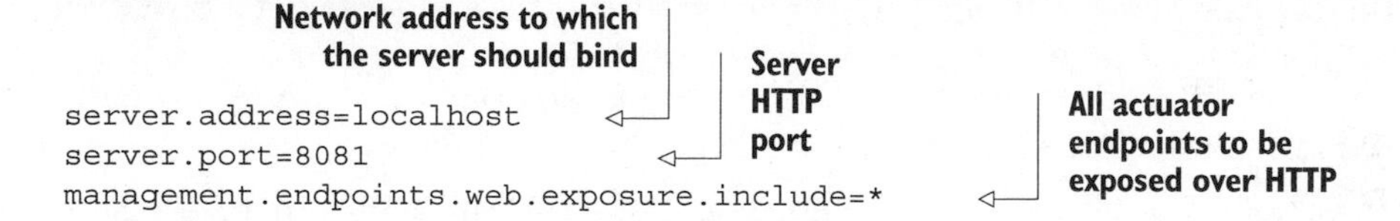

```
server.address=localhost
server.port=8081
management.endpoints.web.exposure.include=*
```


To see the application.properties file in practice, you can modify the `server.port` value in the current application to a different HTTP port value (e.g., to `9090`). If you launch the application after this modification, you can see it starts on the updated HTTP port.

If you are not fond of the property file format, you can alternatively use the YAML (https://yaml.org/spec/1.2/spec.html) file format to configure application properties. YAML allows you to hierarchically define the properties. If you would like to use the YAML file format, you can rename the existing application.properties file to application.yml and specify the properties in YAML format. The following listing shows the equivalent YAML configuration of listing 1.4.

Listing 1.5 The application.yml content to configure the application address and port

```
server:
  address: localhost
  port: 8080
```

```
management:
  endpoints:
    web:
      exposure:
        include: '*'
```

You can refer to the common application properties on the Spring Boot website (http://mng.bz/REJ0) for a list of supported application.properties. As we advance in this book, you'll be surprised to observe how, by simply adding an application configuration property, you can achieve a drastic change in your application behavior.

In this section, you've explored the core components of a Spring Boot application. You should now be familiar with the overall Spring Boot project structure, the pom.xml file components, the @SpringBootApplication annotation, SpringApplication class, and the mighty application.properties that give you the power to control the Spring Boot application behavior through various built-in and custom properties.

1.3.3 Creating an executable JAR file

The easiest way of creating an executable JAR file from your Spring Boot project is by using the mvn package command. Recall that you've selected the packaging type while generating the project. Based on the selection, a JAR file is created in the project's target directory. The generated JAR file can be executed with the java -jar command from your command line to start the application.

By default, the Maven package goal does not generate an executable JAR or WAR file on its own. It's the spring-boot-maven-plugin's repackage goal that binds itself in the package phase and prepares the executable file.

1.3.4 Exploring the JAR file

If you explore the generated jar file, you'll find the following structure as shown in the following listing.

Listing 1.6 Spring Boot generated JAR file structure

```
spring-boot-app-demo.jar
  |
  +-META-INF
  |  +-MANIFEST.MF
  +-org
  |  +-springframework
  |    +-boot
  |      +-loader
  |        +-<spring boot loader classes>
  +-BOOT-INF
    +-classes
    |  +-com
    |    +-manning
    |      +-sbip
    |        +-ch01
    |          +-SpringBootAppDemoApplication.class
```

```
+-lib
| +-dependency1.jar
| +-dependency2.jar
+-classpath.idx
+-layers.idx
```

We can broadly classify the structure into four sections:

- *META-INF*—This section contains the MANIFEST.MF file, which contains much critical information on the JAR that needs to be executed. The two key parameters presented in this file are `Main-Class` and `Start-Class` details.
- *Spring Boot loader components*—Spring Boot loader provides several loader implementations that are used to load the executable file. For instance, the `JarLauncher` class loads a JAR file, a `WarLauncher` loads a WAR file, and the `PropertiesLauncher` lets you customize the class loading through a set of `loader.*` properties.
- *BOOT-INF\classes*—All application class files are packaged in this folder.
- *BOOT-INF\lib*—This folder contains all the dependencies for your application.

One key point to note is the use of `Main-Class` and `Start-Class` parameters in the MANIFEST.MF file. The `Main-Class` contains the `Launcher` class name, which uses the class specified in the `Start-Class` to start the application. In a Spring Boot executable JAR, the `Start-Class` is always your Spring Boot main class.

The classpath.idx file is an index file that lists the dependencies with the order in which the class loader should load them. The layer.idx file is used for JARs that allow the JAR to be segregated into logical layers for Docker or OCI image creation. You'll explore the use of layer.idx in chapter 9 when you create Docker images from your Spring Boot application.

1.3.5 Shutting down a Spring Boot application

You may find shutting down and executing the Spring Boot application quite straightforward. If you are executing the JAR as a foreground process through your command line, you can terminate the Java process with Ctrl-C (in Windows and Linux). Similarly, you can use the appropriate OS-specific command to kill the Java process if the application is running as a background process.

Without any additional configurations, the approaches discussed above terminate the Spring Boot application immediately and do not provide it with any scope to serve the currently executing request if there is any. This might be an issue with your application's user experience. Thus, you need to ensure a graceful shutdown of the application, which should allow the current request to be served, but no new request should be taken before it finally gets terminated.

Spring Boot provides additional configurations to enable the graceful shutdown in your application. You can configure these properties in the application.properties file, as shown in the following listing.

Listing 1.7 Graceful shutdown configuration

```
server.shutdown=graceful
spring.lifecycle.timeout-per-shutdown-phase=1m
```

The default value of the `server.shutdown` property is `immediate`, which indicates an immediate shutdown of the application. Once you configure the graceful shutdown, you can also configure the timeout period the application should wait for the current request to finish. Note that the `spring.lifecycle.timeout-per-shutdown-phase` property has a default value of `30s`. You can configure a custom timeout value if the default value is not suitable for your application. In Listing 1.7, we've configured one minute as the timeout period.

> **NOTE** The above-mentioned graceful shutdown feature was introduced in Spring Boot 2.3.0 release. It's not available for earlier Spring Boot releases.

1.4 Spring Boot additional concepts

In this section, we'll provide a brief introduction to a few useful Spring Boot concepts. Some of these are key concepts of the framework, and we'll provide a detailed discussion in the subsequent chapters.

1.4.1 Spring Boot startup events

Spring framework's event management mechanism promotes decoupling event publishers and subscribers in an application. It allows you to subscribe to the framework's built-in events as well as define your custom events.

The Spring Boot framework also provides several built-in events that you can subscribe to perform certain actions. For instance, there might be a requirement that you need to invoke an external REST API if your Spring Boot application initializes completely. In this section, we'll introduce several Spring Boot events, which are published at various stages of an application startup and initialization:

- `ApplicationStartingEvent`—Published at the beginning of the application startup once the Listeners are registered. Spring Boot's `LoggingSystem` uses this event to perform any action that needs to be taken up before application initialization.
- `ApplicationEnvironmentPreparedEvent`—Published when the application is starting up and the `Environment` is ready for inspection and modification. Spring Boot internally uses this event to preinitialize several services, such as `MessageConverter`, `ConversionService`, Initialize Jackson, and others.
- `ApplicationContextInitializedEvent`—Published when the `ApplicationContext` is prepared, `ApplicationContextInitializers` are executed, but none of the bean definitions are loaded. This event can be used to perform a task before beans are initialized in the Spring container.

- `ApplicationPreparedEvent`—Published when the `ApplicationContext` is prepared, bean definitions are loaded but not refreshed. The `Environment` is ready for use at this stage.
- `ContextRefreshedEvent`—Published when the `ApplicationContext` is refreshed. This event comes from Spring—not Spring Boot. This event does not extend `SpringApplicationEvent`. The Spring Boot `ConditionEvaluationReportLoggingListener` listens to this event and prints the autoconfiguration report once this event is published.
- `WebServerInitializedEvent`—Published when the webserver is ready. This event has two variants based on the type of the application: `ServletWebServerInitializedEvent` for Servlet-based applications and `ReactiveWebServerInitializedEvent` for reactive applications. This event does not extend `SpringApplicationEvent`.
- `ApplicationStartedEvent`—Published when the `ApplicationContext` is refreshed but before the `ApplicationRunner` and `CommandLineRunners` are called.
- `ApplicationReadyEvent`—Published by `SpringApplication` to indicate the application is ready to service requests. It is not advised to change the internal state of the application, as all application initialization steps are finished.
- `ApplicationFailedEvent`—Published when there are some exceptions, and the application has failed to start. This event is useful to perform tasks like script execution or notifying startup failures.

1.4.2 Listening events in a Spring Boot application

Spring Boot events at application startups provide useful information about the various stages of application initialization. These events are useful if you need programmatic control on the application startup behavior. The easiest approach is to subscribe to these events and take necessary actions. For instance, if you need to modify any parameter in the `Environment`, you can subscribe to `ApplicationEnvironmentPreparedEvent` and do so. Spring Boot uses these events internally to initialize several components of the application.

Let's discuss different approaches to subscribe to these events. The easiest way to use Spring Framework's `@EventListener` annotation. For instance, to listen to the `ApplicationReadyEvent`, you can use the code snippet shown in the following listing.

Listing 1.8 Using @EventListener annotation to listen ApplicationReadyEvent

```
@EventListener(ApplicationReadyEvent.class)
public void applicationReadyEvent(ApplicationReadyEvent
➥ applicationReadyEvent) {
    System.out.println("Application Ready Event generated at "+new
➥ Date(applicationReadyEvent.getTimestamp()));
}
```

The above code snippet prints the timestamp of when the `ApplicationReadyEvent` was generated. Although `@EventListener` works well in most circumstances, it does not work for events that are published very early in the application start-up, such as `ApplicationStartingEvent` and `ApplicationEnvironmentPreparedEvent`. In this section, we'll discuss two additional approaches to listening to events in a Spring Boot application.

USING SPRINGAPPLICATION

Typically, in the generated Spring Boot project, the application class invokes the static `run()` method of `SpringApplication` to start the application. However, the `SpringApplication` class also provides several setter methods to customize the application startup behavior. For instance, it lets you add `ApplicationContextInitializer`, set `ApplicationListener`, and many others with the various setter methods. To use `SpringApplication` to listen to events, you can create an appropriate `ApplicationListener` class and implement the `onApplicationEvent()` method. The following listing shows a custom listener that listens to the `ApplicationStartingEvent` of Spring Boot:

Listing 1.9 Creating a custom ApplicationListener

```
public class ApplicationStartingEventListener implements
➥ ApplicationListener<ApplicationStartingEvent> {

    @Override
    public void onApplicationEvent(ApplicationStartingEvent
➥ applicationStartingEvent) {
        System.out.println("Application Starting Event logged at "+new
➥ Date(applicationStartingEvent.getTimestamp()));
    }

}
```

You can then add this listener in the `SpringApplication` so that, once there is an `ApplicationStartingEvent` published, the associated listener is called. The following listing shows the `SpringApplication` implementation.

Listing 1.10 Adding application listener in SpringApplication

```
@SpringBootApplication
public class SpringBootEventsApplication {

    public static void main(String[] args) {
        SpringApplication springApplication = new
➥ SpringApplication(SpringBootEventsApplication.class);
        springApplication.addListeners(new
➥ ApplicationStartingEventListener());
        springApplication.run(args);
    }
}
```

In the listing, you've added the custom listener into the `SpringApplication` instance. The `addListeners(..)` method takes a `varargs`, so you can add any number of listeners using this method.

The `SpringApplication` approach requires you to make code changes in your Spring Boot application class. If this is not convenient, Spring Boot provides another approach through the spring.factories property file to register the custom listeners. Let's explore this in the next section.

USING THE SPRING.FACTORIES FILE

The spring.factories file provides you with an extension point in the Spring Boot framework to configure and customize certain application features. For instance, you can find extensive use of this file by Spring Boot to configure the initializers, application listeners, autoconfiguration, failure analyzers, the template provides, and others. The spring.factories file is a property file consisting of key–value pairs.

In general, the spring.factories file exists even before the Spring Boot, and it is one of the core Spring Framework features. You can find this file inside the `spring-beans` JAR, which is a Spring framework component.

Nonetheless, Spring Boot provides an approach to configure certain custom components, such as the `ApplicationListener`, through this file. The spring.factories is located inside the META-INF folder, which is located inside the src\main\resources folder. The following listing shows a sample spring.factories file.

Listing 1.11 The spring.factories file

```
org.springframework.context.ApplicationListener=com.manning.sbip.ch01.liste
➥ ner.ApplicationStartingEventListener
```

In listing 1.11, the key is the class type of the component you are configuring, and the value is the fully qualified class name of the associated implementation. For instance, as we are configuring an `ApplicationListener`, the key is the fully qualified class type `org.springframework.context.ApplicationListener`, and the value is the custom listener class `com.manning.sbip.ch01.listener.ApplicationStartingEventListener`. You can configure multiple listener implementations separated by a comma. You'll notice the use of the spring.factories file in detail in later chapters while configuring custom autoconfiguration, failure analyzers, and more.

1.4.3 Custom Spring Boot starters

In the earlier example, you likely noticed the use of official Spring Boot starters that are developed and maintained by Spring Boot. Starters are one of the key features of Spring Boot that simplify the dependency management in a Spring Boot application. This concept of starters can be extended to the proprietary code and configurations as well. Spring Boot extends its infrastructure to let you define your custom starters so that you can define and maintain them like other application artifacts. In the latter part of the book, we'll demonstrate how to define a custom starter.

1.4.4 Custom autoconfiguration

In the introduction of this chapter, we mentioned that Spring Boot is opinionated. At the time of application startup, Spring Boot automatically configures various application components based on available dependencies and configurations and other factors. The autoconfiguration strategy lets Spring Boot express its opinion about certain application components and plays a major role in Spring Boot application initialization and execution. For starters, the autoconfiguration feature is also extendable, and you can define your autoconfiguration. Later in the book, we'll demonstrate how to define custom autoconfiguration.

1.4.5 Failure analyzers

Spring Boot uses the notion of failure analyzers that analyzes application failures and provides a detailed diagnostic report about the failure. A `FailureAnalyzer` accepts an exception and provides a detailed `FailureAnalysis`. Figure 1.4 shows the `FailureAnalysis` report printed in the console for the `PortInUseException`. This exception occurs if the port you are using to start the Spring Boot application is not available for use.

```
***************************
APPLICATION FAILED TO START
***************************

Description:

Web server failed to start. Port 8080 was already in use.

Action:

Identify and stop the process that's listening on port 8080 or configure this application to listen on another port.
```

Figure 1.4 Failure analyzer diagnostic report if the port is not available for use

You can extend the concept of `FailureAnalyzer` and define your custom exception and failure analyzers. For instance, it is quite useful, along with custom auto configurations, to define your domain-specific exception and define failure analyzer implementation with a detailed failure analysis report. You'll explore how to create a custom `FailureAnalyzer` later in the book.

1.4.6 Spring Boot actuator

Spring Boot actuator lets you monitor and interact with your Spring Boot application. It is quite common to monitor several health parameters in any production application. For instance, you can perform a health check in an application to determine whether the application is up. Besides, you can also capture the thread dump or heap dump of your application to perform a variety of analyses. Spring Boot provides a plethora of production-ready features with the actuator. To enable the Spring Boot actuator, you need to include the `spring-boot-starter-actuator` dependency in the pom.xml. The following listing shows this dependency.

Listing 1.12 Spring Boot starter actuator dependency

```
<dependency>
   <groupId>org.springframework.boot</groupId>
   <artifactId>spring-boot-starter-actuator</artifactId>
</dependency>
```

By default, Spring Boot exposes the `/actuator` as the base endpoint to access the other endpoints. Only the `/health` and `/info` endpoints are enabled for HTTP by default. For instance, if you access the http://localhost:8080/actuator, you'll see the page as shown in the following listing.

Listing 1.13 Spring Boot actuator endpoints

```
{
   "_links":{
      "self":{
         "href":"http://localhost:8080/actuator",
         "templated":false
      },
      "health":{
         "href":"http://localhost:8080/actuator/health",
         "templated":false
      },
      "health-path":{
         "href":"http://localhost:8080/actuator/health/{*path}",
         "templated":true
      },
      "info":{
         "href":"http://localhost:8080/actuator/info",
         "templated":false
      }
   }
}
```

If you access http://localhost:8080/actuator/health, you can find the application status as `UP` if the application is running. We'll discuss the Spring Boot actuator in detail in chapter 4.

1.4.7 Spring Boot developer tool

To increase developer productivity, Spring Boot provides a set of tools that make the development experience more pleasant. For instance, it monitors the classpath changes and automatically builds the application for any change. Besides, it also provides an embedded LiveReload server that can be used to trigger a browser refresh when a resource is modified. To include developer tools in your Spring Boot project, you need to include the `spring-boot-devtools` dependency in the pom.xml, as shown in the following listing.

Listing 1.14 Spring Boot developer tools

```
<dependency>
    <groupId>org.springframework.boot</groupId>
    <artifactId>spring-boot-devtools</artifactId>
    <optional>true</optional>
</dependency>
```

Summary

Spring Boot enables you to create standalone, production-ready applications that you can run without worrying much about the configuration aspects. Its autoconfiguration and starter-based dependency management perform the heavy lifting of application configuration and let you focus on the business aspect of your application.

In this chapter, we started with an overview of the various Spring Boot features and components. Some of the main areas we explored in this chapter were

- What Spring Boot is and the benefits it offers over a traditional Spring application
- Spring Boot features and its various components
- The structure and the components of a generated Spring Boot project
- How to create an executable JAR file from a Spring Boot project and the structure of the generated JAR file
- How to gracefully shutdown a running Spring Boot application
- Spring Boot startup events and various ways to listen to the events
- An overview of custom starter, autoconfiguration, failure analyzers, and actuators
- An introduction to Spring Boot developer tools to increase development productivity

The remainder of this book is dedicated to presenting the real-world techniques for solving common problems you'll encounter when working with Spring Boot. You'll be introduced to a broad spectrum of subject areas, starting with Spring Boot application development, security, reactive application development, and cloud-based deployments.

Part 2

Part 2 of the book consists of six chapters, which discuss several parts of Spring Boot application development.

Chapter 2 covers several common tasks a developer typically uses in a Spring Boot application. This includes configuration management, logging, using command line runner, data validation, and more.

Chapter 3 shows various techniques for connecting to a database from a Spring Boot application. This chapter also discusses, in depth, multiple approaches to accessing data from a database.

Chapter 4 introduces you to Spring Boot autoconfiguration and Spring Boot Actuator. Spring Boot autoconfiguration is the magic behind Spring Boot's simplicity and opinionated nature. Spring Boot Actuator allows you to monitor various application metrics. These metrics can be visualized in GUI-based tools, such as Grafana.

Chapter 5 and Chapter 6 discuss multiple approaches to securing a Spring Boot application. Chapter 5 covers Spring Security and how it works with Spring Boot. Chapter 6 provides several advanced techniques, including multi-factor authentication, signing in with Google, and reCAPTCHA validation.

Chapter 7 discusses how to develop RESTful APIs with Spring Boot. It also covers techniques for handling exceptions in RESTful APIs, writing unit test cases, documenting APIs with OpenAPI, implementing versioning, and securing RESTful APIs.

2 Common Spring Boot tasks

This chapter covers

- Managing configurations in a Spring Boot application
- Creating custom configurations with `@ConfigurationProperties`
- Exploring the `CommandLineRunner` interface to execute initialization code
- Understanding Spring Boot default logging and configuring `Log4j2` logging
- Validating user data in a Spring Boot application using Bean Validation

By this point, we've learned a bit about what Spring Boot is and its purpose of improving the application development experience by abstracting specific low-level configurations. In this chapter, you'll extend this understanding further by learning a few core concepts, such as how to manage application configuration and create a custom configuration for your application. You'll also use Spring Boot to perform several commonly used tasks that you'll frequently perform while developing Spring Boot applications.

2.1 Managing configurations

Managing application configuration is a key part of any application, and Spring Boot applications are no exception. Depending on how you develop and manage applications, you can have multiple environments (e.g., dev, test, staging, and prod) for an application in your organization. For instance, you can have one environment for development, one for testing, one for staging, and one for production. For all these environments, your application code mostly remains the same, and you need to manage many different configurations based on the environment. As an example, the database configurations or the security configurations are different in all these environments. Besides, as the application grows, and you incorporate new features, it becomes more tedious to manage the configurations.

Spring Boot provides several approaches to let you externalize application configurations without altering the application source code. The various approaches include property files, YAML files, environment variables, and command-line arguments.

In the next sections, you'll explore these approaches and learn how you can configure the application configurations in your Spring Boot application. In all the upcoming subsections, we intend to explain the concepts. If you need to refer to the code, you can download the Spring Boot project from the GitHub repository links.

2.1.1 Using the SpringApplication class

> **Source code**
> The final version of the Spring Boot project is available at http://mng.bz/lag8.

You can use Spring Boot's `SpringApplication` class to define configurations in your Spring Boot application. This class provides a method named `setDefaultProperties()` that accepts a `java.util.Properties` or a `java.util.Map<String, Object>` instance to let you set the configurations. You can configure all your application properties in the `Properties` or `Map` instance. This approach is useful for configurations that are one-time configurations, and you need not change them. Let's explain this using the following example.

In your application.properties file, you can import additional configuration files (e.g., `properties` or `yml` files containing other configurations) using the Spring Boot's `spring.config.import` property. For instance, you can configure `spring.config.import=classpath:additional-application.properties` in your application.properties file, so Spring Boot can load the configuration present in the additional-application.properties file. However, if this file does not exist in the classpath, Spring Boot throws a `ConfigDataLocationNotFoundException`.

Based on your application configuration, you may choose to ignore some configuration files and continue with the application bootstrap. To achieve this, you can configure a property named `spring.config.on-not-found` to `ignore`. The following listing shows this in practice.

Listing 2.1 Using SpringApplication's setDefaultProperties method

```
package com.manning.sbip.ch02;

import java.util.Properties;

import org.springframework.boot.SpringApplication;
import org.springframework.boot.autoconfigure.SpringBootApplication;

@SpringBootApplication
public class SpringBootAppDemoApplication {

    public static void main(String[] args) {

        Properties properties = new Properties();
        properties.setProperty("spring.config.on-not-found", "ignore");

        SpringApplication application = new
➥ SpringApplication(SpringBootAppDemoApplication.class);
        application.setDefaultProperties(properties);
        application.run(args);
    }
}
```

In Listing 2.1 you created an instance of `SpringApplication` class and set the `spring.config.on-not-found` property with a `java.util.Properties` instance through the `setDefaultProperties()` method.

2.1.2 Using @PropertySource

> **Source code**
> The final version of the Spring Boot project is available at http://mng.bz/2jNd.

In your Spring configuration classes, you can specify the `@PropertySource` annotation with the location of the property file to load configurations. The following listing shows this.

Listing 2.2 The DbConfiguration class

```
package com.manning.sbip.ch02;

//imports

@Configuration
@PropertySource("classpath:dbConfig.properties")
public class DbConfiguration {
```

```
    @Autowired
    private Environment env;

    @Override
    public String toString() {
        return "Username: "+env.getProperty("user") +", Password:
➥ "+env.getProperty("password");
    }
}
```

The code snippet in listing 2.2 defines a Spring configuration class that has the `@PropertySource` annotation on it, which reads properties from the `dbConfig.properties` file available in the application classpath. Listing 2.3 shows the `dbConfig.properties` file present in the src\main\resources folder.

Listing 2.3 dbConfig.properties file

```
user=sa
password=p@ssw0rd
```

Besides, you've autowired the Spring `Environment` instance that lets you access the properties available in the dbConfig.properties file. Let us now access the `DbConfiguration` class to get the configured properties, as shown in the following listing.

Listing 2.4 Accessing the DbConfiguration instance

```
package com.manning.sbip.ch02;

//imports

@SpringBootApplication
public class SpringBootAppDemoApplication {

    private static final Logger log =
➥ LoggerFactory.getLogger(SpringBootAppDemoApplication.class);

    public static void main(String[] args) {

        ConfigurableApplicationContext applicationContext =
➥ SpringApplication.run(SpringBootAppDemoApplication.class, args);
        DbConfiguration dbConfiguration =
➥ applicationContext.getBean(DbConfiguration.class);
        log.info(dbConfiguration.toString());
    }
}
```

If you start the application, you'll notice that it prints the `user` and `password` properties in the application console.

@PropertySource

- YML or YAML files are not supported with this annotation like properties files. You need to write additional code to support YML files.
- With Java 8 and above, you can repeat `@PropertySource` annotation with other configuration files. The following code snippet shows `@PropertySource` Java 8 configuration that loads properties from dbConfig.properties and redisConfig.properties files.

```
@Configuration
@PropertySource("classpath:dbConfig.properties")
@PropertySource("classpath:redisConfig.properties")
public class DbConfiguration {
//
}
```

2.1.3 Config data file

Source code

The final version of the Spring Boot project is available at http://mng.bz/1jEV.

Spring Boot lets you specify the application configuration properties in the application.properties or application.yml file. This is the most widely used approach to provide a configuration in a Spring Boot application. By default, the Spring Initializr-generated Spring Boot project includes an empty application.properties file. In case you are comfortable with the YAML or YML files instead of the properties file, you can provide an application.yml file in your application. Configurations specified in the properties or the YML file are loaded into Spring `Environment`, and you can access the `Environment` instance in your application classes. Besides, you can also use them with the `@Value` annotation.

Properties or YML file

Spring Boot lets you specify the application configurations in the properties as well as the YML file. In a property file, you can specify the properties in a key–value pair, as shown below, where the property key is separated from the values with a = separator:

```
server.port=8081
spring.datasource.username=sa
spring.datasource.password=password
```

The similar properties can be configured in a YML in the following manner:

(continued)

```
server:
  port: 8081
spring:
  data source:
    user: sa
    password: password
```

Whether to use properties or YML files is a developer preference. Spring Boot works similarly with both these file types (with a few exceptions). Some people prefer to use YML due to its better clarity and ability to represent hierarchical data more naturally. Besides, it is less repetitive and has enhanced capabilities to support data structures, such as lists, maps, and others.

However, if you choose to use YML files in your application, you should exercise caution to be mindful of its syntax. It is relatively easy to miss an extra space or define an incorrect indentation in the YML file. Additionally, it is much easier to find needed properties by full name if you use the `.properties` format. With YML, you always have to find the needed property manually.

If you need to change the file name from application.properties (or .yml) to other custom names, you can do so easily. You can customize the file name from application.properties with the `spring.config.name` property. In your Spring Boot application, let's create a file named sbip.yml file in the src\main\resources folder and place the `server.port` configuration with value `8081`.

You can build the application using the `mvn package` command from the location of your pom.xml file. In the pom.xml file, we specify the packaging type as JAR. Thus, the `mvn package` command generates a JAR file with the application components. After successfully building the application, run the executable JAR, using the `java -jar <jarName>` command. This is shown in the following listing.

Listing 2.5 Executing the application JAR file

```
java -jar config-data-file-0.0.1-SNAPSHOT.jar
```

You'll notice the application starts in default HTTP port `8080`. Stop the application with the Ctrl-C command, and restart it with the command shown in the following listing.

Listing 2.6 Running a Spring Boot application with a different configuration file name

```
java -jar config-data-file-0.0.1-SNAPSHOT.jar --spring.config.name=sbip
```

You'll notice the application starts with HTTP port `8081`. This is because Spring Boot has read the `server.port` property from the sbip.yml file and started the application in HTTP port `8081`.

By default, Spring Boot reads the application.properties or application.yml file from the following locations:

1 The classpath root
2 The classpath `/config` package
3 The current directory
4 The `/config` subdirectory in the current directory
5 Immediate child directories of the `/config` subdirectory

We leave it as an exercise to try out these configurations in your Spring Boot project. Apart from the above locations, you can also specify a custom location using the `spring.config.location` property. For instance, the `java` command in the following listing reads the configuration file from the path C:\sbip\repo\ch02\config-data-file\data\sbip.yml of my Windows machine.

Listing 2.7 Executing a Spring Boot application with spring.config.location property

```
java -jar target\config-data-file-0.0.1-SNAPSHOT.jar
--spring.config.location=C:\sbip\repo\ch02\config-data-file\data\sbip.yml
```

The command in listing 2.7 starts the Spring Boot application in HTTP port 8081.

From version 2.4.0 onward, Spring Boot throws an error if it could not find any property file you specified. You can use the `optional` prefix to indicate the configuration file is optional. For instance, the command in the following listing continues to start the Spring Boot application even though the property file sbip1.yml is not available in C:\sbip\repo\ch02\config-data-file\data\.

Listing 2.8 Starting a Spring Boot application with an optional property file

```
java -jar target\config-data-file-0.0.1-SNAPSHOT.jar
➥ --spring.config.location=optional:C:\sbip\repo\ch02\config-data-
➥ file\data\sbip1.yml
```

Note on spring.config.name and spring.config.location properties

Spring Boot loads `spring.config.name` and `spring.config.location` in the early phases of application startup. Thus, you can't provide these configurations in the application.properties or applicatiom.yml file. You can use the `SpringApplication.setDefaultProperties()` method, OS environment variable, or command-line arguments to configure these properties. In the above examples, we've used the command-line arguments options.

Command line arguments

Spring Boot lets you specify the configuration as command-line arguments as well. You can create a JAR file of the application and specify the properties as command-line arguments while executing the JAR file. For instance, in this section, you have specified the `spring.config.name` and `spring.config.location` properties as the command line arguments.

Spring Boot also allows you to specify the property files for a specific profile. Spring profiles let you segregate parts of your application configuration and make it available only in a certain environment (e.g., a profile for the `test` environment or a profile for the `production` environment). You can refer to Spring Boot documentation to read more on profiles at http://mng.bz/PWJ9. In this section, we'll keep ourselves focused on the profile features for config data files.

You can define additional config data files dedicated to a profile along with the default application.properties (or .yml) file. You can maintain the profile-specific property files with the application-{profile}.properties (or .yml) file. For instance, if you have two profiles—`dev`, and `test`—you can maintain two different application properties files with the name application-dev.properties and application-test.properties. Let's see this in practice.

In the Spring Boot project, let's create these two property files in the src\main\resources folder. For application-dev.properties, specify `server.port=9090`, and for application-test.properties, specify `server.port=9091`. Thus, if you select profile as the `dev`, the application should start on HTTP port 9090, and for the `test` profile, it should be HTTP port 9091.

You can activate a profile (e.g., `dev` or `test`) using the `spring.profiles.active` Spring Boot property. You can specify it in your application.properties file. For instance, if you specify spring.profiles.active=dev, then profile `dev` is active, and the properties specified in `application-dev.properties` are loaded. Similarly, you can activate the `test` profile by configuring the spring.profiles.active=test property.

Config data files are loaded in the following order:

1. The application properties (properties or the yml file) files packaged *inside* the application JAR
2. Profile-specific application properties packaged *inside* the application JAR
3. The application properties (properties or the yml file) files packaged *outside* the application JAR
4. Profile-specific application properties packaged *outside* the application JAR

2.1.4 OS environment variable

> **Source code**
> The final version of the Spring Boot project is available at http://mng.bz/J1JO.

You can specify the configurations as an environment variable and use the variable name in the config data file. Let us demonstrate this with an example. In the application.properties file, we've declared the following custom property called `app.timeout`, as shown in the following listing.

Listing 2.9 Spring Boot datasource username and password property configuration

```
app.timeout=${APP_TIMEOUT}
```

The `APP_TIMEOUT` is an environment variable configured with the value `30`. In Windows, you can set an environment variable using the `set <VAR>=<value>` command through the command prompt, where `VAR` is the environment variable name, and the value is the associated value. In Linux-based OS, you can use `export <VAR>=<value>` through a terminal. Setting the environment variables with this approach makes the variables available only for that command prompt/terminal session. Thus, you need to run the Spring Boot application in the same command prompt/terminal window. Let's now access the `app.timeout` property in the application code, as shown in the following listing.

Listing 2.10 Accessing the Spring Boot properties

```
package com.manning.sbip.ch02;

//imports

@SpringBootApplication
public class SpringBootAppDemoApplication {

    private static final Logger log =
     LoggerFactory.getLogger(SpringBootAppDemoApplication.class);

    public static void main(String[] args) {
        ConfigurableApplicationContext applicationContext =
     SpringApplication.run(SpringBootAppDemoApplication.class, args);
        Environment env = applicationContext.getBean(Environment.class);
        log.info("Configured application timeout value: "+
     env.getProperty("app.timeout"));
    }
}
```

In listing 2.10, we accessed the `ConfigurableApplicationContext` instance and then accessed the Spring `Environment` bean from it. The `Environment` let you access the properties configured in the application.properties file. We then access and print the properties in the application console. Notice that Spring Boot has accessed the environment variable for you and replaced the placeholders with the actual value at run time.

Additionally, note that it is a common practice to define the properties with the default values in the application.properties file. You can then override these property values using the environment variables if needed. For instance, you can define the `server.port` property in the application.properties file. You can override this value to a different port number using the environment variable.

In this section, you've learned various approaches to configuring application properties in a Spring Boot application. We'll wrap this discussion by understanding the order in which the properties are loaded if a property is present in multiple places. For instance, what happens if you have configured the `server.port` property in the application.properties config data file as well as passed it through as a command-line argument? Following is the order in which properties get precedence. The higher sequence number overrides the properties of the lower sequence number:

1. `SpringApplication`
2. `@PropertySource`
3. Config data file
4. OS environment variable
5. Command line arguments

Thus, a property specified in the command line arguments has the highest precedence over a property specified in the config data file. You can refer to Spring Boot documentation available at http://mng.bz/wnWq for an in-depth understanding of various features on configuration management in your Spring Boot application.

2.2 Creating custom properties with @ConfigurationProperties

In the previous section, you've seen several approaches to configuring properties in a Spring Boot application. The configurations we use can be classified into two categories—Spring Boot built-in properties and custom properties. Spring Boot provides a myriad number of built-in properties to configure various features of your Spring Boot application. The easiest example is the `server.port` property that you've used in the previous section to define the HTTP port your Spring Boot application should run. The `server.port` property is a Spring Boot built-in property. You can find a list of Spring Boot built-in properties in Spring Boot reference documentation available at http://mng.bz/q2Gw.

In this section, we'll discuss custom properties that are specific to your application. Based on the complexity and features available in your application, you may need to configure custom properties. For instance, you can configure an external REST web service URL or a `boolean` flag to enable or disable a specific feature in your application.

The good part is that you can configure any number of properties in your application configuration file(s), and Spring Boot will ensure that it is loaded and available to you at runtime. In the previous section, you've seen how Spring Boot binds the configured properties in the Spring's `Environment` instance that you can autowire to your class and access the properties.

Although this approach works perfectly well, it has several drawbacks:

- There is no type-safety of the configured properties, and we encounter issues at runtime. For instance, let's assume you are capturing a URL or an email address in your property file. You can't enforce the type-safety of these properties, as there is no validation.

- You need to access the property values individually with the `@Value` annotation or through the Spring `Environment` instance.

Spring Boot provides you with an alternative approach that lets you define strongly typed bean definitions that manage the type-safety as well as validate your application configuration. Let's discuss this in the next technique.

2.2.1 Technique: Defining custom properties with @ConfigurationProperties in a Spring Boot application

In this technique, we will introduce defining custom properties with `@ConfigurationProperties` in a Spring Boot application.

Problem

You need to define custom properties in your Spring Boot application that are type-safe and can be validated.

Solution

> **Source code**
> The final version of the Spring Boot project is available at http://mng.bz/7Wr9.

In this technique, we'll discuss how to define custom properties in your Spring Boot application and access these properties in your application classes without using the `@Value` annotation or `Environment` instance. To continue with this technique, you can use the Spring Boot project used previously. You need to add the following additional configuration in the pom.xml file, as shown in the following listing.

Listing 2.11 Spring Boot configuration processor

```
<dependency>
    <groupId>org.springframework.boot</groupId>
    <artifactId>spring-boot-configuration-processor</artifactId>
    <optional>true</optional>
</dependency>
```

You need a Spring Boot configuration processor to generate metadata about classes that are annotated with `@ConfigurationProperties` annotation. This metadata is then used by the IDEs to provide autocompletion and documentation support for the properties in the application.properties or application.yml file. You'll learn more about `@ConfigurationProperties` annotation shortly. Next, let us define the following custom properties in our Spring Boot application, as shown in the following listing.

Listing 2.12 Custom application properties

```
app.sbip.ct.name=CourseTracker
app.sbip.ct.ip=127.0.0.1
```

```
app.sbip.ct.port=9090
app.sbip.ct.security.enabled=true
app.sbip.ct.security.token=asddf998hhyqthgtYYtggghg9908jjh7ttr
app.sbip.ct.security.roles=USER,ADMIN
```

Notice that these are not Spring Boot built-in properties and are custom properties specific to our application. You need to specify these properties in your application.properties file. Let's define a Java class that represents these properties, as shown in the following listing.

Listing 2.13 AppProperties class

```
package com.manning.sbip.ch02.configurationproperties;

import java.util.List;

import org.springframework.boot.context.properties.ConfigurationProperties;
import org.springframework.boot.context.properties.ConstructorBinding;

@ConstructorBinding
@ConfigurationProperties("app.sbip.ct")
public class AppProperties {

    private final String name;          <- Application Name

    private final String ip;            <- Application IP

    private final int port;             <- Application IP

    private final Security security;    <- Application Security configuration

    public String getName() {
        return name;
    }

    public String getIp() {
        return ip;
    }

    public int getPort() {
        return port;
    }

    public Security getSecurity() {
        return security;
    }

    public AppProperties(String name, String ip, int port, Security security) {
        this.name = name;
        this.ip = ip;
        this.port = port;
        this.security = security;
    }
```

```
    @Override
    public String toString() {
        return "AppProperties{" +
                "name='" + name + '\'' +
                ", ip='" + ip + '\'' +
                ", port='" + port + '\'' +
                ", security=" + security +
                '}';
    }

    public static class Security {

        private boolean enabled;                    <-- Enable Security.
                                                        Possible values
Token Value --> private final String token;             true/false.

        private final List<String> roles;           <-- Available roles

        public Security(boolean enabled, String token, List<String> roles) {
            this.enabled = enabled;
            this.token = token;
            this.roles = roles;
        }

        public boolean isEnabled() {
            return enabled;
        }

        public String getToken() {
            return token;
        }

        public List<String> getRoles() {
            return roles;
        }

        @Override
        public String toString() {
            return "Security{" +
                    "enabled=" + enabled +
                    ", token='" + token + '\'' +
                    ", roles=" + roles +
                    '}';
        }
    }

}
```

Let's explain the changes in the `AppProperties` class of listing 2.13:

- This class is annotated with the `@ConstructorBinding` and `@ConfigurationProperties` annotations. We'll provide more details regarding these two annotations in the discussion section. Besides, you've set the prefix for the properties as the `app.sbip.ct`.

- You've defined a few variables with the name of the properties (e.g., name, ip, and port). For the security-related properties, we've defined the `Security` static class inside the `AppProperties` class. This is because the properties are nested in this fashion. For instance, the property named `app.sbip.ct.security.enabled` is represented by the enabled property in the `Security` class.
- You have provided Java documentation to these variables so that IDEs can show this documentation in the application.properties file.

So far, we've defined our properties and the associated class that maps to the properties. Let us now define another class that uses the configured properties, as shown in the following listing.

Listing 2.14 AppService class

```
package com.manning.sbip.ch02;

//imports

@Service
public class AppService {

    private final AppProperties appProperties;

    @Autowired
    public AppService(AppProperties appProperties) {
        this.appProperties = appProperties;
    }

    public AppProperties getAppProperties() {
        return this.appProperties;
    }
}
```

The class defined in listing 2.14 is annotated with Spring `@Service` annotation to define it as a service and should be autoscanned by Spring Boot. The most notable change is that we've autowired the `AppProperties` instance in this class. Spring Boot ensures that all properties are configured in the `application.properties` file are read, validated, and bound to the `AppProperties` instance. This instance is then autowired to the service class. Let's use this service class and access the `AppProperties` instance, as shown in the following listing.

Listing 2.15 Spring Boot application class

```
package com.manning.sbip.ch02;

//imports

@SpringBootApplication
@EnableConfigurationProperties(AppProperties.class)
public class SpringBootAppDemoApplication {
```

```
    private static final Logger log =
➥ LoggerFactory.getLogger(SpringBootAppDemoApplication.class);

    public static void main(String[] args) {
        ConfigurableApplicationContext applicationContext =
➥ SpringApplication.run(SpringBootAppDemoApplication.class, args);
        AppService appService =
➥ applicationContext.getBean(AppService.class);
        log.info(appService.getAppProperties().toString());

    }
}
```

In listing 2.15, we used the `@EnableConfigurationProperties(AppProperties.class)` annotation. This annotation ensures that classes with `@ConfigurationProperties` are registered in the Spring container. One drawback with this annotation is that you need to specify your `@ConfigurationProperties` annotated classes with the annotation.

If you have more classes annotated with `@ConfigurationProperties`, you can use the alternative `@ConfigurationPropertiesScan` and specify a base package so that Spring Boot can scan and find the classes annotated with `@ConfigurationProperties`. In this case, you need not explicitly specify the `@ConfigurationProperties` classes. Note that this annotation does not pick classes that are additionally annotated or meta-annotated with the `@Component` annotation. If you start the application, you can find that configured properties are printed in the application console.

DISCUSSION

Spring Boot's `@ConfigurationProperties` provides a type-safe and structured approach to configure custom application properties. You've already noticed how easily you can configure, validate, and use a set of properties in your Spring Boot application. Along with `spring.config.import` and `@ConfigurationProperties` annotation, you can logically segregate your application properties into various files based on their category.

The `@ConfigurationProperties` annotation lets you externalize configurations in a type-safe and structured fashion. You can add this annotation to a class definition (demonstrated in this technique) or to a method annotated with `@Bean` annotation in a Spring `@Configuration` class. The property binding to the class can be done either with setter methods for the member variables or through constructor binding. In this example, you've provided a prefix named `app.sbip.ct`. This prefix is used along with the properties you've defined in the class. Thus, the property `name` is used as `app.sbip.ct.name` property.

In this example, you've used the `@ConstructorBinding` by explicitly specifying this annotation in the POJO class. This annotation indicates that the configuration properties should be bound using the constructor arguments, rather than by calling setters. This annotation can be specified at the class level as well as the specific constructor. If there is only one constructor, you can specify the annotation at the class level. However, if you have multiple constructors, you can use the annotation at a specific constructor level.

In case you need to use a setter binding other than the constructor binding, you can specify the setter methods for the member variables. If you are looking for the immutability of your property configuration class, you should use `@ConstrcutorBinding` without providing the setter methods. Thus, once the properties bind to the POJO instance, there is no way to modify them. You can optionally use the `@DefaultValue` annotation in the parameter if you need to define a default value for one or more properties. The following listing shows this.

Listing 2.16 AppProperties class constructor with @DefaultValue annotation

```
public AppProperties(String name, String ip, @DefaultValue("8080") int port,
     Security security) {
    this.name = name;
    this.ip = ip;
    this.port = port;
    this.security = security;
}
```

In listing 2.16, you provided a default value of `8080` for the property port. Thus, if this `app.sbip.ct.port` property is not configured in the application, this default value is used. To learn more about `@ConfigurationProperties` annotation, you can refer to Spring Boot documentation available at http://mng.bz/mxer.

2.3 Executing code on Spring Boot application startup

At times, you'll need to execute custom code at Spring Boot application startup. For instance, you may want to execute a database initialization script before the application finishes its initialization or consume a REST service to load data for your application.

The `CommandLineRunner` and `ApplicationRunner` are two Spring Boot interfaces that provide a single `run(..)` method and are invoked just before a Spring Boot application finishes its initialization. These methods are invoked only once at the time of the Spring Boot application startup.

In this section, you'll explore the use of the `CommandLineRunner` interface in a Spring Boot application. The `ApplicationRunner` interface is quite similar to the `CommandLineRunner` interface, and we will leave it as an exercise for you to try yourself.

2.3.1 Technique: Using CommandLineRunner to execute code at Spring Boot application startup

In this technique, we'll introduce you to the `CommandLineRunner`.

PROBLEM

You want to use `CommandLineRunner` to execute some application initialization code at the Spring Boot application startup.

SOLUTION

You can configure `CommandLineRunner` in several ways. The following list shows the approaches to configure a `CommandLineRunner` in a Spring Boot application:

- In the Spring Boot main class that implements the `CommandLineRunner` interface
- By providing the `CommandLineRunner` implementation as a bean definition using the `@Bean` annotation
- By providing the `CommandLineRunner` as a Spring Component using the `@Component` annotation

> **Source code**
> The final version of the Spring Boot project is available at http://mng.bz/5KBB.

In this technique, you'll see the aforementioned `CommandLineRunner` configuration approaches with examples. After creating or importing the Spring Boot project, implement the `CommandLineRunner` interface in your Spring Boot main class, as shown in the following listing.

Listing 2.17 The CommandLineRunner implementation in Spring Boot Main Class

```
package com.manning.sbip.ch02;
//imports

@SpringBootApplication
public class CourseTrackerApplication implements CommandLineRunner  {

    protected final Log logger = LogFactory.getLog(getClass());

    public static void main(String[] args) {
        SpringApplication.run(CourseTrackerApplication.class, args);
    }
    @Override
    public void run(String... args) throws Exception {
        logger.info("CourseTrackerApplication CommandLineRunner has
➥ executed");
    }
}
```

Provides an implementation of the run(..) method of ComandLineRunner interface and prints a log statement in the console

To keep the example simple, you are logging a statement in the console. Once the Spring Boot application starts, it logs the statement in the console, as shown in figure 2.1.

You can also define a `CommandLineRunner` as a Spring `@Bean` definition, as shown in listing 2.18.

```
main] c.m.sbip.ch02.CourseTrackerApplication   : Starting CourseTrackerApplication using Java 17.0.1 on DESKTOP-VBH5P79 with
main] c.m.sbip.ch02.CourseTrackerApplication   : No active profile set, falling back to default profiles: default
main] o.s.b.w.embedded.tomcat.TomcatWebServer  : Tomcat initialized with port(s): 8080 (http)
main] o.apache.catalina.core.StandardService   : Starting service [Tomcat]
main] org.apache.catalina.core.StandardEngine  : Starting Servlet engine: [Apache Tomcat/9.0.56]
main] o.a.c.c.C.[Tomcat].[localhost].[/]       : Initializing Spring embedded WebApplicationContext
main] w.s.c.ServletWebServerApplicationContext : Root WebApplicationContext: initialization completed in 1905 ms
main] o.s.b.w.embedded.tomcat.TomcatWebServer  : Tomcat started on port(s): 8080 (http) with context path ''
main] c.m.sbip.ch02.CourseTrackerApplication   : Started CourseTrackerApplication in 3.307 seconds (JVM running for 3.981)
main] c.m.s.c.commandline.MyCommandLineRunner  : MyCommandLineRunner executed as a Spring Component
main] c.m.s.c.c.AnotherCommandLineRunner       : AnotherCommandLineRunner executed as a Spring Component
main] ication$$EnhancerBySpringCGLIB$$2ad733de : CourseTrackerApplication CommandLineRunner has executed
main] ication$$EnhancerBySpringCGLIB$$2ad733de : CommandLineRunner executed as a bean definition with 0 arguments
```

Figure 2.1 The log statement defined in the CommandLineRunner is printed in the IntelliJ IDEA console log.

Listing 2.18 CommandLineRunner implementation as a Spring Bean

```
package com.manning.sbip.ch02;

//imports

@SpringBootApplication
public class CourseTrackerApplication {

    protected final Logger logger = LoggerFactory.getLogger(getClass());

    public static void main(String[] args) {
        SpringApplication.run(CourseTrackerApplication.class, args);
    }
    @Bean
    public CommandLineRunner commandLineRunner() {
        return args -> {
            logger.info("CommandLineRunner executed as a bean definition with
     "+args.length+" arguments");
            for(int i=0; i<args.length;i++){
                logger.info("Argument: "+args[i]);
            }
        };

    }
}
```

Defines a CommandLineRunner bean. Once the application starts, this bean is loaded and prints the log statement in the console.

In listing 2.18, you defined a Spring bean that provides an implementation of the `CommandLineRunner` interface through a Java lambda expression. This is possible because `CommandLineRunner` is a functional interface with a single method called `run(String... args)`. The `run()` method accepts a String `varargs`. You can supply the command line arguments and access these inside the `commandLineRunner` bean implementation. To supply arguments, you can use the IDE to pass the arguments. Besides, you can package the application using the `mvn package` command and run using the `java -jar <appname> <args>` command. For instance, you can run the `java`

-jar command-line-runner-0.0.1-SNAPSHOT.jar Spring command where Spring is the argument that will be passed to the CommandLineRunner.

This @Bean implementation produces the same result as the previous implements alternative shown in listing 2.17. The benefit of this approach is that you are not forced to implement the CommandLineRunner interface.

So far, you've provided the CommandLineRunner implementation in the Spring Boot main class. However, you can also provide a CommandLineRunner implementation in a separate class and annotate it with Spring's @Component annotation. This approach ensures that the CommandLineRunner specific code is segregated in a separate Java file and not cluttered in the Spring Boot main class.

> **The @Bean and @Component annotation**
>
> Both @Bean and @Component annotation let you instruct Spring to create instances of the annotated class, but their usage is slightly different. You typically use @Bean annotation for the classes for which you don't have access to the source code. Thus, you define a bean and return a new instance of the class. For @Component annotation, as you have access to the source Java file, you can simply annotate the class with this annotation.

The following listing shows a simple CommandLineRunner implementation that logs a statement in the console log.

Listing 2.19 CommandLineRunner implementation as a Spring Component

```
package com.manning.sbip.ch02.commandline;

//imports

@Order(1)
@Component
public class MyCommandLineRunner implements CommandLineRunner {

    protected final Logger logger = LogFactory.getLogger(getClass());

    @Override
    public void run(String... args) throws Exception {
        logger.info("MyCommandLineRunner executed as a Spring Component");
    }
}
```

The Order annotation defines the sorting order of the annotated component. For instance, if you have multiple CommandLineRunner instances, you can use the Order annotation to specify their execution order.

The Spring Boot component scan can detect this component and create an instance of MyCommandLineRunner class. If you start the application, you can see the configured log statement in the console.

You can also configure multiple CommandLineRunner implementations and decide the execution order based on the @Order annotation. Notice that the Order(1) annotation is specified in listing 2.19. For instance, the following listing shows another `CommandLineRunner` implementation that is ordered with order value two.

Listing 2.20 CommandLineRunner implementation with execution order two

```
package com.manning.sbip.ch02.commandline;

//imports

@Order(2)
@Component
public class AnotherCommandLineRunner implements CommandLineRunner {

    protected final Logger logger = LogFactory.getLogger(getClass());

    @Override
    public void run(String... args) throws Exception {
        logger.info("AnotherCommandLineRunner executed as a Spring
➥ Component");
    }
}
```

If you start the application, you can see that both the log statements are printed in the console based on their defined order, as shown in figure 2.2.

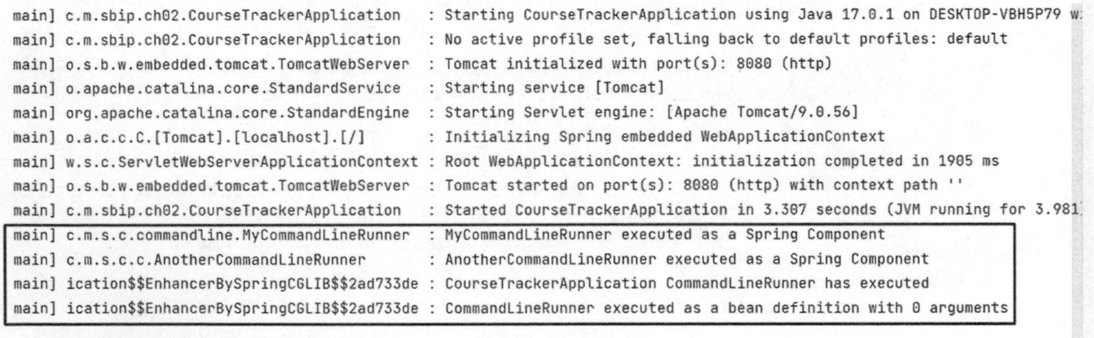

```
main] c.m.sbip.ch02.CourseTrackerApplication    : Starting CourseTrackerApplication using Java 17.0.1 on DESKTOP-VBH5P79 w
main] c.m.sbip.ch02.CourseTrackerApplication    : No active profile set, falling back to default profiles: default
main] o.s.b.w.embedded.tomcat.TomcatWebServer   : Tomcat initialized with port(s): 8080 (http)
main] o.apache.catalina.core.StandardService    : Starting service [Tomcat]
main] org.apache.catalina.core.StandardEngine   : Starting Servlet engine: [Apache Tomcat/9.0.56]
main] o.a.c.c.C.[Tomcat].[localhost].[/]        : Initializing Spring embedded WebApplicationContext
main] w.s.c.ServletWebServerApplicationContext : Root WebApplicationContext: initialization completed in 1905 ms
main] o.s.b.w.embedded.tomcat.TomcatWebServer   : Tomcat started on port(s): 8080 (http) with context path ''
main] c.m.sbip.ch02.CourseTrackerApplication    : Started CourseTrackerApplication in 3.307 seconds (JVM running for 3.981
main] c.m.s.c.commandline.MyCommandLineRunner   : MyCommandLineRunner executed as a Spring Component
main] c.m.s.c.c.AnotherCommandLineRunner        : AnotherCommandLineRunner executed as a Spring Component
main] ication$$EnhancerBySpringCGLIB$$2ad733de : CourseTrackerApplication CommandLineRunner has executed
main] ication$$EnhancerBySpringCGLIB$$2ad733de : CommandLineRunner executed as a bean definition with 0 arguments
```

Figure 2.2 Log statements printed in the IntelliJ IDEA console log, as defined in multiple CommandLineRunner implementations

DISCUSSION

The `CommandLineRunner` is a useful feature that is frequently used to perform several application initialization activities. In a `CommandLineRunner` implementation, you also have access to the command line arguments through the `args` parameter. Thus, you can control the `CommandLineRunner` implementation behavior externally through the supplied arguments.

In a `CommandLineRunner` implementation you can also autowire any dependency using Spring's dependency injection mechanism. Since a `CommandLineRunner` implementation runs when the Spring Boot application almost finishes its initialization, all bean definitions are available for autowire. Hence, you can autowire any bean dependency in your `CommandLineRunner` implementation.

For example, in the upcoming techniques when you'll learn the Spring Data repository, you'll see the use of the `CourseRepository` interface as a dependency on the `CommandLineRunner` implementation. The following listing shows an example.

Listing 2.21 CommandLineRunner implementation from the Spring Boot main class

```
@Bean
public CommandLineRunner printCourses(CourseRepository courseRepository) {
    return args -> {
        System.out.println("============ Course Details
➥ ================");
        courseRepository.findAll().forEach(System.out::println);
    };
}
```

CommandLineRunner Bean definition. The CourseRepository is injected via Spring dependency injection.

We'll explain the Spring Data repository in detail in chapter 3. For now, understand that an instance of `CourseRepository` will be automatically provided by Spring Boot in `printCourses()` method.

SUMMARY

With this technique, you've seen three variations on the usage of a `CommandLineRunner` implementation:

- By implementing the `CommandLineRunner` interface directly in the Spring Boot application and providing an implementation of the `run()` method
- By defining the `CommandLineRunner` as a Spring bean definition using the `@Bean` annotation
- By defining the `CommandLineRunner` as a Spring component using the `@Component` annotation

The first approach is limited, as it lets you define only one `CommandLineRunner` implementation, and there are no execution ordering capabilities. The other two approaches are flexible, as they let you specify the execution order. The third approach allows you to segregate the `CommandLineRunner` implementation away from the Spring Boot main class and provides better code organization.

2.4 Customizing logging in a Spring Boot application

Logging is an essential aspect of an application. A log contains important events of application activity and provides useful information on application behavior. Based on the logging configuration, log statements can be logged in various mediums, such as in the console, files, and database. However, console and file-based logging are the dominant logging types and are most frequently used in an application.

In this section, you'll first understand and explore the default Spring Boot logging mechanism. We'll then explore how to customize the logging in your Spring Boot application with other logging frameworks.

2.4.1 Technique: Understanding and customizing default Spring Boot logging in a Spring Boot application

In this technique, we'll discuss Spring Boot default logging mechanisms and configurations for customizing logging in a Spring Boot application.

PROBLEM

You want to understand and customize the default logging in a Spring Boot application.

SOLUTION

By default, Spring Boot provides a console logging facility for all Spring Boot applications. This console log prints the log statements in the command prompt or terminal at application startup or when you perform any other activity in the application for which logging is enabled.

> **Source code**
> The final version of the Spring Boot project is available at http://mng.bz/6Zdo.

Spring Boot uses the Apache commons logging framework (https://commons.apache.org/proper/commons-logging/) for its internal logging purposes. It also supports other popular logging frameworks, such as Logback (http://logback.qos.ch/), Log4j2 (https://logging.apache.org/log4j/2.x/), and java.util.logging.

If you are using any of the Spring Boot starter dependencies, then by default Spring Boot uses the Logback logging framework. This is because Spring Boot starter dependencies have a transitive dependency with `spring-boot-starter-logging` starter dependency, which includes the Logback dependencies. The following listing shows the Logback dependencies internally used by Spring Boot.

Listing 2.22 Spring Boot starter logging dependencies

```
<dependencies>                                  <-- Spring Boot Starter
    <dependency>                                    Logging dependencies
        <groupId>ch.qos.logback</groupId>
        <artifactId>logback-classic</artifactId>
    </dependency>
    <dependency>
        <groupId>org.slf4j</groupId>
        <artifactId>jul-to-slf4j</artifactId>
    </dependency>
    <dependency>
        <groupId>org.slf4j</groupId>
```

```
        <artifactId>log4j-over-slf4j</artifactId>
    </dependency>
</dependencies>
```

Once the project setup is done, you can start the application using the IDE's launch option or by using the `mvn spring-boot:run` Maven command. You can see the startup log in the console, as shown in figure 2.3.

```
  .   ____          _            __ _ _
 /\\ / ___'_ __ _ _(_)_ __  __ _ \ \ \ \
( ( )\___ | '_ | '_| | '_ \/ _` | \ \ \ \
 \\/  ___)| |_)| | | | | || (_| |  ) ) ) )
  '  |____| .__|_| |_|_| |_\__, | / / / /
 =========|_|==============|___/=/_/_/_/
 :: Spring Boot ::                (v2.6.3)

27-02-2022 17:42:52.145 28504 [main] [INFO ] c.m.sbip.ch02.CourseTrackerApplication   Starting CourseTrackerApplication usin
27-02-2022 17:42:52.161 28504 [main] [INFO ] c.m.sbip.ch02.CourseTrackerApplication   No active profile set, falling back to
27-02-2022 17:42:53.669 28504 [main] [INFO ] o.s.b.w.embedded.tomcat.TomcatWebServer  Tomcat initialized with port(s): 8080
27-02-2022 17:42:53.682 28504 [main] [INFO ] o.apache.catalina.core.StandardService   Starting service [Tomcat]
27-02-2022 17:42:53.687 28504 [main] [INFO ] org.apache.catalina.core.StandardEngine  Starting Servlet engine: [Apache Tomca
27-02-2022 17:42:53.788 28504 [main] [INFO ] o.a.c.c.C.[Tomcat].[localhost].[/]       Initializing Spring embedded WebApplic
27-02-2022 17:42:53.788 28504 [main] [INFO ] w.s.c.ServletWebServerApplicationContext Root WebApplicationContext: initializa
27-02-2022 17:42:54.617 28504 [main] [INFO ] o.s.b.w.embedded.tomcat.TomcatWebServer  Tomcat started on port(s): 8080 (http)
27-02-2022 17:42:54.640 28504 [main] [INFO ] c.m.sbip.ch02.CourseTrackerApplication   Started CourseTrackerApplication in 3.
```

Figure 2.3 Various components of Spring Boot startup logs logged in the console

This console log should be familiar to you if you are following any of the techniques discussed so far. Let us now understand various parts of the console log. Figure 2.3 shows the different elements of the logged message.

Following are the various elements of a log statement:

- *Date and time*—Date and time of logging.
- *Log level*—Logging level. Possible values include `FATAL`, `ERROR`, `WARN`, `INFO`, `DEBUG`, and `TRACE`. A logging level demonstrates the importance of the log statement. For instance, any log statement logged with `FATAL` or `ERROR` indicate some serious issues in the application processing, whereas `INFO` or `DEBUG`, for example, indicate typical regular application activities, which you can likely ignore.
- *Process ID*—Process ID of the application.
- *Separator*—A separator (`---`) to indicate the start of the actual log messages.
- *Thread name*—Name of a thread performing the logging. A Spring Boot application contains multiple threads. Some of the threads could be application threads, and you might be starting a few threads for various reasons. For instance, if you are executing asynchronous processing capabilities of Spring Boot, you can create a `TaskExecutor` and assign a name for the threads of the underlying

thread pool. Thus, in such cases, you'll see the custom thread name as you've configured.

- *Logger name*—Abbreviated source class name.
- *Message*—The actual log message.

Now that you've seen various parts of a log statement, let's understand how these parts are configured. The following listing shows the logging pattern used in figure 2.3.

Listing 2.23 Default logging pattern

```
%clr(%d{${LOG_DATEFORMAT_PATTERN:yyyy-MM-dd HH:mm:ss.SSS}}){faint}
%clr(${LOG_LEVEL_PATTERN:-%5p}) %clr(${PID:- }){magenta} %clr(---){faint}
%clr([%15.15t]){faint} %clr(%-40.40logger{39}){cyan} %clr(:){faint}
%m%n${LOG_EXCEPTION_CONVERSION_WORD:%wEx}
```

Default logging pattern used in Spring Boot console logging

The `%clr` is a conversion word that is used to configure the color-coding. Spring Boot uses the `org.springframework.boot.logging.logback.ColorConverter` class for this purpose. For example, `%clr(${PID:- }){magenta}` prints the process ID in `magenta` color. This default logging pattern is specified in the Spring Boot Logback logging configuration file.

You can customize the default logging pattern with a different logging format. For example, the following listing shows a custom logging pattern by configuring the `logging.pattern.console` property in the application.properties file.

Listing 2.24 Custom logging pattern in the application.properties file

```
logging.pattern.console=%clr(%d{dd-MM-yyyy HH:mm:ss.SSS}){yellow}
%clr(${PID:- }){green} %magenta([%thread]) %highlight([%-5level])
%clr(%-40.40logger{39}){cyan} %msg%n
```

Configuring a custom logging pattern in a Spring Boot application

If you restart the application, you will notice a different logging format printed in the console.

Appender and logger in logging

If you are new to logging, there are a few terminologies you should be aware of:

- *Logger*—A logger is a logging framework component that is responsible for logging the log messages using one or more appenders. You can define several loggers with various logging levels based on your need.

- *Appender*—An appender in a logging framework primarily decides two main things: where the log messages should go and what should be the logging format. Based on the destination of the log messages, there are several appender types. For example, a console appender logs the messages in the underlying application's console. A file appender allows the log messages to be written into a file. A special type of file appender, RollingFileAppender performs additional tasks, such as managing the log file by rolling it over based on time and date. An SMTP appender lets you email the log messages to an email address.

By default, Spring Boot logs statements with `INFO`, `WARN`, and `ERROR` levels. If you need other logging levels, such as `TRACE`, or `DEBUG`, you can configure the associated properties in the application.properties file. For instance, to enable `debug` statements, you can configure `debug=true` in the application.properties file. Similarly, you can enable `trace` mode by configuring `trace=true` in the application.properties file.

Although console logging works well in development time, in a production application, you need the application log statements in a file, so the file can be referred to in the future. Moreover, logging into a file is not enough. You also need to maintain the log files based on the file `size` and `duration` (i.e., what should be the size of a log file and how long you would continue writing into an existing log file).

There are the size- and time-based policies to roll over the log file to a new file. For example, you may decide to roll over to a new log file once your current log file reaches a certain size (e.g., 10 MB). You could also roll over to a new log file daily irrespective of the log file size. You'll see an example of such policies shortly, but before that, let's see how to write the log contents into a file in a Spring Boot application.

The easiest way to configure logging in a file is by configuring the `logging.file.name` or `logging.file.path` properties in the application.properties file. The `logging.file.name` property lets you specify a log file name where the logging should be made. Let's configure the `logging.file.name=application.log` property in the application.properties file.

If you want to configure the log file into a directory other than the project root directory, you can specify the `logging.file.path` property with the path value. For example, configuring `logging.file.path=C:/sbip/logs` generates a log file named spring.log into C:/sbip/logs directory. Note that you can configure the `logging.file.name` or `logging.file.path` properties at any point in time. Let's configure the `logging.file.path` in the application.properties file, as shown in the following listing.

Listing 2.25 Updated application.properties file

```
logging.pattern.console=%clr(%d{dd-MM-yyyy HH:mm:ss.SSS}){yellow}
%clr(${PID:- }){green} %magenta([%thread]) %highlight([%-5level])
%clr(%-40.40logger{39}){cyan} %msg%n

logging.file.path=C:\\sbip\\logs
```

Custom logging pattern (annotates the `logging.pattern.console` lines)

Log file path (annotates the `logging.file.path` line)

By default, Spring Boot backs up the current log file and rolls over to the next log file when the file size reaches 10 MB or the log file is seven days old. You can control these behaviors using the `logging.logback.rollingpolicy.max-file-size` and `logging.logback.rollingpolicy.max-history` properties, respectively. We encourage you to configure these parameters in the application.properties file and notice the changes in the log file.

DISCUSSION

Using this technique, you've learned the default logging configurations in Spring Boot. You've seen how to configure and manage file-based logging with Spring Boot-provided parameters. You can read more about Spring Boot logging features in the Spring Boot documentation available at http://mng.bz/oaOd.

Although Logback logging works fine with a Spring Boot project, you might be interested to configure other major logging frameworks in your Spring Boot application. There could be various reasons to do this. For instance, you are comfortable and familiar with other logging frameworks such as Log4j2 (https://logging.apache.org/log4j/2.x/), or your organization might have a preference towards a specific logging framework. Let us demonstrate how you can exclude the default Logback configuration and configure an alternate logging framework. In the next technique, you'll configure the Log4j2 logging framework in your Spring Boot application.

2.4.2 Technique: Using Log4j2 to configure logging in a Spring Boot application

In this technique, we'll demonstrate how to use Log4j2 logging in a Spring Boot application.

PROBLEM

You need to configure Log4j2 as the logging framework in your Spring Boot application.

SOLUTION

Configuring Log4j2 in a Spring Boot application is straightforward. To start with, you need to exclude the default `spring-boot-starter-logging` dependency and provide the Log4j2 starter dependency in your build configuration file. You can then provide the Log4j2 logging configuration either in properties, XML, YAML, or JSON format for Spring Boot to load and configure the logging. Using this technique, we'll use XML to define the logging configuration.

> **Source code**
>
> The final version of the Spring Boot project is available at http://mng.bz/nYpa.

If you are continuing with the Spring Boot project from the previous technique, then you need to perform two additional changes to start with the Log4j2 logging configuration:

- Remove all the logging configurations you've added to the application.properties file. You can remove all properties that start with the logging prefix.
- You also need to exclude the `spring-boot-starter-logging` dependency from the `spring-boot-starter-web` dependency in the pom.xml file. You then need to add the `spring-boot-starter-log4j2` dependency. The following listing shows these configuration changes.

Listing 2.26 Adding Log4j2 starter dependency and excluding default starter logging

```
<dependencies>                    <-- Excluding the default Logback dependency
    <dependency>                      and including the Log4j2 dependency
        <groupId>org.springframework.boot</groupId>
        <artifactId>spring-boot-starter-web</artifactId>
        <exclusions>
            <exclusion>
                <groupId>org.springframework.boot</groupId>
                <artifactId>spring-boot-starter-logging</artifactId>
            </exclusion>
        </exclusions>
    </dependency>
    <dependency>
        <groupId>org.springframework.boot</groupId>
        <artifactId>spring-boot-starter-log4j2</artifactId>
    </dependency>

    // Other dependencies
</dependencies>
```

The above pom.xml changes ensure that Logback-related dependencies are removed and Log4j2 dependencies are available in the classpath.

You can provide Log4j2 configurations, such as appender, loggers, and associated configurations, in an XML or a YML file. This XML configuration needs to be created in the src\main\resources folder with the name log4j2.xml or log4j2-spring.xml. This configuration file wraps the complete logging configuration to be used in your Spring Boot application. Although Spring Boot provides both the options to define the configurations with either log4j2.xml or log4j2-spring.xml files, it recommends using the latter one wherever possible. This is because Spring Boot can have better control over the logging initialization (http://mng.bz/vom7). The following listing shows a sample log4j2.xml configuration.

Listing 2.27 Sample Log4j2 XML configuration

```
<?xml version="1.0" encoding="UTF-8"?>
<Configuration status="WARN">        <-- The root element of a Log4j2 configuration
                                         file. The status attribute represents the level
                                         of internal log4j2 events. It is set to WARN
                                         in this configuration.
```

A file appender configuration that logs the log statements in a file with a provided file name and pattern. It also provides additional configuration, such as how to manage the file over a period.

Defines common placeholders that can be used in other places in the XML file. You've defined the LOG_PATTERN property here.

```
    <Properties>
        <Property name="LOG_PATTERN">
            %d{yyyy-MM-dd HH:mm:ss.SSS} [%5p] [%15.15t] %-40.40c{1.} :
➥ %m%n%ex
        </Property>
    </Properties>

    <Appenders>
        <Console name="ConsoleAppender" target="SYSTEM_OUT">
            <PatternLayout pattern="${LOG_PATTERN}" />
       </Console>

        <RollingFile name="FileAppender"

                         fileName="logs/application-log4j2.log"
                         filePattern="logs/application-log4j2-%d{yyyy-MM-dd}-
➥ %i.log">
            <PatternLayout>
                <Pattern>${LOG_PATTERN}</Pattern>
            </PatternLayout>
            <Policies>
                <SizeBasedTriggeringPolicy size="10MB" />
                <TimeBasedTriggeringPolicy interval="7" />
            </Policies>
            <DefaultRolloverStrategy max="10"/>
        </RollingFile>
    </Appenders>
    <Loggers>
        <Logger name="com.manning.sbip" level="debug" additivity="false">
            <AppenderRef ref="FileAppender"/>
        </Logger>
        <Logger name="org.springframework.boot" level="info"
 additivity="false">
            <AppenderRef ref="ConsoleAppender"/>
        </Logger>
        <Root level="info">
            <AppenderRef ref="FileAppender"/>
            <AppenderRef ref="ConsoleAppender"/>
        </Root>
    </Loggers>
</Configuration>
```

List of appenders

A console appender configuration that logs the log statements in console/terminal/command prompt.

Rolls the current log file once its size reaches 10 MB

Rolls the current log file after 7 days

Maximum 10 backup log files can be kept

The list of loggers that logs the log statements using the provide appender

A logger that runs in DEBUG logging level. It uses the underlying file appender to log all log events generated from com.manning.sbip and its subpackages.

A logger that runs in INFO logging level and logs events from org.springframeworg.boot and its subpackages

Root logger runs in INFO logging level

You can refer to the inline documentation to understand various configuration parameters. Log4j2 is a powerful and feature-rich logging framework. The above configuration represents the basic logging configuration that is needed to demonstrate Log4j2 integration with Spring Boot.

Let us add the `CommandLineRunner` implementation in the Spring Boot main class to include log statements instead of the system out statements. The following listing shows the modified Spring Boot main class.

Listing 2.28 Spring Boot main class with updated CommandLineRunner implementation

```
package com.manning.sbip.ch02;

//imports

@SpringBootApplication
public class CourseTrackerApplication {

    private static Logger logger =
➥ LoggerFactory.getLogger(CourseTrackerApplication.class);

    public static void main(String[] args) {
        SpringApplication.run(CourseTrackerApplication.class, args);
        logger.info("CourseTrackerApplication started successfully with
➥ Log4j2 configuration");
    }
}
```

You can find the modified code in bold font. There are two main changes you've achieved with this code:

- The first change you've made is creating a logger instance using the `getLogger` method of `LoggerFactory` class. If you look into the import statements, you can find that the imported `LoggerFactory` class is from the SLF4j library. Simple Logging Facade for Java (SLF4J) provides an abstraction for various logging frameworks that allows you to plug in the preferred logging framework (e.g., Log4j2) at build time. You can learn more about SLF4j at http://www.slf4j.org/.
- The next change is that, instead of using the system out statements, you are using the newly created logger instance to log the messages.

If you start the application, you can find the application-log4j2.log log file is generated in the logs folder of your project's root directory. You can see that the configured log message is printed along with other application startup log statements.

DISCUSSION

In this technique, you've learned to configure one of the most popular and widely used logging frameworks of the Java ecosystem. The Log4j2 logging framework is one of the stable logging frameworks and offers a lot of useful features. You can refer to the Log4j2 reference manual (https://logging.apache.org/log4j/2.x/manual) to learn more about this logging framework.

As an exercise, we encourage you to play around with the Log4j2 configuration; its various parameters, such as log levels; various other appender types, such as JDBC appender; filters; and other offerings. For instance, to see how the size-based trigger policy and default rollover strategy works, you can change the `SizeBasedTriggeringPolicy` to a smaller size in the Log4j2 XML configuration file. You can then generate more log messages from your Java files. You'll notice how log files are rolled over once they meet the defined criteria.

2.5 Validate user data using Bean Validation

It is often a requirement to validate the user input data to make sure it meets the business requirement. For instance, you may want to validate certain fields for nonempty or check the minimum and the maximum lengths of the values allowed for that field. You may also want to implement a custom validation on the user data. For example, it might be possible that you want to implement a custom password validation rule for the user-supplied password.

Bean Validation (https://beanvalidation.org/) is the de facto standard for implementing such validations in the Java ecosystem. This Java specification allows you to express validations in terms of simple annotations. Moreover, it also allows you to define custom validators in an extensible manner. Hibernate Validator (http://hibernate.org/validator) is the reference implementation of the Bean Validation specification.

Spring Boot provides seamless integration with the Bean Validation framework with a Spring Boot starter dependency. It provides a `spring-boot-starter-validation` dependency that allows you to use Hibernate Validator in your application.

2.5.1 Technique: Using built-in Bean Validation annotations to validate business entity in a Spring Boot application

In this technique, we'll discuss how to use bean validation to validate the business entities.

Problem

You want to validate business entities using the Java Bean Validation framework in your Spring Boot application.

Solution

Let us demonstrate the usage of bean validation in Spring Boot with an example.

> **Source Code**
>
> The final version of the Spring Boot project is available at http://mng.bz/4jlw.

In this Maven project, we've added the `spring-boot-starter-validation` dependency, as shown in the following listing.

Listing 2.29 Spring Boot starter validation Maven dependency

```
<dependency>
    <groupId>org.springframework.boot</groupId>
    <artifactId>spring-boot-starter-validation</artifactId>
</dependency>
```

To start with, let us add a new entity named `Course`. A course contains an `id`, `name`, `category`, `rating`, and `description`, as shown in the following listing.

Listing 2.30 The course entity

```
package com.manning.sbip.ch02.model;

import javax.validation.constraints.Min;
import javax.validation.constraints.Max;

public class Course {

    private long id;
    private String name;
    private String category;

    @Min(value = 1, message = "A course should have a minimum of 1 rating")
    @Max(value = 5, message = "A course should have a maximum of 5 rating")
    private int rating;

    private String description;

    // Constructor, Getter, and Setters
}
```

We've additionally added two validations for the `rating` field. A rating can have a minimum value of `1` and a maximum value of `5`. If these constraints are not satisfied, then the message defined in the annotation is displayed as an error message. Let's validate these constraints by defining a `CommandLineRunner`, as shown in the following listing.

Listing 2.31 The Spring Boot main class with CommandLineRunner implementation

```
package com.manning.sbip.ch02;

//imports

@SpringBootApplication
public class CourseTrackerApplication implements CommandLineRunner {

    private static Logger logger =
➥ LoggerFactory.getLogger(CourseTrackerApplication.class);
    public static void main(String[] args) {
        SpringApplication.run(CourseTrackerApplication.class, args);
    }

    @Override
    public void run(String... args) throws Exception {
        Course course = new Course();
        course.setId(1);
        course.setRating(0);
        Validator validator =
➥ Validation.buildDefaultValidatorFactory().getValidator();
        Set<ConstraintViolation<Course>> violations =
➥ validator.validate(course);
```

Create a course with a rating of 0, which violates the minimum constraint defined for the rating field.

Get an instance of Validator that validates the bean instances. In this example, it will validate the course entity.

Validate all defined constraints in the course object and return the constraint violations if any.

```
        violations.forEach(courseConstraintViolation -> logger.error("A
➥ constraint violation has occurred. Violation details: [{}].",
➥ courseConstraintViolation));
    }
}
```

Log each constraint violation in the console.

In listing 2.31, you created a course and set the course `rating` value to `0`. Besides, you are obtaining an instance of the `validator` and supplying the course instance to it for constraint validation. The validator validates and returns the set of constraint violations in the supplied object. In this example, the `@Min` constraint validation is violated, and the associated `ConstraintViolation` is returned. We then log this validation error in the console.

If you run the application, you can find that, once the application starts successfully, the `CommandLineRunner` is executed, and the `ConstraintViolation` error message is logged in the console, as shown in figure 2.4.

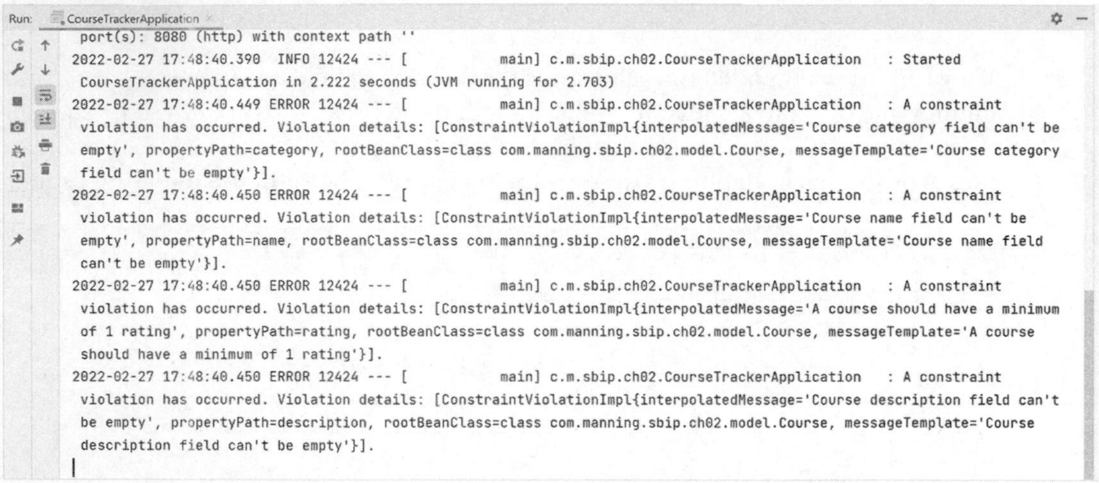

```
Run: CourseTrackerApplication
port(s): 8080 (http) with context path ''
2022-02-27 17:48:40.390  INFO 12424 --- [           main] c.m.sbip.ch02.CourseTrackerApplication   : Started
CourseTrackerApplication in 2.222 seconds (JVM running for 2.703)
2022-02-27 17:48:40.449 ERROR 12424 --- [           main] c.m.sbip.ch02.CourseTrackerApplication   : A constraint
violation has occurred. Violation details: [ConstraintViolationImpl{interpolatedMessage='Course category field can't be
empty', propertyPath=category, rootBeanClass=class com.manning.sbip.ch02.model.Course, messageTemplate='Course category
field can't be empty'}].
2022-02-27 17:48:40.450 ERROR 12424 --- [           main] c.m.sbip.ch02.CourseTrackerApplication   : A constraint
violation has occurred. Violation details: [ConstraintViolationImpl{interpolatedMessage='Course name field can't be
empty', propertyPath=name, rootBeanClass=class com.manning.sbip.ch02.model.Course, messageTemplate='Course name field
can't be empty'}].
2022-02-27 17:48:40.450 ERROR 12424 --- [           main] c.m.sbip.ch02.CourseTrackerApplication   : A constraint
violation has occurred. Violation details: [ConstraintViolationImpl{interpolatedMessage='A course should have a minimum
of 1 rating', propertyPath=rating, rootBeanClass=class com.manning.sbip.ch02.model.Course, messageTemplate='A course
should have a minimum of 1 rating'}].
2022-02-27 17:48:40.450 ERROR 12424 --- [           main] c.m.sbip.ch02.CourseTrackerApplication   : A constraint
violation has occurred. Violation details: [ConstraintViolationImpl{interpolatedMessage='Course description field can't
be empty', propertyPath=description, rootBeanClass=class com.manning.sbip.ch02.model.Course, messageTemplate='Course
description field can't be empty'}].
```

Figure 2.4 The @min constraint violation error message

DISCUSSION

Bean Validation allows you to specify and validate application constraints. You've already noticed how it allows you to specify the constraints in terms of annotations with the ability to configure custom error messages. Table 2.1 provides some of the commonly used annotations defined in the Hibernate Validator API. Note that Hibernate Validator (https://hibernate.org/validator) is the Bean Validation reference implementation and used by Spring Boot for bean validation.

Refer to http://mng.bz/QWJG for a list of supported Hibernate Validator constraints and their usage.

Table 2.1 Hibernate Validator annotations to validate field-level constraints

Annotation	Purpose
`@NotBlank`	Checks for non-null of the annotated character sequence. Supported only in a `CharSequence` field.
`@NotEmpty`	Checks for non-null or empty of the annotated character sequence. Supported only in `CharSequence`, `Collection`, `Map`, and `arrays`.
`@NotNull`	Checks whether the annotated value is non-null. Supported in any data type.
`@Min(value=)`	Checks whether the annotated value is higher than or equal to the specified minimum value.
`@Max(value=)`	Checks whether the annotated value is lower than or equal to the specified maximum value.
`@Pattern(regex=, flags=)`	Checks if the annotated string matches the regular expression `regex` considering the given `flags` match.
`@Size(min=, max=)`	Checks if the annotated element's size is between min and max (inclusive) value.
`@Email`	Checks whether the specified character sequence is a valid email address.

Although built-in annotations work well in most of the scenarios, sometimes you might need custom constraint validations. For instance, you might need to check whether a supplied character sequence is a valid IP address. You can also apply additional constraints for a password supplied by your application users. In the next technique, you'll learn how to implement and use a custom constraint using the Bean Validation framework in your Spring Boot application.

2.5.2 *Technique: Defining and using custom Bean Validation annotation to validate a POJO in a Spring Boot application*

In this technique, we'll learn how to define custom annotations and use those to perform validation of business entities.

PROBLEM

You want to define a custom annotation and use it to validate a POJO in a Spring Boot application.

SOLUTION

In the previous technique, you used the built-in Bean Validation annotations to apply constraints in business entities. In this technique, you'll learn how to implement a custom annotation with a custom validator to implement business-specific constraints in your entities.

To demonstrate how to define a custom constraint, you'll use a `User` POJO that has a username and a password. Typically, organizations define custom password policies that their users need to adhere to. In this example, you'll implement a custom annotation that validates the passwords against the predefined password policy. In this example, you'll use the Passay (https://www.passay.org/) library to enforce the password rules.

> **Source code**
> The final version of the Spring Boot project is available at http://mng.bz/XWJv.

In this project, we've added the Passay Maven dependency in the pom.xml, as shown in the following listing.

Listing 2.32 Passay Maven dependency

```
<dependency>
    <groupId>org.passay</groupId>
    <artifactId>passay</artifactId>
    <version>1.6.0</version>
</dependency>
```

Before defining the custom validation annotation, you need to define the `ConstraintValidator` that is invoked to enforce the constraint. Let us define the `PasswordRuleValidator` class that contains the actual password validation logic, as shown in the following listing.

Listing 2.33 The PasswordRuleValidator

```
package com.manning.sbip.ch02.validation;
//imports

public class PasswordRuleValidator implements ConstraintValidator<Password,
➥ String> {

    private static final int MIN_COMPLEX_RULES = 2;
    private static final int MAX_REPETITIVE_CHARS = 3;
    private static final int MIN_SPECIAL_CASE_CHARS = 1;
    private static final int MIN_UPPER_CASE_CHARS = 1;
    private static final int MIN_LOWER_CASE_CHARS = 1;
    private static final int MIN_DIGIT_CASE_CHARS = 1;

    @Override
    public boolean isValid(String password, ConstraintValidatorContext
➥ context) {
        List<Rule> passwordRules = new ArrayList<>();
        passwordRules.add(new LengthRule(8, 30));
        CharacterCharacteristicsRule characterCharacteristicsRule  =
                new CharacterCharacteristicsRule(MIN_COMPLEX_RULES,
                        new CharacterRule(EnglishCharacterData.Special,
➥ MIN_SPECIAL_CASE_CHARS),
                        new CharacterRule(EnglishCharacterData.UpperCase,
➥ MIN_UPPER_CASE_CHARS),
```

```
                            new CharacterRule(EnglishCharacterData.LowerCase,
➥ MIN_LOWER_CASE_CHARS),
                            new CharacterRule(EnglishCharacterData.Digit,
➥ MIN_DIGIT_CASE_CHARS));
        passwordRules.add(characterCharacteristicsRule);
        passwordRules.add(new
➥ RepeatCharacterRegexRule(MAX_REPETITIVE_CHARS));
        PasswordValidator passwordValidator = new
➥ PasswordValidator(passwordRules);
        PasswordData passwordData = new PasswordData(password);
        RuleResult ruleResult = passwordValidator.validate(passwordData);
        return ruleResult.isValid();
    }
}
```

Let's discuss the code snippet shown in listing 2.33.

- This class implements the `ConstraintValidator` interface and provides an implementation of the `isValid()` method that contains the custom password validation logic. The `ConstraintValidator` interface is typed and accepts two arguments. The first argument defines the annotation (e.g., `Password`) on which the custom validator should be used. The second argument takes the data type of the value on which the custom annotation is applied. Thus, we've defined the `ConstraintValidator<Password, String>`.
- In the `isValid()` method, you've defined the custom policy against which the password should be validated. We've kept the password policy fairly simple. There is a length-based rule that enforces that the password length should be a minimum of 8 characters and a maximum of 30 characters. Besides, the policy expects the password should contain an upper case, a lower case, a digit, and should not be repetitive of a character more than three times.
- The `isValid()` method returns either `true` or `false` based on the defined validation logic.

Let's now define the `@Password` annotation that uses the `PasswordRuleValidator`, as shown in the following listing.

Listing 2.34 The @Password annotation

```
package com.manning.sbip.ch02.validation;

import javax.validation.Constraint;
import javax.validation.Payload;
import java.lang.annotation.ElementType;
import java.lang.annotation.Retention;
import java.lang.annotation.RetentionPolicy;
import java.lang.annotation.Target;

@Target({ElementType.METHOD, ElementType.FIELD})
@Retention(RetentionPolicy.RUNTIME)
@Constraint(validatedBy = PasswordRuleValidator.class)
```

```
public @interface Password {
    String message() default "Password do not adhere to the specified rule";
    Class<?>[] groups() default {};
    Class<? extends Payload>[] payload() default {};
}
```

Let's explore various parts of this annotation definition:

- The `@Target` annotation defines that this annotation applies to the `Method` and `Field`.
- The `@Retention` annotation defines how the `@Password` annotation is stored. You've used `RUNTIME`, so it can be used by the runtime environment.
- The `@Constraint` indicates that this annotation is a Bean Validation constraint. The element `validatedBy` specifies the classes implementing the constraint.
- The `message()` defines the message that needs to be displayed if the input data validation fails.
- The `Class<?>[] groups()` allow the developer to select to split the annotations into different groups to apply different validations to each group. We haven't defined any groups in this example.
- The `Class<? extends PayLoad>[] payLoad()` is typically used to carry metadata information consumed by a validation client. We haven't defined any payload in this example.

Let's now define the business model on which the `@Password` annotation is applied. The following listing shows the `User` POJO.

Listing 2.35 The User business entity

```
package com.manning.sbip.ch02.model;

import com.manning.sbip.ch02.validation.Password;

public class User {

    private String userName;

    @Password
    private String password;

    public User(String userName, String password) {
        this.userName = userName;
        this.password = password;
    }

    public String getUserName() {
        return userName;
    }

    public String getPassword() {
        return password;
    }
```

```
    @Override
    public String toString() {
        return "User{" +
                "userName='" + userName + '\'' +
                ", password='" + password + '\'' +
                '}';
    }
}
```

The User business entity has two fields: a username and password. The password field is annotated with the custom @Password annotation. Let us now create a few users and see how the custom annotation works. The following listing shows a CommandLine-Runner implementation that creates several users.

Listing 2.36 Spring Boot main class with a CommandLineRunner implementation

```
package com.manning.sbip.ch02;

//imports

@SpringBootApplication
public class CourseTrackerApplication implements CommandLineRunner {

    private static Logger logger =
➥ LoggerFactory.getLogger(CourseTrackerApplication.class);

    public static void main(String[] args) {
        SpringApplication.run(CourseTrackerApplication.class, args);
    }

    @Override
    public void run(String... args) throws Exception {
        User user1 = new User("sbip01", "sbip");
        Validator validator =
➥ Validation.buildDefaultValidatorFactory().getValidator();
        Set<ConstraintViolation<User>> violations =
➥ validator.validate(user1);
        logger.error("Password for user1 do not adhere to the password
➥ policy");
        violations.forEach(constraintViolation -> logger.error("Violation
➥ details: [{}].", constraintViolation.getMessage()));

        User user2 = new User("sbip02", "Sbip01$4UDfg");
        violations = validator.validate(user2);
        if(violations.isEmpty()) {
            logger.info("Password for user2 adhere to the password
➥ policy");
        }

        User user3 = new User("sbip03", "Sbip01$4UDfgggg");
        violations = validator.validate(user3);
        logger.error("Password for user3 violates maximum repetitive
➥ rule");
```

```
        violations.forEach(constraintViolation -> logger.error("Violation
➥ details: [{}].", constraintViolation.getMessage()));

        User user4 = new User("sbip04", "Sbip014UDfgggg");
        violations = validator.validate(user4);
        logger.error("Password for user4 violates special character rule");
        violations.forEach(constraintViolation -> logger.error("Violation
➥ details: [{}].", constraintViolation.getMessage()));

    }
}
```

In listing 2.36, you created four users. Apart from `user2`, all other users do not adhere to the defined password policy. For instance, there are multiple password policy violations for `user1`. For `user3` and `user4` there are maximum repetitive rules and special character rule violations. Let us start the application to see these validation issues. Figure 2.5 shows the error message for password violations.

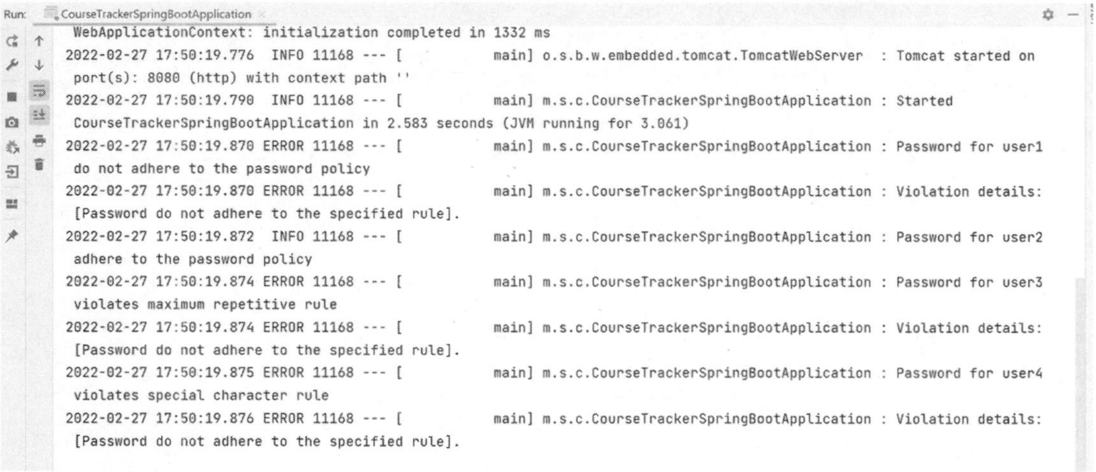

```
Run: CourseTrackerSpringBootApplication
WebApplicationContext: initialization completed in 1332 ms
2022-02-27 17:50:19.776  INFO 11168 --- [           main] o.s.b.w.embedded.tomcat.TomcatWebServer  : Tomcat started on
port(s): 8080 (http) with context path ''
2022-02-27 17:50:19.790  INFO 11168 --- [           main] m.s.c.CourseTrackerSpringBootApplication : Started
CourseTrackerSpringBootApplication in 2.583 seconds (JVM running for 3.061)
2022-02-27 17:50:19.870 ERROR 11168 --- [           main] m.s.c.CourseTrackerSpringBootApplication : Password for user1
do not adhere to the password policy
2022-02-27 17:50:19.870 ERROR 11168 --- [           main] m.s.c.CourseTrackerSpringBootApplication : Violation details:
[Password do not adhere to the specified rule].
2022-02-27 17:50:19.872  INFO 11168 --- [           main] m.s.c.CourseTrackerSpringBootApplication : Password for user2
adhere to the password policy
2022-02-27 17:50:19.874 ERROR 11168 --- [           main] m.s.c.CourseTrackerSpringBootApplication : Password for user3
violates maximum repetitive rule
2022-02-27 17:50:19.874 ERROR 11168 --- [           main] m.s.c.CourseTrackerSpringBootApplication : Violation details:
[Password do not adhere to the specified rule].
2022-02-27 17:50:19.875 ERROR 11168 --- [           main] m.s.c.CourseTrackerSpringBootApplication : Password for user4
violates special character rule
2022-02-27 17:50:19.876 ERROR 11168 --- [           main] m.s.c.CourseTrackerSpringBootApplication : Violation details:
[Password do not adhere to the specified rule].
```

Figure 2.5 The custom constraint violation error message

DISCUSSION

With this technique, you've seen how to define a custom annotation to implement business-specific constraints in your Spring Boot application. To implement a custom constraint, you need to implement the `ConstraintValidator` interface and define the `isValid()` method. In this method, you need to define the business logic that decides whether the input data is valid or not. Once the validator is defined, you need to define the custom annotation that uses the defined validator.

You can then use the annotation in the fields that need to be validated. In this example, we've explicitly used the validator from the `ValidatorFactory` to validate the objects. Later in the book, you'll see much better and more effective uses of the

Bean Validation's built-in and custom annotations while designing the REST API with a Spring Boot application.

Summary

In this chapter, you've explored several core techniques that need to be mastered by any Spring Boot developer. Some of the major topics we've explored in this chapter are:

- Several approaches to managing application properties in a Spring Boot application
- How to use `@ConfigurationProperties` to define properties in a type-safe manner
- How to configure `CommandLineRunner` to execute one-time executable code at Spring Boot application startup
- Default Spring Boot console logging, additional configurations, and how to use Log4j2 logging in a Spring Boot application
- How to use Bean Validation API to validate POJOs in your Spring Boot application with built-in annotations as well as with custom annotations

In chapter 3, the next stop of your Spring Boot journey, you'll learn to access the database from a Spring Boot application.

3 Database access with Spring Data

This chapter covers

- Introducing Spring Data, its needs, and various Spring Data modules
- Configuring a relational database, NoSQL database (MongoDB), and access data in a Spring Boot application
- Enabling Spring Data JPA to manage business domain objects with relational databases
- Various techniques to access data from a relational database using `@NamedQuery`, `@Query`, Criteria API, and `Querydsl`

You've already explored a variety of topics on Spring Boot in the last two chapters. With a solid overview of Spring Boot, you've learned a few common tasks that you may use in your Spring Boot applications quite frequently. So what's next? In today's world, most applications are incomplete without a database that stores the application data. Spring Boot applications are no exception. In this chapter, you'll boot your journey by interacting with the database from your Spring Boot application. You'll explore how seamless it is to perform database configuration, complete initialization, access data, and manage business objects in the database with Spring Boot!

3.1 Introducing Spring Data

Spring Data (https://spring.io/projects/spring-data) lets you access data from a variety of data sources (e.g., relational and nonrelational databases, MapReduce databases, and cloud-based data services). It attempts to provide a uniform, easy-to-use, and familiar programming model through the Spring Framework.

It is an umbrella project under the Spring Framework that contains several subprojects, each of which targeting a specific database. For instance, the Spring Data JPA module is specific to relational databases (e.g., H2, MySQL, PostgreSQL). Similarly, Spring Data MongoDB aims to provide support for the MongoDB database.

Java Persistence API (JPA)

Most applications in today's world need to communicate with the database to store and retrieve application data. And to achieve this interaction developers generally need to write a lot of boilerplate code. For instance, in the standard Java Database Connectivity (JDBC) approach, you need to obtain a database connection, define a `PreparedStatement`, set the bind variables, execute the query, and perform resource management.

The Java Persistence API (JPA) takes away most of these burdens and provides the developers with a bridge between the Java object model (e.g., business objects) and the relational database model (e.g., database tables). This mapping between Java objects and the relational model is popularly known as object-relational mapping (ORM) as illustrated in figure 3.1.

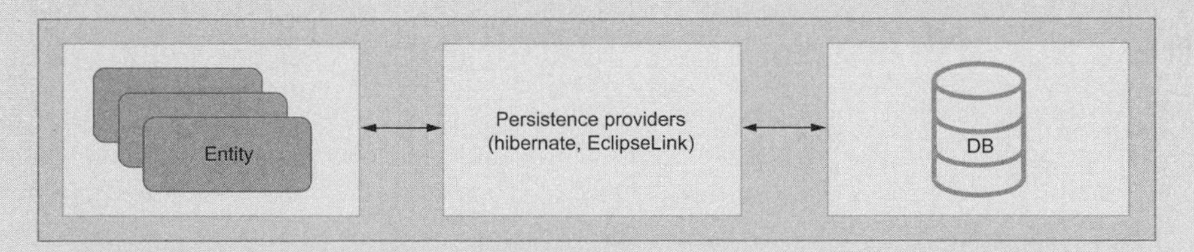

Figure 3.1 An overview of object-relational mapping. An entity represents a business object to be persisted. A persistence provider implements the JPA specification.

JPA is a specification that provides a set of interfaces, classes, and annotations to persist and retrieve application objects easily and concisely. Note that it is just a specification and outlines the standards for the ORM techniques. There are several third-party vendors, such as Hibernate (https://hibernate.org/orm/) and EclipseLink (https://www.eclipse.org/eclipselink/#jpa) that provide a concrete implementation of this specification.

3.1.1 *Why Spring Data?*

One of the core themes of Spring Data is to provide a consistent programming model to access various data sources. Thus, it provides a convenient API that lets you specify the metadata to the domain objects that need to be persisted and ensures that business domain objects are eligible to be persisted in the specific datastore. For instance, you can use a relational database and Spring Data JPA to manage business objects. You can provide the JPA annotations in business objects, and Spring Data JPA ensures the domain object is persisted in the database table. Later in this chapter, you'll see many of these annotations and their use in business objects.

Spring Data modules also expose APIs in the form of templates similar to popular `JdbcTemplate` and `JmsTemplate` template design patterns. For instance, if you use MongoDB, you can use MongoTemplate to perform various operations in the MongoDB database. These template classes provide several helper methods that manage store-specific resource management and exception translations.

> **Spring templates**
>
> Spring templates eliminate the need for boilerplate code that is otherwise required to correctly use some of the commonly used APIs, such as Java Database Connectivity (JDBC), Java Message Service (JMS), and Java Naming and Directory Interface (JNDI). The boilerplate code is typically the setup, error handling, and resource management code that you additionally need to write to achieve the task. For instance, in the previously discussed JDBC example, you need to obtain a database connection, create a `PreparedStatement`, execute the query, handle the exception, and close the `PreparedStatement` and database connection.
>
> The Spring templates take care of most of these boilerplate codes and let you only focus on the actual business logic. For example, the `JdbcTemplate` lets you supply the query you need to run, and the rest is managed by the template.

Spring Data provides a repository abstraction layer across the supported databases as a common programming model. The abstraction is contained in the Spring Data Commons module, and it provides several useful interfaces that let you perform the standard create, read, update, and delete (CRUD) operations as well as executing queries. This abstraction layer is the topmost layer and acts as the foundation for other Spring Data modules.

3.1.2 *Spring Data modules*

In the previous section, you've seen the role of Spring Data. In this section, you'll learn more about Spring Data modules. You can refer to the Spring Data Modules sidebar for the list of major subprojects available under Spring Data.

Spring Data modules

Spring Data is an umbrella project that provides support for several mainstream data stores. Table 3.1 summarizes a few of the commonly used modules.

Table 3.1 Spring Data modules and their purposes

Module Name	Purpose
Spring Data Commons	It contains the foundational components used in all Spring Data projects.
Spring Data JDBC	This module provides repository support for JDBC.
Spring Data JPA	It provides repository support for JPA.
Spring Data MongoDB	It provides support for documents-based MongoDB database.
Spring Data REDIS	It provides the necessary support for Redis datastore.
Spring Data REST	It lets you access Spring data repositories as REST resources.
Spring Data for Apache Cassandra	This module provides the necessary support for Apache Cassandra.

You can refer to the Spring Data reference document (https://spring.io/projects/spring-data) for a full list of Spring Data projects.

Of all Spring Data modules, the Spring Data Commons module is one of the most important. It consists of foundational and data source agnostic components of Spring Data that are used in other Spring Data modules. For instance, the Spring Data JPA module relies on the interfaces defined in the Spring Data Commons module. Spring Data JPA's `JpaRepository` interface is a subinterface of the Spring Data Commons module's `PagingAndSortingRepository` interface and inherits CRUD, pagination, and sorting support from the Spring Data Commons module.

As shown in figure 3.2, the Spring Data Commons module provides three core repository interfaces: `Repository`, `CrudRepository`, and `PagingAndSortingRepository`. As the name suggests, the `CrudRepository` interface allows you to use the CRUD operations. Similarly, the `PagingAndSortingRepository` interface, which is a subinterface of `CrudRepository`, allows you to perform CRUD operations as well as the pagination and sorting of data returned from the database. You'll explore some of these interfaces in detail in section 3.3.

The Spring Data submodules contain database technology-specific Spring Data implementations that provide supports for specific database families (e.g., Spring Data JDBC or Spring Data JPA focus on relational databases) or vendor-specific databases (e.g., Spring Data MongoDB focuses on MongoDB database). These submodules leverage the core framework features offered in the Spring Data Commons module.

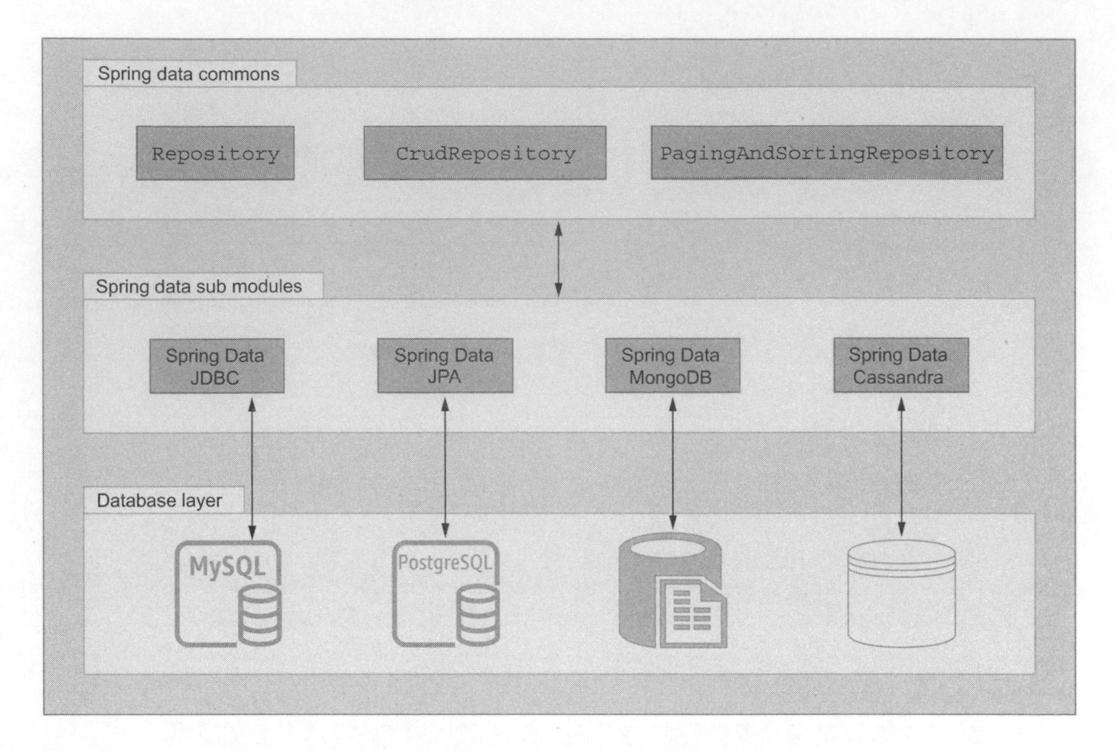

Figure 3.2 Spring Data modules. The Spring Data Commons module provides a foundation upon which other submodules are based. Each submodule targets a specific type of database. The Repository, CrudRepository, and PagingAndSortingRepository are interfaces of the Spring Data Commons module.

3.2 Configuring a database in a Spring Boot application

Configuring and accessing a database is one of the fundamental operations in any application, and Spring Boot applications are no exception to it. Spring Boot provides various techniques to configure and access a database from your Spring Boot application. Let's understand how to configure and access a relational database in a Spring Boot application.

3.2.1 Technique: Configuring a relational database in a Spring Boot application

In this technique, we'll demonstrate how to configure a relational database in a Spring Boot application.

Problem

Most applications need to interact with a database to store and retrieve application data. However, before communicating with the database, you need to configure the database in the application. You need to configure and access a relational database in your Spring Boot application.

SOLUTION

To configure a relational database with Spring Boot, you can add `spring-boot-starter-data-jpa` and the relational database driver dependency in the pom.xml of your application. Additionally, you need to supply the database details, such as database username, password, driver class, and connection URL.

> **Which relational database to use?**
>
> In the demonstration, you'll use an in-memory relational database named H2 (https://www.h2database.com/html/main.html). However, you can use any relational database to continue with this technique. For example, you can use MySQL (https://www.mysql.com/), Oracle (http://mng.bz/y4xB), or PostgreSQL (https:// www.postgresql.org/) databases as well. In case you are using a database other than H2, the configuration technique will be the same, and only the database driver and other supporting configuration parameters will change.
>
> Besides, you need to ensure you have a running instance of the database you are using, so the Spring Boot application can connect to the database. You can either install and configure the database in your development machine or use a database instance from the cloud service providers, such as AWS or Azure. In the latter case, ensure that you have connectivity to the database from your machine. Note that whatever approach (i.e., local or cloud) you use, only the database connection URL changes, and the rest of the configuration remains the same. In this example, we are using the embedded version of the H2 in-memory database.

> **Source code**
>
> You can find the base version of the Spring Boot project used in this technique in the book's companion GitHub repository at http://mng.bz/M2mW. The finished version of the project is available at http://mng.bz/aDy7.

To configure a relational database, you need to add two additional dependencies in the existing pom.xml file, as shown in the following listing. You can copy and paste these dependencies anywhere inside the `dependencies` tag in the pom.xml file.

Listing 3.1 Spring Data JPA starter and H2 dependency

```
<dependency>
    <groupId>org.springframework.boot</groupId>
    <artifactId>spring-boot-starter-data-jpa</artifactId>
</dependency>
<dependency>
    <groupId>com.h2database</groupId>
    <artifactId>h2</artifactId>
    <scope>runtime</scope>
</dependency>
```

Spring Boot Data JPA dependency for JPA support (first dependency)

H2 database driver dependency. This dependency is configured with runtime scope to ensure it is available at the application runtime and not needed at the time of compilation. (second dependency)

In listing 3.1, the first dependency incorporates Spring Data JPA, and the other one includes the H2 database driver in the Spring Boot project. If you are using a database other than H2, you need to use the associated database driver dependency in the pom.xml file. For instance, if you are using MySQL or PostgreSQL database, you can find the corresponding Maven dependency in the Maven central repository.

Among the dependencies, Spring Data JPA lets you manage your business domain objects through ORM techniques without defining SQL queries explicitly. The H2 in-memory dependency allows you to use an embedded H2 database in the Spring Boot application. As this is an in-memory database, the data inside this database is lost each time you restart the application.

Let's now proceed with the H2 database details in the Spring Boot application. If you recall, every Spring Boot application contains an application.properties file that lets you configure various application properties to control its behavior. Let's add the H2 database configurations to the application.properties file. The following listing shows the configuration needed to do this.

Listing 3.2 Application properties with H2 database configuration

```
spring.datasource.url=jdbc:h2:mem:sbipdb
spring.datasource.driverClassName=org.h2.Driver
spring.datasource.username=sa
spring.datasource.password=password
spring.h2.console.enabled=true
```

- **Database URL. We are using a schema called sbipdb in this demonstration.**
- **H2 Driver class**
- **Database Username**
- **Database Password**
- **Enable H2 console. This property is specific to H2 database only.**

In listing 3.2, you've provided the H2 database connection URL, driver class, username, and password and enabled the H2 console. The H2 console provides you with a UI that lets you execute SQL queries in the in-memory H2 database. The provided details are sufficient for Spring Boot to configure the data source in the application.

To validate the created data source, you'll define a test case that asserts the data source type and the underlying database, as shown in listing 3.3. If you are not familiar with the test, you can refer to the book's companion GitHub wiki page at http://mng.bz/jyez.

> **NOTE** If you are interested in unit testing, Manning has a few excellent texts with detailed coverage of the subject. You can refer to *Unit Testing Principles, Practices, and Patterns* by Vladimir Khorikov, available at https://www.manning.com/books/unit-testing.

Listing 3.3 Unit test to validate the data source details

```
package com.manning.sbip.ch03;

// Import Statements are excluded as a matter of readability
```

```
@SpringBootTest
class CourseTrackerSpringBootApplicationTests {

    @Autowired
    private DataSource dataSource;

    @Test
    public void givenDatasourceAvailableWhenAccessDetailsThenExpectDetails()
     throws SQLException {
        assertThat(dataSource.getClass().getName()).isEqualTo("com.zaxxer
     .hikari.HikariDataSource");
        assertThat(dataSource.getConnection().getMetaData().getDatabasePro-
     ductName()).isEqualTo("H2");
    }
}
```

In this test case, you've autowired the `DataSource` instance and asserted that the data source class name is `com.zaxxer.hikari.HikariDataSource` and the database product name is `H2`. You'll learn more about the role of HikariCP in the discussion section of this technique. If you execute this test case, you can see both assertions are true, as shown in figure 3.3.

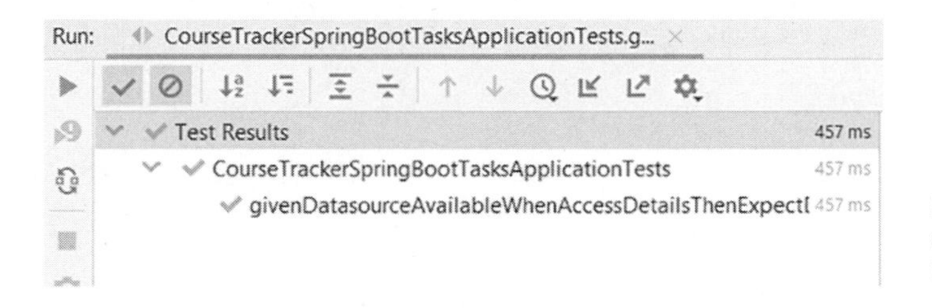

Figure 3.3 Unit test case executed successfully in IntelliJ IDEA

DISCUSSION

With this technique, you've learned how you can configure a relational database in your Spring Boot application with a few configurations. For instance, the presence of database configuration details in the application.properties file, and the Spring Data JPA and H2 driver jars in the classpath enable Spring Boot to configure an H2 data source in the application. You can use this data source for database communication.

As part of the database configuration, Spring Boot automatically configures the HikariCP (https://github.com/brettwooldridge/HikariCP) database connection pool. A database connection pool contains one or more database connections that are generally created at the time of application startup and available for use by the application. The benefit of a database connection pool is that a set of database connections are created at the application startup and available for use by the application. Thus, you don't create a new connection each time you need a database connection and close it once done. The application can take a connection from the pool, use it, and return to the pool. Spring Boot uses HikariCP as the default database connection pool library.

If you are curious to know where the HikariCP dependency is located, you can inspect the `spring-boot-starter-data-jpa` dependency by looking at its associated pom.xml file. Browse to the pom.xml file of the sample application in your IDE, and click on the `spring-boot-starter-data-jpa` dependency. You can observe that `spring-boot-starter-data-jpa` has a dependency on `spring-boot-starter-jdbc`, and that, in turn, has a dependency on the HikariCP library. Figure 3.4 shows this dependency hierarchy.

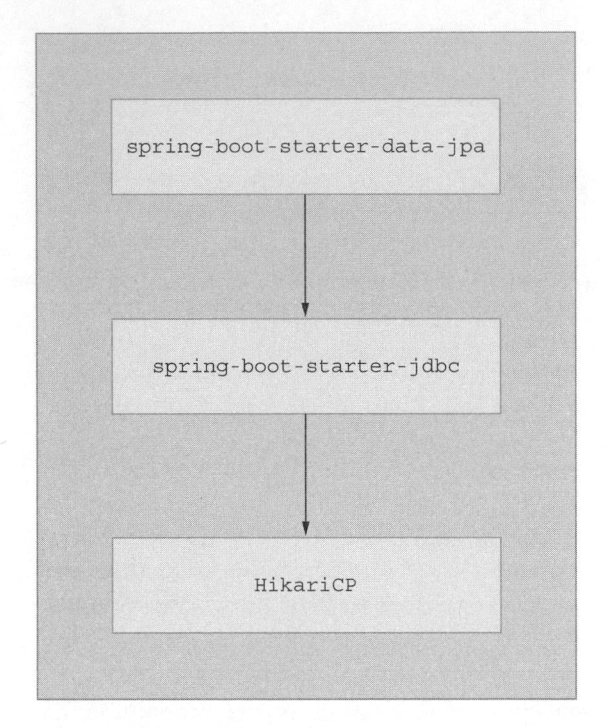

Figure 3.4 HikariCP connection pool library transitive dependency

If you need to use a database connection pooling library other than HikariCP, you can achieve this by excluding the HikariCP dependency from the `spring-boot-starter-data-jpa` dependency and including your preferred database connection pooling library (e.g., Oracle UCP, Tomcat JDBC, DBCP2, etc.). Listing 3.4 shows the configuration to exclude HikariCP and use the `tomcat-jdbc` connection pooling library.

Listing 3.4 POM XML changes to exclude HikariCP and include Tomcat connection pool

```
...
<dependency>
    <groupId>org.springframework.boot</groupId>
    <artifactId>spring-boot-starter-data-jpa</artifactId>
    <exclusions>
        <exclusion>
            <groupId>com.zaxxer</groupId>
```

Default connection pool HikariCP is excluded from Spring Data JPA dependency (annotation pointing to `<exclusion>`)

```
            <artifactId>HikariCP</artifactId>
        </exclusion>
    </exclusions>
</dependency>
<dependency>
    <groupId>org.apache.tomcat</groupId>
    <artifactId>tomcat-jdbc</artifactId>
</dependency>
...
```

Tomcat JDBC connection pool is added explicitly as the connection pool of choice

Spring Boot uses the following strategies to detect the database connection pool library based on the configuration defined in listing 3.4:

1. If HikariCP is not available, then Spring Boot attempts to use Apache Tomcat database connection pooling if it is available in the classpath.
2. If both HikariCP and Apache Tomcat connection pool dependencies are not available, then Spring Boot attempts to use Apache Commons DBCP2 library (https://commons.apache.org/proper/commons-dbcp).
3. If DBCP2 is also not available, Spring Boot configures the JDK's default data source (`javax.sql.DataSource`).

In this technique, you've configured the H2 database in your Spring Boot application by configuring a few parameters in the application.properties file. In this demonstration, you've used only a handful of parameters to enable the database configuration. Spring Boot provides several additional configuration parameters to fine-tune the database configuration.

For instance, if you are using the default HikariCP configuration, you might want to customize the HikariCP connection pool configuration. You can configure a custom maximum number of connections per pool—namely, the maximum connection pool size by configuring the `spring.datasource.hikari.maximum-pool-size` property in the application.properties. If you are using a connection pool library other than HikariCP, you need to configure the property specific to the library.

If you are curious to explore the available database configuration parameters, you can browse Spring Boot application.properties documentation at http://mng.bz/g4OV.

3.2.2 Technique: Configuring MongoDB database in a Spring Boot application

In this technique, we'll demonstrate how to configure MongoDB database in a Spring Boot application.

Problem

You've already explored configuring a relational database in a Spring Boot application. Along with relational databases, NoSQL databases are also gaining popularity. You need to configure the popular NoSQL database MongoDB in a Spring Boot application.

SOLUTION

MongoDB is a popular NoSQL database that stores the data as documents in JSON-like format. Spring Boot provides an easy approach to integrate with the MongoDB database through `spring-boot-starter-data-mongodb` dependency. In this technique, you'll learn how to connect to a MongoDB database from your Spring Boot application.

> **Source code**
>
> You can find the base version of the Spring Boot project used in this technique in the book's companion GitHub repository at http://mng.bz/eneQ. The finished version of the project is available at http://mng.bz/p28z.

To configure MongoDB in a Spring Boot application, you've included the following dependencies in your Spring Boot application, as shown in the following listing.

Listing 3.5 MongoDB Maven dependencies

```
<dependency>
    <groupId>org.springframework.boot</groupId>
    <artifactId>spring-boot-starter-data-mongodb</artifactId>
</dependency>
<dependency>
    <groupId>de.flapdoodle.embed</groupId>
    <artifactId>de.flapdoodle.embed.mongo</artifactId>
</dependency>
```

> **Flapdoodle-embedded MongoDB**
>
> In this section, for demonstration purposes, we have used the Flapdoodle-embedded MongoDB database (http://mng.bz/OGlE). In production or complex applications, you should avoid using it due to the various issues the library has. Refer to http://mng.bz/Yg5A for additional details. Use a real MongoDB instance for production or complex applications or consider using testcontainers (https://www.testcontainers.org/) for testing purposes.

The first dependency provides Spring Data MongoDB support in the Spring Boot application. The second dependency adds the Flapdoodle-embedded MongoDB database to our application. You can find more details on this database at http://mng.bz/GGKO. If you are using a real MongoDB instance, then you don't need the embedded MongoDB database dependency. Let's define a test case to validate how to use MongoDB, as shown in the following listing.

Listing 3.6 Unit test to validate the use of MongoDB in Spring Data

```
package com.manning.sbip.ch03;

// Import statements are excluded as a matter of readability
```

```
import static org.assertj.core.api.Assertions.assertThat;

@DataMongoTest
@ExtendWith(SpringExtension.class)
class CourseTrackerSpringBootApplicationTests {

    @Autowired
    private MongoTemplate mongoTemplate;

    @Test
    public void givenObjectAvailableWhenSaveToCollectionThenExpectValue() {
        // given
        DBObject object = BasicDBObjectBuilder.start().add("Manning", "Spring
➥ Boot In Practice").get();
        // when
        mongoTemplate.save(object, "collection");
        // then
        assertThat(mongoTemplate.findAll(DBObject.class, "collection"))
                .extracting("Manning")
                .containsOnly("Spring Boot In Practice");

    }
}
```

Let's explore the activities performed in this test case:

- You've autowired the `MongoTemplate` in the test class. An instance of `MongoTemplate` is created by Spring Boot. `MongoTemplate` is a helper class that lets you perform various MongoDB operations.
- You then create a document as the key–value pair with the key as *Manning* and the value as *Spring Boot in Practice*. MongoDB stores the documents as part of collections. Thus, you add the document to a collection named *Collection*.
- Finally, you find the document to extract the key and assert the returned value.

DISCUSSION

A relational database stores data in a tabular format in terms of rows and columns. However, not all data is suitable to be stored in a tabular format. There are several use cases in which data is unstructured and treated as a document. The NoSQL databases store the data in terms of a document and are popularly known as document databases. MongoDB is one of the most popular and leading document databases.

With this technique, you've used an in-memory instance of MongoDB. An in-memory instance lets you quickly bootstrap the application and does not require a local or remote database installation.

If you have a local or remote instance (e.g., in a remote server or cloud provider), you can remove the embedded configuration and provide your actual database configuration. The following listing shows the MongoDB database configurations you can provide in the application.properties file to customize the database details.

Listing 3.7 MongoDB properties

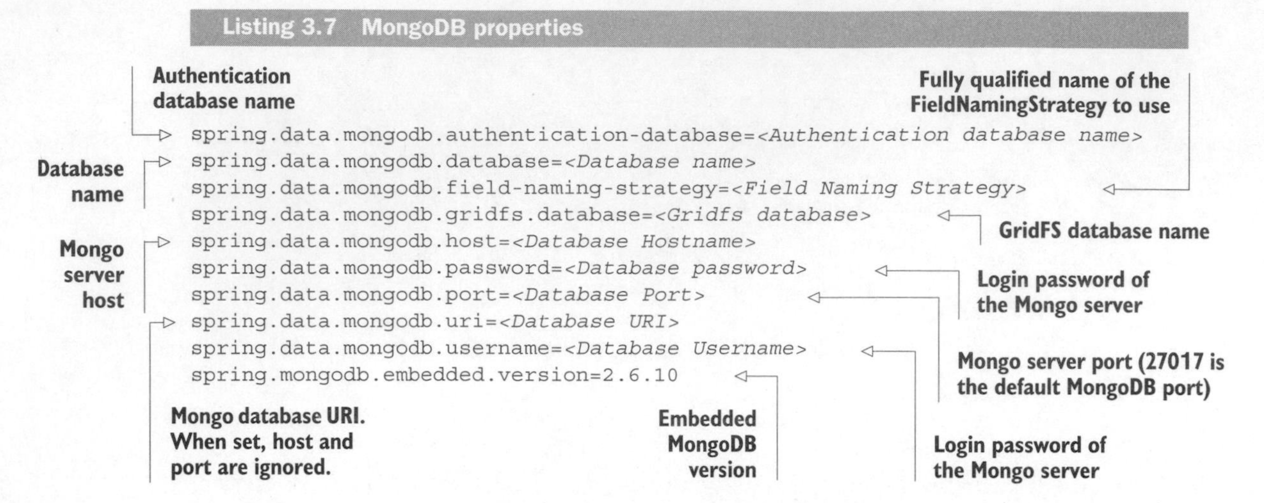

```
spring.data.mongodb.authentication-database=<Authentication database name>
spring.data.mongodb.database=<Database name>
spring.data.mongodb.field-naming-strategy=<Field Naming Strategy>
spring.data.mongodb.gridfs.database=<Gridfs database>
spring.data.mongodb.host=<Database Hostname>
spring.data.mongodb.password=<Database password>
spring.data.mongodb.port=<Database Port>
spring.data.mongodb.uri=<Database URI>
spring.data.mongodb.username=<Database Username>
spring.mongodb.embedded.version=2.6.10
```


NOTE You can refer to Spring Boot reference documentation available at http://mng.bz/zQAQ for all supported properties.

If you are new to MongoDB, you can refer to the book's companion GitHub wiki page for a beginner's guide on MongoDB available at http://mng.bz/0wA6.

3.2.3 *Technique: Initializing a relational database schema with a Spring Boot application*

In this technique, we'll discuss how to initialize a relational database schema in a Spring Boot application.

PROBLEM

In the configuring a relational database in a spring boot application technique, you saw how to configure a relational database in your Spring Boot application. However, before you start accessing the database, you need to ensure the database schema is initialized properly. For instance, all the required tables and indexes are created, and associated insert scripts are executed. You need to initialize the database schema at the application startup.

SOLUTION

Spring Boot allows you to initialize a database schema with built-in solutions as well as third-party libraries (ORM solutions). In this technique, you'll learn how to initialize the database using Spring Data's built-in `schema.sql` and `data.sql` scripts.

Spring Boot can load the SQL scripts from the classpath (e.g., the src/main/resources folder) or a preconfigured location. By default, you define the schema.sql file to provide all DDL scripts and define the data.sql file to include the DML scripts and place it inside the src\main\resources folder for Spring Boot to detect and execute these files. Further, you can also use the `spring.datasource.schema` and `spring.datasource.data` properties to customize the default behavior. You'll examine this in this technique.

DDL and DML in a nutshell

Data definition language (DDL) is used to define database structures, such as database users, schemas, tables, indexes, constraints in a relational database. For example, in H2 you can use the following DDL statement to create a table named `AUTHORS`:

```
create table AUTHORS (
  id bigint not null,
  name varchar(255),
  primary key (id)
);
```

Data manipulation language (DML) is used to manipulate data. For example, DML statements allow you to `INSERT`, `UPDATE`, and `DELETE` data in relational database tables. For example, the following DML script `INSERTS` data into the `AUTHORS` table:

```
INSERT INTO AUTHORS(id, name) VALUES(1, 'John Doe') ;
```

Source code

To start with this technique, you can use the base Spring Boot project from the book's GitHub repository available at http://mng.bz/KB80. The final version of the project is available at http://mng.bz/9K41.

To begin with, if you are using a database other than an embedded (in-memory) database, you need to set `spring.sql.init.mode` to `always` be in the application .properties file, as shown in listing 3.8. This property instructs Spring Boot to always initialize the database schema. It supports three values—`embedded`, `always`, and `never`. By default, this property is set to the value `embedded`. This means Spring Boot automatically initializes the database schema for embedded database types (e.g., H2 in-memory database available at https://www.h2database.com/html/main.html). To initialize MySQL or other actual databases, you need to explicitly configure the value to `always`. Since you are using the H2 database in this technique, you may ignore this property.

In this schema initialization-based approach, Spring Boot re-creates the schema each time you restart the application. There is no database schema versioning done by Spring Boot. For example, in the above example, Spring Boot drops and re-creates the `COURSES` table in each application restart and executes the DML statements provided in the `data.sql` script. The following listing shows the updated application .properties file.

Listing 3.8 Updated application.properties file

```
spring.sql.init.mode=always

// Other data source properties such as username, password, driver name, and
    connection URL
```

Instructs Spring Boot to initialize the database schema. Supported values are embedded, always, and never. By default, it is set to embedded, which means if you use an embedded database, then automatically the database is initialized. For other database types, it always needs to be configured to configure the database.

Let's now define the schema.sql and the data.sql files. However, before that let's recap the business model we are working on within this application. In this example, you are managing `Course` details in the sample application. Thus, the `Course` is the business domain object in the application. The schema.sql creates the `COURSES` table, and the data.sql inserts a few sample courses into the `COURSES` table. The following listing shows the database schema configuration located at src/main/resources/schema.sql.

Listing 3.9 Database schema.sql configuration

```
CREATE TABLE COURSES
(
    id int(15) NOT NULL,
    name varchar(100) NOT NULL,
    category varchar(20) NOT NULL,
    rating int(1) NOT NULL,
    description varchar(1000) NOT NULL,
    PRIMARY KEY (id)
);
```

Listing 3.10 shows the database initialization SQL script provided in the `data.sql` configuration file located at src/main/resources/data.sql. This is a DML script that contains the `INSERT` statements to populate the `COURSES` table.

Listing 3.10 Database initialization scripts

```
INSERT INTO COURSES(ID, NAME, CATEGORY, RATING, DESCRIPTION)
VALUES(1, 'Rapid Spring Boot Application Development',
'Spring', 4, 'Spring Boot gives all the power of the
 Spring Framework without all of the complexities');
INSERT INTO COURSES(ID, NAME, CATEGORY, RATING, DESCRIPTION)
VALUES(2, 'Getting Started with Spring Security DSL',
'Spring', 3,  'Learn Spring Security DSL in easy steps');
INSERT INTO COURSES(ID, NAME, CATEGORY, RATING, DESCRIPTION)
VALUES(3, 'Scalable, Cloud Native Data Applications',
'Spring', 4,  'Manage Cloud based applications with Spring Boot');
INSERT INTO COURSES(ID, NAME, CATEGORY, RATING, DESCRIPTION)
VALUES(4, 'Fully Reactive: Spring, Kotlin, and JavaFX Playing Together',
'Spring', 3,'Unleash the power of Reactive Spring
with Kotlin and Spring Boot');
```

```
INSERT INTO COURSES(ID, NAME, CATEGORY, RATING, DESCRIPTION)
VALUES(5, 'Getting Started with Spring Cloud Kubernetes',
'Spring', 5, 'Master Spring Boot application deployment
 with Kubernetes');
```

Database-specific schema and data SQL files

In addition to the schema.sql and data.sql files, Spring Boot also supports database-specific SQLs. For instance, if your application supports multiple database types, and there are SQL syntax differences, you can use schema-${platform}.sql and data-${platform}.sql files. Thus, you can define a schema-h2.sql and data-h2.sql if you need to support the H2 database. You can specify the database platform by defining spring.datasource.platform=h2 in the `application.properties` file. Note that at any point only one database is active. Thus, you can maintain multiple schema-${platform}.sql and data-${platform}.sql files, but you can configure the `spring.datasource.platform` to a specific database at any time.

To validate whether Spring Boot initializes the database schema, let us write a test case. This simple test case counts the number of courses available in the `COURSES` table in the database, as shown in the following listing.

Listing 3.11 Unit test to validate database schema initialization

```
package com.manning.sbip.ch03;

// Import Statements are excluded as a matter of readability

@SpringBootTest
class CourseTrackerSpringBootApplicationTests {

    @Autowired
    private DataSource dataSource;

    @Test
    public void whenCountAllCoursesThenExpectFiveCourses()
➥ throws SQLException {
        ResultSet rs = null;
        int noOfCourses = 0;
        try(PreparedStatement ps =
➥ dataSource.getConnection().prepareStatement("SELECT COUNT(1) FROM
➥ COURSES")) {
            rs = ps.executeQuery();
            while(rs.next()) {
                noOfCourses = rs.getInt(1);

            }
            assertThat(noOfCourses).isEqualTo(5L);
        }
        finally {
            if(rs != null) {
                rs.close();
```

```
            }
        }
    }
}
```

In listing 3.11, you've autowired the `DataSource` and used basic JDBC code to count the courses from the `COURSES` table. Don't be scared by all this boilerplate code, as in the next section, you'll learn how to perform SQL queries with JPA repositories. In this example, you've created five courses using the `INSERT` queries defined in the data.sql file. Thus, in the test case you are asserting for five courses.

You can also specify a different schema and data file name with a different location. For instance, listing 3.12 shows the configuration for sbip-schema.sql and sbip-data.sql files available at the src\main\resources\sql\schema and src\main\resources\sql\data folders, respectively.

Listing 3.12 Custom schema and data file location

```
spring.sql.init.schema-locations=classpath:sql/schema/sbip-schema.sql
spring.sql.init.data-locations=classpath:sql/data/sbip-data.sql
```

Specifying a different schema file location

Specifying a different data file location

Other than classpath, you can also provide a file system location (with file://<absolute path>) if your schema and data files are in the file system. Further, you can specify more than one schema or data file separated by the comma. For instance, spring.sql.init.data-locations=classpath:sql/data/sbip-data.sql,file://c:/sql/data/reference-data.sql loads both files.

DISCUSSION

In this technique, you've learned how to use Spring Boot's built-in techniques to initialize a database by defining a few SQL files. To recap, you can define the schema.sql file to provide all your DDL scripts that define the database schema. Furthermore, you can use the data.sql file to provide DML scripts that populate the database. You've also learned to maintain database platform-specific SQLs in the same application. This is useful if your application supports multiple databases.

So far, you've used the basic Spring Boot techniques to configure and communicate to the database. In the next section, you'll learn to use Spring Data JPA to manage your database communication in a much more concise and effective manner. Let's proceed to discussing Spring Data's `CrudRepository` interface, which provides support for standard CRUD operations as well as upon which most of the Spring Data submodules are based.

3.3 Understanding the CrudRepository interface

Before starting with the `CrudRepository` interface, you need to know about the `Repository` interface. Spring Data repository uses this generic interface as the primary abstraction for a data source. It takes a business domain class that needs to be managed and an identifier type of the class as the type attribute. A business domain class is a Java class that represents a business entity and needs to be persisted. For instance, in the CourseTracker application, you are managing the course details that are represented in the Course class and have an identifier of the long data type.

The Repository is a marker interface and is primarily used to capture the domain class and its ID type information. A marker interface has no methods or constants and provides runtime type information about objects. The following listing shows the Repository interface from the spring-data-commons module.

Listing 3.13 Spring Data repository interface

```
public interface Repository<T, ID> {}
```

The CrudRepository is a subinterface of the Repository interface and provides CRUD operations. Listing 3.14 shows the CrudRepository interface from the spring-data-commons module. You can find the source code of this interface at http://mng.bz/jyzP.

Listing 3.14 Spring Data CrudRepository methods

```
public interface CrudRepository<T, ID> extends Repository<T, ID> {
  <S extends T> S save(S entity);
  Optional<T> findById(ID id);
  Iterable<T> findAll();
  long count();
  void deleteById(ID id);
  // Additional Methods excluded for brevity
}
```

- The interface definition. The generic type T represents the domain class, and the ID type represents the identifier of the domain class.
- Saves a given entity
- Finds an entity by the given ID
- Finds all entities
- Returns the number of entities available
- Deletes the entity with the given ID

In addition to the CrudRepository, Spring Data also provides a PagingAndSortingRepository, which extends the CrudRepository and provides additional support for *pagination* and *sorting* of the entities. Figure 3.5 shows the relationship between the core interfaces of the Spring Data Commons module.

To manage a business domain class persistence, you typically create an interface that extends either CrudRepository or the PagingAndSortingRepository interface and provides the entity class and its identifier type information. The custom repository interface (e.g., CourseRepository) extends all the methods available in the extended interface (e.g., CrudRepository). Let's explore the use of the CrudRepository interface in the next technique.

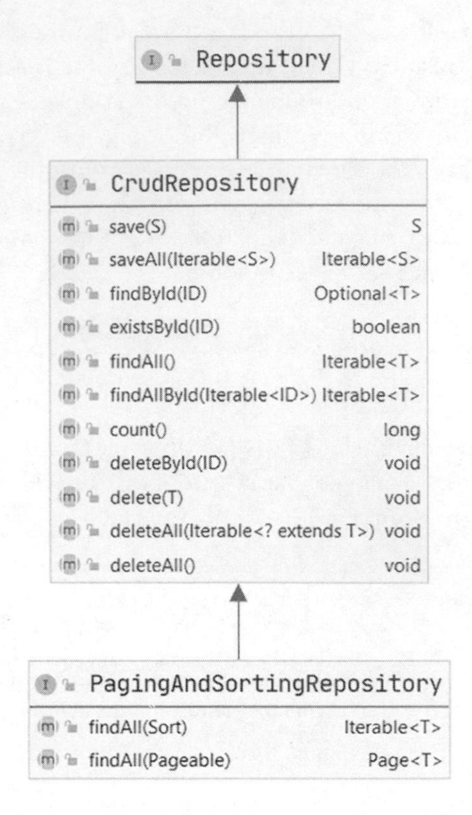

Figure 3.5 Spring Data Commons repository hierarchy class diagram

3.3.1 Technique: Managing domain objects in a relational database with Spring Data JPA

In this section, we'll explore how to manage business domain objects in a relational database with Spring Data JPA.

Problem

You need to use Spring Data JPA to manage domain objects in a relational database in your Spring Boot application.

Solution

In the previous section, you've learned the Spring Data repository interfaces `Repository`, `CrudRepository`, and `PagingAndSortingRepository` that lets you manage domain objects in a Spring Boot application. In this technique, you'll learn how to use the `CrudRepository` interface to perform the create, read, update, and delete operations in an application.

> **Source code**
>
> You can find the base Spring Boot project used in this technique at http://mng.bz/W7R1. The final version of the project is available at http://mng.bz/8lvw.

Let's start by modifying the Course domain class by providing a few JPA annotations so that Spring Data JPA can manage this class. This is shown in the following listing.

Listing 3.15 The Course entity with @Id, @Column, and @GeneratedValue annotations

```
import javax.persistence.*;

@Entity
@Table(name = "COURSES")
public class Course {

    @Id
    @Column(name = "ID")
    @GeneratedValue(strategy = GenerationType.IDENTITY)
    private Long id;

    @Column(name = "NAME")
    private String name;

       @Column(name = "CATEGORY")
    private String category;

       @Column(name = "RATING")
    private int rating;

    @Column(name = "DESCRIPTION")
    private String description;

       public Course(String name, String category,
➥ int rating, String description) {
            this.name = name;
           this.category = category;
            this.rating = rating;
            this.description = description;
       }
    // Getter/setters, and toString is omitted
```

Let's discuss the changes you've made:

- You have annotated the class with the `@Entity` and the `@Table` annotations. The first annotation marks the Java class as a JPA entity, and the other annotation provides the database table details in which the entity needs to be managed.
- You have annotated the Java fields with the `@Column` annotation. This provides mapping information between the Java fields and the associated column name in the table.
- You have annotated the `id` field with the `@Id` annotation to indicate that this field is the primary key of the table. You've also provided details to indicate that the values for this field should be generated using the provided strategy. Refer to the discussion section for more information about the available strategies.
- The course constructor does not have the `id` field. The ID is managed by JPA and is auto-generated.

You'll now define a custom Spring Data repository by extending the `CrudRepository` interface that lets you manage the `Course` details. Recall that the `CrudRepository` interface provides support for the standard CRUD operations. Thus, `CourseRepository` inherits the CRUD operation support from this extended interface. The following listing shows the `CourseRepository` interface.

Listing 3.16 The CourseRepository interface

```
package com.manning.sbip.ch03.repository;

import org.springframework.data.repository.CrudRepository;
import org.springframework.stereotype.Repository;

import com.manning.sbip.ch03.model.Course;

@Repository
public interface CourseRepository extends CrudRepository<Course, Long> {
    // The interface body is actually empty
}
```

You've annotated the `CourseRepository` interface with the `@Repository` annotation to indicate this is a Spring repository. Notice that, although it seems to be an empty interface, at runtime its concrete method implementation is provided by Spring Data JPA, which is then used to perform the CRUD operations.

The last change you need to perform is to update the application.properties file with the `spring.jpa.hibernate.ddl-auto` property with the `create` value. This property instructs the Hibernate (the default JPA provider in Spring Data JPA) to manage the database tables for the entities. Note that this property is specific to Hibernate and is not applicable if any other JPA provider is used. Let's now write a test case to see the CRUD operations in practice, as shown in the following listing.

Listing 3.17 Unit test to validate CrudRepository methods

```
package com.manning.sbip.ch03;

// Import Statements are excluded as a matter of readability

@SpringBootTest
class CourseTrackerSpringBootApplicationTests {

    @Autowired
    private CourseRepository courseRepository;

    @Test
    public void givenCreateCourseWhenLoadTheCourseThenExpectSameCourse() {
        Course course =
➥ new Course("Rapid Spring Boot Application Development",
➥ "Spring", 4, "'Spring Boot gives all the power of the
➥ Spring Framework without all of the complexities");
        Course savedCourse = courseRepository.save(course);
```

```
        assertThat(courseRepository.findById(savedCourse.getId())
➥ .get()).isEqualTo(course);
    }

    @Test
    public void givenUpdateCourseWhenLoadTheCourseThenExpectUpdatedCourse() {
        Course course =
➥ new Course("Rapid Spring Boot Application Development",
➥ "Spring", 4, "'Spring Boot gives all the power of the
➥ Spring Framework without all of the complexities");
        courseRepository.save(course);
        course.setRating(5);
        Course savedCourse = courseRepository.save(course);
assertThat(courseRepository.findById(savedCourse.getId())
➥ .get().getRating()).isEqualTo(5);
    }

    @Test
    public void givenDeleteCourseWhenLoadTheCourseThenExpectNoCourse() {
        Course course =
➥ new Course("Rapid Spring Boot Application Development",
➥ "Spring", 4, "'Spring Boot gives all the power of the
➥ Spring Framework without all of the complexities");
        Course savedCourse  = courseRepository.save(course);
    assertThat(courseRepository.findById(savedCourse.getId())
➥ .get()).isEqualTo(course);
    courseRepository.delete(course);
    assertThat(courseRepository.findById(savedCourse.getId())
➥ .isPresent()).isFalse();
    }
}
```

In the unit test of listing 3.17, you've autowired the `CourseRepository` and defined three test cases:

- The first test case creates a new course and saves it into the database. We then find the course by its ID and assert that it is the same course we've created.
- The second test case creates and saves a course in the database. It then updates the course rating of the course and asserts whether the update is successful.
- The last test case creates and deletes a course. It asserts whether the course deletion is successful.

DISCUSSION

In this technique, you've learned to manage business domain objects through Spring Data JPA. To start with, you've updated the business domain class with JPA annotations. Spring Data JPA uses these annotations to manage the domain objects. Let's explore the JPA annotations in detail:

- `@Entity`—You've annotated the `Course` class with the `@Entity` annotation to indicate that this class is a JPA entity. A JPA entity is a POJO class representing the business domain object that needs to be persisted in a database table. As a default configuration, Spring Data uses the class name as the entity name. However, you can specify a custom entity name with the name attribute of `@Entity` annotation (e.g., `@Entity(name = "COURSE")`).

- `@Table`—By default, the entity class name also represents the name of the database table in which the entity data should be persisted. Thus, the `Course` POJO class name (i.e., `Course`) ensures that course details should be persisted in a table named `COURSE` in the database. Spring Data uses this as the default strategy if there is no table information provided in the class. However, in this example, you've customized the table name as `COURSES` with the `@Table` annotation. You can also specify several other tables-related information, such as the database schema name, unique constraints and indexes for the table, and a custom table name.
- `@Id`—An entity requires an identifier to identify each row in the underlying database table uniquely. The `@Id` annotation on a Java field in the business domain class specifies the property as the primary key of the table. Based on the application, a primary key can be a simple ID with a single field, or it can be a composite ID with multiple fields. To see the use of the composite key in Spring Data JPA, you can refer to http://mng.bz/ExzO.
- `@Column`—By default, Spring Data uses the class field names as the column names in the database table. For example, the field name `id` represents the column `ID` in the database table. Besides, if you have a property with more than one word in the `camelCase` format in your Java class, then the `camelCase` property name in the class is represented as the `camel_case` in the database table field. The words in the field are connected by an underscore `(_)`. Thus, if you've defined a property named `courseId`, it is represented as `course_id` in the table column.

Although the default column naming strategy works well in most scenarios, you can't use it all the time. For example, your organization might have a predefined column naming convention for the database table columns. Thus, you have a database column name different from the generated column name. You can address this name mismatch by specifying the corresponding database column name in the `@Column` annotation in the POJO field. For instance, `@Column(name= "COURSE_ID")` uses `COURSE_ID` as the column name in the `COURSES` table instead of the default generated name `ID`. Besides, you have also noticed that the `id` field is annotated with the `@GeneratedValue` annotation. This annotation indicates that the value of the annotated property is generated. The `GeneratedValue` annotation accepts a `GenerationType` strategy that defines how the property value should be generated. The supported values are `Table`, `Identity`, `Sequence`, and `Auto`. Let's discuss these options briefly:

- *Table*—This option indicates that the persistence provider should assign primary keys for an entity using a database table.
- *Identity*—Identity indicates that the persistence provider should assign the primary keys for an entity using a database identity column.

- *Sequence*—As the name suggests, this option allows the persistence provider to assign the primary keys using a database sequence.
- *Auto*—This option allows the persistence provider to determine the ID-generation scheme.

You've annotated the `CourseRepository` interface with the `@Repository` annotation. This annotation serves two important purposes:

- *Auto detection*—The `@Repository` annotation is meta-annotated with the `@Component` annotation. Thus, the Spring component scan can autodetect the repository interfaces through the classpath scanning, and you can autowire in other classes.
- *Exception translation*—One major benefit of using Spring Data JPA is that it provides flexibility to switch the underlying persistence provider. For instance, you can instruct Spring Boot to use `EclipseLink` as the JPA provider instead of `Hibernate`. However, this also brings the overhead of handling `EclipseLink` specific exceptions.

The `@Repository` annotation assists you in managing this overhead through its support for exception translation. An exception translation in this context means converting a technology-specific exception type (e.g., `SQLException`, `EclipseLinkException`, or `HibernateException`) to a generic Spring exception type (e.g., `DataAccessException`). Spring Data provides `DataAccessException` and a set of its child exception classes, which are runtime exceptions. These exceptions wrap the original technology-specific checked exceptions and enables you to define a consistent exception handling strategy through the `DataAccessException`.

Service and data access object (DAO) layer

Typically, you don't use a repository or the DAO implementations directly in the application. There should be a business service layer that acts as a bridge between the controller and the repository or the DAO layer. However, for simplicity and teaching purposes, in this demonstration, we've directly used the repository inside the test case.

JPA provides you with the flexibility to automatically infer the DDLs from the `@Entity` classes and execute them in a database. The `spring.jpa.hibernate.ddl-auto` property decides how to manage the DDLs in your application. The possible values for this property are `none`, `validate`, `update`, `create`, and `create-drop`. The following list provides a brief discussion on these options:

- `none`—Disables the automatic DDL management. It is the default value for nonembedded databases.
- `validate`—Validates the schema but does not make any changes to the database. Spring Boot throws an error if the database schema is not in expected structure.
- `update`—Updates the already-existing schema if necessary.

- `create`—Creates the schema and destroys already-existing data
- `create-drop`—Creates the schema and destroys at the end of the session. It is the default value for embedded databases.

The property `spring.jpa.hibernate.ddl-auto` is specific to Hibernate, which is the default persistence provider in Spring Boot. If you are using another persistent provider, you can use the more generic property `spring.jpa.generate-ddl`, which accepts a `boolean` value.

> **schema.sql or spring.jpa.hibernate.ddl-auto**
>
> In the previous technique, you've explored that you can use the `schema.sql` to create the database schema. In the current technique, you've learned the `spring.jpa.hibernate.ddl-auto` property that can also instruct Spring Data JPA to create the database schema based on the JPA annotations.
>
> You'll need to ensure that you choose either of the approaches to create the database schema. If you choose to use `schema.sql`, then configure `spring.jpa.hibernate.ddl-auto` property to `none` in the application.properties file.

In this technique, you've explored that you can use the `CrudRepository` interface to perform the CRUD operations in your application. However, at times you might need to control the exposure of the CRUD methods. For instance, you may not want to expose the `delete(..)` method that deletes business entities due to your application design. For instance, many organizations won't delete the application data and instead choose to update the details as inactive in the database. In the next technique, you'll learn to control the exposure of the CRUD methods by defining a custom Spring Data repository.

3.3.2 *Technique: Creating a custom Spring Data repository with Spring Data JPA to manage domain objects in a relational database*

In this technique, we will demonstrate how to create custom Spring Data repositories.

PROBLEM

You want to use Spring Data repository interfaces to manage your application domain objects but don't want to expose all CRUD methods.

SOLUTION

Spring Data repository interfaces provide an excellent and easy way to manage the business domain objects. It also lets you define your custom repository interfaces if the framework provided does not meet your need. With this technique, you'll define a custom Spring Data repository interface and use it in your Spring Boot application.

> **Source code**
>
> You can find the base version of the Spring Boot project at http://mng.bz/NxD1. The completed version of the Spring Boot project is available at http://mng.bz/DxGw.

To create a custom repository, you need to define a base repository interface that extends the Spring Data's `Repository` interface. You can then selectively specify the `CrudRepository` methods you want to expose. Let's define an interface called `BaseRepository` that exposes only the `save()` and `findAll()` methods of the `CrudRepository` interface, as shown in the following listing.

Listing 3.18 Defining the BaseRepository interface

```
package com.manning.sbip.ch03.repository;

import org.springframework.data.repository.NoRepositoryBean;
import org.springframework.data.repository.Repository;

@NoRepositoryBean
public interface BaseRepository<T, ID> extends Repository<T, ID> {

    <S extends T> S save(S entity);

    Iterable<T> findAll();

}
```

You've annotated this interface with `@NoRepositoryBean` annotation. As this is a base interface, you don't want Spring Data infrastructure to pick up this interface and create a concrete instance of it. The `@NoRepositoryBean` annotation ensures that the `BaseRepository` interface is excluded from the proxy object creation. You've also provided the `CrudRepository` method signatures that you want to expose in the `BaseRepository` interface. For these method invocations, Spring Data routes the runtime calls to the actual JPA implementation class, as they match the `CrudRepository` method signature.

Let's define a custom interface that extends the `BaseRepository` interface, as shown in listing 3.19. This ensures that the custom repository has access to only the methods defined in the `BaseRepository` interface.

Listing 3.19 Defining CustomizedCourseRepository interface

```
package com.manning.sbip.ch03.repository;

import com.manning.sbip.ch03.model.Course;
import org.springframework.stereotype.Repository;

@Repository
public interface CustomizedCourseRepository
➥ extends BaseRepository<Course, Long> {
}
```

The `CustomizedCourseRepository` interface is similar to the `CourseRepository` interface with the exception that it extends the `BaseRepository` interface and lets you access only the `save(..)` and `findAll()` methods.

Let's define a test case that uses the custom CustomizedCourseRepository interface, as shown in listing 3.20. Notice that you can only invoke the save(..) and findAll() methods. Trying to access other CrudRepository methods will result in a compile-time error, since that method signature is not available in the BaseRepository interface.

Listing 3.20 Unit test to validate the custom repository

```
package com.manning.sbip.ch03;

// Import Statements are excluded as a matter of readability

@DataJpaTest
class CourseTrackerSpringBootApplicationTests {

    @Autowired
    private CustomizedCourseRepository customizedCourseRepository;

    @Test
    public void givenCreateCourseWhenFindAllCoursesThenExpectOneCourse() {
        Course course =
➥ new Course("Rapid Spring Boot Application Development",
➥ "Spring", 4, "'Spring Boot gives all the power of the
➥ Spring Framework without all of the complexities");
        customizedCourseRepository.save(course);
        assertThat(Arrays.asList(customizedCourseRepository.findAll())
➥ .size()).isEqualTo(1);
    }
}
```

In listing 3.20, you've autowired the CustomizedCourseRepository and used it to create a course. You then assert that one course has been created.

DISCUSSION

In this technique, you've learned how to define a custom repository interface in your application. Although the CrudRepository interface is suitable in most of the scenarios, sometimes it is useful to control the CRUD operations. With the @NoRepositoryBean annotation, Spring Data lets you achieve this.

> **@SpringBootTest vs. @DataJpaTest**
>
> In the previous technique, we've used the @DataJpaTest annotation instead of the @SpringBootTest. The @SpringBootTest annotation is useful when you need to bootstrap the entire Spring IoC container. Thus, this annotation creates the ApplicationContext that is used in the tests. However, at times loading the complete container is overkill. For instance, when you test the DAO layer, you are only interested to load the related beans—not the entire ApplicationContext. To achieve this, Spring Boot provides several annotations to *slice* the testing into different layers and tests only the layer you are interested in. For instance, the @DataJpaTest annotation is provided to

test only the JPA components. Similarly, the `@WebMvcTest` focuses only on the Spring MVC components. It is recommended that you use these feature-specific annotations wherever applicable. You can find more information about feature-specific testing at http://mng.bz/laK8.

3.4 Retrieve data from a database using Spring Data

In the previous sections, you've learned how to configure databases and manage business domain objects or entities. In this section, you'll learn several techniques to efficiently access data from a database in a Spring Boot application.

3.4.1 Defining query methods

In previous techniques, you've seen how to use the `CrudRepository` interface to manage business domain objects. Although this interface provides standard CRUD operations, sometimes these generic methods are not sufficient. Instead, you may need more fine-grained control to manage domain objects. For instance, you might need to query entities based on entity properties instead of only relying on the entity ID (i.e., default `findById(..)`method).

You may also need to query entities after applying some *conditions* on the entity properties (e.g., `Like`, `StartsWith`, `Containing`, etc.). Further, you may also be interested in ordering (i.e., ascending or descending) the fetched entities based on one or more entity properties.

Spring Data JPA provides two ways to define custom query methods that can meet most of these custom requirements:

- Defining custom methods in the repository interfaces with specific naming patterns. Spring Data can internally parse these methods and generate the query from it.
- Defining custom methods and providing an SQL query that is directly used by the Spring Data to query the entities.

In this section, you'll learn the first option to define query method signatures so that Spring Data can parse the provided methods and generate the queries. Spring Data has a predefined method naming pattern that is understood by its method parser. It supports the following commonly used patterns:

- *Query*—For querying entities, it lets you define `find..By`, `read..By`, `get..By`, `query..By`, `stream..By`, and `search..By` methods.
- *Count*—This pattern is used to define `count..By()` methods to count the entities.
- *Exists*—This pattern is used to define `exists..By()` methods that check the existence of an entity.
- *Delete*—To delete entities, it lets you define `delete...By()` and `remove...By()` methods.

Additionally, you can also use additional clauses to fine-tune the methods. For instance, you can use `Distinct` or `All` expression in the method. Further, you can also use the `And` and `Or` expressions to concatenate additional entity properties.

Spring Data uses the concept of a `Subject` and `Predicate` to parse the methods. It splits the method signature based on the `By` clause and treats the first half as the subject and the remaining part as the predicate. Thus, if you define a method named `findDistinctCourseByCategoryOrderByName()`, then the part `DistinctCourse` is the subject, and the `CategoryOrderByName` is the predicate. This is demonstrated in figure 3.6. Let's use a technique to learn how you can define query methods to retrieve data from the database.

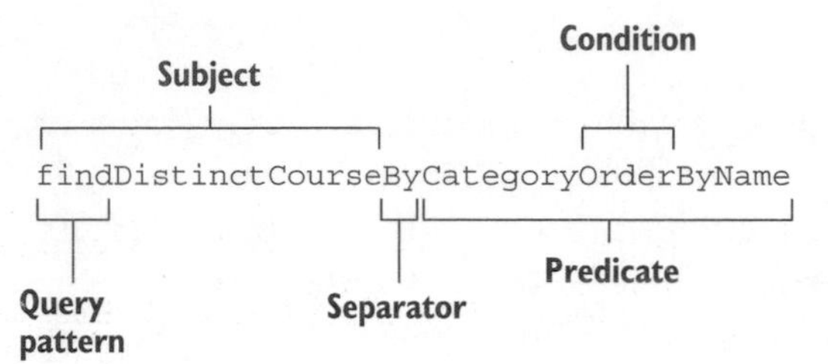

Figure 3.6 Query method structure

3.4.2 *Technique: Defining custom query methods to retrieve domain objects from a relational database with Spring Data JPA*

In this technique, we'll explore how to create custom query methods to retrieve entities from a relational database.

PROBLEM

You need to use Spring Data JPA to define custom query methods to retrieve entities from a relational database in your Spring Boot application.

SOLUTION

Spring Data JPA lets you define custom query methods to retrieve business entity details from the database. In this exercise, you'll learn to use this technique by defining a few custom query methods in the `CourseTracker` application.

> **Source code**
> You can find the base version of the Spring Boot project in the book's companion GitHub repository at http://mng.bz/Bx08. The final version of the project is available at http://mng.bz/dogO.

In the previous technique, you've used the `CourseRepository` interface to extend the `CrudRepository` interface and accessed methods defined in it. Let's modify the `CourseRepository` interface to provide a few query method signatures, as shown in the following listing.

Listing 3.21 CourseRepository interface with custom query methods

```
package com.manning.sbip.ch03.repository;

// Import Statements are excluded as a matter of readability

@Repository
public interface CourseRepository extends CrudRepository<Course, Long> {


    Iterable<Course> findAllByCategory(String category);
    Iterable<Course> findAllByCategoryOrderByName(String category);
    boolean existsByName(String name);
    long countByCategory(String category);
    Iterable<Course> findByNameOrCategory(String name, String category);
    Iterable<Course> findByNameStartsWith(String name);
    Stream<Course> streamAllByCategory(String category);
}
```

- findAllByCategory: Finds all courses by category. A find query returns an Iterable type.
- findAllByCategoryOrderByName: Finds all courses by category and orders the entities by name
- existsByName: Checks if a course with the supplied name exists. Returns true if course exists and false otherwise. Exists queries return the Boolean type.
- countByCategory: Returns the count of courses for the supplied category. Count queries can return an integer or long type.
- findByNameOrCategory: Finds all courses that match the supplied course name or the course category
- findByNameStartsWith: Finds all courses that start with the supplied course name string
- streamAllByCategory: Finds all courses by category and returns a Java 8 Stream

You've defined seven custom query methods that find the course details and related information from the database. Let's explain these methods in detail. Note that you've only defined the method signatures and not provided any implementation for these methods. Spring Data JPA parses the method signatures and ensures a concrete implementation internally:

- `findAllByCategory`—This is the simplest query method you've defined in the `CourseRepository` interface. You can relate it with the `findById(..)` method defined in the `CrudRepository` interface that finds an entity with the supplied entity ID. This method takes the same concept a step further and lets you define a custom method that finds a list of entities that belongs to a category. You can define more custom query methods that use other entity properties. For instance, to find a course that matches the supplied course description, you can define a method named `findByDescription(String description)`.
- `findAllByCategoryOrderByName`—This is an extension to the `findAllByCategory(..)` method with the exception that it returns courses in ascending order of the course name.
- `existsByName`—This method checks if a course with the supplied name exists. It returns `true` if the course exists or `false` otherwise.
- `countByCategory`—This method returns the count of courses for the supplied category.

- `findByNameOrCategory`—Finds all courses that match the supplied course name *or* the course category. Like the `OR` clause, you can also use the `AND` clause if you need to define a query that requires both properties to be available.
- `findByNameStartsWith`—Finds all courses that start with the supplied course name string. The supplied course name method parameter can be a substring of the actual course name.
- `streamAllByCategory`—Finds all courses by category and returns a Java 8 Stream. A `Stream` return type is different from the `Iterable` return type, which you've seen in the previous methods. An `Iterable` is a data structure that contains the returned data that you can iterate. A Stream is not a data structure; instead, it points to a data source from which the data can be streamed.

Let us define a test case to use these query methods in practice, as shown in the following listing.

Listing 3.22 Unit test to validate custom query methods

```
package com.manning.sbip.ch03;

// Import Statements are excluded as a matter of readability

@SpringBootTest
class CourseTrackerSpringBootApplicationTests {

    @Autowired
    private CourseRepository courseRepository;

    @Test
    public void givenCreateCourseWhenLoadTheCourseThenExpectSameCourse() {
        // Saving a list of courses
        courseRepository.saveAll(getCourseList());
        assertThat(courseRepository.findAllByCategory("Spring")).hasSize(3);
        assertThat(courseRepository.existsByName
➥ ("JavaScript for All")).isTrue();
        assertThat(courseRepository.existsByName
➥ ("Mastering JavaScript")).isFalse();
        assertThat(courseRepository.countByCategory("Python"))
➥ .isEqualTo(2);
        assertThat(courseRepository.findByNameStartsWith
➥ ("Getting Started")).hasSize(3);
    }

    private List<Course> getCourseList() {
        // Get Course List
    }
}
```

In the test case of listing 3.22, you have created a few courses and saved them into the database table. You then used the custom query methods and asserted their outcome. If you execute this test case, you'll find that all assertions are true.

DISCUSSION

In this section, you've learned a couple of important concepts of Spring Data JPA. Let's summarize the concepts you've explored so far:

- You have learned how to define custom repository query methods based on the entity properties. You've also seen how you can use various patterns, such as `Or`, `StartsWith`, and `OrderBy`, to control the query and the returned result ordering. These are only a few expressions we've demonstrated in this example. You can refer to http://mng.bz/raND to learn more about the other expressions you can use in the query method name.
- You've seen how to define a repository method with a Java 8 Stream in the repository interface and subsequently use the returned stream in your application. This contrasts with the `Iterable` return type through which you return a collection. You can leverage the Stream features, such as `map-filter-reduce` techniques, using the defined repository Stream method. Refer to the Java 8 Stream to learn more about how to leverage the Stream features.

3.4.3 *Implementing pagination with PagingAndSortingRepository*

Pagination is a technique to break a large set of data into multiple pages. It is an effective and server-friendly way to return the results to your user. Typically, application users will not look beyond the first few results, irrespective of the number of results shown to them. Thus, retrieving, processing, and returning a large set of data, at times, result in a waste of bandwidth and CPU time. Besides, if the returned data contains resources such as images, it can slow down the application loading and impact the user experience. Imagine showing a product catalogue with hundreds of items and each catalogue item containing an image.

Spring Data provides the `PagingAndSortingRepository` interface that provides you with the ability to page and sort the returned data. And since this interface extends `CrudRepository`, you can also access the core CRUD features provided in the `CrudRepository` interface. Let's explore the use of the `PagingAndSortingRepository` interface in the next technique.

3.4.4 *Technique: Using PagingAndSortingRepository interface to paginate and sort the data*

In this technique, we'll demonstrate how to use Spring's `PagingAndSortingRepository` interface for pagination and sorting.

PROBLEM

Loading, sorting, and returning a large set of data to the application users waste the server resources and impact the application user experience. You need to return the data into a smaller subset in terms of pages.

SOLUTION

Pagination is the technique to split the data into a smaller chunk, known as a page. You can configure the size of the page that determines the number of records or data contained in a page. For a better user experience, you can optionally sort the data in ascending or descending order.

In this technique, you'll use Spring Data's built-in `PagingAndSortingRepository` to implement pagination. In this technique, we'll load a few courses and return the courses to the users in terms of pages.

> **Source code**
>
> You can find the base version of the Spring Boot project in the book's companion GitHub repository at http://mng.bz/VIZ0. The final version of the project is available at http://mng.bz/xvVe.

Let's define the `CourseRepository` interface that extends the `PagingAndSortingRepository` interface, as shown in the following listing. We'll look into the `PagingAndSortingRepository` interface shortly.

Listing 3.23 Extending PagingAndSortingRepository

```
@Repository
public interface CourseRepository extends PagingAndSortingRepository<Course,
     Long> {

}
```

Next, let's define a test case that uses the `PagingAndSortingRepository` interface, as shown in the following listing.

Listing 3.24 Unit test to use PagingAndSortingRepository

```
@Test
void givenDataAvailableWhenLoadFirstPageThenGetFiveRecords() {
    Pageable pageable = PageRequest.of(0,5);
    assertThat(courseRepository.findAll(pageable)).hasSize(5);
    assertThat(pageable.getPageNumber()).isEqualTo(0);

    Pageable nextPageable = pageable.next();
    assertThat(courseRepository.findAll(nextPageable)).hasSize(4);
    assertThat(nextPageable.getPageNumber()).isEqualTo(1);
}
```

We are performing the following activities:

- Creating a `PageRequest` instance using the static `of` method by specifying the page number and the number of records on the page. You've specified the page number `0` and the record size on the page as `5`.

- Using a pageable instance in the `findAll()` method of the `CourseRespository` to load the first page. This `findAll()` method is from the `PagingAndSortingRepository` interface.
- Using the various methods of Pageable instances to assert on the values, such as next page and page number.

Let's now explore the use of sorting facilities provided in the `PagingAndSortingRepository` interface, as shown in the following listing.

Listing 3.25 Pagination usage example

```
@Test
void givenDataAvailableWhenSortsFirstPageThenGetSortedSData() {
    Pageable pageable = PageRequest.of(0,5, Sort.by(Sort.Order.asc("Name")));
    Condition<Course> sortedFirstCourseCondition = new Condition<Course>() {
        @Override
        public boolean matches(Course course) {
            return course.getId() == 4
➥ && course.getName().equals("Cloud Native
➥ Spring Boot Application Development");
        }
    };
    assertThat(courseRepository.findAll(pageable))
➥ .first().has(sortedFirstCourseCondition);
}

@Test
void givenDataAvailableWhenApplyCustomSortThenGetSortedResult() {
    Pageable customSortPageable = PageRequest.of(0,5, Sort.by("Rating")
     .descending().and(Sort.by("Name")));
    Condition<Course> customSortFirstCourseCondition = new
     Condition<Course>() {
        @Override
        public boolean matches(Course course) {
            return course.getId() == 2
➥ && course.getName().equals("Getting Started
➥ with Spring Security DSL");
        }
    };
    assertThat(courseRepository.findAll(customSortPageable))
➥ .first().has(customSortFirstCourseCondition);
}
```

In the above code snippet, you've performed sorting of the data:

- First, with the custom sort order with the course name in ascending order
- Second, defining a custom sorting order with descending sorting order on course rating and ascending sorting on course name

DISCUSSION

The PagingAndSortingRepository is a useful interface that lets you achieve custom pagination and sorting features in your application. The following listing shows this interface from the Spring Data codebase.

Listing 3.26 The PagingAndSortingRepository interface definition

```
@NoRepositoryBean
public interface PagingAndSortingRepository<T, ID> extends
➥ CrudRepository<T, ID> {

    Page<T> findAll(Pageable pageable);

    Iterable<T> findAll(Sort sort);

}
```

The first `findAll(..)` method takes an instance of `Pageable`. The `Pageable` interface provides several useful methods to construct page requests as well as access the page information. For instance, you've used the `of(..)` method to construct the page request that lets you specify the page number with the number of records in it. Further, it also allows you to access the previous and next pages.

The second `findAll(..)` method takes an instance of `Sort`. The `Sort` class is flexible and provides myriad ways to construct a sorting order. For instance, in the second test case, you have constructed a custom sort order with rating in descending and name in ascending order.

3.4.5 Specifying query using @NamedQuery

In section 3.4.1, you saw there are two approaches to defining query methods. You learned the first approach in the defining custom query methods to retrieve domain objects from a relational database with Spring Data JPA technique, where we explained how to define custom query method signatures from which Spring Data generates the queries. In this section, you'll learn the other approach to manually define custom queries directly in your repository methods, so Spring Data can use them as is instead of deriving them through the names of the methods.

Although the method name-based query approach works fine in most circumstances, sometimes you would like to define the queries explicitly that should be used by Spring Data. Let's discuss the scenarios in which you might want to use this alternative approach:

- If you have defined a fine-tuned query and leveraged datastore-specific features.
- If there is a requirement to access more than one table with table joins. In this scenario, you might have defined a query that joins multiple tables.

In this section, you'll learn several features to manually specify the query using Spring Data's `NamedQuery`, `Query`, and `QueryDSL` features. In this section, let's start with the `NamedQuery` feature.

A NamedQuery is a predefined query that is associated with a business entity. It uses Jakarta Persistence Query Language (JPQL; see http://mng.bz/AxpK) to define the query. You can define a NamedQuery in an entity or its superclass. You'll see an example of this shortly.

You can define a named query with the @NamedQuery annotation in your entity class. This annotation has four arguments: name, query, lockMode, and hints. The name and query attributes of the @NamedQuery annotations are mandatory, whereas the remaining two attributes are optional. Let's start with the next technique that shows the usage of NamedQuery in your Spring Boot application.

3.4.6 Technique: Using a named query to manage domain objects in a relational database with Spring Data JPA

In this technique, we'll discuss how to use named query to manage domain objects.

Problem

You need to use named query with Spring Data JPA to define custom queries in repository interface methods to manage domain objects in a relational database.

Solution

Although the query methods with query method signature definition approach work well enough in most scenarios, there are cases in which it has some limitations. For instance, if you need to join multiple tables and retrieve the data, there is no easy way to define the method signatures. With the named query, you can provide the query along with the method signature so that the same can be used to retrieve the data.

> **Source code**
> You can find the base version of the Spring Boot project in the book's companion GitHub repository at http://mng.bz/Zz6O. The final version of the project is available at http://mng.bz/RErO.

To begin with, let's modify the Course class to add the @NamedQuery annotation, as shown in the following listing.

Listing 3.27 Course interface with @NamedQuery annotation

```
package com.manning.sbip.ch03.model;

import javax.persistence.*;

@Entity
@Table(name = "COURSES")
@NamedQuery(name = "Course.findAllByCategoryAndRating",
➥ query = "select c from Course c where c.category=?1
➥ and c.rating=?2")
public class Course {
```

The @NamedQuery annotation lets you specify the query for the repository method in JPQL format.

```
    @Id
    @GeneratedValue(strategy = GenerationType.IDENTITY)
    private long id;
    private String name;

    // Remaining parts omitted for brevity
}
```

In the Course POJO, you've provided the query details that fetch all courses by the supplied category in the @NamedQuery annotation. The name attribute contains the entity and method name concatenated with a dot(.). In the query, you've provided the query along with two positional parameters: ?1 and ?2. It uses the supplied parameter values when the repository method is invoked.

Further, you can use @NamedQuery annotation more than once in the entity if you need to define more than one repository method for which you want to use the @NamedQuery feature, which is shown in the following listing.

Listing 3.28 Use of @NamedQueries annotation to include multiple @NamedQuery annotation

```
@Entity
@Table(name = "COURSES")
@NamedQueries({
    @NamedQuery(name = "Course.findAllByRating",
➥ query = "select c from Course c where c.rating=?1"),
    @NamedQuery(name = "Course.findAllByCategoryAndRating",
➥ query = "select c from Course c
➥ where c.category=?1 and c.rating=?2"),
})
public class Course {

// other members are excluded as a matter of readability
}
```

Let us redefine the CourseRepository interface, which now contains a custom method with the same method name provided in the @NamedQuery annotation in the Course entity. The following listing shows the updated CourseRepository interface.

Listing 3.29 CourseRepository interface with the method defined in @NamedQuery annotation

```
package com.manning.sbip.ch03.repository;

// Import Statements are excluded as a matter of readability

@Repository
public interface CourseRepository extends CrudRepository<Course, Long> {

    Iterable<Course> findAllByCategoryAndRating(String category, int rating);
}
```

The repository method is defined in the @NamedQuery annotation. It is defined here, so you can use it with CourseRepository instance.

Let's validate the use of the `findAllByCategoryAndRating(..)` method by defining a test case, as shown in the following listing.

Listing 3.30 Unit test to use @NamedQuery annotation

```
package com.manning.sbip.ch03;

// Import Statements are excluded as a matter of readability

@SpringBootTest
class CourseTrackerSpringBootApplicationTests {

    @Autowired
    private CourseRepository courseRepository;

    @Test
    public void givenCoursesCreatedWhenLoadCoursesBySpringCategory
➥ ThenExpectThreeCourses(){
        courseRepository.saveAll(getCourseList());
        assertThat(courseRepository
➥ .findAllByCategoryAndRating("Spring", 4)).hasSize(1);
    }

    private List<Course> getCourseList() {
        // get course list
    }
}
```

If you run the test case, you'll see it executes successfully. In the next section, let's discuss the `@Query` annotation.

3.5 Specifying query using @Query

Although the named queries to declare queries in the entity class work fine, they unnecessarily add persistence information in the business domain class (recall that you added the `@NamedQuery` annotation in the `Course` class). This can be a concern, as it tightly couples the persistence details in the business domain classes.

As an alternative, you can provide the query information in the repository interface. This co-locates the query method and the JPQL query together. You can use the `@Query` annotation in the repository interface methods to do this. Besides, the benefit of using the `@Query` annotation over the named queries is that the `@Query` annotation lets you use the native SQL queries as well. Thus, you can use both JPQL as well as native SQL queries with the `@Query` annotation. Let's explore the use of `@Query` annotation in the next technique.

3.5.1 Technique: Using @Query annotation to define queries and retrieve domain objects in a relational database with Spring Data JPA

In this technique, we'll discuss how to use `@Query` annotation to define and retrieve domain objects.

PROBLEM

You want to use @Query annotation with Spring Data JPA to define custom queries in repository interface methods to manage domain objects in a relational database.

SOLUTION

The @Query annotation allows you to provide the queries along with the method signature in the repository interface. This is considered a better approach, as the business domain objects are kept free from persistence-related information.

> **Source code**
>
> You can find the base version of the Spring Boot project in the book's companion GitHub repository at http://mng.bz/2jRd. The final version of the project is available at http://mng.bz/1jZV.

Let's redefine the CourseRepository interface in which you'll provide three repository methods using the @Query annotation, as shown in the following listing.

Listing 3.31 Updated CourseRepository with custom query methods with @Query annotation

```
package com.manning.sbip.ch03.repository;

// Import Statements are excluded as a matter of readability

@Repository
public interface CourseRepository extends CrudRepository<Course, Long> {

    @Query("select c from Course c where c.category=?1")
    Iterable<Course> findAllByCategory(String category);
    @Query("select c from Course c where
  ➥ c.category=:category and c.rating >:rating")
    Iterable<Course>
  ➥ findAllByCategoryAndRatingGreaterThan(@Param("category")
  ➥ String category, @Param("rating") int rating);

    @Query(value = "select * from COURSE where rating=?1",
  ➥ nativeQuery = true)
    Iterable<Course> findAllByRating(int rating);

    @Modifying
    @Transactional
```

The repository method that finds all the courses belong to the supplied category. The @Query annotation lets you specify the JPQL Query. You have used a positional argument with ?1, which is replaced by the supplied category in this example.

The repository method finds all the courses that belong to the supplied category and has a rating value greater than the one supplied in the rating parameter. You have used named parameters in this example. These named parameters are replaced by the supplied category and rating values in this example.

The repository method that finds all the courses for a given rating. This is not a JPQL query, and we've set the nativeQuery to true to indicate this query is a native SQL database query.

```
    @Query("update Course c set c.rating=:rating
➥ where c.name=:name")
    int updateCourseRatingByName(@Param("rating") int rating,
➥ @Param("name") String name);
}
```

The repository method lets you update a course rating. The @Modifying annotation indicates that the query specified in the @Query annotation is a modifying query. The @Transactional annotation bounds the method execution in a transaction context as it is performing a database update.

There is quite a lot happening in the updated `CourseRepository` interface. Let us examine what it's achieved in detail:

- You've used the `@Query` annotation to define the JPQL query that should be used by Spring Data to fetch the courses. This query is similar to what you've used in the named queries technique in section 3.4.6. This query also uses positional arguments to use the supplied argument. In this query, you are retrieving all courses that belong to the provided category.
- In the next query, you've used the `@Query` annotation to define the query to be used by Spring Data. However, there are a few notable differences in the syntax. Instead of the positional argument-based approach, you've used *named parameters*. Although the positional-based approach works well, at times it is error-prone if the position of the parameter changes while performing code refactoring. To avoid this issue, you are using the `@Param` annotation to provide the parameter with a name and binding the name in the query.
- In the third query, you've specified an SQL query and set the `nativeQuery` flag to `true` to indicate the query is a native SQL query. Typically, different database vendors offer database-specific features that are native to the specific database. Thus, if you need to leverage database-specific features, you can define the SQL query with `nativeQuery` flag set to `true`.
- The fourth query is quite interesting. So far, most of the queries in the earlier demonstrations have been used to retrieve data from the database. Unlike those queries, the fourth query is a data manipulation query that updates content in the database. Along with the `@Query` annotation, this method also specified two additional annotations and a different return type. Let's explain these in detail:
  - The `@Transactional` annotation is used to bound the method execution in a transaction context, as it is performing a database update. Note that we are not performing any transaction explicitly; instead, Spring is managing the transaction via aspect-oriented programming.
  - The `@Modifying` annotation indicates that the query specified in the `@Query` annotation is a modifying query. This annotation only works in conjunction with the `@Query` annotation. In addition to the `UPDATE` statements, you can also specify `INSERT`, `DELETE`, and other DDL statements in the `@Query` annotation. Note that we'll get an `InvalidDataAccessApiUsageException` if this annotation is not specified.

  - The return type of the query must be either `int/Integer` or `void`, as it is a modifying query. If the return type is `int/Integer`, it returns the number of rows modified by the query.

To understand the supported return types in the query methods, you can refer to Spring Data JPA documentation at http://mng.bz/W7Z4 for a list of supported return types. Let's now define a test case to see these methods in practice, as shown in the following listing.

Listing 3.32 Unit test to examine the use of the @Query annotation

```
package com.manning.sbip.ch03;

// Import Statements are excluded as a matter of readability

@DataJpaTest
class CourseTrackerSpringBootApplicationTests {

    @Autowired
    private CourseRepository courseRepository;

    @Test
    public void givenCoursesCreatedWhenLoadCoursesWithQuery
➥ ThenExpectCorrectCourseDetails() {
        saveMockCourses();
        assertThat(courseRepository.findAllByCategory("Spring"))
➥ .hasSize(3);
        assertThat(courseRepository.findAllByRating(3)).hasSize(2);
        assertThat(courseRepository.findAllByCategory
➥ AndRatingGreaterThan("Spring", 3)).hasSize(2);
        courseRepository.updateCourseRatingByName(4,
➥ "Getting Started with Spring Cloud Kubernetes");
        assertThat(courseRepository.findAllByCategory
➥ AndRatingGreaterThan("Spring", 3)).hasSize(3);
    }

    private void saveMockCourses() {
        // Save List of Courses
    }
}
```

If you execute this test case, you'll find that all the assertions are true.

DESCRIPTION

The `@Query` mechanism is an excellent feature that lets you specify the JPQL and the SQL queries directly in the repository query methods. It offers several benefits compared to the other two approaches (e.g., query methods and named query).

The Spring Data query method has a limitation when you need to fetch data from multiple tables and when you wish to use any native database feature. The `@Query` approach is useful if you need to fetch data from multiple tables with a complex table join query. You can define the query and let the Spring Data repository use the query to retrieve the data. You can also use native SQL features of the underlying database if required.

Although similar, the named query approach introduces persistence details with `@NamedQuery` annotation, which is not always considered a best practice. An attentive reader might counter that the `@Query` approach also specifies native SQL queries inside the Java class, which also is not considered as a best practice. To overcome this problem, Spring Data also lets you externalize the queries in a property file. You can create a folder named META-INF inside the src\main\resources folder. Add a file named jpa-named-queries.properties inside the META-INF folder. You can then externalize the queries in the `Entity.finderMethod=Query` format. For example, you can externalize the query for the `findAllByCategory(..)` method, as shown here: `Course.findAllByCategory = select c from Course c where c.category=?1`. Spring Data automatically refers to this externalized query when it needs to execute the `findAllByCategory(..)` method.

Although the named query and the query approaches seem like excellent alternatives to control how to fetch data, both techniques suffer from a major drawback. In these approaches, there is no syntax check of the provided query at compile time, and any syntax issue in the query only surfaces at run time. In the next section, you'll learn two different techniques to programmatically define queries in a type-safe manner.

3.6 Using Criteria API with Spring Data JPA

One of the major drawbacks of using JPQL is the lack of its type safety and absence of static query checking. This is because JPQL queries are not validated at compile time. Thus, any error in the query can only be detected at execution time.

The Criteria API (http://mng.bz/8lnZ) introduced in JPA 2.0 adds a type-safe way to create queries. It lets you express a query in a programmatic and type-safe manner. The type safety of a query is achieved using the interfaces and classes that represent various parts of the query, such as the select clause, order-by, and others. Type safety is also achieved in terms of referencing attributes of an entity. Let's define a technique to see the use of Criteria API in conjunction with Spring Data JPA.

3.6.1 Technique: Using Criteria API to manage domain objects in a relational database with Spring Data JPA

In this technique, we'll demonstrate the use of Criteria API.

Problem

Previously, you've used JPQL or native SQL queries to access data from the database. However, both JPQL and SQL do not provide any mechanism to validate the correctness of the queries at compile time. Instead, all query syntax issues are detected at runtime. You need to implement a technique that lets you define queries programmatically in a type-safe manner to reduce execution-time errors in the queries.

SOLUTION

Criteria API is a native API of JPA specification. Thus, you don't need additional libraries to use in your Spring Boot application.

> **Source code**
>
> You can find the base version of the Spring Boot project in the book's companion GitHub repository at http://mng.bz/PWB9. The final version of the project is available at http://mng.bz/J1WO.

Most of the components in the `CourseTracker` application require no change to use Criteria API. Thus, the previously defined `Course` class, `CourseRepository` interface, and other configurations remain unchanged. Let's define a test case to see the use of Criteria API in practice, as shown in the following listing.

Listing 3.33 Unit test to demonstrate the use of Criteria API

```
package com.manning.sbip.ch03;

// Import Statements are excluded as a matter of readability

@SpringBootTest
class CourseTrackerSpringBootApplicationTests {

    @Autowired
    private CourseRepository courseRepository;

    @Autowired
    private EntityManager entityManager;

    @Test
    public void givenCoursesCreatedWhenLoadCoursesWithQuery
➥ ThenExpectCorrectCourseDetails() {
        courseRepository.saveAll(getCourseList());

        CriteriaBuilder criteriaBuilder =
➥ entityManager.getCriteriaBuilder();

        CriteriaQuery<Course> courseCriteriaQuery =
➥ criteriaBuilder.createQuery(Course.class);

        Root<Course> courseRoot = courseCriteriaQuery
➥ .from(Course.class);

        Predicate courseCategoryPredicate =
➥ criteriaBuilder.equal(
➥ courseRoot.get("category"), "Spring");

        courseCriteriaQuery.where(courseCategoryPredicate);

        TypedQuery<Course> query =
➥ entityManager.createQuery(courseCriteriaQuery);
```

```
        Assertions.assertThat(query.getResultList()
➥ .size()).isEqualTo(3);

    }

    private List<Course> getCourseList() {
        // Get Courses
    }
}
```

You perform the following activities in the test case:

- Autowire the `EntityManager` in the test class and use it to create an instance of `CriteriaBuilder`. An `EntityManager` instance is associated with a persistence context, which is a set of entity instances. Within the persistence context, the entity instances and their lifecycle are managed. The `CriteriaBuilder` instance allows you to construct criteria queries, selections, ordering, and more.
- The returned `CriteriaBuilder` is used to define a `CriteriaQuery`, and its type is bound to the `Course` type.
- You then define the `Root` of the query using the returned `CriteriaQuery`.
- Subsequently, you define a `Predicate` that defines a condition. In this example, the predicate represents the category as `Spring`.
- Lastly, you used the predicate in the previously defined `CriteriaQuery` and define a `TypedQuery`, which provides the query output.

DISCUSSION

To use Criteria API in your application, you need to follow a series of steps to construct the query. At first, you define an instance of `CriteriaBuilder` instance through the `EntityManager`. Subsequently, you use this `CriteriaBuilder` instance to create any of the `CriteriaQuery`, `CriteriaUpdate`, `CriteriaDelete` instances based on your need. `CriteriaQuery` provides you with the functionalities to construct a query. The `CriteriaUpdate` and `CriteriaDelete` allow you to define queries to perform bulk updates and deletes, respectively.

You then use `CriteriaQuery` to construct various query parts using methods, such as `from(..)`, `where(..)`, `groupBy()`, `orderBy()`, and others. A `CriteriaQuery` instance is typed, as you use the entity type in the `CriteriaBuilder` interface to create it. For instance, in the test case shown earlier, you've used the `Course` type to bound the type. You use `CriteriaQuery` to define the query root, which is always the reference entities (e.g., `Course` in our example).

The obtained `Root` is used to define the expressions. For instance, we have defined the expression that the course category is `Spring`. This expression is used to define a `Predicate`, which is used in `CriteriaQuery`. You use the `EntityManager` instance to create a `TypedQuery` from the already created `CriteriaQuery`. The `TypedQuery` interface controls the execution of the types of queries. You used the methods provided in the `TypedQuery` instance to obtain the query result. For example, we've used the `getResultList(..)` method to execute the query and retrieve the result.

Providing an in-depth guide to Criteria API is beyond the scope of this book. You can refer to chapter 6 of the JPA specification, which is available at http://mng.bz/wnrq, to learn more about this API.

3.7 Using QueryDSL with Spring Data JPA

In section 3.6 you explored the use of Criteria API with Spring Data JPA. Although Criteria API is a native JPA API, one of the major challenges is its verbose nature. To execute even a simple `SELECT` query, you need to write quite a few lines of code.

The `Querydsl` (http://www.querydsl.com/) is an alternative third-party library that also lets you build type-safe queries more concisely using its fluent API. Like Criteria API, it also ensures that the following checks are made at compilation time:

- Entity types specified in a query exist and can be persisted in the database.
- All properties used in a query exist in the entity and can be persisted in the database.
- All SQL operators receive values of expectant type.
- The resulting query is syntactically correct.

Spring Data provides a `QuerydslPredicateExecutor` interface to leverage QueryDSL features in Spring Data modules. In the next technique, let's examine the use of `Querydsl` with JPA.

3.7.1 Technique: Using QueryDSL to manage domain objects in a relational database with Spring Data JPA

In this technique, we'll discuss the use of QueryDSL.

PROBLEM

Criteria API is a native JPA API and provides a means to build queries in a type-safe manner. However, this API is often criticized for being verbose, as you need to perform too many tasks to even execute a simple query. You need a relatively simple alternative.

SOLUTION

QueryDSL is an alternative to Criteria API that provides a fluent and concise API. Like Criteria API, it allows you to define the queries programmatically in a type-safe manner. In this technique, you'll see the use of QuerydDSL API with Spring Data JPA to manage domain objects in a relational database.

> **Source code**
>
> You can find the base version of the Spring Boot project in the book's companion GitHub repository at http://mng.bz/q2Ew. The final version of the project is available at http://mng.bz/7Wn9.

To use QueryDSL, we need to add the `querydsl-apt`, `querydsl-jpa` Maven dependencies and the `apt-maven-plugin` plugin in the pom.xml to enable the `Querydsl` capabilities in the application, as shown in the following listing.

Listing 3.34 Updated pom.xml file with QueryDSL dependencies and apt-maven-plugin

```
<?xml version="1.0" encoding="UTF-8"?>
<project xmlns="http://maven.apache.org/POM/4.0.0"
➥ xmlns:xsi="http://www.w3.org/2001/XMLSchema-instance"
      xsi:schemaLocation="http://maven.apache.org/POM/4.0.0
➥ https://maven.apache.org/xsd/maven-4.0.0.xsd">
    <modelVersion>4.0.0</modelVersion>

    // Other pom.xml components

    <dependencies>
        // Other dependencies
        <dependency>
            <groupId>com.querydsl</groupId>
            <artifactId>querydsl-apt</artifactId>
        </dependency>
        <dependency>
            <groupId>com.querydsl</groupId>
            <artifactId>querydsl-jpa</artifactId>
        </dependency>
    </dependencies>

    <build>
        <plugins>
            <plugin>
                <groupId>org.springframework.boot</groupId>
                <artifactId>spring-boot-maven-plugin</artifactId>
            </plugin>
            <plugin>
                <groupId>com.mysema.maven</groupId>
                <artifactId>apt-maven-plugin</artifactId>
                <version>1.1.3</version>
                <executions>
                    <execution>
                        <phase>generate-sources</phase>
                        <goals>
                            <goal>process</goal>
                        </goals>
                        <configuration>
                            <outputDirectory>
➥ target/generated-sources/java</outputDirectory>
                            <processor>com.querydsl.apt.jpa.JPAAnnotationPro-
    cessor</processor>
                        </configuration>
                    </execution>
                </executions>
            </plugin>
        </plugins>
    </build>

</project>
```

Let's explore the use of these additional Maven dependencies and the plugin:

- The `querydsl-apt` library is an annotation processing tool (APT) that enables the processing of the annotation in the source files before they move to the compilation stage. This tool generates the so-called `Q-types` classes that are related to the entity classes present in the application. These `Q-types` are classes that are directly related to the entity classes of your application but are prefixed with the letter `Q`. For example, for the `Course` entity, you'll see a QCourse.java source file created by this tool.
- The `querydsl-jpa` is the `Querydsl` library designed to be working alongside a JPA application. Similarly, if you would like to use QueryDSL with MongoDB database, you need to use `querydsl-mongodb` Maven dependency.
- The `apt-maven-plugin` ensures that the `Q-types` are generated at the time of the process goal of the Maven build. Besides, as the name indicates, the `outputDirectory` property is the place where the generated `Q-types` are kept. Furthermore, this directory needs to be included as the source folder of the project, as you'll use these generated Java files in your application.

Let's now focus on the `CourseRepository` interface, as shown in the following listing.

Listing 3.35 Updated CourseRepository interface with QuerydslPredicateExecutor

```
package com.manning.sbip.ch03.repository;

// Import Statements are excluded as a matter of readability

@Repository
public interface CourseRepository
➥ extends CrudRepository<Course, Long>,
➥ QuerydslPredicateExecutor<Course> {
}
```

You can notice that, along with the `CrudRepository` interface, `CourseRepository` now also extends the `QuerydslPredicateExecutor` interface. Although this interface is not compulsory to be implemented to use `Querydsl`, it provides several overloaded methods that let you use `Querydsl` instances with the familiar query methods (e.g., `Iterable<T> findAll(OrderSpecifier<?>... orders);`). Note that the query method from the `CrudRepository` interface does not take any argument. You'll see the usage of the methods from this interface shortly.

For this demonstration, there is no change in the `Course` POJO. Since the common IDEs are automatically configured to process annotations, you should find the generated QCourse.java Java file in the configured `outputDirectory`, as configured in the `apt-maven-plugin` plugin in the pom.xml file. For this demonstration, you've configured the target/generated-sources/java directory where this QCourse.java file is generated. If the sources are not generated automatically, then you can run the `mvn generate-sources` command from the root directory of your project to generate the source code.

Ensure that the root package of the generated java file is marked as the source directory. Otherwise, you won't be able to use this Java file in your application. In IntelliJ IDEA, you can right-click on the `java` folder inside the generated-sources folder and click on `Mark Directory` as and then `Generated Sources Root` options.

You'll now use the generated `QCourse` class to define the queries in our application codebase. Typically, you'll use the Q-classes inside the service layer to define the queries. To keep things simple, we will define a test case and use the `QCourse` class to define the queries, which is demonstrated in the following listing.

Listing 3.36 Unit test to examine the use of QueryDSL

```
package com.manning.sbip.ch03;

// Imports excluded as a matter of readability

@SpringBootTest
class CourseTrackerSpringBootApplicationTests {

    @Autowired
    private CourseRepository courseRepository;

    @Autowired
    private EntityManager entityManager;

    @Test
    public void givenCoursesCreatedWhenLoadCoursesWithQuery
➥ ThenExpectCorrectCourseDetails() {
        courseRepository.saveAll(getCourseList());

        QCourse course = QCourse.course;
        JPAQuery query1 = new JPAQuery(entityManager);
        query1.from(course).where(course.category.eq("Spring"));

        assertThat(query1.fetch().size()).isEqualTo(3);

        JPAQuery query2 = new JPAQuery(entityManager);
        query2
➥ .from(course)
➥ .where(course.category.eq("Spring")
➥ .and(course.rating.gt(3)));
        assertThat(query2.fetch().size()).isEqualTo(2);
        OrderSpecifier<Integer> descOrderSpecifier =
➥ course.rating.desc();
        assertThat(Lists.newArrayList(
➥ courseRepository.findAll(descOrderSpecifier))
➥ .get(0).getName())
➥ .isEqualTo("Getting Started with Spring Security DSL");
    }

    private List<Course> getCourseList() {
        // getCourseList implementation goes here. Method body is excluded as
      a matter of readability
    }
}
```

Defines a course instance

Creates a JPAQuery instance

Builds the query using the from and where clauses. Notice the use of DSL (e.g., the use of from and where).

Executes the query and retrieves the courses

OrderSpecifier represents the order-by instance in the course. In this case, we are creating a descending order-by instance with the course rating.

Let's discuss the test case in detail:

- It has a dependency on the `CourseRepository` and the `EntityManager`. The `EntityManager` is used to create the JPA query instances.
- You have defined a local variable named course and initialized it with the `QCourse.course` static instance.
- Subsequently, you have created an instance of `JPAQuery` using the EntityManager. It is the default implementation of the `JPQLQuery` interface for JPA in `Querydsl`.
- You then start building the query using Querydsl's fluent API. You pass the course instance to the `from()` method of `JPAQuery` and build the conditional clause of the query using the `where()` method.
- Following that, you invoke the `fetch()` method on the created query to fetch courses from the database and assert the result.
- Subsequently, in the next `JPAQuery` (query2), you've used the `and(..)` method in the `where()` method to provide additional criteria in the query.
- You then invoke `fetch()` on the generated query and assert the result.
- Lastly, you've created an instance of `OrderSpecifier`, which represents the `order-by` instance in the `Course`. It defines the descending order based on the rating property of the `Course` entity.
- You then use the `findAll(..)` method of `CourseRepository` that accepts the `OrderSpecifier` instance. It returns all courses ordered as per the `OrderSpecifier` instance.

Note that this `findAll(..)` method is from `QuerydslPredicateExecutor`. Since `CourseRepository` extends this interface, you can invoke using the `CourseRepository` instance.

DISCUSSION

With this technique, you've seen the use of `Querydsl` API with Spring Data JPA. `Querydsl` is a popular framework that enables you to construct statically typed SQL-like queries for several data sources. One of the major reasons for this library's popularity is its static type checking, fluent API, and concise nature. This static type check ensures that queries are syntactically correct at compilation time.

QueryDSL was introduced to maintain Hibernate Query Language (HQL) queries in a type-safe way. Incorrect string concatenation and reference to domain types and properties in HQL queries often lead to runtime query execution issues. QueryDSL reduces these errors by performing static type checking at query compilation time. In QueryDSL, queries are constructed based on the generated query types, which are essentially the properties of the business domain class. In the QueryDSL method invocations are also done in a type-safe manner. You can refer to the QueryDSL reference manual at http://mng.bz/mx9r for further details.

Criteria API vs. QueryDSL

In the previous two techniques, you've seen the usage of both Criteria API and the QueryDSL library. The next question that comes to mind is: which one should you use in your application? Well, both APIs are popular and widely used. Following are a few points to consider when deciding which API to use:

- The Criteria API is a native JPA library and, thus, has native support in JPA, whereas the QueryDSL is an open-source, third-party library.
- The Criteria API is criticized for its verbosity and complex nature of the API. You need to write more to even execute a simple query. The QueryDSL has a more approachable API due to the simpler and English-like API.
- Criteria API is only applicable for JPA. QueryDSL has integration with other data stores, such as MongoDB, Lucene, and JDO.

3.8 Managing domain object relationships

Accessing data from a single table is relatively simple, but this is seldom the case for modern enterprise applications. In most scenarios, you are likely to use more than one table to retrieve the required data.

In the relational database nomenclature, retrieving the required columns from different tables is known as *projection*. Spring Data lets you use projections either through interface-based projection or class-based projection.

An *interface-based projection* allows you to limit the attributes of an entity by declaring an interface that exposes accessor methods for the properties to be read. For instance, if you want to read only the description field of the `Course` entity when finding the courses by course name, you can first define an interface that returns the only description, as shown in the following listing.

Listing 3.37 Interface-based projection

```
package com.manning.sbip.ch03.ibp;

public interface DescriptionOnly {
    String getDescription();
}
```

You can then add a query method in the `CourseRepository` interface that returns a collection of `DescriptionOnly` types, as shown in the following listing.

Listing 3.38 Query method with interface-based projection

```
package com.manning.sbip.ch03.repository;

// Import Statements are excluded as a matter of readability

@Repository
public interface CourseRepository extends CrudRepository<Course, Long> {
```

```
    Iterable<DescriptionOnly> getCourseByName(String name);
}
```

The test case presented in the following listing validates the interface-based projection.

Listing 3.39 Unit test to validate interface-based projection

```
@Test
public void givenACourseAvailableWhenGetCourseByName
➥ ThenGetCourseDescription() {
    Iterable<DescriptionOnly> result =
     courseRepository.getCourseByName("Rapid Spring Boot
➥ Application Development");

assertThat(result)
            .extracting("description").contains("Spring Boot
➥ gives all the power of the Spring Framework without all
➥ of the complexity");
}
```

The `getCourseByName(..)` method returns an `Iterable` of type `DescriptionOnly`, and we retrieve the description. Next, we assert the returned description with the actual description.

A *class-based projection* is also referred to as a data transfer object (DTO). A DTO is a Java POJO class that contains the selected properties returned by the query. As the name suggests, the main purpose of this object is to transfer data from the DAO layer to a higher layer, such as the service layer. You may recall that, as a best practice, a service layer bridges the DAO layer, and the Spring controllers and DAO layers are not accessed directly. You'll examine an example of class-based projection shortly.

Another important concept to understand while dealing with more than one entity is the relationship between them. Based on their association, this relationship is classified into the following categories:

- `One-to-One`—This relationship type indicates that one entity is associated with exactly one entity of the other type. For example, in our `Course` entity example, let's assume we have another entity named `CourseDetails` that captures the additional details about a `Course`. Thus, we can say that the `Course` and `CourseDetails` entities have a `One-to-One` relationship, as a `Course` can have only one `CourseDetails`.
- `One-to-Many`—This relationship type indicates that one entity is associated with more than one entity of the other type. For instance, an entity `Person` can have more than one `Address`. Thus, the relationship between the `Person` and the `Address` is `One-to-Many`.
- `Many-to-One`—This relationship type indicates that many entities of one type are associated with one entity of the other type. For instance, the relationship between the entity `Book` and entity `Publisher` is of `Many-to-One`, as multiple `Books` can be published by a `Publisher`.

- `Many-to-Many`—This relationship type indicates that more than one entity of one type is associated with more than one type of the other entity type. For instance, in the course management example, one `Course` may be authored by multiple `Authors`. Similarly, one `Author` can author multiple `Courses`. The relationship in this context is `Many-to-Many` between the author and course entities.

Let's demonstrate the use of DTO and the implementation of a many-to-many relationship in the following technique.

3.8.1 *Technique: Managing domain objects with many-to-many relationships in a relational database with Spring Data JPA*

In this technique, we'll demonstrate how to manage many-to-many relationships in domain objects.

PROBLEM

While managing object relationships in your application, you often encounter scenarios in which objects maintain many-to-many relationships. For instance, in the `Course-Tracker` application, entities `Author` and `Course` maintain a many-to-many relationship. You need to manage the many-to-many relationship among two entities using Spring Data JPA.

SOLUTION

Many-to-many relationships are some of the most-used relationships for managing between entities. For instance, the `Course` and `Author` entities have a many-to-many relationship among them. In such a scenario, you must maintain the author and course details along with the relationship between course and author. For example, an author can author multiple courses, and many authors can collaborate on a course. Thus, in this case, you need to maintain the author and course information as well as their relationship details. Hence, you need to maintain three tables: one for the `Author` details, another for the `Course` details, and one for their related information. Figure 3.7 shows the entity–relationship (ER) diagram:

Before continuing further, let us understand the data model you'll use in this technique. The `Author` entity is represented by the `AUTHOR` table in the database.

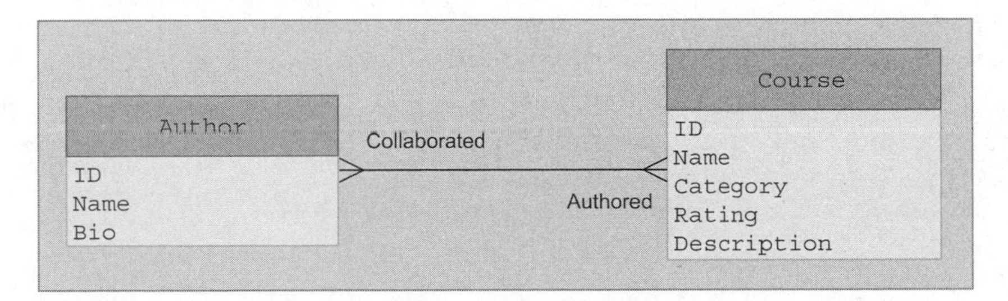

Figure 3.7 Author and Course entity–relationship diagram. In an ER diagram, the relationship table is represented by the relationship arrow itself. Thus, the relationship table is not present in the diagram.

Source code

You can find the base version of the Spring Boot project in the book's companion GitHub repository at http://mng.bz/5K6B. The final version of the project is available at http://mng.bz/6Zoo.

The mapping table between the Author and the Course entities is represented by the AUTHORS_COURSES table. To represent a relationship on Relational Database Management System, the rule is to use relationship tables in which the relationship between author and course is represented with a DB entry containing the corresponding unique identifiers of the two tables. For example, the AUTHORS_COURSES table contains the mapping information of authors and courses based on author_id and course_id. The following listing shows the schema.sql DDL scripts used in this technique.

Listing 3.40 The Schema.sql

```
CREATE TABLE authors (
  id   BIGINT NOT NULL,
  bio  VARCHAR(255),
  name VARCHAR(255),
  PRIMARY KEY (id)
);

CREATE TABLE authors_courses (
  author_id BIGINT NOT NULL,
  course_id BIGINT NOT NULL,
  PRIMARY KEY (author_id, course_id)
);

CREATE TABLE courses (
  id          BIGINT NOT NULL,
  category    VARCHAR(255),
  description VARCHAR(255),
  name        VARCHAR(255),
  rating      INTEGER NOT NULL,
  PRIMARY KEY (id)
);

ALTER TABLE authors_courses
  ADD CONSTRAINT course_id_fk FOREIGN KEY
➥ (course_id) REFERENCES courses (id);

ALTER TABLE authors_courses
  ADD CONSTRAINT author_id_fk FOREIGN KEY (author_id)
➥ REFERENCES authors (id);
```

A foreign key constraint to ensure that the course_id in the authors_courses table is a valid course ID from the courses table

A foreign key constraint to ensure that the author_id in the authors_courses table is a valid author ID from the authors table

Let's now define the INSERT scripts in the data.sql file, as shown in listing 3.41. We've created three courses and two authors. Besides, we've added the author and course relationship by mapping courses 1 and 2 with author 1 and courses 1, 2, and 3 with author 2. Thus, courses 1 and 2 are co-authored by both author 1 and author 2.

Listing 3.41 The data.sql script

```
INSERT INTO COURSES(ID, NAME, CATEGORY, RATING, DESCRIPTION)
➥ VALUES(1, 'Rapid Spring Boot Application Development',
➥ 'Spring', 4, 'Spring Boot gives all the power of the
➥ Spring Framework without all of the complexity');
INSERT INTO COURSES(ID, NAME, CATEGORY, RATING, DESCRIPTION)
➥ VALUES(2, 'Getting Started with Spring Security DSL',
➥ 'Spring', 5, 'Learn Spring Security DSL in easy steps');
INSERT INTO COURSES(ID, NAME, CATEGORY, RATING, DESCRIPTION)
➥ VALUES(3, 'Getting Started with Spring Cloud Kubernetes',
➥ 'Python', 3, 'Master Spring Boot application deployment
➥ with Kubernetes');
INSERT INTO AUTHORS(ID, NAME, BIO)
➥ VALUES(1, 'John Doe',
➥ 'Author of several Spring Boot courses');
INSERT INTO AUTHORS(ID, NAME, BIO)
➥ VALUES(2, 'Steve Muller', 'Author of several
➥ popular Spring and Python courses');
INSERT INTO AUTHORS_COURSES(AUTHOR_ID, COURSE_ID) VALUES(1, 1);
INSERT INTO AUTHORS_COURSES(AUTHOR_ID, COURSE_ID) VALUES(1, 2);
INSERT INTO AUTHORS_COURSES(AUTHOR_ID, COURSE_ID) VALUES(2, 1);
INSERT INTO AUTHORS_COURSES(AUTHOR_ID, COURSE_ID) VALUES(2, 2);
INSERT INTO AUTHORS_COURSES(AUTHOR_ID, COURSE_ID) VALUES(2, 3);
```

To automatically execute the schema.sql and the data.sql we have added the following additional properties in the application.properties file, as shown in the following listing.

Listing 3.42 Additional properties in the application.properties file

```
spring.jpa.hibernate.ddl-auto=none
spring.datasource.initialization-mode=always
```

This is to indicate Spring Boot to execute the schema.sql in our H2 database. (spring.datasource.initialization-mode=always)

We are using schema.sql to initialize schema; thus, we are instructing JPA not to manage the schema. (spring.jpa.hibernate.ddl-auto=none)

Let's now start by defining the `Author` entity, as shown in the following listing.

Listing 3.43 The Author entity

```
package com.manning.sbip.ch03.model;

// Import Statements are excluded as a matter of readability

@Entity(name = "AUTHOR")
@Table(name="AUTHORS")
public class Author {

    @Id
    @GeneratedValue(strategy = GenerationType.IDENTITY)
    private long id;
    private String name;
    private String bio;
```

```
    @ManyToMany
    @JoinTable(name = "AUTHORS_COURSES",
            joinColumns = {
      @JoinColumn(name="author_id",
➥ referencedColumnName = "id", nullable = false,
➥ updatable = false)},
            inverseJoinColumns = {
      @JoinColumn(name="course_id",
➥ referencedColumnName = "id", nullable = false,
➥ updatable = false)}
    )
    private Set<Course> courses = new HashSet<>();

    public Author() {}

    public Author(String name, String bio) {
        this.name = name;
        this.bio = bio;
    }

    public long getId() {
        return id;
    }

    public String getName() {
        return name;
    }

    public String getBio() {
        return bio;
    }

    public Set<Course> getCourses() {
        return courses;
    }

    @Override
    public String toString() {
        return "Author{" +
                "id=" + id +
                ", name='" + name + '\'' +
                ", bio='" + bio + '\'' +
                '}';
    }
}
```

In the Author class, you've initialized an empty set of courses to store the relationship between Author and Course. The following listing shows the Course entity.

Listing 3.44 The updated Course entity

```
package com.manning.sbip.ch03.model;

// Import Statements are excluded as a matter of readability
```

```
@Entity(name = "COURSE")
@Table(name = "COURSES")
public class Course {

    @Id
    @GeneratedValue(strategy = GenerationType.IDENTITY)
    private long id;
    private String name;
    private String category;
    private int rating;
    private String description;

    @ManyToMany(mappedBy = "courses")
    private Set<Author> authors = new HashSet<>();

    // Constructor, getter, setters are excluded as a matter of readability

}
```

The mappedBy attribute of @ManyToMany annotation in the non-owning side of the relationship

The `Course` entity contains information related to a course and specifies the many-to-many relationship with the authors. Note that you've specified the `mappedBy` attribute of `@ManyToMany` annotation in the non-owning side of the relationship. We can create the courses and map to the authors who created it, as shown in the following listing.

Listing 3.45 Mapping course details with authors

```
Course rapidSpringBootCourse =
➥ new Course("Rapid Spring Boot Application Development",
➥ "Spring", 4,"Spring Boot gives all the power of the
➥ Spring Framework without all of the complexity");

Course springSecurityDslCourse =
➥ new Course("Getting Started with Spring Security DSL",
➥ "Spring", 5, "Learn Spring Security DSL in easy steps");

Author author1 = new Author("John Doe",
➥ "Author of several Spring Boot courses");

author1.getCourses().addAll(Arrays
➥ .asList(rapidSpringBootCourse, springSecurityDslCourse));
```

Also, besides the core annotations, such as `@Entity`, `@Table`, and `@Id`, there are other annotations specified to capture the relationship information with the `Course` entity. Let's explore these annotations.

@MANYTOMANY

The `@ManyToMany` annotation specifies the many-valued association with many-to-many multiplicity. Each such association has two sides—the owning side and the non-owning side. The owning side indicates the entity that owns the relationship, and the non-owning side is the inverse side of the relationship.

In the case of a one-to-many relationship, the *many* part of the relationship is the owning side. This is because every object of the many sides can easily have a reference to the *one* side. Otherwise, you need to maintain many references from the single object (i.e., the one part) to the many objects.

For many-to-many relationships, you can choose which side should be declared as the owning side, since both sides can own the relationship. For instance, in this demonstration, we have selected the `Author` entity as the owning side. This is chosen based on the understanding that an author *owns* its courses.

You additionally specify the `@JoinTable` annotation on the owning side of the relationship. As discussed, since an author owns a course, you have specified `@JoinTable` annotation on the `Author` entity. In the case of the non-owning side, you specify the `mappedBy` parameter in `@ManyToMany` annotation to specify the field of the owning side. You'll see the use of the `mappedBy` parameter in the `Course` entity.

@JoinTable

This annotation is specified on the owning side of the relationship and is typically used in the mapping of many-to-many and unidirectional one-to-many associations. You've specified this annotation to define the `AUTHORS_COURSES` join table. If this annotation is not provided, then the default values of the annotation are applied. For example, if the table name is not provided, then the table names of the entities are concatenated together with an underscore character, where the owning side table is used first. Besides, you have specified the `joinColumns` and `inverseJoinColumns` attributes with `@JoinTable` annotation. The `joinColumns` specifies the foreign key columns of the join table (e.g., `AUTHORS_COURSES`), which references the primary table (e.g., `AUTHORS`), which owns the association. The `inverseJoinColumns` specify the foreign key columns of the join table, which reference the primary table (e.g., `COURSES`) of the non-owning side.

@JoinColumn

This annotation lets you specify a column for joining an entity association. To recap, the following is the usage of the `JoinColumn` attribute:

```
@JoinColumn(name="author_id", referencedColumnName = "id",
➥ nullable = false, updatable = false)
```

The `name` attribute specifies the name of the foreign key column of the relationship table. The `referencedColumnName` attribute allows you to specify the database column that should be referenced by the foreign key column. The `nullable` attribute indicates whether the foreign column is nullable. The `updatable` attribute specifies whether the column is included in SQL UPDATE statements of the relationship table generated by the persistence provider. Let's define the `AuthorCourse` entity, as shown in the following listing.

Listing 3.46 The AuthorCourse entity

```
package com.manning.sbip.ch03.model;

// Import Statements are excluded as a matter of readability
```

```
@Entity(name = "AUTHOR_COURSE")
@Table(name = "AUTHORS_COURSES")
public class AuthorCourse {
    @Id
    @Column(name = "author_id")
    private long authorId;
    @Column(name = "course_id")
    private long courseId;

    // Constructor, Getter, and Setters excluded as a matter of readability
}
```

This class stores the relationship information of `Author` and `Course` entities and contains the primary keys of both tables. Besides, this entity also represents the `AUTHORS_COURSES` table, as you've annotated it with the `@Table` entity. You'll see the use of this `AUTHORS_COURSES` table when we define join query to retrieve data in our repository interface. Let's now discuss the `AuthorCourseDto` DTO class presented in the following listing.

Listing 3.47 The AuthorCourseDto entity

```
package com.manning.sbip.ch03.dto;

public class AuthorCourseDto {

    private long id;
    private String authorName;
    private String courseName;
    private String description;

    public AuthorCourseDto(long id, String authorName,
➥  String courseName, String description) {
        this.id = id;
        this.authorName = authorName;
        this.courseName = courseName;
        this.description = description;
    }

    @Override
    public String toString() {
        return "{" +
                "id=" + id +
                ", authorName='" + authorName + '\'' +
                ", courseName='" + courseName + '\'' +
                ", description='" + description + '\'' +
                '}';
    }
}
```

If you recall, a DTO class (the class-based projection) allows you to retrieve data from different tables through projection that might not be represented by an existing entity. Thus, a DTO is an object-oriented representation of the tuple data projection from the repository method. You can use a DTO class as the repository return type for queries with joins, as shown in the next listing.

Listing 3.48 The AuthorRepository interface

```
package com.manning.sbip.ch03.repository;

// Import Statements are excluded as a matter of readability

@Repository
public interface AuthorRepository extends CrudRepository<Author, Long> {

    @Query("SELECT
➥ new com.manning.sbip.ch03.dto.AuthorCourseDto
➥ (c.id, a.name, c.name, c.description) from AUTHOR a,
➥ COURSES c, AUTHORS_COURSES ac where a.id = ac.authorId
➥ and c.id=ac.courseId and ac.authorId=?1")
    Iterable<AuthorCourseDto> getAuthorCourseInfo(long authorId);
}
```

In the `AuthorRepository` interface presented in listing 3.48, there is a query method that fetches data from the `AUTHORS`, `COURSES`, and `AUTHORS_COURSES` tables. Since the data obtained through the projection do not represent either the `Author` or `Course` entity, it is represented with the `AuthorCourseDto` class.

The `AuthorRepository` interface extends the `CrudRepository` to access the basic CRUD features. It also defines a custom finder method to fetch the course details authored by an author through the `authorId`. As you've seen in the earlier techniques, the `@Query` annotation allows you to specify the query that should be used to fetch the data from the database tables. Notice the query specified in the `@Query` annotation is not an SQL query. It is a JPQL query that joins all three tables to fetch the data and map to the provided DTO instance. In figure 3.8, there are three tables, namely `AUTHORS`, `AUTHORS_COURSES`, and `COURSES`. You've defined a query method with the query that joins `AUTHORS`, `COURSES`, and `AUTHORS_COURSES` tables and fetches data based on the criteria specified in the query. Thus, you've created the `AuthorCourseDto` Java POJO that represents the columns in the returned projection.

Now, we'll add a test case to see the usage of the `getAuthorCourseInfo(..)` method of `AuthorRepository` in practice, as shown in the following listing.

Listing 3.49 Unit test to validate many-to-many relationship

```
package com.manning.sbip.ch03;

// Import Statements are excluded as a matter of readability

@SpringBootTest
class CourseTrackerSpringBootApplicationTests {

    @Autowired
    private AuthorRepository authorRepository;

    @Test
    public void whenCountAllCoursesThenExpectFiveCourses() {
        assertThat(authorRepository.getAuthorCourseInfo(2)).hasSize(3));
    }
}
```

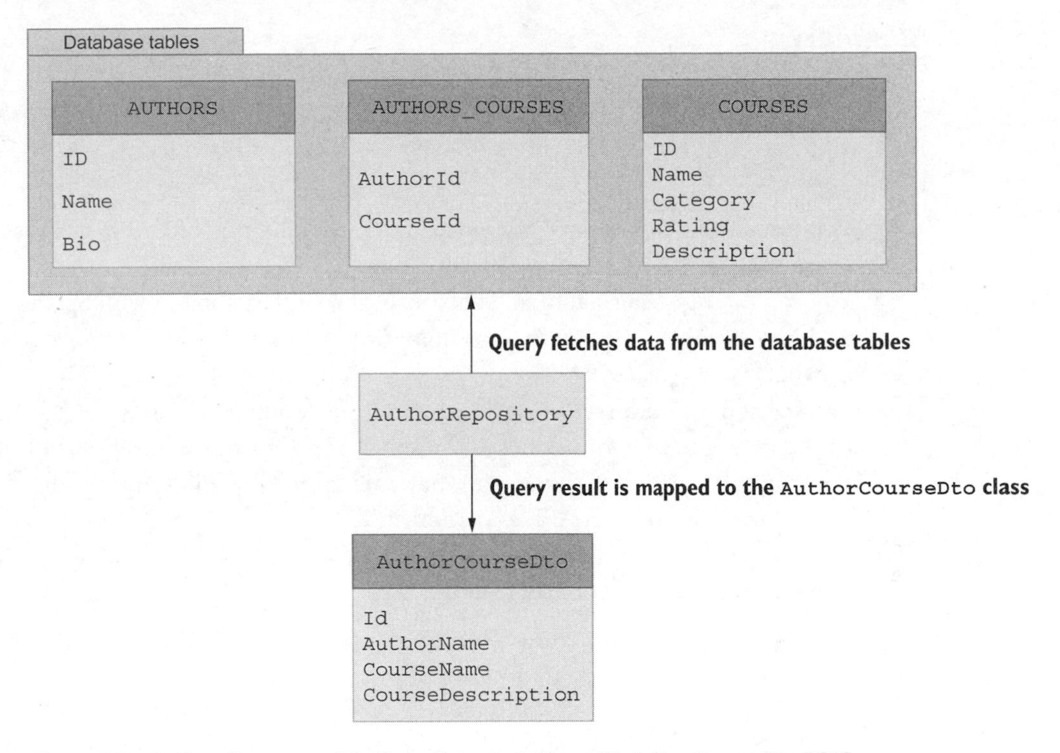

Figure 3.8 Author, Course, and Authors_Courses tables with AuthorCourseDto POJO

In listing 3.49 you defined a test case that fetches courses authored by author ID 2. In this example, the author ID has authored three courses. Thus, you've asserted the number of courses to 3. If you execute this test case, you'll see that it runs successfully and asserts that 3 courses are authored by author ID 2.

DISCUSSION

In this section, you've seen an example of how to manage the many-to-many relationship among the entities. Although the presented example is a very basic one, it demonstrated the features offered by Spring Data JPA to establish and maintain many-to-many relationships between your business domain objects. For instance, you've seen the use of `@ManyToMany` annotation in both the entities maintaining the many-to-many relationship.

Besides, you've also learned the concept of projection. We've explored both the interface and class-based projections with examples. An interface-based projection allows you to selectively fetch columns from an entity, whereas a class-based projection with the notion of DTOs allows you to access data that belongs to multiple entities.

Discussing all the relationship types with code examples is beyond the scope of the book. We encourage you to implement the other relationship types once you are comfortable with the concepts described in this technique.

Summary

In this chapter, you've explored a variety of topics related to database communication from a Spring Boot application. Many of these features are used extensively in Spring Boot application development. Let's quickly summarize the concepts you've learned in this chapter:

- You have been introduced to Spring Data, why it's needed, and various Spring Data modules.
- You can configure a relational database and NoSQL databases with Spring Boot.
- You can initialize the database schema with schema.sql and data.sql as well as through Spring Data JPA.
- You gained an understanding of Spring Data `CrudRepository` and `PagingAndSortingRepository` interfaces and their use in a Spring Boot application.
- You can access data from a relational database using query methods, `@NamedQuery`, `@Query`, Criteria API, and `Querydsl`.
- You know how to manage the many-to-many relationship between domain objects in a Spring Boot application.

In chapter 4, you'll dive into two important concepts of Spring Boot: autoconfiguration and actuator. Spring Boot autoconfiguration performs a lot of automatic configuration under the hood for us and makes it relatively simple to start developing applications. Spring Boot Actuator provides an infrastructure that lets you monitor and interact with a Spring Boot application. Let's discuss these in the next chapter!

4 Spring Boot: Autoconfiguration and Actuator

This chapter covers

- Introducing Spring Boot autoconfiguration, various types of conditional annotation, and in-depth discussion
- An overview of Spring Boot DevTools, how to configure it, and its various purposes
- Introducing Spring Boot FailureAnalyzer and how to define a custom application-specific FailureAnalyzer
- An in-depth discussion on Spring Boot Actuator and how to define custom metrics

You've already learned so much about Spring Boot in the last three chapters. You now have a solid foundation in Spring Boot, having already seen various features of the framework and several common tasks that you need to perform on daily basis. You've also learned how to communicate and use a database in a Spring Boot application.

In this chapter, you'll explore two major concepts of Spring Boot: the Spring Boot autoconfiguration and Spring Boot actuator. You'll learn various building blocks of Spring Boot autoconfiguration and explore how it works in an application.

We'll explore the various conditional annotation, which is the foundation of Spring Boot autoconfiguration. You'll then explore the Spring Boot actuator, which lets you monitor your application health and let you interact with it.

4.1 Understanding Spring Boot autoconfiguration

Spring Boot autoconfiguration is probably the single most important feature of the framework and one of the main reasons behind Spring Boot's popularity. As the name suggests, autoconfiguration automatically configures application components that you would require while developing a Spring application. It makes a sensible guess about the application components and attempts to provide a default configuration with which it initializes the application. For instance, if you include the `spring-boot-starter-web` dependency in your build configuration file, then Spring Boot assumes you need a webserver to run the web application. Thus, it automatically configures the Apache Tomcat web server for you.

Another interesting feature of autoconfiguration is its flexibility. If the autoconfiguration determines that the developer has explicitly configured an application component, then it simply backs away from automatically configuring the specific application component and uses the configuration provided by the developer. For instance, when you use the `spring-boot-starter-web` dependency, Spring Boot uses Apache Tomcat as the default web server. However, if you configure a different web server and exclude Apache Tomcat, Spring Boot backs off its default Tomcat configuration and configures the user-defined web server. The following listing shows the configuration for Jetty web server in a Spring Boot application over Spring Boot default Tomcat.

Listing 4.1 Configuring Jetty web server in a Spring Boot application

```
<dependency>
    <groupId>org.springframework.boot</groupId>
    <artifactId>spring-boot-starter-web</artifactId>
    <exclusions>
        <exclusion>
            <groupId>org.springframework.boot</groupId>
            <artifactId>spring-boot-starter-tomcat</artifactId>
        </exclusion>
    </exclusions>
</dependency>
<dependency>
    <groupId>org.springframework.boot</groupId>
    <artifactId>spring-boot-starter-jetty</artifactId>
</dependency>
```

Imagine you are working in an organization where development teams are working on various projects using the Spring framework. At one point, one of the developers notices that a few Spring configuration beans are used by all the teams and are duplicated across the teams. Accordingly, the developer may decide to extract those duplicate configurations into a common application context configuration, as shown in the following listing.

Listing 4.2 CommonApplicationContextConfiguration class

```
package com.manning.sbip.ch04;

import org.springframework.context.annotation.Bean;
import org.springframework.context.annotation.Configuration;
@Configuration
public class CommonApplicationContextConfiguration {

    #Creates a Spring Bean of type RelationalDataSourceConfiguration
    @Bean
    public RelationalDataSourceConfiguration dataSourceConfiguration() {
        return new RelationalDataSourceConfiguration();
    }

    // Other commonly used Spring bean definitions
}
```

The @Configuration annotation indicates this is a Spring configuration class.

Listing 4.2 shows a sample configuration of the `CommonApplicationContextConfiguration`:

- The `CommonApplicationContextConfiguration` configuration class resides in a separate project and is published as an independent Maven or Gradle component. Thus, other teams can use this as a dependency in their projects.
- The `RelationalDataSourceConfiguration` class provides a relational data source configuration that initializes the database and returns a data source. Since most teams use a relational database, it makes sense to extract and keep this as a separate configuration. Also, for simplicity, we've provided only one configuration, but the `CommonApplicationContextConfiguration` class can contain other common configurations, such as Spring transaction manager bean definition.

Other teams that need to use `CommonApplicationContextConfiguration` can import this common configuration in their specific configuration classes, as shown in the following listing.

Listing 4.3 CommonPaymentContextConfiguration uses CommonApplicationContextConfiguration class

```
import org.springframework.context.annotation.Configuration;
import org.springframework.context.annotation.Import;

@Configuration
@Import(CommonApplicationContextConfiguration.class)
public class CommonPaymentContextConfiguration {

    // Payment teams bean definitions
}
```

Imports the Spring beans defined in the CommonApplicationContextConfiguration class

Teams can define project-specific bean definitions in their respective configuration files. This approach works fine in most scenarios, but there is one problem. What if a team wishes to use all the beans defined in the `CommonApplicationContextConfiguration`, except a specific bean definition? For instance, one team wishes to use all beans defined in the `CommonApplicationContextConfiguration` but not the `RelationalDataSourceConfiguration`, as they don't use a relational database. Thus, there should be some way to tell Spring that importing the `CommonApplicationContextConfiguration` configuration is fine but doesn't create the `RelationalDataSourceConfiguration` bean. How can you achieve this? Spring's `@Conditional` annotation has an answer to this question. We'll look at this in detail in the next section.

4.1.1 Understanding @Conditional annotation

Spring framework provides a `@Conditional` annotation that you can place in the `@Bean`, `@Component`, and `@Configuration` to influence the creation of the Spring-managed components. The `@Conditional` annotation accepts a `Condition` class parameter. The `Condition` interface has a method called `matches(..)` that returns a `boolean` value. A `true` value indicates to further evaluate or create a `@Bean`, `@Component`, or `@Configuration`. A value `false` means not to proceed with the `@Bean`, `@Component`, or `@Configuration` creation. In your custom Condition implementations, you implement the `Condition` interface and define the `matches(..)` method.

Let's now examine how to use the `@Conditional` annotation in the `RelationalDataSourceConfiguration` bean. The following listing shows the modified `CommonApplicationContextConfiguration` configuration class that uses the `@Conditional` annotation.

Listing 4.4 Updated CommonApplicationContextConfiguration

```
import org.springframework.context.annotation.*;
import org.springframework.core.type.AnnotatedTypeMetadata;

@Configuration
public class CommonApplicationContextConfiguration {


    @Bean
    @Conditional(RelationDatabaseCondition.class)
    public RelationalDataSourceConfiguration dataSourceConfiguration() {
        return new RelationalDataSourceConfiguration();
    }
}
```

The Conditional annotation ensures that the bean is only created if the RelationalDatabaseCondtion evaluates it as true.

This configuration is similar to what you've seen in listing 4.2 with the exception that the `DataSourceConfiguration` bean creation now depends on the `RelationDatabaseCondition` condition. The following listing defines this condition.

Listing 4.5 Condition to check a relational database

```
public class RelationDatabaseCondition implements Condition {

    @Override
    public boolean matches(ConditionContext conditionContext,
➥ AnnotatedTypeMetadata annotatedTypeMetadata) {
        return isMySQLDatabase();
    }

    private boolean isMySQLDatabase() {
        try {
            Class.forName("com.mysql.jdbc.Driver");
            return true;
        }
        catch(ClassNotFoundException e) {
           return false;
        }
    }
}
```

This method returns true if the MySQL database driver class is present in the classpath.

Evaluates if the MySQL driver class is present in the classpath. Availability of the class indicates that the MySQL database is being used in the application. We've used MySQL driver for demonstration purposes only.

In listing 4.5, you've made the following changes:

- Providing an implementation of the `Condition` interface. This interface has a `matches(..)` method that returns a `boolean` value.
- Validating whether the MySQL driver class is present in the application classpath. If the driver class is available, then the condition returns `true` to indicate that a relational database is available.

For simplicity, we've kept the `RelationDatabaseCondition` straightforward with only one validation. This one validation should be enough to convey the idea behind the `@Condition` annotation. You can implement more such checks to evaluate a condition and return the Boolean value accordingly. Typically, you can implement a condition to create beans in two different ways:

1. Evaluate the classpath for the presence of specific libraries.
2. Validate whether certain properties are configured in the application. In the `matches(..)` method, you have an instance of `ConditionContext`, which gives access to the configured application properties. Thus, you can access all of the properties configured in the application.properties file.

Although `@Conditional` annotation works just fine, it is a low-level annotation. Spring Boot provides several high-level `@Conditional` annotations that target a specific type of condition. Table 4.1 summarizes a few of the popular `@Conditonal` annotations (the most frequently used annotations are highlighted in bold).

In the next section, you'll explore the use of some of these annotations in detail.

Table 4.1 List of Spring Boot conditional annotations. Refer to the Spring Boot API documentation at http://mng.bz/ExGo for the list of annotations.

Annotation	Example	Example explanation
`@ConditionalOnBean`	`@ConditionalOnBean(DataSource.class)`	This condition is true if the user specifies a `DataSource` bean in a configuration.
`@ConditionalOnClass`	`@ConditionalOnClass(DataSource.class)`	This condition is true if the class `DataSource` is available in the classpath.
`@ConditionalOnProperty`	`@ConditionalOnProperty("some.property")`	This condition is true if `some.property` is configured.
`@ConditionalOnCloudPlatform`	`@ConditionalOnCloudPlatform(CloudPlatform.KUBERNETES)`	This condition is true if the CloudPlatform is set to `KUBERNETES`.
`@ConditionalOnExpression`	`@ConditionalOnExpression("SPEL Expression")`	This condition is true if the SPEL expression is true.
`@ConditionalOnJava`	`@ConditionalOnJava(JavaVersion.EIGHT)`	This condition is true if the supported Java version is `8`.
`@ConditionalOnJndi`	`@ConditionalOnJndi("java:/comp/env/jdbc/MyLocalDB")`	This condition is true if the specified JNDI context exists.
`@ConditionalOnMissingBean`	`@ConditionalOnMissingBean(DataSource.class)`	This condition is true if there is no `DataSource` bean in any configuration.
`@ConditionalOnMissingClass`	`@ConditionalOnMissingClass(DataSource.class)`	This condition is true if there is no `DataSource` class present in the classpath.
`@ConditionalOnNotWebApplication`	`@ConditionalOnNotWebApplication`	This condition is true if the application is not a Web application.
`@ConditionalOnResource`	`@ConditionalOnResource("classpath:some.properties")`	This condition is true if `some.properties` file is present in the classpath.
`@ConditionalOnSingleCandidate`	`@ConditionalOnSingleCandidate(DataSource.class)`	Matches if there is exactly one primary `DataSource` bean present in the application.
`@ConditionalOnWebApplication`	`@ConditionalOnWebApplication`	This condition is true if the application is a Web application.

4.1.2 Deep dive into autoconfiguration

Now that you've learned about the various `@Conditional` annotations, let us explore how Spring Boot uses these annotations in practice. Every Spring Boot project has a dependency on the `spring-boot-autoconfigure` module. It contains the key to Spring Boot's autoconfiguration magic. This JAR contains a file called spring.factories under the META-INF folder. The following listing shows a few of the autoconfiguration classes.

Listing 4.6 Autoconfiguration classes in the spring.factories file

```
# Auto Configure
org.springframework.boot.autoconfigure.EnableAutoConfiguration=\
org.springframework.boot.autoconfigure.admin.SpringApplicationAdminJmxAutoCon
    figuration,\
org.springframework.boot.autoconfigure.aop.AopAutoConfiguration,\
org.springframework.boot.autoconfigure.amqp.RabbitAutoConfiguration,\
org.springframework.boot.autoconfigure.batch.BatchAutoConfiguration,\
org.springframework.boot.autoconfigure.cache.CacheAutoConfiguration,\
org.springframework.boot.autoconfigure.cassandra.CassandraAutoConfiguration,\
org.springframework.boot.autoconfigure.
➥ context.ConfigurationPropertiesAutoConfiguration,\
org.springframework.boot.autoconfigure
➥ .context.LifecycleAutoConfiguration,\
org.springframework.boot.autoconfigure
➥ .context.MessageSourceAutoConfiguration,\
org.springframework.boot.autoconfigure
➥ .context.PropertyPlaceholderAutoConfiguration,\
org.springframework.boot.autoconfigure.
➥ couchbase.CouchbaseAutoConfiguration,\
org.springframework.boot.autoconfigure.
➥ dao.PersistenceExceptionTranslationAutoConfiguration,\
org.springframework.boot.autoconfigure
➥ .data.cassandra.CassandraDataAutoConfiguration,\

// Other autoconfiguration classes
```

If you explore the spring.factories file in the spring-boot-autoconfigure JAR file, you'll find a section called *Auto Configure*, which contains autoconfiguration details for several Spring Boot components and the third-party libraries Spring Boot integrates with. These autoconfiguration classes are Spring configuration files with the `@Conditional` annotations, which you have seen in table 4.1.

To understand this concept further, let's analyze one of the autoconfiguration configurations. In the next section, you'll explore the `DataSourceAutoConfiguration` that configures a data source in a Spring Boot application. Listing 4.7 shows a code snippet from the `DataSourceAutoConfiguration` class. This class is available at http://mng.bz/g4jV.

Listing 4.7 DataSourceAutoConfiguration class

```
@Configuration
@ConditionalOnClass({ DataSource.class, EmbeddedDatabaseType.class })
@EnableConfigurationProperties(DataSourceProperties.class)
@Import({ DataSourcePoolMetadataProvidersConfiguration.class,
```

This configuration is loaded if DataSource and EmbeddedDatabaseType classes are present in the classpath.

```
DataSourceInitializationConfiguration.class })
➥ public class DataSourceAutoConfiguration {

  @Configuration

  @Conditional(EmbeddedDatabaseCondition.class)
  @ConditionalOnMissingBean({ DataSource.class, XADataSource.class })
  @Import(EmbeddedDataSourceConfiguration.class)
  protected static class EmbeddedDatabaseConfiguration {

  }

  @Configuration
  @Conditional(PooledDataSourceCondition.class)
  @ConditionalOnMissingBean({ DataSource.class, XADataSource.class })
  @Import({ DataSourceConfiguration.Hikari.class,
➥ DataSourceConfiguration.Tomcat.class,
         DataSourceConfiguration.Dbcp2.class,
➥ DataSourceConfiguration.Generic.class,
         DataSourceJmxConfiguration.class })
  protected static class PooledDataSourceConfiguration {

  }

// Additional Code
```

DataSourceAutoConfiguration also imports DataSourcePoolMetadataProvidersConfiguration and DataSourceInitializationConfiguration classes.

This configuration is loaded if the EmbeddedDatabaseCondtion evaluates as true, and there are no beans of type DataSource and XADataSource.

This configuration is loaded if the PooledDataSourceCondition evaluates to true, and there are no beans of type DataSource and XADataSource.

There are many annotations configured in the `DataSourceAutoConfiguration` class shown in listing 4.7. Let's explore these annotations one by one:

- This `DataSourceAutoConfiguration` class is configured with `@Configuration` annotation. This indicates that this is a standard Spring configuration class.
- It uses `@ConditionalOnClass` annotation to indicate that `DataSourceAutoConfiguration` configuration should only be evaluated if `DataSource.class` and `EmbeddedDatabaseType.class` are present in the classpath.
- The `@EnableConfigurationProperties(DataSourceProperties.class)` ensures that data source-specific properties provided in the application.properties file are automatically converted to an instance of the `DataSourceProperties` class. For instance, the `spring.datasource.*` properties configured in the application.properties files are automatically mapped to `DataSourceProperties`. In section 2.2 of chapter 2, we discussed the use of the `@EnableConfigurationProperties` annotation in detail.
- The `@Import` annotation pulls two additional configurations into the current class: `DataSourcePoolMetadataProvidersConfiguration` and `DataSourceInitializationConfiguration` to the `DataSourceAutoConfiguration`.
- In the `DataSourceAutoConfiguration` class, there are two inner configurations: `EmbeddedDatabaseConfiguration` and `PooledDataSourceConfiguration`. The first one creates an embedded database configuration if `EmbeddedDatabaseCondition` evaluates to `true` and if you haven't configured a `DataSource` or

`XADataSource` bean explicitly. The `PooledDataSourceConfiguration` creates a database connection pool if `PooledDataSourceCondition` is evaluated to `true` and there is no `DataSource` or `XADataSource` bean configured.

- The `PooledDataSourceConfiguration` imports other data store-specific configurations for the supported connection pool libraries: HikariCP, Tomcat, DBCP2, and Generic.

You can explore these configurations to understand further how the autoconfiguration is implemented. However, the above example demonstrates the foundational concept behind Spring Boot autoconfiguration. As an exercise, you can explore the `EmbeddedWebServerFactoryCustomizerAutoConfiguration`, `JpaRepositoriesAutoConfiguration` and `H2ConsoleAutoConfiguration` classes for further understanding.

4.2 Using Spring Boot DevTools

Spring Boot provides a developer toolkit that provides an additional set of development time features. These tools can be used for a more pleasant Spring Boot application development experience and increased developer productivity. In short, this toolkit is popularly known as Spring Boot DevTools. You can enable DevTools support in your application by adding the following dependency in the pom.xml file, as shown in the following listing.

Listing 4.8 The Spring Boot DevTools Maven dependency

```
<dependency>
    <groupId>org.springframework.boot</groupId>
    <artifactId>spring-boot-devtools</artifactId>
    <optional>true</optional>
</dependency>
```

Notice that DevTools is added as an optional dependency. This is to prevent DevTools dependency from being transitively applied to other modules that depend on your project. In the remainder of this section, you'll explore various features offered by DevTools.

4.2.1 Property defaults

Spring Boot and some of its supporting libraries support caching for improved performance. For instance, the Thymeleaf template engine can cache the HTML templates to avoid reparsing. Although caching works well in production applications, it can be counter-productive at development time, as you need to see your latest changes. Spring Boot DevTools disables all the caching options by default. You can find a list of items for which Spring Boot disables caching in the `DevToolsPropertyDefaultsPostProcessor` class available in the `org.springframework.boot.devtools.env` package of the `spring-boot-devtools` JAR.

4.2.2 Automatic restart

In a typical development setup you make changes to your application, and to view those changes, you restart the application. Spring Boot DevTools makes developer life a little easier by automatically restarting the application whenever there is an application classpath change. This provides a quick feedback loop for the code changes, as you can almost immediately validate your latest changes.

Spring Boot uses two separate class loaders to implement automatic restart functionality. The first one, known as the base class loader, loads classes, which are less likely to change. For instance, the third-party libraries on your application have a dependency that does not change. The other class loader, known as the restart class loader, loads the classes that you are developing. This restart class loader is discarded whenever there is a class change and a new one is created.

4.2.3 Live reload

Spring Boot DevTools provides an embedded `LiveReload` server that can be used to trigger a browser refresh when a resource is changed. To use this feature, the browser needs to have the `LiveReload` extension installed. For a detailed discussion on Spring Boot DevTools, refer to the documentation available at http://mng.bz/5KMa.

4.3 Creating a custom failure analyzer

In chapter 1, you learned the concept of a `FailureAnalyzer` in Spring Boot. As the name indicates, it detects a failure/exception in the application and provides a detailed message that is useful for the developer to further understand the issue. For instance, it is a common occurrence that we try to start multiple instances of a Spring Boot application that uses the same HTTP port. In this case, Spring Boot provides a nicely formatted error message stating you can't start the second instance on the same HTTP port, as it is already in use. Spring Boot does this with the help of a built-in failure analysis infrastructure. Further, it also lets you extend the concept of a failure analyzer, so you can leverage the benefit of it.

There are two reasons a failure analyzer is useful:

- It allows you to provide a detailed error message on the actual error and determine what action you can take to resolve the issue and the root cause of the issue.
- It provides an opportunity to perform validations at application startup and report any errors as early as possible. For instance, let's assume that your application is depending on an external REST service that provides critical business data for your application to function. It may be useful to validate the accessibility of the service at the application startup and ensure your application can operate as expected. However, if the service is not reachable, you may choose not to start the application, as without the REST service your application might not function in an expected manner.

In the next technique, we'll demonstrate how to create a custom failure analyzer in a Spring Boot application.

4.3.1 Technique: Creating a custom Spring Boot FailureAnalyzer

In this technique, we'll demonstrate how to create a custom FailureAnalyzer.

PROBLEM

Your application has a dependency on an external REST service. You need to ensure its reachability at the time of application startup. You also need to provide a detailed message if the service is not accessible.

SOLUTION

Spring Boot provides a failure analysis infrastructure that allows you to define custom logic to perform your business-specific validations and also allows you to report the validation errors. Thus, you can leverage this infrastructure to perform the accessibility of the REST API and report any error at the application startup.

To demonstrate how to create a custom failure analyzer, let's consider the following scenario. Let's assume your application fetches dog details from an external API called https://dog.ceo/dog-api/ and displays them in the application UI. You would like to validate if this URL is accessible at the application startup. You'll perform the following activities:

- You will use Spring Boot's `ContextRefreshedEvent` to trigger the validation. Spring Boot publishes this event once the `ApplicationContext` is refreshed.
- If the API is not accessible, you'll throw a custom `RuntimeException` called `UrlNotAccessibleException`.
- Subsequently, you will define a custom `FailureAnalyzer` called `UrlNotAccessibleFailureAnalyzer` that should be invoked if `UrlNotAccessibleException` occurs.
- Lastly, you'll register `UrlNotAccessibleFailureAnalyzer` through the spring.factories file so that Spring Boot registers the custom `FailureAnalyzer`. The spring.factories is a special file that is located at the src\main\java\META-INF folder of your application and automatically loaded by Spring on application boot time. This file contains a reference to many configuration classes.

Source code

To start with this technique, you can use any of the Spring Boot projects you've used previously. You can also find the base version of the Spring Boot project used in this technique at http://mng.bz/6ZaA. The final version of this Spring Boot project is available at http://mng.bz/oadp.

Let's begin by defining the `UrlNotAccessibleException` exception, as shown in the following listing.

Listing 4.9 The UrlNotAccessibleException exception

```
package com.manning.sbip.ch04.exception;

import lombok.Getter;

@Getter
public class UrlNotAccessibleException extends RuntimeException {

    private String url;

    public UrlNotAccessibleException(String url) {
        this(url, null);
    }

    public UrlNotAccessibleException(String url, Throwable cause) {
        super("URL " + url + " is not accessible", cause);
        this.url = url;
    }
}
```

In the listing, you are defining a RuntimeException that you'll use in case the URL is not accessible. Next, let us define the UrlAccessibilityHandler class, as shown in the following listing.

Listing 4.10 The UrlAccessiblityHandler class

```
package com.manning.sbip.ch04.listener;

//imports

@Component
public class UrlAccessibilityHandler {

    @Value("${api.url:https://dog.ceo/}")
    private String url;

    @EventListener(classes = ContextRefreshedEvent.class)
    public void listen() {
        // For demonstration purpose, we are throwing
        // the exception assuming the site is not reachable
        throw new UrlNotAccessibleException(url);
    }
}
```

In listing 4.10, you've defined the class UrlAccessibilityHandler as a Spring component. Further, you've defined an event listener that is invoked once Spring Boot publishes the ContextRefreshedEvent event. For simplicity and demonstration purposes, you are throwing the UrlNotAccessibleException assuming it is not reachable. Let's now define the UrlNotAccessibleFailureAnalyzer class, as shown in the following listing.

Listing 4.11 The UrlNotAccessibleFailureAnalyzer class

```
package com.manning.sbip.ch04.exception;

//imports

public class UrlNotAccessibleFailureAnalyzer extends
➥ AbstractFailureAnalyzer<UrlNotAccessibleException> {

    @Override
    protected FailureAnalysis analyze(Throwable rootFailure,
➥ UrlNotAccessibleException cause) {
➥ return new FailureAnalysis("Unable to access the URL
➥ "+cause.getUrl(),
➥ "Validate the URL and ensure it is accessible", cause);
    }

}
```

Spring Boot invokes this `FailureAnalyzer` instance when an `UrlNotAccessible-Exception` occurs. However, you need to indicate Spring Boot that you've defined a `FailureAnalyzer` to handle the exception. You can do this by adding the META-INF\spring.factories file in the src\main\java directory. The following listing shows the content of this file.

Listing 4.12 Registering the FailureAnalyzer through spring.factories file

```
org.springframework.boot.diagnostics.FailureAnalyzer=\
com.manning.sbip.ch04.exception.UrlNotAccessibleFailureAnalyzer
```

In the listing, you specify the type of the class (i.e., `FailureAnalyzer`) in this case and specify the fully qualified class name of the `FailureAnalyzer` implementation. The type of class indicates which type of configuration the associated value refers to. If you configure more than one failure analyzer, you can configure a comma-separated list, as shown in the following listing.

Listing 4.13 Registering the FailureAnalyzer through spring.factories file

```
org.springframework.boot.diagnostics.FailureAnalyzer=\
com.manning.sbip.ch04.exception.UrlNotAccessibleFailureAnalyzer,
com.manning.sbip.ch04.exception.AdditionalFailureAnalyzer,
com.manning.sbip.ch04.exception.AnotherFailureAnalyzer
```

You can start the application and find that it failed to start. In the console log, you can notice the nicely formatted failure message, as shown in figure 4.1.

DISCUSSION

Spring Boot uses `FailureAnalyzer` internally to perform several types of failure analysis. For instance, the `NoSuchBeanDefinitionFailureAnalyzer` is invoked when a `NoSuchBeanDefinitionException` exception occurs. Similarly, there is another

```
***************************
APPLICATION FAILED TO START
***************************

Description:

Unable to access the URL https://dog.ceo/dog-api/

Action:

Validate the URL and ensure it is accessible
```

Figure 4.1 Custom FailureAnalyzer with the error description and the action message

analyzer, such as `DataSourceBeanCreationFailureAnalyzer`, which is invoked whenever a `DataSourceBeanCreationException` occurs.

Spring Boot exposes this infrastructure and lets the developer use it to define application-specific analyzers. In this technique, you've seen an example of it. The steps to use a failure analyzer are as follows:

1. Define a custom exception with the required fields that can carry the relevant error messages.
2. Define a `FailureAnalyzer` by extending the `AbstractFailureAnalyzer` class. This class has a type parameter that accepts any subclass of `Throwable`.
3. In the `FailureAnalyzer` implementation return a `FailureAnalysis` that contains the issue, possible resolution, and the issue root cause details.
4. Subsequently, you need to register this `FailureAnalyzer` instance, so Spring Boot is aware of it.
5. Lastly, you need to perform the validation at an appropriate phase of the application startup. You can use various Spring Boot lifecycle events to invoke your application's failure analyzers. For instance, in this technique we've used the `ContextRefreshedEvent` to invoke the `UrlNotAccessibleFailureAnalyzer`.

This summarizes the discussion on `FailureAnalyzer` and how you can define a custom one in your application. In the next section, we'll discuss Spring Boot Actuator.

4.4 Spring Boot Actuator

In addition to the core features to develop applications, Spring Boot also provides a set of additional features for your application's operational support. An application is considered operational when it is in production and serving your customers or users. To manage a seamless service for your customers, you need to monitor and manage your application. This monitoring and managing includes understanding application health, performance, inbound and outbound traffic, auditing, various application metrics (more on this later), restarting the application, changing application log level, and more. The various monitoring inputs and metric details let you analyze application behavior and act on a need basis.

Spring Boot actuator brings these monitoring and managing capabilities to your Spring Boot application. The main benefit of Spring Boot Actuator is that you get a lot of production-ready features in your application without explicitly implementing them in your application.

4.4.1 Technique: Configuring Spring Boot Actuator in a Spring Boot application

In this technique, we'll demonstrate how to configure Spring Boot Actuator.

PROBLEM

You have your application deployed and running in production. You need to monitor the application health status by configuring the Spring Boot Actuator in your Spring Boot application.

SOLUTION

You can enable Spring Boot actuator support in your Spring Boot application by adding the `spring-boot-starter-actuator` dependency in the application pom.xml configuration file, as shown in the following listing.

Listing 4.14 The Spring Boot Starter Actuator dependency

```
<dependency>
    <groupId>org.springframework.boot</groupId>
    <artifactId>spring-boot-starter-actuator</artifactId>
</dependency>
```

The dependency shown in listing 4.14 incorporates `spring-boot-actuator-autoconfigure` and `micrometer-core` dependencies to the application. The first dependency provides the core actuator support and the other one provides additional support for Micrometer (https://micrometer.io/) to capture various matrices. We'll discuss Micrometer in greater detail later in this chapter.

> **Source code**
>
> To start with this technique, you can find the base version of the Spring Boot project used in this technique at http://mng.bz/nYB2. The final version of this Spring Boot project is available at http://mng.bz/vo24.

In the application.properties file, include the `management.endpoints.web.exposure.include=*` property. This property indicates to enable all actuator endpoints over the Web (HTTP). If you do not wish to expose all actuator endpoints, you can provide comma separated actuator endpoint names as well. For instance, `management.endpoints.web.exposure.include=info,health property` exposes only `info` and `health` endpoints.

Start the application and browse the following URL at http://localhost:8080/actuator/health either through your Web browser or the terminal to access the application `/health` endpoint. Figure 4.2 shows the output.

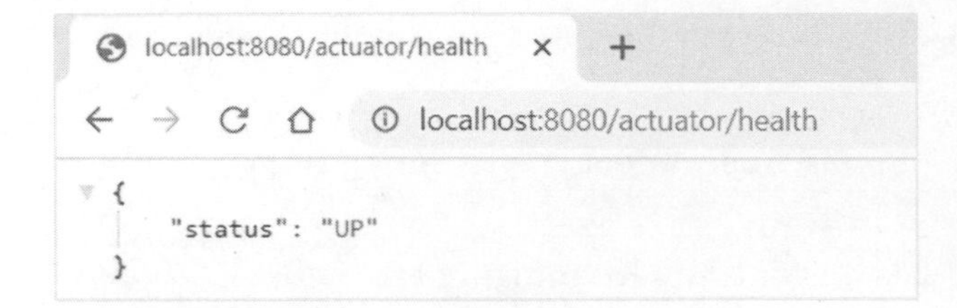

Figure 4.2 The /health endpoint outcome

The health endpoint returns with the status as `UP`. The `UP` status indicates the overall health status of the application is good, and all components of the application are accessible. Later in this chapter, we'll discuss more on the other health statuses and how to write a custom `HealthIndicator` in a Spring Boot application. You'll learn more about the other available endpoints and various other customizations in the subsequent sections.

4.4.2 *Understanding Spring Boot Actuator endpoints*

An actuator endpoint allows you to monitor and manage your application. In the previous technique, you saw the usage of the `health` actuator endpoint that lets you monitor the health status of the application. Spring Boot provides several built-in endpoints you can use out-of-the-box. You can also add your custom endpoint specific to your application.

The actuator endpoints can be accessed either over the Web (HTTP) or JMX (Java Management Extensions), and you can make the endpoints enabled, disabled, or exposed. The enabled or disabled options indicate that you can control whether to allow a specific actuator endpoint in the application. For instance, by default the `shutdown` endpoint that lets you shut down a running application is disabled for security reasons. You can override this default behavior and enable it in your application. The expose option indicates whether a specific endpoint is exposed to be accessed through an access mode (e.g., over the HTTP or JMX). For instance, by default only the `health` and `info` endpoints are exposed over HTTP, and the rest of the endpoints are not exposed over HTTP. However, all Spring Boot built-in actuator endpoints are exposed over JMX by default. JMX is considered more secure than HTTP and is the reason built-in endpoints are exposed by default over JMX.

Spring Boot provides a discovery page that contains all available actuator endpoints. By default, this discovery page is available at /actuator and always accessible. Thus, you can get the list of available actuator endpoints by accessing the URL http://localhost:8080/actuator/, as shown in figure 4.3. Table 4.2 shows the built-in Spring Boot actuator endpoints.

localhost:8080/actuator/

localhost:8080/actuator/


```
{
  "_links": {
    "self": {
      "href": "http://localhost:8080/actuator",
      "templated": false
    },
    "beans": {
      "href": "http://localhost:8080/actuator/beans",
      "templated": false
    },
    "caches-cache": {
      "href": "http://localhost:8080/actuator/caches/{cache}",
      "templated": true
    },
    "caches": {
      "href": "http://localhost:8080/actuator/caches",
      "templated": false
    },
    "info": {
      "href": "http://localhost:8080/actuator/info",
      "templated": false
    },
    "conditions": {
      "href": "http://localhost:8080/actuator/conditions",
      "templated": false
    },
    "configprops": {
      "href": "http://localhost:8080/actuator/configprops",
      "templated": false
    },
    "env": {
      "href": "http://localhost:8080/actuator/env",
      "templated": false
    },
    "env-toMatch": {
      "href": "http://localhost:8080/actuator/env/{toMatch}",
      "templated": true
    },
    "loggers": {
      "href": "http://localhost:8080/actuator/loggers",
      "templated": false
    },
```


Figure 4.3 The Spring Boot Actuator discovery page. This page contains a list of endpoints you can access. The templated field is true if the endpoint URL has a template that needs to be replaced with an appropriate value. For instance, in the URL http://localhost:8080/actuator/caches/{cache} you can retrieve details of a particular cache by replacing the {cache} with the actual cache name.

Table 4.2 Spring Boot Actuator built-in endpoints

Endpoint Id	Purpose	Expose over HTTP	Expose over JMX
`auditevents`	Security audit information, such as user login/logout	No	Yes
`beans`	Lists all available beans in the `BeanFactory`	No	Yes
`caches`	Lists all the caches in the application	No	Yes
`conditions`	Reports all the autoconfiguration conditions	No	Yes
`configprops`	Shows all `@ConfigurationProperties` beans	No	Yes
`env`	Shows current environment properties	No	Yes
`flyway`	Shows details of the Flyway (https://flywaydb.org/) database configurations if Flyway is configured in the application	No	Yes
`health`	Health status of the application	Yes	Yes
`heapdump`	Build and return the heap dump of the JVM used by the application.	No	Yes
`httptrace`	Provides the details of HTTP requests and responses. To view the HTTP traces you need to configure an `HttpTraceRepository` bean.	No	Yes
`info`	General application information such as custom data, build information, and latest commit details	Yes	Yes
`integrationgraph`	Exposes a graph containing all Spring Integration components	No	Yes
`logfile`	Provides access to the contents of the application's log file	No	N/A
`loggers`	Provides access to the application's loggers and the configuration of their levels	No	Yes
`liquibase`	Provides detail of Liquibase (https://www.liquibase.org/) database configurations if Liquibase is configured in the application	No	Yes
`metrics`	Provides details of various application metrics	No	Yes
`mappings`	Provides information about the application's request mappings	No	Yes
`prometheus`	Provides Spring Boot application's metrics in the format required for scraping by a Prometheus server	No	N/A

Table 4.2 Spring Boot Actuator built-in endpoints *(continued)*

Endpoint Id	Purpose	Expose over HTTP	Expose over JMX
`scheduledtasks`	Provides information about the application's scheduled tasks	No	Yes
`sessions`	Provides information about the application's HTTP sessions that are managed by Spring Session	No	Yes
`shutdown`	Shut down the application.	No	Yes
`startup`	Provides information about the application's startup sequence	No	Yes
`threaddump`	Provides a thread dump from the application's JVM	No	Yes

4.4.3 Managing Spring Boot Actuator endpoints

In section 4.4.2, you've seen by default Spring Boot exposes the `health` and `info` endpoints over the HTTP. You can expose other built-in endpoints by configuring the `management.endpoints.web.exposure.include` property in the application.properties file. You can selectively specify the endpoint names you wish to expose over the Web, or you can use the wildcard character (i.e., `*`) to expose all the actuator endpoints. The following listing shows the configurations to enable actuator endpoints over the Web.

Listing 4.15 Actuator Web Endpoints include property

```
management.endpoints.web.exposure.include=beans,threaddump
management.endpoints.web.exposure.include=*
```

In listing 4.15, the first configuration enables only `beans` and `threaddump` endpoints over the Web (HTTP). The second configuration enables all available actuator endpoints over the Web (HTTP).

Further, you can also use the exclude property to control the exposure of actuator endpoints. For instance, you may wish to expose all actuator endpoints except the `threaddump`, `heapdump`, and `health` endpoints. The following listing shows this configuration.

Listing 4.16 Actuator Web endpoints include and exclude property

```
management.endpoints.web.exposure.include=*
management.endpoints.web.exposure.exclude=threaddump,heapdump,health
```

In listing 4.16, you've exposed all actuator endpoints with the `*` wildcard but excluded the `threaddump`, `heapdump` and `health` endpoints.

In the previous sections, you've seen that the context root of all actuator endpoints is always set to the `actuator`. For instance, to access the `health` actuator endpoint, you used the URL http://localhost:8080/actuator/health. Spring Boot allows you to customize the endpoint context root with the custom values. This is useful if you already use the /actuator endpoint for some other purposes and need to choose a different context root. For instance, configuring the `management.endpoints.web.base-path=/sbip` property in the application.properties file changes the actuator context root from `actuator` to `sbip`.

You can also change the management server port to a different HTTP port than the actual application HTTP port. For instance, our Spring Boot application is running on HTTP port `8080`, and by default this is used as the management port for actuator endpoints. You can change the management port to `8081` by configuring the property `management.server.port=8081` in the application.properties file, as shown in figure 4.4.

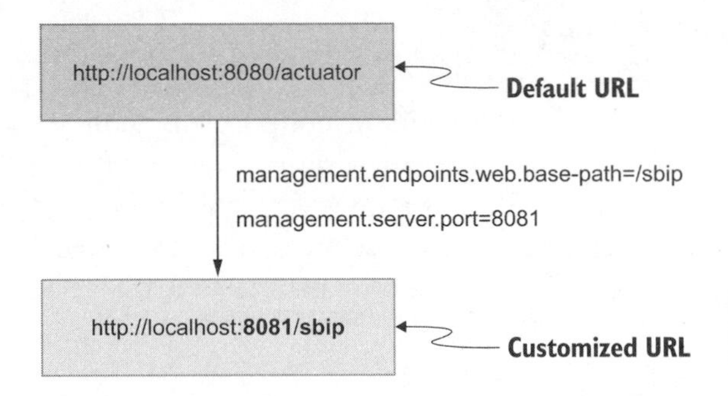

Figure 4.4 Customizing the Spring Boot actuator URL with different HTTP port and context root

You can also customize the specific actuator endpoint name. For instance, you can customize the default `/health` endpoint to `/apphealth` by configuring the `management.endpoints.web.path-mapping.health=apphealth` property in the application.properties file, as shown in figure 4.5.

4.4.4 Health endpoint deep dive

In section 4.4.2, you learned about the use of the `health` Spring Boot actuator endpoint. As the name indicates, it provides the health status of the application and various other components of it. For instance, you can retrieve the health status of the database component of the application through the `health` actuator endpoint.

Out of the box, Spring Boot provides several `HealthIndicator` implementations that provide the health status of a particular application component. Some of these `HealthIndicators` are provided by Spring Boot and are always configured. For instance, Spring Boot always configures the `DiskSpaceHealthIndicator` and `PingHealthIndicator`.

Earlier, you learned that the `health` endpoint only provides the aggregated health status (e.g., `UP`). Let us configure the following property to retrieve the disk space and

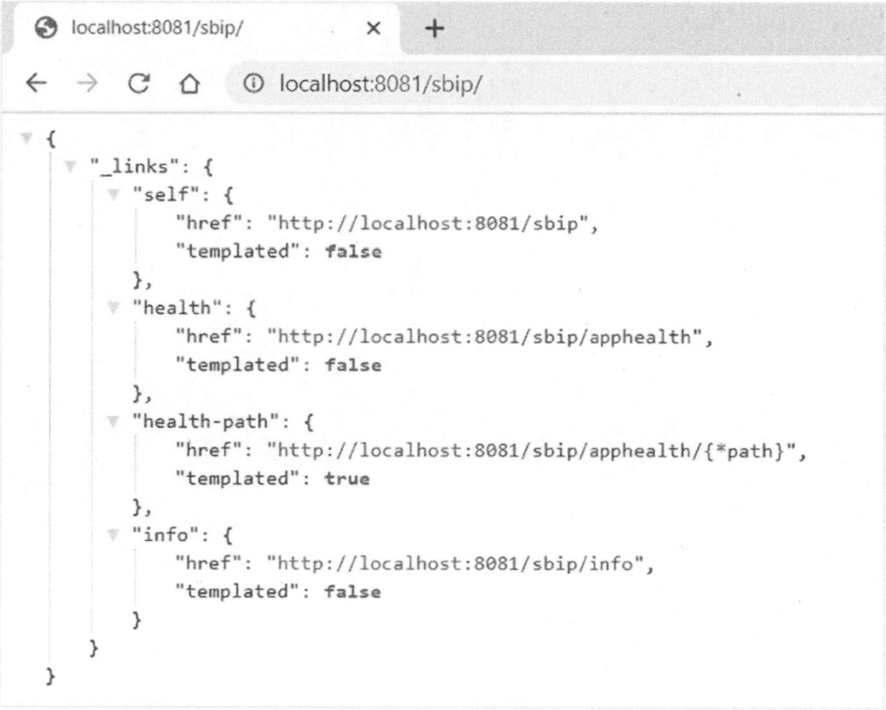

localhost:8081/sbip/


```
{
  "_links": {
    "self": {
      "href": "http://localhost:8081/sbip",
      "templated": false
    },
    "health": {
      "href": "http://localhost:8081/sbip/apphealth",
      "templated": false
    },
    "health-path": {
      "href": "http://localhost:8081/sbip/apphealth/{*path}",
      "templated": true
    },
    "info": {
      "href": "http://localhost:8081/sbip/info",
      "templated": false
    }
  }
}
```


Figure 4.5 Spring Boot Actuator endpoint discovery page with custom content. In this example, the /actuator context is customized to /sbip. The management server port is 8081, whereas the application port is 8080.

the ping status along with the aggregated application health status. Let's configure the following property in the application.properties file, as shown in the following listing.

Listing 4.17 Property to display detailed health status

```
management.endpoint.health.show-details=always
```

The property in the listing can be configured with the following three values:

- `always`—Indicates to always display the detailed health status.
- `never`—Indicates only to provide the health status without any additional details. This is the default value.
- `when-authorized`—Indicates only to provide details of the user or API authorized to access the health endpoint. A user is considered authorized if they are authenticated in the application and have the roles defined in the `management.endpoint.health.roles` property in the application.properties file.

If you restart the application and access the http://localhost:8080/actuator/health URL, you'll notice that the diskspace and ping health status are also provided, as shown in figure 4.6.

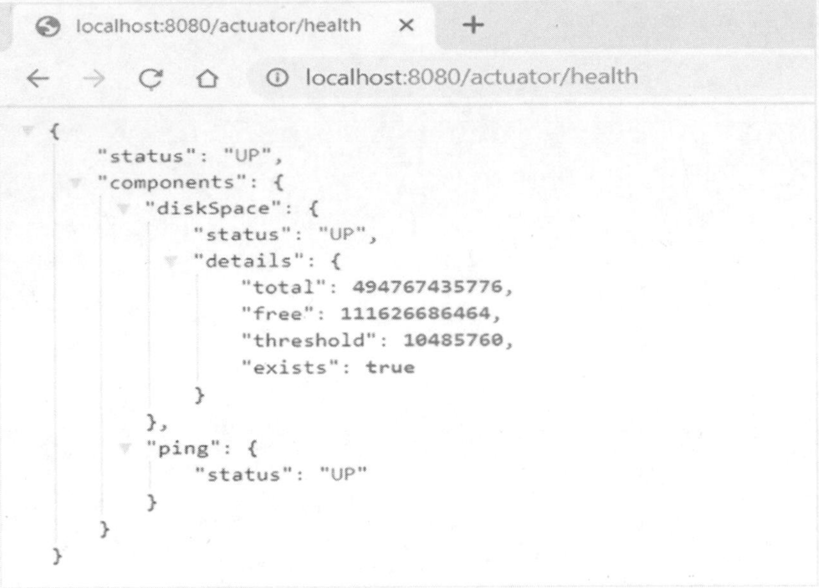

localhost:8080/actuator/health

localhost:8080/actuator/health


```
{
    "status": "UP",
    "components": {
        "diskSpace": {
            "status": "UP",
            "details": {
                "total": 494767435776,
                "free": 111626686464,
                "threshold": 10485760,
                "exists": true
            }
        },
        "ping": {
            "status": "UP"
        }
    }
}
```


Figure 4.6 Spring Boot Actuator health endpoint with show-details *always* configuration

Sometimes, Spring Boot enables `HealthIndicator` conditionally. These conditions could be due to the presence of a particular dependency in the application classpath. For instance, if you are using a relational database, Spring Boot automatically configures the `DataSourceHealthIndicator` and provides the underlying database health status. Note that these additional details are made available under the health endpoint only if `management.endpoint.health.show-details` property is configured to `always`, as shown in listing 4.17. Let's include the `H2` database dependency in the application pom.xml file, as shown in the following listing.

Listing 4.18 The H2 database dependency

```
<dependency>
    <groupId>com.h2database</groupId>
    <artifactId>h2</artifactId>
    <scope>runtime</scope>
</dependency>
```

If you restart the application and access the `/health` endpoint, you'll notice that database health status is included along with other components' health status, as shown in figure 4.7.

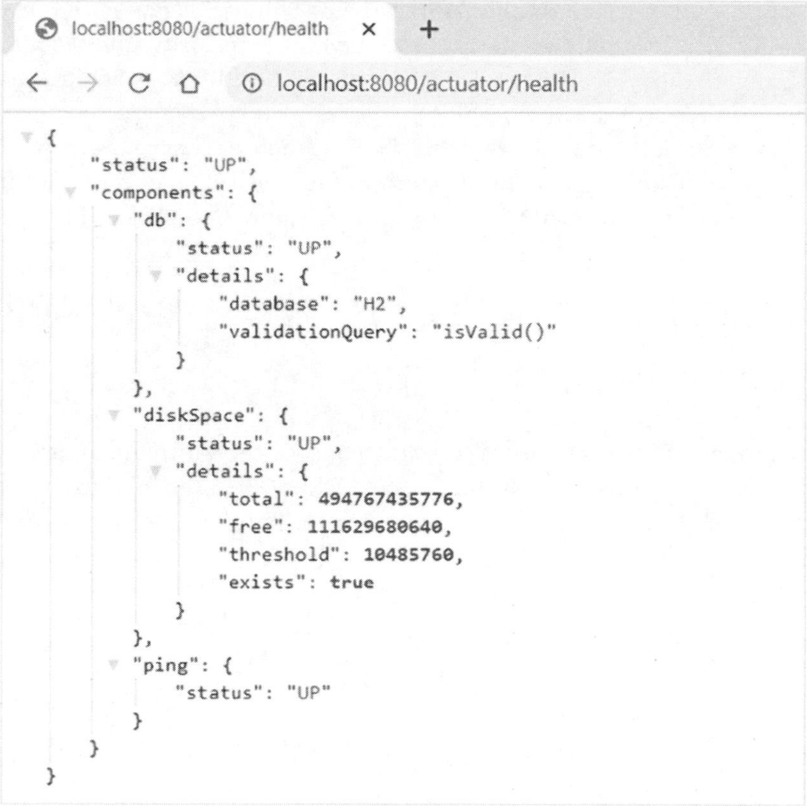
localhost:8080/actuator/health
localhost:8080/actuator/health
{
"status": "UP",
"components": {
"db": {
"status": "UP",
"details": {
"database": "H2",
"validationQuery": "isValid()"
}
},
"diskSpace": {
"status": "UP",
"details": {
"total": 494767435776,
"free": 111629680640,
"threshold": 10485760,
"exists": true
}
},
"ping": {
"status": "UP"
}
}
}

Figure 4.7 Spring Boot Actuator /health endpoint with database health status

In figure 4.7, the root status shows the aggregated health status of your application. By default, Spring Boot provides the following four health statuses:

1. `DOWN`: The component is not available.
2. `OUT-OF-SERVICE`: The component is temporarily out of service.
3. `UP`: The component is working as expected.
4. `UNKNOWN`: The component status is unknown.

If you need other statuses in your application, you can define custom statuses as well. You can use the `status(..)` method of the `Health` class to define a custom status. Listing 4.19 creates a new status called `FATAL`. You'll learn more about this in the next section.

Listing 4.19 Creating a custom health status

```
public Health health() {
    return Health.status("FATAL").build();
}
```

Spring Boot uses the specified status order to determine the aggregated health status of the application. Thus, the status `DOWN` has the highest priority, and `UNKNOWN` has the lowest. If any of the `HealthIndicators` return the health status as `DOWN`, the aggregated application status is `DOWN`.

You can customize this order with the `management.endpoint.health.status.order` property in the application.properties file. For instance, the following listing shows a custom status order in which the custom status `FATAL` is configured with the highest order.

Listing 4.20 Defining a custom health status order

```
management.endpoint.health.status.order=
➥ FATAL,DOWN,OUT-OF-SERVICE,UNKNOWN,UP
```

These health statuses affect the `HTTP` status code of the endpoint. For instance, by default Spring Boot maps the `DOWN` and `OUT-OF-SERVICE` status code to the `HTTP` status code 503 (`Service Unavailable`). The `UP` status and other statuses are mapped to the `HTTP` status code 200 (`OK`).

If you need to customize the health status mapping to different HTTP status code, you can configure the `management.endpoint.health.status.http-mapping.<status>` property. The following listing shows the mapping for the `down` and `out_of_service` statuses.

Listing 4.21 Health status mapping

```
management.endpoint.health.status.http-mapping.down=500
management.endpoint.health.status.http-mapping.out_of_service=503
```

You can also customize the mapping programmatically by providing an implementation of the `HttpCodeStatusMapper` interface and defining the `getStatusCode()` method.

> **Source code**
>
> You can refer to the Spring Boot available at http://mng.bz/4jyj for more details.

4.4.5 Creating a custom Spring Boot HealthIndicator

In the previous section, you explored the use of the `health` actuator endpoint. You saw some of the Spring Boot built-in `HealthIndicators`, such as `DiskSpaceHealthIndicator` and `DataSourceHealthIndicator`, which provide the disk space and data source status, respectively. Looking at these, you may think it would be useful to define your own custom `HealthIndicator` to provide the health status to your application or any subsystem your application is integrated with—by allowing your application to load data from an external REST API, for example. You may want to validate the health status of the REST API system. As you may have correctly guessed, Spring

Boot allows you to define a custom HealthIndicator and automatically integrates the health status through the health endpoint. Let's explore this in the next technique.

4.4.6 Technique: Defining a custom Spring Boot actuator HealthIndicator

In this technique, we'll discuss how to define a custom Spring Boot actuator HealthIndicator.

PROBLEM

Spring Boot's built-in HealthIndicator does not allow you to inquire about the health status of your application-specific components. You need to define a custom HealthIndicator that allows you to monitor the health status of the critical REST API system your application is integrated with.

SOLUTION

Spring Boot provides the HealthIndicator interface that lets you define any number of custom HealthIndicators for your application. These HealthIndicator implementations are treated as regular Spring components and automatically discovered by the Spring Boot component scanning and automatically integrated with the Spring Boot actuator /health endpoint data. To demonstrate how to define a custom HealthIndicator, we will monitor the health status of a REST API with which our Spring Boot application is integrated. We'll use https://dog.ceo/dog-api/ as our REST API that returns beautiful dog images.

> **Source code**
>
> To start with this technique, you can use the Spring Boot project available at http://mng.bz/QW1v. You can find the completed Spring Boot project used in this technique at http://mng.bz/XWQa.

Once you are done with the project setup, you'll provide an implementation of HealthIndicator called DogsApiHealthIndicator. Note that it is a convention to use the HealthIndicator suffix in the custom HealthIndicator class. The following listing shows this implementation.

Listing 4.22 The DogsApiHealthIndicator class

```
package com.manning.sbip.ch04.health.indicator;

// imports

@Component
public class DogsApiHealthIndicator implements HealthIndicator {

    @Override
    public Health health() {
```

```
        try {
            ParameterizedTypeReference<Map<String, String>> reference
➥ = new ParameterizedTypeReference<Map<String, String>>() {};
            ResponseEntity<Map<String, String>> result
➥ = new RestTemplate().exchange
➥ ("https://dog.ceo/api/breeds/image/random",
➥ HttpMethod.GET, null, reference);
            if (result.getStatusCode().is2xxSuccessful() &&
➥ result.getBody() != null) {
                return Health.up().withDetails(result.getBody()).build();
            }
            else {
                return Health.down().withDetail("status",
➥ result.getStatusCode()).build();
            }
        }
        catch(RestClientException ex) {
             return Health.down().withException(ex).build();
        }
    }
}
```

We are doing the following activities in this class:

- This class implements the `HealthIndicator` interface. It implies that this class provides the health status of some application component.
- It is annotated with `@Component` annotation, so it can be discovered by Spring Boot component scanning.
- We've used Spring's `RestTemplate` class to call the `https://dog.ceo` API. `RestTemplate` allows you to invoke the REST APIs from your application.
- We then evaluate the HTTP response status. If the status code is HTTP 2XX series (e.g., 200, 201) and the response body is not null, we define the health status as `UP` and return the REST service response body, so it can be shown in the `/health` endpoint.
- If we encounter any exception, we return the actuator health status as down and provide the exception, so it can be shown in the `/health` endpoint result.

That's all. You just need to define the `HealthIndicator`, and Spring Boot will discover it to collect the health status and provide the output in `/health` endpoint. You can start the application and access the http://localhost:8080/actuator/health/ endpoint. Figure 4.8 shows the output.

Note that you need to have an active internet connection to get the result shown above. To see the custom health indicator failing, you can disconnect your computer from the network and access the same URL. Figure 4.9 shows the outcome.

Discussion

With this technique, we've discussed how to define a custom `HealthIndicator` that enquires the health status of a REST API. As you've seen, it is straightforward to define a custom health indicator and return the health status. In the next section,

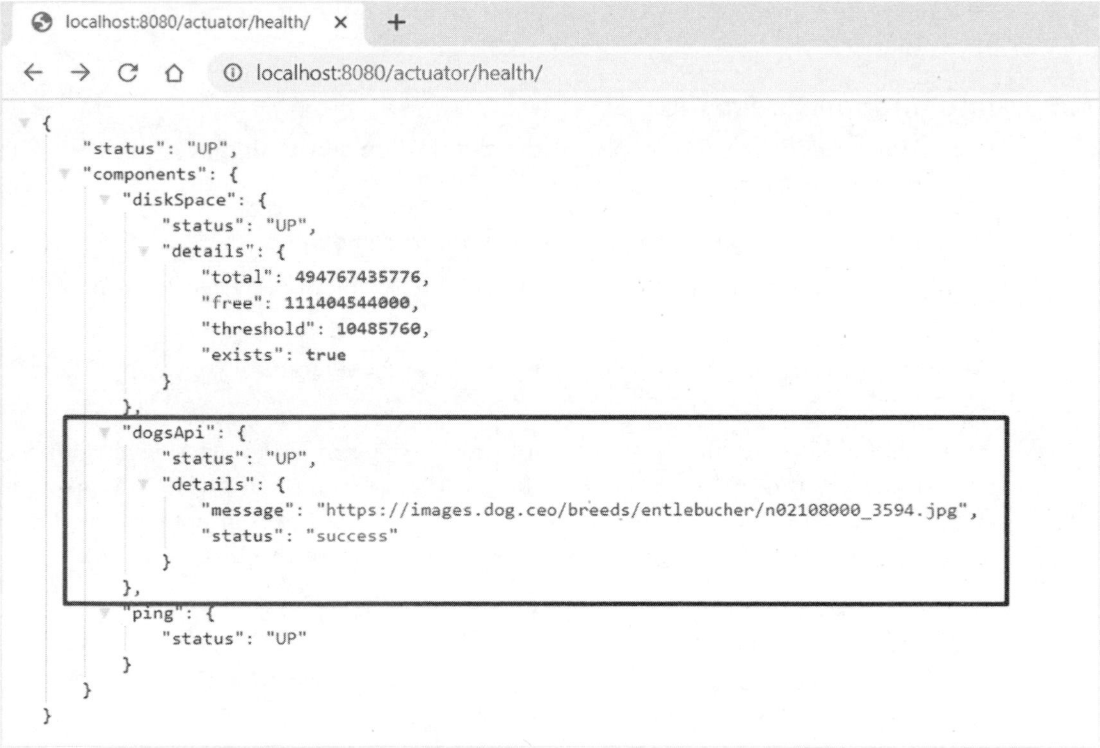

localhost:8080/actuator/health/

```
{
    "status": "UP",
    "components": {
        "diskSpace": {
            "status": "UP",
            "details": {
                "total": 494767435776,
                "free": 111404544000,
                "threshold": 10485760,
                "exists": true
            }
        },
        "dogsApi": {
            "status": "UP",
            "details": {
                "message": "https://images.dog.ceo/breeds/entlebucher/n02108000_3594.jpg",
                "status": "success"
            }
        },
        "ping": {
            "status": "UP"
        }
    }
}
```

Figure 4.8 Spring Boot Actuator health endpoint with custom HealthContributor

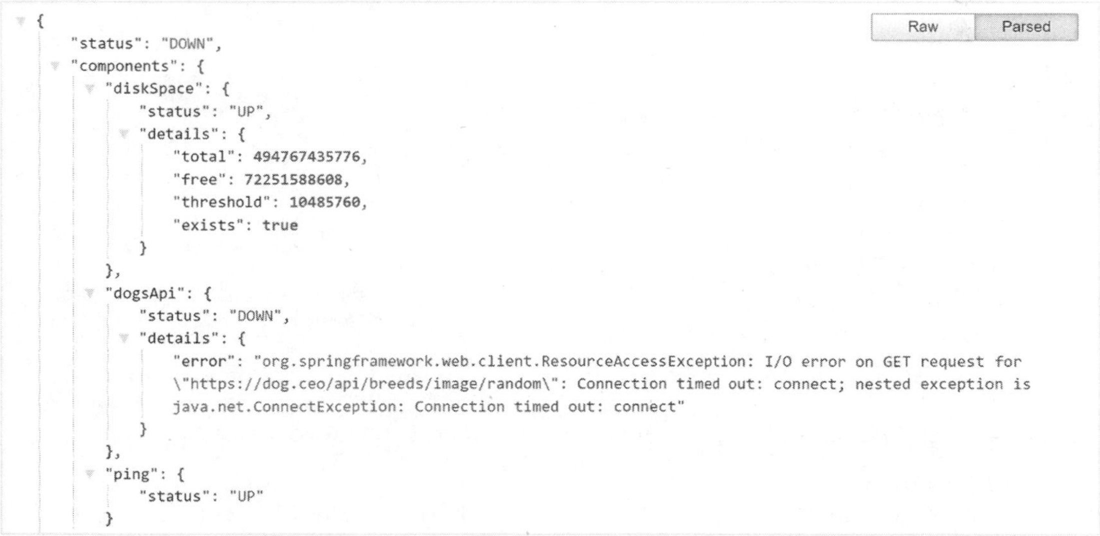

Raw Parsed

```
{
    "status": "DOWN",
    "components": {
        "diskSpace": {
            "status": "UP",
            "details": {
                "total": 494767435776,
                "free": 72251588608,
                "threshold": 10485760,
                "exists": true
            }
        },
        "dogsApi": {
            "status": "DOWN",
            "details": {
                "error": "org.springframework.web.client.ResourceAccessException: I/O error on GET request for
                \"https://dog.ceo/api/breeds/image/random\": Connection timed out: connect; nested exception is
                java.net.ConnectException: Connection timed out: connect"
            }
        },
        "ping": {
            "status": "UP"
        }
```

Figure 4.9 Spring Boot Actuator health endpoint with failed health status for custom HealthIndicator

let us explore more on the /info endpoint and learn how to define a custom InfoContributor.

4.5 Info endpoint deep dive

In previous sections, you've explored the health actuator endpoint. In this section, you'll dive into the info actuator endpoint.

4.5.1 Technique: Configuring info Spring Boot Actuator endpoint

In this technique, we'll discuss how to configure a Spring Boot Actuator endpoint.

PROBLEM

You need to configure the info Spring Boot Actuator endpoint in your application.

SOLUTION

As the name indicates, the info endpoint provides information related to the application. By default, the info endpoint does not provide any information. However, you can customize this behavior to return some information related to your application. There are two modes through which you can configure the data for the info endpoint.

> **Source code**
>
> You can find the completed Spring Boot project used in this technique available at http://mng.bz/y46d.

First, you can configure the properties in the application.properties file by setting the info.* properties. For instance, you can configure the following properties in the application.properties in your Spring Boot application, as shown in the following listing.

Listing 4.23 The info properties

```
info.app.name= Spring Boot Actuator Info Application
info.app.description=Spring Boot application that explores the /info endpoint
info.app.version=1.0.0

management.endpoints.web.exposure.include=*      <-- To expose all actuator endpoints over Web
management.info.env.enabled=true      <-- Enable the Info environment contributor (needed for Spring Boot 2.6.x and above)
```

You can configure any number of properties with the info.* prefix in the application.properties file, and these properties will be rendered at /info. Restart the application, and access the http://localhost:8080/actuator/info endpoint. Figure 4.10 shows the output.

You can also print the project details, such as artifactId, groupId, and version, through the info endpoint. For instance, configure the following properties as shown in listing 4.24.

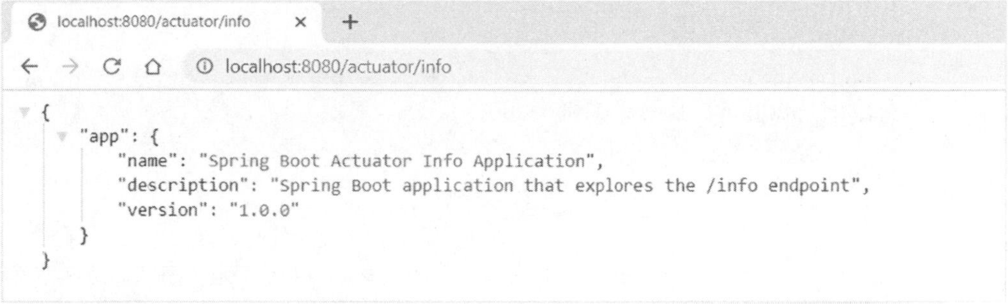

localhost:8080/actuator/info

```
{
  "app": {
    "name": "Spring Boot Actuator Info Application",
    "description": "Spring Boot application that explores the /info endpoint",
    "version": "1.0.0"
  }
}
```


Figure 4.10 The Spring Boot Actuator info endpoint shows the application name, description, and version as configured in the application.properties file.

Listing 4.24 The info properties

```
info.build.artifact=@project.artifactId@
info.build.name=@project.name@
info.build.description=@project.description@
info.build.version=@project.version@
info.build.properties.java.version=@java.version@
```

In listing 4.24, the values are configured as `@..@`. Spring Boot automatically expands the properties from the Maven project. If you restart the application and access the http://localhost:8080/actuator/info endpoint again, you will find the output shown in figure 4.11.

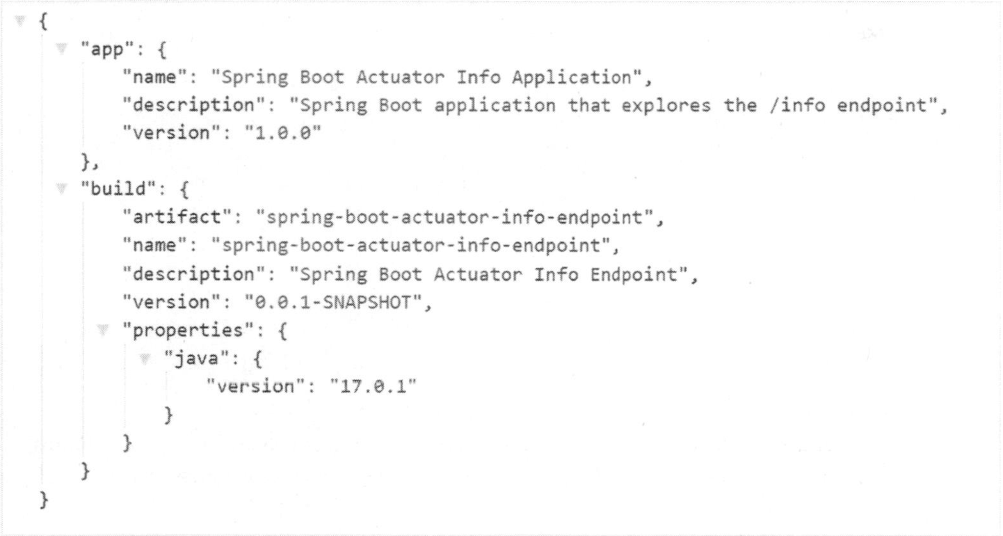

```
{
  "app": {
    "name": "Spring Boot Actuator Info Application",
    "description": "Spring Boot application that explores the /info endpoint",
    "version": "1.0.0"
  },
  "build": {
    "artifact": "spring-boot-actuator-info-endpoint",
    "name": "spring-boot-actuator-info-endpoint",
    "description": "Spring Boot Actuator Info Endpoint",
    "version": "0.0.1-SNAPSHOT",
    "properties": {
      "java": {
        "version": "17.0.1"
      }
    }
  }
}
```


Figure 4.11 Spring Boot Actuator info endpoint with the application details. These details are sourced from the pom.xml file of the application.

Gradle users

If you are using Gradle, you can also retrieve the details. Add the following in the build.gradle file of your application:

```
springBoot {
  buildInfo()
}
```

Start the application using the `gradlew bootRun` command and access the http://localhost:8080/actuator/info endpoint, and you will notice the details shown in figure 4.12.

localhost:8080/actuator/info

```
{
  "build": {
    "artifact": "info-endpoint-gradle",
    "name": "info-endpoint-gradle",
    "time": "2021-05-02T14:08:23.664Z",
    "version": "0.0.1-SNAPSHOT",
    "group": "com.manning.sbip.ch04.endpoint"
  }
}
```

Figure 4.12 Accessing build information in a Spring Boot Gradle application through info endpoint

Second, the `/info` endpoint allows you to fetch your application's git repository, environment, and build details. The git repository details are automatically displayed if a git.properties file is available in the classpath. You can refer to http://mng.bz/M2AB to learn how to generate a git.properties file.

Similarly, the build details are also available if the build-info.properties file is available inside the META-INF folder in the classpath. The git repository and the build information are managed through the `GitInfoContributor` and `BuildInfoContributor` classes, respectively. You'll shortly learn more about the `InfoContributor` interface. To generate these files, you can perform the changes to the application's pom.xml file shown in the following listing.

Listing 4.25 The pom.xml changes to generate the build.info and git.properties file

```
<build>
  <plugins>
    <plugin>
      <groupId>org.springframework.boot</groupId>
      <artifactId>spring-boot-maven-plugin</artifactId>
```

```
        <executions>
          <execution>
            <goals>
              <goal>build-info</goal>
            </goals>
          </execution>
        </executions>
      </plugin>
      <plugin>
        <groupId>pl.project13.maven</groupId>
        <artifactId>git-commit-id-plugin</artifactId>
      </plugin>
    </plugins>
  </build>
```

The changes to the listing do the following:

- The `build-info` goal in the `spring-boot-maven-plugin` generates the build-info.properties file.
- The `git-commit-id-plugin` generates the git.properties file. This file contains git repository information, such as git commit, build, and branch details. Note that this is not a Spring Boot plugin; instead, it is a third party one.

Open a command line or terminal window and start the application. If you access the http://localhost:8080/actuator/info, you'll find the details shown in figure 4.13.

localhost:8080/actuator/info

localhost:8080/actuator/info


```
{
  "git": {
    "commit": {
      "time": "2021-03-27T11:31:00Z",
      "id": "3f436f9"
    },
    "branch": "main"
  },
  "build": {
    "version": "0.0.1-SNAPSHOT",
    "artifact": "spring-boot-actuator-info-endpoint",
    "name": "spring-boot-actuator-info-endpoint",
    "group": "com.manning.sbip.ch04",
    "time": "2021-04-01T06:29:00.265Z"
  }
}
```


Figure 4.13 Spring Boot Actuator info endpoint with git and build details. The git details are sourced from the git.properties file. The build details are sourced from the build-info.properties file. You can control the git details with the management.info .git.mode property in the application.properties file with values full or simple. Setting the property to full displays complete git details. By default, this default value of this property is simple, and it only shows git commit time and ID.

Lastly, you can provide a custom `InfoContributor` that can provide application details. Previously, we mentioned that the `GitInfoContributor` provides the information regarding your git repository. This class reads the git.properties file and presents the related data through the `info` endpoint.

4.5.2 Technique: Configuring a custom info contributor to provide custom application info in the Spring Boot Actuator endpoint

In this technique, we'll explore how to configure a custom info contributor.

PROBLEM

You need to provide custom application details through the info Spring Boot Actuator endpoint in your application.

SOLUTION

Spring Boot provides the `InfoContributor` interface that lets you expose application information through the Spring Boot Actuator built-in `info` endpoint.

> **Source code**
> You can find the completed Spring Boot project used in this technique at http://mng.bz/aDYm.

With this technique, you'll create a custom implementation of `InfoContributor` named `CourseInfoContributor` in the course tracker application. This custom `InfoContributor` provides the course name and the course ratings through the `info` endpoint. The following listing shows this class.

Listing 4.26 Defining a custom InfoContributor

```
package com.manning.sbip.ch04.info;

import org.springframework.boot.actuate.info.InfoContributor;
// Other Imports

@Component
public class CourseInfoContributor implements InfoContributor {

    @Autowired
    private CourseService courseService;

    @Override
    public void contribute(Info.Builder builder) {
        Map<String, Integer> courseNameRatingMap = new HashMap<>();
        List<CourseNameRating> courseNameRatingList = new ArrayList<>();
        for(Course course : courseService.getAvailableCourses()) {
            courseNameRatingList.add(CourseNameRating.builder()
➥ .name(course.getName()).rating(course.getRating()).build());
        }
        builder.withDetail("courses", courseNameRatingList);
    }
```

```
    @Builder
    @Data
    private static class CourseNameRating {
        String name;
        int rating;

    }
}
```

In the listing, you've done the following:

- First, you've implemented the Spring Boot `InfoContributor` interface and defined the `contribute(..)` method.
- Second, you've used the course service that returns all available courses in the application.
- Lastly, you've mapped the course name and rating information from the course, and you've added the list of course names and ratings to the `Info.Builder` instance. As the name indicates, the `Info.Builder` allows you to build the info details.

Start the application, and you'll notice the output shown in figure 4.14.

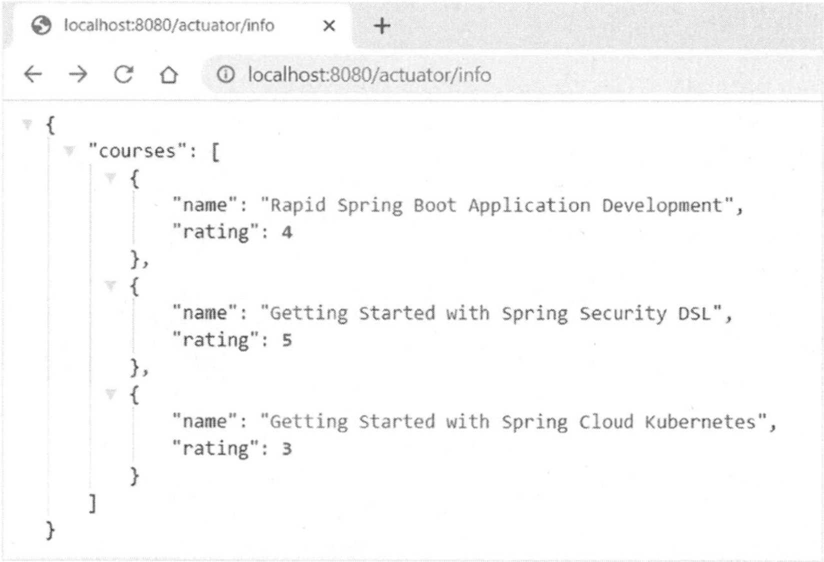

localhost:8080/actuator/info


```
{
    "courses": [
        {
            "name": "Rapid Spring Boot Application Development",
            "rating": 4
        },
        {
            "name": "Getting Started with Spring Security DSL",
            "rating": 5
        },
        {
            "name": "Getting Started with Spring Cloud Kubernetes",
            "rating": 3
        }
    ]
}
```


Figure 4.14 Showing application-specific custom details with the info endpoint.

NOTE In this technique, you may notice that we are using the application business domain details in the Spring Boot Actuator endpoint. You'll notice the use of application business domain details in several other techniques as well. Ideally, Spring Boot Actuator endpoints are intended to be used for application monitoring and interaction purposes and not to expose or alter business domain details. A RESTful Web service is more appropriate to manage business domain details. For demonstration purposes and to keep the examples simple, we've used the business domain details in the Spring Boot Actuator endpoints.

4.6 Creating a custom Spring Boot Actuator endpoint

In the previous section, you've seen the built-in Spring Boot actuator endpoints, such as `/health` and `/info`. However, sometimes you may need to define custom endpoints specific to your application that can provide your application-specific data. The custom endpoints are an easy and useful way to get some insight into your application. In the next technique, we'll explore how to define a custom Spring Boot actuator endpoint.

4.6.1 Technique: Creating a custom Spring Boot actuator endpoint

In this technique, we'll create a custom Spring Boot Actuator endpoint.

Problem

Spring Boot built-in actuator endpoints are generic and do not provide application-specific business details. You need to define an actuator endpoint that lets you monitor and interact with application business details.

Solution

To demonstrate how to define and use a custom Spring Boot actuator endpoint, you'll use the course tracker application you've used in the previous techniques. You'll define a `releaseNotes` endpoint that provides the application release details. A release consists of release version, date, commit tag, new release, and bug fix details. We'll also enable viewing a specific release detail through the `version`. You'll also enable delete operations through the actuator endpoint. The `delete` operation allows us to delete a specific release version. Let's implement this in the course tracker application.

> **Source code**
> To start with this technique, you can use the Spring Boot project available at http://mng.bz/g4jv. You can find the completed Spring Boot project used in this technique at http://mng.bz/enKV.

To create a new actuator endpoint, you need to create a Java class, annotate with the `@Endpoint` annotation and define the methods that support the `@ReadOperation`, `@WriteOperation`, and `@DeleteOperation`. We'll discuss these annotations in detail in the discussion section.

Let's first create a collection of release notes by defining a bean definition in the `CourseTrackerApplication` class, as shown in the following listing.

Listing 4.27 Creating a collection of ReleaseNote bean definitions

```
@Bean(name = "releaseNotes")
public Collection<ReleaseNote> loadReleaseNotes() {
    Set<ReleaseNote> releaseNotes = new LinkedHashSet<>();
    ReleaseNote releaseNote1 = ReleaseNote.builder()
            .version("v1.2.1")
            .releaseDate(LocalDate.of(2021, 12, 30))
            .commitTag("a7d2ea3")
            .bugFixes(Set.of(
                    getReleaseItem("SBIP-123",
➥ "The name of the matching-strategy property is
➥ incorrect in the action message of the failure
➥ analysis for a PatternParseException #28839"),
                    getReleaseItem("SBIP-124",
➥ "ErrorPageSecurityFilter prevents deployment
➥ to a Servlet 3.1 compatible container #28790")))
            .build();

    ReleaseNote releaseNote2 = ReleaseNote.builder()
            .version("v1.2.0")
            .releaseDate(LocalDate.of(2021, 11, 20))
            .commitTag("44047f3")
            .newReleases(Set.of(getReleaseItem("SBIP-125",
➥ "Support both kebab-case and camelCase as Spring init
➥ CLI Options #28138")))
            .bugFixes(Set.of(getReleaseItem("SBIP-126",
➥ "Profiles added using @ActiveProfiles have
➥ different precedence #28724")))
            .build();
    releaseNotes.addAll(Set.of(releaseNote1, releaseNote2));
    return releaseNotes;
}
```

The `ReleaseNote` and `ReleaseItem` classes are defined in the following listing.

Listing 4.28 The ReleaseNote and ReleaseItem classes

```
package com.manning.sbip.ch04.model;

//imports

@Builder
@Getter
@Setter
public class ReleaseNote {

    private String version;
    private LocalDate releaseDate;
    private String commitTag;
    private Set<ReleaseItem> newReleases;
    private Set<ReleaseItem> bugFixes;
}
```

```
package com.manning.sbip.ch04.model;

//imports

@Builder
@Getter
@Setter
@NoArgsConstructor
@AllArgsConstructor
public class ReleaseItem {

    private String itemId;
    private String itemDescription;
}
```

Next, let's create a class called `ReleaseNotesEndpoint` that provides the details of all available releases in the application. The following listing shows this class.

Listing 4.29 The ReleaseNotesEndpoint class

```
package com.manning.sbip.ch04.endpoint;

import java.util.Collection;
import java.util.Optional;

import org.springframework.beans.factory.annotation.Autowired;
import org.springframework.boot.actuate.endpoint.annotation.DeleteOperation;
import org.springframework.boot.actuate.endpoint.annotation.Endpoint;
import org.springframework.boot.actuate.endpoint.annotation.ReadOperation;
import org.springframework.boot.actuate.endpoint.annotation.Selector;
import org.springframework.stereotype.Component;

import com.manning.sbip.ch04.model.ReleaseNote;

@Component
@Endpoint(id = "releaseNotes")
public class ReleaseNotesEndpoint {

    private final Collection<ReleaseNote> releaseNotes;

    @Autowired
    public ReleaseNotesEndpoint(Collection<ReleaseNote> releaseNotes) {
        this.releaseNotes = releaseNotes;
    }

    @ReadOperation
    public Iterable<ReleaseNote> releaseNotes() {
        return releaseNotes;
    }
}
```

We've performed the following actions in this class:

- Annotated the class with `@Component` annotation, so Spring Boot component scanning can detect this class and create the bean.

- Annotated the class with `@Endpoint` annotation that indicates this class is an actuator endpoint. We've also provided an ID named `releaseNotes` to uniquely identify the endpoint.
- Autowired the `releaseNotes` in this class, so it can be used to get the release details.
- Defined a method with `@ReadOperation` annotation that returns all releases.

To access the `releaseNotes` endpoint, you need to configure the `management.endpoints.web.exposure.include` property with the value `releaseNotes` or with the value `*`. The following listing shows this property with the `releaseNotes` endpoint.

Listing 4.30 Expose the custom endpoint

```
management.endpoints.web.exposure.include=releaseNotes
```

If you start the application and access the actuator discovery page http://localhost:8080/actuator/ from your browser, you will notice the endpoint is listed as shown in figure 4.15.

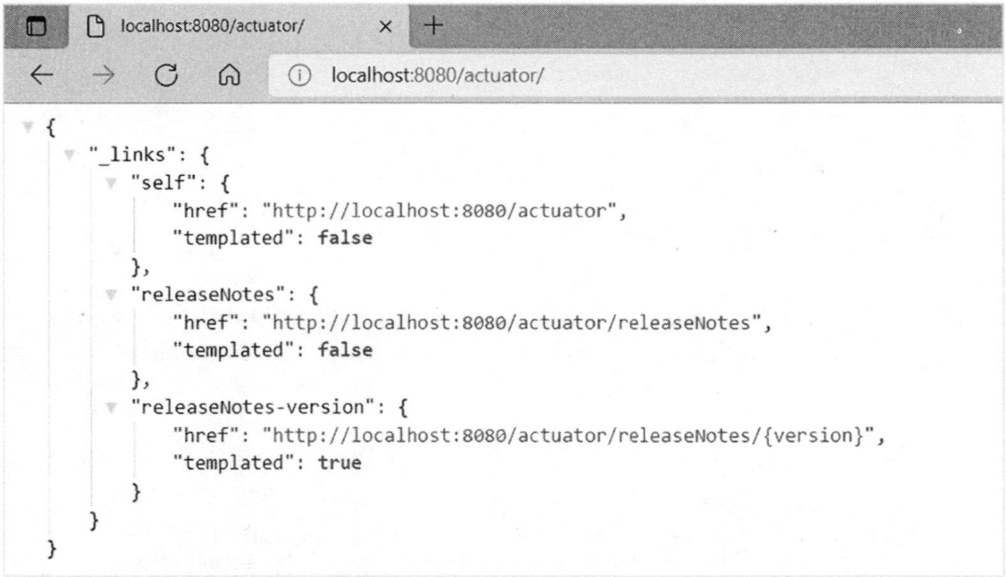

localhost:8080/actuator/

{
  "_links": {
    "self": {
      "href": "http://localhost:8080/actuator",
      "templated": false
    },
    "releaseNotes": {
      "href": "http://localhost:8080/actuator/releaseNotes",
      "templated": false
    },
    "releaseNotes-version": {
      "href": "http://localhost:8080/actuator/releaseNotes/{version}",
      "templated": true
    }
  }
}

Figure 4.15 Defining custom endpoint /releaseNotes and exposing it through the Actuator discovery page

If you access the http://localhost:8080/actuator/releaseNotes endpoint, you'll notice that it provides the list of releases available in the application, as shown in figure 4.16.

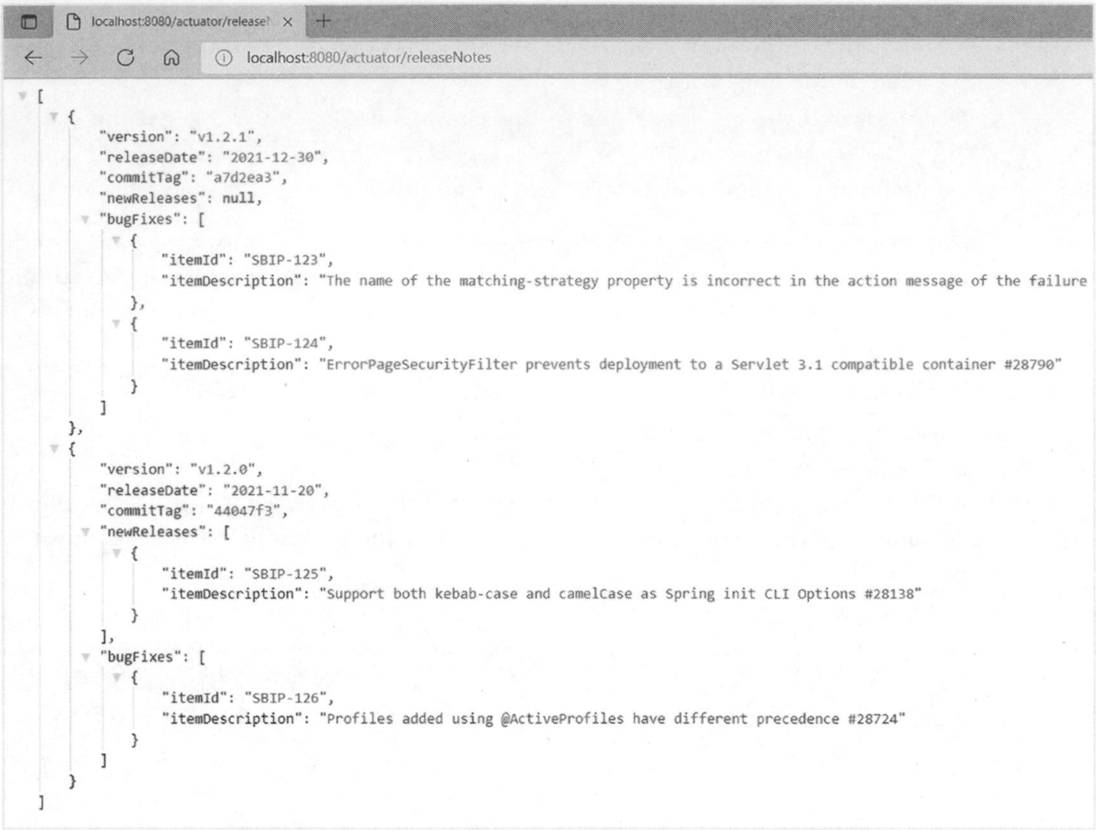

localhost:8080/actuator/releaseNotes

```
[
  {
    "version": "v1.2.1",
    "releaseDate": "2021-12-30",
    "commitTag": "a7d2ea3",
    "newReleases": null,
    "bugFixes": [
      {
        "itemId": "SBIP-123",
        "itemDescription": "The name of the matching-strategy property is incorrect in the action message of the failure
      },
      {
        "itemId": "SBIP-124",
        "itemDescription": "ErrorPageSecurityFilter prevents deployment to a Servlet 3.1 compatible container #28790"
      }
    ]
  },
  {
    "version": "v1.2.0",
    "releaseDate": "2021-11-20",
    "commitTag": "44047f3",
    "newReleases": [
      {
        "itemId": "SBIP-125",
        "itemDescription": "Support both kebab-case and camelCase as Spring init CLI Options #28138"
      }
    ],
    "bugFixes": [
      {
        "itemId": "SBIP-126",
        "itemDescription": "Profiles added using @ActiveProfiles have different precedence #28724"
      }
    ]
  }
]
```


Figure 4.16 The releaseNotes endpoint with the release details

Let us now implement the endpoint that lets you find specific release details through the release `version`. The following listing shows this in the `ReleaseNotesEndpoint` class.

Listing 4.31 Defining the Read operation

```
@ReadOperation
public Object selectCourse(@Selector String version) {
    Optional<ReleaseNote> releaseNoteOptional = releaseNotes
            .stream()
            .filter(releaseNote -> version.equals(releaseNote.getVersion()))
            .findFirst();
    if(releaseNoteOptional.isPresent()) {
        return releaseNoteOptional.get();
    }
    return String.format("No such release version exists : %s", version);
}
```

In listing 4.31, we implemented another `@ReadOperation` that lets you specify a release `version` as the `@Selector` and return only the release specific details. If there is an invalid release version, it returns the following error message: *No such release version exists.*

The next operation you'll implement is to delete release details. The following listing shows this operation.

Listing 4.32 Defining the delete operation

```
@DeleteOperation
public void removeReleaseVersion(@Selector String version) {
    Optional<ReleaseNote> releaseNoteOptional = releaseNotes
            .stream()
            .filter(releaseNote -> version.equals(releaseNote.getVersion()))
            .findFirst();
    if(releaseNoteOptional.isPresent()) {
        releaseNotes.remove(releaseNoteOptional.get());
    }
}
```

In the code snippet in listing 4.32, you are first checking if there is a release available for the supplied version. If a release detail is found, the same is removed from the collection. The following listing shows the `cURL` command to delete the course.

Listing 4.33 Performing the delete operation for a single course with cURL

```
curl -i -X DELETE http://localhost:8080/actuator/releaseNotes/v1.2.1
```

You can access the http://localhost:8080/actuator/releaseNotes URL from your browser, and you'll notice that the release with `version` v1.2.1 is deleted.

There is another annotation named `@WriteOperation` that lets you perform create/update operations for the endpoint. We've skipped it in this example, as a write operation does not fit well in the above example.

DISCUSSION

With this technique, you've learned how to define a custom Spring Boot actuator endpoint. It is straightforward to define a custom endpoint with the `@Endpoint`, `@ReadOperation`, `@WriteOperation`, `@DeleteOperation`, and `@Selector` annotations.

The `@Endpoint` annotation indicates that the annotated class is a Spring Boot actuator endpoint and able to provide or mutate information in the running application. It takes two arguments: `id` and `enablebyDefault`. In this example, you've configured the `id` as `/releaseNotes`. By default, the `enableByDefault` parameter is set to true. However, to expose it over a specific technology (e.g., JMX or Web), you need to configure the associated `management.endpoints.<web/jmx>.exposure.include` parameter in the application.properties file.

Spring Boot also provides two technology-specific endpoint annotations: `@Jmx-Endpoint` and `@WebEndpoint`. The first one lets you define an endpoint that is only exposed over JMX, and the latter one exposes the endpoint over HTTP only. For instance, in listing 4.29 you can change the `@Endpoint` to `@JmxEndpoint` and notice that the `/releaseNotes` endpoint is not available on the discovery page at http://localhost:8080/actuator. You can use the `JConsole` tool (http://mng.bz/p2rK) to view the JMX endpoints, as shown in figure 4.17.

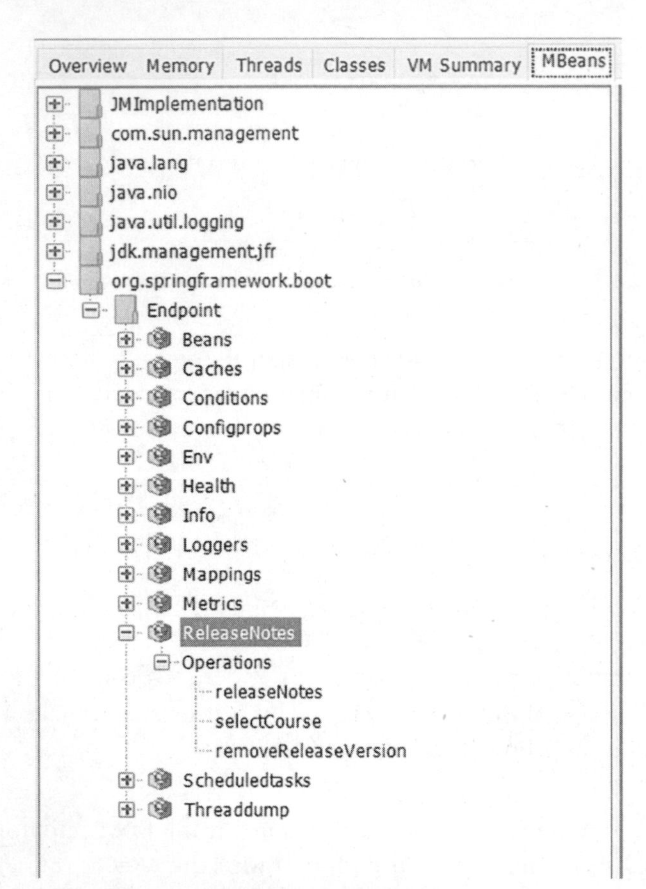

Figure 4.17 The Spring Boot Actuator endpoints exposed through JMX

4.6.2 Spring Boot actuator metrics

In addition to other endpoints, Spring Boot provides the `metrics` actuator endpoint that provides various application metrics. For instance, if you start the `spring-boot-actuator-metrics` application and access the http://localhost:8080/actuator/metrics endpoint, you'll see the output shown in figure 4.18.

Each one of these is an application metric that provides application-related information. For example, if you need to know how much time the application was paused

localhost:8080/actuator/metrics/


```
{
  "names": [
    "http.server.requests",
    "jvm.buffer.count",
    "jvm.buffer.memory.used",
    "jvm.buffer.total.capacity",
    "jvm.classes.loaded",
    "jvm.classes.unloaded",
    "jvm.gc.live.data.size",
    "jvm.gc.max.data.size",
    "jvm.gc.memory.allocated",
    "jvm.gc.memory.promoted",
    "jvm.gc.pause",
    "jvm.memory.committed",
    "jvm.memory.max",
    "jvm.memory.used",
    "jvm.threads.daemon",
    "jvm.threads.live",
    "jvm.threads.peak",
    "jvm.threads.states",
    "logback.events",
    "process.cpu.usage",
    "process.start.time",
    "process.uptime",
    "system.cpu.count",
    "system.cpu.usage",
    "tomcat.sessions.active.current",
    "tomcat.sessions.active.max",
    "tomcat.sessions.alive.max",
    "tomcat.sessions.created",
    "tomcat.sessions.expired",
    "tomcat.sessions.rejected"
  ]
}
```


Figure 4.18 List of available Spring Boot actuator metrics

for garbage collection, you can use the `jvm.gc.pause` metric through the http://localhost:8080/actuator/metrics/jvm.gc.pause URL, as shown in figure 4.19.

In this example, the application was paused 10 times, and the total pause duration was 0.031 seconds. Under the hood, the Spring Boot actuator uses Micrometer framework (https://micrometer.io/) to configure the metrics. It also lets us define custom metrics, such as counters, timers, gauges, and distribution summaries. Shortly, you'll learn how to create these metrics in a Spring Boot application. Let us now provide a brief overview of the Micrometer framework.

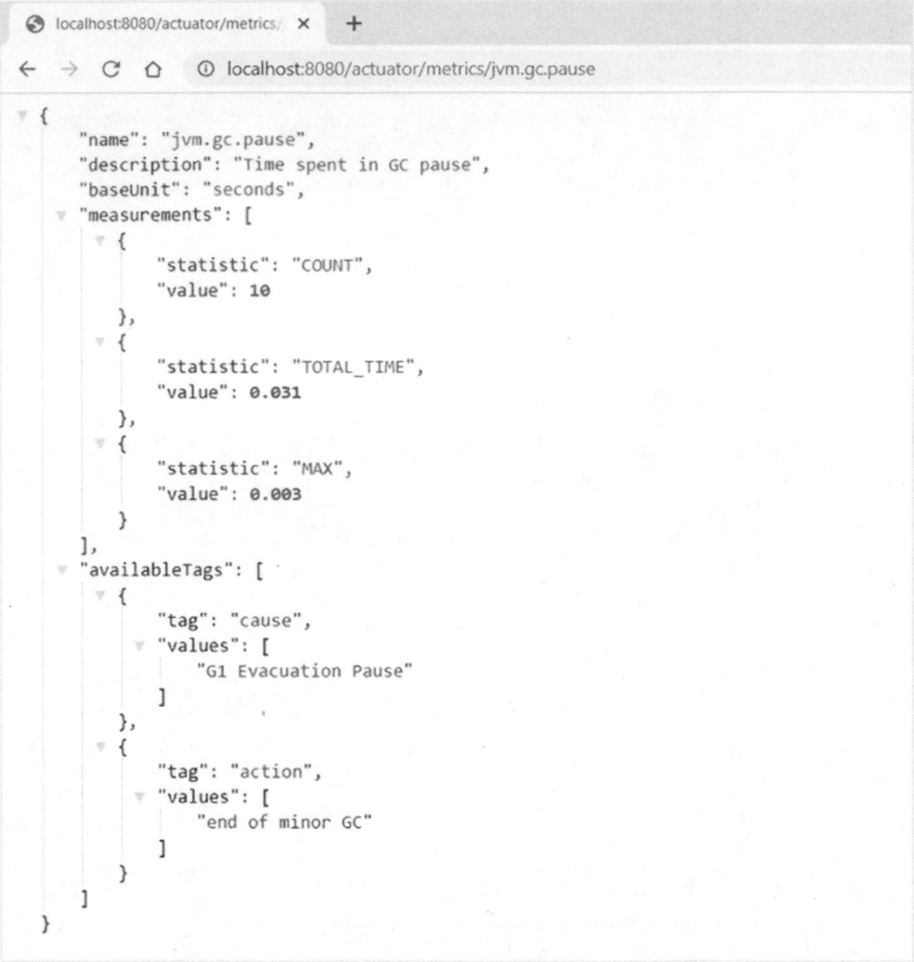
localhost:8080/actuator/metrics/
localhost:8080/actuator/metrics/jvm.gc.pause
{
"name": "jvm.gc.pause",
"description": "Time spent in GC pause",
"baseUnit": "seconds",
"measurements": [
{
"statistic": "COUNT",
"value": 10
},
{
"statistic": "TOTAL_TIME",
"value": 0.031
},
{
"statistic": "MAX",
"value": 0.003
}
],
"availableTags": [
{
"tag": "cause",
"values": [
"G1 Evacuation Pause"
]
},
{
"tag": "action",
"values": [
"end of minor GC"
]
}
]
}

Figure 4.19 Details of the jvm.gc.pause metric

> **NOTE** An in-depth discussion on the Micrometer framework or other monitoring systems is beyond the scope of this text. You can refer to Micrometer documentation (https://micrometer.io/docs) or the respective monitoring system documentation for further references. You can also refer to http://mng.bz/NxNN for more insight on Micrometer with Spring Boot. For a list of supporting monitoring systems, you can refer to the Spring Boot documentation at http://mng.bz/OGRw. In this book, we'll show you how to use the monitoring tool Prometheus, which collects the metrics, and the observability platform Grafana, which lets you visualize these metrics.

The Micrometer is a metrics collection facade intended to collect various types of metrics in a vendor-neutral way. It allows you to plug in the various concrete implementations of monitor systems (e.g., Prometheus, Graphite, New Relic, etc.). Spring Boot can select various monitoring systems through configuration and classpath to export metrics data.

Micrometer provides a vendor-neutral metrics collection API (`io.micrometer.core.instrument.MeterRegistry` and its subclasses) and provides implementations for other monitoring frameworks, such as Prometheus (`io.micrometer.prometheus.PrometheusMeterRegistry`). To configure a different monitoring system, you can provide the corresponding dependency `micrometer-registry-{monitoring_system}`, and Spring Boot will automatically configure the registry for you. For instance, to configure Prometheus, you need to configure the `micrometer-registry-prometheus` dependency in the pom.xml file. Further, Spring Boot also provides several properties to control these features. The following listing shows some of these properties.

Listing 4.34 Exposing the metrics

```
management.metrics.export.<registry>.enabled=false
management.metrics.export.defaults.enabled=false
```

The first command indicates whether exporting metrics to the registry (e.g., Graphite) is enabled. The second command indicates whether to enable default metrics exporters. For instance, setting `management.metrics.export.defaults.enabled` to `false` does not expose any metrics. You can validate that by accessing http://localhost:8080/actuator/metrics URL.

Spring Boot autoconfigures a composite `MeterRegistry` that lets you add any number of registry implementations. Thus, you can ship your metrics to more than one monitoring system. Besides, you configure the registries with `MeterRegistryCustomizer`. For instance, you can ship your application metrics to both Prometheus and New Relic. You can then configure a common set of tags for both registries. Tags, in this context, are used as an identifier. For instance, if multiple applications publish metrics data, they can use a tag to identify the application name. Let's say you need to add a tag in your metrics that adds the `application` name to all metrics. Listing 4.35 shows how you can customize the `MeterRegistry` using the `MeterRegistryCustomizer` with a Spring bean definition in a Spring configuration file.

Listing 4.35 Customizing MeterRegistry with MeterRegistryCustomizer

```
@Bean
MeterRegistryCustomizer<MeterRegistry> metricsCommonTags() {
    return registry -> registry.config()
➥ .commonTags("application", "course-tracker");
}
```

Open a browser window and access any of the metrics; you'll find the application tag is present in the metrics data. You can then use the custom tag to filter the metric data. You can append the query string `?tag=tagName:tagValue` in the metric URL to achieve this. For instance, figure 4.20 shows this in an example.

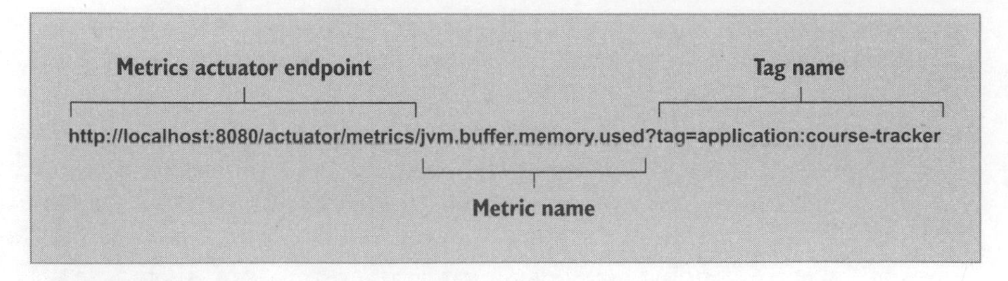

Figure 4.20 Using the tag to filter the metric output

This summarizes the overview of the Spring Boot metrics. In the next section, you'll learn how to create custom metrics in a Spring Boot application.

4.6.3 Creating custom metrics

In the previous section, you explored the `/metrics` endpoint that exposes critical application and system information worth monitoring for application performance and overall health. The metrics you've seen so far are built-in to the Micrometer, and Spring Boot autoconfigures those for us. For instance, the Micrometer framework provides `JvmGcMetrics`, `JvmMemoryMetrics`, and `JvmThreadMetrics` classes that expose JVM garbage collection, memory, and thread details, respectively. All these metrics are autoconfigured by the Spring Boot `JvmMetricsAutoConfiguration` class.

Spring Boot lets you create custom metrics that expose application-specific data you may need to monitor. Let's discuss this in terms of the `CourseTracker` application. In this application, you may be interested to monitor the number of courses created in the application on a real-time basis. You may also track the time that is being taken to create a new course or the time taken within the SLAs.

The micrometer framework provides several types of the meters, such as `Counter`, `Gauge`, `Timer`, and `DistributionSummary`, that you can use to create custom metrics. Let's explore some of these. We'll define the following additional metrics in the `CourseTracker` application:

- Counting the number of courses created using the `Counter` metric.
- Counting the number of courses created using the `Gauge` metric. We'll discuss the difference between `Counter` and `Gauge` metrics.
- Capturing the time taken to create the course using the `Timer` metric.
- Capturing the distribution summary of the course ratings using the `Distribution-Summary` metric.

> **Source code**
>
> To continue with this exercise, you can download the initial version of the Spring Boot project from GitHub at http://mng.bz/YgXz. The final version of the application can be accessed at http://mng.bz/GGID.

COUNTER

The `Counter` is the first type of metric we'll explore. A `Counter` represents a single numeric value that can be incremented. For instance, we can use it to count the number of times a method was invoked. Thus, if we need to count the total number of courses created, we can use the `Counter` in the course creation method to keep track. Let's first create a Counter instance and then use it in the `DefaultCourseService` to count the number of courses. The following listing shows the `createCourseCounter` bean definition in the `CourseTrackerMetricsConfiguration` class.

Listing 4.36 The createCourseCounter bean

```
@Configuration
public class CourseTrackerMetricsConfiguration {

    @Bean
    public Counter createCourseCounter(MeterRegistry meterRegistry) {
        return Counter.builder("api.courses.created.count")
                .description("Total number of courses created")
                .register(meterRegistry);
    }
}
```

In the listing, you created a `Counter` instance with the name `api.courses.created.count` and provided a description indicating its purpose. Finally, you registered it to the `MeterRegistry`, so it can be exposed in the metrics list.

Let's now use this `Counter` instance in the `createCourse(..)` method of the `DefaultCourseService` class, so each time this service method is invoked, the `Counter` value can be incremented, as shown in the following listing.

Listing 4.37 Count the number of courses created

```
@Autowired
private final Counter createCourseCounter;

public Course createCourse(Course course) {
    createCourseCounter.increment();
    return courseRepository.save(course);
}
```

Start the application, and access the http://localhost:8080/actuator/metrics URL. You'll notice that a new metric endpoint is added. Access this http://localhost:8080/actuator/metrics/api.courses.created.count endpoint URL, and you'll notice it is displaying the total number of courses created so far. However, as we haven't created any courses yet, it shows the count value is `0`.

> **NOTE** In listing 4.37, we used the `Counter` metric directly inside the Spring Boot service class. Although this approach works, it tightly couples the metric code with the actual business logic. As a better design, you can use Spring's event listener mechanism to decouple the use of the `Counter` metric.

Open a browser window, and access the http://localhost:8080/index URL to create a new course. Post that, and access the http://localhost:8080/actuator/metrics/api.courses.created.count endpoint again. This time you'll notice that the course count is increased to `1`. Figure 4.21 shows the output.

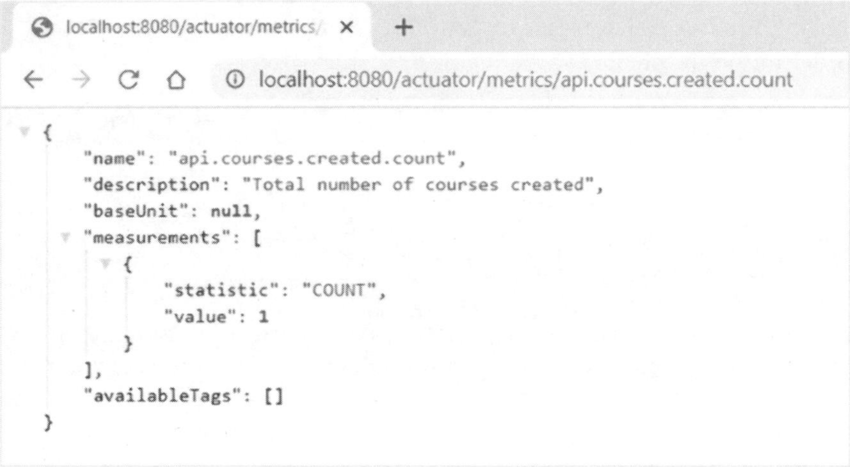

localhost:8080/actuator/metrics/api.courses.created.count

```
{
    "name": "api.courses.created.count",
    "description": "Total number of courses created",
    "baseUnit": null,
    "measurements": [
        {
            "statistic": "COUNT",
            "value": 1
        }
    ],
    "availableTags": []
}
```

Figure 4.21 Outcome of the api.courses.created.count custom metric

4.6.4 Gauge

The drawback of the `Counter` metric is that it can't persist the counter value once there is an application restart. The counter value is set to `0` after the restart. Thus, if you need to keep track of the total number of courses created in the application irrespective of the application restart, a `Counter` is not the right metric.

A gauge is the other metric that is more suitable to find the total number of courses available. For instance, in a production application, you'll use a database that can persist the application data. Thus, you can query the database on the total number of courses available and expose it through a `Gauge` metric. Let's demonstrate how to implement this with a `Gauge`.

Let's begin by defining a `Gauge` metric that retrieves the total number of courses available in the database. Add the following bean definition in the previously created `CourseTrackerMetricsConfiguration` class. The following listing shows the `createCoursesGauge` bean definition.

Listing 4.38 The createCoursesGauge bean definition

```
@Bean
public Gauge createCoursesGauge(MeterRegistry meterRegistry, CourseService
➥ courseService) {
    return Gauge.builder
```

```
➥ ("api.courses.created.gauge", courseService::count)
➥             .description("Total courses available")
➥             .register(meterRegistry);
}
```

In the listing, you've created a Gauge metric named api.courses.created.gauge with a suitable description and registered it with the MeterRegistry. The metric data is fetched from the database using the count(..) method defined in the CourseService.

As the data required by the Gauge metric is supplied from the database, you need not incorporate it in the createCourse(..) service. Besides, as the api.courses.created.gauge metric is already registered with the MeterRegistry, it is already exposed in the /metrics endpoint.

Start the application, create a few courses, and access the http://localhost:8080/actuator/metrics/api.courses.created.gauge URL. You'll find the total number of courses available in the application.

NOTE In this example, you are using the H2 in-memory database, and it is restarted each time there is an application restart. Thus, you'll notice that the Gauge metric is behaving similarly to the Counter metric. To explore the data persistence across application restart, use a database that persists the data in the disk. For instance, you can use MySQL to explore this.

TIMER

The previous two metrics, Counter and Gauge, let you measure the count of *something* (e.g., courses) in your application. Further, at times you may be interested to measure the time taken to perform an operation in your application. For instance, you may need to measure the time taken to create a course. Additionally, in time-critical applications, you can measure whether the operation is completed within the SLA. A Timer allows you achieve this. Let's define a timer that allows you to measure the time taken to create a course in the CourseTracker application. We'll define a Timer metric in the CourseTrackerMetricsConfiguration class in the following listing.

Listing 4.39 The createCoursesTimer bean definition

```
@Bean
public Timer createCoursesTimer(MeterRegistry meterRegistry) {
    return Timer.builder("api.courses.creation.time")
        .description("Course creation time")
        .register(meterRegistry);
 }
```

In the listing, you defined a metric called api.courses.creation.time with a suitable description and registered it with the MeterRegistry. Let's now use this metric in the createCourse(..) method of DefaultCourseService to capture the time taken to create a course, as shown in the following listing.

Listing 4.40 Using the createCoursesTimer

```
@Autowired
private Timer createCoursesTimer;

@SneakyThrows
public Course createCourse(Course course) {
    return createCoursesTimer.recordCallable(() ->
➥ courseRepository.save(course));
}
```

In the listing, you are using the `recordCallable(..)` method of the `Timer` interface. This method accepts a `java.util.concurrent.Callable` instance. In this demonstration, we've represented it with a lambda expression in which we invoke the repository to save the course details. Internally, the timer uses this callable instance to capture the total time taken to invoke the repository `save(..)` method. The `recordCallable(..)` method throws an exception. We've used Lombok's `@SneakyThrows` annotation that wraps the checked exception to an unchecked one.

You can restart the application, create a few courses, and then access the http://localhost:8080/actuator/metrics/api.courses.creation.time URL. The `api.courses.creation.time` provides the details, such as total courses created, total time taken to create the courses, and maximum time taken to create a course, as shown in Figure 4.22.

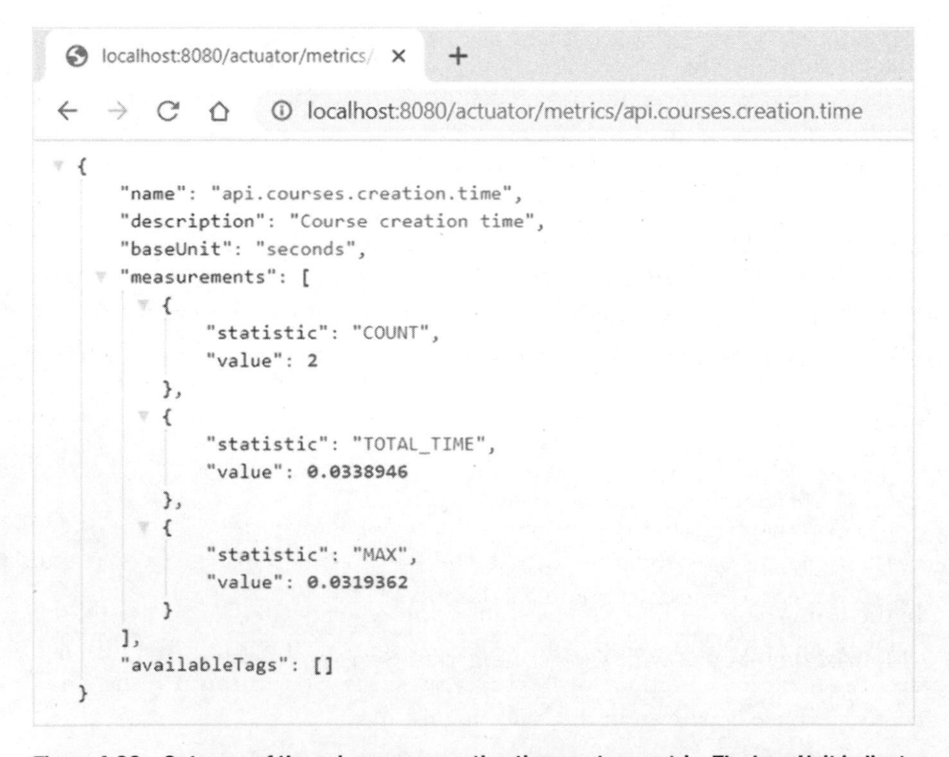

Figure 4.22 Outcome of the api.courses.creation.time custom metric. The baseUnit indicates the unit for the metric and provides an option to customize the unit for the metric.

DISTRIBUTION SUMMARY

A distribution summary allows you to measure the distribution of events. It is similar to a `Timer` structurally but is used to record values that do not represent a unit of time. For example, a distribution summary could be used to measure the course ratings in the `CourseTracker` application.

Let's define a `DistributionSummary` metric in the `CourseTrackerMetrics-Configuration` class, as shown in the following listing.

Listing 4.41 Defining a distribution summary

```
@Bean
public DistributionSummary createDistributionSummary(MeterRegistry
➥ meterRegistry) {
    return DistributionSummary
➥  .builder("api.courses.rating.distribution.summary")
➥            .description("Rating distribution summary")
➥            .register(meterRegistry);
}
```

Like other metrics, in the listing you've defined a `DistributionSummary` metric with a name and description and registered it with the `MeterRegistry`. Let's now use this metric in the `createCourse(..)` method of `DefaultCourseService`, as shown in the following listing.

Listing 4.42 Using DistributionSummary in CreateCourse method

```
@Autowired
private DistributionSummary distributionSummary;
@SneakyThrows
public Course createCourse(Course course) {
    distributionSummary.record(course.getRating());
➥      return createCoursesTimer.recordCallable(() ->
➥  courseRepository.save(course));
}
```

Restart the application, and create a few courses with different course ratings. Post that, and navigate to the http://localhost:8080/actuator/metrics/api.courses.rating .distribution.summary URL to access the newly defined distribution summary endpoint. Figure 4.23 shows the output.

This completes the discussion of the major metrics that you may need to use in your application. In the next section, you'll learn how to use Prometheus and Grafana to view these metrics in a graphical dashboard.

4.6.5 Metrics dashboard with Prometheus and Grafana

In this section, you'll learn how to use Prometheus to collect the metrics you've defined so far. Note that Prometheus is a monitoring solution, and Spring Boot publishes all metrics (built-in and custom) if Prometheus libraries are present in the

localhost:8080/actuator/metrics/api.courses.rating.distribution.summary

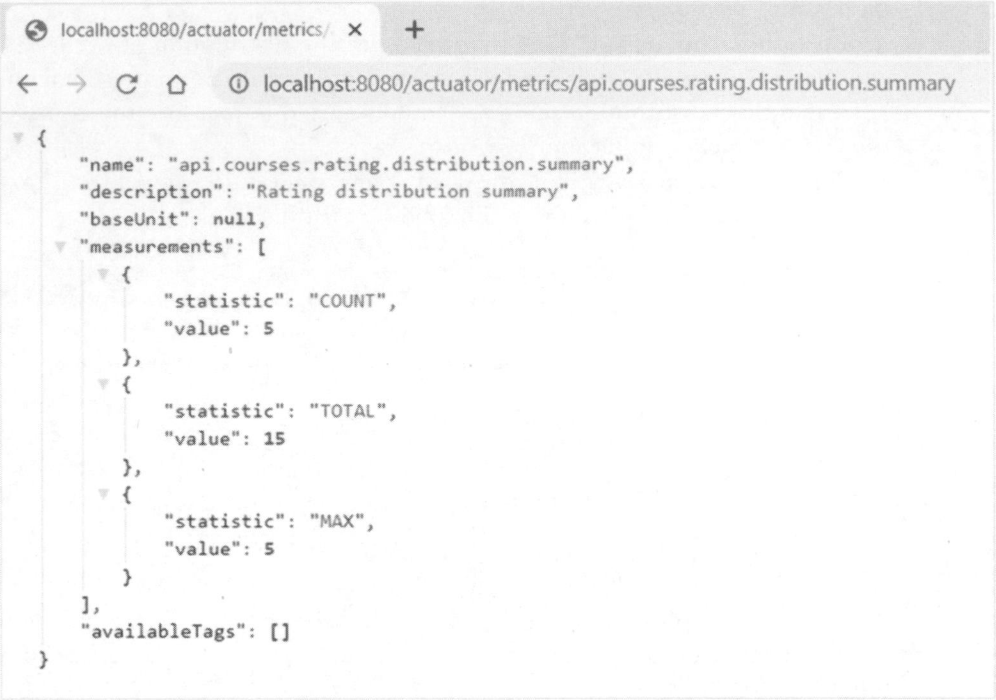

```
{
    "name": "api.courses.rating.distribution.summary",
    "description": "Rating distribution summary",
    "baseUnit": null,
    "measurements": [
        {
            "statistic": "COUNT",
            "value": 5
        },
        {
            "statistic": "TOTAL",
            "value": 15
        },
        {
            "statistic": "MAX",
            "value": 5
        }
    ],
    "availableTags": []
}
```


Figure 4.23 Outcome of the api.courses.rating.distribution.summary custom metric. The COUNT property indicates how many courses have been created. The TOTAL provides information regarding the aggregated value of the rating. Lastly, the MAX property shows the maximum value of a course rating. For demonstration, we've used the course rating in this example. We can also use other details, such as time in units of second and length to capture distribution summary.

application classpath. Prometheus uses a different format to represent metrics. Refer to http://mng.bz/aJMz for a list of Prometheus metrics. Further, you'll configure Grafana to visualize the Prometheus metrics.

> **NOTE** Prometheus (https://prometheus.io/) is an open-source system-monitoring and alerting toolkit originally built at SoundCloud. You can find more information about Prometheus by viewing their documentation at https://prometheus.io/docs/introduction/overview/. Grafana (https://grafana.com/) provides a graphical toolkit that allows you to collect and visualize the metrics in dashboards in the form of various graphical representations, such as `Graph`, `Time Series`, `Gauge Table`, and more. You can use Prometheus and Grafana either by installing them in your local machine or running the Docker images. Refer to the GitHub wiki, available at http://mng.bz/0wvJ, for a quick guide on setting up these applications. You can refer to the Prometheus and Grafana documentation for more details.

Spring Boot provides an easy integration with Prometheus and publishes all the metrics under the /actuator/prometheus endpoint. Add the following dependency to the pom.xml of your project, as shown in the following listing.

Listing 4.43 Prometheus dependency

```
<dependency>
    <groupId>io.micrometer</groupId>
    <artifactId>micrometer-registry-prometheus</artifactId>
    <scope>runtime</scope>
</dependency>
```

We discussed previously that Spring Boot autoconfiguration can configure one or more systems in a Spring Boot application, based on the presence of libraries in the application classpath. Adding this dependency enables the PrometheusMetricsExportAutoConfiguration class, which in turn configures the PrometheusMeterRegistry bean. This bean is the Prometheus registry plugged in the metrics facade.

Restart the application and access the http://localhost:8080/actuator/prometheus endpoint URL to view the available metrics. Notice that the metrics are published in a slightly different format.

To proceed with the remaining part of this section, you need to ensure that you've installed and configured Prometheus and Grafana. Refer to http://mng.bz/0wvJ for a quick discussion on how to set up these applications. Once you've installed Prometheus, you should be able to access the server and view the metrics. For instance, in this demonstration, we've installed Prometheus in the local machine and can access it through the http://localhost:9090 URL. Prometheus provides a functional query language named PromQL (Prometheus Query Language) that lets you select and aggregate metric data. You can view the result either in tabular or graphical format in Prometheus's expression browser. We'll leave it to the reader to explore how to select and view various metric data through PromQL (http://mng.bz/KBVX).

Although Prometheus allows you to view the data in graphical format through the table and simple graphs, the visualization capability of Prometheus is limited. To present data with better visualization, we'll use Grafana, as it has a rich set of visualization toolkits. Grafana can pull the metric data from the Prometheus server and present it in the Grafana dashboard. You can use the PromQL to select the metric and present the metric data in the dashboard.

To use Grafana, you first need to create a data source. In this demonstration, the data source is the Prometheus server. You can then proceed by creating an empty dashboard and adding one or more panels to it. Each panel can represent one metric of data. Grafana allows you to choose the type of UI toolkit (e.g., graph, table, heatmap, gauge, etc.) you would like to use to present the data in the dashboard. Refer to Grafana documentation, available at http://mng.bz/9Kpj, for more information about how to create a Grafana dashboard. Figure 4.24 shows a sample dashboard created for the demonstration.

Figure 4.24 Spring Boot Actuator metric in the Grafana dashboard

In figure 4.24, we have shown four panels in the dashboard. The *Courses Created* panel shows the number of courses created. The second panel, *Course Creation Rate*, shows the rate of courses created per minute. The third panel, *JVM Thread Status*, shows the threads in the application in various states. The last panel, *System CPU Usage*, shows the use of the CPU over a period. The above is a basic dashboard created for demonstration purposes. You can explore the various metrics and present them in a variety of visualizations (e.g., bar, chart, table, heatmap, etc.) in Grafana.

Summary

We've come along a long way in our Spring Boot Journey. You can now develop and monitor Spring Boot applications with the concepts covered so far. Let's quickly summarize the concepts you've learned in this chapter:

- We had an in-depth discussion on Spring Boot autoconfiguration. We explored various conditional annotations that play a critical role in implementing autoconfiguration and explored a built-in class, `DataSourceAutoConfiguration`, to understand how it works in a Spring Boot application.
- We discussed Spring Boot DevTools, which provides a suite of features for a pleasant development experience. Automatic application restart, disabling caching, and browser refresh are a few notable features.
- We explored Spring Boot `FailureAnalyzer` and its role in validating various application startup issues. We also discussed how to implement a custom `FailureAnalyzer`.

- We had an in-depth discussion on the Spring Boot actuator and its various endpoints. We then explored the `/info` and `/health` endpoints in further detail. We also learned several techniques on how to define and include custom application information and health status in these endpoints.
- We explored the built-in metrics exposed by Spring Boot. We also discussed how to create custom metrics, such as `Counter`, `Gauge`, `Timer`, and `Distribution Summary`. Lastly, we demonstrated how to use Prometheus and Grafana to monitor and view the metrics in a GUI console in real-time.

In chapter 5, you'll learn to secure your Spring Boot applications with Spring Security. You'll explore Spring Security basic concepts and various fundamental security techniques, such as basic and JDBC authentication. Let's get started!

5 Securing Spring Boot applications

This chapter covers

- An overview of Spring Security and common security threats
- Enabling Spring Security in a Spring Boot application and understanding Spring Security autoconfiguration
- Customizing Spring Security with in-memory, JDBC, and LDAP authentication
- Implementing HTTP basic authentication in a Spring Boot project

In past chapters, you learned several essential techniques to build Spring Boot applications, and you are now well-versed in core Spring Boot concepts, understand several techniques to communicate to the database, can monitor Spring Boot applications with Spring Boot Actuator, and are in a position to start building enterprise-grade Spring Boot applications. However, before you get super excited and announce to the world your newly acquired skills, there is another essential technique that you need to master. *What about the security of our Spring Boot applications?*

In this chapter, you'll explore several techniques to secure Spring Boot applications with Spring Security.

5.1 Introducing Spring Security

In previous chapters, you've seen the use of some of the core Spring modules, such as Spring MVC and Spring Data and features such as Spring Boot Actuator and DevTools. Spring Framework provides a dedicated module called Spring Security that focuses on the security aspects of the Spring applications. Spring Boot provides easy integration with Spring Security with the `spring-boot-starter-security` dependency. In this chapter, we'll demonstrate the use of Spring Security in Spring Boot applications.

However, before we deep-dive into techniques for implementing various security features offered by Spring Security, let's explore some of the default security features offered by Spring Security in a Spring Boot application:

- Spring Security enforces the application users to be authenticated before accessing it.
- If the application does not have a `login` page, Spring Security generates a default login page for user login and allows the user to log out from the application.
- Spring Security provides a default user named `user` and generates a default password (printed in the console log) for form-based login.
- Spring Security provides several password encoders to encode the plain-text password and store it in the persistence storage.
- Spring Security prevents session fixation attacks by changing the session ID after successful user authentication.
- Spring Security provides default protection from cross-site request forgery (CSRF) attacks. It does so by including a randomly generated token in the HTTP response. It expects this token to be available in all subsequent form-based requests that intend to perform a state-changing operation in the application. A malicious user won't have access to the token and, thus, can't make CSRF attacks. Figure 5.1 demonstrates the CSRF protection with Spring Security.
- By default, Spring Security includes several HTTP response headers that prevent many common types of attacks. These headers are shown in the following listing.

Listing 5.1 Default Spring Security HTTP response headers

```
Cache-Control: no-cache, no-store, max-age=0, must-revalidate
Pragma: no-cache
Expires: 0
X-Content-Type-Options: nosniff
Strict-Transport-Security: max-age=31536000 ; includeSubDomains
X-Frame-Options: DENY
X-XSS-Protection: 1; mode=block
```

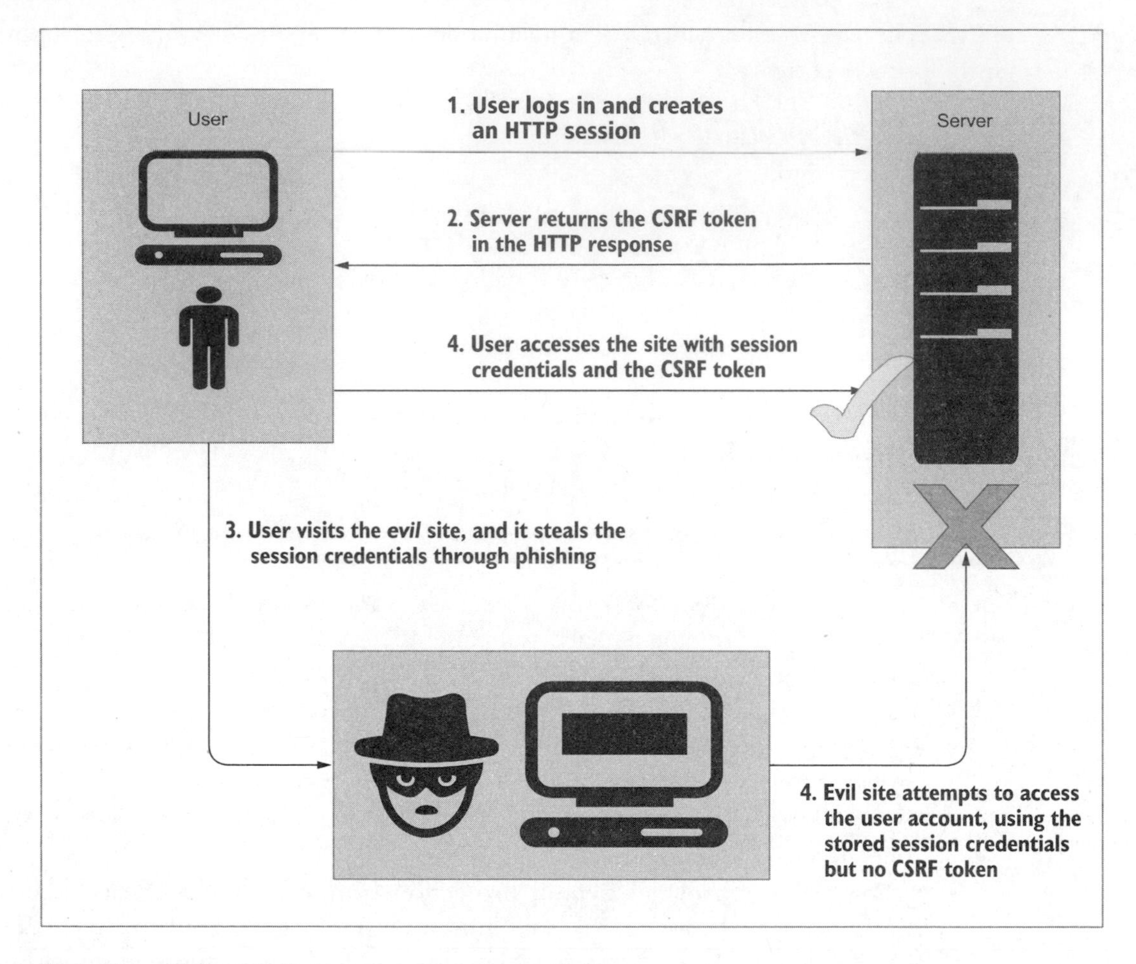

Figure 5.1 CSRF protection in a Spring Security application

Let's explore these headers and their role in protecting a Spring Boot application:

- The `Cache-Control` header instructs the browser to disable the browser caching completely.
- The `X-Content-Type-Options` header prevents the browser from attempting to guess the content type of a request when the `Content-Type` header is missing in the request.
- The `Strict-Transport-Security` header enforces the `HTTP Strict Transport Security (HSTS)`. Refer to the Spring Security reference documentation at http://mng.bz/jyEa to learn more about `HSTS`.
- The `X-Frame-Options` HTTP header with `DENY` configuration instructs the browser not to load application pages in a `frame`, `iframe`, or `embed`. This prevents clickjacking attacks in a Web application.

- The `X-XSS-Protection` HTTP header with `1; mode=block` prevents reflective `Cross-Site-Scripting` attacks. The value `1` enables the browser's built-in XSS filtering, and the option `mode=block` allows the browser to prevent loading a page if an XSS attack is detected.

You can find a detailed discussion on these and other HTTP response headers in the Spring Security reference document available at http://mng.bz/W74g.

5.2 Hello Spring Security with Spring Boot

In this section, we'll introduce Spring Security in the course tracker application that we've been building in previous chapters. Let's explore this in the next technique.

5.2.1 Technique: Enabling application security with Spring Security in a Spring Boot application

In this technique, we'll demonstrate how to enable application security with Spring Security.

Problem

You've developed a Web application with Spring Boot. However, there is no application security implemented in the application. You need to implement basic application security in the application.

Solution

> **Source code**
>
> To begin using this technique, you can use the base version of the Spring Boot project used throughout it, which is available at http://mng.bz/8leK. The final version of this Spring Boot project is available at http://mng.bz/ExNq.

The simplest way to provide security in a Spring Boot application is to introduce the `spring-boot-starter-security` dependency in the application's pom.xml file. This dependency is shown in the following listing.

Listing 5.2 Spring Security starter dependency

```
<dependency>
    <groupId>org.springframework.boot</groupId>
    <artifactId>spring-boot-starter-security</artifactId>
</dependency>
```

The `spring-boot-starter-security` dependency brings all the necessary libraries and enables Spring Security in the Spring Boot application. Spring Boot starter dependency includes core Spring Security libraries, such as `spring-security-config` and `spring-security-web`, into the application.

You can start the application using the IDE's run configuration option. Once the application successfully starts, let's access the `index` page of the application by accessing the URL http://localhost:8080/index. To your surprise, you'll find a `login` page asking you to sign in instead of presenting the application `index` page. This happens because you've incorporated Spring Security in the application, and it has automatically enabled a form-based login in the application. By default, Spring Security displays the login page, as shown in figure 5.2 to sign in to the application.

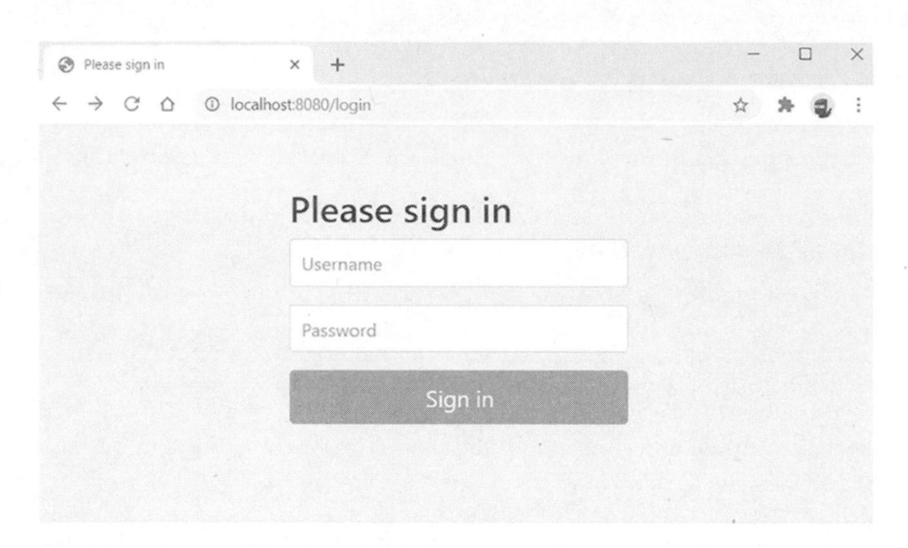

Figure 5.2 Default login page for user sign in. This login page is generated by Spring Security in the absence of a custom login page in the application. You can customize this login page to configure a custom page.

The default username for the application is `user`. Spring Boot generates and prints a password in the console log. This password changes each time the application is restarted. This default password might not be convenient for a production application in which you would need the user to configure their passwords. Later in this chapter, you'll notice Spring Boot is flexible enough and lets you achieve the same. However, for now, we'll proceed with the default password printed in the console, as shown in figure 5.3.

```
2022-02-26 08:40:22.935  INFO 36700 --- [           main] org.hibernate.dialect.Dialect            : HHH000400: Using dialec
2022-02-26 08:40:23.587  INFO 36700 --- [           main] o.h.e.t.j.p.i.JtaPlatformInitiator       : HHH000490: Using JtaPla
2022-02-26 08:40:23.596  INFO 36700 --- [           main] j.LocalContainerEntityManagerFactoryBean : Initialized JPA EntityM
2022-02-26 08:40:24.041  WARN 36700 --- [           main] JpaBaseConfiguration$JpaWebConfiguration : spring.jpa.open-in-view
2022-02-26 08:40:24.305  INFO 36700 --- [           main] o.s.b.a.w.s.WelcomePageHandlerMapping    : Adding welcome page tem
2022-02-26 08:40:25.178  INFO 36700 --- [           main] .s.s.UserDetailsServiceAutoConfiguration :

Using generated security password: 2bb6de24-58ed-4453-b20d-915832113818

2022-02-26 08:40:25.547  INFO 36700 --- [           main] o.s.s.web.DefaultSecurityFilterChain     : Will secure any request
2022-02-26 08:40:25.786  INFO 36700 --- [           main] o.s.b.w.embedded.tomcat.TomcatWebServer  : Tomcat started on port(
2022-02-26 08:40:25.806  INFO 36700 --- [           main] m.s.c.CourseTrackerSpringBootApplication : Started CourseTrackerSp
```

Figure 5.3 Spring Security-generated password printed in the console log

Log in to the application with the username as the user and the password as printed in the console. For instance, in this example the password is d9bbec60-e3ce-4cb9-b4a7-3ee35d3dc0f1. After successful login, you'll be redirected to the application index page, as shown in figure 5.4.

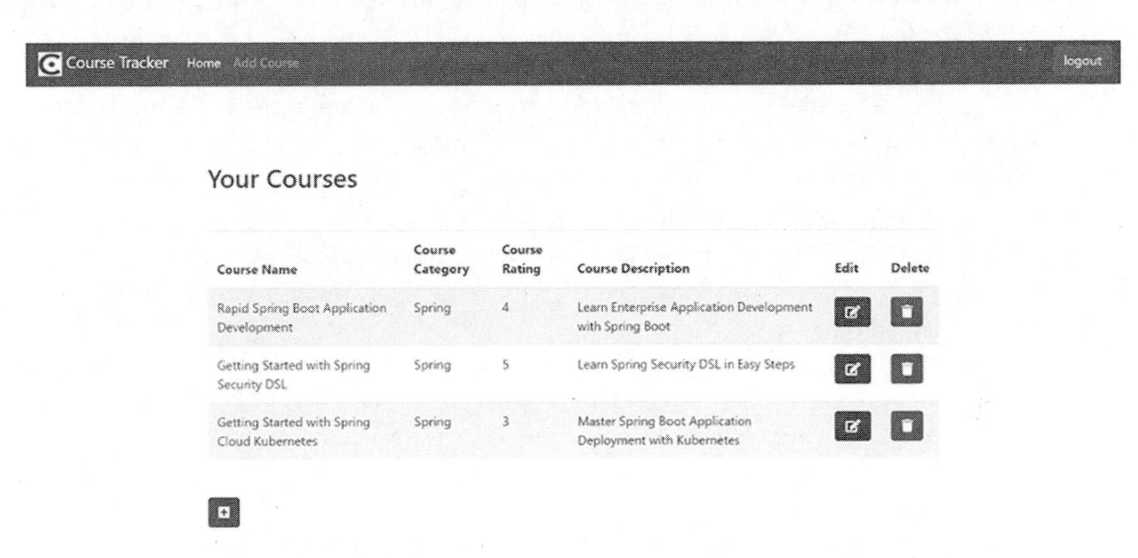

Figure 5.4 Course Tracker application index page. On application startup, we've initialized the database schema and created three courses. Thus, three courses are shown in the course list.

You are now logged in to the application and can access all application features, such as adding a new course, editing an existing course, and deleting an existing course. You can also log out from the application by clicking the logout button at the top right corner of the application. Once logged out, you will be redirected to the login page and can't access any of the application features unless you log in again. By default, Spring Security exposes the /logout endpoint. In the course tracker example, we've included the logout button on the index page of the application. Once you click on the logout button, the /logout endpoint is invoked, and you are logged out of the application.

DISCUSSION

With this technique, you've learned how to enable default application security in a Spring Boot application with Spring Security. You've observed that introducing spring-boot-starter-security dependency in the pom.xml file magically enables some level of application security through a form-based login in the application. Spring Boot also generates a password to log in to the application.

The introduction of spring-boot-starter-security dependency integrates the Spring Security ecosystem to the application. You can inspect the spring-boot-starter-security dependency in the pom.xml file and find that it has transitive dependencies to `spring-security-config` and `spring-security-web` libraries. Together, these two libraries provide the necessary support for Spring Security.

As you've seen before with Spring Boot autoconfiguration, the presence of Spring Security libraries in the application classpath enables Spring Boot to configure necessary security components in the application. You'll shortly examine what these components are and how they are configured in the Spring Security autoconfiguration section.

Before we make ourselves familiar with the internal workings of Spring Security, let's provide a very high-level overview of the authentication process in a typical Web application. The sequence diagram in figure 5.5 provides the sequence of steps:

1. You attempt to access the home page of an application by accessing a Web URL (e.g., http://localhost:8080/ in the course tracker application).
2. The request reaches the server, and it finds that you are trying to access a protected resource.
3. As you are not presently authenticated, the server responds indicating that you need to be authenticated. The response could be an HTTP response code or redirect to a Web page based on the security implementation at the server.
4. Based on the authentication mechanisms implemented in the server, the browser will either redirect you to a login page or retrieve the credentials through other modes, such as the HTTP basic authentication dialogue box or a cookie. You'll learn how to configure the authentication mechanisms in the server in later techniques.
5. The credentials are then sent back to the server. Browsers can either use an HTTP POST request (e.g., for a login page) or an HTTP header (e.g., for BASIC authentication) to pass the credentials to the server.
6. The server validates the credentials. If the credentials are valid, the login is considered successful, and the server moves to the next step. However, if the credentials are invalid, the browser typically asks to try again, so you return to step 3.
7. If the login is successful and logged in with sufficient authorities, then the request will be successful. Otherwise, the server returns with an HTTP error code 403, which indicates `forbidden`.
8. If the user logs out from the application, the server clears the session and other login credentials from the server and logs out the user. It then redirects the user to the login page or the index page of the application based on the security configuration of the server.

In the next section, you'll begin with Spring Security architecture and learn how the above steps are implemented in Spring Security.

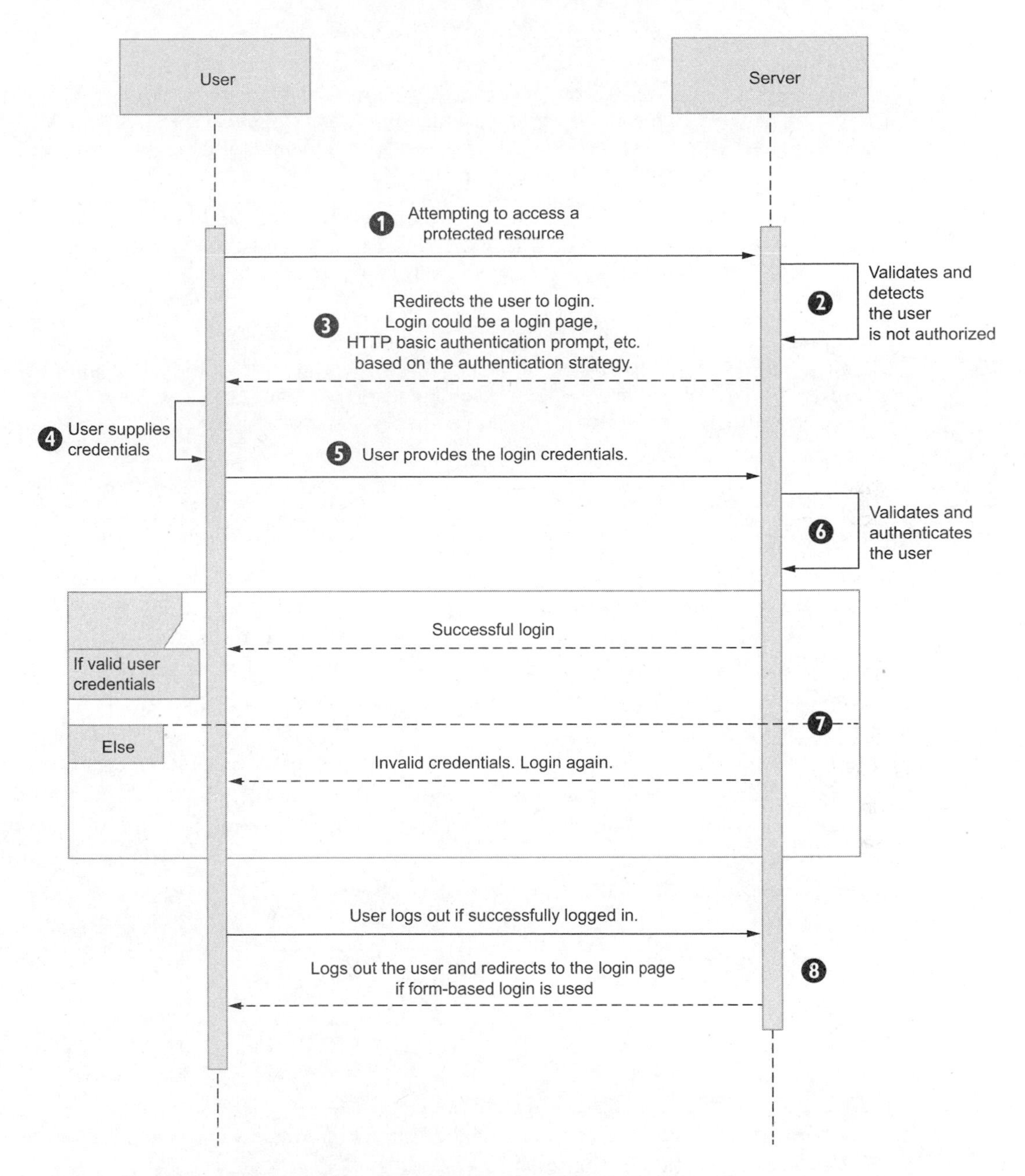

Figure 5.5 Sequence diagram of user authentication in a Web application

Note

Spring Security is a large topic and contains numerous features. It is beyond the scope of this text to provide in-depth coverage on Spring Security concepts and various features it offers. In this book, we'll cover the bare minimum Spring Security concepts you need to understand to continue with the subsequent techniques.

In this chapter and the next, you'll learn several techniques that show how to implement various security features leveraging Spring Security. Since this is a Spring Boot book, we'll keep our focus limited to the use of Spring Security in the context of Spring Boot.

For an in-depth understanding of Spring Security, we recommend referring to dedicated Spring Security books or the Spring Security reference material available at http://mng.bz/DxYn. Manning has a book dedicated to Spring Security, *Spring Security in Action* by Laurențiu Spilcă, available at http://mng.bz/NxZE.

5.2.2 Filter, FilterChain, and Spring Security

In a typical Java Web application, a client requests the server to access a resource through HTTP or HTTPS protocol. The client request in the server is handled by a servlet. The servlet processes the HTTP request and provides an HTTP response. This response is sent back to the client. In a Spring Web application, this servlet is the `DispatcherServlet`, which handles all incoming requests to the application.

A major component of Servlet specification that plays a pivotal role in request–response processing is a `Filter`. A `Filter` sits before a `Servlet` and intercepts the request–response. It can make changes to the request–response objects, as shown in figure 5.6. One or more filters can be configured through a `FilterChain`, and all filters that are part of the chain can intercept and modify the request–response objects. Many of the Spring Security features are based on these filters. Both `Filter` and `FilterChain` are interfaces from `javax.servlet` package.

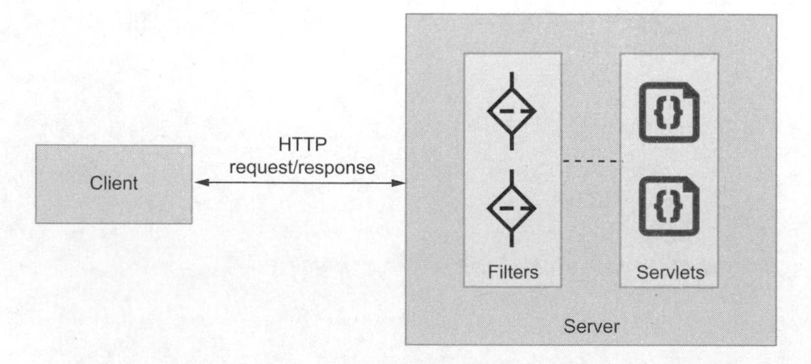

Figure 5.6 High-level overview of request–response processing in a Spring Security application

Like how a special servlet named `DispatcherServlet` handles all incoming requests in a Spring Web application, a special filter named `DelegatingFilterProxy` is used to enable Spring Security. This filter is registered to the servlet container, and it starts intercepting the incoming requests. In a Spring Boot application, this registration is done by Spring Boot's Spring Security autoconfiguration. Let's now take a look into the `Filter` interface, as shown in the following listing.

Listing 5.3 The Filter interface

```
public interface Filter {

    public default void init(FilterConfig filterConfig) throws
➥ ServletException {}

    public void doFilter(ServletRequest request, ServletResponse response,
            ➥ FilterChain chain) throws IOException, ServletException;

    public default void destroy() {}
}
```

Contains the logic that the filter needs to perform

A `Filter` implementation needs to implement three methods (`init()`, `doFilter()`, and `destroy(..)`), as shown in figure 5.7.

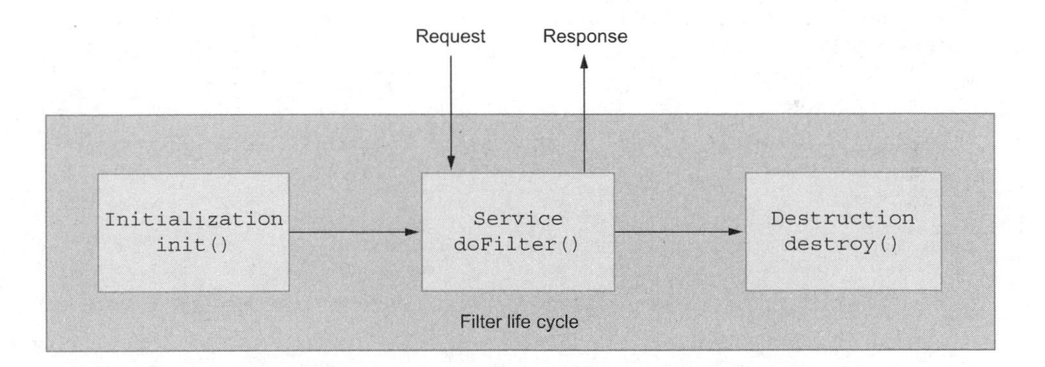

Figure 5.7 Filter life cycle methods. The init(..) method contains a code snippet that is invoked at the time of the filter initialization and destroy (..) method contains code that is invoked when the filter is about to go out of service from the container. The doFilter(..) method performs the request handling and returns a response to the caller.

The three filter methods are discussed below:

- The `init(..)` is invoked by the Web container to indicate to a filter that it is being placed into service.
- The `doFilter(..)` is the main method where the actual action of the filter is done. It has access to the request, response, and `FilterChain` objects. The

FilterChain allows the current filter to invoke the next filter in the chain once its processing is over.

- The destroy() is called when the container takes the filter out of service.

A FilterChain is another component provided by the servlet container that provides a view into the invocation chain of a filtered request. Figure 5.8 shows a sample filter chain. Filters use the FilterChain to invoke the next filter in the chain or the actual resource (e.g., the servlet) if the filter is the last in the chain. A FilterChain has only one method named doFilter(). If you revisit listing 5.3, you'll notice the doFilter() method in the Filter interface has access to the FilterChain along with the ServletRequest and ServletResponse instances. Thus, a Filter can perform its assigned task and access the FilterChain to invoke the next filter in the chain. Listing 5.4 shows the FilterChain interface.

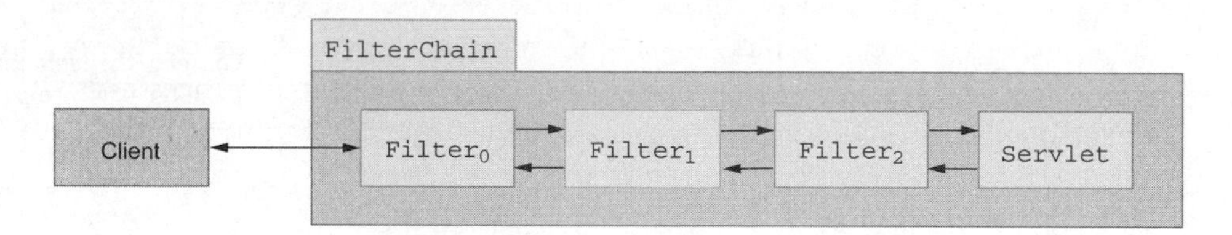

Figure 5.8 Representation of a FilterChain. A Client invokes the first filter in the chain. This filter then invokes the subsequent filter in the chain. Lastly, the request reaches a servlet that is at the end of the FilterChain.

Listing 5.4 The FilterChain interface

```
public interface FilterChain {
    public void doFilter(ServletRequest request, ServletResponse response)
➥ throws IOException, ServletException;
}
```

Spring Security makes heavy use of the filters to implement various security features. The core foundation of Spring Security is based on these filters. For instance, if Spring Security needs to perform a username and password-based authentication, it delegates the request to a filter named UsernamePasswordAuthenticationFilter that is responsible for authenticating the user based on the supplied credentials. Similarly, for HTTP basic authentication Spring Security uses BasicAuthenticationFilter.

Now, let's discuss two major filter implementations in Spring Security, DelegatingFilterProxy and the FilterChainProxy, that act as the entry point for an HTTP request into the Spring Security infrastructure. Further, you'll also explore the SecurityFilterChain interface.

5.2.3 Spring Security architecture

In the previous section, we've provided a high-level overview of `Filter` and `FilterChain` and discussed how Spring Security leverages the features provided by these components. In this section, let us discuss the `DelegatingFilterProxy`, the `FilterChainProxy` filter, and the `SecurityFilterChain` class.

A `Filter` is a very useful component in the Servlet specification. Spring Security uses it to implement several of its core functionalities and authentication strategies. Although useful, a `Filter` instance is a servlet container component, and it is managed by the servlet container. The container instantiates, initializes, and destroys it. The servlet specification doesn't require any kind of Spring integration to deal with a `Filter`.

Spring Security provides a filter called `DelegatingFilterProxy` to bridge this gap. You configure this filter with the servlet container, so its life cycle is managed by the servlet container. We then define a separate `Filter` implementation and make it a Spring bean managed by Spring. This Spring-managed bean is configured as a delegate in the `DelegatingFilterProxy`. At runtime, `DelegatingFilterProxy` finds out this actual Spring-managed filter and delegates the request for processing.

The `FilterChainProxy` class is the other filter implementation that the `DelegatingFilterProxy` delegates the HTTP requests. It contains one or more `SecurityFilterChains` that process the HTTP request. Figure 5.9 shows a high-level overview of these components.

The `SecurityFilterChain` interface has two methods: `matches(..)` and `getFilters(..)`. The first method allows Spring Security to evaluate whether the current `SecurityFilterChain` matches the incoming request. Spring Security provides the `RequestMatcher` interface and provides several implementations to perform the match. For instance, to match any request it provides the `AnyRequestMatcher` that matches all HTTP requests. Spring Security also provides an ant-style matcher `AntPathRequestMatcher` that matches the URL paths.

If there is a match, the `getFilters(..)` method returns the list of filters that needs to be applied to the incoming request. If you continue with Spring Security default configurations, then it configures a default `SecurityFilterChain` called `DefaultSecurityFilterChain` and configures a list of required filters. It also ensures that all HTTP requests pass through this filter chain.

Based on the application design and other security requirements, you may choose to override the default security configurations and configure one or more `SecurityFilterChains` in an application. For instance, you might configure one `SecurityFilterChain` for a set of application URLs (e.g., `/courses`) that has access to one module of the application. Similarly, you can configure another `SecurityFilterChain` for another set of URLs (e.g., `/users`). Since `SecurityFilterChain` consists of a list of filters that provides security, this approach provides better flexibility in your security implementation. For example, you may choose to implement form-based authentication for the user controller of the application, whereas for the courses controller, you can use HTTP basic authentication.

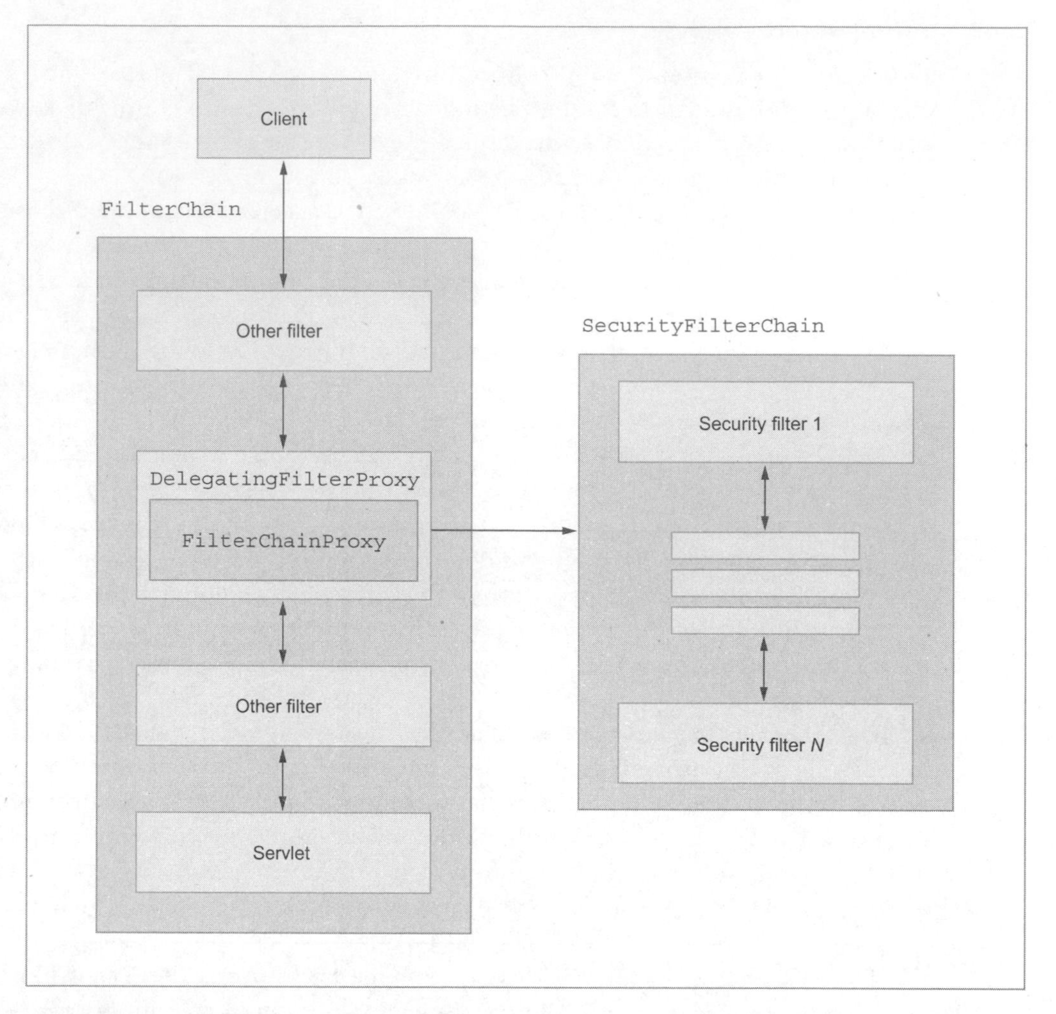

Figure 5.9 Position of DelegatingFilterProxy, FilterChainProxy, and the SecurityFilterChain while accessing a resource in the server. One or more filter sits behind the actual servlet that serves the client request. DelegatingFilterProxy is a special filter that delegates the request processing to FilterChainProxy, which, in turn, leverages the filters in the SecurityFilterChain.

Implementing multiple SecurityFilterChains

If you are configuring multiple `SecurityFilterChains` in your application, you need to ensure the order of the chains. You can use Spring's `@Order` annotation to order the `SecurityFilterChains`. The `SecurityFilterChain` for a more specific application URL should be ordered before the generic ones. Otherwise, the generic `SecurityFilterChain` will always match the incoming requests, and the specific `SecurityFilterChain` will never invoke. For instance, if you have two filter chains (for the URLs, `/admin` and `/*`), you need to ensure that `/admin` specific filter chain orders before the `/*`, as the latter one is generic and matches all requests.

5.2.4 Authenticating a user

Before discussing authentication steps in detail, let us first discuss a few of the notable classes and concepts that play an important role in authentication:

- SecurityContextHolder—This class associates the SecurityContext instance to the current execution thread. A SecurityContext contains information about an authenticated principal, such as username, user authorities, and other user identification details. The SecurityContextPersistenceFilter manages the SecurityContext instance. This filter tries to retrieve the SecurityContext from a SecurityContextRepository. In a Web application, the HttpSessionSecurityContextRepository implementation tries to load the SecurityContext from the HTTP Session. In the beginning, as we are not authenticated, an empty security context is added to the SecurityContextHolder. Figure 5.10 shows a block diagram of SecurityContextHolder.

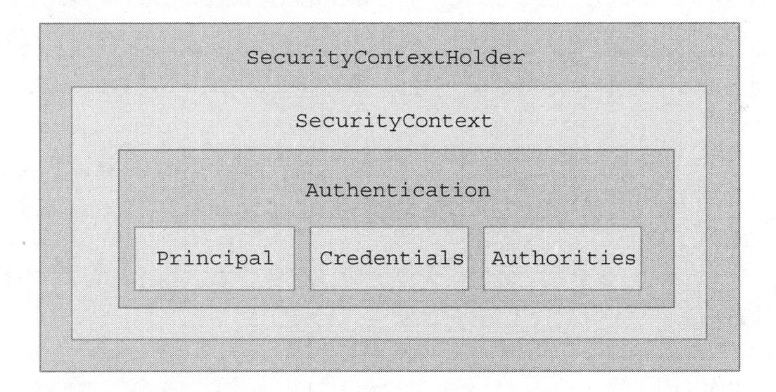

Figure 5.10 A SecurityContextHolder holds a SecurityContext, which, in turn, holds the Authentication details.

- AuthenticationFilters—These filters are used to authenticate a principal and Spring Security provides several authentication filters. For instance, the BasicAuthenticationFilter performs HTTP basic authentication, the DigestAuthenticationFilter performs Digest authentication. Once an authentication filter authenticates a principal, it places an authentication token in the SecurityContext. This authentication token then can be used by other filters in the filter chain.
- ExceptionTranslationFilter—The ExceptionTranslationFilter plays a key role in the authentication process. Based on whether the user is already authenticated or the user has the necessary access to a resource, there are two exception types: AuthenticationException and AccessDeniedException. The ExceptionTranslationFilter addresses both these exception types. For an AuthenticationException, this filter redirects to an AuthenticationEntryPoint

to initiate the authentication process. Based on the configured authentication mechanisms, Spring Security provides several AuthenticationEntryPoint implementations. For an AccessDeniedException, the request is redirected to an appropriate AccessDeniedHandler implementation. One key benefit of the Spring Security architecture is that it is extremely flexible and allows you to define custom implementations if the framework-defined implementations do not meet your requirement or you need further customizations.

- UserDetailsService—The UserDetailsService provides the necessary abstractions to map user-specific data to Spring Security's UserDetails, which contains the core user information. You can either choose to use Spring Security's implementations or provide a custom implementation.
- AuthenticationProvider—The AuthenticationProvider processes a specific authentication implementation. It accepts an authentication request object, performs the authentication, and returns a fully authenticated instance. It throws AuthenticationException if the authentication fails.

Let's now discuss how the authentication process is implemented in Spring Security. Figure 5.11 shows this process through a block diagram. The following are the high level steps:

1. The initial request is handled by the authentication filters. Based on the security strategy configured in the server (you'll see how you can configure this shortly), an appropriate authentication filter handles the request. For instance, the BasicAuthenticationFilter processes the request if the HTTP basic authentication is configured.
2. The authentication filter creates an authentication token from the incoming request.
3. It then invokes an AuthenticationManager to authenticate the request.
4. The AuthenticationManager contains a list of AuthenticationProvider instances. An AuthenticationProvider has two methods: supports(..) and authenticate(..). The supports(..) method decides whether the AuthenticationProvider supports the authentication type. The authenticate(..) performs the actual authentication.
5. The AuthenticationProvider uses the UserDetailsService implementation to perform the authentication. The UserDetailsService loads the UserDetails from an identity store that contains user account details, such as user authorities, username, password, and other account-related statistics. The AuthenticationProvider uses the loaded UserDetails instance and performs the actual authentication. The authenticated principal is then returned to the AuthenticationManager, and the returned Authentication object is stored in the SecurityContext for later usage by other filters.

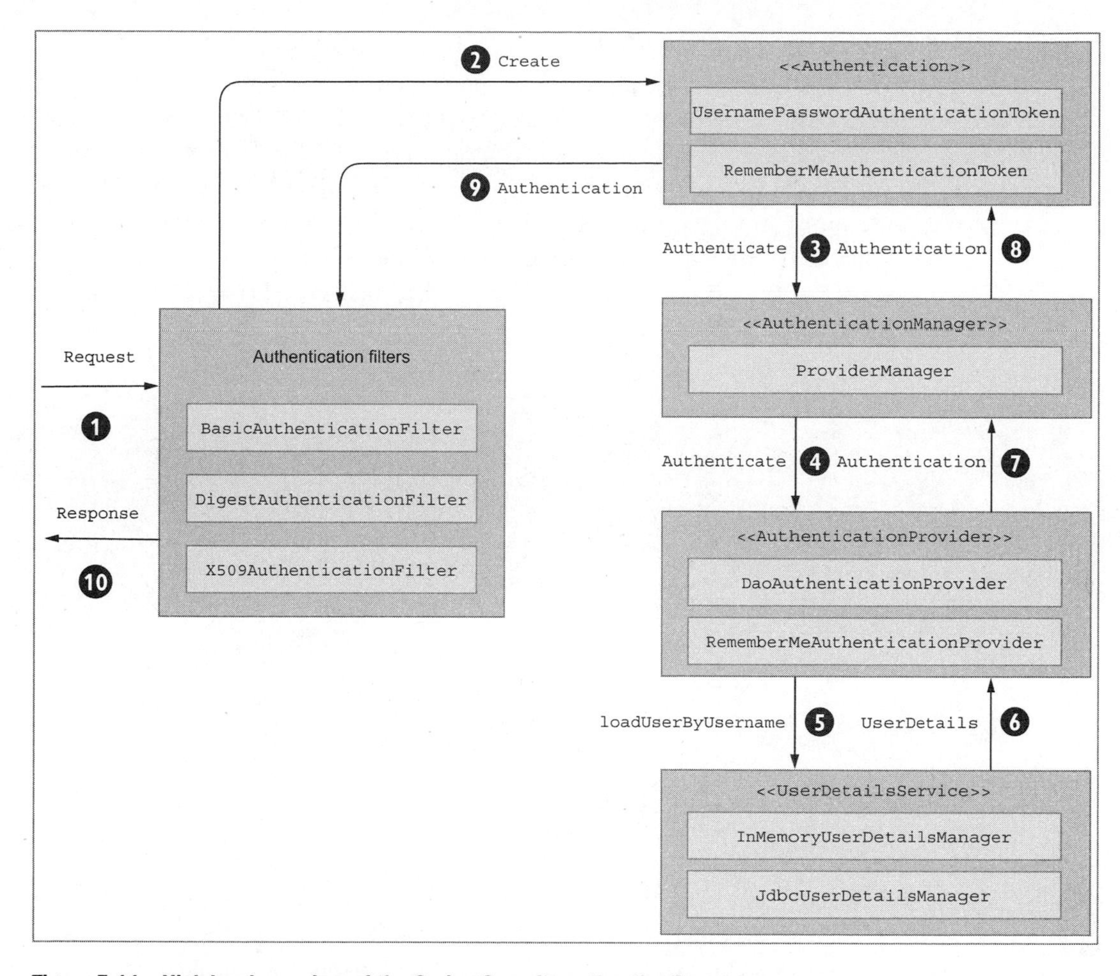

Figure 5.11 High-level overview of the Spring Security authentication steps

UserDetailsService

The `UserDetailsService` interface performs a crucial role by bridging the application-specific user details to Spring's `UserDetails` implantations. The `UserDetails` interface represents an application user in a Spring application and contains various user account-related information. The `UserDetailsService` exposes a `loadUserByUsername(String username)` method that lets you connect to the application-specific identity store and load the user account details by the supplied username. Spring Security provides several implementations of this interface, such as `InMemoryUserDetailsManager` and `JdbcUserDetailsManager`. Besides, you can also provide your custom implementations of this interface by defining the `loadUserByUsername(..)` method. We'll discuss the custom implementation in a later technique.

5.2.5 Spring Security autoconfiguration

By now, you've acquired the foundational knowledge in Spring Security and understand various building blocks, such as `DelegatingFilterProxy`, `FilterChainProxy`, `SecurityFilterChain`, list of filters, and several other components. However, the last piece of the puzzle is how these components are configured and work together in a Spring Boot application. As you might have already anticipated, Spring Boot does this with its smart and efficient autoconfiguration strategies. Let's explore how Spring Security autoconfiguration is implemented in Spring Boot. Figure 5.12 shows the main autoconfiguration classes.

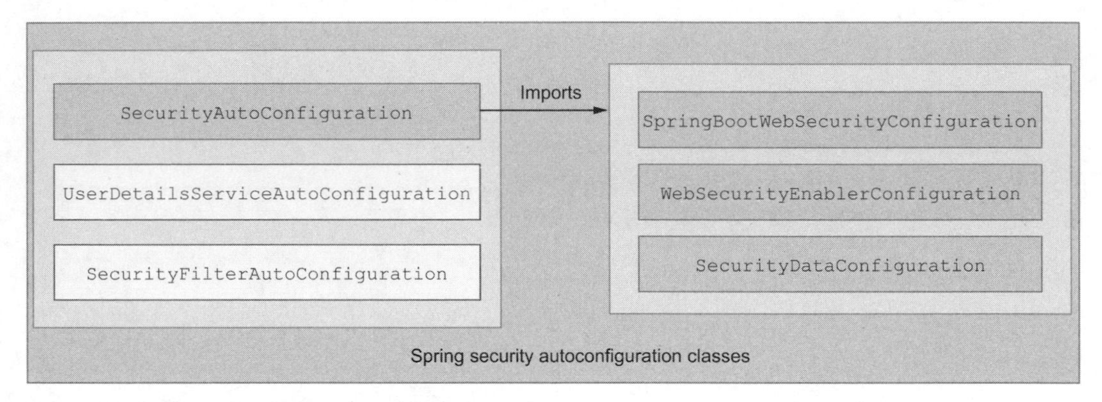

Figure 5.12 Spring Security autoconfiguration classes

Spring Boot uses three configuration classes: `SecurityAutoConfiguration`, `UserDetailsServiceAutoConfiguration`, and `SecurityFilterAutoConfiguration` to autoconfigure the core Spring Security components in a Spring Boot application.

SecurityAutoConfiguration

The `SecurityAutoConfiguration` is at the heart of Spring Security autoconfiguration. It leverages three other classes, `SpringBootWebSecurityConfiguration`, `WebSecurityEnablerConfiguration`, and `SecurityDataConfiguration`, to perform the autoconfiguration. The following listing shows this class.

Listing 5.5 SecurityAutoConfiguration

```
package org.springframework.boot.autoconfigure.security.servlet;

// Imports ommitted

@Configuration(proxyBeanMethods = false)
@ConditionalOnClass(DefaultAuthenticationEventPublisher.class)
@EnableConfigurationProperties(SecurityProperties.class)
@Import({ SpringBootWebSecurityConfiguration.class,
➥ WebSecurityEnablerConfiguration.class,
```

```
        SecurityDataConfiguration.class })
public class SecurityAutoConfiguration {

    @Bean
    @ConditionalOnMissingBean(AuthenticationEventPublisher.class)
    public DefaultAuthenticationEventPublisher
➥ authenticationEventPublisher(ApplicationEventPublisher publisher) {
        return new DefaultAuthenticationEventPublisher(publisher);
    }

}
```

Let's discuss these classes briefly. The `SpringBootWebSecurityConfiguration` class is loaded if security is available and we haven't defined our configuration. The following listing shows the `WebSecurityEnablerConfiguration` class.

Listing 5.6 WebSecurityEnablerConfiguration

```
package org.springframework.boot.autoconfigure.security.servlet;
// imports omitted

@Configuration(proxyBeanMethods = false)
@ConditionalOnMissingBean(name = BeanIds.SPRING_SECURITY_FILTER_CHAIN)
@ConditionalOnClass(EnableWebSecurity.class)
@ConditionalOnWebApplication(type = ConditionalOnWebApplication.Type.SERVLET)
@EnableWebSecurity
class WebSecurityEnablerConfiguration {

}
```

The `WebSecurityEnablerConfiguration` is a configuration class that adds the `@EnableWebSecurity` annotation in the Spring configuration if Spring Security is present in the classpath. This is to ensure that the `@EnableWebSecurity` annotation is present in the default Spring Security autoconfiguration. However, if we explicitly add this annotation to our Spring Security configuration file or define a bean with the name `springSecurityFilterChain`, this configuration backs off and does nothing.

The `@EnableWebSecurity` annotation performs a pivotal role in Spring Security configuration. It provides three key configurations along with other functionalities. It provides default `WebSecurityConfiguration` and `HttpSecurityConfiguration` and enables `@EnableGlobalAuthentication`. The `WebSecurityConfiguration` creates the `WebSecurity` instance that performs the Web-based security in Spring Security. Web Security allows you to manage the security of Web components in your application (e.g., images, CSS, and JS files). The `HttpSecurityConfiguration` creates the `HttpSecurity` bean that allows us to configure Web security for the HTTP requests. The `@EnableGlobalAuthentication` annotation provides the necessary configuration to configure the `AuthenticationManagerBuilder` instance. We use this instance to configure the `AuthenticationManager`.

If you need to customize the default configuration provided in the above configuration classes, you can easily do that by defining a class that extends the `WebSecurityConfigurerAdapter` or implementing the `WebSecurityConfigurer` interface. When we discuss the upcoming techniques, you'll notice we heavily use the `WebSecurityConfigurerAdapter` class to customize `WebSecurity` and `HttpSecurity` implementations and use the `AuthenticationManagerBuilder` to configure various types of authentications in our Spring Boot application.

The `SecurityDataConfiguration` class provides support for Spring Data integration with Spring Security. It defines a bean called `SecurityEvaluationContextExtension`, which allows Spring Security to be exposed as `SpEL` expressions to create Spring Data queries. Refer to the Java Documentation of this class, available at http://mng.bz/DxEy, for a better understanding of how this works.

USERDETAILSSERVICEAUTOCONFIGURATION

The `UserDetailsServiceAutoConfiguration` class automatically configures `InMemoryUserDetailsManager` if an instance of `UserDetailsService` is not configured in the application. The default implementation contains a user with the default username as a `user` and a generated password, which is a random UUID. In the previous technique, you saw this generated password printed in the application console. You can customize and provide your implementation of the `UserDetailsService` interface, so Spring Security's default configuration can back off, and the custom implementation can take effect. You'll see this in practice in the upcoming techniques.

The last autoconfiguration we'll discuss is the `SecurityFilterAutoConfiguration` class that configures the `DelegatingFilterProxyRegistrationBean`. This is a `ServletContextInitializer` that registers the Spring Security filter `DelegatingFilterProxy`. This autoconfiguration class is invoked after the `SecurityAutoConfiguration`.

5.3 Using Spring Security

In the previous sections, you've learned several concepts related to Spring Security architecture, its authentication mechanism, and the Spring Security autoconfiguration by Spring Boot. In this section, you'll implement several techniques that explain the use of various Spring Security features in a Spring Boot-based Web application. In the next technique, we'll customize the login page of the course tracker application.

5.3.1 Technique: Customizing the default Spring Security login page of a Spring Boot application

In this technique, we'll discuss how to customize the Spring Security provided default login page to an application-specific custom login page.

PROBLEM

In the previous technique, you introduced Spring Security in the course tracker application and noticed that Spring Security has enabled user login in the application with a default `login` page. You want to customize the login page with a custom login page.

SOLUTION

The default login page generated and provided by Spring Security is a basic one and just does the job. However, there are several reasons you'll be interested in customizing this page. For instance, you might want to keep the application login page in line with your application's Web page design. You might also implement additional authentication strategies, such as an additional security pin along with the regular login, a one-time password (OTP), or a captcha.

> **Source code**
>
> To begin using this technique, you can use the base version of the Spring Boot project used throughout it, which is available at http://mng.bz/laDj. The final version of this Spring Boot project is available at http://mng.bz/BxWv.

Let's first add a new login page to the application that is in line with the course tracker application design. Place this page inside the templates folder under src\main\resources folder. The following listing shows the `login.html` page.

Listing 5.7 Course Tracker application login page

```
<!DOCTYPE html>
<html xmlns:th="http://www.thymeleaf.org">
<head>
<meta charset="utf-8">
<meta http-equiv="x-ua-compatible" content="ie=edge">
<title>Login</title>
<meta name="viewport" content="width=device-width, initial-scale=1">

<link rel="stylesheet" type="text/css"
➥ href="http://cdn.jsdelivr.net/webjars/bootstrap/4.1.0/css/bootstrap.min.c
➥ ss" th:href="@{/webjars/bootstrap/css/bootstrap.min.css}" />
<script src="http://cdn.jsdelivr.net/webjars/bootstrap/4.1.0/js/
     bootstrap.min.js"
➥ th:src="@{/webjars/bootstrap/js/bootstrap.min.js}"></script>
<script src="http://cdn.jsdelivr.net/webjars/jquery/3.3.1/jquery.min.js"
➥ th:src="@{/webjars/jquery/jquery.min.js}"></script>
</head>

<body>
    <nav class="navbar navbar-dark bg-dark navbar-expand-sm">
        <a class="navbar-brand brand-text" href="#">
            <img src="/images/logo.png" width="30" height="30" alt="logo">
            Course Tracker
        </a>
        <button class="navbar-toggler" type="button" data-toggle="collapse"
➥ data-target="#navbar-list" aria-controls="navbarNav" aria-
➥ expanded="false" aria-label="Toggle navigation">
            <span class="navbar-toggler-icon"></span>
        </button>
```

```
        <div class="collapse navbar-collapse justify-content-between"
➥ id="navbar-list">
            <ul class="navbar-nav">
                <li class="nav-item">
                    <a class="nav-link" href="#" th:href="@{/index}">Home</a>
                </li>
                <li class="nav-item">
                    <a class="nav-link" href="#" th:href="@{/addcourse}">Add
  Course</a>
                </li>
            </ul>
        </div>
    </nav>
    <div class="container my-5">
        <div class="row">
            <div class="col-md-3"></div>
            <div class="col-md-6">
                <h2 class="mb-1 text-center">Login</h2>
            </div>
            <div class="col-md-3"></div>
        </div>
        <div class="row">
            <div class="col-md-3"></div>
            <div class="col-md-6">
                <form th:action="@{/login}" method="post">
                    <div class="form-group">
                        <label for="username">Username</label>
                        <input type="text" class="form-control"
➥ name="username" placeholder="Enter Username" required autofocus>
                    </div>
                    <div class="form-group">
                        <label for="password">Password</label>
                        <input type="password" class="form-control"
➥ name="password" placeholder="Enter Password" required autofocus>
                    </div>
                    <button type="submit" class="btn btn-
➥ dark">Submit</button>
                </form>
            </div>
            <div class="col-md-3"></div>
        </div>
    </div>
</body>
</html>
```

This is a basic HTML page designed with Bootstrap. There is a login form that accepts the username and password of the user and invokes the `login` HTTP endpoint. Now, let's define a `LoginController` that exposes this `login` endpoint. The following listing shows the `LoginController`.

Listing 5.8 The LoginController class

```
package com.manning.sbip.ch05.controller;

// imports

@Controller
public class LoginController {

    @GetMapping("/login")
    public String login() {
        return "login";
    }
}
```

This endpoint ensures whenever there is an invocation to the `login` URL (e.g., http://localhost:8080/login), the `login.html` page is presented to the user. Let's now customize the Spring Security `HTTPSecurity` configuration to instruct Spring to redirect to the `login` endpoint for user login. If you recall, Spring Security provides the default security configuration in the `WebSecurityConfigurerAdapter` class. Thus, to provide a custom configuration, you need to override this method. The following listing shows the `SecurityConfiguration` class that provides a custom security configuration.

Listing 5.9 The SecurityConfiguration class

```
package com.manning.sbip.ch05.security;

import org.springframework.context.annotation.Configuration;
import
➥ org.springframework.security.config.annotation.web.builders.HttpSecurity;
import
➥ org.springframework.security.config.annotation.web.builders.WebSecurity;
import
➥ org.springframework.security.config.annotation.web.configuration.WebSec
➥ urityConfigurerAdapter;

@Configuration
public class SecurityConfiguration extends WebSecurityConfigurerAdapter {


    @Override
    protected void configure(HttpSecurity http) throws Exception {
        http.authorizeRequests()
                .antMatchers("/login").permitAll()
                .anyRequest().authenticated()
                .and()
                .formLogin().loginPage("/login");
    }

    @Override
    public void configure(WebSecurity web) throws Exception {
```

Customizing the HTTPSecurity to configure the custom login page. We have excluded the login page from authentication and enforced login for all other URLs.

```
        web.ignoring().antMatchers("/webjars/**", "/images/**", "/css/**",
➥ "/h2-console/**");
    }
}
```

We've made the following configuration changes:

- We've defined this class as the Spring configuration, so the Spring Boot component scanning can find this class.
- The `SecurityConfiguration` class extends the `WebSecurityConfigurerAdapter` class. It allows you to customize the Spring Security configuration.
- We've overridden the `configure(HttpSecurity http)` method and provided a custom implementation to include the custom login page.
- We've also overridden the `configure(WebSecurity web)` method to allow static content, such as CSS and images, to be excluded from authentication. Otherwise, Web components, such as images, CSS, and JavaScript files, will not be rendered for the pages that do not require authentication.

Let's now start the application and access the index page by accessing the URL http://localhost:8080/index. As you are not yet logged in to the application, you'll be redirected to the login page at the URL http://localhost:8080/login. Figure 5.13 shows the custom login page of our application.

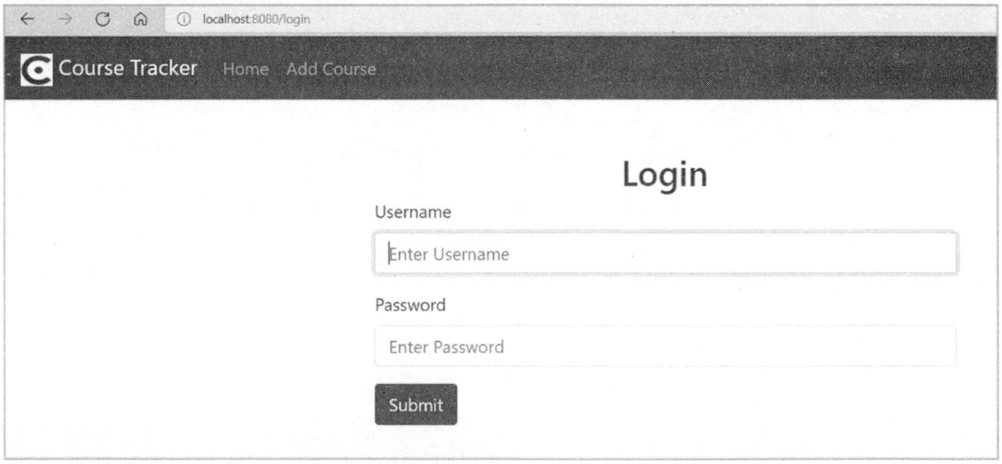

Figure 5.13 Course Tracker custom login page

You may notice that this is not the same login page you used previously. You can use the username as a `user` and the password as printed in the application console. Once successfully logged in, you'll be redirected to the http://localhost:8080/index page, which shows the list of available courses.

DISCUSSION

With this technique, you've explored how to customize the login page of a Spring Boot application with Spring Security. As part of this technique, we've added the `login.html` page and a `LoginController`, which contains an HTTP GET endpoint `login`. Once this endpoint is accessed, it returns the logical view name `login`, and it is rendered in the browser as `login.html`.

The most notable change is the induction of the `SecurityConfiguration` class in the application. The first thing to notice here is that it extends the `WebSecurityConfigurerAdapter` class. If you recall, the `WebSecurityConfigurerAdapter` class is the base class that provides the default Spring Security configurations in your Spring Boot application. You can extend this class to customize various security settings in Spring Security. As we will notice later in this chapter, we'll heavily use this class to customize or configure several features of Spring Security.

The second change to notice is that you've overridden the `configure(HttpSecurity http)` method that allows us to customize the security configuration in the application. The following listing shows the changes inside the method.

Listing 5.10 Security configuration

```
http.authorizeRequests()
                .antMatchers("/login").permitAll()
                .anyRequest().authenticated()
                .and()
                .formLogin().loginPage("/login");
```

The `antMatchers` allows us to specify an application URL or an URL pattern. In the above code snippet, we are ensuring that the `login` endpoint is permitted to be accessed by all users and does not require to be authenticated. This is obvious, as the login page allows us to log in. Next, we are enforcing that all other requests (i.e., `anyRequest()`) to the application need to be authenticated. The authentication type is form-login (i.e., `formLogin()`), and the associated login page is available at the `login` endpoint.

You've also overridden the `configure(WebSecurity web)` method to ensure the static Web resources, such as the images and stylesheet files, are accessible without any form of authentication. Otherwise, the stylesheets or the images for the login page will not be accessible.

5.3.2 *Technique: Configuring in-memory authentication with custom users in Spring Security in a Spring Boot application*

In this technique, we'll demonstrate how to use Spring Security in-memory authentication in a Spring Boot application.

PROBLEM

Although the application in the previous technique works just fine, there is one major issue with the user login. The password is a random `UUID` that is changed each time the application is restarted. You'll need to enhance the application login experience by configuring a few custom users.

SOLUTION

In earlier techniques, we relied on Spring Boot's default `InMemoryUserDetailsManager` configuration to configure the user in our application. This default configuration creates an in-memory user with a username as a `user` and a password as a random `UUID`. Let's now change this to provide our custom `InMemoryUserDetailsManager` implementation.

If you recall from earlier chapters, Spring Boot backs off with the default configurations if it finds a user-defined implementation. Thus, Spring Boot-provided `InMemoryUserDetailsManager` implementation will no longer be used if we provide our implementation.

> **Source code**
> To start using technique, you can use the base version of the Spring Boot project used throughout it, which is available at http://mng.bz/doOD. The final version of this Spring Boot project is available at http://mng.bz/raxg.

Let's enhance the `SecurityConfiguration` class by defining the `InMemoryUserDetails-Manager`, as shown in the following listing.

Listing 5.11 Updated SecurityConfiguration

```
package com.manning.sbip.ch05.security;

import org.springframework.beans.factory.annotation.Autowired;
import org.springframework.context.annotation.Bean;
import org.springframework.context.annotation.Configuration;
import
➥ org.springframework.security.config.annotation.authentication.builders.
➥ AuthenticationManagerBuilder;
import
➥ org.springframework.security.config.annotation.web.builders.HttpSecurity;
import
➥ org.springframework.security.config.annotation.web.builders.WebSecurity;
import
➥ org.springframework.security.config.annotation.web.configuration.WebSec
➥ urityConfigurerAdapter;
import org.springframework.security.crypto.bcrypt.BCryptPasswordEncoder;
import org.springframework.security.crypto.password.PasswordEncoder;
import org.springframework.security.web.access.AccessDeniedHandler;

@Configuration
public class SecurityConfiguration extends WebSecurityConfigurerAdapter {

    @Autowired
    private AccessDeniedHandler customAccessDeniedHandler;

    @Override
    protected void configure(AuthenticationManagerBuilder auth) throws
➥ Exception {
```

```
        auth.inMemoryAuthentication().passwordEncoder(passwordEncoder())
                .withUser("user")
                .password(passwordEncoder().encode("p@ssw0rd"))
                .roles("USER")
                .and()
                .withUser("admin")
                .password(passwordEncoder().encode("pa$$w0rd"))
                .roles("ADMIN");
    }

    @Override
    protected void configure(HttpSecurity http) throws Exception {
        http.authorizeRequests()
                .antMatchers("/login").permitAll()
                .antMatchers("/delete/**").hasRole("ADMIN")
                .anyRequest().authenticated()
                .and()
                .formLogin().loginPage("/login")
                .and()
                .exceptionHandling().accessDeniedHandler(customAccessDenied-
     Handler);
    }
    @Override
    public void configure(WebSecurity web) throws Exception {
        web
        .ignoring()
        .antMatchers("/webjars/**", "/images/**", "/css/**", "/h2-
➥ console/**");
    }

    @Bean
    public PasswordEncoder passwordEncoder() {
        return new BCryptPasswordEncoder();
    }
}
```

In listing 5.11, we've performed the following activities:

- We've overridden the `configure(AuthenticationManagerBuilder auth)` method to define the `InMemoryUserDetailsManager` configuration. In this method, we have created two custom users, named `user` and `admin`, with their respective passwords and roles `USER` and `ADMIN`. A role is an important aspect in controlling user authorization in the application.
- In the `HttpSecurity` configuration, we've done the following:
  - The login page does not require any authentication, and it is available at the `login` endpoint.
  - The `delete` endpoint can only be invoked by a user with the role of `ADMIN`. Note how we are leveraging the user roles to control user actions in the application. Spring Security throws an `AccessDeniedException` if any user without the `ADMIN` role attempts to invoke the `delete` endpoint.

  - If there is an access denied exception, we've configured a custom `AccessDeniedHandler` that lets us perform the actions when an `AccessDeniedException` occurs. Note that we've autowired the `CustomAccessDeniedHandler`.
- We've provided an implementation for a `PasswordEncoder`. A password encoder encodes a password from a plain text format to an encoded format. We'll discuss `PasswordEncoder` in greater detail shortly. In this example, we've used the `BCryptPasswordEncoder` to encode the password.

The following listing shows the `CustomAccessDeniedHandler` class.

Listing 5.12 The CustomAccessDeniedHandler implementation

```
package com.manning.sbip.ch05.security;

//imports
@Component
public class CustomAccessDeniedHandler implements AccessDeniedHandler {

    @Override
    public void handle(HttpServletRequest request, HttpServletResponse
➥ response,
            AccessDeniedException accessDeniedException) throws
➥ IOException, ServletException {
        // log unauthorized access

      response.sendRedirect(request.getContextPath() + "/accessDenied");

    }
}
```

In the `CustomAccessDeniedHandler` class, we are redirecting the user to the `accessDenied` endpoint, which redirects the user to an error page. The `AccessDeniedHandler` provides the flexibility to perform custom actions if there is an `AccessDeniedException`. For instance, you can log the unauthorized access details, such as the user who attempts the unauthorized access on which resource, in your application for auditing purposes.

The last change you'll perform is adding a `LogoutController` that is invoked when you click on the logout button. The following listing shows this controller.

Listing 5.13 The LogoutController

```
package com.manning.sbip.ch05.controller;

//imports

@Controller
public class LogoutController {

    @PostMapping("/doLogout")
    public String logout(HttpServletRequest request, HttpServletResponse
➥ response) {
```

```
        Authentication authentication =
➥ SecurityContextHolder.getContext().getAuthentication();
        if(authentication != null) {
➥           new SecurityContextLogoutHandler().logout(request, response,
➥ authentication);
        }
        return "redirect:/login";
    }
}
```

We've executed the following operations in listing 5.13:

- We've created an HTTP POST endpoint that handles the user logout from the application. Note that it is recommended to use the HTTP POST method instead of the HTTP GET method for logout to avoid a CSRF attack.
- We've invoked the `SecurityContextLogoutHandler` for the user to log out of the application. This class invalidates the existing `HttpSession`, clears the authentication in the `SecurityContext`, and completes the logout.

Let's now start the application and access the index page by accessing the URL http://localhost:8080/index. Since you are not yet logged in to the application, you'll be redirected to the custom login page at the URL http://localhost:8080/login. You can log in to the application using the username `user` and the password `p@ssw0rd` or with the username `admin` and the password `pa$$w0rd`. After you log in successfully, you'll be redirected to the `index` page containing the list of courses.

If you notice the application console log, you won't find the Spring Security-generated password anymore. This is because you've configured custom `InMemoryUserDetailsManager` implementation, and there is no default `InMemoryUserDetailsManager` configuration provided by Spring Boot.

If you login to the application with the user as a `user` and attempt to delete a course, you'll be redirected to the error page, as shown in figure 5.14.

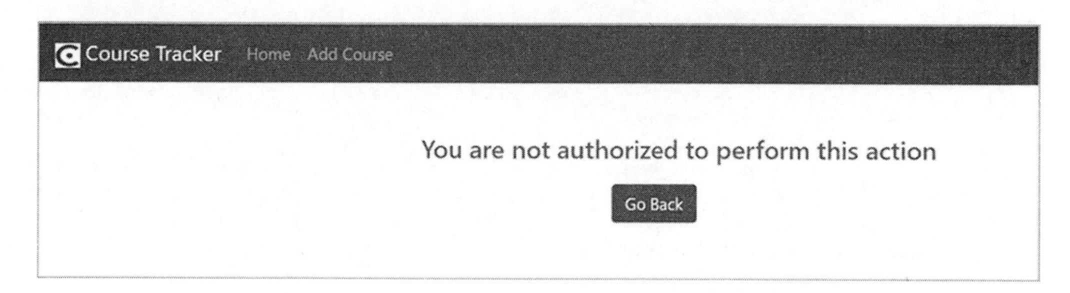

Figure 5.14 Error page for unauthorized access

DISCUSSION

Using this technique, you've learned to customize a Spring Boot application with custom users through Spring Security's `AuthenticationManagerBuilder` class. This class provides easy access for configuring various types of authentications, such as in-memory, JDBC, and LDAP. For instance, you've used the `inMemoryAuthentication(..)` method to configure the in-memory authentication. Similarly, you can also use the `jdbcAuthentication(..)` and `ldapAuthentication(..)` methods to configure JDBC- and LDAP-based authentication, respectively. You'll learn more about JDBC and LDAP authentication in later techniques.

Let us now focus on the `PasswordEncoder` bean definition. A `PasswordEncoder` encodes the plain-text password on a string to protect it. Spring Security provides several `PasswordEncoder` implementations, such as `NoOpPasswordEncoder`, `BCryptPasswordEncoder`, `Pbkdf2PasswordEncoder` and `SCryptPasswordEncoder` to name a few. In this example, for demonstration, we've used the `BCryptPasswordEncoder`.

Spring Security provides a factory class named `PasswordEncoderFactories`, which allows you to create an instance of a `DelegatingPasswordEncoder` instance. A `DelegatingPasswordEncoder` instance delegates the password encoding to an actual `PasswordEncoder`, such as `BCryptPasswordEncoder`, which performs the actual encoding.

In general, the password of a user is encoded using the configured `PasswordEncoder`, and the encoded password is stored in the persistence store if a persistence store-based identity store is used. Later, while the password is supplied for authentication, the supplied password is provided to the encoder, and it matches the user-supplied password with the previously encoded password retrieved from the identity store. This is shown in figure 5.15.

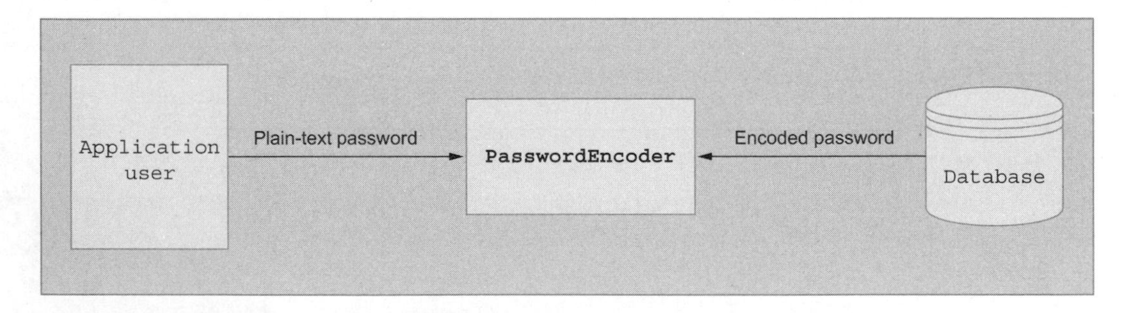

Figure 5.15 PasswordEncoder's password comparison process. A PasswordEncoder takes the plain-text password supplied by the user, and the encoded password is retrieved from the database. Based on the type of PasswordEncoder used, it applies an internal algorithm to compare the password. If there is a match, the comparison is successful. If the passwords do not match, the comparison is marked as failed.

After authentication, the supplied plain-text password is erased from the application. This prevents the plain-text password from being available in the application.

We'll now provide an alternative approach to creating an `InMemoryUserDetailsManager` that uses the `DelegatingPasswordEncoder` instance to encode the password. The following listing shows this configuration.

Listing 5.14 The SecurityConfiguration class

```
package com.manning.sbip.ch05.security;

import org.springframework.beans.factory.annotation.Autowired;
import org.springframework.context.annotation.Bean;
import org.springframework.context.annotation.Configuration;
import
➥ org.springframework.security.config.annotation.web.builders.HttpSecurity;
import
➥ org.springframework.security.config.annotation.web.builders.WebSecurity;
import
➥ org.springframework.security.config.annotation.web.configuration.WebSec
➥ urityConfigurerAdapter;
import org.springframework.security.core.userdetails.User;
import org.springframework.security.core.userdetails.UserDetails;
import org.springframework.security.core.userdetails.UserDetailsService;
import
➥ org.springframework.security.crypto.factory.PasswordEncoderFactories;
import org.springframework.security.crypto.password.PasswordEncoder;
import
➥ org.springframework.security.provisioning.InMemoryUserDetailsManager;
@Configuration
public class SecurityConfiguration extends WebSecurityConfigurerAdapter {

    @Autowired
    private PasswordEncoder passwordEncoder;

    @Override
    protected void configure(HttpSecurity http) throws Exception {
        http.authorizeRequests()
                .antMatchers("/login").permitAll()
                .antMatchers("/delete/**").hasRole("ADMIN")
                .anyRequest().authenticated()
                .and()
                .formLogin().loginPage("/login")
                .and()
              .exceptionHandling().accessDeniedHandler(customAccessDenied
➥ Handler);
    }

    @Override
    public void configure(WebSecurity web) throws Exception {
        web.ignoring().antMatchers("/webjars/**", "/images/*", "/css/*",
➥ "/h2-console/**");
    }


    @Bean
    @Override
    public UserDetailsService userDetailsService() {    <-- Defining the UserDetailsService as a Spring Bean definition

        UserDetails user = User.withUsername("user")
                .passwordEncoder(passwordEncoder::encode)
                .password("p@ssw0rd").roles("USER").build();
```

```
        UserDetails admin = User.withUsername("admin")
                .passwordEncoder(passwordEncoder::encode)
                .password("pa$$w0rd").roles("ADMIN").build();

        InMemoryUserDetailsManager userDetailsManager = new
➥ InMemoryUserDetailsManager();

        userDetailsManager.createUser(user);
        userDetailsManager.createUser(admin);

        return userDetailsManager;
    }

    @Bean
    public PasswordEncoder passwordEncoder() {
        return PasswordEncoderFactories.createDelegatingPasswordEncoder();
    }
}
```

In listing 5.14, you defined an instance of `UserDetailsService`. First, you created the builder methods of the `User` class and built the instance of `UserDetails` instance. Recall that the `UserDetails` represents a user in the Spring Security context. Notice that you've used Java 8's method reference with the password encoder to encode the supplied password.

Also, you've created an instance of `DelegatingPasswordEncoder` that internally uses the `BCryptPasswordEncoder`. A `BCryptPasswordEncoder` is an actual password encoder and considered more secure. Start the application with this configuration, and you'll notice that it works in the same way it worked previously. The major difference in this approach is the way you have initialized the `InMemoryUserDetailsManager` and used an appropriate password encoder.

Authentication, authorization, and roles

In the previous technique, you learned that while creating the application users, along with the user details, we've also defined user roles. When dealing with security, you need to understand the concepts of authentication and authorization.

Authentication is the process of ensuring that a user is the one they claim to be. This is done through some sort of user identification mechanism, such as the user's username and password, certificates, biometric information, or other information. *Authorization* defines what an authenticated user is allowed to perform once they are logged in to the application. Let's explore this using the analogy of traveling through an airport. To catch a flight, you reach the airport and present your identity document to get access to the airport terminal. The identity document authenticates you as the right traveler. Once you are inside the terminal you are only authorized to board the airplane as recorded in your boarding pass. The boarding pass defines your travel authority. Even though you are inside the terminal, you can't board any flight of your choice, as you are not authorized to board any flight you don't have a boarding pass for. A similar concept is applied to the users in an application. They can only perform the activities they are authorized for in the application.

In a Spring Security application, you use the notion of *roles* to control what a logged-in user is authorized to view and perform in the application. You can think of a role as the permission or right of a user. Refer to http://mng.bz/la06 for more details about using roles in a Spring Boot application.

5.3.3 Technique: Configuring JDBC authentication with Spring Security in a Spring Boot application

In this technique, we'll discuss how to use Spring Security JDBC authentication in a Spring Boot application.

PROBLEM

Storing user credentials in the source code is a bad idea, as it can be retrieved by anyone with access to the source code. Storing user credentials in a database table is a relatively better approach. You need to configure JDBC authentication in a Spring Boot application.

SOLUTION

The application you've developed in the previous technique is slightly better than its previous version, as you have the option to configure the custom users in the application. However, this is not enough because you will rarely be interested in keeping the user credentials hardcoded in your source code. This defeats the purpose of enabling the security altogether, since anyone with access to the source code can easily retrieve the user credentials. Besides, if your application allows the registration of new users, it will be a challenge to let them log in to the application with this approach.

A better alternative is to store the user credentials in a persistent store, such as a database. A database table, in most production applications, is secure, and only authorized persons can access it. Thus, this technique allows us to explore how to store the user credentials in a database table and use it for user authentication.

Source code

To start using this technique, you can use the base version of the Spring Boot project used throughout it, which is available at http://mng.bz/VlvX. The final version of this Spring Boot project is available at http://mng.bz/xv58.

The first change you'll need to perform is introducing two tables: `USERS` and `AUTHORITIES`. As the names suggest, the `USERS` table contains the user details, and the `AUTHORITIES` table contains the user authorities. Note that authorities in broader terms define what a user is authorized to do in the application. Previously, we defined the user role in the same manner. Note that the core difference between these two is the semantics of how we use these features. In the Spring Security context, the differences are minimal and mostly work in the same way. Providing an in-depth discussion on the differences between roles and authorities is beyond the scope of this book. You can refer to Spring Security documentation or Manning's *Spring Security in Action* by Laurențiu Spilcă for a detailed understanding of this subject.

USERS and AUTHORITIES are the default table names used by Spring JDBC, and to use the default JDBC authentication provided by Spring Security, we need to use these table names. In the latter technique, you'll learn how to customize these table names and the table structure. Listing 5.15 shows the modified schema.sql located in the src/main/resources folder.

Listing 5.15 Modified schema.sql

```
// Users and Authorities DDL

create table users(
    username varchar(50) not null primary key,
    password varchar(500) not null,
    enabled boolean not null
);                                       <-- The USERS table stores the application user details.

create table authorities (
    username varchar(50) not null,
    authority varchar(50) not null,
    constraint fk_authorities_users foreign key(username) references
➥  users(username)
);                          <-- The AUTHORITIES table stores the user authorities.

create unique index ix_auth_username on authorities (username,authority);  <-- Unique index to ensure the unique username and authority mappings
```

Listing 5.16 shows the modified data.sql file.

Listing 5.16 The data.sql file

```
// Users insert queries
INSERT into USERS(username, password, enabled) values ('user','p@ssw0rd',
➥ true);
INSERT into USERS(username, password, enabled) values ('admin','pa$$w0rd',
➥ true);                                    <-- Application Users

INSERT into AUTHORITIES(username, authority) values ('user','USER');
INSERT into AUTHORITIES(username, authority) values ('admin','ADMIN');  <-- Application user Authorities
```

Upon application startup, Spring Boot will execute the queries provided in the above listings. Recall from chapter 3 that Spring Boot automatically executes these scripts on startup. Let's now move on to the SecurityConfiguration changes, as shown in the following listing.

Listing 5.17 The security configuration

```
package com.manning.sbip.ch05.security;

import org.springframework.beans.factory.annotation.Autowired;
import org.springframework.context.annotation.Bean;
import org.springframework.context.annotation.Configuration;
import
➥ org.springframework.security.config.annotation.authentication.builders.
➥ AuthenticationManagerBuilder;
import
➥ org.springframework.security.config.annotation.web.builders.HttpSecurity;
import
➥ org.springframework.security.config.annotation.web.builders.WebSecurity;
import
➥ org.springframework.security.config.annotation.web.configuration.WebSec
➥ urityConfigurerAdapter;
import org.springframework.security.crypto.password.NoOpPasswordEncoder;
import org.springframework.security.crypto.password.PasswordEncoder;

import javax.sql.DataSource;

@Configuration
public class SecurityConfiguration extends WebSecurityConfigurerAdapter {

    @Autowired
    private DataSource dataSource;

    @Override
    protected void configure(HttpSecurity http) throws Exception {
        http.authorizeRequests()
                .antMatchers("/login").permitAll()
                .anyRequest().authenticated()
                .and()
                .formLogin().loginPage("/login");
    }

    @Override
    public void configure(WebSecurity web) throws Exception {
        web.ignoring().antMatchers("/webjars/**", "/images/**", "/css/**",
➥ "/h2-console/**");
    }

    @Override
    protected void configure(AuthenticationManagerBuilder auth) throws
➥ Exception {
        auth.jdbcAuthentication().dataSource(dataSource);
    }

    @Bean
    public PasswordEncoder passwordEncoder() {
        return NoOpPasswordEncoder.getInstance();
    }
}
```

Implementing JDBC authentication. By default Spring Security uses the supplied data source (autowired above) to connect to the database and loads the user details and authorities from USERS and AUTHORITIES tables, respectively.

The first change you've made is autowiring the `DataSource` into the class. You've updated the authentication strategy to JDBC authentication in the `configure (Authentication-ManagerBuilder auth)` method. You then configured the JDBC authentication with this data source, so Spring Boot can perform the necessary database lookup for user authentication.

Note that you've just specified the data source in JDBC authentication. By default, Spring Security executes the queries listed in listing 5.18 to load the user details and its authorities. It then uses these details to authenticate the users and validate their authority to access the resource (e.g., if the user is authorized to access the index page).

Listing 5.18 Queries used by Spring Security to load user details and authorities

```
select username, password, enabled from users where username =?
select username, authority from authorities where username =?
```

Queries to fetch the user's details and authorities from the supplied username to perform authentication

Let's now start the application and access the index page by navigating to the URL http://localhost:8080/index. You'll be redirected to the login page at the URL http://localhost:8080/login. You can log in to the application using the username `user` and password `p@ssw0rd` or with the username `admin` and password `pa$$w0rd`. After successful login, you'll be redirected to the index page containing the list of courses.

DISCUSSION

With this technique, you've learned to perform JDBC authentication in the application. This approach is much better than the previous authentication strategies, as the user credentials are stored in a database table.

For JDBC authentication, Spring Security provides the `JdbcDaoImpl` class that implements the `UserDetailsService` and defines the `loadUserByUsername(..)` method. This method loads the user details using the database. Besides, as shown in figure 5.16, the `JdbcUserDetailsManager` class extends the `JdbcDaoImpl` and provides more extensive support for user management services through JDBC. For instance, this class allows performing CRUD operations for a user. Thus, if your application supports user management, you can use this class to create or delete a user in the application.

Although this technique works fine, it has a certain limitation, as it forces you to use the Spring default tables (`USERS` and `AUTHORITIES`) for authentication. But your application might have its database tables to store user details, and you would like to use that table for the JDBC authentication. In the next technique, we'll demonstrate how to use custom tables for JDBC authentication.

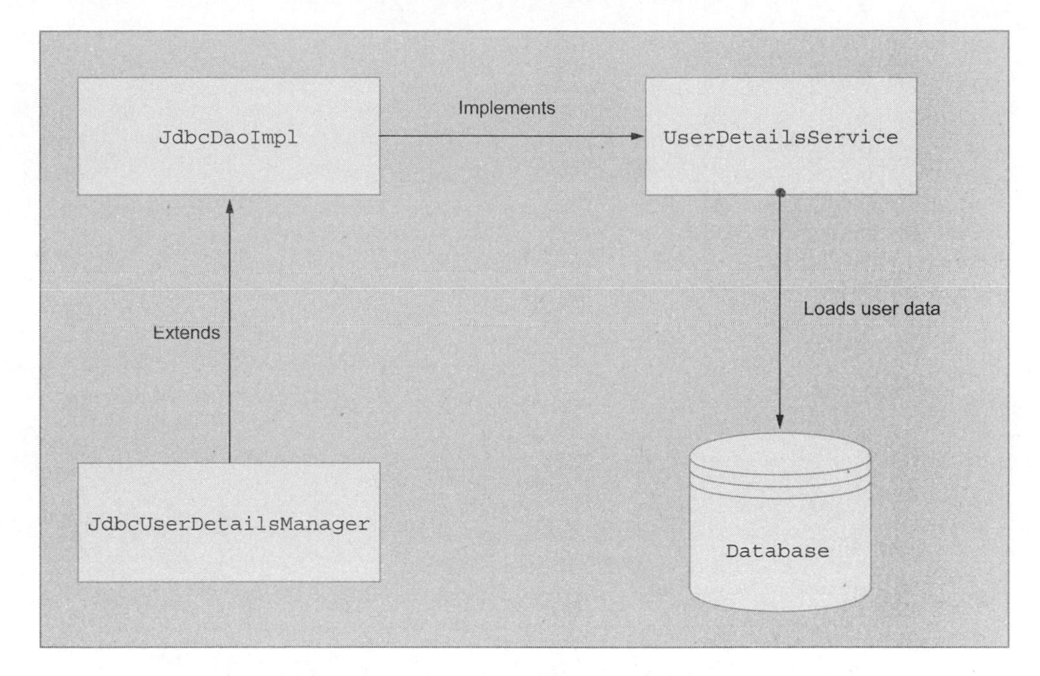

Figure 5.16 Spring Security class and interfaces for JDBC authentication

5.3.4 *Technique: Implementing JDBC authentication with custom UserDetailsService in a Spring Boot application*

In this technique, we'll discuss how to implement Spring Security JDBC authentication with a custom `UserDetailsService`.

PROBLEM

Implementing JDBC authentication with custom queries does not provide complete control of the user account management. Features such as user account locking, account expiry, and user credentials expiry are not available.

SOLUTION

Spring Security provides a `UserDetailsService` interface that acts as a bridge between the application user implementation and the Spring Security `UserDetails`. If you have a custom user management module and user details that do not conform to the Spring Security user implementation, you can provide an implementation of this interface.

The `UserDetailsService` interface is straightforward and provides only one method `loadUserByUsername()` that allows you to load the user details from the identity store and return a Spring Security's `UserDetails` implementation.

Source code

To start using this technique, you can use the base version of the Spring Boot project used throughout it, which is available at http://mng.bz/Axjp. The final version of this Spring Boot project is available at http://mng.bz/Zzmm.

In this technique, we are talking about application-specific users. Therefore, we will model an application user entity, as shown in the following listing.

Listing 5.19 Custom user in the Course Tracker application

```
package com.manning.sbip.ch05.model;

import lombok.Data;

import javax.persistence.*;

@Entity
@Table(name = "CT_USERS")
@Data
public class ApplicationUser {

    @Id
    @GeneratedValue(strategy = GenerationType.IDENTITY)
    private Long id;
    private String firstName;
    private String lastName;
    private String username;
    private String email;
    private String password;
    private boolean verified;
    private boolean locked;
    @Column(name = "ACC_CRED_EXPIRED")
    private boolean accountCredentialsExpired;
}
```

The details in listing 5.19 are straightforward. It contains user details, such as `first_name`, `last_name`, `username`, and other user account details. We've named the table that stores user details as `CT_USERS`.

We need a Spring Data repository interface implementation for the `ApplicationUser`, so we can manage the user details in the database. The following listing shows the `ApplicationUserRepository` interface.

Listing 5.20 The ApplicationUserRepository interface

```
package com.manning.sbip.ch05.repository;

@Repository
public interface ApplicationUserRepository extends
➥ CrudRepository<ApplicationUser, Long> {
```

```
    ApplicationUser findByUsername(String username);
}
```

In listing 5.20, we've added the method `findByUsername()` that finds the `ApplicationUser` from the database with the supplied username. We need this method, as we need to load the user details in the `UserDetailsService` implementation. Let's provide the custom `UserDetailsService` implementation, as shown in the following listing.

Listing 5.21 Custom UserDetailsService implementation

```
package com.manning.sbip.ch05.service;

import com.manning.sbip.ch05.model.ApplicationUser;
import com.manning.sbip.ch05.repository.ApplicationUserRepository;
import org.springframework.beans.factory.annotation.Autowired;
import org.springframework.security.core.userdetails.User;
import org.springframework.security.core.userdetails.UserDetails;
import org.springframework.security.core.userdetails.UserDetailsService;
import
➥ org.springframework.security.core.userdetails.UsernameNotFoundException;

@Service
public class CustomUserDetailsService implements UserDetailsService {

    @Autowired
    private ApplicationUserRepository applicationUserRepository;

    @Override
    public UserDetails loadUserByUsername(String username) throws
➥ UsernameNotFoundException {
        ApplicationUser applicationUser =
➥ applicationUserRepository.findByUsername(username);
        if(applicationUser == null) {
            throw new UsernameNotFoundException("No user with "+username+"
➥ exists in the system");
        }
        return User.builder()
                .username(applicationUser.getUsername())
                .password(applicationUser.getPassword())
                .disabled(!applicationUser.isVerified())
                .accountExpired(applicationUser.isAccountCredentialsExpired())
                .accountLocked(applicationUser.isLocked())
                .roles("USER")
                .build();
    }
}
```

Providing implementation of loadUserByUsername(..) method that maps application-specific user details to Spring Security-specific UserDetails. We first load the user from the database and then use the Spring Security's builder method to construct the UserDetails instance. If the user is not available, we throw the UsernameNotFoundException exception.

Let's discuss the changes in listing 5.21:

- The `CustomUserDetailsService` class provides an implementation of the `UserDetailsService` interface.
- It autowires the `ApplicationUserRepository` interface implementation, as this is used to load the user details from the database.
- Lastly, in the `loadUserByUsername()` method, we are doing the following:
  - We are finding the user details from the database.
  - If there is no user with the supplied username, we are throwing the `UsernameNotFoundException`. This is a Spring Security exception to indicate the user is not available.
  - If the user exists, then we will build the Spring Security user with the `ApplicationUser` details.

In this example, we mark a user as disabled if the user account is not verified. Similarly, `accountExpired()` and `accountLocked()` can be used to control the user account status. For instance, you can implement the account as locked after a configurable number of incorrect login attempts. In fact, you can also implement account expiry to force the user to change their password after a period. Besides, we've set the user role as `USER` to indicate they have the role as user. Spring Security forces you to configure either the role or the authorities of the user.

The last change we need to perform is using this custom `UserDetailsService` in the `SecurityConfiguration` class, so the custom implementation can be used by Spring Security. The following listing shows the updated `SecurityConfiguration` class.

Listing 5.22 SecurityConfiguration class

```
package com.manning.sbip.ch05.security;

import com.manning.sbip.ch05.service.CustomUserDetailsService;
import org.springframework.context.annotation.Bean;
import org.springframework.context.annotation.Configuration;
import
➥ org.springframework.security.config.annotation.web.builders.HttpSecurity;
import
➥ org.springframework.security.config.annotation.web.builders.WebSecurity;
import
➥ org.springframework.security.config.annotation.web.configuration.WebSec
➥ urityConfigurerAdapter;
import org.springframework.security.core.userdetails.UserDetailsService;
import org.springframework.security.crypto.password.NoOpPasswordEncoder;
import org.springframework.security.crypto.password.PasswordEncoder;

@Configuration
public class SecurityConfiguration extends WebSecurityConfigurerAdapter {

    @Override
    protected void configure(HttpSecurity http) throws Exception {
```

```
        http
                .authorizeRequests()
                .antMatchers("/login").permitAll()
                .anyRequest().authenticated()
                .and()
                .formLogin().loginPage("/login");
    }

    @Override
    public void configure(WebSecurity web) throws Exception {
        web
                .ignoring()
                .antMatchers("/webjars/**", "/images/*", "/css/*", "/h2-
➥ console/**");
    }

    @Bean
    public PasswordEncoder passwordEncoder() {
        return NoOpPasswordEncoder.getInstance();
    }
    @Bean
    public UserDetailsService userDetailsService() {
        return new CustomUserDetailsService();
    }
}
```

Defining custom UserDetailsService implementation as a Spring bean

In listing 5.22, you've made two additional changes: adding the `UserDetailsService` bean definition and removing the `configure(AuthenticationManagerBuilder auth)` method. The last method is no longer necessary, as you are providing the `UserDetails-Service` implementation.

The last change you'll perform is creating the `CT_USERS` table and adding a few user details to it. Listing 5.23 shows the schema.sql changes.

Listing 5.23 The CT_USERS table definition

```
create table ct_users(
  ID    BIGINT(19)    NOT NULL,
  EMAIL    VARCHAR(255)    NOT NULL,
  FIRST_NAME    VARCHAR(255) NOT NULL,
  LAST_NAME    VARCHAR(255) NOT NULL,
  PASSWORD    VARCHAR(255) NOT NULL,
  USERNAME    VARCHAR(255) NOT NULL,
  VERIFIED    BOOLEAN(1) NOT NULL,
  LOCKED BOOLEAN(1) NOT NULL,
  ACC_CRED_EXPIRED BOOLEAN(1) NOT NULL,
  PRIMARY KEY (ID)
);
```

The following listing shows the data.sql changes that contain two user details.

Listing 5.24 CT_USERS INSERT queries

```
INSERT INTO CT_USERS(ID, FIRST_NAME, LAST_NAME, USERNAME, PASSWORD, EMAIL,
➥ VERIFIED, LOCKED, ACC_CRED_EXPIRED) VALUES(1, 'John', 'Socket',
➥ 'jsocket', 'password', 'jsocket@example.com', TRUE, FALSE, FALSE);

INSERT INTO CT_USERS(ID, FIRST_NAME, LAST_NAME, USERNAME, PASSWORD, EMAIL,
➥ VERIFIED, LOCKED, ACC_CRED_EXPIRED) VALUES(2, 'Steve', 'Smith',
➥ 'smith', 'password', 'smith@example.com', FALSE, FALSE, FALSE);
```

In listing 5.24, we created two users with usernames of `jsocket` and `smith`, respectively. The first user account is enabled, and the last one is disabled. You can start the application and try logging in with both the users. You'll notice that you can successfully log in with the `jsocket` user but not with the `smith` user.

DISCUSSION

Many applications store their application user details in the database and use them to authenticate the users. Spring Security provides several approaches to using JDBC authentication based on the complexity of the application user set up in the application.

In the last techniques, we discussed these approaches to perform JDBC-based user authentication. In the first technique, you saw the default use of basic JDBC authentication where you need to implement the tables, as Spring Security requires you to configure. In the next technique, you used the custom SQL queries, which is better than the previous one, as it removes the restriction of using Spring Security-specific tables. The third approach provides you with more control over how you need to manage your users and user account configuration.

Although storing user details in the database works well, many organizations store user details and roles in an LDAP (Lightweight Directory Access Protocol) server for better user management and authentication. Let's discuss this in the next technique.

5.3.5 Technique: Implementing LDAP authentication in a Spring Boot application

In this technique, we'll demonstrate how to perform LDAP authentication in a Spring Boot application.

PROBLEM

Many organizations manage LDAP to store user details and use it for authenticating users. In the course tracker application, you need to enable LDAP authentication.

SOLUTION

Most major organizations use LDAP as the central repository for storing user details, their roles, and authentication purposes. An LDAP server is typically fast for reading and query operations. As user details are changed less frequently and are queried for purposes, such as authentication and validation on their roles, LDAP is the suitable protocol to manage user details.

Since LDAP is important and is often used by organizations, Spring Security provides built-in support for performing user authentication. In this technique, you'll first learn how to use LDAP authentication in a Spring Boot application.

> **Source code**
> To start using this technique, you can use the base version of the Spring Boot project used throughout it, which is available at http://mng.bz/RE5j. The final version of this Spring Boot project is available at http://mng.bz/2jQ8.

The first change you need to perform is including the Maven dependencies required to include LDAP support in the course tracker project. Listing 5.25 shows the Maven dependencies to be included in the pom.xml file.

Listing 5.25 LDAP dependencies

```
<dependency>
    <groupId>org.springframework.ldap</groupId>
    <artifactId>spring-ldap-core</artifactId>
</dependency>
<dependency>
    <groupId>org.springframework.security</groupId>
    <artifactId>spring-security-ldap</artifactId>
</dependency>
<dependency>
    <groupId>com.unboundid</groupId>
    <artifactId>unboundid-ldapsdk</artifactId>
</dependency>
```

In listing 5.25, the `spring-ldap-core` and `spring-security-ldap` dependencies provide the necessary support to enable LDAP features in the Spring Boot application. Besides, to use LDAP you need an LDAP server. For simplicity, in this example you've used an embedded LDAP server called UnboundID (https://ldap.com/unboundid-ldap-sdk-for-java/).

The next change you'll need to perform is adding the user data that will be accessed by the LDAP server. By default, an LDAP server does not store the data; it is stored in an underlying data storage. In this example, we'll use an LDAP Data Interchange Format (LDIF) (https://ldap.com/ldif-the-ldap-data-interchange-format/) file that stores the user records. The following listing shows the users.ldif file stored inside the src\main\resources folder.

Listing 5.26 The users.ldif file

```
dn: dc=manning,dc=com
objectclass: top
objectclass: domain
objectclass: extensibleObject
dc: manning
```

```
dn: ou=people,dc=manning,dc=com
objectclass: top
objectclass: organizationalUnit
ou: people
```

These acronyms will be explained later in the discussion section.

```
dn: uid=steve,ou=people,dc=manning,dc=com
objectclass: top
objectclass: person
objectclass: organizationalPerson
objectclass: inetOrgPerson
cn: Steve Smith
sn: Smith
uid: steve
userPassword: password
```

Defines user Steve Smith

```
dn: uid=jsocket,ou=people,dc=manning,dc=com
objectclass: top
objectclass: person
objectclass: organizationalPerson
objectclass: inetOrgPerson
cn: John Socket
sn: Socket
uid: jsocket
userPassword: password
```

Defines user John Socket

We'll provide a brief explanation of the users.ldif file in the discussion section. For now, understand that you've two user details with the username `steve` and `jsocket`. The password for both users is set to `password`. Lets now include the LDAP server configuration in the application.properties file, as shown in the following listing.

Listing 5.27 Embedded LDAP server configuration

```
spring.ldap.embedded.port=8389
spring.ldap.embedded.ldif=classpath:users.ldif
spring.ldap.embedded.base-dn=dc=manning,dc=com
```

Embedded LDAP server port

Embedded LDIF file location

Embedded LDAP server distinguished name

In the listing, you specify the embedded LDAP server port and the LDIF file location. You also specify the base distinguished name (DN) of the LDAP server, which acts as the root entity in the LDAP server.

The next and last change you'll need to make is configuring the `SecurityConfiguration` class to instruct Spring Security to perform an LDAP authentication. The following listing shows the updated `SecurityConfiguration` class.

Listing 5.28 The SecurityConfiguration class

```
package com.manning.sbip.ch05.security;

import org.springframework.context.annotation.Bean;
import org.springframework.context.annotation.Configuration;
import
➥ org.springframework.security.config.annotation.authentication.builders.
➥ AuthenticationManagerBuilder;
import
➥ org.springframework.security.config.annotation.web.builders.HttpSecurity;
import
➥ org.springframework.security.config.annotation.web.builders.WebSecurity;
import
➥ org.springframework.security.config.annotation.web.configuration.WebSec
➥ urityConfigurerAdapter;
import org.springframework.security.crypto.password.NoOpPasswordEncoder;
import org.springframework.security.crypto.password.PasswordEncoder;

@Configuration
public class SecurityConfiguration extends WebSecurityConfigurerAdapter {

    @Override
    protected void configure(HttpSecurity http) throws Exception {
        http
                .authorizeRequests()
                .antMatchers("/login").permitAll()
                .anyRequest().authenticated()
                .and()
                .formLogin().loginPage("/login");
    }
    @Override
    protected void configure(AuthenticationManagerBuilder auth) throws
➥ Exception {
        auth
                .ldapAuthentication()
                .userDnPatterns("uid={0},ou=people")
                .contextSource()
                .url("ldap://localhost:8389/dc=manning,dc=com")
                .and()
                .passwordCompare()
                .passwordEncoder(NoOpPasswordEncoder.getInstance())
                .passwordAttribute("userPassword");
    }

    @Override
    public void configure(WebSecurity web) throws Exception {
        web
                .ignoring()
                .antMatchers("/webjars/**", "/images/*", "/css/*", "/h2-
     console/**");
    }
}
```

Defining LDAP configuration through Authentication-ManagerBuilder

Let's discuss the changes made for LDAP authentication:

- We've used the `AuthenticationManagerBuilder` to configure the LDAP authentication.
- We've set the DN to `uid={0}` and `ou=people`. In the `uid={0}`, the `{0}` is replaced with the user ID (e.g., `steve`), while performing the authentication. Besides, the `ou=people` indicate the user belongs to the people organization unit.
- We then perform the `contextSource` to configure Spring Security to point to the LDAP server that should be used to authenticate users.
- The next operation we perform is doing a password comparison. Unlike a database table, LDAP servers do not allow fetching the user password. Thus, while authenticating Spring Security takes the password supplied by the user and does an LDAP compare operation by supplying the user password to the LDAP server.
- While performing password comparison, we specify the password encoder and the LDAP entity attribute name that represents the password in the LDAP server. In this example, we are supplying a `NoOpsPasswordEncoder`, as we are using a plain text password. We also set the password attribute to `userPassword`, as in our LDIF file, we've used this attribute to represent the user password.

You can start the application and access the index page of the application. You'll be redirected to the familiar login page. You can log in with the users configured in the LDAP server. You can use the username `steve` and password `password` to log in.

DISCUSSION

In this technique, we've discussed how to implement LDAP authentication through Spring Security in a Spring Boot application. LDAP is an extremely popular directory access protocol, and most major organizations manage their users and other organizational details through LDAP servers.

In this example, we've kept the LDAP implementation as minimal as possible to keep the example simple and clear. If you are not familiar with LDAP and its purpose, you can find an in-depth LDAP guide at http://www.zytrax.com/books/ldap/.

Next, we'll provide a brief explanation of the users.ldif file you've used in this technique to store the user details. Figure 5.17 provides a high-level overview of this file. In listing 5.26, you first created a root entry with `dc=manning,dc=com`. You then created the organizational unit (`ou`) with `ou=people`. Lastly, you stored two user details: Steve Smith with `uid smith` and John Socket with `uid jsocket`. Figure 5.17 shows these details.

In the previous technique, you learned that the use of `UserDetailsService` plays a major role in user authentication. In LDAP authentication we can't use the `UserDetailsService`, as the LDAP server does not allow reading user passwords. Spring Security provides a `LdapAuthenticator` interface that is responsible for performing the LDAP authentication.

In Spring Security, you can perform LDAP authentication in two ways: bind authentication and password authentication. In password authentication, the user-supplied password is *compared* with the one present in the LDAP server. In this exam-

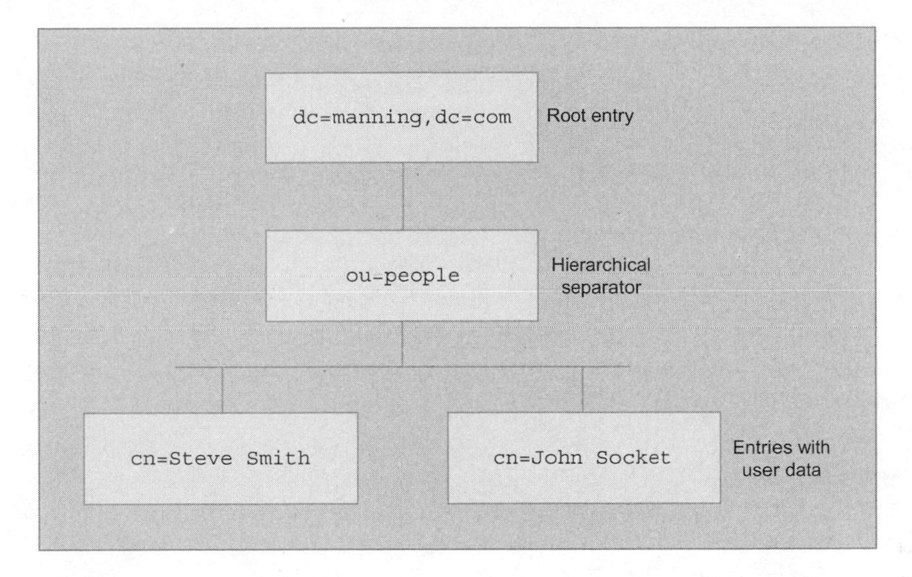

Figure 5.17 The users.ldif file structure. Its shows the root entries, the separator, and the user data

ple, you used the password comparison to authenticate the users. In bind authentication, users are authenticated to establish an authorization identity that is used in subsequent operations to the LDAP server. To authenticate, the users provide identity proof, such as a password. Refer to https://ldap.com/the-ldap-bind-operation/ to read more about LDAP bind operation.

In all these techniques, you've seen the use of form-based user authentication. In form-based authentication, a login form is presented to the user to enter the user credentials. Once the user attempts to log in, these credentials are read by the server, and user authentication is performed. Another popular form of authentication is HTTP basic authentication that lets the user agent (e.g., the browser) accept the user credentials and do the user authentication. The HTTP basic authentication technique is useful when you don't have an option to perform form-based authentication.

5.3.6 Technique: Implementing HTTP basic authentication in a Spring Boot application

In this technique, we'll discuss how to implement HTTP basic authentication in a Spring Boot application.

PROBLEM

In the previous techniques, you've explored form-based user authentication for the users to allow access to the application. However, some applications prefer to use HTTP basic authentication instead of form-based login. You need to implement HTTP basic authentication in your application.

SOLUTION

NOTE It is not recommended to use HTTP basic authentication in production applications due to its limitations. This authentication mode encodes the plain-text password with Base64 encoding, which can easily be decoded. A production application prefers using techniques, such as token-based authentication.

HTTP basic authentication is an alternative authentication approach used in applications to authenticate the users. Like form-based login, it also accepts the user credentials and allows the server to authenticate the user. In this technique, we'll first demonstrate the use of HTTP basic authentication in the course tracker application. In the discussion section, we'll provide more information on the HTTP basic authentication and how it works.

> **Source code**
>
> To start using this technique, you can use the base version of the Spring Boot project used throughout it, which is available at http://mng.bz/J1rK. The final version of this Spring Boot project is available at http://mng.bz/wnK2.

In this technique, we'll use the default JDBC-based HTTP basic authentication. Thus, we'll remove the form-based login, as used in the previous techniques, and define HTTP basic authentication in the `SecurityConfiguration` class, as shown in the following listing.

Listing 5.29 The SecurityConfiguration class for HTTP basic authentication with JDBC

```
package com.manning.sbip.ch05.security;

import org.springframework.beans.factory.annotation.Autowired;
import org.springframework.context.annotation.Bean;
import org.springframework.context.annotation.Configuration;
import
➥ org.springframework.security.config.annotation.authentication.builders.
➥ AuthenticationManagerBuilder;
import
➥ org.springframework.security.config.annotation.web.builders.HttpSecurity;
import
➥ org.springframework.security.config.annotation.web.builders.WebSecurity;
import
➥ org.springframework.security.config.annotation.web.configuration.WebSec
➥ urityConfigurerAdapter;
import org.springframework.security.crypto.password.NoOpPasswordEncoder;
import org.springframework.security.crypto.password.PasswordEncoder;

import javax.sql.DataSource;

@Configuration
public class SecurityConfiguration extends WebSecurityConfigurerAdapter {

    @Autowired
    private DataSource dataSource;
```

```
    @Override
    protected void configure(HttpSecurity http) throws Exception {
        http
                .authorizeRequests()
                .anyRequest()
                .authenticated()
                .and()
                .httpBasic();
    }

    @Override
    protected void configure(AuthenticationManagerBuilder auth) throws
     Exception {
        auth.jdbcAuthentication().dataSource(dataSource);
    }

    @Override
    public void configure(WebSecurity web) throws Exception {
        web
                .ignoring()
                .antMatchers("/webjars/**", "/images/**", "/css/**", "/h2-
➥ console/**");
    }

    @Bean
    public PasswordEncoder passwordEncoder() {
        return NoOpPasswordEncoder.getInstance();
    }
}
```

The configure method indicates that all requests to the application need to be authenticated, and the authentication needs to be performed by HTTP Basic Authentication.

In listing 5.29, you've defined that any requests to the application need to be authenticated, and the authentication scheme is HTTP basic authentication. These are the only changes you've made to implement HTTP basic authentication in the application.

Let's start the application and access the http://localhost:8080/index from the browser. You won't find the familiar login page; instead, there will be a dialogue box from the browser prompting you to enter the username and password, as shown in figure 5.18. Provide the same credentials used earlier, as there is no change in the users

Sign in
http://localhost:8080
Username
Password
Sign in Cancel

Figure 5.18 HTTP basic authentication dialogue box for user authentication in Google Chrome browser

you have created previously. For example, you can use the username `user` and the password `p@ssw0rd` to log in.

After successfully logging in, you'll be redirected to the index page of the application. You'll notice there is no logout button available on any of the pages. This is because there is no logout function in HTTP basic authentication. To log out from the application, you'll need to close all instances of the browser.

DISCUSSION

HTTP basic authentication is one of the simplest forms of authentication available in HTTP. When you request the index page, the server detects that basic authentication is enabled and does two things:

- It adds an HTTP response header called `WWW-Authenticate` with the value `Basic realm="Realm"`.
- It sends an HTTP status code `401` indicating the `Unauthorized` request.

A realm can be interpreted as an area (e.g., a group of Web pages) for which the user credentials are shared. On receipt of the HTTP `401` error, the browser understands that it needs to supply the username and password. Thus, it opens the dialogue box for the user to enter the credentials, as shown in figure 5.18. Once the credentials are provided, the browser concatenates the details in `username:password` format and performs Base64 encoding on the concatenated data. It then inserts the `Authorization` HTTP header in the request in the following format: `Authorization: Basic <Base64 encoded data>`.

The browser remembers the credentials, and on all subsequent requests, it inserts the `Authorization` header with the encoded credentials. You need to close the browser for it to discard the remembered credentials.

Summary

Let's summarize the key takeaways of this chapter:

- We learned about Spring Security, its architecture, and Spring Boot autoconfiguration for Spring Security.
- We discussed how to implement Spring Security in a Spring Boot application and customize the user login page.
- We explored how to implement in-memory, JDBC, and LDAP authentication with Spring Security.
- We discussed how to implement role-based access control in a Spring Boot application.
- We learned how to implement HTTP basic authentication to authenticate users in a Spring Boot application.

In the next chapter, you'll extend your understanding of Spring Security by implementing a few more advanced application security features.

6 Implementing additional security with Spring Security

This chapter covers

- Configuring advanced security configurations, including securing passwords with Spring Cloud Vault, Remember Me, and Google reCAPTCHA
- Enabling multi-factor authentication, including email verification and two-factor authentication with Google Authenticator
- Implementing login with OAuth2 in a Spring Boot application
- Securing Spring Boot Actuator endpoints with Spring Security

In chapter 5, we introduced you to Spring Security and provided an introduction to various Spring Security concepts. Further, we've explored several techniques for using Spring Security in a Spring Boot application. In this chapter, you'll use the foundational concepts from the previous chapter and implement several advanced security features in your Spring Boot application using Spring Security. Some of these features include enabling HTTPS; storing passwords in HashiCorp Vault; and implementing Remember Me, reCAPTCHA, email verification, two-factor authentication, and more.

You can use Spring Security to implement several advanced application security features in a Spring Boot application. Some of these features are widely used in production applications, and implementing these in your Spring Boot application can certainly enhance application security. Let's summarize the features you'll implement in this chapter:

- *Enabling HTTPS*—The interaction between client and server over the HTTP protocol poses a serious security risk. This is because the HTTP protocol transfers data in plain text. Therefore, malicious users can intercept the network traffic and can access application data. HTTPS protocol encrypts the interaction between client and server and protects application data.
- *Secret management*—Managing application secrets (e.g., password, API keys, etc.) is a key concern in any application. In a Spring Boot application, it is a common occurrence to place secrets in the application.properties (or application.yml) file; however, this defeats the purpose of the actual use of the secret. We'll demonstrate how to use Spring Cloud Vault to manage application secrets.
- *User registration*—Most Web applications deal with users. Therefore, effectively managing users in an application is one of the key tasks. You'll learn this by implementing a user registration module in the Course Tracker application.
- *Email verification*—While registering users in an application, the users must provide a valid email address. You'll learn how to verify user email by implementing email verification in the user registration in the Course Tracker application.
- *Locking user account*—It is a common practice to lock user accounts in case there are multiple failed log in attempts. These features can protect user accounts from brute-force attacks by malicious users or internet bots.
- *Remember Me*—Remembering users in a trusted device can save users time. Spring Security provides built-in support for enabling the Remember Me feature in a Spring application.
- *Enabling reCAPTCHA*—Internet bots can cause severe damage to an application, as they can overwhelm the application by creating fictitious users. It can drain the computing resources for the application and provide poor or no service to the real application user. You can prevent this by enabling CAPTCHA. You'll implement Google reCAPTCHA in the Course Tracker application.
- *Two-factor authentication*—The two-factor authentication provides added security to the applications, as it requires the user to provide additional authentication. You'll implement two-factor authentication in the Course Tracker application, which requires users to submit a one-time password (OTP) from the Google Authenticator application.
- *Logging in with Google*—Most users these days have user accounts on websites like Google, Facebook, GitHub, and many others. The ability for users to use these existing accounts to access an application, such as Course Tracker, provides an added convenience, as it does not require the user to go through the

lengthy user registration and account activation process in third-party applications. In the Course Tracker application, you'll let the users log in with their Google account.

NOTE In this chapter, we intend to show you how to implement several advanced security features that are often used in enterprise or production applications. Thus, in this chapter, you'll see a lot of code examples and comparatively fewer theoretical explanations. Further, as some of these techniques are lengthy, at times we'll refer you to the book's GitHub repository for the relevant code snippets.

6.1 Enabling HTTPS in a Spring Boot application

In modern-day applications, it is a common practice to serve the users through HTTPS instead of the HTTP protocol. HTTPS is the HTTP with TLS encryption. With HTTPS, the HTTP request and response are encrypted and are more safe and secure. It is relatively easy to enable HTTPS in a Spring Boot application. Let's explore this in the next technique.

6.1.1 Technique: Enabling HTTPS in a Spring Boot application

In this technique, we'll show how to enable HTTPS support in a Spring Boot application.

Problem

HTTPS provides better security for a Web application. You need to enable HTTPS in the Course Tracker application.

Solution

Enabling HTTPS in a Spring Boot application is a two-step process. First, you need to obtain a TLS certificate, then you need to configure the certificate in your Spring Boot application. A TLS certificate contains information, including the public and private keys of the certificate owner. These details serve two purposes: encrypting the data and providing identity assurance of the certificate owner. For the first step, you can obtain a certificate in two ways. You can obtain it via a trusted certificate authority (CA), such as Verisign, Entrust, or Let's Encrypt or by generating a self-signed certificate via utilities like `keytool` or `openssl`. For a production application, it is always recommended to use a certificate obtained from a trusted CA. For demonstration purposes, we'll generate a self-signed certificate using the JDK's `keytool` utility. You can refer to the GitHub wiki (see http://mng.bz/q2pJ) for the steps for generating a self-signed certificate.

> **Source code**
>
> To begin this technique, you can use the base version of the Spring Boot project used in this technique, which is available at http://mng.bz/7WAe. The final version of this Spring Boot project is available at http://mng.bz/mxM4.

Once you have the certificate, you can proceed with the HTTPS configuration in the Spring Boot application. The first step is to place the keystore file (which contains the certificate) inside the Spring Boot application. We'll keep the file inside a folder called keystore in the src\main\resources folder. The next step is to configure the Spring Boot application to use the provided keystore and then enable HTTPS.

Next, to enable the HTTPS in the Spring Boot application, let's open the application.properties (or application.yml) file and define the properties, as shown in the following listing.

Listing 6.1 HTTPS properties

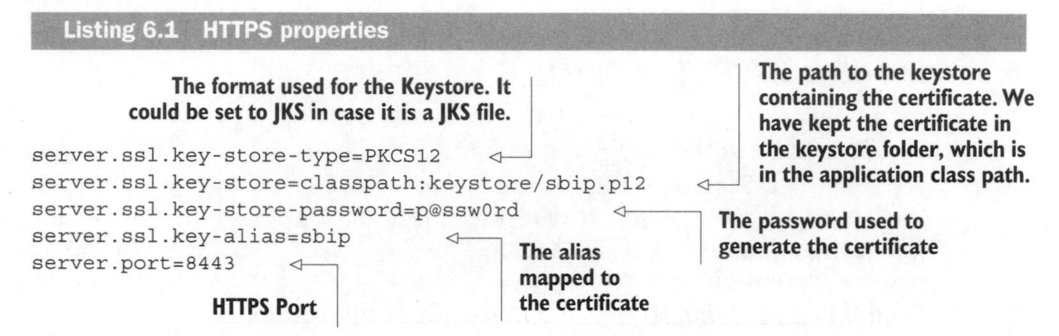

The format used for the Keystore. It could be set to JKS in case it is a JKS file.
The path to the keystore containing the certificate. We have kept the certificate in the keystore folder, which is in the application class path.
server.ssl.key-store-type=PKCS12
server.ssl.key-store=classpath:keystore/sbip.p12
server.ssl.key-store-password=p@ssw0rd
server.ssl.key-alias=sbip
server.port=8443
The password used to generate the certificate
The alias mapped to the certificate
HTTPS Port

The next change we'll implement is enforcing HTTPS for every request. This can be done in the `SecurityConfiguration` class that extends the `WebSecurityConfigurerAdapter` class (we introduced this Spring Security class in chapter 5). The following listing shows the changes.

Listing 6.2 Updated SecurityConfiguration class

```
@Configuration
public class SecurityConfiguration extends WebSecurityConfigurerAdapter {

       @Override
    protected void configure(HttpSecurity http) throws Exception {
        http.requiresChannel().anyRequest().requiresSecure()
        .and()
        .authorizeRequests().antMatchers("/login").permitAll()
        .anyRequest().authenticated().and().formLogin().loginPage("/login");
    }


    @Override
    protected void configure(AuthenticationManagerBuilder auth) throws
➥ Exception {
        auth.inMemoryAuthentication().passwordEncoder(passwordEncoder())
   .withUser("
➥ user")
                .password(passwordEncoder().encode("pass")).roles("USER");
    }

    @Override
    public void configure(WebSecurity web) throws Exception {
```

```
        web.ignoring().antMatchers("/webjars/**", "/images/*", "/css/*",
➥ "/h2-console/**");
    }

    @Bean
    public PasswordEncoder passwordEncoder() {
        return new BCryptPasswordEncoder();
    }
}
```

In listing 6.2, the bold code snippet indicates that all requests need to be secure (i.e., over HTTPS). You can start the application and access the login page by accessing https://localhost:8443/login URL. Notice that we are using the `HTTPS` protocol and associated port `8443` instead of the default HTTP port `8080`.

Now that we've implemented HTTPS, and the application blocks all HTTP requests, we need to redirect all traffic to `HTTPS` automatically. In the application.properties file, you've already configured the HTTPS configuration (through the `server.port =8443` property). Thus, you won't be able to configure HTTP anymore through properties configuration, as Spring Boot supports only one of the protocol configurations at a time in the application.properties file.

We'll configure the HTTP connector for the Tomcat server programmatically, so all incoming HTTP requests can be automatically redirected to HTTPS. The following lisitng shows the code snippet added in the `CourseTrackerSpringBootApplication` class.

Listing 6.3 Configuration redirect HTTP request to HTTPS

```
@Bean
public ServletWebServerFactory servletContainer() {
    TomcatServletWebServerFactory tomcat = new
➥ TomcatServletWebServerFactory() {
        @Override
        protected void postProcessContext(Context context) {
            SecurityConstraint securityConstraint = new
➥ SecurityConstraint();
            securityConstraint.setUserConstraint("CONFIDENTIAL");
            SecurityCollection collection = new SecurityCollection();

            collection.addPattern("/*");
            securityConstraint.addCollection(collection);
            context.addConstraint(securityConstraint);
        }
    };
    tomcat.addAdditionalTomcatConnectors(redirectConnector());
    return tomcat;
}

private Connector redirectConnector() {
    Connector connector = new
➥ Connector("org.apache.coyote.http11.Http11NioProtocol");
    connector.setScheme("http");
```

We have provided the pattern of /* to include all incoming requests.

```
        connector.setPort(8080);
        connector.setRedirectPort(8443);
        return connector;
}
```

Default HTTP port is set to 8080, and the redirect port is configured to HTTPS port 8443.

In listing 6.3, you've made the following changes:

- Defined the `TomcatServletWebServerFactory` class, created the security constraint, and included it in the context
- Defined the redirect connector that redirects `HTTP` requests at 8080 requests to `HTTPS` port 8443

Restart the application and access the http://localhost:8080/login URL. You'll notice you are automatically redirected to the https://localhost:8443/login URL.

DISCUSSION

In any production-grade application, it is always recommended to use HTTPS over HTTP. In HTTP the request and response are transferred in plain-text mode, and your application is vulnerable to exposing sensitive application information. For example, imagine that your social account password or credit card details are transferred in plain text and can be accessed by malicious users.

HTTPS encrypts the request and response and prevents exposing the application data in transit. Thus, applications using HTTPS are trustworthy to the users. Besides, it provides security to both application users and application owners.

Spring Boot provides built-in support to configure HTTPS, and in this technique, you've explored how easily you can configure it in a Spring Boot application. You've also learned how to block the HTTP requests using Spring Security and implemented auto redirection of HTTP requests to HTTPS.

You may notice that the HTTPS URL of the Course Tracker Spring Boot application shows a *Not secure* message in the browser. This is due to the use of a self-signed certificate we are using in our example. Self-signed certificates are not trusted by browsers, as these can be generated by anyone and do not have any credibility. However, self-signed certificates are useful for development and demonstration purposes. In a production application, you must use certificates issued from a trusted CA.

In this technique, we've shown you how to enable HTTPS in the Spring Boot application. In a production or enterprise setup, it is a common practice to use load balancers that frontend the Spring Boot applications. Typically, the HTTPS is managed in the load balancer layer—not in the Spring Boot application. The demonstrated technique is useful if you don't use a load balancer or would like to enable HTTPS in the Spring Boot application as a last resort or as a quick hack in an internal company project.

6.2 Securing secrets in Spring Cloud Vault

Managing application secrets is one of the key challenges for any application, and Spring Boot applications are no exception. An application can contain verities of secrets, such as passwords, API Keys, TLS certificates, and encryption keys to name a few. Exposing these secrets to malicious actors can cause catastrophic damage to an application. For instance, imagine the consequences if the database password of a banking application is exposed to malicious users.

Spring Boot allows you to manage the application properties (including secrets) through the application.properties (or the application.yml) file for a smooth application configuration. Although this approach is developer-friendly, it can leave room for developers to accidentally place secrets in plain text and expose them to the outside. It is a common occurrence that developers accidentally check-in secrets in public repositories and compromise overall application security. For instance, in the previous technique, you stored the keystore password in the application.properties file.

In this section, we'll introduce you to HashiCorp's Vault (https://www.vaultproject.io/). It is a popular tool that allows you to manage the secrets of an application securely and efficiently. You'll also explore how to integrate Vault into a Spring Boot project and manage the application secrets in the vault. Before we start discussing Vault concepts, let's first use it in the next technique and then provide a discussion on it.

> **A note on HashiCorp Vault**
> HashiCorp Vault provides plenty of configurations and options to manage and use the vault. Some of these configurations include configuring the vault persistence storage, cloud integration, dynamic secret generation, and others. It is beyond the scope of this text to provide in-depth coverage on this topic. In this section, we aim to show how to configure a basic vault and use it in a Spring Boot application. For further details on various vault features, refer to the documentation at https://www.vaultproject.io/docs.

6.2.1 *Technique: Managing application secrets with HashiCorp Vault in a Spring Boot application*

In this technique, we'll demonstrate how to manage application secrets (e.g., passwords, API keys, etc.) with HashiCorp Vault in a Spring Boot application.

PROBLEM

Your application contains sensitive application information, such as database passwords or external API keys. You need to secure those with HashiCorp Vault.

SOLUTION

With this technique, we'll demonstrate storing application secrets in the Hashicorp Vault and using the secrets in a Spring Boot application. Presently, in the Course Tracker application, we are storing the keystore password as plain text in the application.properties file. We'll externalize this secret to the vault and make the necessary configuration changes in the application to refer it from the vault.

> **Source code**
> To begin this technique, you can use the base version of the Spring Boot project used in this technique, which is available at http://mng.bz/5KVa. The final version of this Spring Boot project is available at http://mng.bz/6ZxA.

Before we proceed with this technique, you'll need to set up the vault server and configure it to store your secrets. You can refer to http://mng.bz/oagp for setting this up in your machine.

Next, let's perform the pom.xml changes to include the Spring Cloud config support in the Course Tracker application. The following listing shows the updated pom.xml changes.

Listing 6.4 Updated pom.xml

```
<?xml version="1.0" encoding="UTF-8"?>
<project xmlns="http://maven.apache.org/POM/4.0.0"
    xmlns:xsi="http://www.w3.org/2001/XMLSchema-instance"
    xsi:schemaLocation="http://maven.apache.org/POM/4.0.0
➥ https://maven.apache.org/xsd/maven-4.0.0.xsd">
    <modelVersion>4.0.0</modelVersion>
    <parent>
        <groupId>org.springframework.boot</groupId>
        <artifactId>spring-boot-starter-parent</artifactId>
        <version>2.6.3</version>
        <relativePath /> <!-- lookup parent from repository -->
    </parent>
    <groupId>com.manning.sbip.ch06</groupId>
    <artifactId>course-tracker-implementing-vault-final</artifactId>
    <version>1.0.0</version>
    <name>course-tracker-implementing-vault-final</name>
    <description>Spring Boot application for Chapter 06</description>

    <properties>
        <java.version>17</java.version>
        <spring-cloud.version>2021.0.0</spring-cloud.version>
    </properties>

    <dependencies>
        // additional configurations
        <dependency>
            <groupId>org.springframework.cloud</groupId>
            <artifactId>spring-cloud-starter-vault-config</artifactId>
        </dependency>
    </dependencies>

    <dependencyManagement>
        <dependencies>
            <dependency>
                <groupId>org.springframework.cloud</groupId>
                <artifactId>spring-cloud-dependencies</artifactId>
```

```
                <version>${spring-cloud.version}</version>
                <type>pom</type>
                <scope>import</scope>
            </dependency>
        </dependencies>
    </dependencyManagement>
    // additional configurations
</project>
```

Next, let's provide the vault configuration in the application.properties file, as shown in the following listing.

Listing 6.5 Application.properties changes

```
spring.cloud.vault.token=s.YGgzy5qOtEf4d6XoOi6qqQGL
spring.cloud.vault.authentication=token
spring.cloud.vault.host=localhost
spring.cloud.vault.port=8200
spring.cloud.vault.scheme=http
spring.config.import=vault://secret/coursetracker
spring.application.name=coursetracker

server.ssl.key-store-password=${keystore}
```

Spring configuration to refer to the secret/coursetracker in the vault

Replace the server.ssl.key-store-password=p@ssw0rd property with this configuration.

Let's discuss the changes made in listing 6.5:

1. We included the initial root token obtained while initializing the vault. The token value for your configuration will be different. This token is required for the Course Tracker application to authenticate itself to the vault.
2. We used the authentication mode as a token. Vault supports several other authentication modes.
3. We supplied the vault host, port, and scheme. We are using HTTP, as we have configured the Vault to run with HTTP. This is solely to keep the example simple, and in a production application you should always use the HTTPS scheme.
4. We provided the secret configuration. Note that we used the `secret/coursetracker` in the Vault to store the keystore password. We also provided the application name as `coursetracker`.
5. We replaced the keystore password with the vault key, which is configured as a `keystore` in the vault.

You can start the application and access the https://localhost:8443 URL. You'll find the application is running as usual.

Discussion

With this technique, you've explored using the Hashicorp Vault to store application secrets and using it in a Spring Boot application. Hashicorp Vault is a powerful and feature-rich vault that is flexible and allows you to configure the vault per your requirements.

Figure 6.1 shows the interaction between the user, Spring Boot application, and vault:

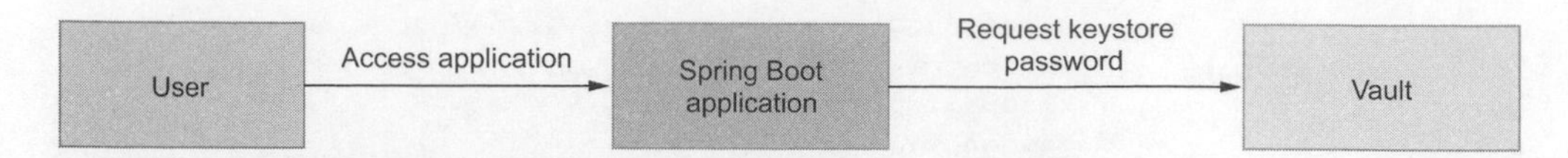

Figure 6.1 Interaction between user, Spring Boot application, and Hashicorp Vault

With this technique, we've placed the initial root token in the application.properties file. Vault generates this token when you initialize the vault with the `vault operator init` command. In a production application, you should refer to it from an environment variable or use some other means to supply it to the application. We are using HTTP to communicate with the vault, which can compromise secrets. It is recommended to configure HTTPS to use the vault in a production application.

6.3 Implementing user registration

Registering and managing users is one of the key features of a Web application. In this section, we'll discuss how we can create new users in the Course Tracker application. Let's implement this in the next technique.

6.3.1 Technique: Implementing user registration with Spring Security in a Spring Boot application

In this technique, we will discuss implementing user registration in a Spring Boot application.

PROBLEM

You need to implement a user registration module in the Course Tracker application. The new user details should be persisted in the application, and the user should be able to log in to the application.

SOLUTION

Before we deep dive into the actual implementation of the user registration, let's provide an outline of the changes you'll perform in the existing Course Tracker application:

- Defining a user registration HTML page (`add-user.html`) to capture the new user details.
- Creating a `UserDto` data transfer object (DTO) class that captures the details submitted through the HTML page.
- Defining the `ApplicationUser` domain entity class that represents the user in the Course Tracker application. Note that `UserDto` class represents the data captured in the HTML page and might contain additional parameters, which might not be required to be part of actual `ApplicationUser` details (e.g., the `ConfirmPassword` field in the `UserDto` class).
- Creating the associated service implementations and Spring Data repositories.

> **Source code**
> To begin this technique, you can use the base version of the Spring Boot project used in this technique, which is available at http://mng.bz/nYa2. The final version of this Spring Boot project is available at http://mng.bz/vo04.

To add a new user, let's begin by defining a user registration page. You can find the HTML page at http://mng.bz/4jrj.

This user registration page is similar to the previous HTML pages you've used earlier. It has an HTML form that allows users to enter basic user details and register themselves in the application. Let's now add a Java POJO class that captures these details. The following listing shows the `UserDto` class, which captures the user data entered by the user on the registration page.

Listing 6.6 The UserDto class

```
package com.manning.sbip.ch06.dto;

import javax.validation.constraints.*;

@Data
@NoArgsConstructor
@AllArgsConstructor
public class UserDto {

    @NotEmpty(message="Enter your firstname")
    private String firstName;

    @NotEmpty(message="Enter your lastname")
    private String lastName;
    @NotEmpty(message="Enter a username")

    private String username;
    @NotEmpty(message="Enter an email")
    @Email(message="Email is not valid")
    private String email;

    @NotEmpty(message="Enter a password")
    private String password;

    @NotEmpty(message="Confirm your password")
    private String confirmPassword;

    // Getter, Setter, and Constructors omitted
}
```

The `UserDto` is a plain Java class containing fields that are the same as the registration page with `javax.validation.constraints` annotations that are used to perform the validations. Note that you've named this class `UserDto`. This is because it is transferring the data from the HTML page to the controller. Typically, you need to have a different user class that represents the actual user in the application. For instance, you might have additional details in the UserDto class that might not be useful to store for the actual user. For instance, in the example in listing 6.6, you have the password and confirmPassword fields, which are required to ensure the passwords provided are the same. However, for the actual application entity, using only the password field is enough. The following listing shows the ApplicationUser class.

Listing 6.7 ApplicationUser Java class

```
package com.manning.sbip.ch06.model;

import javax.persistence.*;

@Data
@Entity
@Table(name = "CT_USERS")
@NoArgsConstructor
public class ApplicationUser {

    @Id
    @GeneratedValue(strategy = GenerationType.IDENTITY)
    private Long id;

    private String firstName;
    private String lastName;
    private String username;
    private String email;
    private String password;

    // Getter, Setter, and Constructors omitted
}
```

This class is a JPA entity, and you are using a custom table named CT_USERS to store application user details. It is a common practice to append the acronym of the application module (e.g., CT for the CourseTracker application) in the table name. The following listing shows the table details located in src\main\resources\script.ddl file.

Listing 6.8 The CT_USERS table DDL

```
create table CT_USERS (
    id BIGINT NOT NULL auto_increment,
    first_name varchar(50),
    last_name varchar(50),
    email varchar(50),
    username varchar(50),
    password varchar(100),
    PRIMARY KEY (id)
);
```

Let's define the UserRepository interface that lets us manage the ApplicationUser details in the application, as shown in the following listing.

Listing 6.9 UserRepository interface

```
package com.manning.sbip.ch06.repository;

//imports

@Repository
public interface UserRepository extends CrudRepository<ApplicationUser,
➥ Long> {

    ApplicationUser findByUsername(String username);
}
```

Listing 6.9 defines a custom method that lets us find the `ApplicationUser` based on the supplied `username`. In chapter 3, we discussed in detail how Spring Data uses these custom methods and retrieves data from the database. Next, let's define a `UserService` interface that provides the operations you can perform to maintain the users in the application, as shown in the following listing.

Listing 6.10 The UserService interface

```
package com.manning.sbip.ch06.service;

//imports

public interface UserService {
    ApplicationUser createUser(UserDto userDto);          // Create a new user in the application.
    ApplicationUser findByUsername(String username);      // Finds a user from the supplied username
}
```

In listing 6.10, you've defined two operations:

- The `createUser(..)` method, which lets you create a new user.
- The `findByUsername(..)` method, which finds the user from the supplied username.

The following listing provides an implementation to this interface.

Listing 6.11 The default implementation of the UserService interface

```
package com.manning.sbip.ch06.service.impl;

//imports

@Service
public class DefaultUserService implements UserService {

    @Autowired
    private UserRepository userRepository;

    @Autowired
    private PasswordEncoder passwordEncoder;
```

```
    public ApplicationUser createUser(UserDto userDto) {
        ApplicationUser applicationUser = new ApplicationUser();
        applicationUser.setFirstName(userDto.getFirstName());
        applicationUser.setLastName(userDto.getLastName());
        applicationUser.setEmail(userDto.getEmail());
        applicationUser.setUserName(userDto.getUsername());
        applicationUser.setPassword(passwordEncoder.encode(userDto.getPass-
     word()));

        return userRepository.save(applicationUser);
    }

    public ApplicationUser findByUsername(String username) {
        return userRepository.findByUsername(username);
    }
}
```

Maps the UserDto details captured from the HTML page to the actual ApplicationUser instance that is persisted into the database. Notice the use of a password encoder that encodes the plain-text password into an encoded password.

In listing 6.11, you've implemented the `createUser(..)` method. You created an instance of the `applicationUser` and populated the object using the details from the `userDto` object. You then saved the application object details in the `CT_USERS` table using the `userRepository`. Notice that you've used the password encoder to encode the password so that the encoded password is stored in the database table.

You've also provided an implementation of the `findByUsername(..)` method, which finds the `ApplicationUser` using the supplied username. You'll see the use of this method while we implement our custom `UserDetailsService` to load data from the `CT_USERS` table.

If you recall from chapter 5, the `UserDetailsService` interface provides a bridge between the custom identity store and Spring Security user management. The next thing you'll do is provide an implementation of the `UserDetailsService`, as shown in the following listing.

Listing 6.12 UserDetailsService implementation

```
package com.manning.sbip.ch06.service.impl;

//import

@Service
public class CustomUserDetailsService implements UserDetailsService {

    @Autowired
    private UserService userService;

    public UserDetails loadUserByUsername(String username) throws
➥ UsernameNotFoundException {

        ApplicationUser applicationUser =
➥ userService.findByUsername(username);
        if(applicationUser == null) {
```

```
            throw new UsernameNotFoundException("User with username
➥ "+username+" does not exists");
        }
        UserDetails userDetails  =
➥ User.withUsername(username).password(applicationUser.getPassword()).roles
➥ ("USER").disabled(false).build();     <---
return userDetails;
    }
}
```

We are returning a Spring Security UserDetails instance created from the custom ApplicationUser class.

With this technique, you are using a custom table (i.e., `CT_USERS`) to manage the users. Thus, you need to provide a mapping between your custom user details and the Spring Security user.

In the `CustomUserDetailsService` class, you use the `UserService` implementation to find the `ApplicationUser` instance from the `CT_USERS` table. If no such user exists, you return a `UsernameNotFoundException` exception. However, if there is a user with the supplied username, you map the `ApplicationUser` instance to Spring Security `UserDetails`.

Let's now add a Spring controller that manages the user registration. The following listing shows this.

Listing 6.13 RegistrationController

```
package com.manning.sbip.ch06.controller;

//imports

@Controller
public class RegistrationController {

    @Autowired
    private UserService userService;
    @GetMapping("/adduser")
    public String register(Model model) {     <---
        model.addAttribute("user", new UserDto());
        return "add-user";
    }

    @PostMapping("/adduser")
    public String register(@Valid @ModelAttribute("user") UserDto userDto,
➥ BindingResult result) {     <---
        if(result.hasErrors()) {
            return "add-user";
        }
        userService.createUser(userDto);
        return "redirect:adduser?success";
    }
}
```

The HTTP GET mapping that returns the caller to the add-user.html page. We also add an empty instance of the UserDto class that is used to bind the data entered into the HTML page.

The HTTP POST mapping that performs the user registration. In the UserDto class, you've used validation (using annotations such as @NotEmpty) to ensure that the UserDto fields are not empty. Thus, we check if the BindingResult has any error.

In the listing, you added two endpoints: the `adduser` HTTP GET endpoint, which returns the `add-user.html` page and the `adduser` HTTP POST endpoint, which checks if the UserDto object is valid and all necessary details are provided. This endpoint is the one bound in the submit attribute of the add-user.html page. If it is invalid, you return to the add-user.html page with the list of errors. If it is valid, the user is created in the CT_USERS table.

Let's now handle the user login failure in the LoginController class. As we discussed in chapter 5, this controller displays the login page to the user. Let's add a new HTTP GET endpoint login-error that displays a login error message to the user in case of an unsuccessful login. The following listing shows the updated LoginController class.

Listing 6.14 The login controller

```
package com.manning.sbip.ch06.controller;

//imports

@Controller
public class LoginController {

    @GetMapping("/login")
    public String login() {
        return "login";
    }

    @GetMapping("/login-error")
    public String loginError(Model model) {
        model.addAttribute("loginError", true);
        return "login";
    }
}
```

For login error, this endpoint is invoked. It set the loginError flag to true and based on this the login page displays the login error issue to the user. Notice that you are using Spring MVC's model instance to transport the loginError attribute to the login.html page.

The last change you'll perform is updating the SecurityConfiguration class. The listing 6.15 shows the updated class.

Listing 6.15 The SecurityConfiguration class

```
package com.manning.sbip.ch06.security;
//imports

@Configuration
public class SecurityConfiguration extends WebSecurityConfigurerAdapter {

    @Override
    protected void configure(HttpSecurity http) throws Exception {
        http.authorizeRequests()
        .antMatchers("/adduser", "/login", "/login-error").permitAll()
        .anyRequest().authenticated()
    .and()
    .formLogin().loginPage("/login").failureUrl("/login-error");
    }
```

```
    @Override
    public void configure(WebSecurity web) throws Exception {
        web.ignoring().antMatchers("/webjars/**", "/images/*", "/css/*");
    }

    @Bean
    public PasswordEncoder passwordEncoder() {
        return new BCryptPasswordEncoder();
    }
}
```

We made the following changes in this class:

- We added the `login-error` endpoint to the list of endpoints accessible without any authentication.
- We added the login `failureUrl` to the `login-error` endpoint to redirect the user to relogin for an unsuccessful login. Spring Security internally redirects the users to the `login-error` endpoint in case of a login failure.
- We defined the `BCryptPasswordEncoder` to encode the password. Recall that, in the `DefaultUserService` class, you've used this encoder to encode the passwords before storing them in the database.

You can start the application, access the http://localhost:8080 URL, and click on the Register menu to add a new user. You'll see the user registration page, as shown in figure 6.2.

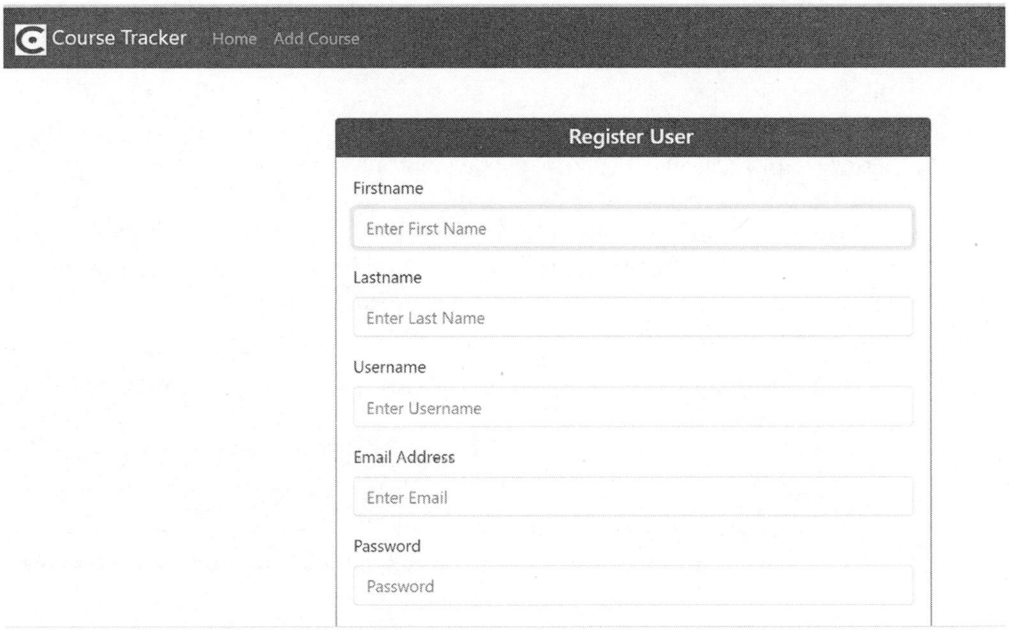

Figure 6.2 User registration page. This page contains basic user details, which are saved into the CT_USERS table.

Once you fill in the details and click on Sign Up, you'll see a successful user registration message and a link for login. At this stage, if you query to the `CT_USERS` table in the `h2-console`, you'll notice a new user is created, and the password is stored in an encoded text.

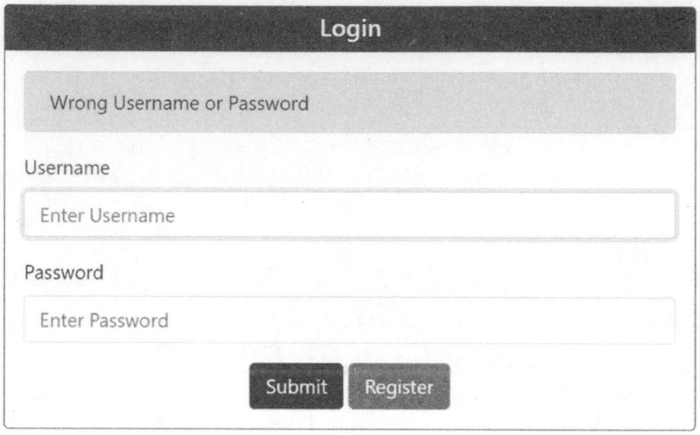

Figure 6.3 User login failed. The user is presented with an error message for invalid credentials.

If you click on the sign in link, you'll be redirected to the login page. You can log in with your username and password. If the login is successful, you'll be redirected to the index page, containing the list of available courses. For an unsuccessful login, you'll notice an error message, as shown in figure 6.3. Notice that this error page is the one appearing when the `loginError` is set to `true`.

DISCUSSION

With this technique, you've implemented a user registration module in the Course Tracker application. The Course Tracker application is now able to register new users, and the newly created users can log in with their credentials.

You've introduced a few components in the application to enable the user registration capability in the application. Notice that in this technique, we've used a handful of already-discussed technical concepts to implement this feature. Let's recap the major changes we've made in this technique:

- Introducing a user registration HTML page and the associated `RegistrationController`.
- Inducting the `UserDto` and `ApplicationUser`. The `UserDto` class transfers data from the HTML page to the controller. The `ApplicationUser` class represents the users in the application.
- Creating a new `UserRepository` service and the corresponding `UserService` class to perform operations on the `User` class.
- Providing an implementation of the `UserDetailsService` and changing the `SecurityConfiguration` and `LoginController` classes to additionally handle login failures.

Although this user registration module works fine, a few additional validations need to be handled. For instance, you need to ensure that the `Password` and `Confirm-Password` filed data is the same. The email address and username values also need to be unique across the application. Further, there is no password policy implemented, and most production applications should have a defined password policy (e.g., minimum password length, usage of special characters, etc.). We leave these activities as an exercise for the reader. You can refer to section 2.5 in chapter 2 for more information about implementing these features.

6.4 Implementing email verification at user registration

In the previous section, while registering a user, you collected the user email address. On the registration page, you enforced email validation that ensures the user is providing a structurally valid email address. However, you haven't validated whether the provided email address exists or if it belongs to the user. Validating user email is an important action performed by most Web applications. There are several reasons for this:

- You are validating that the user is who they are claiming to be and not impersonating anyone else.
- The user is not an internet bot (http://mng.bz/KxG0) but a legitimate user that wants to register to the application.
- A valid email is also useful to inform the user of various marketing, promotions, and product offerings.

Let's demonstrate how to validate the user email address by sending a verification link to the provided email address. We'll discuss this in the next technique.

6.4.1 Technique: Validating user email addresses in a Spring Boot application

In this technique, we'll demonstrate how to validate a user email address while registering a new user in a Spring Boot application.

Problem

While registering a new user, you need to validate the user email address by sending a verification link to the supplied email address.

Solution

With this technique, you'll learn how to validate a user email address in a Spring Boot application. You'll do this by sending a verification link to the user's email address. Until the user verifies their email address through the verification link, the associated user account will be disabled. Once the user confirms the email address by clicking the verification link, the user account is activated.

Source code

To begin this technique, you can use the base version of the Spring Boot project used in this technique, which is available at http://mng.bz/QW9v. The final version of this Spring Boot project is available at http://mng.bz/XWla.

Let's begin by providing a high-level outline of the changes you'll be performing in this technique.

A user registers to the course application by creating a new user account. The Course Tracker application successfully records the user details in the `CT_USERS` table. However, it marks the user account as disabled, as the user email ID is not yet verified. As part of the registration process, the Course Tracker application sends an email to the registered email ID with a verification link to activate the account. If the user attempts to access the account before activation, they are redirected to an error page, which asks the user to activate the account. After successful verification, the account is activated in the application, and the user can log in.

NOTE In this example, we've used Gmail as the preferred email server for demonstration purposes. You can use other email service providers as well as your custom email server. If you choose to do so, ensure to provide relevant email server configuration in place of Gmail. You'll see how to configure these details in listing 6.17.

Let's now begin with the necessary code changes to implement this feature. The first change you need to make is adding the `spring-boot-starter-mail` dependency in the application's pom.xml file. This dependency contains necessary libraries, which allow you to send an email to the user's email address. The following listing shows the dependency.

Listing 6.16 The spring-boot-starter-mail dependency

```
<dependency>
    <groupId>org.springframework.boot</groupId>
    <artifactId>spring-boot-starter-mail</artifactId>
</dependency>
```

Let's also update the application.properties file to provide the email server details that should be used to send the email. In this demonstration, we'll use Gmail as our email server. You can use any other email server (e.g., Outlook or your custom email server configuration). If you use an email server other than Gmail, ensure that you provide the necessary configurations. The following listing shows the Gmail email server configuration in the application.properties file.

Listing 6.17 Updated application.properties file with Gmail email server configuration

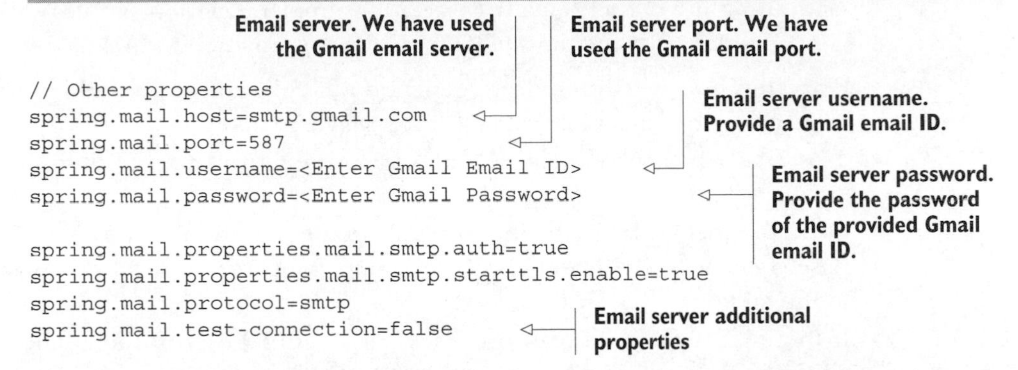
Email server. We have used the Gmail email server.
Email server port. We have used the Gmail email port.
Email server username. Provide a Gmail email ID.
Email server password. Provide the password of the provided Gmail email ID.
Email server additional properties

```
// Other properties
spring.mail.host=smtp.gmail.com
spring.mail.port=587
spring.mail.username=<Enter Gmail Email ID>
spring.mail.password=<Enter Gmail Password>

spring.mail.properties.mail.smtp.auth=true
spring.mail.properties.mail.smtp.starttls.enable=true
spring.mail.protocol=smtp
spring.mail.test-connection=false
```

In the listing 6.17, you've provided the Gmail email server configuration. By default, Gmail does not allow sending emails from less secure applications. The Course Tracker is treated as a less secure application by Gmail. Thus, you need to enable the Less Secure App Access option in your Gmail account security settings.

> **NOTE** In listing 6.17, you included the Gmail username and password in the application.properties file. The application.properties file is part of your application codebase and eventually moved to the source code repository. *It is strongly discouraged to configure any type of application secrets in the application.properties (or application.yml) file*, as doing so risks exposing the secrets to a wider audience. Imagine you pushed the configurations with the email address and password to a public repository in GitHub, and it is forked by other users. Your credentials will sprawl to all these forked repositories, and let others gain access to your email account. A better alternative is to use solutions, such as a vault, to keep application secrets, which we have discussed in one of the previous techniques.

The next change you need to make in the `ApplicationUser` class is ensuring whether the user account is verified. Add a new `boolean` variable named `verified` and the associated getter/setter methods in the `ApplicationUser` class.

Since we are changing the entity class, we need to change the `CT_USERS` table as well to add the new column verified. The following listing shows this.

Listing 6.18 The updated CT_USERS table with verified column

```
create table CT_USERS (
    id BIGINT NOT NULL auto_increment,
    first_name varchar(50),
    last_name varchar(50),
    email varchar(50),
    username varchar(50),
    password varchar(100),
    verified smallint(1),
    PRIMARY KEY (id)
);
```

With this technique, you are attempting to validate the newly registered user by sending an activation link to their email. To keep this implementation simple, we'll use a Base64 encoded UUID as the unique ID for a given username. It works as follows:

- Once the user is registered, we generate a UUID, and store it along with the user's username in a table called `CT_EMAIL_VERIFICATIONS`.
- This UUID is Base64 encoded and sent to the user as part of their activation email.
- Once the user clicks on the link available in the activation email, we retrieve the Base64 encoded UUID value, decode it, and compare it against the stored value in the table.
- If there is a match, we record the user as a verified user in the application by updating the verified flag in the `CT_USERS` table to `true`.

Let's define the `EmailVerification` entity class that contains the `verificationId` and the `username` of the users, as shown in the following listing.

Listing 6.19 EmailVerification POJO class

```
package com.manning.sbip.ch04.model;

//imports

@Entity
@Table(name = "CT_EMAIL_VERIFICATIONS")
public class EmailVerification {
    @Id
    @GeneratedValue(generator = "UUID_GENERATOR")
    @GenericGenerator(name = "UUID_GENERATOR", strategy =
     "org.hibernate.id.UUIDGenerator")
    private String verificationId;          <-- The UUID-based verification ID
    private String username;        <-- The username of the registered user
}
```

Let's define the `CT_EMAIL_VERIFICATIONS` table that stores the verification ID and username, as shown in listing 6.20. You can append this table DDL in the script.ddl file located in the src\main\resources folder. This table contains the binding between usernames and their validation identifiers.

Listing 6.20 CT_EMAIL_VERIFICATIONS table

```
create table CT_EMAIL_VERIFICATIONS (
    verification_id varchar(50),
    username varchar(50),
    PRIMARY KEY (verification_id)
);
```

Let us now define a Spring service class that manages the `EmailVerfication` entity services. The following listing shows the `EmailVerificationService` class.

Listing 6.21 The EmailVerificationService class

```
package com.manning.sbip.ch04.service;

//imports
@Service
public class EmailVerificationService {

    private final EmailVerificationRepository repository;

    @Autowired
    public EmailVerificationService(EmailVerificationRepository repository) {
        this.repository = repository;
    }
    public String generateVerification(String username) {              ◁ Generates a verification ID for a supplied username
        if (!repository.existsByUsername(username)) {
            EmailVerification verification = new
➥ EmailVerification(username);
            verification = repository.save(verification);
            return verification.getVerificationId();
        }
        return getVerificationIdByUsername(username);
    }

    public String getVerificationIdByUsername(String username) {        ◁ Provides the verification ID for a supplied username
        EmailVerification verification =
➥ repository.findByUsername(username);
        if(verification != null) {
            return verification.getVerificationId();
        }
        return null;
    }

    public String getUsernameForVerificationId(String verificationId) { ◁ Provides the username for a supplied verification ID
        Optional<EmailVerification> verification =
➥ repository.findById(verificationId);
        if(verification.isPresent()) {
            return verification.get().getUsername();
        }
        return null;
    }
}
```

Let's now shift our focus to generating the verification email when a new user registers in the application. You'll leverage Spring's `ApplicationEvent` and `ApplicationListener` for this purpose. The `ApplicationEvent` class represents an event in the application. The `ApplicationListener` class allows you to listen to the published events and perform some action once the events are emitted.

With this technique, you'll generate a `UserRegistrationEvent` whenever a new user is created in the application. Then, you'll define an `EmailVerificationListener` that listens to this event and allows you to compose and send an email with the verification link.

You might wonder whether we could send the email in the `RegistrationController` class itself while registering the user. The benefit of using Spring's `ApplicationEvent` is that it allows you to decouple the email-sending activity from the actual user registration process. The usage of this observer pattern is generally a best practice, especially in distributed microservices scenarios. Refer to http://mng.bz/y4jd for the `UserRegistrationEvent` class. The following listing shows the `EmailVerificationListener` class.

Listing 6.22 EmailVerificationListener class

```
package com.manning.sbip.ch06.listener;

//imports

@Service
public class EmailVerificationListener implements
➥ ApplicationListener<UserRegistrationEvent> {

    @Autowired
    private final JavaMailSender mailSender;

    @Autowired
    private final EmailVerificationService verificationService;

    public void onApplicationEvent(UserRegistrationEvent event) {
         ApplicationUser user = event.getUser();
        String username = user.getUsername();
        String verificationId =
➥ verificationService.generateVerification(username);
        String email = event.getUser().getEmail();

        SimpleMailMessage message = new SimpleMailMessage();
        message.setSubject("Course Tracker Account Verification");
        message.setText(getText(user, verificationId));
        message.setTo(email);
        mailSender.send(message);
    }

    private String getText(ApplicationUser user, String verificationId) {
        String encodedVerificationId = new
➥ []String(Base64.getEncoder().encode(verificationId.getBytes()));
StringBuffer buffer = new StringBuffer();
buffer.append("Dear ").append(user.getFirstName()).append("
➥ ").append(user.getLastName()).append(",").append(System.lineSeparator()
➥ ).append(System.lineSeparator());
buffer.append("Your account has been successfully created in the Course
➥ Tracker application. ");

buffer.append("Activate your account by clicking the following link:
➥ http://localhost:8080/verify/email?id=").append(encodedVerificationId);
buffer.append(System.lineSeparator()).append(System.lineSeparator());
```

```
buffer.append("Regards,").append(System.lineSeparator()).append("Course
➥ Tracker Team");
return buffer.toString();
    }
}
```

In the `EmailVerificationListener` class, upon receiving a `UserRegistrationEvent` (which is created at the time of user registration in the `RegistrationController`) you retrieve the `username` and use the `EmailVerificationSevice` to generate the verification ID. You then create an instance of Spring's `SimpleMailMessage` class and compose the email message. Finally, you send the email with the verification link to the configured email ID.

Note

Notice that, by default, the event publisher and listener are executed by the same thread. Thus, the user registration is not completed unless the event listener sends the email. If you need to handle the email generation and sending as an asynchronous task, you can use Spring's `SimpleApplicationEventMulticaster`. The following listing shows this configuration.

Listing 6.23 SimpleApplicationEventMulticaster bean definition

```
package com.manning.sbip.ch06.config;

// imports

@Configuration
public class EventConfiguration {

    @Bean(name = "applicationEventMulticaster")
    public ApplicationEventMulticaster
            simpleApplicationEventMulticaster() {
        SimpleApplicationEventMulticaster eventMulticaster = new
➥   SimpleApplicationEventMulticaster();

        eventMulticaster.setTaskExecutor(new SimpleAsyncTaskExecutor());
        return eventMulticaster;
    }
}
```

In listing 6.23, you've defined an instance of `SimpleApplicationEventMulticaster` and provided it with an instance of `SimpleAsyncTaskExecutor` that handles the published event asynchronously.

Let's now define the `EmailVerificationController` class that is invoked once the user clicks on the verification link, as shown in the following listing.

Listing 6.24 The EmailVerificationController class

```
package com.manning.sbip.ch04.controller;

//imports

@Controller
public class EmailVerificationController {

    @Autowired
    private EmailVerificationService verificationService;
    @Autowired
    private UserService userService;

    @GetMapping("/verify/email")
    public String verifyEmail(@RequestParam String id) {
        byte[] actualId = Base64.getDecoder().decode(id.getBytes());
       String username =
➥ verificationService.getUsernameForVerificationId(new String(actualId));
       if(username != null) {
            ApplicationUser user = userService.findByUsername(username);
            user.setVerified(true);
            userService.save(user);
            return "redirect:/login-verified";
        }
        return "redirect:/login-error";
    }
}
```

In listing 6.24, you first retrieve the verificationId and find the associated username. If there is a user found against the username, you load the user and update the account as verified. Otherwise, the user is redirected to a login error page. Let's explore the changes you need to perform in the SecurityConfiguration class, as shown in the following listing.

Listing 6.25 The SecurityConfiguration class

```
package com.manning.sbip.ch06.security;

//import

@Configuration
public class SecurityConfiguration extends WebSecurityConfigurerAdapter {

    @Autowired
    private CustomAuthenticationFailureHandler
➥ customAuthenticationFailureHandler;

    @Override
    protected void configure(HttpSecurity http) throws Exception {

       http.requiresChannel().anyRequest().requiresSecure()
       .and()
```

```
        .antMatchers("/adduser", "/login", "/login-error", "/login-
➥ verified", "/login-disabled", "/verify/email").permitAll()
        .anyRequest().authenticated()
        .and()
        .formLogin().loginPage("/login").failureHandler(customAuthentication-
      Failure
➥ Handler);
    }

    // Additional code
}
```

In listing 6.25, you've made the following changes:

- Allowing the "/adduser", /login", /login-error", /login-verified", /login-disabled", and "/verify/email" endpoints to be accessed without any form of authentication. This is obvious, as these endpoints deal with actions that either allow a user to log in or a new user register to the application.
- Leveraging Spring Security's AuthenticationFailureHandler interface to provide a custom failure handler implementation that handles login failure. Recall in previous techniques, you had used a failureUrl to forward the request to a failure page. The AuthenticationFailureHandler implementation provides better control, as you can place additional logic on what needs to be done in case of a login failure.

Let's define the CustomAuthenticationFailureHandler class, as shown in the following listing.

Listing 6.26 CustomAuthenticationFailureHandler class

```
package com.manning.sbip.ch06.handler;

import org.springframework.security.authentication.DisabledException;
//Other imports

@Service
public class CustomAuthenticationFailureHandler implements
➥ AuthenticationFailureHandler {

    private DefaultRedirectStrategy defaultRedirectStrategy = new
➥ DefaultRedirectStrategy();

    public void onAuthenticationFailure(HttpServletRequest request,
➥ HttpServletResponse response, AuthenticationException exception) throws
➥ IOException, ServletException {

        if(exception instanceof DisabledException) {
            defaultRedirectStrategy.sendRedirect(request, response,
➥ "/login-disabled");
            return;
        }
```

```
        defaultRedirectStrategy.sendRedirect(request, response, "/login-
➥ error");
    }
}
```

In case of an authentication failure, Spring Security throws the actual exception that indicates the type of authentication failure. Using this technique, there could be a situation in which a user can attempt to access their account without activating it. However, the user account is disabled in the application, unless the account is activated through the activation link. Spring Security automatically throws a `DisabledException`, indicating that the user account is disabled. If that happens, we redirect the user to the `/login-disabled` endpoint. You've used Spring's `DefaultRedirectStrategy` class to redirect the response to the appropriate endpoint.

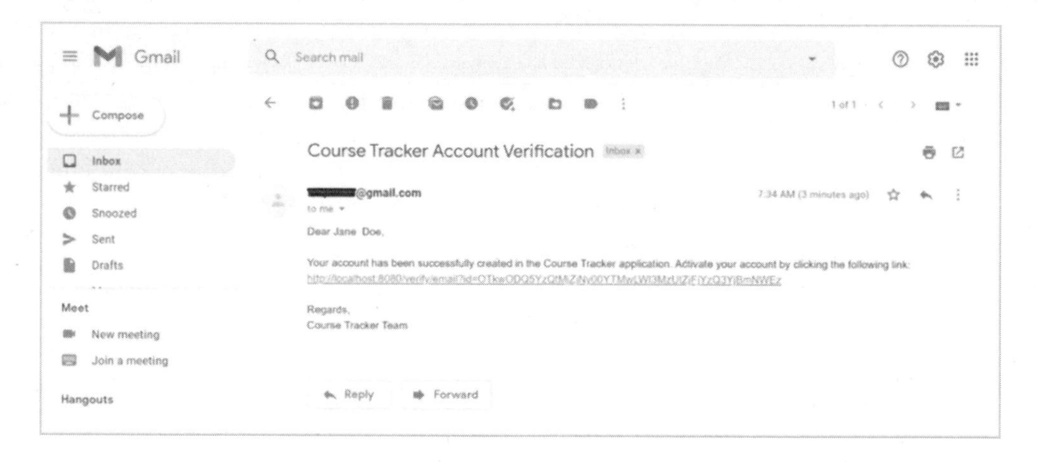

Figure 6.4 Account verification email for a newly registered user in the Course Tracker application

If you start the application and create a new user using the `Register` option, you'll notice that an email is sent out to the configured email, as shown in figure 6.4. You need to ensure that you have an active internet connection for the application to send the email. After successful registration of the user, you'll receive an email similar to the one shown in the figure.

DISCUSSION

With this technique, we've learned how to effectively implement a user registration through a verification email. We've leveraged some of the core Spring features, such as Spring event management, and used Spring Security features, such as `AuthenticationFailureHandler`. We recommend you try out the following scenarios:

- Register a new user in the application. Upon successful registration, you'll notice there is an activation link.

- At this stage, if you try to login into the application, you'll receive an error message stating the user account is disabled.
- Once you click on the activation link, you'll notice a confirmation message that the account is activated, and you can log in.
- At this stage, you can try login with valid credentials, and you will be redirected to the index page that shows the available courses.

Using this technique, you've shared a verification link in the user email and asked the users to click on it to activate the user account. You can further enhance this implementation by imposing an expiry time on the verification link. This will prevent any malicious actor from sending randomly generated IDs and misusing the application. We leave this task as an exercise for the reader. If you decide to proceed with this task, consider including an expiry time in the verification link and storing this expiry time in the `CT_EMAIL_VERIFICATIONS` table. Once the user clicks on the verification link, along with the verification token, validate whether the expiry time provided in the link is still valid. Further, clear the verification link details from the `CT_EMAIL_VERIFICATIONS` table for any misuse.

6.5 Controlling multiple incorrect login attempts

In many applications, it is a common practice to temporarily suspend user access if there are multiple incorrect login attempts. This is one of the security measures taken by applications to prevent brute-force attacks on an application to gain unauthorized access to the application. In this section, you'll learn how to implement this in the Course Tracker application.

6.5.1 Technique: Controlling multiple incorrect login attempts in a Spring Boot application

In this technique, we'll demonstrate how to temporarily block a user account in case there are multiple incorrect login attempts.

Problem

In the current implementation, the Course Tracker application allows users to make any number of login attempts. You need to temporarily suspend user access for 24 hours if the user performs three incorrect login attempts.

Solution

Spring Security publishes several Spring events while it performs various security activities in an application. For instance, once a user is successfully authenticated Spring Security publishes `AuthenticationSuccessEvent`. Similarly, Spring publishes `AuthenticationFailureBadCredentialsEvent` if the authentication fails due to invalid credentials. There are many such events published by Spring Security that applications can listen to and perform necessary actions.

Let's provide an outline on how we can use the aforementioned Spring Security events to suspend user access if there are multiple incorrect login attempts:

- We will define a cache that maintains the number of failed login attempts.
- We will use the aforementioned events to manage the user status in the cache.
- We will block the user access if the cache indicates the user has more than three failed login attempts.
- The cache will automatically expire the user login attempts status after 24 hours.

> **Source code**
> To begin this technique, you can use the base version of the Spring Boot project used in this technique, which is available at http://mng.bz/M2GB. The final version of this Spring Boot project is available at http://mng.bz/aD2m.

We'll use the Google Guava library to implement the cache. Therefore, let's add the Guava dependency in the pom.xml file, as shown in the following listing.

Listing 6.27 Guava dependency

```
<dependency>
    <groupId>com.google.guava</groupId>
    <artifactId>guava</artifactId>
    <version>30.1.1-jre</version>
</dependency>
```

Next, let's define the `LoginAttemptService` class that defines the cache and a few useful methods to maintain the cache and user login attempt status. The following listing shows this in action.

Listing 6.28 LoginAttemptService class

```
package com.manning.sbip.ch06.service;

//imports

@Service
public class LoginAttemptService {

    private static final int MAX_ATTEMPTS_COUNT = 3;

    private LoadingCache<String, Integer> loginAttemptCache;

    public LoginAttemptService() {
        loginAttemptCache = CacheBuilder.newBuilder().expireAfterWrite(1,
➥ TimeUnit.DAYS)
                .build(new CacheLoader<String, Integer>() {
                    @Override
                    public Integer load(final String key) {
                        return 0;
                    }
                });
    }
```

In this cache, the String type represents a username, and the Integer type represents the failed login attempts.

Creates the cache and expires the cache contents after one day

```
    public void loginSuccess(String username) {
        loginAttemptCache.invalidate(username);
    }

    public void loginFailed(String username) {
        int failedAttemptCounter = 0;

        try {
            failedAttemptCounter = loginAttemptCache.get(username);
        }
        catch (ExecutionException e) {
            failedAttemptCounter = 0;
        }
        failedAttemptCounter++;
        loginAttemptCache.put(username, failedAttemptCounter);
    }
    public boolean isBlocked(String username) {
        try {
            return loginAttemptCache.get(username) >= MAX_ATTEMPTS_COUNT;
        }
        catch (ExecutionException e) {
            return false;
        }
    }
}
```

Increments the failed login attempt counter for the specified username

Indicates whether the user has exceeded the maximum number of allowed login attempts

We'll now define two event listeners: one that listens to the `AuthenticationFailureBadCredentialsEvent` and one that invokes the `LoginAttemptService` to update the cache with the failed login attempt count, as shown in the following listing.

Listing 6.29 AuthenticationFailureEventListener class

```
package com.manning.sbip.ch06.listener;

//imports

@Service
public class AuthenticationFailureEventListener implements
➥ ApplicationListener<AuthenticationFailureBadCredentialsEvent> {

    @Autowired
    private LoginAttemptService loginAttemptService;

    @Override
    public void onApplicationEvent(AuthenticationFailureBadCredentialsEvent
➥ authenticationFailureBadCredentialsEvent) {
        String username = (String)
➥ authenticationFailureBadCredentialsEvent.getAuthentication().getPrincipal
();
        loginAttemptService.loginFailed(username);
    }
}
```

Next, we'll define the `AuthenticationSuccessEventListener` class that listens to `AuthenticationSuccessEvent` and invalidate the cache for the user. The following listing shows this.

Listing 6.30 AuthenticationSuccessEventListener class

```
package com.manning.sbip.ch06.listener;

//imports

@Component
public class AuthenticationSuccessEventListener implements
➥ ApplicationListener<AuthenticationSuccessEvent> {

    @Autowired
    private LoginAttemptService loginAttemptService;

    @Override
    public void onApplicationEvent(AuthenticationSuccessEvent
➥ authenticationSuccessEvent) {
        User user = (User)
➥ authenticationSuccessEvent.getAuthentication().getPrincipal();
        loginAttemptService.loginSuccess(user.getUsername());
    }
}
```

In listing 6.30, we retrieve the username of the user from the `AuthenticationSuccess-Event` and invalidate the cache for the username. Thus, previous incorrect login attempts are removed from the cache, as the user logs in to the application successfully.

Next, we'll update the `CustomUserDetailsService` class to validate whether the user is blocked. Recall that the `isBlocked(..)` method from the `LoginAttemptService` class checks if the user has exceeded the maximum allowed incorrect login attempts, as shown in the following listing.

Listing 6.31 CustomUserDetailsService class

```
package com.manning.sbip.ch06.service.impl;

//imports

@Service
public class CustomUserDetailsService implements UserDetailsService {

    @Autowired
    private LoginAttemptService loginAttemptService;


    public UserDetails loadUserByUsername(String username) throws
➥ UsernameNotFoundException {
```

```
        if(loginAttemptService.isBlocked(username)) {
➥            throw new LockedException("User Account is Locked");
        }

        // other parts are omitted

    }
}
```

In listing 6.31, you are returning Spring Security's `LockedException` if the user account is blocked. This exception indicates there is an error in the login attempt, and the login has failed. Recall that we invoke the `CustomAuthenticationFailureHandler` to identify the login failure type and redirect the user to the appropriate login endpoint. Listing 6.32 shows the updated `CustomAuthenticationFailureHandler` class.

Listing 6.32 CustomAuthenticationFailureHandler class

```
package com.manning.sbip.ch06.handler;

//imports

@Service
public class CustomAuthenticationFailureHandler implements
➥ AuthenticationFailureHandler {

    private DefaultRedirectStrategy defaultRedirectStrategy = new
➥ DefaultRedirectStrategy();

    public void onAuthenticationFailure(HttpServletRequest request,
➥ HttpServletResponse response, AuthenticationException exception) throws
➥ IOException, ServletException {

        if(exception instanceof DisabledException) {
            defaultRedirectStrategy.sendRedirect(request, response,
➥ "/login-disabled");
            return;
        }
        if(exception.getCause() instanceof LockedException) {
            defaultRedirectStrategy.sendRedirect(request, response,
➥ "/login-locked");
            return;
        }
        defaultRedirectStrategy.sendRedirect(request, response, "/login-
➥ error");
    }
}
```

In listing 6.32, we modified the `CustomAuthenticationFailureHandler` already implemented in the previous technique with the addition of another redirect for `LockedException` instances. We redirected the user to the `login-locked` endpoint if there is a `LockedException`. Define the `login-locked` endpoint that redirects the user to the login page with an error message specifying the user account is locked. Listing 6.33 shows this endpoint defined in the `LoginController`.

Listing 6.33 The login-locked endpoint

```
@GetMapping("/login-locked")
    public String loginLocked(Model model) {
        model.addAttribute("loginLocked", true);
        return "login";
    }
```

You need to use the `loginLocked` flag in the `login.html` page to display the error message that the user account is locked. It is available at http://mng.bz/g4nv. Lastly, you need to permit this endpoint to be accessed without any authentication, as shown in listing 6.34.

Listing 6.34 Updated SecurityConfiguration

```
package com.manning.sbip.ch06.security;

//imports

@Configuration
public class SecurityConfiguration extends WebSecurityConfigurerAdapter {

    @Override
    protected void configure(HttpSecurity http) throws Exception {
        http.requiresChannel()
.anyRequest()
.requiresSecure()
.and()
.authorizeRequests()
               .antMatchers("/adduser", "/login", "/login-error", "/login-
➥ verified", "/login-disabled", "/verify/email", "/login-
➥ locked").permitAll()
.anyRequest().authenticated().and().formLogin().loginPage("/login").failure
➥ Handler(customAuthenticationFailureHandler);
    }

    // Other code snippets are omitted
}
```

In listing 6.34, we included the `login-locked` endpoint in the existing `antMatchers` list.

You can start the application and register and activate a new user, then try to make incorrect login attempts multiple times. After three failed login attempts, you'll find that the user account is suspended, and the following error is displayed, as shown in figure 6.5.

DISCUSSION

With this technique, you've learned how to temporarily suspend a user account if there are multiple incorrect login attempts. The key takeaway from this technique is

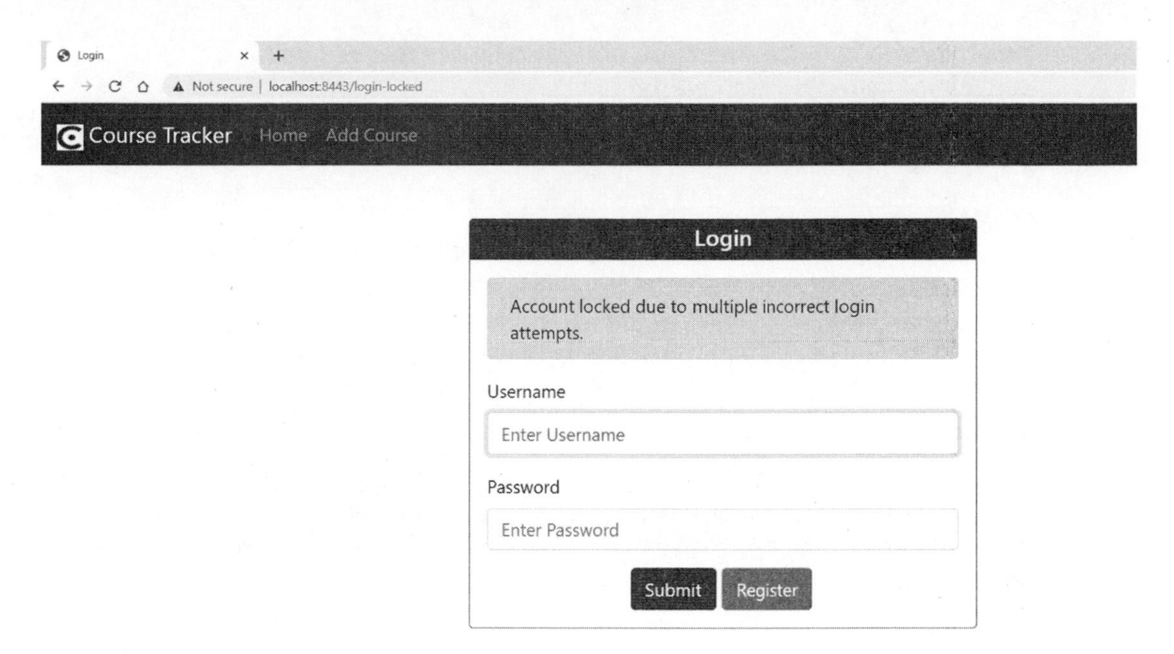

Figure 6.5 User account is locked due to multiple incorrect login attempts. The red tag appearing in the form here is the one showing when the loginLocked flag is set to true.

the use of Spring Security built-in security events to identify the user authentication status. Note that we use the cache to manage the user login attempt statistics. The cache automatically clears the login statistics after 24 hours and makes the user eligible for login.

6.6 Implementing a Remember Me feature

Although you'll make every effort to secure your application, you also need to be mindful of the user experience. If you make your application too secure that the users need to make a great deal of effort to access the application, it can easily discourage them from accessing the application. Thus, you need to maintain a careful balance between user experience and application security. For instance, many applications provide a `remember-me` feature that allows the application to remember the identity of the user between sessions. Spring Security supports this with an additional cookie to the user's browser, which is included in all subsequent requests to the server. In case the session cookie is expired, Spring uses the `remember-me` cookie to authenticate the user.

Spring Security provides two built-in approaches to implement `remember-me` services: a hash-based token approach and a persistent token approach. The first one stores user identity in a browser cookie, which makes it less secure. The persistent token approach stores the details in a database. Let's first implement the hash-based token approach in the Course Tracker application.

6.6.1 Technique: Enabling a Remember Me feature in a Spring Boot application with Spring Security

In this technique, we'll demonstrate how to implement the Remember Me feature in a Spring Boot-based Web application.

PROBLEM

For a better user experience, many applications provide a `remember-me` feature. You need to implement this feature in the Course Tracker application.

SOLUTION

Spring Security provides built-in support for the `remember-me` feature and provides sensible defaults for most of the configurations. To enable `remember-me`, you'll need to perform two changes in the application:

- Adding an HTML checkbox to the login page with the name `remember-me`. The checkbox name in the HTML page must be `remember-me`, as Spring Security checks the HTTP request to validate whether there is a parameter with this name.
- In the `SecurityConfiguration` class, you've to enable the `remember-me` configuration, so Spring Security can include necessary configurations.

> **Source code**
>
> To begin this technique, you can use the base version of the Spring Boot project used in this technique, which is available at http://mng.bz/Bx60. The final version of this Spring Boot project is available at http://mng.bz/doRN.

The following listing shows the changes in the `login.html` page.

Listing 6.35 The Login.html changes

```
<div class="form-group">
    <label for="password">Password</label>
    <input type="password" class="form-control" name="password"
➥ placeholder="Enter Password" required autofocus>
</div>
<div class="form-check">
    <input type="checkbox" class="form-check-input" name="remember-me">
    <label for="remember-me" class="form-check-label">Remember me</label>
</div>
<div class="text-center mt-1">
    <button type="submit" class="btn btn-dark">Submit</button>
    <a class="btn btn-success" href="#" th:href="@{/adduser}">Register</a>
</div>
```

You've added the checkbox to the login page. The key part here is that the input parameter name must be `remember-me`. Listing 6.36 shows the `SecurityConfiguraton` changes.

Listing 6.36 The SecurityConfiguraton class changes

```
@Override
protected void configure(HttpSecurity http) throws Exception {

    http.authorizeRequests()
    .antMatchers("/adduser", "/login", "/login-error", "/login-verified",
➥ "/login-disabled", "/verify/email").permitAll()
    .anyRequest().authenticated()
    .and()
    .formLogin().loginPage("/login").failureHandler(customAuthenticationFailure
➥ Handler)
    .and()
    .rememberMe().key("remember-me-key").rememberMeCookieName("course-
tracker-remember-me")
    .and()
    .logout().deleteCookies("course-tracker-remember-me");
}

@Override
protected UserDetailsService userDetailsService() {
  return this.customUserDetailsService;
}
```

In listing 6.36, we made two changes:

- Invoke the `rememberMe()` method in the `HttpSecurity` configuration for Spring Security to enable the Remember Me services. Further, you've customized the key and the cookie name, both of which are optional, and Spring provides default values as `remember-me` if you don't configure these parameters.
- We also need to ensure we override the `userDetailsService()` method and return the `UserDetailsService` implementation. This is needed, as `RememberMeServices` loads the `UserDetails` based on this implementation to load the user details and create the authentication instance.

If you start the application and attempt to log in, you'll find a new checkbox option for `remember-me`. If this is enabled, after successful login you'll find an additional cookie in your browser with the name `course-tracker-remember-me`.

DISCUSSION

Let's discuss how a hash-based token approach works. When the user ticks the checkbox in the login page while logging in to the application, Spring Security sends an additional cookie to the user browser, which is included in all subsequent requests to the server. Thus, even if the session cookie is expired, the `remember-me` cookie is available and not expired. The server can fetch the user details from the `remember-me` cookie and reauthenticate the user automatically.

If you inspect the `course-tracker-remember-me` cookie in your browser, you'll find it has lots of scrambled text. These are the Base64 encoded details Spring Security stores inside the cookie. The cookie has the details in the format shown in the following listing.

Listing 6.37 The hash-based token format

```
Base64(username:expirationTime:md5Hex(username:tokenExpiryTime:password:key))
```

Following are the details used in the token:

- `username`—As identifiable to the `UserDetailsService`.
- `expirationTime`—The date and time when the `remember-me` token expires, expressed in milliseconds. By default, it is set to two weeks.
- `md5Hex`—Calculates the MD5 hash of the `username`, `tokenExpiry`, `password`, and `key`. The generated hash value is represented in hexadecimal.
- `password`—That matches the one retrieved in the `UserDetails`.
- `key`—A private key to prevent modification of the `remember-me` token. By default, Spring Security generates the key if you haven't configured one. However, the drawback with this generated key is that if the application shuts down, then all `remember-me` cookies will be invalidated, as the key will be different after restarting the application. In our example, we've used the `remember-me-key` as the key name.

Although the hash-based `remember-me` token approach makes it a lot easier for a user to access the application, it has several shortcomings:

- If the `remember-me` cookie is stolen or accessed by malicious users, it can be used to gain unauthorized access to the application if the expiry time in the cookie is valid.
- Even if the cookie is expired, malicious users can use the details present in the cookie to gain access to the `key` and the `password` through brute force attacks. If the key or password is poorly chosen, malicious users can perform dictionary attacks (http://mng.bz/95Yl) to retrieve them.

The weakness of the hash-based `remember-me` token approach can be improved if it is used with two-factor authentication. With this, even if the `remember-me` cookie is compromised, the second level of login can prevent unauthorized access. Spring Security provides another alternative with a persistent token approach that uses a database table to store confidential information.

6.7 Implementing reCAPTCHA

CAPTCHA stands for *completely automated public Turing test to tell computers and humans apart*. It is a computer program or application that distinguishes human inputs from machine inputs as a measure to prevent bot spam. CAPTCHAs can be available in many formats. It could be as simple as clicking a checkbox or as complicated as clicking on certain image types or entering some text.

Although CAPTCHAs might be annoying to the users, it serves a purpose to protect the application. For instance, these days internet bots are used to spam applications a lot. In the Course Tracker application, internet bots may create fictitious users and exhaust the application resources resulting in a denial-of-service (DoS) attack. CAPTCHAs help applications prevent bot spamming to a certain degree.

There are several providers of CAPTCHA: reCAPTCHA (https://www.google.com/recaptcha/about/) from Google is a popular choice for many. HCAPTCHA (https://www.hcaptcha.com/) is another alternative. Let's secure the Course Tracker application registration page with Google's reCAPTCHA in the next technique.

6.7.1 Technique: Enabling Google reCAPTCHA in a Spring Boot application with Spring Security

In this technique, we'll demonstrate how to implement Google reCAPTCHA in a Spring Boot-based Web application.

Problem

Internet bot spamming is a growing concern for Web application owners, as it creates fictitious users and exhausts the application resources. You need to implement CAPTCHA to prevent bot spamming in the Course Tracker application.

Solution

Using this technique, you'll implement Google reCAPTCHA services at the time of user registration. This will ensure that only a human user can register successfully in the Course Tracker application. You'll find the steps to set up Google reCAPTCHA documented at http://mng.bz/en6V.

After this setup is done, you'll have two keys: the site key and the secret key. You'll need these keys in your Spring Boot application. The site key is to be specified on the HTML page, and the secret key is to be used to validate the CAPTCHA response captured from the user. You'll explore this shortly.

> **Source code**
>
> To begin this technique, you can use the base version of the Spring Boot project used throughout, which is available at http://mng.bz/p2eK. The final version of this Spring Boot project is available at http://mng.bz/OGOw.

The first change you'll need to make is to include the link for the CAPTCHA on the registration page. Add the following in the `add-user.html` page before the sign-up form group, as shown in the following listing.

Listing 6.38 Sitekey in the add-user.html page

```
// Additional Code
<div class="form-group">
 <label for="confirmPassword">Confirm Password</label>
 <input type="password" th:field="*{confirmPassword}" class="form-control"
➥ id="confirmPassword" placeholder="Confirm Password">
 <span th:if="${#fields.hasErrors('confirmPassword')}"
➥ th:errors="*{confirmPassword}" class="text-danger"></span>
```

```
</div>
<div class="g-recaptcha mb-2" data-sitekey="<Your Site Key>"></div>
<div class="form-group text-center">
    <input type="submit" class="btn btn-dark center" value="Sign Up" />
    <p>Already have an account? <a href="/login">Sign in</a></p>
</div>

// Additional Code
```

In listing 6.38, the highlighted code (in bold) enables the CAPTCHA verification checkbox on the user registration page. Further, add the following script tag inside the head section of the page, as shown in the following listing.

Listing 6.39 ReCAPTCHA API Script tag

```
<script src="https://www.google.com/recaptcha/api.js"></script>
```

The code snippet in the previous two listings enables the Google reCAPTCHA option on the registration page. Let's now define a reCAPTCHA verification service that validates the reCAPTCHA response from the user, as shown in the following listing.

Listing 6.40 Google reCAPTCHA verification service

This is the secret key defined in the application.properties file with the key captcha.secret.key. Secrets are placed in the application.properties only for demonstration purpose.

We are using the RestTemplate to validate the user response with Google. The RecaptchaDto contains the success (and errors, if any). In listing 6.42, you are using this RecaptchaDto POJO.

```
package com.manning.sbip.ch06.service.impl;

//imports

@Service
public class GoogleRecaptchaService {

    private static final String VERIFY_URL =
➥ "https://www.google.com/recaptcha/api/siteverify"
            + "?secret={secret}&remoteip={remoteip}&response={response}";
    private final RestTemplate restTemplate;

    @Value("${captcha.secret.key}")
    private String secretKey;

    public GoogleRecaptchaService(RestTemplate restTemplate) {
        this.restTemplate=restTemplate;
    }

    public RecaptchaDto verify(String ip, String recaptchaResponse) {
        Map<String, String> request = new HashMap<>();
        request.put("remoteip", ip);
        request.put("secret", secretKey);
        request.put("response", recaptchaResponse);
        ResponseEntity<Map> response =
➥ restTemplate.getForEntity(VERIFY_URL, Map.class, request);
```

```
        Map<String, Object> body = response.getBody();
        boolean success = (Boolean)body.get("success");
        RecaptchaDto recaptchaDto = new RecaptchaDto();
        recaptchaDto.setSuccess(success);
        if(!success) {
            recaptchaDto.setErrors((List)body.get("error-codes"));
        }
        return recaptchaDto;
    }
}
```

The code in the listing validates the user provided CAPTCHA response with the Google reCAPTCHA verification service hosted at https://www.google.com/recaptcha/api/siteverify. You've supplied your secret key, the server IP address (localhost in this example), and the CAPTCHA response. The secret is added in the application.properties with the key name `captcha.secret.key`. If these details are correct, you get a successful response. For failures, you get the list of error codes. For instance, for an incorrect response, the error code is `invalid-input-response`. We've also added a `RestTemplate` configuration to invoke the Google reCAPTCHA service, as shown in the following listing.

Listing 6.41 RestTemplate configuration

```
package com.manning.sbip.ch04.configuration;

//imports

@Configuration
public class CommonConfiguration {

    @Bean
    public RestTemplate restTemplate(RestTemplateBuilder
➥ restTemplateBuilder) {
        return restTemplateBuilder.build();
    }
}
```

The following listing shows the `RecaptchaDto` class that captures the CAPTCHA validation response.

Listing 6.42 ReCAPTCHADto class

```
package com.manning.sbip.ch04.dto;

import java.util.List;

public class RecaptchaDto {

    private boolean success;
    private List<String> errors;

    // Getter and Setters
}
```

In the listing, the success captures whether the user response is correct. The errors list stores the errors if there is a failure in validating the user provided CAPTCHA response.

In the RegistrationController class you need to validate that the user provided CAPTCHA response is valid. For a valid response, you continue and create the user in the application. Otherwise, an error message is shown to the user in the user registration page. The following listing shows the updated adduser endpoint.

Listing 6.43 Updated adduser endpoint

```
@PostMapping("/adduser")
public String register(@Valid @ModelAttribute("user") UserDto userDto,
➥ HttpServletRequest httpServletRequest, BindingResult result) {
    if(result.hasErrors()) {
        return "add-user";
    }
    String response = httpServletRequest.getParameter("g-recaptcha-
➥ response");
    if(response == null) {
        return "add-user";
    }

    String ip = httpServletRequest.getRemoteAddr();
    RecaptchaDto recaptchaDto = captchaService.verify(ip, response);
    if(!recaptchaDto.isSuccess()) {
        return "redirect:adduser?incorrectCAPTCHA";
    }

    ApplicationUser applicationUser = userService.createUser(userDto);
    if("Y".equalsIgnoreCase(emailVerification)) {
        eventPublisher.publishEvent(new
➥ UserRegistrationEvent(applicationUser));
        return "redirect:adduser?validate";
    }
    return "redirect:adduser?success";
}
```

The following statements validate whether the user has provided any response in the CAPTCHA checkbox in the user registration page. If not, we redirect them to the add-user.html page again.

If the user has provided a response in the CAPTCHA checkbox, we use the CAPTCHA service to validate with Google whether the response is correct. For incorrect response, the user is redirected to the CAPTCHA error page.

Let's start the application and browse to the Register option to add a new user. You'll be redirected to the user registration page and notice a CAPTCHA option above the Sign Up button. Fill in all the details and click on the I'm Not a Robot checkbox. You'll be presented with a graphic challenge that will ask you to select the tiles that belong to a specific category. Figure 6.6 shows the user registration page with a sample CAPTCHA. Note that the CAPTCHA images change each time you perform a user registration.

DISCUSSION

To be precise, this is not a Spring Boot or Spring Security technique, as we have not used any specific features from these technologies. However, in the era of machine learning and artificial intelligence, this is a useful feature to protect applications from internet bot spamming.

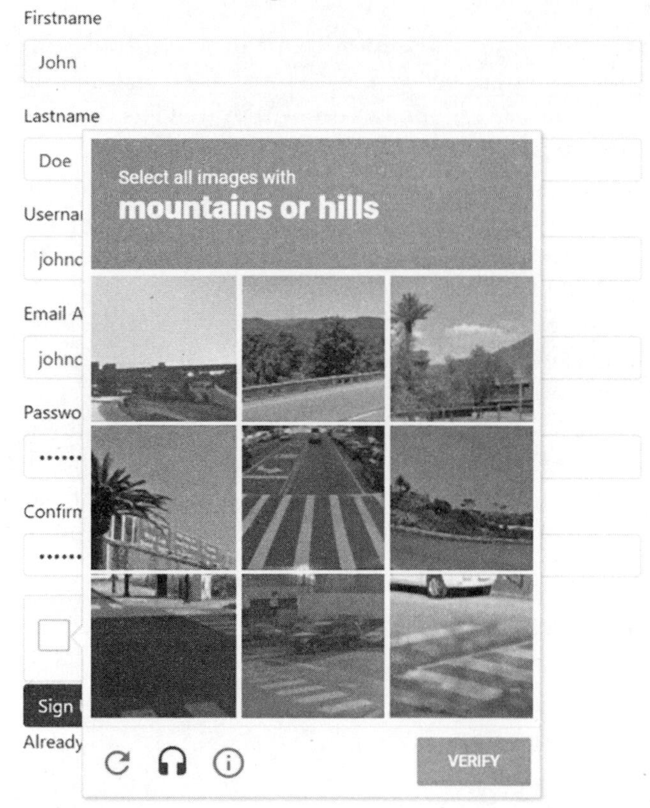

Figure 6.6 Google reCAPTCHA while performing user registration

There are several variations of CAPTCHA implementations these days. As the bots are getting smarter day by day, there is a growing need to improve the CAPTCHA technologies as well. Using this technique, we've implemented Google reCAPTCHA version 2, which is relatively old, and there are newer versions available as well.

Further, in this technique, we've used the CAPTCHA secret in the application .properties file. In a production application, use a safer solution, such as a vault.

Before we conclude this technique, I'll give a word of caution. As discussed previously, application security needs to be balanced against user experience. This applies to CAPTCHA-based application security as well. For instance, many applications only start displaying CAPTCHA if it detects multiple login failures. This is a balanced approach, as the application becomes suspicious against the repeated failed login attempts and automatically increases the application security by enabling additional security measures, such as CAPTCHA. We leave this as an exercise to the reader. As a hint, you can use a cache to store the login failure attempts and enable the CAPTCHA once there are three or more incorrect failure attempts.

6.8 Enabling two-factor authentication with Google Authenticator

Multi-factor authentication (MFA) is an authentication pattern that forces the users to undergo multiple authentication steps before the user is allowed to access the application. *Two-factor authentication* (or 2FA) is one variant of MFA that lets the user undergo two different levels of authentication steps.

Most Web applications use username- and password-based authentication to authenticate the application users. Although this authentication pattern works perfectly well in most circumstances, it may make the users vulnerable if the user's username and password are compromised. An additional level authentication with a different authentication mode ensures greater security to the users. For instance, along with the regular username and password, a random OTP is often used in the majority of the applications.

In this section, you'll learn to enable two-factor authentication in the Course Tracker application. You'll use the regular username and password as the first level of authentication. Next, you'll use an OTP as the second level of authentication. We'll use the Google Authenticator app to generate the OTP. Let's explore this in the next technique.

6.8.1 Technique: Enabling two-factor authentication in a Spring Boot application

In this section, we'll demonstrate how to implement two-factor authentication in a Spring Boot application.

PROBLEM

The Course Tracker application currently uses username- and password-based authentication. For better application security, you need to implement two-factor authentication in the application.

SOLUTION

In this technique, you'll use the Google Authenticator app to enable two-factor authentication in the Course Tracker application. You need to download this application on a smartphone from the Google Play store (http://mng.bz/YgBz) or Apple store (http://mng.bz/GGaD). This app will generate a time-based one-time password (TOTP), and we'll use this to perform the second level authentication. We'll provide a brief discussion on how the TOTP algorithm works in the discussion section.

> **Source code**
>
> To begin this technique, you can use the base version of the Spring Boot project used in this technique available at http://mng.bz/zQW1. The final version of this Spring Boot project is available at http://mng.bz/OwDJ.

You may notice that two-factor authentication is not a mandatory authentication strategy. Applications provide a choice to users of whether they would like to opt for this feature. In the Course Tracker application, we'll provide the users with the same choice. Following is the outline for implementing 2FA in the Course Tracker application:

1. The user registers, and the user account is created in the application.
2. Upon first logging in to the application, we'll ask the user whether they would like to enable 2FA. If they are not interested, they can skip and redirect to the application index page.
3. If the user opts for 2FA, we'll then generate a quick reference (QR) code and let the user scan the code in the Google Authenticator app on their smartphone.
4. Once the app configures the Course Tracker application, we'll ask the user to enter the OTP from the smartphone app on the 2FA registration page. This process completes the 2FA registration for the user. For all subsequent logins, the user needs to enter the OTP from the Google Authenticator app to proceed with application access.
5. If the user has not enabled 2FA at the time of registration, we'll prompt the user to enable 2FA on each successful login. Note that this is for demonstration purposes only. Most applications provide an option in their application security settings to the users to enable it at their convenience.

To start with, let's add the following dependency in the pom.xml file, as shown in the following listing.

Listing 6.44 Google Auth dependency

```
<dependency>
    <groupId>com.warrenstrange</groupId>
    <artifactId>googleauth</artifactId>
    <version>1.4.0</version>
</dependency>
```

The Google Auth dependency in the listing provides the necessary support to implement the TOTP-based 2FA in the application. You can refer to https://github.com/wstrange/GoogleAuth for further details on this library.

Next, while the user registers for 2FA, we share a QR code with the user. This QR code contains a secret that needs to be stored against the username for further usage. Let's define a Java POJO entity that allows us to capture these details and persist them into the `CT_TOTP_DETAILS` table. The following listing shows the `TotpDetails` class.

Listing 6.45 TOTP details

```
package com.manning.sbip.ch06.model;

// imports
```

```
@Entity
@Data
@NoArgsConstructor
@AllArgsConstructor
@Table(name = "CT_TOTP_DETAILS")
public class TotpDetails {

    @Id
    @GeneratedValue(strategy = GenerationType.IDENTITY)
    private long id;
    private String username;
    private String secret;

    public TotpDetails(String username, String secret) {
        this.username = username;
        this.secret = secret;
    }
}
```

The following listing shows the `CT_TOTP_DETAILS` table DDL located in the src/main/resources/script.ddl file.

Listing 6.46 CT_TOTP_DETAILS table DDL

```
create table CT_TOTP_DETAILS (
  id BIGINT NOT NULL auto_increment,
  secret    varchar(255),
  username    varchar(255),
  PRIMARY KEY (id)
);
```

Recall from the outline that after a successful login, we need to ask the user whether they would like to opt for 2FA. From the previous techniques, you have seen Spring Security provides an `AuthenticationSuccessHandler` interface you can implement to define post-successful login actions. Let's define the `DefaultAuthenticationSuccessHandler` class that implements the `AuthenticationSuccessHandler` interface, as shown in the following listing.

Listing 6.47 DefaultAuthenticationSuccessHandler class

```
package com.manning.sbip.ch06.service;

//imports

@Component
public class DefaultAuthenticationSuccessHandler implements
➥ AuthenticationSuccessHandler {

    private RedirectStrategy redirectStrategy = new
➥ DefaultRedirectStrategy();

    public void onAuthenticationSuccess(HttpServletRequest request,
➥ HttpServletResponse response, Authentication authentication) throws
```

```
➥ IOException, ServletException {
        if(isTotpAuthRequired(authentication)) {
            redirectStrategy.sendRedirect(request, response, "/totp-
➥ login");
        }
        else {
            redirectStrategy.sendRedirect(request, response, "/account");
        }
    }

    private boolean isTotpAuthRequired(Authentication authentication) {
        Set<String> authorities =
AuthorityUtils.authorityListToSet(authentication.getAuthorities());
        return authorities.contains("TOTP_AUTH_AUTHORITY");
    }
}
```

We'll discuss this snippet in greater detail later. Specifically, the TOTP_AUTH_AUTHORITY and its use.

In listing 6.47, you are validating whether the user has 2FA configured by checking whether the user has the role `TOTP_AUTH_AUTHORITY`; if the user has 2FA configured, you redirect the user to the `totp-login` endpoint. Otherwise, the user is redirected to the account endpoint. Note that `TOTP_AUTH_AUTHORITY` is a custom authority in the application that is assigned to the users enabled 2FA. You'll explore this shortly. The `totp-login` redirects the user to the 2FA login page that allows the user to enter the OTP from their Google Authenticator app. The `account` endpoint redirects the user to the 2FA setup page if the user has not configured 2FA already. The following listing shows the `AccountController` class.

Listing 6.48 AccountController class

```
package com.manning.sbip.ch06.controller;

//imports

@Controller
@RequiredArgsConstructor
public class AccountController {

    private final TotpService totpService;

    @GetMapping("/account")
    public String getAccount(Model model, @AuthenticationPrincipal
➥ CustomUser customUser) {
        if (customUser != null && !customUser.isTotpEnabled()) {
            model.addAttribute("totpEnabled", false);
            model.addAttribute("configureTotp", true);
        } else {
            model.addAttribute("totpEnabled", true);
        }
        return "account";
    }
```

This service class provides services to generate and validate TOTP for a user.

Redirects the user to the 2FA set up page. Sets the totpEnabled and configureTotp parameters used in the account.html page. The account.html page lets you enable 2FA.

This endpoint let the user set up 2FA. If the user does not have TOTP configured, it invokes the TOTP service and generates the QR code that lets the user configure the Course Tracker application in the Google Authenticator app.

```
    @GetMapping("/setup-totp")
    public String getGoogleAuthenticatorQrUrl(Model model,
➥ @AuthenticationPrincipal CustomUser customUser) {
        String username = customUser.getUsername();
        boolean isTotp = customUser.isTotpEnabled();

         if (!isTotp) {
            model.addAttribute("qrUrl",
➥ totpService.generateAuthenticationQrUrl(username));
            model.addAttribute("code", new TotpCode());
            return "account";
        }
        model.addAttribute("totpEnabled", true);
        return "account";
    }
    @PostMapping("/confirm-totp")
    public String confirmGoogleAuthenticatorSetup(Model model,
➥ @AuthenticationPrincipal CustomUser customUser,
            TotpCode totpCode) {
        boolean isTotp = customUser.isTotpEnabled();
        if (!isTotp) {
            try {
                totpService.enableTotpForUser(customUser.getUsername(),
➥ Integer.valueOf(totpCode.getCode()));
            } catch (InvalidVerificationCode ex) {
                model.addAttribute("totpEnabled",
  customUser.isTotpEnabled());
                model.addAttribute("confirmError", true);
                model.addAttribute("configureTotp", false);
                model.addAttribute("code", new TotpCode());
                return "account";
            }

            model.addAttribute("totpEnabled", true);
        }
        customUser.setTotpEnabled(true);
        return "redirect:/logout";
    }
}
```

This conditional branch happens when the QR code needs to be created. The TotpCode is used to capture the verification OTP in the account.html page.

This endpoint enables the TOTP for the user.

Next, let's define the TotpService class, as shown in the following listing.

Listing 6.49 TotpService

```
package com.manning.sbip.ch06.service;

//imports

@Service
public class TotpService {
```

```
    private final GoogleAuthenticator googleAuth = new
➥ GoogleAuthenticator();
    private final TotpRepository totpRepository;
    private final UserRepository userRepository;
    private static final String ISSUER = "CourseTracker";

    public TotpService(TotpRepository totpRepository, UserRepository
➥ userRepository) {
        this.totpRepository = totpRepository;
        this.userRepository = userRepository;
    }

    @Transactional
    public String generateAuthenticationQrUrl(String username){      <-- Generates the QR URL for the supplied username
        GoogleAuthenticatorKey authenticationKey =
➥ googleAuth.createCredentials();
        String secret = authenticationKey.getKey();
        totpRepository.deleteByUsername(username);
        totpRepository.save(new TotpDetails(username, secret));
        return GoogleAuthenticatorQRGenerator.getOtpAuthURL(ISSUER,
➥ username, authenticationKey);
    }

    public boolean isTotpEnabled(String userName) {
        return userRepository.findByUsername(userName).isTotpEnabled();
    }

    public void enableTotpForUser(String username, int code){        <-- Validates whether the supplied OTP is correct and valid and ensures that the user has configured 2FA
        if(!verifyCode(username, code)) {
            throw new InvalidVerificationCode("Invalid verification code");
        }

        User user = userRepository.findByUsername(username);
        user.setTotpEnabled(true);
        userRepository.save(user);
    }

    public boolean verifyCode(String userName, int verificationCode) {
        TotpDetails totpDetails = totpRepository.findByUsername(userName);
        return googleAuth.authorize(totpDetails.getSecret(),
➥ verificationCode);
    }
}
```

The `TotpService` class contains several useful methods related to 2FA. For instance, it contains the method for generating the QR code, enabling TOTP for users, or verifying the supplied verification code.

Next, let's perform the necessary changes to the `CustomUserDetailsService` class that assigns the `TOTP_AUTH_AUTHORITY` authority to users based on whether they have enabled 2FA, as shown in the listing 6.50.

Listing 6.50 The CustomUserDetailsService

```
package com.manning.sbip.ch06.service;

//imports

@Service
public class CustomUserDetailsService implements UserDetailsService {

    private UserRepository userRepository;

    @Autowired
    public CustomUserDetailsService(UserRepository userRepository) {
        this.userRepository = userRepository;
    }

    public UserDetails loadUserByUsername(String username) throws
➥ UsernameNotFoundException {
        User user = userRepository.findByUsername(username);
        if(user == null) {
            throw new UsernameNotFoundException(username);
        }
        SimpleGrantedAuthority simpleGrantedAuthority = null;
        if(user.isTotpEnabled()) {
            simpleGrantedAuthority = new
➥ SimpleGrantedAuthority("TOTP_AUTH_AUTHORITY");
        }
        else {
            simpleGrantedAuthority = new
➥ SimpleGrantedAuthority("ROLE_USER");
        }
        CustomUser customUser = new CustomUser(user.getUsername(),
➥ user.getPassword(), true, true, true, true,
➥ Arrays.asList(simpleGrantedAuthority));
        customUser.setTotpEnabled(user.isTotpEnabled());
        return customUser;
    }

}
```

In listing 6.50, if the user has configured TOTP, we assign the `TOTP_AUTH_AUTHORITY` authority to the user. Otherwise, we assign the `ROLE_USER` authority to the user.

Once the user has enabled the TOTP, for all subsequent logins, they need to enter the OTP, which the application verifies. You can complete this verification in several ways. For instance, you can include the OTP verification logic in the associated Spring controller and, based on the verification, redirect the user to the appropriate page.

However, we'll use a different technique. We'll define a custom filter that performs this validation and include this filter in the Spring Security filter chain in an appropriate position so that it gets invoked automatically by Spring Security. The following listing shows the `TotpAuthFilter` class.

Listing 6.51 TotpAuthFilter class

```
package com.manning.sbip.ch06.filter;

 //imports

@Component
public class TotpAuthFilter extends GenericFilterBean {

    private TotpService totpService;
    private static final String ON_SUCCESS_URL = "/index";
    private static final String ON_FAILURE_URL = "/totp-login-error";
    private final RedirectStrategy redirectStrategy = new
➥ DefaultRedirectStrategy();

    @Autowired
    public TotpAuthFilter(TotpService totpService) {
        this.totpService = totpService;
    }

    public void doFilter(ServletRequest request, ServletResponse response,
➥ FilterChain chain) throws IOException, ServletException {

        Authentication authentication =
➥ SecurityContextHolder.getContext().getAuthentication();
        String code = request.getParameter("totp_code");
        if(!requiresTotpAuthentication(authentication) || code == null) {
            chain.doFilter(request, response);
            return;
        }
        if(code != null && totpService.verifyCode(authentication.getName(),
➥ Integer.valueOf(code))) {
            Set<String> authorities =
➥ AuthorityUtils.authorityListToSet(authentication.getAuthorities());
            authorities.remove("TOTP_AUTH_AUTHORITY");
            authorities.add("ROLE_USER");
            authentication = new
➥ UsernamePasswordAuthenticationToken(authentication.getPrincipal(),
➥ authentication.getCredentials(), buildAuthorities(authorities));

      SecurityContextHolder.getContext().setAuthentication(authentication);
            redirectStrategy.sendRedirect((HttpServletRequest) request,
➥ (HttpServletResponse) response, ON_SUCCESS_URL);
        }
        else {
            redirectStrategy.sendRedirect((HttpServletRequest) request,
➥ (HttpServletResponse) response, ON_FAILURE_URL);
        }
    }

    private boolean requiresTotpAuthentication(Authentication
➥ authentication) {
        if (authentication == null) {
            return false;
        }
```

Implementation of the filter. If the user does not require 2FA, this filter is skipped, and the next filter on the filter chain is invoked. However, if 2FA is enabled, then the verification code supplied from the user is validated, and the user is assigned with the USER role.

```
        Set<String> authorities =
➥ AuthorityUtils.authorityListToSet(authentication.getAuthorities());
        boolean hasTotpAutheority =
➥ authorities.contains("TOTP_AUTH_AUTHORITY");
        return hasTotpAutheority && authentication.isAuthenticated();
    }

    private List<GrantedAuthority> buildAuthorities(Collection<String>
➥ authorities) {
        List<GrantedAuthority> authList = new ArrayList<GrantedAuthority>(1);
        for(String authority : authorities) {
            authList.add(new SimpleGrantedAuthority(authority));
        }
        return authList;
    }
}
```

Let's discuss the changes made in the listing:

1. We retrieved the authentication object from the `SecurityContextHolder` class and check if the user is authenticated and has `TOTP_AUTH_AUTHORITY` authority.
2. We validated the user-supplied OTP. If the OTP was not valid, we redirected the user to an error page.
3. If the OTP was valid, we revoked the `TOTP_AUTH_AUTHORITY` authority from the user and assign the `ROLE_USER`. We remove the `TOTP_AUTH_AUTHORITY` authority, as we only need it to enable TOTP. Once the user has enabled TOTP, we removed this and provided an ordinary role, such as `USER`.
4. We created a new `UsernamePasswordAuthenticationToken` token with the new role. As we are changing the user role, we built this token, and updated it in the `SecurityContextHolder`.
5. The user was redirected to the index page.

Next, let us make the necessary changes in the HTTP configuration in the `SecurityConfiguration` class to configure the `TotpAuthFilter`. The following listing shows this.

Listing 6.52 SecurityConfiguration

```
package com.manning.sbip.ch06.security;

//imports

@Configuration
public class SecurityConfiguration extends WebSecurityConfigurerAdapter {

    @Autowired
    private TotpAuthFilter totpAuthFilter;


    @Override
    protected void configure(HttpSecurity http) throws Exception {
```

```
        http.addFilterBefore(totpAuthFilter,
➥ UsernamePasswordAuthenticationFilter.class);

        http.authorizeRequests()
        .antMatchers("/adduser", "/login", "/login-error",  "/setup-totp",
➥ "/confirm-totp").permitAll()
        .antMatchers("/totp-login", "/totp-login-
➥ error").hasAuthority("TOTP_AUTH_AUTHORITY")
        .anyRequest().hasRole("USER").and()
        .formLogin().loginPage("/login")
        .successHandler(new
➥ DefaultAuthenticationSuccessHandler()).failureUrl("/login-error");
    }

    // Other code snippets
}
```

In listing 6.52, we added the `TotpAuthFilter` before the `UsernamePassword-AuthenticationFilter`. This ensures the `TotpAuthFilter` is part of the Spring Security filter chain and is invoked. Recall that the Spring Security filter chain has a list of filters that are invoked in sequence to perform the specific task the filter is assigned with. Further, we are also ensuring that the TOTP related endpoints are only accessed by the users with the `TOTP_AUTH_AUTHORITY` authority.

> **NOTE** As you may notice this technique involves a few code snippets, and we could not accommodate all the code examples, as it will take more pages. We suggest you refer to the completed version of the Spring Boot project in the GitHub repository for all code snippets. Only the important and relevant code snippets are provided in the technique.

You can start the application and register a new user. After login, you'll notice the page for 2FA activation shown in figure 6.7.

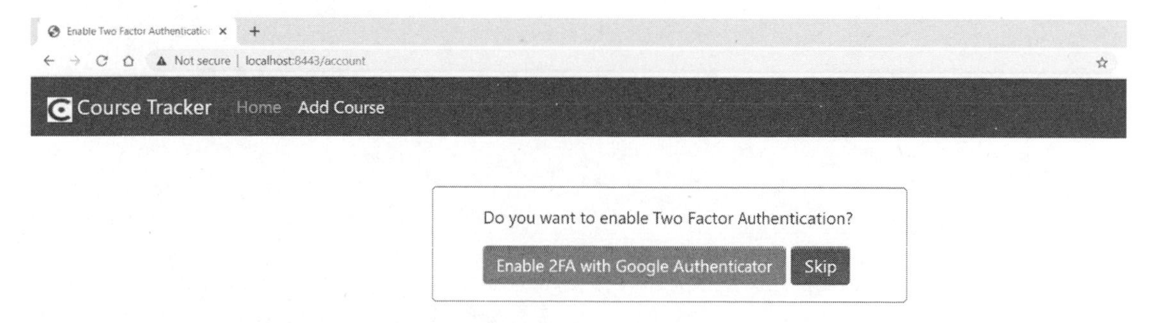

Figure 6.7 Option to enable 2FA with Google Authenticator

You can either opt for the 2FA or skip to the index page. Let's enable 2FA by clicking on the Enable 2FA with Google Authenticator button. Figure 6.8 shows the next page with the QR code.

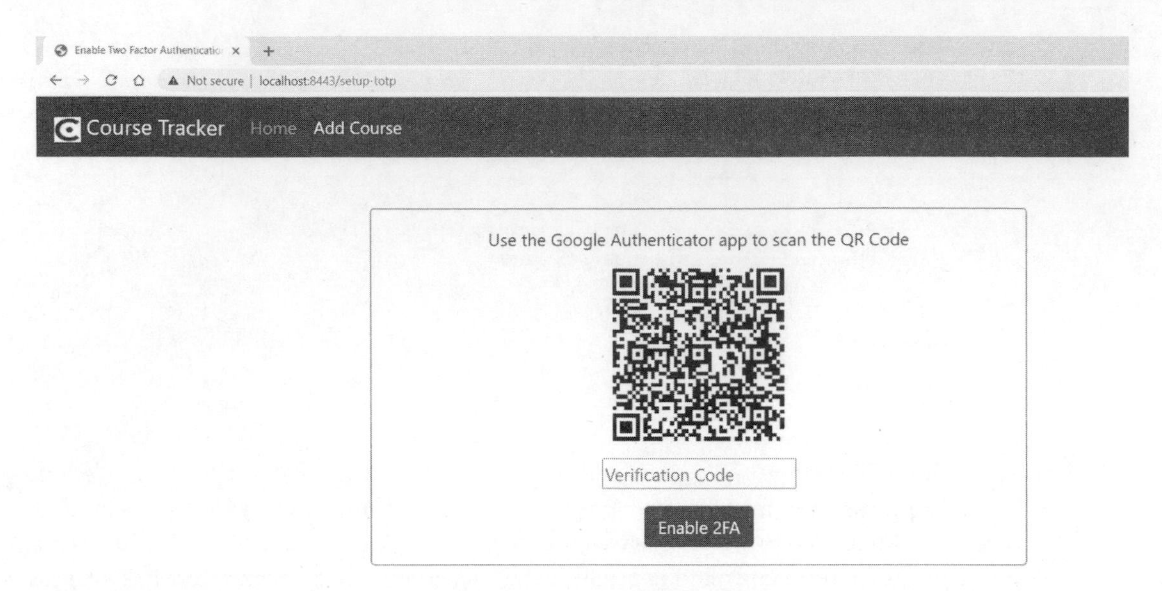

Figure 6.8 QR Code to register for 2FA in the Google Authenticator application. Once the user scans the QR code, they can see the verification code in the smartphone application.

Scan the QR code, as shown in the Google Authenticator code, for your application, and enter the verification code displayed in the app. Don't scan the QR code shown in the figure, as it won't work for you. You need to scan the QR code shown in the Course Tracker application to the smartphone application. You'll notice an entry in the smartphone application with a verification code. Enter this verification code in the text box, as shown in figure 6.8, and click Enable 2FA. For a successful verification code, the Course Tracker application redirects you to the login page. Log in again, and you'll be redirected to the following page to provide the OTP, as shown in figure 6.9.

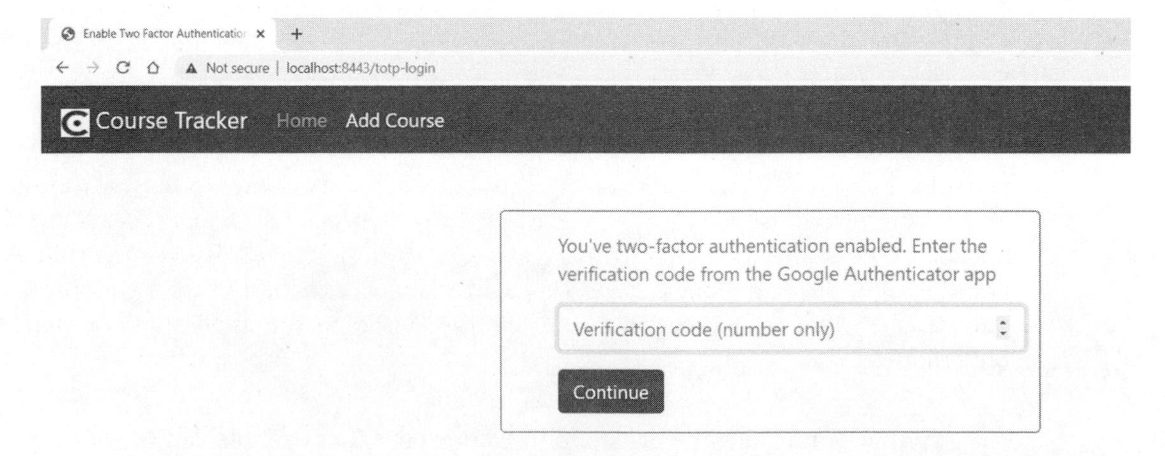

Figure 6.9 For regular logins, the user is prompted to enter the verification code from the Google Authenticator application.

Enter the OTP from the Google Authenticator app, and you'll be redirected to the application index page showing the list of courses. For every login, you need to provide the OTP to access the application.

DISCUSSION

Google Authenticator supports two types of OTP algorithms: a time-based OTP algorithm (TOTP) and an HMAC-based OTP algorithm (HOTP). Using this technique, we've shown how to implement TOTP-based 2FA with Spring Security in a Spring Boot application.

The way the TOTP algorithm works is relatively simple. In this algorithm, both the server (the Course Tracker application) and the client (the Google Authenticator app) use a common secret and the time to generate the OTP. Recall that once you enable the 2FA, the application provides a QR code for you to scan in your Google Authenticator application. The QR code transfers the secret key that is used by the Google Authenticator application to calculate the OTP. Both parties use the secret and the time (that's why it's called time-based OTP) to generate the OTP.

Using this technique, you've also learned to implement custom filters and inserted them into the Spring Security filter chain. For instance, another use case is suspending the user access for incorrect login attempts. The logic presented in listing 6.31 to validate whether the user account is blocked can be implemented through custom filters. You can define any number of custom filters to implement various business features. You've also seen how to define custom authorities and leverage in the application.

Another enhancement that can be performed is limiting the number of invalid guesses that can be entered on the `/confirm-totp` page. We leave this as an exercise for the reader.

6.9 Authentication with OAuth2

Previously, you learned several techniques for letting users log in to the Course Tracker application. We've implemented a user registration module that captures user details, performs email verification to let users activate their account, and, finally, logs in to the application. There is an alternative way to allow users access to your application without requiring them to register in the application.

These days many people have a user account on websites like Google, Facebook, GitHub, and many others. They have already provided their details to these websites at the time of registration. You can leverage these websites to let users access your application. The interesting part is that both your custom user management module and the login through Google, Facebook, or GitHub can co-exist in the application. For instance, https://stackoverflow.com lets you log in to the application through both modes.

As you proceed with this technique, you'll learn that this feature is implemented through an open standard for access delegation. Spring Security provides a separate module that deals with this integration. You'll learn more about this in the upcoming technique. We'll implement user login with Google in the next technique.

6.9.1 Technique: Enabling sign in with Google in a Spring Boot application

In this technique, we'll discuss how to enable sign in with Google in a Spring Boot-based Web application.

PROBLEM

To access the Course Tracker application, users need to register and activate their accounts before they can access the application. However, some users already have a Google account, and they need to log in using their Google account. You need to enable users to log in through their Google account in the Course Tracker application.

SOLUTION

To let the users log in through their Google account, your application first needs to be a client of Google. This can be done by registering your application with Google. Once your application has registered with Google, you'll have a Google client ID and a secret key. We'll discuss the role of these keys later in the technique. You can refer to http://mng.bz/KBOX to register the Course Tracker application with Google.

> **Source code**
>
> To begin this technique, you can use the base version of the Spring Boot project used throughout it, which is available at http://mng.bz/9KRj. The final version of this Spring Boot project is available at http://mng.bz/jyQa.

NOTE In this technique, you'll use OAuth 2.0 to provide login access to the users through Google. The OAuth2.0 is an authorization framework that enables third-party applications (e.g., the Course Tracker) to obtain limited access to a resource (e.g., an HTTP service) either on behalf of a resource owner (e.g., Google), by orchestrating an approval interaction between the resource owner and the HTTP service, or by allowing the third-party application to obtain access on its behalf. Providing a detailed discussion on OAuth2.0 is beyond the scope of this text. You can refer to the OAuth2.0 RFC available at https://datatracker.ietf.org/doc/html/rfc6749 for more details on OAuth2.0 Authorization Framework. Refer to the Spring Security-specific texts to learn more about the use of OAuth2.0 with the Spring framework. You can refer to the Manning Publication's *API Security in Action* by Neil Madden or *Spring Security in Action* by Laurențiu Spilcă for further details

To begin with, let's add the `spring-boot-starter-oauth2-client` dependency to the pom.xml file. This provides necessary support to configure OAuth2 in the application, as shown in the following listing.

Listing 6.53 Spring Boot started OAuth2 client

```
<dependency>
    <groupId>org.springframework.boot</groupId>
    <artifactId>spring-boot-starter-oauth2-client</artifactId>
</dependency>
```

Next, add the following properties in the application.properties file, as shown in the following listing.

Listing 6.54 Google OAuth2 properties

```
spring.security.oauth2.client.registration.google.client-id=<Your client ID>
spring.security.oauth2.client.registration.google.client-secret=<Your Secret>
spring.security.oauth2.client.registration.google.scope=email, profile
```

In listing 6.54, we configured the `client-secret` (obtained from Google) in the application.properties file only for demonstration purposes. In a production application, you should not place it in the code or property file. A better alternative is to use environment variables or use a vault to keep the secret. Next, let's update the HTTP security configuration in the `SecurityConfiguration` file, as shown in listing 6.55.

Listing 6.55 The Updated HTTP configuration

```
@Override
protected void configure(HttpSecurity http) throws Exception {

      http.authorizeRequests()
      .antMatchers("/adduser", "/login", "/login-error", "/login-verified",
➥ "/login-disabled", "/verify/email").permitAll()
      .anyRequest().authenticated()
      .and()
   .formLogin().loginPage("/login").failureHandler(customAuthenticationFailure
➥ Handler)
      .and()
      .oauth2Login().loginPage("/login").successHandler(new
➥ Oauth2AuthenticationSuccessHandler());
}
```

To enable OAuth2 support, you've enabled the `oauth2Login()` in the configuration. This configuration invokes the `OAuth2LoginConfigurer` class and allows you to customize the OAuth2-related features. For instance, we've used a custom login page by configuring the `loginPage("/login")`. This ensures we are redirecting the user to a customized login page instead of the Spring default login page. We've also provided an `AuthenticationSuccessHandler` implementation, which is invoked once the user is authenticated. The following listing shows the `Oauth2AuthenticationSuccessHandler` implementation.

Listing 6.56 Oauth2AuthenticationSuccessHandler

```
package com.manning.sbip.ch06.service.impl;

//imports

@Component
public class Oauth2AuthenticationSuccessHandler implements
➥ AuthenticationSuccessHandler {
```

```
    private RedirectStrategy redirectStrategy = new
➥ DefaultRedirectStrategy();

    public void onAuthenticationSuccess(HttpServletRequest request,
➥ HttpServletResponse response, Authentication authentication) throws
➥ IOException, ServletException {
        redirectStrategy.sendRedirect(request, response, "/index");
    }
}
```

In listing 6.56, you redirected the user to the /index endpoint, which shows the logged-in user the application index page. Note that the authentication parameter is an instance of OAuth2AuthenticationToken, and you can access various user information (e.g., name, email, etc.) from it. To keep the implementation simple, we haven't demonstrated this.

Lastly, let's update the login page to enable a Login with Google button on the login page. You can access the updated login page at http://mng.bz/raXB. Start the application, and you'll find the page shown in figure 6.10.

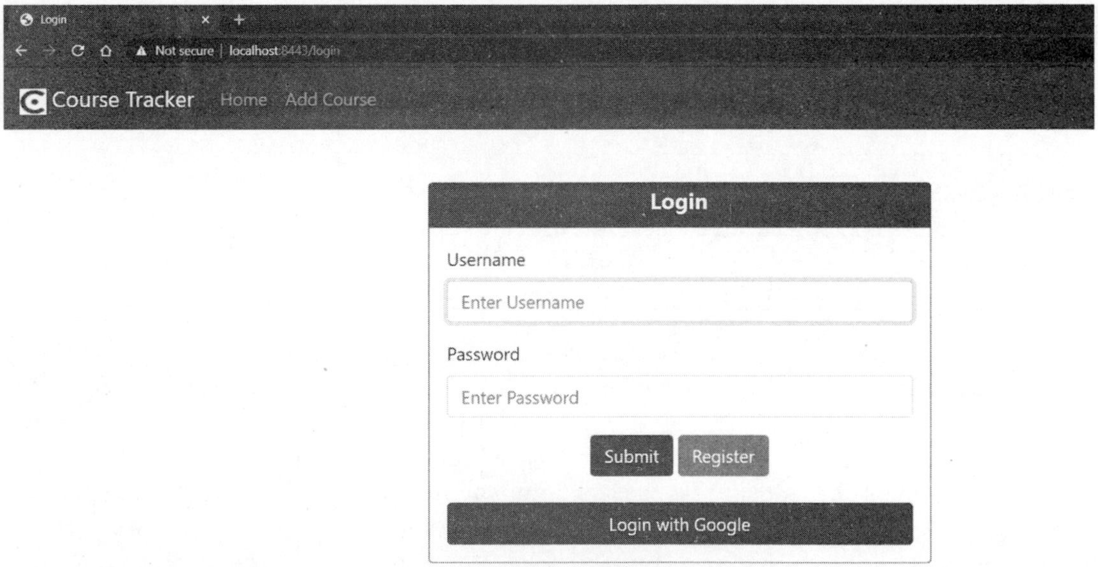

Figure 6.10 User login page with the Login with Google option

Click on the Login with Google button, and you'll be redirected to the Google sign-in page. If you pay attention to the URL, you'll notice it has the application client ID, scope, and redirect URL, as shown in the following listing.

Listing 6.57 Google redirect URL

```
https://accounts.google.com/o/oauth2/v2/auth/identifier?response_type=code&
➥ client_id=81684764817-
➥ lb9qc6bgsb4o73smdkhfkdj72q7pa6ns.apps.googleusercontent.com&scope=email
➥ %20profile&state=judvx4EoF8AnPBLSGbqCdpqZCR6xdkX0hbC8D4ub-
➥ Co%3D&redirect_uri=https%3A%2F%2Flocalhost%3A8443%2Flogin%2Foauth2%2Fco
➥ de%2Fgoogle&flowName=GeneralOAuthFlow
```

Figure 6.11 shows the Google sign in page with a message to continue accessing the Course Tracker. Provide your Google credentials, and you'll be redirected to the application index page.

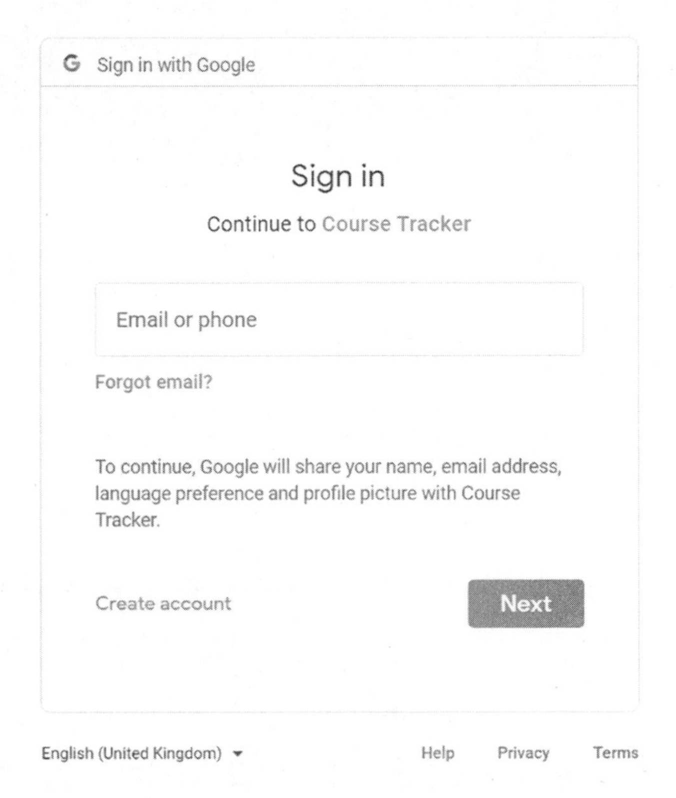

Figure 6.11 Google login page to log in to the Course Tracker application with Oauth2

DISCUSSION

To enable OAuth2 support in the Spring Boot application, you've added the `spring-boot-starter-oauth2-client` to the pom.xml file. Spring Boot provides an autoconfiguration class called `OAuth2ClientAutoConfiguration` that performs several configurations automatically to set up OAuth2 in the Spring application. The presence of `spring-boot-starter-oauth2-client` triggers this autoconfiguration. The authentication for OAuth2 is performed by the `OAuth2LoginAuthenticationFilter` filter. This filter is configured by the `OAuth2LoginConfigurer` class.

Let's now provide a brief overview of how we've used OAuth2, while letting the user sign in with Google. In the beginning, you've registered your application with Google, and you've received a `client_id` and a `secret`. The `client_id` is a unique ID for the Course Tracker application. The secret is a confidential piece of information that is internally used by Google and the Course Tracker application. Figure 6.12 shows the authorization flow in detail.

Let's discuss the steps:

1. The user attempts to log in to the application with Google.
2. The application redirects the user to the Google sign-in page and embedded the `client_id` in the redirect URL.
3. The user signs in to Google with their Google login credentials.
4. Google then displays a confirmation page asking whether the user authorizes the Course Tracker application to access certain details. Notice that while you register your application with Google, you provide certain scopes (e.g., user name, email, etc.) to Google that you will need from the user. On this confirmation page, Google shows the user the same details that the Course Tracker application will access.
5. The user confirms with Google to grant access to the details to the Course Tracker application.
6. Google then sends an authentication code to the user (i.e., to the user browser). Google uses the secret key to encrypt the authentication code.
7. The browser then forwards it to the Course Tracker application. The application uses its secret key to decrypt the authentication code.
8. The application then sends the authentication code to Google, and it is validated by Google.
9. Next, Google shares an access token to the application.
10. The application then uses this access token to retrieve the authenticated user details.
11. The application redirects the user to the application index page.

With this technique, you've learned to allow users to log in with Google. You can also implement this technique with Facebook or GitHub in the same manner. You first need to register your application with these websites and obtain the `client_key` and `secrets`. You can then use these details in the Spring Boot application to implement these login options. We leave it as an exercise for the reader to implement this in the Course Tracker application.

6.10 Securing Actuator endpoints

In chapter 4, we discussed Spring Boot application observability and explored the built-in Spring Boot actuator that exposes various application metrics. Spring Boot

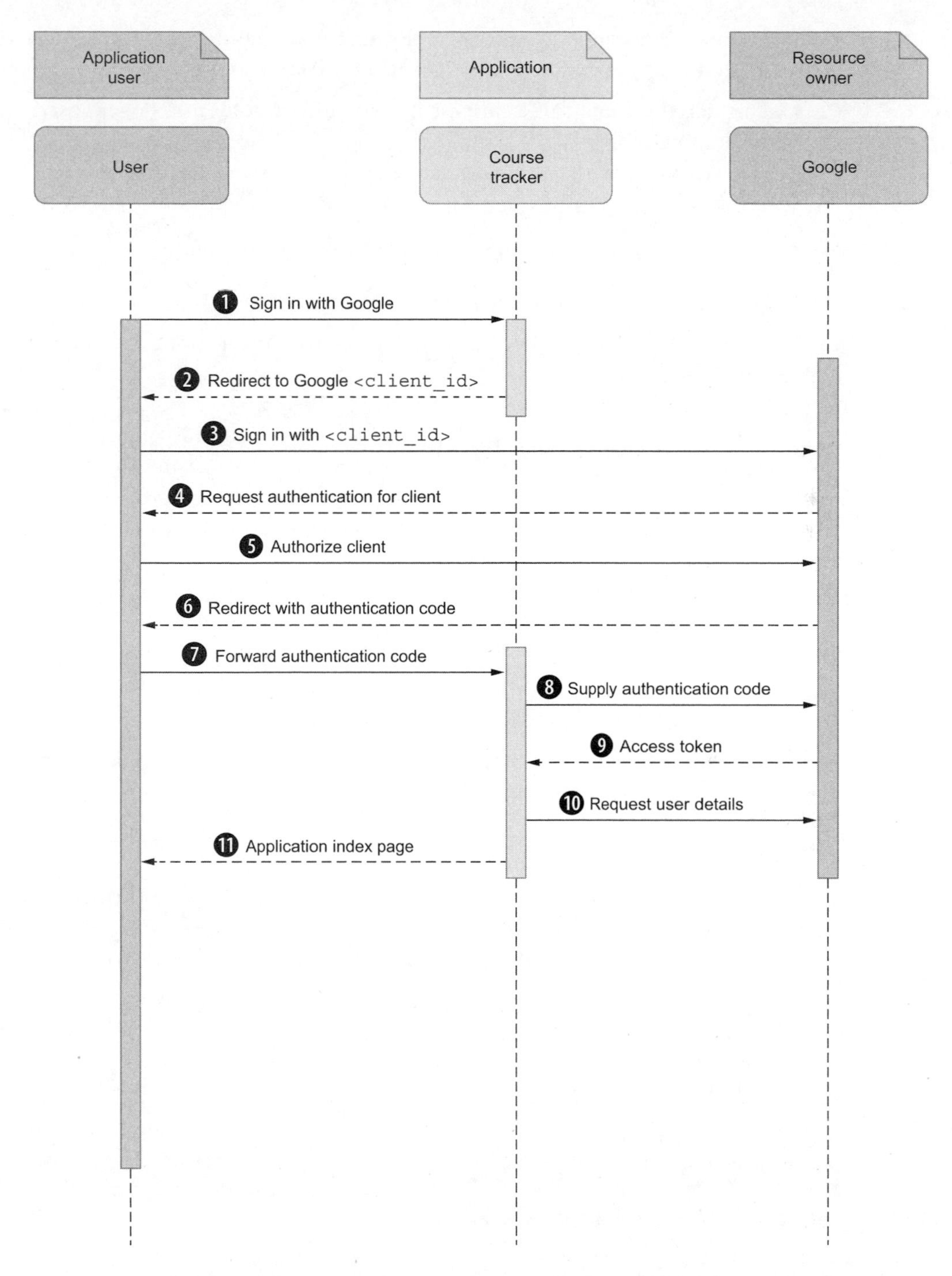

Figure 6.12 OAuth2 authorization flow between the user, Google, and Course Tracker application

Actuator endpoints contain sensitive application details and should be protected from unauthorized access. You need to ensure two things:

- The actuator endpoints are protected and should not be exposed without authentication.
- You are be able to authorize access to endpoints to privileged users, such as application admins or the monitoring team.

Let us explore how to implement these in the next technique.

6.10.1 Technique: Securing Spring Boot Actuator endpoints

In this technique, we'll demonstrate how to secure Spring Boot Actuator endpoints with Spring Security.

PROBLEM

In the Course Tracker application, the actuator endpoint is accessible by ordinary users. However, as actuator endpoints contain sensitive application information, they need to be protected from unauthorized access.

SOLUTION

In the previous chapter as well as this one, you've learned several Spring Security concepts. You'll leverage the same concepts to enable appropriate authentication and authorization to safeguard the actuator endpoints from unauthorized access.

> **Source code**
>
> To begin this technique, you can use the base version of the Spring Boot project used throughout it, which is available at http://mng.bz/W7Dg. The final version of this Spring Boot project is available at http://mng.bz/8lZK.

Using this technique, we'll enable all actuator Web endpoints and provide access to health endpoints to both the user groups with role `USER` and `ENDPOINT_ADMIN`. We are providing health endpoint access to both groups, as it allows users to view the health status of the application and will be useful to find out if the application has any infrastructure issues. All other endpoints are accessible only by the users with the role `ENDPOINT_ADMIN`.

Let's add the security configuration to implement the above feature. The following listing shows Spring Security configurations.

Listing 6.58 Security configuration to safeguard Actuator endpoints

```
package com.manning.sbip.ch06.security;

//imports

@Configuration
public class SecurityConfiguration extends WebSecurityConfigurerAdapter {
```

```
    @Override
    protected void configure(AuthenticationManagerBuilder auth) throws
➥ Exception {
        auth.inMemoryAuthentication().passwordEncoder(passwordEncoder())
.withUser(User.builder().username("user").password(passwordEncoder().encode
➥ ("password")).roles("USER").build())
.withUser(User.builder().username("admin").password(passwordEncoder().encod
➥ e("admin")).roles("ENDPOINT_ADMIN").build());
    }
    @Override
    protected void configure(HttpSecurity http) throws Exception {
        http.authorizeRequests().requestMatchers(EndpointRe-
     quest.to("health")).hasA
➥ nyRole("USER", "ENDPOINT_ADMIN")

.requestMatchers(EndpointRequest.toAnyEndpoint()).hasRole("ENDPOINT_ADMIN")
➥ .and().formLogin();
    }
    @Bean
    public PasswordEncoder passwordEncoder() {
        return new BCryptPasswordEncoder();
    }
}
```

The health endpoint is accessible to users with either of the USER or ENDPOINT_ADMIN role. All other endpoints require ENDPOINT_ADMIN role. Also, we've used a form-based login for authentication.

In listing 6.58, we made the following changes:

- Programmatically defined two users: `user` and `admin`. The user was assigned the role `USER`, and the admin was assigned the role `ENDPOINT_ADMIN`.
- We allowed access to the actuator `health` endpoint to both the user and admin. All other remaining endpoints are accessible only by the users having role `END-POINT_ADMIN`.
- You've used form-based authentication for both user types.

Start the application, and log in with the user as the `user`. You can only access the http://localhost:8080/actuator/health endpoint. For all other endpoints, you'll receive a 403 Forbidden error message. Log out from the application by accessing the http://localhost:8080/logout URL. Next, log in to the application with the user `admin` and password as `admin`, and you'll notice you have access to all endpoints.

Summary

Let's summarize the key takeaways of this chapter:

- We enabled HTTPS in a Spring Boot application with a self-signed certificate and implemented redirection of all HTTP requests to HTTPS.
- We implemented Hashicorp Vault to externalize application secrets in the vault and connected the Spring Boot application to the vault for secret access.
- We implemented a user registration module and enabled user account verification via email.
- We enabled an application feature that temporarily suspends a user's account for multiple incorrect login attempts.

- We enabled the Remember Me feature for quick login from trusted devices.
- We implemented Google reCAPTCHA to prevent internet bot and spam attacks.
- We enabled two-factor authentication with Google Authenticator for additional application security.
- We implemented OAuth2 login in a Spring Boot application with Google.
- We learned how to protect Spring Boot Actuator endpoints from unauthorized access with Spring Security.

7 Developing RESTful Web services with Spring Boot

This chapter covers

- Designing and building RESTful Web services with Spring Boot
- Exception handling in RESTful Web services
- Developing unit test cases to test RESTful Web services
- Documenting the RESTful Web services through OpenAPI
- Implementing different versioning strategies for RESTful Web services
- Techniques for securing RESTful Web services

In the microservice-based architecture, it is a common practice to expose application functionality in terms of RESTful APIs. These APIs can then be accessed via a range of application devices, such as desktop applications, mobile devices, as well as other APIs.

In this chapter, we'll introduce you to designing and building RESTful APIs with Spring Boot. You'll also learn to document the API, so the API consumers can find required details about the API, such as the request, response structures, HTTP return codes, etc. Finally, you'll learn to develop unit test cases to test the API. Lastly, we'll show you how to secure your RESTful API. Let's get started.

7.1 Developing a RESTful API with Spring Boot

A RESTful API (also known as REST API) is an application programming interface that follows the constraints of REST architectural style. REST is an acronym for representational state transfer and was created by Roy Fielding (http://mng.bz/Exyq). In a REST API, when a client requests a resource from the server, the server provides a representation of the state of the requested resource to the client. This representation can be delivered through various formats, such as JSON, plain text, HTML, and others. However, JSON is the most widely used format in the REST API parlance.

Spring Boot provides built-in support in the framework to design and build REST APIs. Spring Boot is one of the most popular frameworks in the Java space for developing REST APIs. In this section, we'll explore developing a RESTful API with Spring Boot.

7.1.1 Technique: Developing a RESTful API using Spring Boot

In this technique, we'll demonstrate how to develop a RESTful API using Spring Boot.

PROBLEM

Previously, you've used the Course Tracker Spring Boot application with Thymeleaf as the frontend. You now need to expose the Course Tracker application as a RESTful API. Exposing application backend functionality as RESTful API allows the decoupling of application backend with the frontend UI. This design approach lets you opt for the application frontend frameworks (e.g., Angular, React, Vue, etc.) of your choice without being tightly coupled with the backend.

SOLUTION

Designing RESTful APIs with Spring Boot is relatively easy, as the framework provides built-in support for it. These days Spring Boot is the de facto choice for Java developers to build RESTful APIs. If you are following the previous chapters, then you are already aware of most of the content for building a RESTful API with Spring Boot.

In chapter 3, we discussed the use of Spring Data and talked about the approaches to configuring and using a database in a Spring Boot application. In chapter 5, we demonstrated building Spring Boot applications by using Spring controllers in conjunction with Spring Data repositories.

> **Source code**
> The final version of the Spring Boot project is available at http://mng.bz/NxzE.

With this technique, you'll build a RESTful API for the Course Tracker application. It will expose the REST endpoints shown in table 7.1.

Table 7.1 REST endpoints exposed by the Course Tracker API

Endpoint	Operation type	Purpose
`/courses/`	`GET`	Returns all available courses from the application
`/courses/{id}`	`GET`	Returns a course with the supplied course ID
`/courses/category/{name}`	`GET`	Returns the list of courses with the supplied course category name
`/courses/`	`POST`	Creates a new course
`/courses/{id}`	`PUT`	Updates the course for the supplied course ID
`/courses/{id}`	`DELETE`	Deletes a course with the supplied course ID
`/courses/`	`DELETE`	Deletes all courses from the application

Table 7.1 contains the REST endpoints that let you perform the CRUD operations in the Course Tracker application. To keep the example simple, we've only introduced a limited number of endpoints. In a production application, you may define more REST endpoints. For instance, you can have a few more GET endpoints that let you filter application data to meet application requirements. However, to demonstrate the concepts, we'll use these REST endpoints throughout this chapter, as this endpoint covers the fundamental operations (CRUD) that most APIs support.

In the Course Tracker application, we are managing `Course` details. Therefore, we will define the course business entity. The following listing shows this class.

Listing 7.1 The course entity

```
package com.manning.sbip.ch07.model;

import javax.persistence.Column;
import javax.persistence.Entity;
import javax.persistence.GeneratedValue;
import javax.persistence.GenerationType;
import javax.persistence.Id;
import javax.persistence.Table;

import lombok.Data;

@Data
@Entity
@Table(name - "COURSES")
public class Course {

    @Id
    @GeneratedValue(strategy = GenerationType.IDENTITY)
    @Column(name = "ID")
    private Long id;

    @Column(name = "NAME")
    private String name;
```

```
    @Column(name = "CATEGORY")
    private String category;

    @Column(name = "RATING")
    private int rating;

    @Column(name = "DESCRIPTION")
    private String description;
}
```

The Course is a Java POJO that models the course details in the application with fields such as course id, name, category, rating, and description. Next, let's define the CourseRepository interface, which lets us manage the courses in the database.

Listing 7.2 The CourseRepository interface

```
package com.manning.sbip.ch07.repository;

import org.springframework.data.repository.CrudRepository;
import org.springframework.stereotype.Repository;

import com.manning.sbip.ch07.model.Course;

@Repository
public interface CourseRepository extends CrudRepository<Course, Long> {

    Iterable<Course> findAllByCategory(String category);
}
```

The CourseRepository interface extends the CrudRepository interface and defines a custom method findAllByCategory(..) that finds all courses belonging to a specific category.

Let's now define the service layer of the application. We define the service layer with an interface that provides the operations supported in the application. The following listing shows the CourseService interface.

Listing 7.3 The CourseService interface

```
package com.manning.sbip.ch07.service;

//imports

public interface CourseService {

    Course createCourse(Course course);

    Optional<Course> getCourseById(long courseId);

    Iterable<Course> getCoursesByCategory(String category);

    Iterable<Course> getCourses();
```

```
    void updateCourse(long courseId, Course course);

    void deleteCourseById(long courseId);

    void deleteCourses();
}
```

The methods defined in listing 7.3 are self-explanatory. It contains the method declarations that allow us to perform the CRUD operations in the application. Let's now provide a default implementation that provides implementations of these methods.

Generally, it is a best practice to define an interface consisting of the operations supported in the API. This interface provides a contract to the controller with the operations supported in the service layer. You can then provide a concrete class that implements these operations. Further, in the controller class, you use the interface name instead of specifying the actual implementation class. This allows you to decouple the controller with the actual implementation. In the future, if you need to provide a different implementation of the service layer, your controller class is not impacted, as it uses the interface and is not tied to a specific implementation. Listing 7.4 shows the `CourseServiceImpl` class.

Listing 7.4 The CourseServiceImpl class

```
package com.manning.sbip.ch07.service;

//imports

@Service                        <-- Annotated with @Service to indicate it's a service
public class CourseServiceImpl implements CourseService {

    @Autowired                  <-- Autowires the CourseRepository to perform the database operations
    private CourseRepository courseRepository;

    @Override
    public Course createCourse(Course course) {
        return courseRepository.save(course);
    }

    @Override
    public Optional<Course> getCourseById(long courseId) {
        return courseRepository.findById(courseId);
    }

    @Override
    public Iterable<Course> getCoursesByCategory(String category) {
        return courseRepository.findAllByCategory(category);
    }

    @Override
    public Iterable<Course> getCourses() {
        return courseRepository.findAll();
    }
```

```
    @Override
    public void updateCourse(Long courseId, Course course) {

        courseRepository.findById(courseId).ifPresent(dbCourse -> {
            dbCourse.setName(course.getName());
            dbCourse.setCategory(course.getCategory());
            dbCourse.setDescription(course.getDescription());
            dbCourse.setRating(course.getRating());

            courseRepository.save(dbCourse);
        });
    }

    @Override
    public void deleteCourses() {
        courseRepository.deleteAll();
    }

    @Override
    public void deleteCourseById(long courseId) {
        courseRepository.deleteById(courseId);
    }

}
```

The `CourseServiceImpl` class is annotated with `@Service` annotation to indicate it's a service. Recall that `@Service` is a Spring stereotype annotation that indicates the annotated class is a service class and contains business logic. Further, it uses the `CourseRepository` to perform the necessary database operations.

We are now left with defining the `CourseController` that defines the REST endpoints. A Spring controller contains one of more endpoints and accepts the client requests. It then, optionally, uses the services offered by the service layer and generates a response. It wraps the response in a model and shares it with the view layer. A `RestContoller` also performs a similar activity. However, instead of wrapping the response in the model and sharing to the view layer, it binds the response to the HTTP response body, which is directly shared with the endpoint requester. The following listing shows the `CourseController` class.

Listing 7.5 The CourseController class

```
package com.manning.sbip.ch07.controller;

import java.util.Optional;

import org.springframework.beans.factory.annotation.Autowired;
import org.springframework.web.bind.annotation.DeleteMapping;
import org.springframework.web.bind.annotation.GetMapping;
import org.springframework.web.bind.annotation.PathVariable;
import org.springframework.web.bind.annotation.PostMapping;
import org.springframework.web.bind.annotation.PutMapping;
import org.springframework.web.bind.annotation.RequestBody;
```

Handles HTTP GET requests for the path /courses/category/{name}. The {name} is a path variable and replaced with an appropriate value (e.g., /courses/category/Spring, where Spring is the value of the path variable name).

The RequestMapping annotation specified the route or the path to the API. In this example, we have defined the path /courses/ so that all HTTP requests to the /courses/ path are redirected to this controller.

```
import org.springframework.web.bind.annotation.RequestMapping;
import org.springframework.web.bind.annotation.RestController;

import com.manning.sbip.ch07.model.Course;
import com.manning.sbip.ch07.service.CourseService;

@RestController
@RequestMapping("/courses/")
public class CourseController {

    @Autowired
    private CourseService courseService;

    @GetMapping
    public Iterable<Course> getAllCourses() {
        return courseService.getCourses();
    }

    @GetMapping("{id}")
    public Optional<Course> getCourseById(@PathVariable("id") long
➥ courseId) {
        return courseService.getCourseById(courseId);
    }

    @GetMapping("category/{name}")
    public Iterable<Course> getCourseByCategory(@PathVariable("name")
➥ String category) {
        return courseService.getCoursesByCategory(category);
    }

    @PostMapping
    public Course createCourse(@RequestBody Course course) {
        return courseService.createCourse(course);
    }

    @PutMapping("{id}")
    public void updateCourse(@PathVariable("id") long courseId,
➥ @RequestBody Course course) {
        courseService.updateCourse(courseId, course);
    }
```

A GetMapping is a special type of RequestMapping that handles only the HTTP GET request. As no path is specified in this endpoint, it is the default endpoint for the HTTP GET /courses/ endpoint.

Handles HTTP GET requests for the path /courses/{id}. The {id} is a path variable and replaced with an appropriate value, e.g. /courses/1, where 1 is the value of the path variable ID.

Handles HTTP POST requests for the path /courses/. An HTTP POST request accepts a request payload. You use the @RequestBody annotation to specify the request body. Note that the requester typically sends a JSON payload, and in the endpoint you expect a Java POJO class that represents the JSON payload. Spring Boot internally performs this deserialization to convert the JSON to the Java type.

Handles the HTTP PUT operations for the path /courses/{id}. The HTTP PUT operation is used to perform the update operations. In this endpoint, we expect the ID of the resource that needs to be updated and the updated representation of the resource in the HTTP request payload. We use the @RequestBody to accept the request payload.

```
    @DeleteMapping("{id}")
    void deleteCourseById(@PathVariable("id") long courseId) {
        courseService.deleteCourseById(courseId);
    }

    @DeleteMapping
    void deleteCourses() {
        courseService.deleteCourses();
    }
}
```

Represents the HTTP DELETE operation for the /courses/{id} path. In this endpoint, we delete the course for the supplied course ID.

Represents the HTTP DELETE operation for the /courses/ path. In this endpoint, we delete all available courses.

Listing 7.5 defines all the endpoints listed in table 7.1. We'll explore this class in greater detail in the discussion section of this technique. However, one thing you should take note of is the use of `@RestController` annotation instead of the previously used `@Controller` annotation.

> **Testing REST endpoints**
>
> Several utilities can be used to test REST endpoints. You can use Postman (https://www.postman.com/) tool, which provides a GUI to test the endpoint. One nice feature of Postman is that you can group related endpoints to create a collection. You can export the collection and share it with others, who can import it in their Postman and test the same endpoints.
>
> If you prefer command-line tools, you can use cURL or HTTPie. The cURL is a Unix built-in utility that can be used to access the REST endpoints. HTTPie is a command-line HTTP client that allows you to access HTTP URLs. We'll use this as an alternative to cURL to test our APIs. You can find more information on HTTPie at https://httpie.io/. You can also refer to http://mng.bz/KxeK for a quick introduction on installing and using HTTPie.

Let us start the application and access the endpoints. First, let's create a course using the `POST /courses/` endpoint. Listing 7.6 shows the HTTPie command to create a course.

Listing 7.6 The HTTPie command to create a new course

```
> http POST :8080/courses/ name="Mastering Spring Boot" rating=4
➥ category=Spring description="Mastering Spring Boot intends to teach
➥ Spring Boot with practical examples"
HTTP/1.1 200
// Other HTTP Response Headers
{
    "category": "Spring",
    "description": "Mastering Spring Boot intends to teach Spring Boot with
➥ practical examples",
    "id": 1,
    "name": "Mastering Spring Boot",
```

```
    "rating": 4
}
```

In listing 7.6, although we've supplied the request body data in key–value pair, the HTTPie tool internally converts it to a JSON payload. Once this command is executed in the terminal, a new course is created in the Course Tracker application. Let's view the course details using the `GET /courses/{id}` endpoint to retrieve course details with a `courseId` obtained in the POST operation of listing 7.6. This is shown in the following listing.

Listing 7.7 The HTTPie command to view a course

```
> http GET :8080/courses/1
HTTP/1.1 200
// Other HTTP Response Headers
{
    "category": "Spring",
    "description": "Mastering Spring Boot intends to teach Spring Boot with
➥ practical examples",
    "id": 1,
    "name": "Mastering Spring Boot",
    "rating": 4
}
```

You can try accessing other endpoints in the same manner and monitor the output.

DISCUSSION

With this technique, you've learned to create a complete RESTful API. We have kept the application extremely simple to demonstrate the concepts. Let's now discuss a few best practices we've followed while designing the REST API.

If you notice, we've used JSON to accept the requests and similarly responded with JSON in the response. It is a best practice that the REST APIs accept request payloads in JSON and provide a response in JSON.

JSON is widely used to store and transfer data. Spring Boot provides built-in support to perform the mapping between JSON and Java POJOs and vice versa. For instance, if you notice in listing 7.6, you've sent a JSON request as the payload to create a new course in the application. However, the POST endpoint accepts a `Course` instance. Spring Boot performs this deserialization internally for us. By default, it uses the Jackson library (https://github.com/FasterXML/jackson) to perform this mapping.

The next thing to notice is the use of nouns while defining the endpoint paths. It is a best practice to use the plural form of the noun (e.g., `Course`, `Person`, `Vehicle`, etc.) to define the routes. We should not use verbs in the route paths as the HTTP request method already has a verb (e.g., GET, POST, etc.) that defines the actions. Letting the developers use the verbs in paths make the paths lengthy and inconsistent. For instance, to get the course details, one developer may use `/getCourses`, whereas another can use `/retrieveCourses`. However, the get or retrieve is already defined through the HTTP GET method. Thus, specifying it in the route path makes it redundant. Hence, `GET /courses/` is the preferred endpoint path to get all courses. Similarly, the `POST /courses/` is the appropriate endpoint to create a new course.

Let's now provide a high-level flow diagram that shows the request and response processing in a REST API in a Spring Boot application. Figure 7.1 shows this diagram.

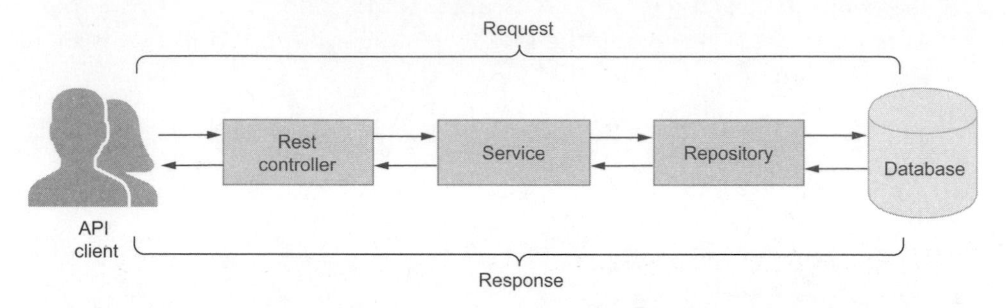

Figure 7.1 The communication flow diagram in a REST API. A user invokes a REST endpoint, which is handled by the REST Controller. The controller then uses the service layer to process the request. The service layer relies on the repository to communicate to the database. Once there is a response from the repository, it is processed by the service layer and forwarded to the controller. The controller may perform additional processing, and the final response is provided to the API client.

In listing 7.5, we've used the `@RestController` annotation in place of the previously used `@Controller` annotation. The `@RestController` annotation is a convenience annotation that is meta-annotated with the `@Controller` and `@ResponseBody` annotations. The `@ResponseBody` annotation indicates that a method's return value should be bound to the HTTP response body.

Although the above API works well and serves the purpose, currently there is no exception handling. For instance, let's try to delete a course that does not exist in the application. You'll notice that you have presented with an error and an ugly looking large stack trace. We'll fix this in the next technique.

7.2 Managing exceptions in a Spring Boot RESTful API

Exceptions are inevitable in software code. Numerous factors could cause an exceptional scenario in your code. For instance, in the RESTful API we've designed, a user could attempt to access or delete a course with a nonexisting course ID. They could also submit a malformed JSON request payload to create a new course through the POST endpoint. All these scenarios cause exceptions in the API. In this section, we'll discuss how to handle these exceptions and provide a meaningful response to the user specifying the exception details.

7.2.1 Technique: Handling exceptions in a RESTful API

In this technique, we'll discuss how to handle exceptions in a RESTful API.

PROBLEM

The previously defined RESTful API is unable to handle errors, as there is no exception handling in place. It presents the user with a large stack trace that is not intuitive and exposes application internal details. You need to handle exceptions and ensure to provide meaningful error responses.

SOLUTION

Exception handling is an important aspect of a RESTful API. Typically, your APIs will be consumed by a variety of consumers and being able to provide a meaningful error response in the event of an exception scenario makes your API robust and user friendly.

> **Source code**
>
> The final version of the Spring Boot project is available at http://mng.bz/layj.

In the API designed in section 7.1, we've not handled the exceptions and the default Spring Boot exception handling mechanism is in place. For instance, deleting a course that does not exist in the application presents the error message, as shown in the following listing.

Listing 7.8 Default exception handling

```
C:\sbip\repo>http DELETE :8080/courses/10
HTTP/1.1 500
{
    "error": "Internal Server Error",
    "message": "No class com.manning.sbip.ch07.model.Course entity with id
➥ 10 exists!",
    "path": "/courses/10",
    "status": 500,
    "timestamp": "2021-06-23T16:38:20.105+00:00",
    "trace": "org.springframework.dao.EmptyResultDataAccessException: No
➥ class com.manning.sbip.ch07.model.Course entity with id 10
➥ exists!\r\n\tat
➥ org.springframework.data.jpa.repository.support.SimpleJpaRepository.lam
➥ bda$deleteById$0(SimpleJpaRepository.java:166)\r\n\tat
➥ java.base/java.util.Optional.orElseThrow(Optional.java:401)\r\n\tat
➥ org.springframework.data.jpa.repository.support.SimpleJpaRepository.del
➥ eteById(SimpleJpaRepository.java:165)\r\n\tat
➥ java.base/jdk.internal.reflect.NativeMethodAccessorImpl.invoke0(Native
➥ Method)\r\n\tat
➥ java.base/jdk.internal.reflect.NativeMethodAccessorImpl.invoke(NativeMe
➥ thodAccessorImpl.java:64)\r\n\tat

// Remaining section of the exception is omitted
```

As you may notice, the above error message is not a desired one and contains details that are not of much use to the API users. It also exposes to the caller information about the tech stack used for the implementation of the API, which is generally considered a security flaw. Further, the HTTP response code is also generic (500 Internal Server Error), which indicates that a server-side error has occurred. In this technique, we'll improve the Course Tracker RESTful API by implementing exception handling in the API.

To begin with, let's first discuss the type of exceptions we may encounter in the application. For this API, we can have only a handful of exception scenarios. For instance, it may be possible that a user attempts to get, update, or delete a course that does not exist in the application. This should result in an HTTP 404 Not Found error, as the requested resource does not exist in the application. It is also possible that the user is submitting an incomplete/incorrect JSON payload, while creating or updating a course. Let's handle these exception scenarios. This results in an HTTP 400 Bad Request status code, as the user request could not be processed because the server is unable to parse the request, since it is malformed. To handle the first scenario, let's create a custom exception called `CourseNotFoundException`, as shown in the following listing.

Listing 7.9 CourseNotFoundException

```
package com.manning.sbip.ch07.exception;

public class CourseNotFoundException extends RuntimeException {

    private static final long serialVersionUID = 5071646428281007896L;

    public CourseNotFoundException(String message) {
        super(message);
    }
}
```

This `CourseNotFoundException` is thrown whenever API users attempt to access a course that does not exist in the application. Let's now redefine the `CourseService-Impl` class, as shown in the following listing.

Listing 7.10 CourseServiceImpl class

```
package com.manning.sbip.ch07.service;
//imports

@Service
public class CourseServiceImpl implements CourseService {

    // Additional Code

    @Override
    public Course updateCourse(long courseId, Course course) {

        Course existingCourse = courseRepository.findById(courseId)
        .orElseThrow(() -> new CourseNotFoundException(String.format("No
```

```
➥ course with id %s is available", courseId)));
        existingCourse.setName(course.getName());
        existingCourse.setCategory(course.getCategory());
        existingCourse.setDescription(course.getDescription());
        existingCourse.setRating(course.getRating());
        return courseRepository.save(existingCourse);
    }


    @Override
    public void deleteCourseById(long courseId) {
    courseRepository.findById(courseId).orElseThrow(() -> new
➥ CourseNotFoundException("No course with id %s is available" +
➥ courseId));
        courseRepository.deleteById(courseId);    }
}
```

Listing 7.10 shows the modified methods of CourseServiceImpl class. For an update or a delete operation, if a course with the supplied courseId does not exist in the application, we throw the CourseNotFoundException.

Now that we've thrown the exception, what's next? We need to define an exception handler that intercepts the thrown exception and executes custom exception handling logic. For instance, for an unhandled exception, the HTTP response code 500 Internal Server Error is returned. However, if a course with the supplied courseid does not exist in the application, the appropriate HTTP error code should be 404 Not Found. The latter HTTP response code tells the API consumer the course they are accessing does not exist. Let's define the GlobalExceptionHandler class that defines the ExceptionHandlers of our application, as shown in the following listing.

Listing 7.11 GlobalExceptionHandler class

```
package com.manning.sbip.ch07.exception.handler;

//imports

@ControllerAdvice
public class CourseTrackerGlobalExceptionHandler extends
➥ ResponseEntityExceptionHandler {

    @ExceptionHandler(value = {CourseNotFoundException.class})
    public ResponseEntity<?> handleCourseNotFound(CourseNotFoundException
➥ courseNotFoundException, WebRequest request) {
        return super.handleExceptionInternal(courseNotFoundException,
                courseNotFoundException.getMessage(), new HttpHeaders(),
➥ HttpStatus.NOT_FOUND, request);
    }
}
```

In the class in listing 7.11, you've defined a few ExceptionHandler implementations that handle the exceptions and can be thrown while processing the requests. Let's explore this class in detail:

- This class is annotated with the `@ControllerAdvice` annotation. This annotation is a specialized `@Component` that allows you to declare the `@ExceptionHandler`. The `@ControllerAdvice` annotation allows writing global code that applies to a range of `controllers` (and `RestControllers`). Thus, the `ExceptionHandler` defined in listing 7.11 applies to all controllers in the application.
- This class extends the `ResponseEntityExceptionHandler` class, which is a base class for `@ControllerAdvice` annotated classes that provide a centralized exception handling across all `@RequestMapping` annotated methods through `@ExceptionHandler` methods. This class provides exception handling logic for a variety of exceptions that can occur in the application. We can extend this class and override the exception handling logic at our convenience.
- We've defined a new `ExceptionHandler` for our custom exception `CourseNotFoundException`. In this implementation, we are setting the HTTP response code to 404 Not Found and the error message retrieved from the custom exception. Finally, we are invoking the superclass method `handleExceptionInternal(..)` with these details.

Let's now start the application and try out replicating a few exceptions scenarios and observing the response. Let's try deleting a course with a course ID that is not present in the application. The HTTPie command and the associated response is shown in the following listing.

Listing 7.12 Delete a course

```
C:\sbip\repo>http DELETE :8080/courses/1
HTTP/1.1 404
// HTTP Response Headers

No course with id 1 is available
```

Notice that we have an appropriate HTTP status code 404 as well as a relevant error message that specifies the error. Moreover, the user does not see any reference to the technology used for the API implementation (i.e., no Spring Boot stack trace appearing anymore).

DISCUSSION

The ability of a RESTful API to handle various user errors and to respond with appropriate HTTP status codes and error messages makes it robust and user friendly. This makes the application more compliant with the RESTful paradigm itself.

While designing APIs, it is a common practice to first identify the possible error scenarios in the application. You can then define custom exception classes that define the identified error scenario. One advantage of designing a custom exception is that it allows you to model the exception in a better manner and provides flexibility to capture various details about the exception. You can then define the `ExceptionHandler` that intercepts these exception classes and allows you to define custom error response. For instance, try defining an exception handler that handles the wrong request payloads and responds with the HTTP 400 bad request. We leave this as an exercise for the readers.

7.3 Testing a RESTful API

In the previous techniques, you've learned to design and build a RESTful API. Once you are done with the development, the next task is to test the endpoints of the API to ensure that the API is working as expected. There are multiple ways to test a REST API, as shown in figure 7.2.

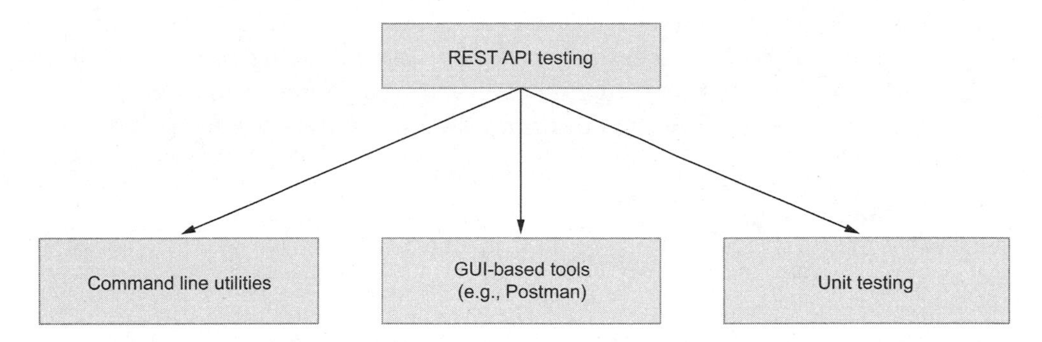

Figure 7.2 Options to test a RESTful API. Command line utilities includes cURL, HTTPie. The GUI-based tools include Postman, SoapUI. Unit testing can be done with Spring Boot MockMVC in conjunction with JUnit.

So far, we've discussed using the command-line tool HTTPie that can be used to access the endpoints. You can also use the cURL utility to test the endpoints. If you are not comfortable with CLI utilities, GUI-based tools are another great alternative. In the REST API testing, Postman (https://www.postman.com/) is extensively used by API developers to test the APIs. Besides, if you are familiar with the Microsoft VS Code editor (https://code.visualstudio.com/), it also provides several extensions to enable testing support for the REST APIs. We won't cover these utilities, as there are enough tutorials and how-to guides for these tools available on the internet.

In the next section, we'll discuss how to test a REST API through integration testing. It is always a best practice to write test cases for the endpoints that are executed while you build the API. Let's explore it in the next technique.

7.3.1 Technique: Testing a RESTful API in a Spring Boot application

In this section, we'll explore how to test a RESTful API.

Problem

We haven't defined any test cases to test the REST API endpoints. To ensure the API endpoints are working correctly and are not broken while introducing new changes in the future, we need to define integration test cases.

SOLUTION

In a typical application, to test your application classes, you either instantiate those and invoke the methods defined in it or use mocking frameworks, such as Mockito to mock the class and other components. In a Spring MVC application, we can similarly define test cases. However, that does not verify a few important MVC framework features, such as request mapping, validation, data binding, @ExceptionHandler, and others.

Spring MVC provides a testing framework that provides comprehensive testing capabilities for Spring MVC-based applications without the need for an actual server. This framework, also known as MockMVC, performs the MVC request handling via mock request and response objects.

In this technique, we'll show you how to use the Spring MockMVC framework in a Spring Boot application to test a REST API. We'll define integration test cases for the API endpoints we've defined in the previous techniques.

> **Source code**
> The final version of the Spring Boot project is available at http://mng.bz/Bx4v.

Let's begin by defining the first test case that creates a course in the Course Tracker application. The following listing shows the class.

Listing 7.13 Integration test case for Course Tracker REST API create course endpoint

```
package com.manning.sbip.ch07;

import static org.hamcrest.Matchers.greaterThan;
import static org.hamcrest.Matchers.hasSize;
import static org.junit.jupiter.api.Assertions.assertNotNull;
import static
➥ org.springframework.test.web.servlet.request.MockMvcRequestBuilders.del
➥ ete;
import static
➥ org.springframework.test.web.servlet.request.MockMvcRequestBuilders.get;
import static
➥ org.springframework.test.web.servlet.request.MockMvcRequestBuilders.post;
import static
➥ org.springframework.test.web.servlet.request.MockMvcRequestBuilders.put;
import static
➥ org.springframework.test.web.servlet.result.MockMvcResultHandlers.print;
import static
➥ org.springframework.test.web.servlet.result.MockMvcResultMatchers.jsonP
➥ ath;
import static
➥ org.springframework.test.web.servlet.result.MockMvcResultMatchers.status;

import org.junit.jupiter.api.Test;
import org.junit.jupiter.api.extension.ExtendWith;
```

```
import org.springframework.beans.factory.annotation.Autowired;
import
➥ org.springframework.boot.test.autoconfigure.web.servlet.AutoConfigureMo
➥ ckMvc;
import org.springframework.boot.test.context.SpringBootTest;
import org.springframework.mock.web.MockHttpServletResponse;
import org.springframework.test.context.junit.jupiter.SpringExtension;
import org.springframework.test.web.servlet.MockMvc;

import com.fasterxml.jackson.databind.ObjectMapper;
import com.jayway.jsonpath.JsonPath;
import com.manning.sbip.ch07.model.Course;
import com.manning.sbip.ch07.service.CourseService;

@SpringBootTest
@AutoConfigureMockMvc
@ExtendWith(SpringExtension.class)
class CourseTrackerApiApplicationTests {

    @Autowired
    private CourseService courseService;

    @Autowired
    private MockMvc mockMvc;

    @Test
    public void testPostCourse() throws Exception {
        Course course = Course.builder()
                .name("Rapid Spring Boot Application Development")
                .category("Spring")
                .rating(5)
                .description("Rapid Spring Boot Application
➥ Development").build();
        ObjectMapper objectMapper = new ObjectMapper();

        MockHttpServletResponse response = mockMvc.perform(post("/courses/")
                .contentType("application/json")
                .content(objectMapper.writeValueAsString(course)))
                .andDo(print())
                .andExpect(jsonPath("$.*", hasSize(5)))
                .andExpect(jsonPath("$.id", greaterThan(0)))
                .andExpect(jsonPath("$.name").value("Rapid Spring Boot
➥ Application Development"))
                .andExpect(jsonPath("$.category").value("Spring"))
                .andExpect(jsonPath("$.rating").value(5))
                .andExpect(status().isCreated()).andReturn().getResponse();

        Integer id =
➥ JsonPath.parse(response.getContentAsString()).read("$.id");
        assertNotNull(courseService.getCourseById(id));

    }
}
```

Let's define various components we used in the class defined in listing 7.13:

- The `@SpringBootTest` annotation indicates the annotated class runs Spring Boot-based tests and provides necessary environmental support to run the test cases. It creates the Spring application context that creates all Spring beans needed to run the test cases.
- The `@AutoConfigureMockMvc` annotation enables and auto-configures the MockMVC framework. This annotation performs the heavy lifting to provide the necessary support, so we can simply autowire an instance of MockMVC and use it in the test.
- The `@ExtendWith(SpringExtension.class)` annotation integrates the Spring TestContext Framework with JUnit 5's Jupiter programming model. `@ExtendWith` is a JUnit 5 annotation that allows you to specify the extension to be used to run the test case.
- We autowired the `CourseService` and the `MockMvc` instance in the class.
- We used the `mockMvc` instance to perform an HTTP POST operation with a sample course.

Once the request is fired, we use the `andExpect` to assert various attributes. We've used the `jsonpath` to extract the values from the JSON response. Lastly, we validate the HTTP response status code. Let's now provide the test case to get the course by ID. The following listing shows this test case.

Listing 7.14 Test case to get a course by a course ID

```
@Test
public void testRetrieveCourse() throws Exception {
     Course course = Course.builder()
                .name("Rapid Spring Boot Application Development")
                .category("Spring")
                .rating(5)
                .description("Rapid Spring Boot Application
➥ Development").build();
    ObjectMapper objectMapper = new ObjectMapper();

    MockHttpServletResponse response = mockMvc.perform(post("/courses/")
            .contentType("application/json")
            .content(objectMapper.writeValueAsString(course)))
            .andDo(print())
            .andExpect(jsonPath("$.*", hasSize(5)))
            .andExpect(jsonPath("$.id", greaterThan(0)))
            .andExpect(jsonPath("$.name").value("Rapid Spring Boot
➥ Application Development"))
            .andExpect(jsonPath("$.category").value("Spring"))
            .andExpect(jsonPath("$.rating").value(5))
            .andExpect(status().isCreated()).andReturn().getResponse();
    Integer id = JsonPath.parse(response.getContentAsString()).read("$.id");

    mockMvc.perform(get("/courses/{id}",id))
            .andDo(print())
```

```
            .andExpect(jsonPath("$.*", hasSize(5)))
            .andExpect(jsonPath("$.id", greaterThan(0)))
            .andExpect(jsonPath("$.name").value("Rapid Spring Boot
➥ Application Development"))
            .andExpect(jsonPath("$.category").value("Spring"))
            .andExpect(jsonPath("$.rating").value(5))
            .andExpect(status().isOk());

}
```

In listing 7.14, we've first created a course through the `post()` method and then used the `get()` method to retrieve the course details. Like the previous test case, we've asserted the various response parameters along with the HTTP response status code. Let's now include the remaining test cases, as shown in the following listing.

Listing 7.15 Test cases for the Invalid Couse ID, Update, and Delete Course endpoints

```
@Test
public void testInvalidCouseId() throws Exception {
    mockMvc.perform(get("/courses/{id}",100))
    .andDo(print())
    .andExpect(status().isNotFound());
}

@Test
public void testUpdateCourse() throws Exception {
     Course course = Course.builder()
                .name("Rapid Spring Boot Application Development")
                .category("Spring")
                .rating(3)
                .description("Rapid Spring Boot Application
➥ Development").build();
    ObjectMapper objectMapper = new ObjectMapper();

    MockHttpServletResponse response = mockMvc.perform(post("/courses/")
            .contentType("application/json")
            .content(objectMapper.writeValueAsString(course)))
            .andDo(print())
            .andExpect(jsonPath("$.*", hasSize(5)))
            .andExpect(jsonPath("$.id", greaterThan(0)))
            .andExpect(jsonPath("$.name").value("Rapid Spring Boot
➥ Application Development"))
            .andExpect(jsonPath("$.category").value("Spring"))
            .andExpect(jsonPath("$.rating").value(3))
            .andExpect(status().isCreated()).andReturn().getResponse();
    Integer id = JsonPath.parse(response.getContentAsString()).read("$.id");

    Course updatedCourse = Course.builder()
            .name("Rapid Spring Boot Application Development")
            .category("Spring")
            .rating(5)
            .description("Rapid Spring Boot Application
➥ Development").build();
```

```
    mockMvc.perform(put("/courses/{id}", id)
            .contentType("application/json")
            .content(objectMapper.writeValueAsString(updatedCourse)))
            .andDo(print())
            .andExpect(jsonPath("$.*", hasSize(5)))
            .andExpect(jsonPath("$.id").value(id))
            .andExpect(jsonPath("$.name").value("Rapid Spring Boot
➥   Application Development"))
            .andExpect(jsonPath("$.category").value("Spring"))
            .andExpect(jsonPath("$.rating").value(5))
            .andExpect(status().isOk());

}

@Test
public void testDeleteCourse() throws Exception {
     Course course = Course.builder()
                .name("Rapid Spring Boot Application Development")
                .category("Spring")
                .rating(5)
                .description("Rapid Spring Boot Application
➥   Development").build();
   ObjectMapper objectMapper = new ObjectMapper();

   MockHttpServletResponse response = mockMvc.perform(post("/courses/")
            .contentType("application/json")
            .content(objectMapper.writeValueAsString(course)))
            .andDo(print())
            .andExpect(jsonPath("$.*", hasSize(5)))
            .andExpect(jsonPath("$.id", greaterThan(0)))
            .andExpect(jsonPath("$.name").value("Rapid Spring Boot
➥   Application Development"))
            .andExpect(jsonPath("$.category").value("Spring"))
            .andExpect(jsonPath("$.rating").value(5))
            .andExpect(status().isCreated()).andReturn().getResponse();
   Integer id = JsonPath.parse(response.getContentAsString()).read("$.id");

   mockMvc.perform(delete("/courses/{id}", id))
            .andDo(print())
            .andExpect(status().isOk());

}
```

In listing 7.15, we've defined three test cases:

- The first test case attempts to get the course details for a course ID that is not available. The application returns an HTTP 404 status code, and we expect the same in the test case.
- The second test case performs an HTTP `PUT` operation to test the update course endpoint.
- The last test case performs the HTTP `DELETE` operation to delete a course with a `courseId`.

DISCUSSION

Spring MockMVC framework provides an excellent way to test Spring MVC-based applications. Moreover, Spring Boot autoconfiguration of MockMVC has simplified defining the test cases even further. With this technique, we've demonstrated how to define test cases for the REST API endpoints with Spring's MockMVC framework. The MockMVC framework provides a fluent API that allows you to perform the assertion of various response parameters. You can find further details regarding MockMVC at http://mng.bz/do5D.

Spring also provides an alternate test client called WebTestClient that lets you verify the response in a much better manner. We'll demonstrate the use of WebTestClient in the next chapter.

7.4 Documenting a RESTful API

As part of modern-day application development, APIs play a critical role in the success of an application. As application features are consumed by a variety of devices, it is important that APIs are documented. Further, an API represents a contract between an API provider and consumers. Therefore, a good API should ensure that the API details are available to its consumers, so consumers can develop their code accordingly. These details include the HTTP request and response structure, HTTP status code that an endpoint returns, security configurations, and various other details. You can refer to https://petstore.swagger.io/ for a quick glimpse of the documentation of the Spring Petclinic application (https://github.com/spring-projects/spring-petclinic). In this section, we'll discuss documenting the RESTful APIs through OpenAPI (https://swagger.io/specification/), which is the most popular and de facto standard of RESTful API documentation.

7.4.1 Technique: Documenting a RESTful API with OpenAPI

In this technique, we'll learn how to document a RESTful API.

PROBLEM

The Course Tracker API is currently undocumented, and there are no means other than exploring the application source code to find out the details regarding the API. We need to document this API with OpenAPI, so the API consumers can find the required details about the API.

SOLUTION

The OpenAPI Specification provides a standard approach to document RESTful APIs, so the API consumers can find out the details and capabilities of the API in a consistent manner.

> **Source code**
> The final version of the Spring Boot project is available at http://mng.bz/raOg.

The OpenAPI specification is language-agnostic, which means it is not only limited to Spring Boot, but it is available for other languages and frameworks as well. For instance, we can use OpenAPI to document the RESTful API developed through a Spring Boot application, and the same is possible for a RESTful API developed through Express JS (https://expressjs.com/).

In this section, we'll demonstrate how to document the Course Tracker API with OpenAPI. To proceed with that, let's first add the following Maven dependency in the pom.xml file, as shown in the following listing.

Listing 7.16 OpenAPI Maven dependency

```
<dependency>
    <groupId>org.springdoc</groupId>
    <artifactId>springdoc-openapi-ui</artifactId>
    <version>1.5.9</version>
</dependency>
```

The `springdoc-openapi` (https://springdoc.org/) library automates the generation of API documentation in a Spring Boot project. It does so by inspecting a Spring Boot application at runtime to infer the API semantics based on Spring configurations, class structure, and other annotations. The `springdoc-openapi-ui` dependency provides integration between Spring Boot and Swagger UI. It automatically deploys the `swagger-ui` to a Spring Boot application and makes it available at http://{server}:{port}/{context-path}/swagger-ui.html.

Notice that we've introduced Swagger in our discussion. Let's clarify the difference between Swagger and OpenAPI. The OpenAPI is the specification that dictates the guidelines for the API documentation. Swagger is the tool that implements this specification. Swagger consists of various components, such as Swagger Editor, Swagger UI, Swagger Codegen, and a few other modules. Please refer to http://mng.bz/VlNX for a detailed discussion on Swagger vs. OpenAPI.

Let's now proceed with documenting the Course Tracker API. To document the API, we annotate the endpoints with various annotations. These annotations contain custom details about the endpoint, such as the purpose of the endpoint, the HTTP status code it returns, and more. The following listing shows the updated `CourseController` annotated with the OpenAPI annotations.

Listing 7.17 The CourseController class

```
package com.manning.sbip.ch07.controller;

// imports

import io.swagger.v3.oas.annotations.Operation;
import io.swagger.v3.oas.annotations.tags.Tag;

@RestController
@RequestMapping("/courses/")
```

```
@Tag(name = "Course Controller", description = "This REST controller
➥ provide services to manage courses in the Course Tracker application")
public class CourseController {

    private CourseService courseService;

    @Autowired
    public CourseController(CourseService courseService) {
        this.courseService = courseService;
    }

    @GetMapping
    @ResponseStatus(code = HttpStatus.OK)
    @Operation(summary = "Provides all courses available in the Course
➥ Tracker application")
    public Iterable<Course> getAllCourses() {
        return courseService.getCourses();
    }

    @GetMapping("{id}")
    @ResponseStatus(code = HttpStatus.OK)
    @Operation(summary = "Provides course details for the supplied course
➥ id from the Course Tracker application")
    public Optional<Course> getCourseById(@PathVariable("id") long courseId)
     {
        return courseService.getCourseById(courseId);
    }

    @GetMapping("category/{name}")
    @ResponseStatus(code = HttpStatus.OK)
    @Operation(summary = "Provides course details for the supplied course
➥ category from the Course Tracker application")
    public Iterable<Course> getCourseByCategory(@PathVariable("name")
String category) {
        return courseService.getCoursesByCategory(category);
    }

    @PostMapping
    @ResponseStatus(code = HttpStatus.CREATED)
    @Operation(summary = "Creates a new course in the Course Tracker
➥ application")
    public Course createCourse(@Valid @RequestBody Course course) {
        return courseService.createCourse(course);
    }

    @PutMapping("{id}")
    @ResponseStatus(code = HttpStatus.NO_CONTENT)
    @Operation(summary = "Updates the course details in the Course Tracker
➥ application for the supplied course id")
    public void updateCourse(@PathVariable("id") long courseId, @Valid
@RequestBody Course course) {
        courseService.updateCourse(courseId, course);
    }
```

```
    @DeleteMapping("{id}")
    @ResponseStatus(code = HttpStatus.NO_CONTENT)
    @Operation(summary = "Deletes the course details for the supplied
➥ course id from the Course Tracker application")
    public void deleteCourseById(@PathVariable("id") long courseId) {
        courseService.deleteCourseById(courseId);
    }

    @DeleteMapping
    @ResponseStatus(code = HttpStatus.NO_CONTENT)
    @Operation(summary = "Deletes all courses from the Course Tracker
➥ application")
    public void deleteCourses() {
        courseService.deleteCourses();
    }

}
```

In listing 7.17, we annotated the class with `@Tag` and the endpoints with `@ResponseStatus` and `@Operation` annotations. The `@Tag` provides information about the controller. The `@ResponseStatus` indicates the HTTP status code the endpoint returns. Notice that the HTTP status code is critical for the API consumer to code their application logic, as it defines the status of the API call. Thus, we must take care while determining the HTTP Status code for the endpoints. Lastly, the `@Operation` annotation captures details regarding the purpose of the endpoint.

Let's now capture a few custom details about the API, such as API version, title, description, license details, and more. You can do this by defining a Spring bean of type OpenAPI. Listing 7.18 shows the OpenAPI bean definition. For simplicity, we've defined this bean in the Spring Boot main class, as shown in the following listing. In a typical application, you should define a separate Spring configuration class that should contain this `@Bean` definition.

Listing 7.18 The OpenAPI bean definition

```
package com.manning.sbip.ch07;

//imports

import io.swagger.v3.oas.models.OpenAPI;
import io.swagger.v3.oas.models.info.Info;
import io.swagger.v3.oas.models.info.License;

@SpringBootApplication
public class CourseTrackerApiApplication {

    public static void main(String[] args) {
        SpringApplication.run(CourseTrackerApiApplication.class, args);
    }

    @Bean
    public OpenAPI customOpenAPI(@Value("${app.description}") String
```

```
➥ appDescription,
            @Value("${app.version}") String appVersion) {

        return new OpenAPI().info(new Info().title("Course Tracker
➥ API").version(appVersion)
                .description(appDescription).termsOfService("http://swag-
   ger.io/terms/")
                .license(new License().name("Apache
➥ 2.0").url("http://springdoc.org")));

    }

}
```

In listing 7.18, we defined the OpenAPI bean, which contains custom API details. In the following listing, we define the `app.description` and `app.version` properties in the application.properties file.

Listing 7.19 The application.properties file

```
app.description=Spring Boot Course Tracker API
app.version=v1
```

That's all. Let's start the application and access the `swagger-ui` to view the API documentation. You can access `swagger-ui` for this application at http://localhost:8080/swagger-ui.html. Figure 7.3 shows the `swagger-ui` for the Course Tracker API.

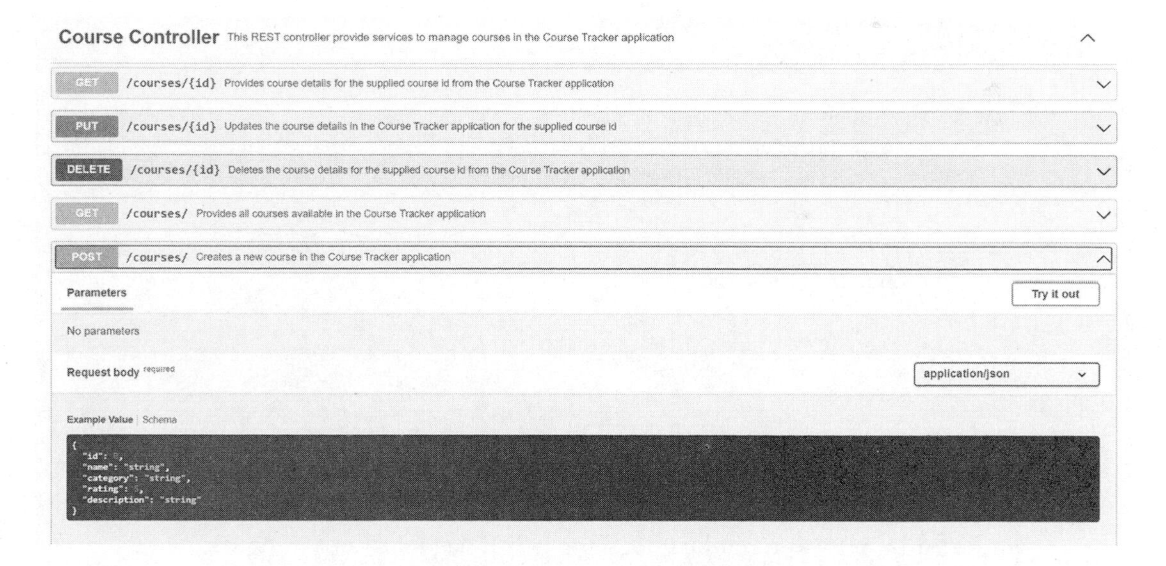

Figure 7.3 The Course Tracker swagger documentation. It contains the API description, controller details, and endpoint details.

DISCUSSION

OpenAPI is the de facto choice to document RESTful APIs. As you've seen in the previous example, by adding a few dependencies you have a nice HTML-based API document that captures the details about the API. However, one issue with the HTML is that it is difficult to share with the API consumers. To handle this, Swagger also lets you extract the API documentation in JSON format. You can retrieve this JSON by accessing the http://localhost:8080/v3/api-docs URL. This is shown in the following listing.

Listing 7.20 The API documentation in JSON format

```
{
   "openapi":"3.0.1",
   "info":{
      "title":"Course Tracker API",
      "description":"Spring Boot Course Tracker API",
      "termsOfService":"http://swagger.io/terms/",
      "license":{
         "name":"Apache 2.0",
         "url":"http://springdoc.org"
      },
      "version":"v1"
   },
   "servers":[
      {
         "url":"http://localhost:8080",
         "description":"Generated server url"
      }
   ],
   "tags":[
      {
         "name":"Course Controller",
         "description":"This REST controller provides services to manage
➥  courses in the Course Tracker application"
      }
   ],
   "paths":{
      "/courses/{id}":{
         "get":{
            "tags":[
               "Course Controller"
            ],

// Remaining part of the JSON is omitted
```

Swagger provides the Swagger Editor (https://editor.swagger.io/), which allows you to import this JSON and renders the same HTML layout shown in figure 7.4.

You can ship this JSON shown in listing 7.20 with API consumers to let them render it through Swagger Editor. To make life even simpler, Swagger also provides a Codegen utility that allows you to generate client applications from this JSON. For

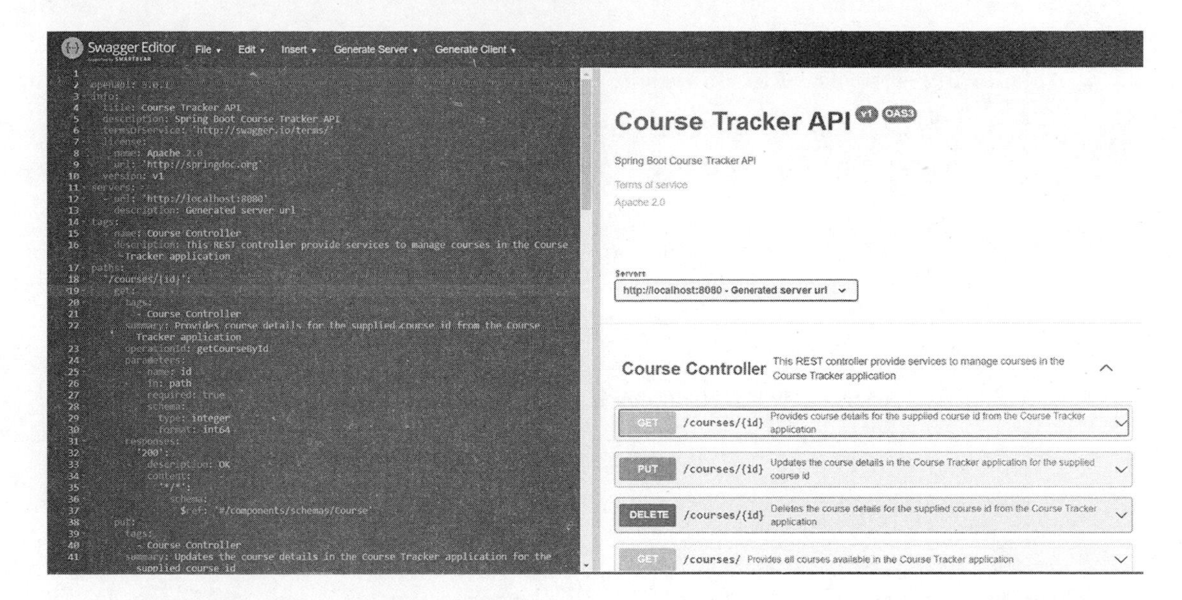

Figure 7.4 Rendering the REST API documentation in the Swagger Editor. The Swagger Editor prefers the YAML version of the JSON data and automatically converts a JSON to YAML while you paste the JSON in the editor.

instance, let's assume that the API client uses Node JS as their preferred language. You can generate this Node JS client stub with Swagger Codegen. Swagger Codegen also allows you to generate the client stub for a lot of different languages. Refer to https://swagger.io/tools/swagger-codegen/ for more details on Swagger Codegen. For further details on Spring Doc and OpenAPI integration, refer to Spring Doc reference documentation available at https://springdoc.org/.

7.5 Implementing RESTful API versioning

In this section, we'll discuss the various approaches to versioning a RESTful API. However, before proceeding with the discussion of various versioning techniques, let's discuss REST API versioning and why it's necessary.

In simple words, versioning a REST API means the ability for the API to support multiple versions. It is a common occurrence to enhance or upgrade the application features over time. Various factors could drive these changes. For instance, it could be the implementation of new business features, adoption of a new technology stack, or refinement of the existing APIs.

However, the issue with a breaking API change is that it directly impacts the API consumers and breaks their application. It also causes a cascading impact on the API invocation chain. One way to resolve this issue is to implement versioning while designing your APIs. This way, you may have a version that is stable and available for your API consumers. For any breaking changes, you can introduce a newer version of the API that can be progressively adopted by various consumers.

In this section, we'll discuss the available techniques to implement API versioning. Following is the list of techniques we'll discuss in this chapter:

- *URI versioning*—Uses a version number in the URI
- *Request parameter versioning*—Uses an HTTP request parameter to identify the version
- *Custom HTTP header versioning*—Uses an HTTP request header to distinguish the version
- *Media type versioning*—Uses the accept header request header in the request to identify the version

We'll demonstrate the different versioning techniques in the next technique. Later, we'll provide an analysis on the merits and demerits of the approaches. To better explain the versioning techniques, we'll simplify the `CourseController` class and only use the `GET/courses/` and `POST /courses/` endpoint for versioning. Let's discuss this in the next technique.

7.5.1 Technique: Implementing versioning in a RESTful API

In this technique, we'll discuss how to implement versioning in a RESTful API.

PROBLEM

The Course Tracker API has not implemented any versioning strategy. We need to implement a versioning technique to ensure that the API can handle any breaking changes.

SOLUTION

In this section, we'll first discuss the URI versioning technique. This is a straightforward approach, as it includes a version identifier in the REST URI. For instance, `/courses/v1` represents version 1 of the API, and `/courses/v2` represents version 2 of the API.

> **Source code**
> The final version of the Spring Boot project is available at http://mng.bz/xv98.

Let's assume we now need to enhance Course Tracker API, and it needs to also support an additional attribute of course `price` along with the previous course details. Introduction of course `price` could also mean that we can have additional REST endpoints, such as finding courses between a price range or retrieving courses based on the price order.

NOTE For simplicity reasons and demonstration purposes we are introducing the price attribute to the `Course` entity to design a new version of the API. In actual scenarios, there should be more appropriate reasons for API versioning.

To demonstrate this change, we'll make changes to the `CourseController` class in the Course Tracker application. We'll rename the existing `CourseController` class to `LegacyCourseController` and keep only `GET /courses/` and `POST /courses/` endpoints in it. The following listing shows the modified class.

Listing 7.21 The LegacyCourseController class

```
package com.manning.sbip.ch07.controller;

// imports

@RestController
@RequestMapping("/courses/v1")
public class LegacyCourseController {

    private CourseService courseService;

    @Autowired
    public LegacyCourseController(CourseService courseService) {
        this.courseService = courseService;
    }

    @GetMapping
    @ResponseStatus(code = HttpStatus.OK)
    public Iterable<Course> getAllCourses() {
        return courseService.getCourses();
    }

    @PostMapping
    @ResponseStatus(code = HttpStatus.CREATED)
    public Course createCourse(@Valid @RequestBody Course course) {
        return courseService.createCourse(course);
    }
}
```

The request mapping URL contains the version number. We've appended version v1 to indicate the first version of the API.

The most notable change in listing 7.21 is that we've updated the `@RequestMapping` URI to `/courses/v1`. This is now the `v1` version of the API. We'll also introduce a new `RestController` called `ModernCourseController`. This controller class contains the changes related to the course `price`. The following listing shows the `ModernCourseController` class.

Listing 7.22 The ModernCourseController class

```
package com.manning.sbip.ch07.controller;

//imports

@RestController
@RequestMapping("/courses/v2")
public class ModernCourseController {

    private ModernCourseRepository modernCourseRepository;
```

```
    @Autowired
    public ModernCourseController(ModernCourseRepository
➥ modernCourseRepository) {
        this.modernCourseRepository = modernCourseRepository;
    }

    @GetMapping
    @ResponseStatus(code = HttpStatus.OK)
    public Iterable<ModernCourse> getAllCourses() {
        return modernCourseRepository.findAll();
    }

    @PostMapping
    @ResponseStatus(code = HttpStatus.CREATED)
    public ModernCourse createCourse(@Valid @RequestBody ModernCourse
➥ modernCourse) {
        return modernCourseRepository.save(modernCourse);
    }
}
```

Listing 7.22 represents the `v2` version of the API, and we have done this by defining the `@RequestMapping` to `/courses/v2` URI. We've also defined a new JPA entity class called `ModernCourse` that contains the new course attribute `price` along with other parameters and a new Spring Data repository interface called `ModernCourseRepository` available at http://mng.bz/Ax5z. For simplicity, we have skipped the service layer in the new version of the API.

That's it. Now, let's start the application and access both versions of the API. Listing 7.23 shows the output of creating and accessing a course with the `v1` version of the API.

Listing 7.23 Creating and retrieving courses with v1 version of Courses Tracker API

```
>http POST :8080/courses/v1 name="Mastering Spring Boot" rating=4
➥ category=Spring description="Mastering Spring Boot intends to teach
➥ Spring Boot with practical examples"
HTTP/1.1 201
// Other HTTP Response Headers

{
    "category": "Spring",
    "description": "Mastering Spring Boot intends to teach Spring Boot with
➥ practical examples",
    "id": 1,
    "name": "Mastering Spring Boot",
    "rating": 4
}


>http GET :8080/courses/v1
HTTP/1.1 200
// Other HTTP Response Headers
```

```
[
    {
        "category": "Spring",
        "description": "Mastering Spring Boot intends to teach Spring Boot
➥ with practical examples",
        "id": 1,
        "name": "Mastering Spring Boot",
        "rating": 4
    }
]
```

Let's now create and retrieve courses with the v2 version of the API. The following listing shows the output.

Listing 7.24 Creating and retrieving courses with v2 version of Course Tracker API

```
>http POST :8080/courses/v2 name="Mastering Spring Boot" rating=4
➥ category=Spring description="Mastering Spring Boot intends to teach
➥ Spring Boot with practical examples" price=42.34
HTTP/1.1 201
// Other HTTP Response Headers

{
    "category": "Spring",
    "description": "Mastering Spring Boot intends to teach Spring Boot with
➥ practical examples",
    "id": 1,
    "name": "Mastering Spring Boot",
    "price": 42.34,
    "rating": 4
}


>http GET :8080/courses/v2
HTTP/1.1 200
// Other HTTP Response Headers
[
    {
        "category": "Spring",
        "description": "Mastering Spring Boot intends to teach Spring Boot
➥ with practical examples",
        "id": 1,
        "name": "Mastering Spring Boot",
        "price": 42.34,
        "rating": 4
    }
]
```

Creating a new course with the new version (/courses/v2) of the course API. Notice that we've included a new field named price in this endpoint.

As you may have noticed, both versions of the APIs are working fine. In the v1 version of the API, there is no price parameter. In the v2 version of the API, the price parameter is shown.

Let's now discuss the second versioning technique of using an HTTP request parameter to determine the version. We'll use the same Course Tracker application to demonstrate this versioning type.

Source code

The final version of the Spring Boot project is available at http://mng.bz/Zzdm.

For the HTTP request parameter-based versioning technique, you'll provide a request parameter in the REST endpoint URI that dictates which version of the API should be invoked. Let's define a new `RestController` class called `RequestParameterVersioningCourseController`. The following listing shows the `RequestParameterVersioningCourseController` class.

Listing 7.25 Implementing the versioning with HTTP request parameter

```
package com.manning.sbip.ch07.controller;

//imports

@RestController
@RequestMapping("/courses/")
public class RequestParameterVersioningCourseController {

    @Autowired
    private CourseService courseService;

    @Autowired
    private ModernCourseRepository modernCourseRepository;

    @GetMapping(params = "version=v1")
    @ResponseStatus(code = HttpStatus.OK)
    public Iterable<Course> getAllLegacyCourses() {
        return courseService.getCourses();
    }

    @PostMapping(params = "version=v1")
    @ResponseStatus(code = HttpStatus.CREATED)
    public Course createCourse(@Valid @RequestBody Course course) {
        return courseService.createCourse(course);
    }

    @GetMapping(params = "version=v2")
    @ResponseStatus(code = HttpStatus.OK)
    public Iterable<ModernCourse> getAllModernCourses() {
        return modernCourseRepository.findAll();
    }

    @PostMapping(params = "version=v2")
    @ResponseStatus(code = HttpStatus.CREATED)
```

```
    public ModernCourse createCourse(@Valid @RequestBody ModernCourse
➥ modernCourse) {
        return modernCourseRepository.save(modernCourse);
    }
}
```

In listing 7.25, notice the use of `version=v1` and `version=v2` request parameters that determines the endpoint to be invoked. Also notice that we've used the `CourseService` class for the `v1` version of the API and `ModernCourseRepository` for the `v2` version of the API. Ideally, we should define a service class to wrap the functionalities of the `ModernCourseRepository` interface for the version `v2` API as well. For simplicity and demonstration purposes, we have skipped this step. In a real production application, you should define a service class for the controller.

You can start the application and access the new endpoints with the `version=v2` parameter. The following listing shows the output.

Listing 7.26 Invoking the v2 version of POST /courses/ endpoint with request parameter

```
>http POST :8080/courses/?version=v2 name="Mastering Spring Boot" rating=4
➥ category=Spring description="Mastering Spring Boot intends to teach
➥ Spring Boot with practical examples" price=42.34
HTTP/1.1 201
// Other HTTP Response Headers
{
    "category": "Spring",
    "description": "Mastering Spring Boot intends to teach Spring Boot with
➥ practical examples",
    "id": 1,
    "name": "Mastering Spring Boot",
    "price": 42.34,
    "rating": 4
}

>http GET :8080/courses/?version=v2
// Other HTTP Response Headers
[
    {
        "category": "Spring",
        "description": "Mastering Spring Boot intends to teach Spring Boot
➥ with practical examples",
        "id": 1,
        "name": "Mastering Spring Boot",
        "price": 42.45,
        "rating": 4
    }
]
```

In the `v1` version of the API, you'll notice that the price parameter is not available.

Let's now discuss the third API versioning technique that uses a custom HTTP header to identify the endpoint that needs to be invoked. This is quite similar to the second technique of using the HTTP request parameter. In this case, instead of an

HTTP request parameter in the URI, we use a custom HTTP header in the HTTP request. Let's define a new class that implements this versioning strategy.

Source code

The final version of the Spring Boot project is available at http://mng.bz/REjj.

Listing 7.27 shows the `CustomHeaderVersioningCourseController` class.

Listing 7.27 Implementing versioning with a custom HTTP header

```
package com.manning.sbip.ch07.controller;
// imports

@RestController
@RequestMapping("/courses/")
public class CustomHeaderVersioningCourseController {

    private CourseService courseService;
    private ModernCourseRepository modernCourseRepository;

    @Autowired
    public CustomHeaderVersioningCourseController(CourseService
➥ courseService, ModernCourseRepository modernCourseRepository) {
        this.courseService = courseService;
        this.modernCourseRepository = modernCourseRepository;
    }

    @GetMapping(headers = "X-API-VERSION=v1")
    @ResponseStatus(code = HttpStatus.OK)
    public Iterable<Course> getAllLegacyCourses() {
        return courseService.getCourses();
    }

    @PostMapping(headers = "X-API-VERSION=v1")
    @ResponseStatus(code = HttpStatus.CREATED)
    public Course createCourse(@Valid @RequestBody Course course) {
        return courseService.createCourse(course);
    }

    @GetMapping(headers = "X-API-VERSION=v2")
    @ResponseStatus(code = HttpStatus.OK)
    public Iterable<ModernCourse> getAllModernCourses() {
        return modernCourseRepository.findAll();
    }

    @PostMapping(headers = "X-API-VERSION=v2")
    @ResponseStatus(code = HttpStatus.CREATED)
    public ModernCourse createCourse(@Valid @RequestBody ModernCourse
➥ modernCourse) {
        return modernCourseRepository.save(modernCourse);
    }
}
```

In listing 7.27, we used a custom HTTP header `X-API-VERSION` to determine the endpoint that needs to be invoked. To invoke a REST endpoint, you need to supply the `X-API-VERSION` header in your HTTP request. The following listing shows the use of this custom HTTP header.

Listing 7.28 Invoking the v2 version of POST /courses/ endpoint with a custom HTTP header

```
>http POST :8080/courses/ X-API-VERSION:v2 name="Mastering Spring Boot"
➥ rating=4 category=Spring description="Mastering Spring Boot intends to
➥ teach Spring Boot with practical examples" price=42.34
HTTP/1.1 201
// Other HTTP Response Headers

{
    "category": "Spring",
    "description": "Mastering Spring Boot intends to teach Spring Boot with
➥ practical examples",
    "id": 1,
    "name": "Mastering Spring Boot",
    "price": 42.34,
    "rating": 4
}

>http GET :8080/courses/ X-API-VERSION:v2

// Other HTTP Response Headers

[
    {
        "category": "Spring",
        "description": "Mastering Spring Boot intends to teach Spring Boot
➥ with practical examples",
        "id": 1,
        "name": "Mastering Spring Boot",
        "price": 42.34,
        "rating": 4
    }
]
```

The last versioning technique we'll discuss in this section is media-type versioning. This is also known as the `Content Negotiation` or `Accept Header` versioning strategy. This is due to the use of the `Accept` HTTP request header. In this technique, instead of using a custom HTTP header, we leverage the built-in `Accept` HTTP header. With the `Accept` HTTP header, a client indicates a server the content types (through MIME types) that the client understands. In the HTTP request, the client provides the `Accept` header. In the content negotiation (http://mng.bz/2jB8) phase, the server uses its internal algorithm to determine one of the `Accept` header values and inform the choice with the `Content-Type` response header.

Source code

The final version of the Spring Boot project is available at http://mng.bz/1jl1.

Let's define the AcceptHeaderVersioningCourseController class that implements the versioning technique with the Accept HTTP header. This implementation is shown in the following listing.

Listing 7.29 Implementing the versioning with Accept HTTP header

```
package com.manning.sbip.ch07.controller;

//imports


@RestController
@RequestMapping("/courses/")
public class AcceptHeaderVersioningCourseController {

    private CourseService courseService;
    private ModernCourseRepository modernCourseRepository;

    @Autowired
    public AcceptHeaderVersioningCourseController(CourseService
➥ courseService, ModernCourseRepository modernCourseRepository) {
        this.courseService = courseService;
        this.modernCourseRepository = modernCourseRepository;
    }

    @GetMapping(produces = "application/vnd.sbip.app-v1+json")
    @ResponseStatus(code = HttpStatus.OK)
    public Iterable<Course> getAllLegacyCourses() {
        return courseService.getCourses();
    }

    @PostMapping(produces = "application/vnd.sbip.app-v1+json")
    @ResponseStatus(code = HttpStatus.CREATED)
    public Course createCourse(@Valid @RequestBody Course course) {
        return courseService.createCourse(course);
    }

    @GetMapping(produces = "application/vnd.sbip.app-v2+json")
    @ResponseStatus(code = HttpStatus.OK)
    public Iterable<ModernCourse> getAllModernCourses() {
        return modernCourseRepository.findAll();
    }

    @PostMapping(produces = "application/vnd.sbip.app-v2+json")
    @ResponseStatus(code = HttpStatus.CREATED)
    public ModernCourse createCourse(@Valid @RequestBody ModernCourse
➥ modernCourse) {
        return modernCourseRepository.save(modernCourse);
    }
}
```

In the following listing, we've used the produces attribute of the @GetMapping and @PostMapping annotations that declares the content the endpoint produces. The application/vnd.sbip.app-v1+json is a custom MIME type that indicates the v1 version of the API, and application/vnd.sbip.app-v2+json specifies the v2 version of the API. The following listing shows the use of the Accept HTTP header.

Listing 7.30 Invoking the v2 version of POST /courses/ endpoint with Accept HTTP header

```
>http POST :8080/courses/ Accept:application/vnd.sbip.app-v2+json
➥ name="Mastering Spring Boot" rating=4 category=Spring
➥ description="Mastering Spring Boot intends to teach Spring Boot with
➥ practical examples" price=42.34
HTTP/1.1 201
Connection: keep-alive
Content-Type: application/vnd.sbip.app-v2+json
Date: Fri, 25 Jun 2021 18:42:15 GMT
Keep-Alive: timeout=60
Transfer-Encoding: chunked

{
    "category": "Spring",
    "description": "Mastering Spring Boot intends to teach Spring Boot with
➥ practical examples",
    "id": 1,
    "name": "Mastering Spring Boot",
    "price": 42.34,
    "rating": 4
}

>http GET :8080/courses/ Accept:application/vnd.sbip.app-v2+json
HTTP/1.1 200
Connection: keep-alive
Content-Type: application/vnd.sbip.app-v2+json
Date: Mon, 08 Nov 2021 02:39:29 GMT
Keep-Alive: timeout=60
Transfer-Encoding: chunked

[
    {
        "category": "Spring",
        "description": "Mastering Spring Boot intends to teach Spring Boot
➥ with practical examples",
        "id": 1,
        "name": "Mastering Spring Boot",
        "price": 42.34,
        "rating": 4
    }
]
```

DISCUSSION

With this technique, we've seen the various techniques to implement versioning in a REST API. Now that you have several choices to implement versioning, the immediate next question that comes to mind is which approach is better and preferable. This is a difficult question, and there is no straightforward answer to it. This is because none of the solutions we've discussed are perfect.

For instance, many developers reject the idea of assigning a version number in the endpoint URI, as it creates URI pollution. Since the version is not part of the actual URI, many argue the presence of the version identifier is a bad practice. Versioning in the URI exposes to the API consumers that there are multiple versions of the API that exist. Many organizations do not expose this fact to the API consumers.

Similarly, many developers reject the idea of using `Accept` header for versioning purposes, as the `Accept` HTTP header is not designed for this purpose. Using `Accept` header for versioning is just a workaround and is not considered a preferred solution to implement versioning. A similar type of counterargument is available for the other two versioning techniques.

If there are multiple versions of the same endpoint available, it causes issues while documenting the API. For instance, the API consumers may get confused if they find two different approaches to invoke the same service.

As you may notice, there are both merits and demerits of the discussed approaches. Thus, selecting a versioning strategy is a design choice of API designers or the organizations after analyzing the pros and cons of the approach before adopting it to practice. The following list shows the API versioning approaches adopted by several major API providers:

- *Amazon*—Request parameter versioning
- *GitHub*—Media type versioning
- *Microsoft*—Custom header versioning
- *Twitter*—URI versioning

7.6 Securing a RESTful API

In previous sections, we discussed various aspects of developing a RESTful API that includes developing an API, its documentation, its testing, and its versioning. We are still left with another core aspect of API development. And it's the security of the API. Presently, this API is not secure, and anyone who knows the API endpoints can access the API.

There are several ways an API can be secured. The most straightforward approach is using HTTP basic authentication to secure the API. This is the simplest one to implement, as it uses a username and password to authenticate the users. You may remember that in chapter 5, we demonstrated how to implement HTTP basic authentication to secure a Spring Boot application. You can refer to section 5.3.6 in chapter 5 to implement HTTP basic authentication in the Course Tracker API.

However, you should limit the use of HTTP basic authentication to the extent possible due to its various shortcomings. Only consider it for your internal testing or development purposes. An attentive reader may ask why we are discussing it here if it is not recommended to use. The use of basic authentication is still widespread (http://mng.bz/PWKY) due to its simplicity and ease of use. Only recently, some organizations are deprecating the use of this authentication strategy (http://mng.bz/J1pK).

Let's discuss the reasons we should not use it in a production application in the first place. First, HTTP basic authentication uses the username and password in plaintext format with Base64 encoding to authenticate the users. The Base64 encoding is not an encryption technique, and it is extremely easy to retrieve the credentials from a Based64 encoded string. Thus, without HTTPS, there is a high chance credentials could be exposed. Second, with HTTP basic authentication technique, both the client application and the server application act as the password keeper and manage the user credentials for authentication and authorization purposes. This is again problematic, as there are chances that credentials could be compromised by either party.

A preferred approach would be managing the user credentials in a centralized authorization server instead of allowing either the server or the client application to deal with the user password. The authorization server can issue a token that could be used for authentication and authorization purposes. Let's discuss this approach in the next technique.

7.6.1 Technique: Using JWT to authorize RESTful API requests

In this technique, we will discuss how to authorize RESTful API requests using JWT.

Problem

The Course Tracker RESTful API has not implemented any security measures that can secure the REST endpoints. Without security configurations, anyone can access the application endpoints.

Solution

With this technique, we'll demonstrate how to secure the endpoint access with the Bearer Token approach. As mentioned previously, we'll use an authorization server for authorizing access. However, before proceeding with the implementation, let's provide a high-level overview of the REST request and response flow between the client, REST API server, and the authorization server. Figure 7.5 shows a block diagram of this flow:

Let's understand the flow discussed in the figure:

- A client requests to get course details from the Course Tracker REST API by invoking the GET `/courses` endpoint.
- As the client is not authenticated, the API responds with 401 Unauthorized and indicates in the HTTP response header that it needs to authenticate itself with a Bearer Token.
- The client then requests the authorization server to get a Bearer Token. While making this request, the client supplied the required details, such as `client_id`, `username`, `password`, `scope`, and others. Note that the user for which the Bearer Token is requested needs to be configured before a token is requested.

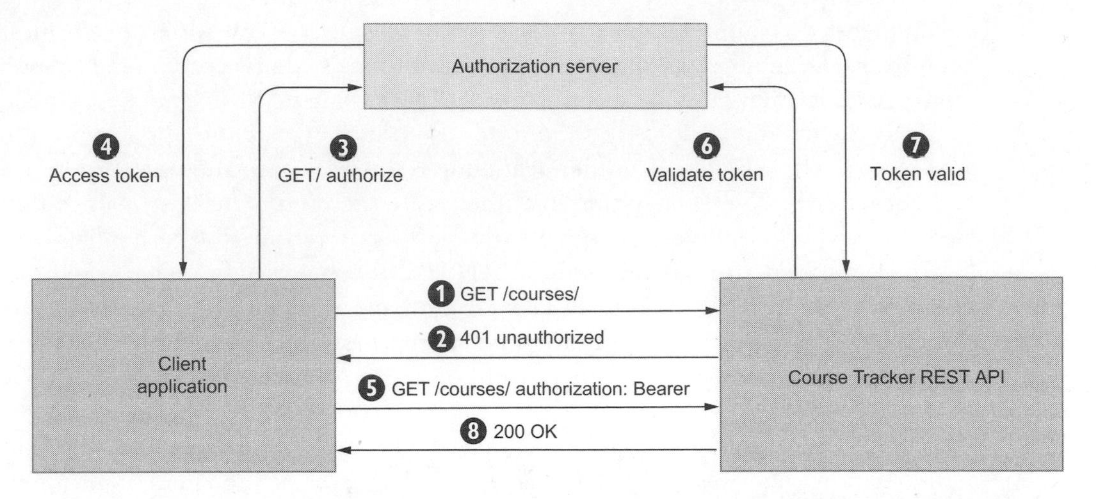

Figure 7.5 The communication between client application, REST API server, and the authorization server to access a REST endpoint by a client. We are using the OAuth2 framework for authentication and authorization.

- For a valid token request, the authorization server returns an `access_token` in JSON Web Token (JWT) format.
- The client application makes a new request to the Course Tracker REST API and supplies the Bearer token in the request.
- The Course Tracker REST API validates the token with the authorization server and receives a response.
- For a valid response, the Course Tracker REST API returns the requested course details. For an invalid response from the authorization server, it returns an error response to the client.

Note that the flow in figure 7.5 is for a new request if the API client attempts to access the endpoint without supplying the JWT token. If the client is supplying the token, the communication starts at step 5.

> **Source code**
> The final version of the Spring Boot project is available at http://mng.bz/wn72.

Let's now begin with the implementation. The first thing that needs to be done is to configure the authorization server. We'll use Keycloak (https://www.keycloak.org/) as the authorization server. We'll configure two users, namely `john` and `steve`, in the authorization server. You can refer to the following GitHub wiki http://mng .bz/q27J to set up the authorization server. It is strongly recommended that you set up the authorization server before continuing with the next steps.

To keep the example simple, we've simplified the Course Tracker application a bit. The course domain entity now contains only three fields: a course ID, a name, and an author. The following listing shows the updated course class.

Listing 7.31 The updated course entity

```
package com.manning.sbip.ch07.model;

// imports

@Entity
@Data
@NoArgsConstructor
@AllArgsConstructor
public class Course {

    @Id
    @GeneratedValue(strategy = GenerationType.IDENTITY)
    @Column(name = "ID")
    private Long id;

    @NotEmpty
    @Column(name = "NAME")
    private String name;

    @NotEmpty
    @Column(name = "AUTHOR")
    private String author;
}
```

We've also simplified the `CourseController` class, and it has the following endpoints:

- Get courses by an author.
- Get course by an ID.
- Create a new course.
- Update an existing course.

To enable JSON Web Token (JWT) support, we need to update the pom.xml with the dependencies shown in the following listing.

Listing 7.32 The Maven depencies for OAuth2 and JWT support

```
<dependency>
    <groupId>org.springframework.boot</groupId>
    <artifactId>spring-boot-starter-oauth2-resource-server</artifactId>
</dependency>
<dependency>
    <groupId>org.springframework.security</groupId>
    <artifactId>spring-security-oauth2-jose</artifactId>
</dependency>
```

The first dependency makes the Course Tracker application an OAuth2 resource server. The second dependency provides support for JWT (https://jwt.io/introduction).

Let's now include the property in the application.properties file shown in the following listing.

Listing 7.33 The JSON Web Token issues URL

```
spring.security.oauth2.resourceserver.jwt.issuer-
➥ uri=http://localhost:9999/auth/realms/master
```

Listing 7.33 configures the Keycloak JWT issuer URL. Let's now explore the updated `CourseController` class, as shown in the following listing.

Listing 7.34 The updated CourseController class

```
package com.manning.sbip.ch07.controller;

//imports

@RestController
@RequestMapping("/courses/")
public class CourseController {

    private CourseRepository courseRepository;

    @Autowired
    public CourseController(CourseRepository courseRepository) {
        this.courseRepository = courseRepository;
    }

    @GetMapping
    public Iterable<Course> getAllCourses(@AuthenticationPrincipal Jwt
➥ jwt) {
        String author = jwt.getClaim("user_name");
        return courseRepository.findByAuthor(author);
    }

    @GetMapping("{id}")
    public Optional<Course> getCourseById(@PathVariable("id") long courseId)
     {
        return courseRepository.findById(courseId);
    }

    @PostMapping
    public Course createCourse(@RequestBody String name,
➥ @AuthenticationPrincipal Jwt jwt) {
        Course course = new Course(null, name, jwt.getClaim("user_name"));
        return courseRepository.save(course);
    }
}
```

The user_name is a custom claim defined in the authorization server. In this context, we use it to get the author name to look up the courses authored by a user.

In listing 7.34, we used the `@AuthenticationPrincipal` annotation to get access to the JWT token. This JWT instance contains the various details about the user request. From the JWT, we retrieve the user_name claim, which is the course author name in this context. Let's now create two courses: one for the author john and another for author steve, as shown in the following listing.

Listing 7.35 Creating courses in the application

```
@Bean
CommandLineRunner createCourse(CourseRepository courseRepository) {
    return (args) -> {
        Course spring = new Course(null, "Spring", "john");
        Course python = new Course(null, "Python", "steve");
        courseRepository.save(spring);
        courseRepository.save(python);
    };
}
```

That's all. Let's now start the application and try accessing the endpoints. Listing 7.36 shows the outcome while we try to access the GET /courses/ endpoint without supplying a JWT token.

Listing 7.36 Accessing GET /courses/ endpoint without a JWT token

```
>http GET :8080/courses
HTTP/1.1 401
WWW-Authenticate: Bearer
// HTTP Response Headers
```

The request is denied with an HTTP 401 unauthorized error response. The API has also responded with the WWW-Authenticate:Bearer response header indicating the client needs to provide a Bearer Token in the HTTP request. This is automatically done by Spring Security. As we are using Bearer Token-based authentication, Spring Security uses the BearerTokenAuthenticationFilter to process the incoming request. It attempts to parse the request and generates a JwtAuthenticationToken, which contains the JWT token details. In the discussion section, we'll provide more details on the classes used to process the request. For now, remember that the BearerTokenAuthenticationFilter is the Spring Security filter that performs the authentication. Let's now try to obtain a Bearer Token for the user john, so the same can be included in the HTTP request. The following listing shows the command to obtain a token.

Listing 7.37 Obtaining a JWT from the Keycloak authorization server

```
C:\Users\musib>http --form POST http://localhost:9999/auth/realms/master/pro-
     tocol/openid-connect/token
➥ grant_type=password client_id=course-tracker scope=course:read
➥ username=john password=password Content-Type:application/x-www-form-
➥ urlencoded
HTTP/1.1 200 OK
// HTTP Response Headers
```

```
{
    "access_token":
➥ "eyJhbGciOiJSUzI1NiIsInR5cCIgOiAiSldUIiwia2lkIiA6ICJxY2lKalIxSWNocTk4Qk
➥ VMcEo5cDJiWDBRaF80MzZ1S0ktbkx4UlF3Zk53In0.eyJleHAiOjE2MjQ3NzczOTgsImlhd
➥ CI6MTYyNDc3Mzc5OCwianRpIjoiYTY4OWM0Y2ItYTVhZC00YTM5LWE1YjQtNjFjNGNhNGZk
➥ MjMzIiwiaXNzIjoiaHR0cDovL2xvY2FsaG9zdDo5OTk5L2F1dGgvcmVhbG1zL21hc3RlciI
➥ sImF1ZCI6ImNvdXJzZS10cmFja2VyIiwic3ViIjoiNmQxMTE4MTktZmF1ZC00NzQzLWFiNT
➥ EtMzk0YmVmNGQ0ZjBlIiwidHlwIjoiQmVhcmVyIiwiYXpwIjoiY291cnNlLXRyYWNrZXIiL
➥ CJzZXNzaW9uX3N0YXRlIjoiOWIyMTdiOTUtOWM1MS00ZGY0LWI3NTYtYTI3NzdmNmI0MDk2
➥ IiwiYWNyIjoiMSIsInNjb3BlIjoiY291cnNlOndyaXRlIGNvdXJzZTpyZWFkIiwidXNlcl9
➥ uYW1lIjoiam9obiIsImF1dGhvcml0aWVzIjpbInVzZXIiXX0.NgBcrpPvDB36sd2ytaeMUk
➥ qM_1_psUDMsHHkB9zZlT_9sIwF3kdPOhSLSmoMqhFtGpOOJI5CmB92WEBu4rVcNa2lnuh16
➥ lkksnC-0ASn23z8TIRtucrQ-
➥ Px2bOgFyducmRH7ec93gOsLKeZSUnjup0YA9FT_0o7eroKFdWrrqoyOiAxOua9nGg307Lkv
➥ _VKXtCB5wSrPFfPQrp6muw-gcREJaBgcYSx-
➥ 5QKC5UK30cFSsWlKXC9i2ov2O3aPA4DlHIqWx06a_M7AKmvgG3fVpyJSztbi0XHDnU9Y_mJ
➥ Vug-WH5MOIpgRUmYYnSL1Ki3PV24tZ11LolyA13XsA859vg",
    "expires_in": 3600,
    "not-before-policy": 0,
    "refresh_expires_in": 1800,
    "refresh_token":
➥ "eyJhbGciOiJIUzI1NiIsInR5cCIgOiAiSldUIiwia2lkIiA6ICIyYzI4MTNiNy05NmIzLT
➥ RkMzctYmUwOS1lMTE0ZTkzZjJlNTcifQ.eyJleHAiOjE2MjQ3NzU1OTgsImlhdCI6MTYyND
➥ c3Mzc5OCwianRpIjoiMTU4Y2E1ZGQtMDMyNy00NTE4LTk4NWItZGQ5ZTliNzcwNjg5Iiwia
➥ XNzIjoiaHR0cDovL2xvY2FsaG9zdDo5OTk5L2F1dGgvcmVhbG1zL21hc3RlciIsImF1ZCI6
➥ Imh0dHA6Ly9sb2NhbGhvc3Q6OTk5OS9hdXRoL3JlYWxtcy9tYXN0ZXIiLCJzdWIiOiI2ZDE
➥ xMTgxOS1mYWVkLTQ3NDMtYWI1MS0zOTRiZWY0ZDRmMGUiLCJ0eXAiOiJSZWZyZXNoIiwiYX
➥ pwIjoiY291cnNlLXRyYWNrZXIiLCJzZXNzaW9uX3N0YXRlIjoiOWIyMTdiOTUtOWM1MS00Z
➥ GY0LWI3NTYtYTI3NzdmNmI0MDk2Iiwic2NvcGUiOiJjb3Vyc2U6d3JpdGUgY291cnNlOnJl
➥ YWQifQ.a1O4SuspoN5u_RvYdXZsb6WLC3INx1smroEIVdYWG_E",
    "scope": "course:write course:read",
    "session_state": "9b217b95-9c51-4df4-b756-a2777f6b4096",
    "token_type": "Bearer"
}
```


In listing 7.37, we used the Keycloak authorization server's token endpoint with the required parameters. If you recall, we've configured all the attributes in the command while setting up and configuring the client application and the users in the Keycloak server. Revisit the GitHub wiki link to understand the purpose of these parameters. Let's explain the various request parameters we've used to access the token details:

- We have used `x-www-form-urlencoded` as the content type, since the Keycloak server understands this request.
- The `grant_type` refers to how an application gets an access token. The `grant_type=password` tells the token endpoint that the application is using the `Password` grant type.
- A `client_id` is generated in the authorization server once an application is registered in the server.
- Scope refers to one or more space-separated strings indicating which permission the application is requesting. In this case, the scope value we are requesting is `course:read`.

- The username and password fields supply the username and password of the user.

In the HTTP response, the Keycloak server returns the access_token and the client scopes configured for the user and token_type. For now, we'll use the access_token from this response to include this token in the HTTP GET request to the Course Tracker API. Note that we've configured the access token to be valid for one hour. Typically, in a production application, tokens are configured to be short-lived for security reasons. For simplicity and testing purposes, we've configured the token to be valid for one hour. In your testing, you should generate a new token and should not use the token provided in listing 7.37. The following listing shows the HTTP GET /courses/ request with the token.

Listing 7.38 Accessing GET /courses/ endpoint with a JWT token

```
C:\Users\musib>http GET :8080/courses/ "Authorization:Bearer
➥ eyJhbGciOiJSUzI1NiIsInR5cCIgOiAi…"
HTTP/1.1 200
// HTTP Response Headers
[
    {
        "author": "john",
        "id": 1,
        "name": "Spring"
    }
]
```

For brevity and readability purposes, we've elided the complete token details.

This time the HTTP status code is 200 OK, and we can retrieve the courses authored by user john.

Although this approach works well, there is a flaw in the implementation. With the current security implementation, we can use the token of one user to get details of the other users. For instance, in this case, we can use the token of john to access the courses authored by steve, as shown in the following lisitng.

Listing 7.39 Accessing author Steve's course details with author John's token

```
>http GET :8080/courses/2 "Authorization:Bearer
➥ eyJhbGciOiJSUzI1NiIsInR5cCIgOiAi…"
HTTP/1.1 200
// HTTP Response Headers

{
    "author": "steve",
    "id": 2,
    "name": "Python"
}
```

Ouch! We can access author Steve's course details (which is course ID 2) with the token of author John. This is an access control issue in the application known as the insecure direct object reference (IDOR) problem (see http://mng.bz/7WBe).

This problem occurred because the token for user `john` is a valid token, and the endpoint `GET /courses/{id}` is not performing any access control check. To avoid this issue, we'll implement method level security with Spring Security. Simply put, the method level security allows you to secure the methods. We'll leverage the Spring Security `@PreAuthorize` or `@PostAuthorize` annotations to implement this. These annotations take Spring Expression Language (SpEL) expression, which is evaluated to make the access control decisions.

Let's demonstrate the use of the `@PostAuthorize` annotation to prevent the `Insecure Direct Object Reference` problem. The access problem happened because there were no checks for whether the supplied token belongs to the author requesting access to the course details performed at the endpoint (with the supplied course ID). We can retrieve the author name (using the `user_name` claim) from the token and compare it with the returned course author name. If there is a mismatch, then we'll forbid this access.

To use the method level security, you need to include the `@EnableGlobalMethodSecurity(prePostEnabled = true)` in the Spring Boot main class. This annotation enabled the method level security in the application, as shown in the following listing.

Listing 7.40 Configuring the EnableGlobalMethodSecurity annotation

```
package com.manning.sbip.ch07;

import
➥ org.springframework.security.config.annotation.method.configuration.Ena
➥ bleGlobalMethodSecurity;

//Other imports

@SpringBootApplication
@EnableGlobalMethodSecurity(prePostEnabled = true)
public class CourseTrackerApiApplication {

    public static void main(String[] args) {
        SpringApplication.run(CourseTrackerApiApplication.class, args);
    }
}
```

Next, you need to include the `@PostAuthorize` annotation on the offending endpoint. The following listing shows the updated endpoint.

Listing 7.41 Implementing @PostAuthorize to secure access control

```
@GetMapping("{id}")
@PostAuthorize("@getAuthor.apply(returnObject,
➥ principal.claims['user_name'])")
public Optional<Course> getCourseById(@PathVariable("id") long courseId) {
    return courseRepository.findById(courseId);
}
```

We supplied two attributes to a `BiFunction` implementation that performs the comparison of the token-supplied author name and the method-returned author name and returns a Boolean value. We've supplied the SpEL expression `@getAuthor.apply(returnObject, principal.claims['user_name'])` to perform the access control. The `returnObject` is the method return object, which is `Optional<Course>`, and the `principal.claims['user_name'])` provides the author name. Listing 7.42 shows this `BiFunction` implementation as a bean definition in the Spring Boot main class. For simplicity, we've included this `@Bean` definition in the Spring Boot main class. In a real application, define a Spring configuration class to define this bean.

Listing 7.42 The BiFunction implementation

```
@Bean
BiFunction<Optional<Course>, String, Boolean> getAuthor() {
    return (course, userId) -> course.filter(c ->
➥ c.getAuthor().equals(userId)).isPresent();
}
```

Let's again try accessing course ID 2 with the access token of author `john`. The following listing shows the outcome.

Listing 7.43 Accessing author Steve's course details with author John's token

```
C:\Users\musib>http GET :8080/courses/2 "Authorization:Bearer
➥ eyJhbGciOiJSUzI1NiIsInR5cCIgOiAi.."
HTTP/1.1 403
// HTTP Response Headers
```

We ended up with the 403 Forbidden HTTP status code. The 403 HTTP return code indicates that the requested user was successfully authenticated to the application but failed in the authorization while accessing the endpoint.

The next thing we'll discuss in this technique is the use of a scope to perform access control in the application. For instance, we can use a scope called `course:read` to ensure that tokens with this scope can access an endpoint.

A scope defines the access level provided in the token to a client application by a user. Imagine, you (as the user) have granted access to a third-party client application to read all the courses authored by you, but you want to restrict that the client application should not be able to perform any write operation. Thus, you can grant (through `grant_type=password`) the third-party client application to obtain a token (by accessing the Keycloak server) only with the `course:read` scope. If the application attempts to perform a write operation for any reason, it will receive a 403 Forbidden error, as the write operation requires a different scope (e.g. `course:write`), which is not provided while granting the token.

We'll use the `@PreAuthorize` annotation to implement this. Let's add the following annotation in the `getCourseById(..)` method to the `CourseController` class, as shown in the following listing.

Listing 7.44 Implementing the scope-based access control

```
@GetMapping("{id}")
@PreAuthorize("hasAuthority('SCOPE_course:read')")
@PostAuthorize("@getAuthor.apply(returnObject,
➥ principal.claims['user_name'])")
public Optional<Course> getCourseById(@PathVariable("id") long courseId) {
    return courseRepository.findById(courseId);
}
```

Spring Security appends the `SCOPE_` prefix in the scope. Thus, we've configured the `course:read` scope as `SCOPE_course:read`. The `@PreAuthorize` annotation checks whether the requester (the client application) has the defined scope and, based on that, decides the access. We leave it as an exercise to the reader to play around with the Keycloak server to configure various scopes and explore the access control outcomes.

DISCUSSION

In this technique, you've explored using JWT with an authorization server to secure REST endpoints. Explaining the OAuth2 and the authorization server in depth is beyond the scope of this text. You can refer to books dedicated to OAuth2 (https://www.manning.com/books/oauth-2-in-action), OpenID connect (https://www.manning.com/books/openid-connect-in-action), and Spring Security (https://www.manning.com/books/spring-security-in-action) for a better understanding of these subjects.

In chapter 5, we demonstrated the use of Spring Security to secure Spring Boot applications. We also discussed that Spring Security uses a `FilterChain` and a list of filters that enforces security in the application. For Bearer Token-based authentication, Spring Security provides `BearerTokenAuthenticationFilter`. Figure 7.6 shows the flow of how the JWT is processed and a final `JwtAuthenticationToken` is generated.

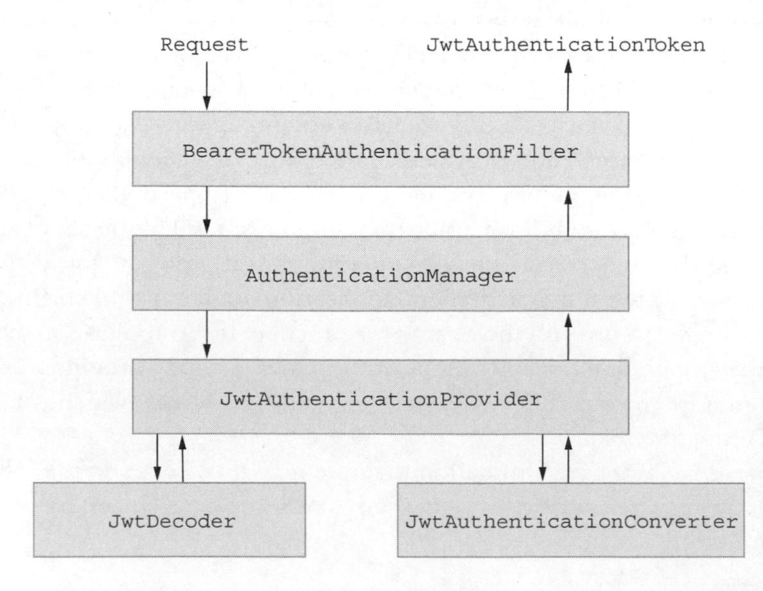

Figure 7.6 The list of classes and the flow to process a JWT and generate a Jwt-AuthenticationToken

The `BearerTokenAuthenticationFilter` delegates the JWT processing to an `AuthenticationManager` to perform the authentication. The `AuthenticationManager` uses `JwtAuthenticationProvider` to perform the actual authentication task. It uses a `JwtDecoder` and `JwtAuthenticationConverter` that process the request and generate the `JwtAuthenticationToken`.

Summary

Let's summarize the key takeaways of this chapter:

- We developed a RESTful API with Spring Boot application and discussed a few best practices for developing an API.
- We explored how to perform exception handling and provide appropriate HTTP response codes.
- We explored the use of OpenAPI to document a REST API.
- We explored various techniques to implement versioning in a REST API. The techniques we discussed are URI versioning, request parameters, custom headers, and `Accept` header-based versioning.
- We implemented Bearer Token-based authentication and authorization techniques to secure the REST API.

Part 3

Part 3 of the book consists of one chapter, which discusses reactive application development with Spring Boot. Chapter 8 provides an overview of reactive programming and covers reactive application development with Spring WebFlux. This chapter shows how to develop reactive APIs with annotated controllers and functional endpoints. It also shows how to test reactive applications. Lastly, this chapter demonstrates using WebSocket and RSocket with Spring Boot.

8 Reactive Spring Boot application development

This chapter covers

- Introducing reactive programming with Spring WebFlux
- Developing reactive RESTful APIs with annotated controller and functional endpoints
- Accessing reactive RESTful APIs with WebClient
- Developing Spring Boot applications with RSocket
- Using WebSocket and Spring Boot to develop applications

In the previous chapter, we explored how to design and develop RESTful API with Spring Boot. Spring Framework offers an alternative technology stack with Spring WebFlux to develop reactive applications. Spring WebFlux, which is based on Project Reactor, offers utilities that allow you to design reactive applications with controls, such as nonblocking, backpressure, and writing code in a declarative manner. It also provides the `WebClient` utility with a fluent API to consume the APIs.

In this chapter, we'll look at RSocket and WebSocket protocols, which offer support for bidirectional communication between the communicating parties. Lastly, we'll demonstrate how to use these protocols in a Spring Boot application. Let's get started.

8.1 Introduction to reactive programming

Reactive programming is programming with asynchronous data streams. Let's cover the *asynchronous data stream* with a discussion of the terms *asynchronous* and *data streams.*

A *data stream* refers here to a stream of data in which data is emitted, one data point after another, within an interval of time. The data stream can be created from a variety of sources: user inputs, properties, caches, databases, and others. Let's learn about this using a comparison between traditional data processing and stream data processing, as shown in figure 8.1.

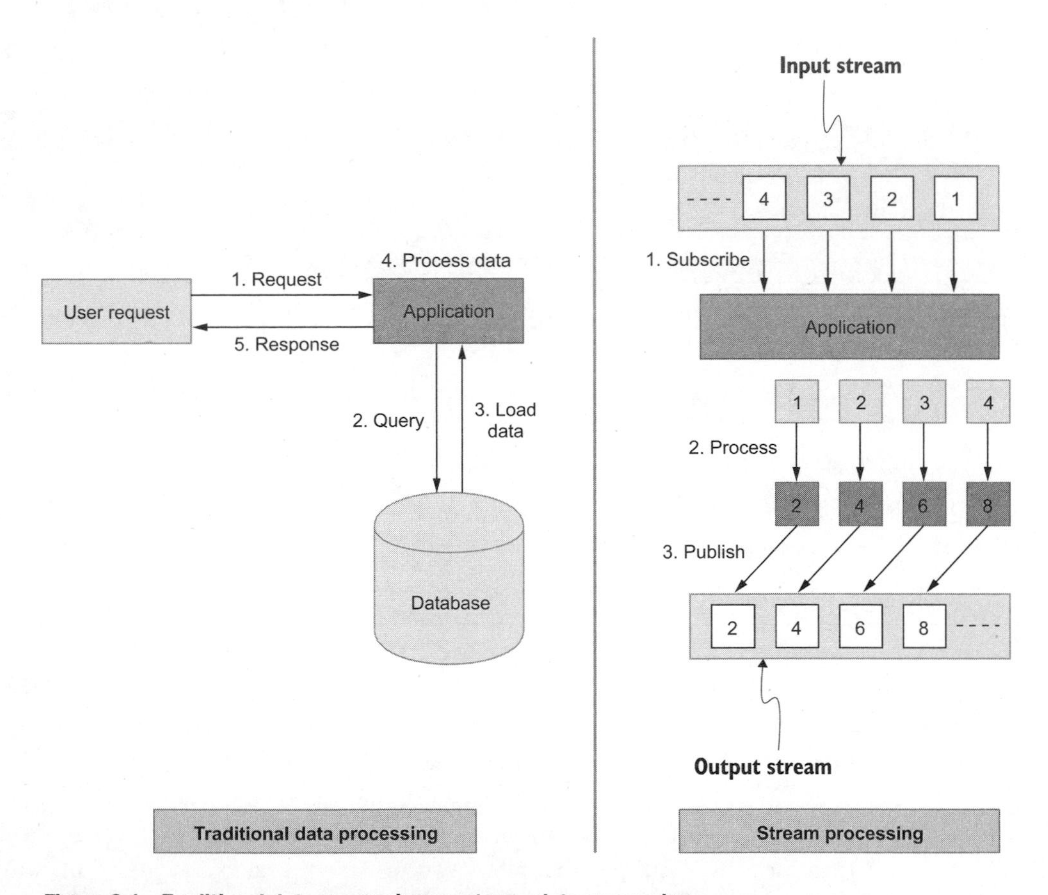

Figure 8.1 Traditional data processing vs. stream data processing

In figure 8.1, on the left side, we've shown the traditional data processing. A user request is received by the application, and the requested data is retrieved from the database by the application. The retrieved data is then processed and returned to the user.

On the right side of figure 8.1, we've demonstrated stream processing. In stream processing, an application subscribes to a data stream and receives data when the data is available. The application processes the data and publishes the processed data into another stream. In figure 8.1, we have a data stream of numbers to which the application has subscribed. As the application receives the data stream, it processes the data elements by multiples of two, and the resultant data is published into another stream.

Let's now discuss the concept of *asynchronous processing*. The term *asynchronous* means that for a request, the associated response appears once it is ready without the calling thread waiting for the response. Figure 8.2 shows a comparison between synchronous and asynchronous processing.

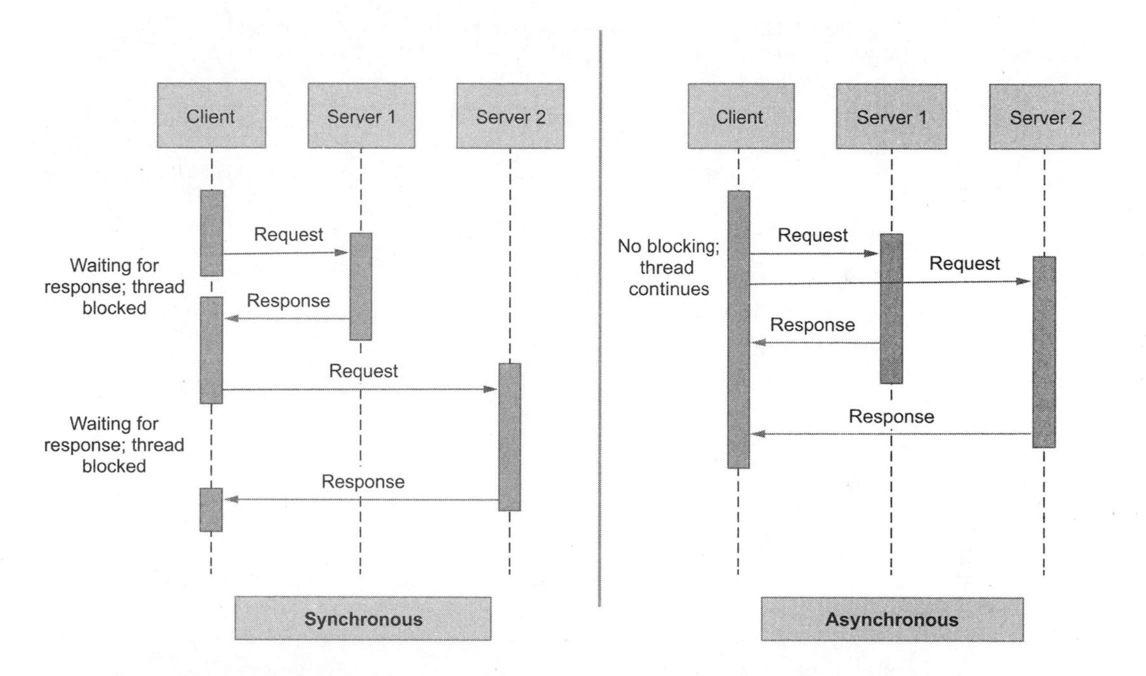

Figure 8.2 Synchronous and asynchronous processing. In synchronous, the calling thread waits for a response from the server before proceeding with the next request. Thus, the thread *blocks.* In asynchronous, the thread makes the request and continues with other activities (e.g., making another request). It does not wait for a response. The server sends the response *asynchronously* once the data is ready.

Before we proceed further, let's discuss a real-world example of asynchronous data streams. The typical mouse click events are an example of it. Application users can click on a button and generate an event, which you can observe and react to by performing an activity in your application. You can imagine these events as a stream of asynchronous events. Let's demonstrate this with the diagram shown in figure 8.3.

As you may notice, a *stream* is an ongoing event ordered in time. A stream can emit three things: a value, an error, or a complete signal. The *value* indicates that the

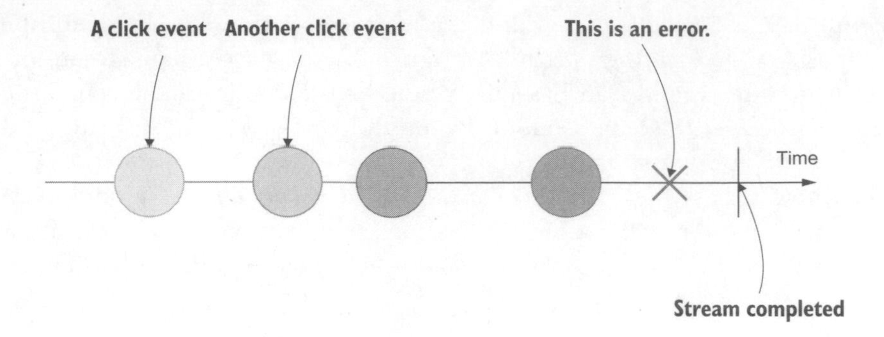

Figure 8.3 An example of asynchronous data stream for the mouse click event. We have a total of four events in the above diagram. After the fourth mouse click event, there is an error, and the stream terminates.

stream has emitted a value on which you can apply a function to take some action. The *error* means the stream has produced an error, and you can invoke some error handling mechanism. Lastly, the *complete signal* marks the end of the stream.

Events are emitted asynchronously, and we listen to those by defining functions. These functions react when the events have been emitted—for instance, one for the emitted data, one for the error, and another for the completion of the stream. In reactive programming, this listening is known as *subscribing*. The functions are the *observers*, and the stream is the *observable*, which is being observed. This is known as the observer design pattern.

Note

Spring WebFlux, and reactive programming in general, is a large topic, and it is beyond the scope of this text to provide an in-depth discussion on this subject. In this chapter, we aim to introduce you to reactive programming and demonstrate how to develop reactive applications with Spring Boot. In this section, we'll briefly introduce you to reactive programming and then discuss Reactive Streams upon which Project Reactor is based. We'll then talk about Spring WebFlux, which primarily uses Project Reactor for its reactive support.

You can refer to the following references for a detailed discussion on this topic:

- Reactive Streams: http://mng.bz/qYOA
- Project Reactor: http://mng.bz/7ydm
- Spring WebFlux: http://mng.bz/mOaP

8.1.1 Backpressure

Let's learn about another important concept in reactive programming: backpressure. However, before discussing it, let's discuss the notion of *push* and *pull* methods in a producer and consumer setup. A consumer subscribes data from a producer, and the producer pushes the data to the consumer. This is shown in figure 8.4.

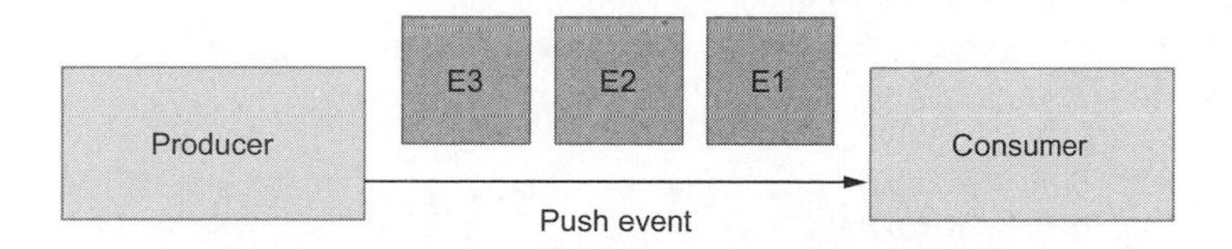

Figure 8.4 A producer pushes events to a consumer using the *push* method.

In figure 8.4, a producer pushes the events to the subscribed consumer. This setup is fine if the consumer's consumption rate is the same as the producer's push rate. However, what if the consumer processes the events at a slower rate than the producer pushes the events? The consumer can queue the events in a buffer. This is shown in figure 8.5.

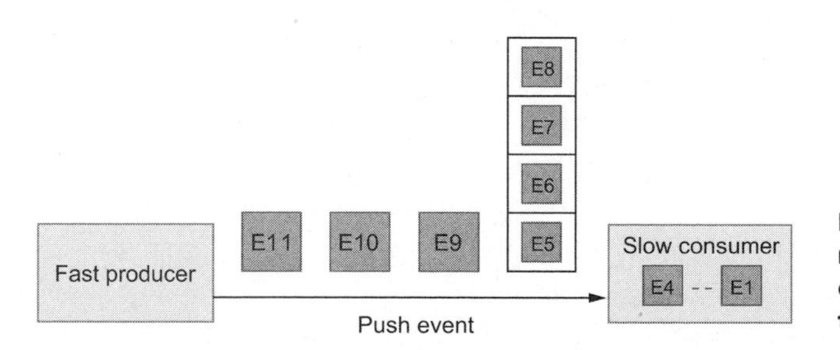

Figure 8.5 A fast producer pushes more events than a slow consumer can consume. The consumer parks the additional events into a buffer.

The consumer can either choose a *bounded* or an *unbounded buffer* to park the additional events. With a *bounded buffer*, some events will be dropped, as the buffer has limited space. The producer may need to resend the dropped events. Resending events requires additional network, CPU processing overhead, and a complex event processing setup. The *unbounded buffer* may lead to an out of memory error in the application if the buffer fills up rapidly with events. This could result in the unavailability of the application.

To avoid this problem, we can opt for the *pull method* instead of the push. In the *pull method*, the consumer requests events from the producer based on its processing capacity, as shown in figure 8.6.

In figure 8.6, the consumer requests three events from the producer, and it returns three events. This process allows the consumer to dynamically decide how many events to pull from the producer based on its capacity and is known as *backpressure*.

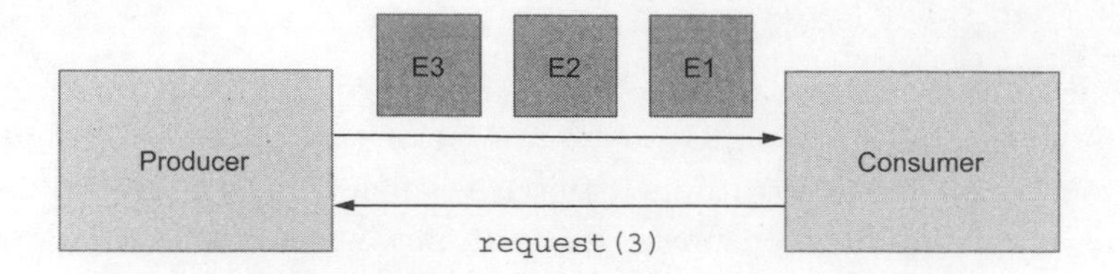

Figure 8.6 A consumer pulls events from a producer using the *pull* method. This approach gives the consumer flexibility to pull events based on their processing capacity.

8.1.2 Benefits of reactive programming

Now that we have some understanding of reactive programming concepts, let's discuss a few of its benefits:

- *No blocking*—Usually with the traditional programming model, developers write blocking codes. For instance, the calling thread waits for the data, while accessing a remote API or makes a database call. Although programs with blocking code work well, it has scalability and performance issues. Besides, it wastes the system resources by simply waiting for the data. The reactive programming model removes these bottlenecks.
- *Better asynchronous programming model in JVM*—Java provides two approaches to perform asynchronous programming: through *callback* and *future.* With *callback,* an asynchronous method takes an extra callback parameter that is invoked when the result is available. With *future,* asynchronous methods immediately return a `Future<T>`. The asynchronous method computes a value T, and this value is wrapped inside the future. The result inside the future is available only when it is ready. Both these approaches have drawbacks. For instance, composing callbacks can be difficult to manage. Nesting of callbacks can quickly get out of hand and is infamously referred to as *callback hell.* Futures are a bit better than callbacks, but they also don't do well in terms of the composition of the asynchronous operations.
- *Additional features*—The reactive programming approach provides a few additional benefits:
  - In the reactive model of programming, the code is declarative. You specify what needs to be done rather than how something is to be done. This leads to better code composition and makes the code more readable.
  - A rich set of operators you can apply to the data stream.
  - The processing or the operations starts only when you invoke the subscribe on the stream.
  - The concept of backpressure is that it lets the consumer signal the producer that the rate of emission is too high.

You'll explore a few of these benefits in practice in the next sections.

8.2 Understanding Project Reactor

The Reactor is a fully nonblocking reactive programming model for the JVM. It is based on Reactive Streams (https://www.reactive-streams.org/). Reactive Streams is a standard and specification for Stream-oriented libraries. It processes a potentially unbounded number of elements in a sequence. It also allows us to asynchronously pass elements between operators with nonblocking backpressure. The Reactive Streams API is relatively simple and provides four major interfaces, as shown in the following listing.

Listing 8.1 Reactive Streams API

```
public interface Publisher<T> {
   public void subscribe(Subscriber<? super T> s);
}

public interface Subscriber<T> {
   public void onSubscribe(Subscription s);
   public void onNext(T t);
   public void onError(Throwable t);
   public void onComplete();
}

public interface Subscription {
   public void request(long n);
   public void cancel();
}

public interface Processor<T, R> extends Subscriber<T>, Publisher<R> {
}
```

Let's provide a brief overview of these interfaces:

- *Publisher*—A *publisher* is a provider of a potentially unbounded number of sequenced elements and publishes them according to the demand from its subscribers. The `subscribe()` method of the `Publisher` interface allows subscribers to subscribe to the producer.
- *Subscriber*—A *subscriber* decides when and how many elements it is able and willing to receive. The `onNext()` method allows the subscriber to process received data, `onError()` to process the error, `onComplete()` to complete tasks, and `onSubscribe()` to subscribe with parameters.
- *Subscription*—A *subscription* represents the relationship between a subscriber and the producer. The subscriber is in control over when elements are requested and when more elements are no longer required. The `request()` method is used to request the data, and the `cancel()` method is used to cancel subscriptions.
- *Processor*—A *processor* represents a processing stage and is bound by both publisher and subscriber specifications.

Figure 8.7 shows the communication between the `Subscriber`, `Publisher`, and `Subscription` interfaces.

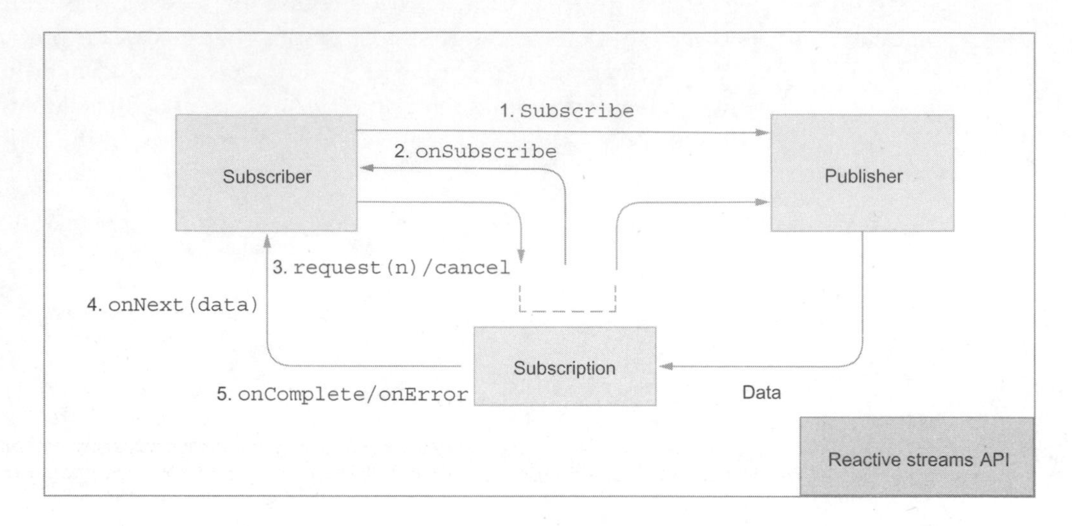

Figure 8.7 Communication between publisher, subscriber, and subscription interfaces in Reactive Streams API

Let's discuss how these APIs communicate with each other:

1. A subscriber uses the `subscribe()` method of the `Publisher` interface to add a subscription to a publisher.
2. A publisher uses the `onSubscribe()` method of `Subscribe` interface to send the `Subscription` to the subscriber.
3. A subscriber uses the `request()` or `cancel()` method of the `Subscription` interface to request or cancel data from the publisher.
4. The publisher uses the `onNext()`, `onComplete()`, and `onError()` methods of the `Subscriber` interface to send data or an error to a subscriber through the subscription.

The main component of the Reactor library is the reactor core module, which is built on top of Reactive Streams specifications and targets Java 8. Reactor provides composable reactive types, such as `Flux` and `Mono`, that implement the `Publisher` interface.

A `Flux` is a standard publisher that represents an asynchronous sequence of `0` to `N` emitted items, optionally terminated by an error or a completion signal. A `Mono` is a specialized publisher that emits at most one item through the `onNext` signal, which is then terminated by an `onComplete` (successful `Mono`) or only emits a single `onError` signal (failed Mono). Figure 8.8 shows the diagrammatic representation of how `Flux` produces items.

Figure 8.9 shows the diagrammatic representation of how Mono transforms items.

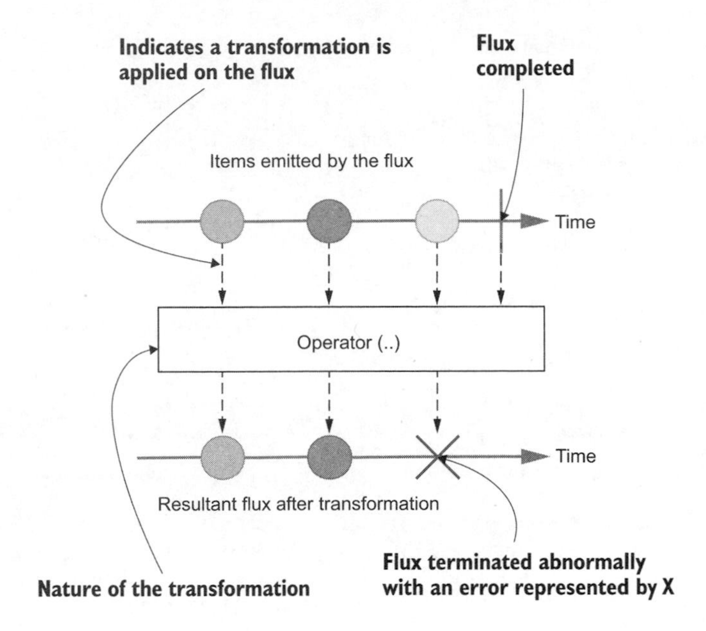

Figure 8.8 The items emitted by the Flux undergo a user-defined transformation. Once the transformation is applied, the items are converted to another Flux. Once the Flux terminates (i.e., it stops producing items), it is represented by a vertical line. An error processing an item is represented with the X symbol.

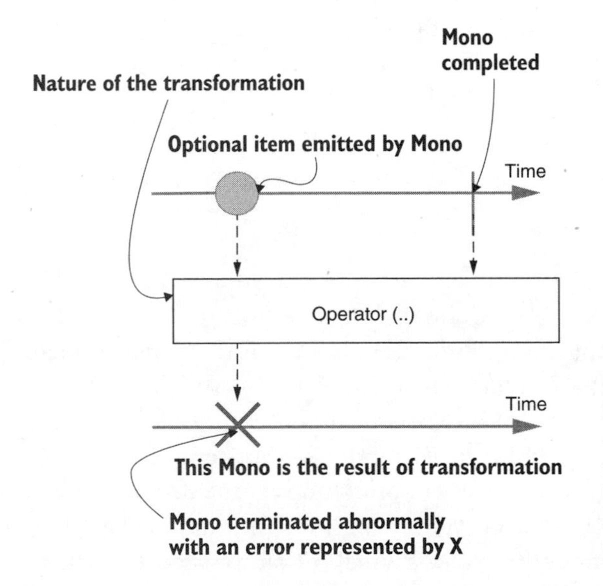

Figure 8.9 A Mono can emit 0..1 element. In case the Mono emits an item, a user-defined transformation can be applied to it, and a new Mono is created. The end of the Mono is represented by a vertical line. Any error processing the Mono is represented by an X symbol.

> **Note**
>
> If you would like to try out the code snippets shown in listing 8.2, create a Spring Boot project with the following Maven dependency and paste the contents of listing 8.2 inside the application's main method.

(continued)

```
<dependency>
  <groupId>org.springframework.boot</groupId>
  <artifactId>spring-boot-starter-webflux</artifactId>
</dependency>
```

We'll discuss WebFlux in greater detail in the next section.

Now that we've discussed what `Flux` and `Mono` are, let's explore several ways to create them.

Listing 8.2 Creating Flux and Mono

```
Flux<Integer> intFlux =  Flux.just(1,2,3);
Flux<Integer> intFluxRange =  Flux.range(1,10);
Flux<String> stringFlux =  Flux.fromIterable(List.of("foo", "bar"));
Flux<String> anotherStringFlux =  Flux.fromArray(new String[] {"foo", "bar"});

Mono<Integer> emptyMono =  Mono.empty();
Mono<Integer> intMono =  Mono.just(1);

intFlux.map(i -> i * 2).subscribe(System.out::println);
```

Creating Flux

Creating Mono

Using Flux. The intFlux consists of number 1,2,3. We map each number to a new number by multiplying by 2, and then we print each number in the console.

We've also shown a very simple way you can use `Flux`. We'll explore ways to create a `Flux` and `Mono` and a way you can use `Flux` in greater detail in subsequent sections.

8.3 Introducing Spring WebFlux

Spring Framework 5.0 introduced a new framework that supports reactive Web application development in Spring. This is done through the Spring WebFlux (http://mng.bz/mOaP). It is a fully nonblocking library and based on the project reactor. It targets Web servers, such as Netty, Undertow, and Servlet 3.1+ containers.

Spring WebFlux provides two programming models: annotated controllers and functional endpoints. The *annotated controller* model is consistent with the Spring MVC framework, and you can use the same set of annotations available in Spring MVC.

The *functional endpoints* model provides a lightweight, lambda-based functional programming model. This model provides a small set of libraries that an application can use to route and handle HTTP requests.

Now, let's discuss how to use the above mentioned reactive programming model to design a RESTful API. We'll use the previously used Course Tracker example to design the APIs. In the next technique, let's demonstrate how to develop a reactive RESTful API with an annotated controller approach.

8.3.1 Technique: Developing a reactive RESTful API with annotated controllers

In this technique, we'll discuss how to develop a reactive RESTful API with annotated controllers.

PROBLEM

The Course Tracker REST API developed previously is a blocking API and uses Spring MVC. You need to use reactive stack to build a nonblocking, scalable API with Spring WebFlux.

SOLUTION

To develop a reactive nonblocking RESTful API, in this technique, we'll use Spring WebFlux annotated controller model. As we've discussed previously, this approach uses the same Spring MVC annotations to build the API. Thus, you can use the familiar `@GetMapping`, `@PostMapping`, and other annotations to design the API.

> **Using MongoDB database**
>
> In this chapter, we'll use a reactive MongoDB database. You need not install and configure MongoDB to continue with this technique, as we'll use an embedded MongoDB database. We only require the Spring Data Reactive MongoDB and Embedded MongoDB dependencies for MongoDB support. Note that you can also continue to use the H2 database along with the Spring Data R2DBC dependency if you don't want to use MongoDB. You need to make necessary changes in the POJO class and the repository interface if you want to stick to the H2 database.

> **Source code**
>
> The final version of the Spring Boot project is available at http://mng.bz/5Qlz.

In this technique, we'll use previously used Course Tracker application. However, as we are using MongoDB database, there are a few changes in the application. Thus, we'll create a new Spring Boot project with the following dependencies, as shown in the following listing.

Listing 8.3 The pom.xml file

```
<?xml version="1.0" encoding="UTF-8"?>
<project xmlns="http://maven.apache.org/POM/4.0.0"
    xmlns:xsi="http://www.w3.org/2001/XMLSchema-instance"
    xsi:schemaLocation="http://maven.apache.org/POM/4.0.0
➥ https://maven.apache.org/xsd/maven-4.0.0.xsd">
    <modelVersion>4.0.0</modelVersion>
    <parent>
        <groupId>org.springframework.boot</groupId>
        <artifactId>spring-boot-starter-parent</artifactId>
```

```
    <version>2.6.3</version>
    <relativePath /> <!-- lookup parent from repository -->
</parent>
<groupId>com.manning.sbip.ch08</groupId>
<artifactId>course-tracker-api-annotated-controller</artifactId>
<version>0.0.1-SNAPSHOT</version>
<name>course-tracker-api-annotated-controller</name>
<description>Course Tracker REST API</description>
<properties>
    <java.version>17</java.version>
</properties>
<dependencies>
    <dependency>
  <groupId>org.springframework.boot</groupId>
  <artifactId>spring-boot-starter-data-mongodb-reactive</artifactId>
</dependency>

<dependency>
  <groupId>org.springframework.boot</groupId>
  <artifactId>spring-boot-starter-webflux</artifactId>
</dependency>

<dependency>
  <groupId>org.springframework.boot</groupId>
  <artifactId>spring-boot-devtools</artifactId>
  <scope>runtime</scope>
  <optional>true</optional>
</dependency>
<dependency>
  <groupId>org.projectlombok</groupId>
  <artifactId>lombok</artifactId>
  <optional>true</optional>
</dependency>
<dependency>
  <groupId>org.springframework.boot</groupId>
  <artifactId>spring-boot-starter-test</artifactId>
  <scope>test</scope>
</dependency>
<dependency>
  <groupId>de.flapdoodle.embed</groupId>
  <artifactId>de.flapdoodle.embed.mongo</artifactId>
</dependency>
<dependency>
  <groupId>io.projectreactor</groupId>
  <artifactId>reactor-test</artifactId>
  <scope>test</scope>
</dependency>
</dependencies>

<build>
    <plugins>
        <plugin>
            <groupId>org.springframework.boot</groupId>
            <artifactId>spring-boot-maven-plugin</artifactId>
        </plugin>
```

```
        </plugins>
    </build>
</project>
```

In listing 8.3, you included `spring-boot-starter-webflux`, `spring-boot-starter-data-mongodb-reactive`, and `de.flapdoodle.embed.mongo`, among other dependencies.

The `spring-boot-starter-webflux` dependency provides necessary support for Spring WebFlux framework. The `mongodb-reactive` dependency provides reactive Spring Data support for MongoDB database. Lastly, the `de.flapdoodle.embed.mongo` dependency allows us to use the embedded instance of a MongoDB database in the application. This ensures you don't need to install and configure MongoDB in your machine. Lastly, the `reactor-test` dependency provides necessary support (classes and methods) to test reactive applications. Next, we'll define the `CourseRepository` interface shown in the following listing.

Listing 8.4 The CourseRepository interface

```
package com.manning.sbip.ch08.repository;

import org.springframework.data.mongodb.repository.ReactiveMongoRepository;
import org.springframework.stereotype.Repository;

import com.manning.sbip.ch08.model.Course;

import reactor.core.publisher.Flux;

@Repository
public interface CourseRepository extends ReactiveMongoRepository<Course,
➥ String> {

    Flux<Course> findAllByCategory(String category);
}
```

Notice in listing 8.4, we used the `ReactiveMongoRepository` interface. This is the MongoDB-specific Spring Data repository with reactive support. We've also defined a custom method `findAllByCategory(String category)` that returns a `Flux` of courses that matches the supplied category. Note that the interface in listing 8.3 is quite similar to the previous repository interfaces, except the method return types are of type `Flux`. If you explore the `ReactiveMongoRepository` interface or its parent interfaces, you'll find that other method return types are either `Flux` or `Mono`, and the input to the repository methods in some cases is an instance of a `Publisher`. Let's now define the `Course` domain model shown in the following listing.

Listing 8.5 The Course domain model

```
package com.manning.sbip.ch08.model;

import org.springframework.data.mongodb.core.mapping.Document;
// Other Imports
```

```
@Data
@Builder
@Document
@NoArgsConstructor
@AllArgsConstructor
public class Course {

    @Id
    private String id;
    private String name;
    private String category;
    private int rating;
    private String description;
}
```

This is the same POJO class we used previously, except this time we are using the `@Document` annotation in place of the `@Entity` annotation, as we are using MongoDB database instead of the H2 database. MongoDB stores data records in a document. Thus, a course detail in MongoDB is a document. Let's now define the Course Controller class, as shown in the following listing.

Listing 8.6 The CourseController class

```
package com.manning.sbip.ch08.controller;

import org.springframework.beans.factory.annotation.Autowired;
import org.springframework.http.ResponseEntity;
import org.springframework.web.bind.annotation.DeleteMapping;
import org.springframework.web.bind.annotation.GetMapping;
import org.springframework.web.bind.annotation.PathVariable;
import org.springframework.web.bind.annotation.PostMapping;
import org.springframework.web.bind.annotation.PutMapping;
import org.springframework.web.bind.annotation.RequestBody;
import org.springframework.web.bind.annotation.RequestMapping;
import org.springframework.web.bind.annotation.RestController;

import com.manning.sbip.ch08.model.Course;
import com.manning.sbip.ch08.repository.CourseRepository;

import lombok.extern.slf4j.Slf4j;
import reactor.core.publisher.Flux;
import reactor.core.publisher.Mono;

@Slf4j
@RestController
@RequestMapping("/courses/")
public class CourseController {

    private CourseRepository courseRepository;

    @Autowired
    public CourseController(CourseRepository courseRepository) {
        this.courseRepository = courseRepository;
    }
```

This endpoint returns a Mono<ResponseEntity <Course>>. As we are getting a course by ID, we may or may not find a course with the supplied course ID. Thus, we are returning a Mono. Recall that a Mono can emit 0..1 element. We are using ResponseEntity to wrap the response with HTTP status 200 OK for a successful response or HTTP status 404 Not Found if the course is not found.

This endpoint returns a Flux of courses. Recall that Flux can emit 0..N elements. Also, notice the use of @GetMapping annotation to define the endpoint route, which is similar to what you've used in Spring MVC.

Note the use of map and defaultIfEmpty operators. If the findById(..) returns a result, then we map the result to a success response. The defaultIfEmpty operator is invoked if the findById returns no course.

```
@GetMapping
public Flux<Course> getAllCourses() {
    return courseRepository.findAll();
}

@GetMapping("{id}")
public Mono<ResponseEntity<Course>> getCourseById(@PathVariable("id")
➥ String courseId) {
    return courseRepository.findById(courseId)
            .map(course -> ResponseEntity.ok(course))
            .defaultIfEmpty(ResponseEntity.notFound().build());
}

@GetMapping("category/{name}")
public Flux<Course> getCourseByCategory(@PathVariable("name") String
➥ category) {
    return courseRepository.findAllByCategory(category)

            .doOnError(e -> log.error("Failed to create course",
➥ e.getMessage()));
}

@PostMapping
public Mono<Course> createCourse(@RequestBody Course course) {
    return courseRepository.save(course)
            .doOnSuccess(updatedCourse -> log.info("Successfully
➥ created course", updatedCourse))
            .doOnError(e -> log.error("Failed to create course",
➥ e.getMessage()));
}


@PutMapping("{id}")
public Mono<ResponseEntity<Course>> updateCourse(@PathVariable("id")
➥ String courseId, @RequestBody Course course) {
```

Updates an existing course; if it exists and returns a 200 OK. If not, it returns a 404 response. The response is wrapped in a Mono instance.

For any error, the doOnError is invoked, and it logs the error message in the console log.

Finds all courses for the supplied category and returns a Flux of courses

Creates a new course in the application. If the course is successfully created, the doOnSuccess is invoked, the success message is logged, and a Mono<Course> is returned. For any error, the doOnError is triggered, and the error message is logged.

```
        return
➥ this.courseRepository.findById(courseId).flatMap(existingCourse -> {
            existingCourse.setName(course.getName());
            existingCourse.setRating(course.getRating());
            existingCourse.setCategory(course.getCategory());
            existingCourse.setDescription(course.getDescription());
            return this.courseRepository.save(existingCourse);
        }).map(updatedCourse ->
➥ ResponseEntity.ok(updatedCourse)).defaultIfEmpty(ResponseEntity.notFound
➥ ().build())
                .doOnError(e -> log.error("Failed to update course",
➥ e.getMessage()));

    }

    @DeleteMapping("{id}")
    public Mono<ResponseEntity<Course>>
➥ deleteCourseById(@PathVariable("id") String courseId) {
        return this.courseRepository.findById(courseId).flatMap(
                course ->
➥ this.courseRepository.deleteById(course.getId()).then(Mono.just(ResponseE
➥ ntity.ok(course))))
                .defaultIfEmpty(ResponseEntity.notFound().build());
    }


    @DeleteMapping
    public Mono<Void> deleteCourses() {
        return courseRepository.deleteAll();
    }

}
```

Deletes all courses from the application and returns a Mono<Void>

Deletes a course with the supplied course ID. If a course with the supplied ID is found, then it is deleted, and an HTTP 200 OK response is created. If a course is not found, then an HTTP 404 Not Found response is created. This response is then returned as Mono<ResponseEntity<Course>>.

Listing 8.6 contains the endpoints to perform the CRUD operations in the Course Tracker application. The endpoints are the same as we defined when we created a REST API with Spring MVC. Notice the declarative style of coding in the endpoints and how various operators are composed (e.g., how the map is used or the `doOnSuccess` and `doOnError` are composed). Lastly, let's define a new Spring `@Configuration` file and a `CommandLineRunner` bean definition to create a few courses, as shown in the following listing.

Listing 8.7 CommandLineRunner bean definition to create a few courses

```
package com.manning.sbip.ch08.config;

import org.springframework.boot.CommandLineRunner;
import org.springframework.context.annotation.Bean;
import org.springframework.context.annotation.Configuration;
```

```
import com.manning.sbip.ch08.model.Course;
import com.manning.sbip.ch08.repository.CourseRepository;

import reactor.core.publisher.Flux;

@Configuration
public class CourseConfig {

    @Bean
    public CommandLineRunner init(CourseRepository courseRepository) {
        return args -> {

            Course course1 = Course.builder().name("Mastering Spring
➥ Boot").category("Spring").rating(4)
                    .description("Mastering Spring Boot").build();
            Course course2 = Course.builder().name("Mastering
➥ Python").category("Python").rating(5)
                    .description("Mastering Python").build();
            Course course3 = Course.builder().name("Mastering
➥ Go").category("Go").rating(3).description("Mastering Go")
                    .build();

            Flux
                .just(course1, course2, course3)
                .flatMap(courseRepository::save)
                .thenMany(courseRepository.findAll())
                .subscribe(System.out::println);
        };
    }
}
```

We are invoking Flux API to declaratively save and then print the output of three courses.

In listing 8.7, we created three sample courses. We then used the static method `just(..)` from the `Flux` class to create a flux with the sample courses. Next, we used the `flatMap(..)` operator to save the courses and then the `thenMany(..)` to find all the courses. Lastly, we subscribed to `Flux` to start the processing and print each course in the console. Note that reactive programming is lazy, and nothing happens until you invoke the `subscribe()` method.

Next, you need to specify the `spring.mongodb.embedded.version=3.6.2` property in the application.properties file. Let's start the application and test the endpoints. We've already created a few courses in listing 8.7; we'll use the `/courses/` endpoint to get those courses. The following listing shows the `HTTPie` command (https://httpie.io/) to get all the courses.

Listing 8.8 Getting all courses

```
C:\Users\musib>http :8080/courses/
HTTP/1.1 200 OK
Content-Type: application/json
transfer-encoding: chunked

[
    {
        "category": "Spring",
```

```
        "description": "Mastering Spring Boot",
        "id": "60fa36d47c237777890dca33",
        "name": "Mastering Spring Boot",
        "rating": 4
    },
    {
        "category": "Python",
        "description": "Mastering Python",
        "id": "60fa36d47c237777890dca34",
        "name": "Mastering Python",
        "rating": 5
    },
    {
        "category": "Go",
        "description": "Mastering Go",
        "id": "60fa36d47c237777890dca35",
        "name": "Mastering Go",
        "rating": 3
    }
]
```

Similarly, let's test the delete endpoint by deleting the course with course ID `60fa36d47c237777890dca35`. The following listing shows the `HTTPie` command to delete a course with a course ID.

Listing 8.9 Delete a course with a course

```
C:\Users\musib>http DELETE :8080/courses/60fa36d47c237777890dca35
HTTP/1.1 200 OK
Content-Length: 111
Content-Type: application/json

{
    "category": "Go",
    "description": "Mastering Go",
    "id": "60fa36d47c237777890dca35",
    "name": "Mastering Go",
    "rating": 3
}
```

Similarly, you can test other endpoints and find that those are also working as expected.

DISCUSSION

With this technique, you've seen how to create a REST API with Spring WebFlux. If you recall, Spring MVC uses a special servlet called `DispatcherServlet` as a front controller servlet that handles the request and delegates other specialized components to process the request and generate a response.

In Spring WebFlux, the `DispatcherHandler` is the central dispatcher for HTTP request handlers. It dispatches the requests to registered mappers and handlers to process the request. The `HandlerMapping` instances are used to map the request to the handler object. The `HandlerAdapter` is used to handle the request with the supported handler object, and it returns a `HandlerResult`. Lastly, a `HandlerResultHandler` is used to handle the `HandlerResult`.

In the `CourseController` class, you used the same annotations as those available in Spring MVC—the `@GetMapping` to get the course details, the `@PostMapping` to create a new course, and so on. Similarly, you have also used the `@PathVariable` and `@RequestBody` annotations in Spring MVC.

If you explore the `CourseRepository` interface or any of its parent interfaces, you'll notice that most method names are consistent with what you have seen in the nonreactive Spring Data interfaces. However, the method arguments and the return types of these methods are of reactive types. For instance, the `findAll(..)` method returns a `Flux` instead of an `Iterable`. In the next technique, we'll explore how to define functional endpoints with Spring WebFlux.

8.3.2 Technique: Developing a reactive RESTful API with functional endpoints

In this technique, we'll discuss how to develop a reactive RESTful API with functional endpoints.

Problem

Another technique for transforming your blocking REST API in a reactive fashion is the adoption of functional endpoints. You need to build a reactive REST API based on functional endpoints.

Solution

In the previous technique, we explored building a reactive REST API with Spring WebFlux using the annotated controller approach. Spring WebFlux provides a lambda-based, lightweight, and functional programming model. This is a different model than what we've used previously with the Spring MVC and WebFlux annotated controller-based approach. The functional model provides you a set of utilities (Java methods), so you can define the routes to handle requests.

To explore the use of the functional endpoints further, let's build a REST API with functional endpoints. With this technique, we'll continue with our Course Tracker application to build a REST API with the functional endpoint.

> **Source code**
> The final version of the Spring Boot project is available at http://mng.bz/6X7y.

For the Spring Boot project in this technique, you can continue with the Spring Boot project used in the previous technique. You can also create a new project with the same set of dependencies as those specified in listing 8.3 and continue with the technique. Create the `CourseRepository` interface and `Course` domain class, as shown in listings 8.4 and 8.5, respectively.

We'll begin by defining the routes. The routes are the URLs to perform the CRUD operations. The following listing shows the RouterContext class.

Listing 8.10 The RouterContext class to define the routes

```
package com.manning.sbip.ch08.configuration;

import static org.springframework.http.MediaType.APPLICATION_JSON;
import static
➥ org.springframework.web.reactive.function.server.RequestPredicates.DELE TE;
import static
➥ org.springframework.web.reactive.function.server.RequestPredicates.GET;
import static
➥ org.springframework.web.reactive.function.server.RequestPredicates.POST;
import static
➥ org.springframework.web.reactive.function.server.RequestPredicates.PUT;
import static
➥ org.springframework.web.reactive.function.server.RequestPredicates.acce pt;
import static
➥ org.springframework.web.reactive.function.server.RouterFunctions.route;

import org.springframework.context.annotation.Bean;
import org.springframework.context.annotation.Configuration;
import org.springframework.web.reactive.function.server.RouterFunction;
import org.springframework.web.reactive.function.server.ServerResponse;

import com.manning.sbip.ch08.component.CourseHandler;

@Configuration
public class RouterContext {

    @Bean
    RouterFunction<ServerResponse> routes(CourseHandler courseHandler) {
        return route(GET("/courses").and(accept(APPLICATION_JSON)),
➥ courseHandler::findAllCourses)
                .andRoute(GET("/courses/{id}").and(accept(APPLICATION_JSON)),
➥ courseHandler::findCourseById)
                .andRoute(POST("/courses").and(accept(APPLICATION_JSON)),
➥ courseHandler::createCourse)
                .andRoute(PUT("/courses").and(accept(APPLICATION_JSON)),
➥ courseHandler::updateCourse)
               .andRoute(DELETE("/courses/{id}").and(accept(APPLICATION_JSON)),
➥ courseHandler::deleteCourse)
                .andRoute(DELETE("/courses").and(accept(APPLICATION_JSON)),
➥ courseHandler::deleteAllCourses);
    }

}
```

Listing 8.10 is a Spring @Configuration class with one RouterFunction bean definition. The RouterFunction defines the routes to perform the CRUD operation in the Course Tracker reactive REST API. This bean definition requires the CourseHandler instance, so once there is a request to any of the routes, it can be forwarded to the handler to handle the request. We have defined two routes with HTTP GET requests—one for each of the POST, PUT requests and two for DELETE requests. For each of the routes, we've delegated the request processing to the appropriate methods of the CourseHandler class.

Next, let's define the CourseHandler class, as shown in the following listing. This class contains the logic to perform the CRUD operations.

Listing 8.11 The CourseHandler class

```
package com.manning.sbip.ch08.component;

import static org.springframework.http.MediaType.APPLICATION_JSON;
import static
➥ org.springframework.web.reactive.function.BodyInserters.fromValue;

import org.springframework.beans.factory.annotation.Autowired;
import org.springframework.http.HttpStatus;
import org.springframework.stereotype.Component;
import org.springframework.web.reactive.function.server.ServerRequest;
import org.springframework.web.reactive.function.server.ServerResponse;

import com.manning.sbip.ch08.model.Course;
import com.manning.sbip.ch08.repository.CourseRepository;

import reactor.core.publisher.Flux;
import reactor.core.publisher.Mono;

@Component
public class CourseHandler {

    private CourseRepository courseRepository;

      @Autowired
      public CourseHandler(CourseRepository courseRepository) {
       this.courseRepository = courseRepository;
      }
    public Mono<ServerResponse> findAllCourses(ServerRequest serverRequest) {
        Flux<Course> courses = this.courseRepository.findAll();
        return
➥ ServerResponse.ok().contentType(APPLICATION_JSON).body(courses,
    Course.class);
    }

    public Mono<ServerResponse> findCourseById(ServerRequest
➥ serverRequest){
        String courseId = serverRequest.pathVariable("id");
        Mono<Course> courseMono = this.courseRepository.findById(courseId);
```

A handler that finds all courses. The ServerRequest represents a server-side HTTP request. We find all courses and prepare a ServerResponse with the content type as application/json and list of courses as the response body. The ServerResponse represents a server side response.

A handler that finds a course by the supplied course ID. We retrieve the course from the ServerRequest instance through the pathVariable method of it, as the course ID was supplied as a path variable. If there is a course found, we return an HTTP 200 OK ServerResponse or 404 Not Found, otherwise.

```
        return courseMono.flatMap(course ->
➥ ServerResponse.ok().contentType(APPLICATION_JSON).body(fromValue(course)))
                .switchIfEmpty(notFound());
    }

    public Mono<ServerResponse> createCourse(
➥ ServerRequest serverRequest) {
        Mono<Course> courseMono = serverRequest.bodyToMono(Course.class);

        return courseMono.flatMap(course ->
➥ ServerResponse.status(HttpStatus.CREATED).contentType(APPLICATION_JSON)
                .body(this.courseRepository.save(course), Course.class));
    }

    public Mono<ServerResponse> updateCourse(
➥ ServerRequest serverRequest) {
        String courseId = serverRequest.pathVariable("id");
        Mono<Course> existingCourseMono =
➥ this.courseRepository.findById(courseId);
        Mono<Course> newCourseMono =
➥ serverRequest.bodyToMono(Course.class);
        return newCourseMono
            .zipWith(existingCourseMono,
        (newCourse, existingCourse) ->
➥ Course.builder().id(existingCourse.getId())
➥ .name(newCourse.getName()).category(newCourse.getCategory())
➥ .rating(newCourse.getRating()).description(newCourse.getDescription()).
➥ build())
        .flatMap(course -> ServerResponse
                    .ok().contentType(APPLICATION_JSON)
                .body(this.courseRepository.save(course), Course.class))
                .switchIfEmpty(notFound());
    }

    public Mono<ServerResponse> deleteCourse(
➥ ServerRequest serverRequest) {
        String courseId = serverRequest.pathVariable("id");
        return this.courseRepository.findById(courseId)
                .flatMap(existingCourse ->
➥ ServerResponse.ok().build(this.courseRepository.deleteById(courseId)))
                .switchIfEmpty(notFound());
    }

    public Mono<ServerResponse> deleteAllCourses(
➥ ServerRequest serverRequest) {
```

Creates a new course. We use the bodyToMono method of ServerRequest to extract the HTTP request body and convert it to a Mono. This Mono is then used to create the course.

Updates an existing course with the supplied new course details. We first fetch the course to be updated, and then extract the existing course and the updated course. We then prepare to update the course and return a ServerResponse. For a successful update, an HTTP 200 OK response is provided or 404 Not Found, otherwise.

Deletes a course with the supplied course ID

Deletes all courses

```
        return
➥   ServerResponse.ok().build(this.courseRepository.deleteAll());
    }

    private Mono<ServerResponse> notFound() {
        return ServerResponse.notFound().build();
    }

}
```

Next, we'll create a few courses and save them in the database. You can follow the same steps as defined in listing 8.7. Additionally, you need to specify the `spring.mongodb.embedded.version=3.6.2` property in the application.properties file.

Let's now start the application and test the endpoints. The following listing shows the HTTPie command to access the /courses/ endpoint with the result.

Listing 8.12 The /courses/ endpoint result

```
C:\Users\musib>http :8080/courses/
HTTP/1.1 200 OK
Content-Type: application/json
transfer-encoding: chunked

[
    {
        "category": "Go",
        "description": "Mastering Go",
        "id": "60fa68a55359e82fcc4c3de9",
        "name": "Mastering Go",
        "rating": 3
    },
    {
        "category": "Spring",
        "description": "Mastering Spring Boot",
        "id": "60fa68a55359e82fcc4c3de7",
        "name": "Mastering Spring Boot",
        "rating": 4
    },
    {
        "category": "Python",
        "description": "Mastering Python",
        "id": "60fa68a55359e82fcc4c3de8",
        "name": "Mastering Python",
        "rating": 5
    }
]
```

If you try accessing the other endpoints, you'll notice those are also working as expected.

DISCUSSION

With this technique, you've seen how to create a REST API with functional endpoints, which are an alternative approach to defining endpoints. Spring WebFlux included this functional programming model, which allows you to define functions to route and handle the request. Other than the programming model, both models run on the same reactive core foundation.

In the functional model, an HTTP request is handled with a `HandlerFunction`, which takes a `ServerRequest` and returns a `Mono<ServerResponse>`. The `HandlerFunction` is equivalent to the body of a `@RequestMapping` method in the annotation-based programming model. We defined all our handler functions in the `CourseHandler` class. The `ServerRequest` provides access to the HTTP method, URI, HTTP headers, and query parameters. The request body is accessed through the various `body` methods, and the `ServerResponse` provides access to the HTTP response.

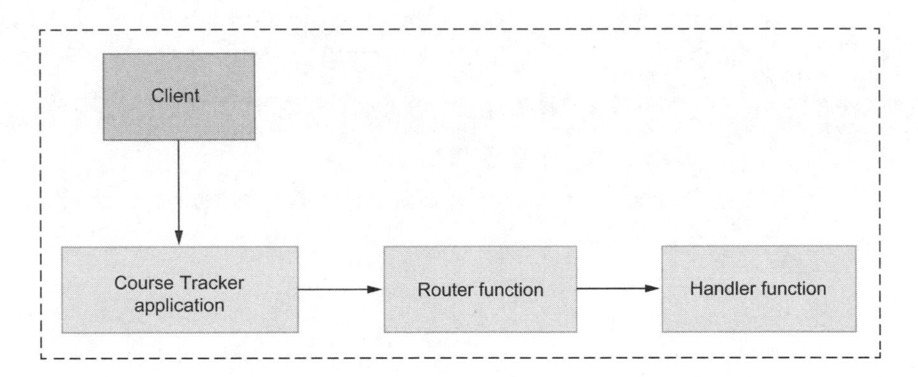

Figure 8.10 Incoming request processing in a Spring WebFlux functional endpoint. A client requests access to the server application with an HTTP endpoint.

As shown in figure 8.10, incoming requests are routed to a `HandlerFunction` through a `RouterFunction` , which takes a `ServerRequest` and returns a `HandlerFunction`. If the router function matches, a handler function is returned; otherwise, an empty `Mono` is returned. To define router functions, you can use the methods from the `RouterFunctions` utility class to create the routes. Spring WebFlux recommends using the `route()` builder method to create a router function.

In listing 8.11, we defined several routes. Spring WebFlux evaluates these routes in order. If the first route does not match, the second route is evaluated, and so on. Thus, you should define the most specific routes before the generic ones.

8.4 Testing reactive applications

In the previous section, you learned two different approaches to designing REST APIs with Spring WebFlux. In this section, you'll learn how to test the APIs. Previously, to test these API endpoints, we used the HTTPie command-line utility. In this section, you'll learn to use the `WebClient` to build an API client to access a REST API.

8.4.1 Technique: Using WebClient to build an API client

In this technique, we'll demonstrate the use of WebClient.

PROBLEM

You have an external REST API, and you need to define an API client to test this API.

SOLUTION

It is a common occurrence to access external REST API. Spring provides a client called `WebClient` to perform HTTP requests. Using this technique, you'll learn to use WebClient to build an API client. Previously, we designed a REST API for the Course Tracker application. We'll build an API client with `WebClient` that will access the Course Tracker REST API.

> **Source code**
> The final version of the Spring Boot project is available at http://mng.bz/o2eM.

To begin with, let's create a Spring Boot project and include the dependencies, as shown in the following listing.

Listing 8.13 The Course Tracker client API pom.xml

```
<?xml version="1.0" encoding="UTF-8"?>
<project xmlns="http://maven.apache.org/POM/4.0.0"
    xmlns:xsi="http://www.w3.org/2001/XMLSchema-instance"
➥      xsi:schemaLocation="http://maven.apache.org/POM/4.0.0
➥ https://maven.apache.org/xsd/maven-4.0.0.xsd">
    <modelVersion>4.0.0</modelVersion>
    <parent>
        <groupId>org.springframework.boot</groupId>
        <artifactId>spring-boot-starter-parent</artifactId>
        <version>2.6.3</version>
        <relativePath /> <!-- lookup parent from repository -->
    </parent>
    <groupId>com.manning.sbip.ch08</groupId>
    <artifactId>course-tracker-client-api</artifactId>
    <version>0.0.1-SNAPSHOT</version>
    <name>course-tracker-client-api</name>
    <description>Course Tracker REST API</description>
    <properties>
        <java.version>17</java.version>
    </properties>
    <dependencies>
        <dependency>
            <groupId>org.springframework.boot</groupId>
            <artifactId>spring-boot-starter-webflux</artifactId>
        </dependency>
        <dependency>
            <groupId>org.projectlombok</groupId>
            <artifactId>lombok</artifactId>
```

```
            <optional>true</optional>
        </dependency>
    </dependencies>

    <build>
        <plugins>
            <plugin>
                <groupId>org.springframework.boot</groupId>
                <artifactId>spring-boot-maven-plugin</artifactId>
            </plugin>
        </plugins>
    </build>

</project>
```

You'll also need to define the `Course` domain model, as we'll be dealing with the courses in the client API. Define the Course Java class as specified in listing 8.5. Let's start building the `WebClientApi` class that contains the client methods to invoke the various REST endpoints. The following listing shows this class.

Listing 8.14 The Course Tracker client API

```
package com.manning.sbip.ch08.api;

import org.springframework.http.ResponseEntity;
import org.springframework.stereotype.Component;
import
➥ org.springframework.web.reactive.function.client.ExchangeFilterFunction;
import org.springframework.web.reactive.function.client.ExchangeStrategies;
import org.springframework.web.reactive.function.client.WebClient;

import com.manning.sbip.ch08.model.Course;

import reactor.core.publisher.Flux;
import reactor.core.publisher.Mono;

@Component
public class WebClientApi {

    private static final String BASE_URL =
➥ "http://localhost:8080/courses/";

    private WebClient webClient;

    public WebClientApi() {
        this.webClient = WebClient.builder().baseUrl(BASE_URL).build();
    }

    public Mono<ResponseEntity<Course>> postNewCourse(Course course) {
        return this.webClient
                .post()
                .body(Mono.just(course), Course.class)
```

Creating the WebClient instance. We are setting the BASE_URL, while building the WebClient, so we can use the relative URLs while invoking an endpoint.

Creating a new course. We use the WebClient's post() method to invoke the HTTP POST endpoint of the Course Tracker API.

```
                .retrieve()
                .toEntity(Course.class)
                .doOnSuccess(result -> System.out.println("POST "+ result));
    }

    public Mono<Course> updateCourse(String id, String name, String
➥ category, int rating, String description) {
        return this.webClient
                .put()
                .uri("{id}", id)
                .body(Mono.just(Course
                                    .builder()
                                    .id(id)
                                    .name(name)
                                    .category(category)
                                    .rating(rating)
                                    .description(description)
                                    .build()), Course.class)
                .retrieve()
                .bodyToMono(Course.class)
                .doOnSuccess(result -> System.out.println("Update Course:
➥ "+result));
    }


    public Mono<Course> getCourseById(String id) {
        return this.webClient
                .get()
                .uri("{id}", id)
                .retrieve()
                .bodyToMono(Course.class)
                .doOnSuccess(c -> System.out.println(c))
                .doOnError((e) -> System.err.println(e.getMessage()));
    }


    public Flux<Course> getAllCourses() {
        return this.webClient
                .get()
                .retrieve()
                .bodyToFlux(Course.class)
                .doOnNext(c -> System.out.println(c))
                .doOnError((e) -> System.err.println(e.getMessage()));
    }
    public Mono<Void> deleteCourse(String id) {
        return this.webClient
                .delete()
                .uri("{id}", id)
                .retrieve()
                .bodyToMono(Void.class)
                .doOnSuccess(result -> System.out.println("DELETE
➥ "+result))
                .doOnError((e) -> System.err.println(e.getMessage()));
    }
}
```

Updating a course. We've used the WebClient's put() method to invoke the HTTP PUT endpoint of the course tracker API. We've also used the uri() method to set the relative URL.

Get a course by the supplied course ID. Notice that we've used the get() method to invoke the HTTP GET endpoint with relative URI {id}.

Get all courses. We've used the get() method to invoke the HTTP GET method.

Delete the course for the supplied course ID. We've used the delete() method to invoke the HTTP DELETE endpoint with relative URI {id}.

Listing 8.14 is a Spring component that defines the API client methods to invoke the Course Tracker REST API. Notice the HTTP methods of the WebClient class. For instance, you use the get() method to perform HTTP GET request post() for an HTTP POST request.

Let's now use some of these client methods to invoke the Course Tracker REST API endpoints. The following listing shows a CommandLineRunner bean definition that creates a new course and then retrieves all courses.

Listing 8.15 Testing Course Tracker API with API client

```
package com.manning.sbip.ch08.client;

import org.springframework.boot.CommandLineRunner;
import org.springframework.context.annotation.Bean;
import org.springframework.context.annotation.Configuration;

import com.manning.sbip.ch08.api.WebClientApi;
import com.manning.sbip.ch08.model.Course;

@Configuration
public class ApiClient {

    @Bean
    public CommandLineRunner invokeCourseTrackerApi(WebClientApi
➥ webClientApi) {
        return args -> {
            Course course = Course
                                .builder()
                                .name("Angular Basics")
                                .category("JavaScript")
                                .rating(3)
                        .description("Learn Angular Fundamentals")
                                .build();

            webClientApi.postNewCourse(course)
            .thenMany(webClientApi.getAllCourses())
            .subscribe();
        };
    }
}
```

In listing 8.15, we created a new course instance and used the WebClientApi to post the course in Course Tracker API. Finally, we are getting all courses from the API. Notice that the postNewCourse() and getAllCourses() methods are chained together through the thenMany operator.

Before we use the client API, we need to ensure the Course Tracker REST API from the previous section is running and accessible. Let's now start the client API Spring Boot project. Once the application started successfully, you'll notice the following output in the application console, as shown in the following listing.

Listing 8.16 Client API execution output

```
POST <201,Course(id=60faacfb400a9a1c3adb1bf7, name=Angular Basics,
➥ category=JavaScript, rating=3, description=Learn Angular
➥ Fundamentals),[Content-Type:"application/json", content-length:"135"]>

Course(id=60faaced400a9a1c3adb1bf5, name=Mastering Python, category=Python,
➥ rating=5, description=Mastering Python)
Course(id=60faaced400a9a1c3adb1bf6, name=Mastering Go, category=Go,
➥ rating=3, description=Mastering Go)
Course(id=60faaced400a9a1c3adb1bf4, name=Mastering Spring Boot,
➥ category=Spring, rating=4, description=Mastering Spring Boot)
Course(id=60faacfb400a9a1c3adb1bf7, name=Angular Basics,
➥ category=JavaScript, rating=3, description=Learn Angular Fundamentals)
```

In listing 8.16, the first block is the output of successful POST request. The next block shows the list of courses.

DISCUSSION

Spring WebFlux includes the `WebClient` to perform an HTTP request. As shown in listing 8.14, WebClient has a functional, fluent API based on Reactor that allows you to compose asynchronous logic without the need for threads and concurrency. It needs an HTTP client library to perform the HTTP requests. By default, it has support for Reactor Netty, Jetty Reactive HttpClient, and Apache HttpComponents.

The easiest way to create an instance of `WebClient` is to use the `create()` static factory method. If you need to use advanced configuration, such as configuring HTTP headers, codecs, or cookies or using a specialized `HttpClient`, you can use the `builder()` method. The following listing shows a more complex example of building a `WebClient` instance using the `builder()` method.

Listing 8.17 Building a WebClient using the builder method

Building a WebClient instance. We've used a custom HTTP client with additional configuration. We are also setting a default HTTP header to set the USER_AGENT. Besides, we are configuring the codecs with a custom maximum memory size. A codec is a component that takes care of the encoding and decoding of the data. Lastly, we are using filters to log the HTTP request and response.

```
private static final String USER_AGENT = "Mozilla/5.0 (Macintosh; Intel Mac
➥ OS X 10_15_7) AppleWebKit/537.36 (KHTML, like Gecko)
➥ Chrome/89.0.4389.114 Safari/537.36";

public WebClientApi() {
    this.webClient = WebClient.builder()
            .baseUrl(BASE_URL)
            .clientConnector(getClientConnector())
            .defaultHeader(HttpHeaders.USER_AGENT, USER_AGENT)

      .exchangeStrategies(ExchangeStrategies.builder().codecs(configurer ->
➥ configurer.defaultCodecs().maxInMemorySize(30 * 1024 * 1024)).build())
            .filter(logRequest()).filter(logResponse()).build();
}
```

Logging the HTTP request. It prints the HTTP request method, URL, and all HTTP headers.

Creating a custom HTTP connector. For requirements, such as timeouts, proxy configuration, and SSL setup, you may need to customize the HTTP connector.

```
public ReactorClientHttpConnector getClientConnector() {
        return new
➥ ReactorClientHttpConnector(HttpClient.create().followRedirect(true).com
➥ press(true).secure()
                .option(ChannelOption.CONNECT_TIMEOUT_MILLIS, 3000));
    }

private static ExchangeFilterFunction logRequest() {
    return ExchangeFilterFunction.ofRequestProcessor(clientRequest -> {
➥          System.out.println("Request: " + clientRequest.method() + " " +
➥ clientRequest.url());
        clientRequest.headers()
                .forEach((name, values) -> values.forEach(value ->
➥ System.out.println(name + " " + value)));
        return Mono.just(clientRequest);
    });
}

private static ExchangeFilterFunction logResponse() {
    return ExchangeFilterFunction.ofResponseProcessor(clientResponse -> {
        System.out.println("Response: " + clientResponse.statusCode());
        clientResponse.headers().asHttpHeaders()
                .forEach((name, values) -> values.forEach(value ->
➥ System.out.println(name + " " + value)));
        return Mono.just(clientResponse);
    });
}
```

Logging the HTTP response. It prints the HTTP response status code and all HTTP response headers.

You can refer to section 2 of Spring WebFlux documentation available at http://mng.bz/mOaP for an in-depth discussion on various supported configurations.

8.5 Introduction to RSocket

In the previous section, we discussed the WebClient and demonstrated its use with Spring Boot. In this section, we'll explore the RSocket protocol and its use with Spring Boot.

RSocket (https://rsocket.io/) is an application protocol for multiplexed, duplex communication over TCP, WebSocket, and other byte stream transports, such as Aeron (https://github.com/real-logic/aeron). RSocket allows the following four communication models shown in figure 8.11.

In RSocket, once the initial handshake between the client and server is done, the *client* versus *server* distinction is lost, as both sides can independently initiate one of the interactions, as specified in figure 8.11.

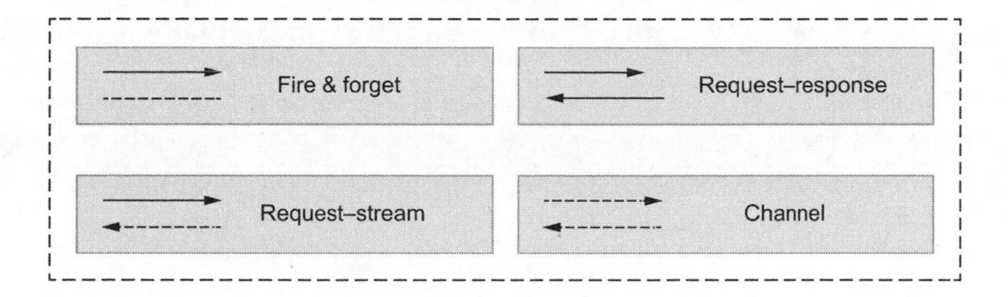

Figure 8.11 Communication models in RSocket protocol. In the fire-and-forget pattern, a client sends one message and expects no response from the server. In the request–response pattern, the client sends one message and receives one back from the server. In the request–stream pattern, a client sends one message and expects a stream of messages in response from the server. In the Channel pattern, the client and server send streams of messages to each other.

The RSocket protocol has a few key features and offers several benefits:

- *Reactive Streams semantics for streaming requests interactions between request-stream and channel and support for backpressure signals between the requester and responder*—This allows a requester to slow down a responder at the source. Thus, it reduces reliance on network layer congestion control and network-level buffering.
- *Support for request throttling to reduce the number of possible messages*—This can be done after sending a `LEASE` frame to limit the total number of requests allowed by other ends for a given time.
- *Fragmentation and reassembly of large messages.*
- *Keepalive through heartbeat messages.*

Next, we'll demonstrate how to use the RSocket protocol in a Spring Boot application. We'll implement all four interaction patterns shown in figure 8.11.

8.5.1 Technique: Developing applications using RSocket and Spring Boot

In this technique we'll discuss the use of RSocket in a Spring Boot application.

Problem

You learned about RSocket protocol and need to use it in a Spring Boot application.

Solution

Spring Framework provides support for RSocket protocol in the `spring-messaging` module. Spring Boot provides the `spring-boot-starter-rsocket` starter dependency that includes the relevant dependencies to using RSocket in a Spring Boot application.

> **Source code**
> The final version of the Spring Boot project is available at http://mng.bz/nNgK.

To begin with, let's create a new Spring Boot project with the dependencies, as shown in the following listing.

Listing 8.18 The pom.xml file

```
<?xml version="1.0" encoding="UTF-8"?>
<project xmlns="http://maven.apache.org/POM/4.0.0"
➥ xmlns:xsi="http://www.w3.org/2001/XMLSchema-instance"
   xsi:schemaLocation="http://maven.apache.org/POM/4.0.0
➥ https://maven.apache.org/xsd/maven-4.0.0.xsd">
    <modelVersion>4.0.0</modelVersion>
    <parent>
        <groupId>org.springframework.boot</groupId>
        <artifactId>spring-boot-starter-parent</artifactId>
        <version>2.6.3</version>
        <relativePath/> <!-- lookup parent from repository -->
    </parent>
    <groupId>com.manning.sbip.ch08</groupId>
    <artifactId>spring-boot-rsocket</artifactId>
    <version>0.0.1-SNAPSHOT</version>
    <name>spring-boot-rsocket</name>
    <description>Spring Boot RSocket</description>
    <properties>
        <java.version>17</java.version>
    </properties>
    <dependencies>
        <dependency>
            <groupId>org.springframework.boot</groupId>
            <artifactId>spring-boot-starter-rsocket</artifactId>
        </dependency>

        <dependency>
            <groupId>org.springframework.boot</groupId>
            <artifactId>spring-boot-devtools</artifactId>
            <scope>runtime</scope>
            <optional>true</optional>
        </dependency>
        <dependency>
            <groupId>org.projectlombok</groupId>
            <artifactId>lombok</artifactId>
            <optional>true</optional>
        </dependency>
        <dependency>
            <groupId>org.springframework.boot</groupId>
            <artifactId>spring-boot-starter-test</artifactId>
            <scope>test</scope>
        </dependency>
        <dependency>
            <groupId>io.projectreactor</groupId>
            <artifactId>reactor-test</artifactId>
            <scope>test</scope>
        </dependency>
    </dependencies>
```

```
    <build>
        <plugins>
            <plugin>
                <groupId>org.springframework.boot</groupId>
                <artifactId>spring-boot-maven-plugin</artifactId>
                <configuration>
                    <excludes>
                        <exclude>
                            <groupId>org.projectlombok</groupId>
                            <artifactId>lombok</artifactId>
                        </exclude>
                    </excludes>
                </configuration>
            </plugin>
        </plugins>
    </build>

</project>
```

The notable dependency in listing 8.18 is the `spring-boot-starter-rsocket` dependency. This transitively includes the other required dependencies, such as `spring-messaging`, `rsocket-core`, and others. In the application.properties file, let's include the properties shown in the following listing.

Listing 8.19 Application.properties configuration

```
spring.rsocket.server.port=7000
spring.main.lazy-initialization=true
```

The first property sets the TCP port for the RSocket server to 7000, and the second property enables the Spring Boot's lazy initialization.

In this Spring Boot application, we'll continue with the `Course` domain object. The updated course model is shown in the following listing.

Listing 8.20 The Course domain class

```
package com.manning.sbip.ch08.model;

import java.time.Instant;
import java.util.UUID;

import lombok.Data;
import lombok.NoArgsConstructor;

@Data
@NoArgsConstructor
public class Course {

    private UUID courseId = UUID.randomUUID();
    private long created = Instant.now().getEpochSecond();
    private String courseName;
```

```
    public Course(String courseName) {
        this.courseName = courseName;
    }
}
```

The Course class has a courseId field, which is a random UUID, a created field that captures the course creation time, and a courseName field that is supplied by the user.

Next, let's define the CourseController class that contains the routes for all four interaction models, as specified in figure 8.11. The following listing shows the Course-Controller class.

Listing 8.21 The CourseController class

```
package com.manning.sbip.ch08.controller;

import java.time.Duration;

import org.springframework.messaging.handler.annotation.MessageMapping;
import org.springframework.stereotype.Controller;

import com.manning.sbip.ch08.model.Course;

import lombok.extern.slf4j.Slf4j;
import reactor.core.publisher.Flux;
import reactor.core.publisher.Mono;

@Slf4j
@Controller
public class CourseController {

    @MessageMapping("request-response")
    public Mono<Course> requestResponse(final Course course) {
        log.info("Received request-response course details {} ", course);
        return Mono.just(new Course("Your course name: " +
➥ course.getCourseName()));
    }

    @MessageMapping("fire-and-forget")
    public Mono<Void> fireAndForget(final Course course) {
        log.info("Received fire-and-forget course details {} ", course);
        return Mono.empty();
    }

    @MessageMapping("request-stream")
    public Flux<Course> requestStream(final Course course) {
        log.info("Received request-stream course details {} ", course);
        return Flux
                    .interval(Duration.ofSeconds(1))
                .map(index -> new Course("Your course name: " +
➥ course.getCourseName() + ". Response #" + index))
```

Implements the request-response interaction pattern. The user is expected to supply a course, and this endpoint echoes it back to the caller.

Implements the fire–forget interaction pattern. The user is expected to supply a course and expects nothing. Thus, we are returning an empty Mono.

Implements the request-stream interaction pattern. The user is expected to supply a course, and this endpoint returns a stream of course with modified course name in an interval of one second.

```
                .log();
    }

    @MessageMapping("stream-stream")
    public Flux<Course> channel(final Flux<Integer> settings) {
        log.info("Received stream-stream (channel) request... ");

        return settings
    .doOnNext(setting -> log.info("Requested interval is {} seconds",
➥ setting))
    .doOnCancel(() -> log.warn("Client cancelled the channel"))
    .switchMap(setting ->
➥ Flux.interval(Duration.ofSeconds(setting)).map(index -> new
➥ Course("Spring. Response #"+index)))
                .log();
    }
}
```

Implements the channel interaction pattern. The user is expected to supply a stream, and this endpoint returns a stream of course with a modified course name in an interval configured by the user. The user can specify the interval by invoking the delayElements() method in the source Flux. Recall that in channel interaction patterns, both sides can send a stream of data.

You can start the application and find that it is running on configured TCP port 7000. We'll demonstrate two approaches to test the application. First, we can use RSocket Client CLI (RSC) to test the routes. It's a command-line utility that allows you to access the endpoints. You can go through https://github.com/making/rsc for the steps to install this in your machine. Once you've installed it, access the `request-response` route using the command, as shown in the following listing.

Listing 8.22 Invoking RSocket endpoint with rsc CLI

```
C:\Users\musib>rsc --debug --request --data "{\"courseName\":\"Spring\"}" -
➥ -route request-response --stacktrace tcp://localhost:7000
2021-07-29 10:27:54.597 DEBUG 17700 --- [actor-tcp-nio-2]
➥ io.rsocket.FrameLogger : sending ->
Frame => Stream ID: 0 Type: SETUP Flags: 0b0 Length: 75
Data:

2021-07-29 10:27:54.607 DEBUG 17700 --- [actor-tcp-nio-2]
➥ io.rsocket.FrameLogger : sending ->
Frame => Stream ID: 1 Type: REQUEST_RESPONSE Flags: 0b100000000 Length: 53
Metadata:
         +-------------------------------------------------+
         |  0  1  2  3  4  5  6  7  8  9  a  b  c  d  e  f |
+--------+-------------------------------------------------+----------------+
|00000000| fe 00 00 11 10 72 65 71 75 65 73 74 2d 72 65 73 |.....request-res|
|00000010| 70 6f 6e 73 65                                  |ponse           |
+--------+-------------------------------------------------+----------------+
Data:
         +-------------------------------------------------+
         |  0  1  2  3  4  5  6  7  8  9  a  b  c  d  e  f |
+--------+-------------------------------------------------+----------------+
|00000000| 7b 22 63 6f 75 72 73 65 4e 61 6d 65 22 3a 22 53 |{"courseName":"S|
|00000010| 70 72 69 6e 67 22 7d                            |pring"}         |
+--------+-------------------------------------------------+----------------+
```

```
2021-07-29 10:27:54.768 DEBUG 17700 --- [actor-tcp-nio-2]
➥ io.rsocket.FrameLogger : receiving ->
Frame => Stream ID: 1 Type: NEXT_COMPLETE Flags: 0b1100000 Length: 118
Data:
         +-------------------------------------------------+
         | 0  1  2  3  4  5  6  7  8  9  a  b  c  d  e  f |
+--------+-------------------------------------------------+----------------+
|00000000| 7b 22 63 6f 75 72 73 65 49 64 22 3a 22 32 33 39 |{"courseId":"239|
|00000010| 66 37 65 64 61 2d 65 31 61 64 2d 34 66 30 36 2d |f7eda-e1ad-4f06-|
|00000020| 62 66 30 64 2d 63 38 31 32 61 66 36 66 65 37 61 |bf0d-c812af6fe7a|
|00000030| 63 22 2c 22 63 72 65 61 74 65 64 22 3a 31 36 32
➥ |c","created":162|
|00000040| 37 35 33 34 36 37 34 2c 22 63 6f 75 72 73 65 4e
➥ |7534674,"courseN|
|00000050| 61 6d 65 22 3a 22 59 6f 75 72 20 63 6f 75 72 73 |ame":"Your cours|
|00000060| 65 20 6e 61 6d 65 3a 20 53 70 72 69 6e 67 22 7d |e name: Spring"}|
+--------+-------------------------------------------------+----------------+
{"courseId":"239f7eda-e1ad-4f06-bf0d-
➥ c812af6fe7ac","created":1627534674,"courseName":"Your course name:
➥ Spring"}
```

We have enabled the debug in the command to print the frame details. As you may notice, the first frame send is SETUP and then REQUEST_RESPONSE with some metadata and the payload. Lastly, it receives the response from the endpoint. In listing 8.22, we've shown how to test request–response with the RSC client. Similarly, you can test other patterns also with RSC. Refer to https://rsocket.io/about/protocol for a detailed understanding of the frame and the protocol in detail.

Next, we can also write the integration test cases to test the endpoint. The following listing shows the test case.

Listing 8.23 Integration test to verify the request–response route

```
package com.manning.sbip.ch08;

import static org.assertj.core.api.Assertions.assertThat;

import java.time.Duration;

import org.junit.jupiter.api.BeforeAll;
import org.junit.jupiter.api.Test;
import org.springframework.beans.factory.annotation.Autowired;
import org.springframework.boot.rsocket.context.LocalRSocketServerPort;
import org.springframework.boot.test.context.SpringBootTest;
import org.springframework.messaging.rsocket.RSocketRequester;
import org.springframework.messaging.rsocket.RSocketStrategies;

import com.manning.sbip.ch08.model.Course;

import reactor.core.publisher.Flux;
import reactor.core.publisher.Mono;
import reactor.test.StepVerifier;
```

```
@SpringBootTest
class SpringBootRsocketApplicationTests {

    private static RSocketRequester requester;


    @BeforeAll
    public static void setUpOnce(@Autowired RSocketRequester.Builder
➥ builder, @LocalRSocketServerPort Integer port,
➥     @Autowired RSocketStrategies rSocketStrategies) {

        requester = builder.tcp("localhost", port);
    }

    @Test
    public void testRequestResponse() {

        Mono<Course> courseMono = requester
                .route("request-response")
                .data(new Course("Spring"))
              .retrieveMono(Course.class);

        StepVerifier.create(courseMono)
            .consumeNextWith(course ->
➥ assertThat(course.getCourseName()).isEqualTo("Your course name:
➥ Spring"))
                .verifyComplete();
    }
}
```

Set up the RsocketRequester instance. The RSocketRequester.Builder interface lets us create a requester by connecting to the server.

Send a request.

Verify the response.

In the `testRequestResponse()` we send a request to the route and validate the expected response. In the requester instance, we set the route path and the data and then retrieve the response. Since this is `request-response` pattern, we expect a single response, and it is captured in a `Mono`. We then use the `StepVerifier` to consume the response and assert the expected value from the response. Once the verification is done, we complete it with `verifyComplete()`.

Let's now define the remaining test cases in the `SpringBootRsocketApplicationTests` class. The following listing shows the `FireAndForget` endpoint.

Listing 8.24 Testing the FireAndForget endpoint

```
@Test
public void testFireAndForget() {
    Mono<Void> courseMono = requester
            .route("fire-and-forget")
            .data(new Course("Spring"))
        .retrieveMono(Void.class);

    StepVerifier
      .create(courseMono)
      .verifyComplete();
}
```

Send a request.

Verify the response.

The following listing shows the test case to test the `RequestStream` endpoint.

Listing 8.25 Testing the RequestStream endpoint

```
@Test
public void testRequestStream() {

    Flux<Course> courseFlux = requester
                .route("request-stream")
                .data(new Course("Spring"))
            .retrieveFlux(Course.class);

    StepVerifier.create(courseFlux)
            .consumeNextWith(course ->
➥ assertThat(course.getCourseName()).isEqualTo("Your course name: Spring.
➥ Response #0"))
            .expectNextCount(0)
            .consumeNextWith(course ->
➥ assertThat(course.getCourseName()).isEqualTo("Your course name: Spring.
➥ Response #1"))
            .thenCancel()
                .verify();
}
```

Send a request, and expect a stream of courses as Flux<Course>.

Use StepVerifier to verify the response. We retrieve two courses from the stream, and then cancel them to indicate we are not interested in further data from the stream.

The following listing shows the test case to test the `channel` endpoint.

Listing 8.26 Testing the channel endpoint

```
@Test
public void testChannel() {
    Mono<Integer> setting1 =
➥ Mono.just(Integer.valueOf(2)).delayElement(Duration.ofSeconds(0));
    Mono<Integer> setting2 =
➥ Mono.just(Integer.valueOf(1)).delayElement(Duration.ofSeconds(3));
    Flux<Integer> settings = Flux.concat(setting1, setting2);
    Flux<Course> stream = requester.route("stream-
➥ stream").data(settings).retrieveFlux(Course.class);
    StepVerifier
    .create(stream)
    .consumeNextWith(course ->
➥ assertThat(course.getCourseName()).isEqualTo("Spring. Response #0"))
    .consumeNextWith(course ->
➥ assertThat(course.getCourseName()).isEqualTo("Spring. Response #0"))
    .thenCancel()
    .verify();
}
```

Create first setting after 0 seconds. The server starts sending after 2 seconds.

Create next setting after 3 seconds. The server starts sending in after 1 second.

Bundle settings into a Flux.

Send a stream of request messages.

DISCUSSION

With this technique, we've demonstrated the use of `RSocket` protocol in a Spring Boot application. We've seen the use of the `spring-boot-starter-rsocket` dependency that brings the necessary dependencies in the application.

The Spring Boot also provides several autoconfiguration classes that configure the RSocket in a Spring Boot application. Figure 8.12 shows these classes.

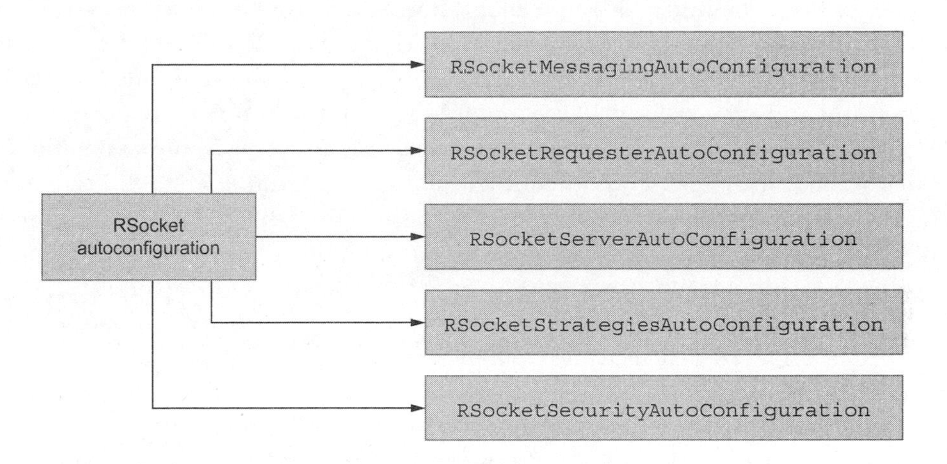

Figure 8.12 Spring Boot RSocket autoconfiguration classes

The `RsocketMessagingAutoConfiguration` autoconfigures the `RsocketMessageHandler`. This class handles RSocket requests for the methods defined with `@ConnectMapping` and `@MessageMapping` annotations.

The `RsocketRequesterAutoConfiguration` autoconfigures the `RsocketRequester`. This class provides a fluent API that can be used to accept and return input and output. It also provides methods to prepare routing and other metadata. We've used this class in our test case in listing 8.23.

The `RsocketServerAutoConfiguration` autoconfigures the RSocket server. We've configured the `spring.rsocket.server.port` property to start the standalone RSocket server at port 7000.

The `RsocketStrategiesAutoConfiguration` autoconfigures the `RsocketStrategies`. This class defines the strategies for use by `RSocket` requester and responder components. Some of the strategies, for instance, are the decoder and encoder for the messages.

Lastly, the `RsocketSecurityAutoConfiguration` autoconfigures Spring Security for an RSocket server. Securing the RSocket server with Spring Security is beyond the scope of this text. You can refer to the internet on this subject.

8.6 Introduction to WebSocket

So far, we've discussed the use of HTTP through which we can access contents from the server. For instance, in the Course Tracker REST API, we initiated an HTTP request from the browser/HTTPie CLI to the server to get the available courses. Although HTTP works perfectly well in most scenarios, and it is the dominant protocol of the Web, it has a major drawback. The communication between client and server can only be initiated by the client. It works in a request–response style; the client should ask the server what it needs by accessing the URLs. The server can't initiate a connection to the client and send data to it. There are workarounds, such as HTTP streaming and long polling, that attempt to reduce this problem to a certain degree. However, these are not permanent solutions. For instance, in the case of an HTTP long polling, the client sends a request to the server, and the server holds the request until there is something to return to the client. Thus, the client polls the server for new data, and the server responds when it has something to return to the client.

In this section, we'll introduce you to the WebSocket protocol (https://datatracker.ietf.org/doc/html/rfc6455) that intends to remove the aforementioned drawbacks of HTTP. This protocol provides a *standardized* way to establish a full-duplex, two-way communication channel between client and server over a single TCP connection. Note the emphasis we put on the standardized part of the definition, as this protocol is designed for two-way communication, and you need not rely on any workarounds. WebSocket is a different protocol than HTTP, but it is designed to work over HTTP and HTTPS, using ports 80 and 443. The client–server communication model in HTTP and WebSocket is shown in figure 8.13.

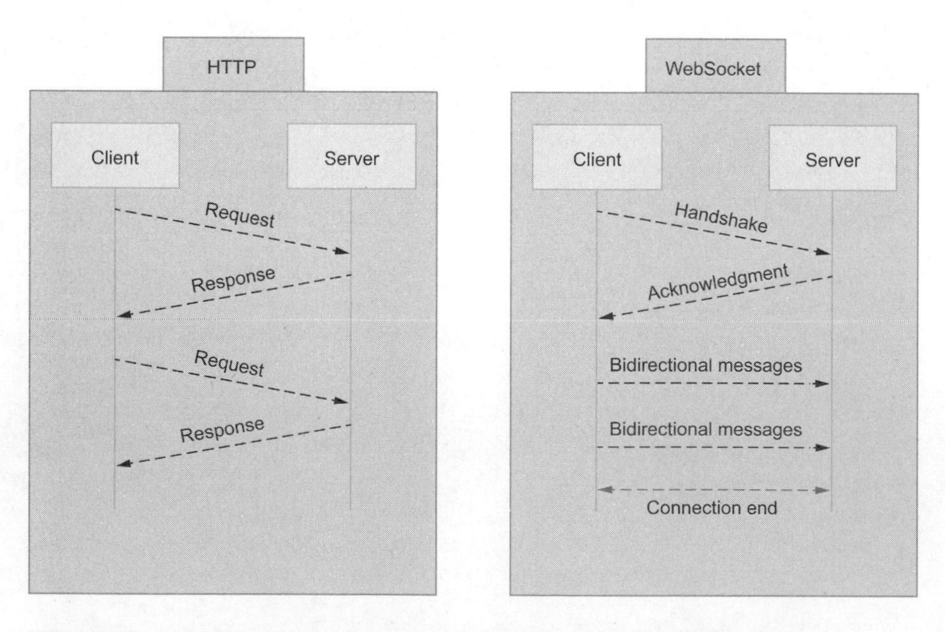

Figure 8.13 The client–server communication in HTTP and WebSocket protocol

In this section, we've introduced you to the WebSocket protocol that facilitates two-way communication between client and server. With WebSocket, once the initial handshake is completed, both client and server can send data to each other. It is important to know that the HTTP is used for the initial handshake, and once that is done, the HTTP connection is upgraded to a newly established TCP/IP connection, which is used by WebSocket.

Further, the WebSocket protocol is a low-level one, and it defines how a stream of bytes is transformed to frames. A frame can contain a binary or text message. However, the message does not carry any additional information related to routing and processing. Thus, it becomes difficult to use raw WebSocket protocol without any additional coding. However, the WebSocket protocol specification allows using higher-level subprotocols that operate on the application level. One such subprotocol supported by Spring is Simple (or Streaming) Text Oriented Messaging Protocol (STOMP).

The Spring Framework provides a WebSocket API we can use to write a client and server-side application that handles WebSocket messages. We'll provide more details on how the WebSocket protocol works in the discussion section. For now, let's explore how to build a Spring Boot application with WebSocket in the next technique.

8.6.1 Technique: Developing an application using WebSocket and Spring Boot

In this technique, we'll discuss how to use WebSocket in a Spring Boot application.

Problem

So far you've built applications that use HTTP. You need to explore the use of WebSocket protocol with Spring Boot for more real-time communication between client and server.

Solution

Let's begin by building a Spring Boot application with WebSocket and STOMP.

> **Source code**
> The final version of the Spring Boot project is available at http://mng.bz/v68M.

In this demonstration, we'll build a really simple chat application that echoes the text provided by the users. Let's create a new Spring Boot application with the dependencies, as shown in listing 8.27.

Listing 8.27 The pom.xml file

```
<?xml version="1.0" encoding="UTF-8"?>
<project xmlns="http://maven.apache.org/POM/4.0.0"
➥ xmlns:xsi="http://www.w3.org/2001/XMLSchema-instance"
➥     xsi:schemaLocation="http://maven.apache.org/POM/4.0.0
➥ https://maven.apache.org/xsd/maven-4.0.0.xsd">
    <modelVersion>4.0.0</modelVersion>
```

```
<parent>
    <groupId>org.springframework.boot</groupId>
    <artifactId>spring-boot-starter-parent</artifactId>
    <version>2.6.3</version>
    <relativePath/> <!-- lookup parent from repository -->
</parent>
<groupId>io.musibs.dev.labs</groupId>
<artifactId>spring-boot-websocket</artifactId>
<version>0.0.1-SNAPSHOT</version>
<name>spring-boot-websocket</name>
<description>Demo project for Spring Boot</description>
<properties>
    <java.version>17</java.version>
</properties>
<dependencies>
    <dependency>
        <groupId>org.springframework.boot</groupId>
        <artifactId>spring-boot-starter-websocket</artifactId>
    </dependency>
    <dependency>
        <groupId>org.projectlombok</groupId>
        <artifactId>lombok</artifactId>
        <optional>true</optional>
    </dependency>
    <dependency>
        <groupId>org.springframework.boot</groupId>
        <artifactId>spring-boot-starter-test</artifactId>
        <scope>test</scope>
    </dependency>
</dependencies>

<build>
    <plugins>
        <plugin>
            <groupId>org.springframework.boot</groupId>
            <artifactId>spring-boot-maven-plugin</artifactId>
            <configuration>
                <excludes>
                    <exclude>
                        <groupId>org.projectlombok</groupId>
                        <artifactId>lombok</artifactId>
                    </exclude>
                </excludes>
            </configuration>
        </plugin>
    </plugins>
</build>

</project>
```

In listing 8.27, we included the `spring-boot-starter-websocket` dependency. The `spring-boot-starter-websocket` dependency provides the necessary support for WebSocket protocol in Spring. Next, let's configure Spring to enable WebSocket and STOMP messaging, as shown in the following listing.

Listing 8.28 Enabling WebSocket and STOMP support

```
package com.manning.sbip.ch08.config;

import org.springframework.context.annotation.Configuration;
import org.springframework.messaging.simp.config.MessageBrokerRegistry;
import
➥ org.springframework.web.socket.config.annotation.EnableWebSocketMessage
➥ Broker;
import
➥ org.springframework.web.socket.config.annotation.StompEndpointRegistry;
import
➥ org.springframework.web.socket.config.annotation.WebSocketMessageBroker
➥ Configurer;

@Configuration
@EnableWebSocketMessageBroker
public class WebSocketConfiguration implements
➥ WebSocketMessageBrokerConfigurer {
    @Override
    public void registerStompEndpoints(StompEndpointRegistry registry) {
        registry.addEndpoint("/ws").withSockJS();
    }

    @Override
    public void configureMessageBroker(MessageBrokerRegistry registry) {
        registry.enableSimpleBroker("/topic");
        registry.setApplicationDestinationPrefixes("/app");
    }
}
```

The StompEndpointRegistry interface lets us register STOMP over WebSocket endpoints.

The MessageBrokerRegistry lets us configure message broker options.

In listing 8.28, the `registerStompEndpoints()` method allows us to register a STOMP endpoint over a WebSocket endpoint at the `/ws` endpoint. Further, the `withSockJS()` enables SockJS fallback options. SockJS (https://github.com/sockjs/sockjs-client) allows our WebSockets to work even if the browser does not support WebSocket protocol.

The `configureMessageBroker` method creates an in-memory message broker with one or more destinations for sending and receiving messages. In listing 8.28, we've created one destination with the prefix as `/topic`. We've also defined the application destination prefix as /app. This is used to filter destinations by methods annotated with `@MessageMapping`. You'll define these methods in a separate controller class. After processing the message, the controller sends the message to the broker. In this example, you've used an in-memory message broker. In a production application, you may choose to use better alternatives, such as RabbitMQ (https://www.rabbitmq.com/). Next, let's define the controller, as shown in the following listing.

Listing 8.29 The MessageController class

```
package com.manning.sbip.ch08.controller;

import java.time.Clock;
import java.time.Instant;
```

```
import org.springframework.messaging.handler.annotation.MessageMapping;
import org.springframework.messaging.handler.annotation.SendTo;
import org.springframework.stereotype.Controller;

import com.manning.sbip.ch08.model.InputMessage;
import com.manning.sbip.ch08.model.OutputMessage;

import lombok.extern.slf4j.Slf4j;

@Slf4j
@Controller
public class MessageController {

    @MessageMapping("/chat")
    @SendTo("/topic/messages")
    public OutputMessage message(InputMessage message) {
        log.info("Input Message "+message);
        return OutputMessage
            .builder()
            .time(Instant.now(Clock.systemDefaultZone()))
            .content(message.getContent())
            .build();
    }
}
```

In listing 8.29, you defined the Spring controller, and you defined an endpoint `/chat` with `@MessageMapping` annotation. The `@SendTo` annotation broadcasts the message to all clients subscribed to the `/topic/messages` endpoint. The `InputMessage` and `OutputMessage` are two Java POJO classes that represent the input message and the output message, respectively. Refer to the GitHub repository for the Java files.

Let's now define the client-side HTML page we will use to send and receive the messages. The index.html file located in the src/main/resources folder is shown in the following listing.

Listing 8.30 The index.html page

```
<!DOCTYPE html>
<html lang="en">

<head>
    <meta charset="UTF-8">
    <meta http-equiv="X-UA-Compatible" content="IE=edge">
    <meta name="viewport" content="width=device-width, initial-scale=1.0">
    <title>Spring Boot WebSocket</title>
</head>

<body>
        <label for="message-input">Enter your message</label>
        <input type="text" class="form-control" id="message-input">
        <button type="submit" onclick="sendMessage()">Send</button>
        <ul id="message-list"></ul>
```

```
    <script src="https://cdnjs.cloudflare.com/ajax/libs/sockjs-
➥ client/1.5.1/sockjs.js"></script>
    <script
➥ src="https://cdnjs.cloudflare.com/ajax/libs/stomp.js/2.3.3/stomp.min.js
➥ "></script>
    <script src="js/main.js"></script>
</body>

</html>
```

We are downloading sock.js and stomp.js from the CDN.

In listing 8.30, we've done the following:

- We've defined a text box and a button, so the user can enter a text message and send it to the server. Clicking the button invokes the `sendMessage()` function.
- We've also defined an empty unordered list with an ID of `message-list`, which is used to print the messages broadcasted by the server.
- Included the SockJS and STOMP JS in the HTML page. You'll notice the use of these JS files in the custom JS file called main.js. The main.js file is used to initiate the WebSocket connection and subscribe to the `/topic/messages` endpoint.

Let's now define the main.js file, which is available at the src\main\resources\js folder. The following listing shows this file.

Listing 8.31 The main.js file

```
let sock = new SockJS('http://localhost:8080/ws');

let client = Stomp.over(sock);

function sendMessage() {
    console.log("Sending message");
    let input = document.getElementById('message-input');
    client.send('/app/chat', {}, JSON.stringify({ content: input.value }));
}


client.connect({}, (frame) => {
    client.subscribe('/topic/messages', (payload) => {
        let message_list = document.getElementById('message-list');
        let message = document.createElement('li');
        let output = JSON.parse(payload.body);
        message.appendChild(document.createTextNode(output.content +" at "
➥ +output.time));
        message_list.appendChild(message);
    });
});
```

Create a WebSocket connection at http://localhost:8080/ws.

Create a new StompClient object (from stomp.min.js library) with the WebSocket endpoint.

Function to send message. This function is invoked while you click on the Send in the HTML page. It takes the value in the "message-input" text field and sends it to the server with empty headers ({}).

Start the STOMP communications; provide a callback for when the CONNECTED (part of WebSocket protocol) frame arrives.

Subscribe to "/topic/messages". Whenever there is a new message, add the text in a list-item element in the unordered list.

Let's now start the application and access http://localhost:8080. You can enter text and notice it is broadcasted back with a timestamp. You can open another tab in your browser and access the same URL http://localhost:8080. Enter text, and you'll notice that the same text message is broadcasted to the first window as well.

DISCUSSION

In this technique, you explored the use of WebSocket protocol in a Spring Boot application with a simple messaging application. Let's now understand how a handshake between the client and server works in a WebSocket application, as shown in figure 8.14.

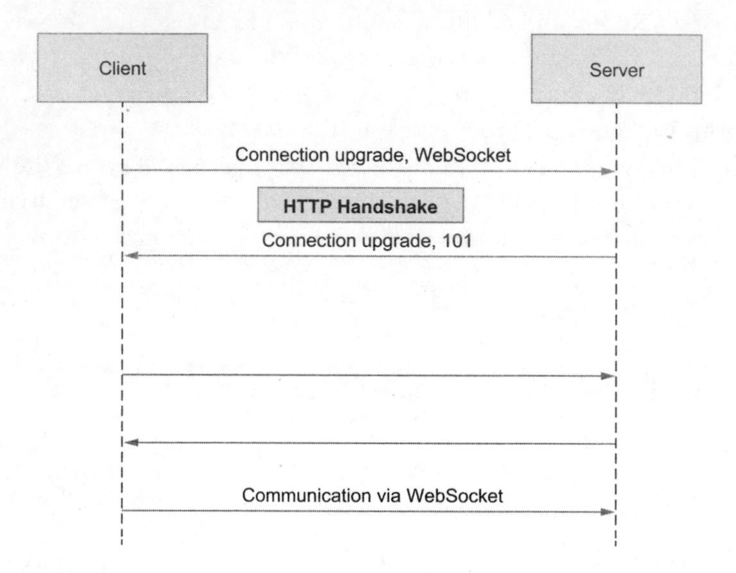

Figure 8.14 Client and server communication through WebSocket protocol

In the initial phase of a connection setup the client sends a few special HTTP headers asking for a WebSocket connection. The HTTP headers are shown in the following listing.

Listing 8.32 HTTP request headers

```
GET ws://localhost:8080/ws/257/vktswatd/websocket HTTP/1.1
Host: localhost:8080
Connection: Upgrade
Upgrade: websocket
Origin: http://localhost:8080
Sec-WebSocket-Version: 13
Accept-Encoding: gzip, deflate, br
Accept-Language: en-US,en;q=0.9
Sec-WebSocket-Key: kVE6ElOMjfIi4bPZzojWzA==
Sec-WebSocket-Extensions: permessage-deflate; client_max_window_bits
```

The initial request needs to be an `HTTP GET` request. Besides, the client begins the interaction with the server with an `HTTP Upgrade` header to upgrade or switch to WebSocket protocol. The client also sends additional `Sec-*` headers for other purposes. For instance, the `Sec-WebSocket-Key` is used for security purposes. Refer to the https://datatracker .ietf.org/doc/html/rfc6455 for more details on these additional headers.

If the server supports WebSocket protocol, it automatically responds with the `HTTP 101 Switching Protocols` response instead of the usual `HTTP 200 OK` status code. The response headers are shown in the following listing.

Listing 8.33 The HTTP response headers

```
HTTP/1.1 101
Vary: Origin
Vary: Access-Control-Request-Method
Vary: Access-Control-Request-Headers
Upgrade: websocket
Connection: upgrade
Sec-WebSocket-Accept: vNLDQJwTllhnlFr6XKRZdjCX2Vk=
Sec-WebSocket-Extensions: permessage-deflate;client_max_window_bits=15
Date: Wed, 28 Jul 2021 10:30:46 GMT
```

After a successful handshake, the TCP socket underlying the HTTP upgrade request remains open for both the client and the server to continue sending and receiving messages.

Summary

- We introduced reactive programming with a focus on asynchronous data streams and the benefits of reactive programming.
- We introduced Reactive Streams, Project Reactor, and Spring WebFlux.
- We discussed designing a reactive restful API with Spring WebFlux annotated controllers and functional endpoints.
- We discussed techniques for accessing a reactive application with WebClient.
- We introduced WebSocket protocol and how to use it in a Spring Boot application.
- We introduced RSocket protocol, its different interaction patterns, and how to use RSocket in a Spring Boot application.

Part 4

Part 4 of the book consists of one chapter, which discusses techniques for deploying Spring Boot applications. Chapter 9 begins with basic JAR- and WAR-based deployment and then proceeds with PaaS-style deployments with Heroku and Cloud Foundry. This chapter then shows how to run Spring Boot applications as containers and deploy them into the Kubernetes cluster as well as into Red Hat OpenShift.

9 Deploying Spring Boot applications

This chapter covers

- Running Spring Boot applications as a JAR file or deploying as a WAR file
- Deploying Spring Boot applications to Cloud Foundry and Heroku
- Running Spring Boot applications as Docker containers
- Developing Spring Boot applications for Kubernetes clusters and the Red Hat OpenShift platform

Once you are done with your application development and testing, you need to deploy the applications into your production server to serve the application users. Spring Boot applications can be deployed through an array of deployment strategies. Based on the application's scalability, availability, and resilience requirements, you can decide on your application deployment strategy.

In this chapter, we'll introduce you to various approaches to deploy the Spring Boot application. You'll learn traditional deployment techniques, such as running the application as an executable JAR or deploying it into an application server as a WAR. We'll then explore deploying into Pivotal Cloud Foundry and Heroku. Later, we'll also learn how to run Spring Boot applications as a Docker container and deploy them into a Kubernetes cluster. Finally, we'll show how to deploy the application into Red Hat OpenShift. Let's get started.

Developing various types of applications with the Spring Boot framework is a popular choice among developers and organizations. Due to the framework's flexibility, ease of use, and popularity, it is often used to develop a diverse category of applications, such as Web applications, REST APIs, microservices, and others. Some of these applications are small and target a limited number of users, whereas some are complex and available across multiple geographies and a broad range of users. The deployment strategies for first-category applications are straightforward. However, the latter category is complex and requires a sophisticated and thoughtful deployment model.

To meet the need for all categories, Spring Boot supports a wide range of deployment techniques. You can package your Spring Boot application as an executable JAR and run it without the need for any application server. Spring Boot provides built-in support for several embedded Web servers. Similarly, if you need to package your application as a WAR file and deploy it to an application server, Spring Boot has built-in support to prepare the WAR file. As you'll explore shortly, it is straightforward to package your Spring Boot application as a WAR file without defining a web.xml and other configurations.

Deploying the applications through the JAR or WAR files approach has a prerequisite you need to build a package for your application. The Pivotal Cloud Foundry (PCF) (https://www.cloudfoundry.org/) offers an alternative approach with which you can use your source code directly to deploy the application, and PCF will perform the required steps. Similarly, if you don't have your on-premises infrastructure, you can leverage cloud providers, such as AWS, Azure, Google Cloud Platform (GCP), and Heroku to deploy your packaged application. In this chapter, we'll demonstrate how to deploy your application on Heroku.

Further, if you need to run your application as a container image, Spring Boot provides built-in support to generate a container image for your application. You can then use the image to run your application locally or deploy it to cloud environments. If you need scalable, high available and fault-tolerant applications, you can deploy your application to Kubernetes. In this chapter, we'll demonstrate how to deploy a Spring Boot application to Kubernetes and Red Hat OpenShift.

NOTE How to deploy an application and serve end-users is a business requirement and is done based on multiple factors, such as application performance, availability, scalability, resilience, compliance needs, and so on. Thus, there are plenty of deployment techniques and strategies available. There are many technical toolkits and platforms out there to facilitate the diverse need of the deployments. In this book, we aim to focus on the Spring Boot application deployment on popular and commonly used platforms. Due to the vastness of this subject, it is beyond the scope of this text to provide an in-depth discussion on the technologies and platforms. However, we'll provide additional references for the specific technology or platform wherever possible and cover the setup steps (if any) in the book's companion GitHub wiki.

9.1 Running Spring Boot applications as executable JAR files

Previously, you've seen that you can package a Spring Boot application as an executable JAR file and execute it in local machines or servers. In this section, we'll explore this step in detail.

9.1.1 Technique: Packaging and executing a Spring Boot application as an executable JAR file

In this technique, we'll demonstrate how to package and execute a Spring Boot application as an executable JAR file.

Problem

You have developed a Spring Boot application and need to execute it as an executable JAR file.

Solution

Once you are done with the application development, you need to execute it to see it in action. Spring Boot provides several options to deploy the application and run it. In this technique, we'll explore Spring Boot's built-in approach to package the application as an executable JAR file and run it. This is one of the popular approaches to package and run a Spring Boot application.

To demonstrate how to package the application components and run the application as an executable JAR file, we'll use the Course Tracker Spring Boot application we've developed in the earlier chapters.

> **Source code**
> The final version of the Spring Boot project is available at http://mng.bz/oa7Z.

To ensure the application is packaged as an executable JAR file, you need to ensure the following two things:

1. The `packaging` type in the pom.xml file needs to be set as a JAR. This ensures the application components will be packaged as a JAR.
2. Configure the `spring-boot-maven-plugin` in the `plugins` section of the pom.xml file, as shown in the following listing.

Listing 9.1 The Spring Boot Maven plugin

```
<plugin>
    <groupId>org.springframework.boot</groupId>
    <artifactId>spring-boot-maven-plugin</artifactId>
</plugin>
```

The spring-boot-maven-plugin prepares the executable JAR file when the Maven package goal is executed. We'll discuss more on this in the discussion section.

Open a terminal window, and browse to the location of the pom.xml file. Next, execute the mvn package command to build and package the application components. This ensures the application is compiled, built, and packaged as a JAR file. The following listing shows the output.

Listing 9.2 The mvn package command

```
$course-tracker-app\target>mvn package
[INFO] Scanning for projects...
[INFO]
[INFO] ------------< com.manning.sbip.ch09:course-tracker-app-jar >------------
[INFO] Building course-tracker-app-jar 1.0.0
[INFO] --------------------------------[ jar ]---------------------------------
[INFO]
[INFO] --- maven-resources-plugin:3.2.0:resources (default-resources) @
➥ course-tracker-app-jar ---
[INFO] Using 'UTF-8' encoding to copy filtered resources.
[INFO] Using 'UTF-8' encoding to copy filtered properties files.
[INFO] Copying 1 resource
[INFO] Copying 7 resources
[INFO]
[INFO] --- maven-compiler-plugin:3.8.1:compile (default-compile) @
➥ course-tracker-app-jar ---
[INFO] Changes detected - recompiling the module!
[INFO] Compiling 6 source files to C:\sbip\repo\ch09\course-tracker-app-
➥ jar\target\classes
[INFO]
[INFO] --- maven-resources-plugin:3.2.0:testResources (default-
➥ testResources) @ course-tracker-app-jar ---
[INFO] Using 'UTF-8' encoding to copy filtered resources.
[INFO] Using 'UTF-8' encoding to copy filtered properties files.
[INFO] skip non existing resourceDirectory C:\sbip\repo\ch09\course-
➥ tracker-app-jar\src\test\resources
[INFO]
[INFO] --- maven-compiler-plugin:3.8.1:testCompile (default-testCompile) @
➥ course-tracker-app-jar ---
[INFO] Changes detected - recompiling the module!
[INFO]
[INFO] --- maven-surefire-plugin:2.22.2:test (default-test) @ course-
➥ tracker-app-jar ---
[INFO]
[INFO] --- maven-jar-plugin:3.2.0:jar (default-jar) @ course-tracker-app-
➥ jar ---
[INFO] Building jar: C:\sbip\repo\ch09\course-tracker-app-
➥ jar\target\course-tracker-app-jar-1.0.0.jar
[INFO]
[INFO] --- spring-boot-maven-plugin:2.5.3:repackage (repackage) @ course-
➥ tracker-app-jar ---
[INFO] Replacing main artifact with repackaged archive
[INFO] ------------------------------------------------------------------------
[INFO] BUILD SUCCESS
[INFO] ------------------------------------------------------------------------
```

After successfully packaging, you'll find there is a target directory created in the same location as the pom.xml file. This target directory contains an executable JAR file. By default, the name of the JAR file is <artifactId>-<version>.jar. In our example, the JAR file name is course-tracker-app-jar.1.0.0.jar. You can execute this JAR file using the java -jar <jarName> command from your terminal from the target directory. This is shown in the following listing.

Listing 9.3 Executing the Spring Boot executable JAR file

```
$course-tracker-app\target>java -jar course-tracker-app-jar.1.0.0.jar
```

You'll notice the application starts up and is successfully initialized. In this example, the application starts on default HTTP port 8080. Open a Web browser, and access http://localhost:8080, then you'll see the Course Tracker application index page.

DISCUSSION

In this section, we discussed how to create and run an executable JAR file from your Spring Boot application. In chapter 1, sections 1.3.3 and 1.3.4, we briefly discussed how the JAR file is created and explored the structure of the JAR file. We discussed that the repackage goal of spring-boot-maven-plugin hooks in at the Maven package phase and prepares the executable JAR file. Previously, we discussed that Spring Boot projects have a parent POM called spring-boot-starter-parent. This POM file includes the necessary configuration to define the repackage goal. Further, in the same target directory, you'll notice that there is another JAR file with naming format <artifactId>-<version>.jar.original. In our example, this JAR name is course-tracker-app-jar-1.0.0.jar.original. This is the original JAR file prepared by Maven. Note that this is not an executable JAR. The contents of this JAR file are subsequently packaged by the spring-boot-maven-plugin to create the executable JAR file. The following listing shows the structure of the Spring Boot-packaged JAR file.

Listing 9.4 Spring Boot-packaged JAR file structure

```
course-tracker-app-jar-1.0.0.jar
  |
  +-META-INF
  |   +-MANIFEST.MF
  +-org
  |   +-springframework
  |     +-boot
  |       +-loader
  |         +-<spring boot loader classes>
  +-BOOT-INF
    +-classes
    |   +-com
    |     +-manning
    |       +-sbip
    |         +-ch09
    |           +-CourseTrackerSpringBootApplication.class
```

These loader classes are used to launch a Spring Boot application.

```
+-lib
| +-dependency1.jar
| +-dependency2.jar
+-classpath.idx
+-layers.idx
```

Third-party libraries required for the Spring Boot application to run (e.g., Spring JARs, logging JARs, etc.)

The META-INF folder contains the MANIFEST.MF manifest file. A manifest is a special file that contains meta-information about the files packaged in the JAR file. The following listing shows the sample contents of a manifest file.

Listing 9.5 The MANIFEST.MF file for the Course Tracker JAR file

```
Manifest-Version: 1.0
Created-By: Maven Jar Plugin 3.2.0
Build-Jdk-Spec: 17
Implementation-Title: course-tracker-app-jar
Implementation-Version: 1.0.0
Main-Class: org.springframework.boot.loader.JarLauncher
Start-Class: com.manning.sbip.ch09.CourseTrackerSpringBootApplication
Spring-Boot-Version: 2.6.3
Spring-Boot-Classes: BOOT-INF/classes/
Spring-Boot-Lib: BOOT-INF/lib/
Spring-Boot-Classpath-Index: BOOT-INF/classpath.idx
Spring-Boot-Layers-Index: BOOT-INF/layers.idx
```

Listing 9.5 contains various meta-information about the JAR file. The `Main-Class` property contains the `org.springframework.boot.loader.JarLauncher` class, which is the entry point of the execution of the JAR. The `Start-Class` property contains the actual Spring Boot application class that begins the initialization of the Spring Boot application. The `JarLauncher` class launches this class specified in `Start-Class` property.

The application-specific class files are packaged inside the `BOOT-INF\classes`, and the dependencies are packaged inside the BOOT-INF\lib folder. These are the third-party libraries required by the Spring Boot application to function.

In addition, the JAR also includes two index files: classpath.idx and layers.idx. The classpath.idx file contains a list of JAR names (including the directories) in the order they should be added to the classpath.

The layers.idx files contain a list of layers and parts of the JAR that should be contained within them. The layers play a crucial role if you need to build a Docker image from the contents of the JAR file. While creating the Docker file these layers are written into different layers in the Docker image. We'll discuss this in greater depth while discussing the creation of a Docker image of a Spring Boot application.

By default, Spring Boot defines the following layers:

- `dependencies`—Contains all dependencies with a version that does not contain `SNAPSHOT`.
- `spring-boot-loader`—Spring Boot loader classes. For instance, the `JarLauncher` class is part of this layer.

- `snapshot-dependencies`—Contains all dependencies with a version that contains `SNAPSHOT`.
- `application`—Contains application classes and resources.

The last thing we will discuss in this section is to view and extract the aforementioned layers through `layertools` JAR mode. Previously, you noticed that you can execute the executable JAR via the `java -jar <jarName>` command. You can specify the `-Djarmode=layertools` to view the `layertools` options. The following listing shows the use of `layertools`.

Listing 9.6 Using layertools JAR mode

```
$course-tracker-app\target>java -Djarmode=layertools -jar course-tracker-
➥ app-jar-1.0.0.jar
Usage:
  java -Djarmode=layertools -jar course-tracker-app-jar-1.0.0.jar

Available commands:
  list     List layers from the jar that can be extracted
  extract  Extracts layers from the jar for image creation
  help     Help about any command
```

The `layertools` provides three options: `list` the layers, `extract` the layers, and the `help` command for which `help` is the default option. When you execute the command, the `JarLauncher` class is invoked as it is the entry point of the JAR execution. However, as the `jarmode` flag is configured, instead of starting the application, it executes any of the available commands of `layertools`. These commands are provided by another launcher: `JarModeLauncher`. It is used whenever we invoke `java -jar` with `-Djarmode=layertools`.

Further, by default Spring Boot packages the layers.idx file. When an executable JAR with this file is created, Spring Boot automatically provides and packages the `spring-boot-jarmode-layertools` JAR. The `spring-boot-jarmode-layertools` JAR includes the `LayerToolsJarMode` class, which provides the necessary support for the `layertools` jarmode feature. Let's now discuss the use of `list` and `extract` commands along with `layertools` jarmode. The following listing shows the use of the `list` command.

Listing 9.7 Use of list command in jarmode layertools to view the layers

```
$course-tracker-app\target> java -Djarmode=layertools -jar course-tracker-
➥ app-jar-1.0.0.jar list
dependencies
spring-boot-loader
snapshot-dependencies
application
```

Listing 9.7 shows the layers present inside the course-tracker-app-jar-1.0.0.jar file. You can extract these layers into the file system using the `extract` command, as shown in the following listing.

Listing 9.8 Use of extract command in jarmode layertools to extract the layers in the file system

```
$course-tracker-app\target>java -Djarmode=layertools -jar course-tracker-
➥ app-jar-1.0.0.jar extract --destination layers

C:\sbip\repo\ch09\course-tracker-app-jar\target>dir layers
 Volume in drive C is OS
 Volume Serial Number is 8EF3-F5B9

 Directory of C:\sbip\repo\ch09\course-tracker-app-jar\target\layers

04/03/2022  01:20 PM    <DIR>          .
04/03/2022  01:20 PM    <DIR>          ..
04/03/2022  01:20 PM    <DIR>          application
04/03/2022  01:20 PM    <DIR>          dependencies
04/03/2022  01:20 PM    <DIR>          snapshot-dependencies
04/03/2022  01:20 PM    <DIR>          spring-boot-loader
```

In listing 9.8, we first used the extract command and specified a destination folder called layers to extract the layers. We then use the `dir` command to show the created directories. If you browse these directories, you'll notice the contents of the `course-tracker-app-jar-1.0.0.jar` JAR is extracted inside these folders.

If you are wondering what the need for these layers is and why we are discussing these in this section, wait until we demonstrate creating Docker images for Spring Boot applications. You'll notice that these layers help us to build an optimized docker image. As we've discussed the executable JAR creation and structure in this section, for continuity purposes, we have provided the layers discussion in the same section.

9.2 Deploying Spring Boot applications as WAR in the WildFly application server

In the previous section, we explored how to package Spring Boot application components in an executable JAR and run it. Although it works fine, at times, you need to package your application components into a WAR file and deploy them into a Web server or application servers.

Before containerization and Kubernetes, deploying applications into a Web server or application servers were the de facto standards. Application servers offer a lot of enterprise features that help developers and application architects to leverage those features and plan application deployment strategies. For instance, most application servers provide features, such as support for database connection, session replication, sticky sessions, clustering, and more. For application server-based deployments, it is a common scenario to deploy the same instance of the application into multiple servers and use a load balancer to balance the incoming requests among the application instances.

Figure 9.1 shows a high-level diagram with the use of application server clustering to deploy Spring Boot applications. This cluster deployment provides capabilities,

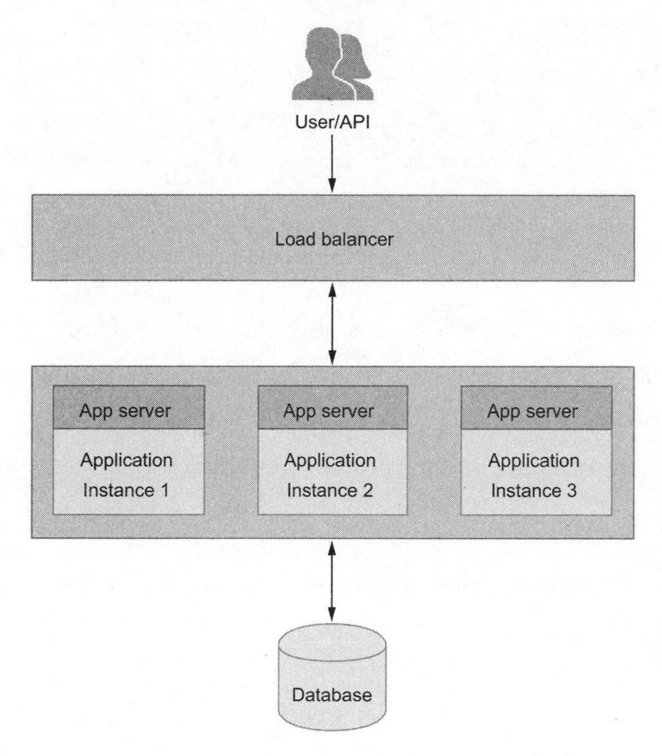

Figure 9.1 Deploying Spring Boot application in an application server cluster. The user request is received by a load balancer that front ends the application servers. Based on the load balancer configuration, the request is routed to one of the application server instances, and a response is provided back to the user.

such as load balancing and high availability. Note that we've provided this design for a high-level understanding and allow you to visualize how the typical application server-based production deployments work.

In the following section, you'll learn how to package your application as a WAR file and deploy it into a standalone WildFly server (https://www.wildfly.org/). WildFly is the community edition of the popular Red Hat JBoss Enterprise Application Platform server and is available free of cost.

9.2.1 Technique: Packaging and deploying a Spring Boot application as WAR in the WildFly application server

In this technique, we'll discuss how to package a Spring Boot application as a WAR file and deploy into WildFly application server.

Problem

You have developed a Spring Boot application and need to package it as a WAR file and deploy it in the WildFly application server.

Solution

In this section, we'll demonstrate how to package a Spring Boot application and deploy it in the WildFly server (https://www.wildfly.org/). You can refer to the version-specific installation document available at https://docs.wildfly.org/. To demonstrate how to package the application components as a WAR file and deploy it in the WildFly application server, we'll use the Course Tracker Spring Boot application we developed in the earlier chapters.

Source code

The final version of the Spring Boot project is available at http://mng.bz/nY75.

To package the components as WAR files, you need to make two changes:

1. In the pom.xml file, the packaging type should be `war`, as shown in the following listing.

Listing 9.9 Package type as WAR type in pom.xml file

```
...
<groupId>com.manning.sbip.ch09</groupId>
<artifactId>course-tracker-app-war</artifactId>
<version>1.0.0</version>
<packaging>war</packaging>
<name>course-tracker-app-war</name>
...
```

2. Define an instance of a `WebApplicationInitializer` to run the application from a WAR deployment. The `WebApplicationInitializer` allows us to configure the `ServletContext` programmatically in a Servlet 3.0+ environment. If you create your Spring Boot application through Spring Initializr (available at https://start.spring.io) with the packaging type as `war`, then by default Spring Boot provides a class called `ServletInitializer`. This class extends the `SpringBootServletInitializer` class, which is an instance of `WebApplicationInitializer`. The `SpringBootServletInitializer` class is an opinionated `WebApplicationInitializer` implementation provided by Spring Boot to run a Spring Boot application in a WAR deployment. If you are not creating your Spring Boot application from Spring Initializr, you have to perform this step manually.

The following listing shows the `ServletInitializer` class.

Listing 9.10 The ServletInitializer class

```
package com.manning.sbip.ch09;

import org.springframework.boot.builder.SpringApplicationBuilder;
import
➥ org.springframework.boot.web.servlet.support.SpringBootServletInitial
➥ izer;

public class ServletInitializer extends SpringBootServletInitializer {
```

```
  @Override
  protected SpringApplicationBuilder configure(SpringApplicationBuilder
➥ application) {
    return application.sources(CourseTrackerSpringBootApplication.class);
  }

}
```

In listing 9.10, we added the `CourseTrackerSpringBootApplication` class in `SpringApplicationBuilder`. Later on, this `SpringApplicationBuilder` is used to build an instance of `SpringApplication`, which is run to start the Spring Boot application.

Next, let's exclude the `logback-starter` dependency from the `spring-boot-starter-web` dependency in the pom.xml, as shown in the following listing.

Listing 9.11 Excluding the logback-classic dependency from spring-boot-starter-web

```
<dependency>
    <groupId>org.springframework.boot</groupId>
    <artifactId>spring-boot-starter-web</artifactId>
    <exclusions>
        <exclusion>
            <groupId>ch.qos.logback</groupId>
            <artifactId>logback-classic</artifactId>
        </exclusion>
    </exclusions>
</dependency>
```

We excluded this dependency, as it conflicts with the `slf4j-jboss-logmanager-1.1.0.Final.jar` of the WildFly server. Next, let's define the context root of the application to "/". The following listing shows the associated configuration for jboss-web.xml file located in the src\main\webapp\WEB-INF folder.

Listing 9.12 The jboss-web.xml file

```
<?xml version="1.0" encoding="UTF-8"?>
<jboss-web>
    <context-root>/</context-root>
</jboss-web>
```

We are done with all the configurations. Let's now package the application and deploy it into the WildFly server. To package the application, you need to execute the `mvn package` command from a terminal from the directory where the application's pom.xml file is located. After successfully building, you'll notice that the application is packaged as a WAR file. You can deploy this WAR file on the WildFly server.

Before starting deployment, you need to ensure an instance of the WildFly application server is running. You can then open a browser window and access the http://localhost:9990 URL, and you'll notice the WildFly server management console. Click on the Deployments menu and then the Upload Deployment button, as shown in figure 9.2.

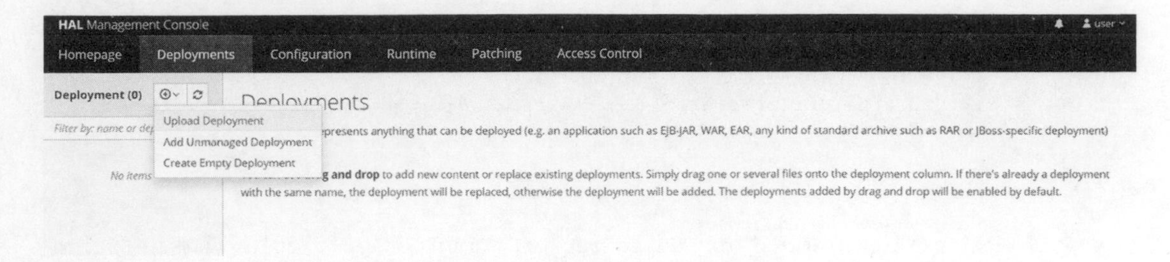

Figure 9.2 WildFly server Upload Deployment screen to upload a deployment

In the next window, upload the previously generated WAR file (e.g. course-tracker-app-war-1.0.0.war) from the target directory, and click the Next button and then in the next screen click the Finish button. After successful deployment, you'll notice the successful deployment message, as shown in figure 9.3.

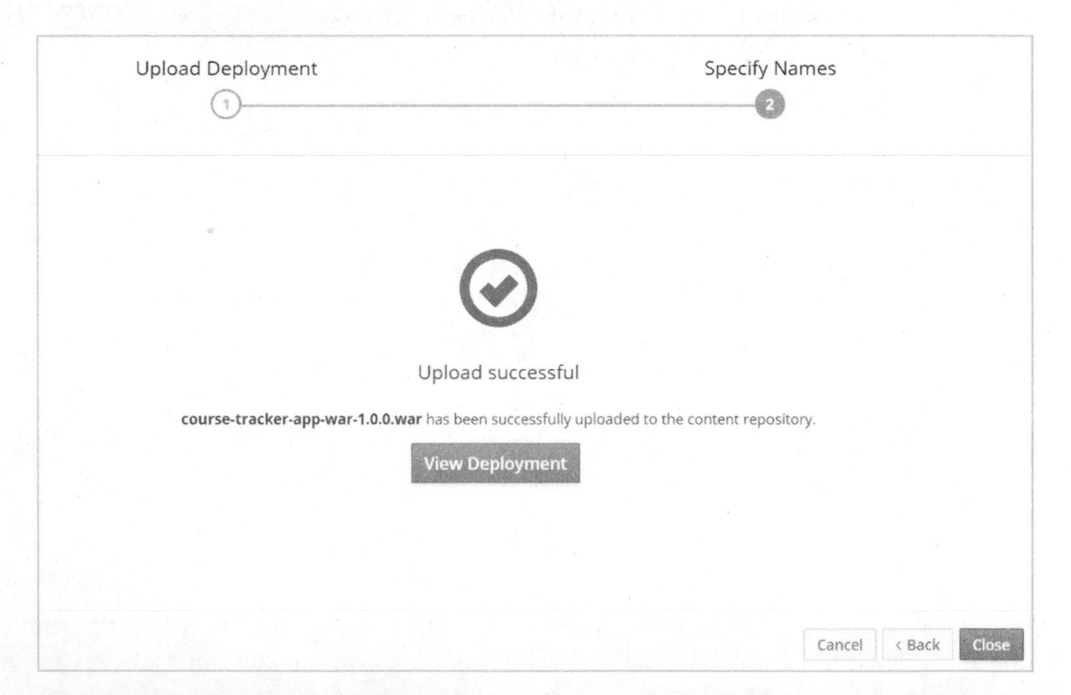

Figure 9.3 The Course Tracker WAR file uploaded successfully into the server. This indicates the application deployed successfully and can be accessed.

Click on the Close button, and the Course Tracker application is ready to be accessed. Let's open a browser window and access the http://localhost:8080 URL. You'll notice the index page of the Course Tracker application, as shown in figure 9.4.

Your Courses

Course Name	Course Category	Course Rating	Course Description	Edit	Delete
Rapid Spring Boot Application Development	Spring	4	Learn Enterprise Application Development with Spring Boot		
Getting Started with Spring Security DSL	Spring	5	Learn Spring Security DSL in Easy Steps		
Getting Started with Spring Cloud Kubernetes	Spring	3	Master Spring Boot Application Deployment with Kubernetes		

Figure 9.4 The Course Tracker application index page. This page is served by the WildFly server.

If you are performing frequent deployments and need to automate the deployment process, you can use the `wildfly-maven-plugin` Maven plugin to automatically deploy the generated WAR file.

> **Source code**
> The final version of the Spring Boot project with `wildfly-maven-plugin` is available at http://mng.bz/44JV.

To use the `wildfly-maven-plugin`, you need to add the associated configuration in the Course Tracker pom.xml file. Following is the summary of the changes. The following listing shows the updated pom.xml file.

Listing 9.13 Updated pom.xml file with `wildfly-maven-plugin` configuration

```
<?xml version="1.0" encoding="UTF-8"?>
<project xmlns="http:/ /maven.apache.org/POM/4.0.0"
➥ xmlns:xsi="http:/ /www.w3.org/2001/XMLSchema-instance"
➥ xsi:schemaLocation="http:/ /maven.apache.org/POM/4.0.0
➥ https:/ /maven.apache.org/xsd/maven-4.0.0.xsd">
    <modelVersion>4.0.0</modelVersion>
```

```
<parent>
    <groupId>org.springframework.boot</groupId>
    <artifactId>spring-boot-starter-parent</artifactId>
    <version>2.6.3</version>
    <relativePath/>
    <!-- lookup parent from repository -->
</parent>
<groupId>com.manning.sbip.ch09</groupId>
<artifactId>course-tracker-app-war-mvn-plugin</artifactId>
<version>1.0.0</version>
<packaging>war</packaging>
<name>course-tracker-app-war-mvn-plugin</name>
<description>Spring Boot application for Chapter 09</description>
<properties>
    <java.version>17</java.version>
 <wildfly.deploy.user>${ct.deploy.user}</wildfly.deploy.user>
 <wildfly.deploy.pass>${ct.deploy.pass}</wildfly.deploy.pass>
 <plugin.war.warName>${project.build.finalName}</plugin.war.warName>
</properties>
<dependencies>
    <dependency>
        <groupId>org.springframework.boot</groupId>
        <artifactId>spring-boot-starter-web</artifactId>
        <exclusions>
            <exclusion>
                <groupId>ch.qos.logback</groupId>
                <artifactId>logback-classic</artifactId>
            </exclusion>
        </exclusions>
    </dependency>
    <dependency>
        <groupId>org.springframework.boot</groupId>
        <artifactId>spring-boot-starter-tomcat</artifactId>
        <scope>provided</scope>
    </dependency>
    <dependency>
        <groupId>org.springframework.boot</groupId>
        <artifactId>spring-boot-starter-data-jpa</artifactId>
    </dependency>
    <dependency>
        <groupId>com.h2database</groupId>
        <artifactId>h2</artifactId>
        <scope>runtime</scope>
    </dependency>
    <dependency>
        <groupId>org.projectlombok</groupId>
        <artifactId>lombok</artifactId>
    </dependency>
    <dependency>
        <groupId>org.springframework.boot</groupId>
        <artifactId>spring-boot-starter-validation</artifactId>
    </dependency>
    <dependency>
        <groupId>org.springframework.boot</groupId>
        <artifactId>spring-boot-starter-thymeleaf</artifactId>
```

To deploy the Spring Boot application WAR file through the plugin, you need to configure the server username, password, and the WAR file name that needs to be deployed. We are referring these properties from settings.xml file. We've provided relevant settings.xml in the next listing.

```
        </dependency>
        <dependency>
            <groupId>org.webjars</groupId>
            <artifactId>bootstrap</artifactId>
            <version>4.4.1</version>
        </dependency>
        <dependency>
            <groupId>org.webjars</groupId>
            <artifactId>jquery</artifactId>
            <version>3.4.1</version>
        </dependency>
        <dependency>
            <groupId>org.webjars</groupId>
            <artifactId>webjars-locator</artifactId>
            <version>0.38</version>
        </dependency>
        <dependency>
            <groupId>org.springframework.boot</groupId>
            <artifactId>spring-boot-starter-test</artifactId>
            <scope>test</scope>
            <exclusions>
                <exclusion>
                    <groupId>org.junit.vintage</groupId>
                    <artifactId>junit-vintage-engine</artifactId>
                </exclusion>
            </exclusions>
        </dependency>
    </dependencies>
    <build>
        <plugins>
            <plugin>
                <groupId>org.springframework.boot</groupId>
                <artifactId>spring-boot-maven-plugin</artifactId>
            </plugin>
            <plugin>
                <groupId>org.wildfly.plugins</groupId>
                <artifactId>wildfly-maven-plugin</artifactId>
                <version>2.1.0.Beta1</version>
                <configuration>
                    <hostname>localhost</hostname>
                    <port>9990</port>
                    <username>${wildfly.deploy.user}</username>
                    <password>${wildfly.deploy.pass}</password>
                    <name>${project.build.finalName}.${project.packaging}</name>
                </configuration>
                <executions>
                    <execution>
                        <id>undeploy</id>
                        <phase>clean</phase>
                        <goals>
                            <goal>undeploy</goal>
                        </goals>
                        <configuration>
                            <ignoreMissingDeployment>true</ignoreMissingDeployment>
                        </configuration>
                    </execution>
```

Properties defined in the properties section of this pom.xml

```
                <execution>
                    <id>deploy</id>
                    <phase>install</phase>
                    <goals>
                        <goal>deploy</goal>
                    </goals>
                </execution>
            </executions>
        </plugin>
    </plugins>
  </build>
</project>
```

To use the `wildfly-maven-plugin`, you've defined the server configuration, including `host`, `port`, `username`, and `password`. We've also defined two execution configurations: one to perform the deployment in the Maven `install` phase and one to perform undeployment in the Maven `clean` phase. For security reasons, we haven't configured the username and password in the pom.xml file. We're referring those from the Maven settings.xml file. The following listing shows the Maven settings.xml profile configuration.

Listing 9.14 Maven settings.xml profile configuration inside profiles section

```
...
<profile>
      <id>course-tracker-prod</id>
          <activation>
            <activeByDefault>true</activeByDefault>
          </activation>
          <properties>
            <ct.deploy.user>user</ct.deploy.user>
            <ct.deploy.pass>password</ct.deploy.pass>
          </properties>
    </profile>
...
```

We refer to the properties `ct.deploy.user` and `ct.deploy.pass` in the pom.xml properties configuration in listing 9.13, so the username and password could be used by `wildfly-maven-plugin` to perform the deploy and undeploy operations.

Open a terminal window to browse to the `course-tracker-app-war-mvn-plugin` application's pom.xml directory, and execute the `mvn install` command. You'll notice that the application deployed successfully. The following listing shows the `mvn install` command's output.

Listing 9.15 The mvn install command output for successful deployment

```
...
...
[INFO] --- spring-boot-maven-plugin:2.5.3:repackage (repackage) @ course-
➥ tracker-app-war-mvn-plugin ---
[INFO] Replacing main artifact with repackaged archive
[INFO]
```

```
[INFO] <<< wildfly-maven-plugin:2.1.0.Beta1:deploy (deploy) < package @
➥ course-tracker-app-war-mvn-plugin <<<
[INFO]
[INFO]
[INFO] --- wildfly-maven-plugin:2.1.0.Beta1:deploy (deploy) @ course-
➥ tracker-app-war-mvn-plugin ---
[INFO] JBoss Threads version 2.3.3.Final
[INFO] JBoss Remoting version 5.0.12.Final
[INFO] XNIO version 3.7.2.Final
[INFO] XNIO NIO Implementation Version 3.7.2.Final
[INFO] ELY00001: WildFly Elytron version 1.9.1.Final
[INFO] ------------------------------------------------------------------------
[INFO] BUILD SUCCESS
```

You can now open a browser window and access the http://localhost:8080/ URL to use the Course Tracker application. You'll notice the Course Tracker application index page. If you need to undeploy the application, you can execute the `mvn clean` command, and the application will be undeployed, as shown in the following listing.

Listing 9.16 Mvn clean to undeploy the deployed WAR file

```
$course-tracker-app\target>mvn clean
[INFO] Scanning for projects...
[INFO]
[INFO] ------< com.manning.sbip.ch09:course-tracker-app-war-mvn-plugin >---
[INFO] Building course-tracker-app-war-mvn-plugin 1.0.0
[INFO] --------------------------------[ war ]---------------------------------
[INFO]
[INFO] --- maven-clean-plugin:3.1.0:clean (default-clean) @ course-tracker-
➥ app-war-m
[INFO] Deleting C:\sbip\repo\ch09\course-tracker-app-war-mvn-plugin\target
[INFO]
[INFO] --- wildfly-maven-plugin:2.1.0.Beta1:undeploy (undeploy) @ course-
➥ tracker-app
[INFO] JBoss Threads version 2.3.3.Final
[INFO] JBoss Remoting version 5.0.12.Final
[INFO] XNIO version 3.7.2.Final
[INFO] XNIO NIO Implementation Version 3.7.2.Final
[INFO] ELY00001: WildFly Elytron version 1.9.1.Final
[INFO] ------------------------------------------------------------------------
[INFO] BUILD SUCCESS
```

Discussion

With this technique, you've learned to deploy a Spring Boot application in an application server. We've discussed two approaches to achieve this. In the first approach, you build the WAR file via the `mvn install` command and then manually deploy the WAR file via the application server's Web interface. With the second approach, you've used the `wildfly-maven-plugin` to automatically deploy the generated WAR file in the application server.

Now that you've explored both approaches, you may wonder which approach is better. I would recommend the `wildfly-maven-plugin`-based approach, as it enables a more automated way of deployment and requires less manual intervention.

9.3 Deploying Spring Boot applications in Cloud Foundry

In the previous sections, we've discussed two traditional approaches with JAR and WAR files to package and deploy a Spring Boot application. In this section, we'll look into an alternative application deployment approach through Cloud Foundry.

> **NOTE** Cloud Foundry provides a much more straightforward and easier model to build, test, and deploy applications. As you'll notice shortly, Cloud Foundry allows you to push your source code to the Cloud Foundry server and perform the build and deployment from the source code. Finally, it makes the application available to the end users. Cloud Foundry is a large topic and offers several features. It is beyond the scope of this text to provide in-depth coverage of this. Refer to the Cloud Foundry documentation available at https://docs.cloudfoundry.org/ for more information.

These days, cloud platforms allow us to deploy applications and make them available across the globe in a short period. The cloud platforms also allow us to scale the application on demand without worrying much about infrastructure and its scalability. Figure 9.5 shows various layers of technology stacks used in an application.

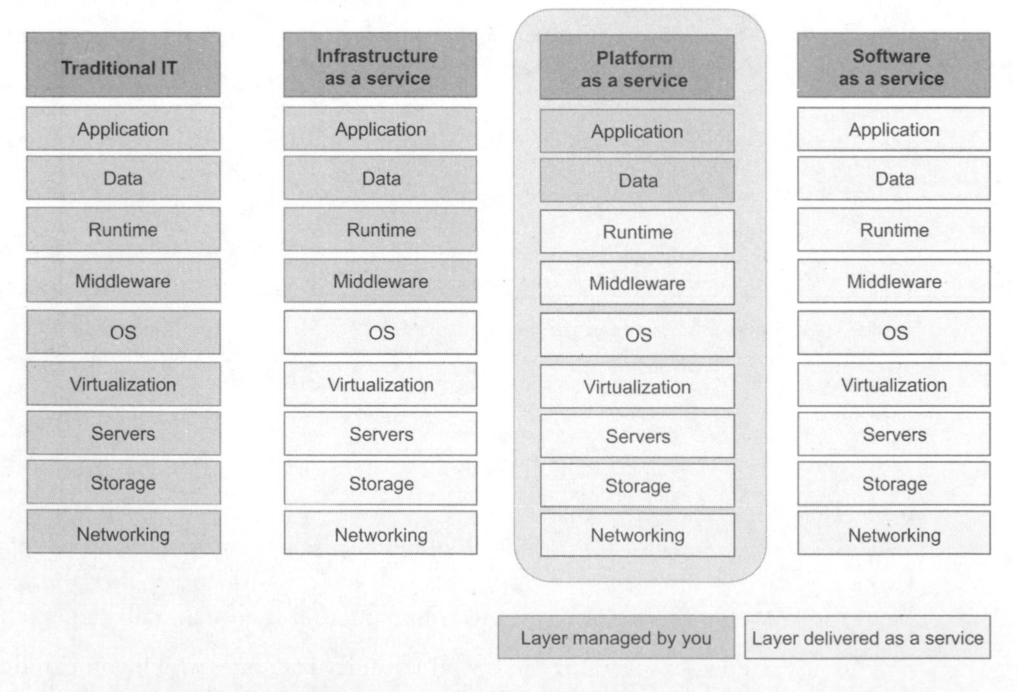

Figure 9.5 Layers of technology stacks required by an application. In traditional IT, all layers of infrastructure are managed by you. In the IaaS model, the core infrastructure is delivered as a service. In the PaaS model, only the application and data need to be managed by you, and the rest of all layers are delivered as a service. In the SaaS model, all layers are delivered as a service. We've highlighted the PaaS model, as Cloud Foundry belongs to this model.

Cloud Foundry belongs to the platform-as-a-service model, where only the data and application are managed by you, and all remaining layers are managed by the Cloud Foundry. But what is Cloud Foundry in the first place? It is an open-source cloud application platform that allows you to select the cloud platform you want to use, offers several developer frameworks, and offers other application services. One of the major benefits of Cloud Foundry over the traditional deployments is that it makes application building, testing, deployment, and scaling faster and easier. In the next technique, we'll explore how to deploy a Spring Boot application to Cloud Foundry.

9.3.1 Technique: Deploying a Spring Boot application to Cloud Foundry

In this technique, we'll discuss how to deploy a Spring Boot application to Cloud Foundry.

Problem

Your Spring Boot application is currently running as a standalone JAR file in a Unix server. You need to deploy it to a cloud platform through Cloud Foundry.

Solution

Using this technique, we'll explore how to deploy a Spring Boot application in a Cloud Foundry cloud platform. To deploy your application in Cloud Foundry, you need a Cloud Foundry instance. You can either run Cloud Foundry yourself, use a company-provided Cloud Foundry instance, or use a hosted solution. There are several hosted solutions available, such as anynines (https://paas.anynines.com/) and SAP (http://mng.bz/vo7p), which provides a trial version of the Cloud Foundry instance. In this technique, we'll use the SAP Cloud Foundry instance. You can browse the SAP link and follow the steps to set up your trial account.

> **Source code**
>
> The final version of the Spring Boot project is available at http://mng.bz/4jNR.

Once you are done with the Cloud Foundry instance set up, you'll need to install the Cloud Foundry command-line interface (CLI). You'll use this CLI tool to interact with the Cloud Foundry instance. The CLI runs on a terminal window and makes REST calls to the Cloud Foundry API. Browse to the https://github.com/cloudfoundry/cli#downloads link to install CLI on your computer. Once the installation is completed successfully, run the `cf version` command from your terminal, and it should return the installed Cloud Foundry CLI version.

The next step is to log in to the Cloud Foundry instance, which you can do using the `cf login` command. The following listing shows the complete login command.

Listing 9.17 Cloud Foundry login

```
cf login -a <CLOUDFOUNDRY_API_ENDPOINT> -u <USERNAME>
```

The CLOUDFOUNDRY_API_ENDPOINT is the Cloud Foundry instance URL. If you are using SAP, you'll find this on the SAP account page. The USERNAME is your login ID. For SAP, this is the email ID of the SAP account you just created.

Invoking the command of listing 9.17 with the API endpoint and the username will prompt you to enter the password. Enter your SAP account login password. The following listing shows a sample command and the associated output.

Listing 9.18 Login to Cloud Foundry

```
cf login -a https://api.cf.eu10.hana.ondemand.com/ -u ****@gmail.com
API endpoint: https://api.cf.eu10.hana.ondemand.com/

Password:

Authenticating...
OK

Targeted org 6****986trial.

Targeted space dev.

API endpoint:    https://api.cf.eu10.hana.ondemand.com
API version:     3.102.0
user:            ****@gmail.com
org:             6****86trial
space:           dev
```

Next, let's build the Course Tracker Spring Boot application using the mvn clean install command. We'll use the generated JAR file to push to the Cloud Foundry instance. Instead of pushing the raw JAR file, we'll define a manifest.yml file in the application root directory, so Cloud Foundry CLI can read it and perform the deployment. The following listing shows the manifest.yml file.

Listing 9.19 The manifest.yml file to deploy into Cloud Foundry

```
applications:
- name: course-tracker-app-cf
  instances: 1
  memory: 1024M
  path: target/course-tracker-app-cf-1.0.0.jar
  random-route: true
  buildpacks:
  - java_buildpack
```

This is a relatively simple configuration file with minimal details. We've specified the application name, the number of instances required, the memory that needs to be allocated, and the application executable path. The route details indicate Cloud Foundry to assign a random route for the deployed application. The buildpacks configuration allows Cloud Foundry to select a Java buildpack to run the application. You can now run the cf push command (from any OS user) to start the deployment, as shown in the following listing.

Listing 9.20 Cloud Foundry push command to start deployment

```
cf push
```

The command takes a while to upload the artifacts, and the deployment begins. Once the command returns, you can execute the cf apps command to find the running application and the associated URL. The following listing shows a sample output of the cf apps command.

Listing 9.21 Sample output of the cf apps command

```
> cf apps
Getting apps in org 6****986trial / space dev as ****@gmail.com...

name                    requested state   processes           routes
course-tracker-app-cf   started           web:1/1, task:0/0   course-
➥ tracker-app-cf-active-genet-qh.cfapps.eu10.hana.ondemand.com
```

In the above example, the course-tracker-app-cf-active-genet-qh.cfapps.eu10 .hana.ondemand.com is the application route (URL). In your case, you might notice a different routes name. You can copy the routes and access the URL in a browser window. You'll notice you are redirected to the Course Tracker application index page.

DISCUSSION

With this technique, we've demonstrated how to deploy your Spring Boot application to Cloud Foundry. To keep things simple, we've used the Course Tracker application with an in-memory database. In a production application, you'll also have other application components, such as database, messaging, caching, and others.

Based on the Cloud Foundry service provider, you can use the offerings from the provider. To find the list of offerings, you can execute the cf marketplace command, and it will return the available services and their details. Based on the need, you can enable one or more services. To know more about a service offering, you can execute the cf marketplace -e <SERVICE_OFFERING> command. Replace the SERVICE_OFFERING placeholder with the actual service name.

To create a new service, you can use the cf create-service <SERVICE> <SERVICE_PLAN> <SERVICE_INSTANCE> command. Further, you can find the list of services by invoking the cf services command. You can bind service with your application using the cf bind-service <APP_NAME> <SERVICE_INSTANCE> command.

Lastly, once you have the services defined, you may need to access the service-specific environment variables. For instance, if you've created a database, you need the database URL, username, password, and more to connect and access it. Spring provides the CloudFoundryVcapEnvironmentPostProcessor (http://mng.bz/QWO6) class that takes all the Cloud Foundry environment variables and provides in form of

Spring `Environment`. If you have configured Spring `spring-boot-starter-actuator` and enabled the `env` actuator endpoint, you'll find the Cloud Foundry properties through `/actuator/env` endpoint. You can also refer to the `java-cfenv` library (https://github.com/pivotal-cf/java-cfenv) for more information on using Cloud Foundry environment variables.

9.4 Deploying Spring Boot applications in Heroku

In the previous section, you've seen how to deploy an application in Cloud Foundry. In this section, we'll discuss deploying a Spring Boot application in Heroku (https://www.heroku.com/). Heroku is another PaaS solution that allows you to build, run, and execute applications in the cloud. It can run applications written in Ruby, Node.js, Java, Python, Clojure, Scala, Go, and PHP.

Heroku takes the application source code along with the dependencies the application requires and prepares an artifact that can be executed. For instance, a Spring Boot application takes the Spring Boot application source code and the pom.xml for the required dependencies. Heroku uses Git distributed version control system for deploying the application. Lastly, Heroku uses Dynos (https://devcenter.heroku.com/articles/dynos) to execute the applications. Dynos are lightweight Linux containers in which Heroku runs the application. In the next technique, let's explore how to deploy a Spring Boot application in Heroku.

9.4.1 Technique: Deploying a Spring Boot application in Heroku

In this technique, we'll discuss how to deploy a Spring Boot application in Heroku.

Problem

You need to deploy the application in the Heroku cloud platform.

Solution

Heroku is a PaaS solution that allows you to deploy a Spring Boot application in the Heroku cloud platform with a few steps. To demonstrate this, we'll use the previously used Course Tracker Spring Boot application to deploy into Heroku.

> **Source code**
> The final version of the Spring Boot project is available at http://mng.bz/XWj9.

To begin with, you need to create a user account in Heroku. You can navigate to https://signup.heroku.com/ and sign up for a new account. Next, you need to install Heroku Command Line Interface (CLI) tool on your machine. This CLI provides a set of commands to interact with the Heroku cloud platform and also allows you to deploy the application. Refer to https://devcenter.heroku.com/articles/heroku-cli for more information on installing the CLI in your machine. You are now ready to start deploying your application.

First, log in to Heroku from your terminal, so that you can execute the next set of commands to proceed with your deployment. Open a terminal and type `heroku login`. This command provides an option to authenticate yourself through a browser-based login. Once authenticated, you will find output similar to the following listing.

Listing 9.22 Login to Heroku

```
heroku login
heroku: Press any key to open up the browser to login or q to exit:
➥ Opening browser to https://cli-
➥ auth.heroku.com/auth/cli/browser/d4da08df-3725-44b6-bf28-
➥ c0a78fbe54e3?requestor=SFMyNTY.g2gDbQAAAA8xMDMuMjE1LjIyNC4xNTFuBgDw-
➥ iCkewFiAAFRgA.6fS4ju_OBxvr9_YQNkSn5Z7UK68CQNULUhh9VEzCVxQ
Logging in... done
Logged in as *****@gmail.com
```

Next, as mentioned earlier, Heroku uses a Git-distributed version control system for deployment. Thus, we need to create a Git repository for the Course Tracker application. Browse to the root directory of the Course Tracker application and execute the commands, as shown in the following listing.

Listing 9.23 Creating a Git repository for the Course Tracker application

```
git init                                   <-- Initializes an empty local Git repository
git add .                                  <-- Add all the files to the repository.
git commit -am "Course Tracker first commit"   <-- Commits the changes in the local Git repository
```

Next, to deploy the application in Heroku, we need to provision a new Heroku application. We will do that by executing the `heroku create` command, as shown in the following listing.

Listing 9.24 Provisioning the Heroku application

```
heroku create
Creating app... done, ⬢ secure-journey-03985
➥ https://secure-journey-03985.herokuapp.com/ |
➥ https://git.heroku.com/secure-journey-03985.git
```

The command in the listing also creates a remote repository called Heroku and adds its reference in your local Git repo. Heroku generates a random name (in this case `secure-journey-03985`) for your Spring Boot application.

In the Course Tracker application, to keep the example simple and easy to execute, we've used the H2 in-memory database. However, it is seldom the case in a production application. To demonstrate how to use a mainstream database, we used PostgreSQL in the application. Refer to the application pom.xml file for related configuration. Before we proceed with the deployment, let's attach a PostgreSQL database to the application. Execute the `heroku addons:create heroku-postgresql` command from your terminal to create a PostgreSQL database add-on. Once the add-on is created, Heroku will automatically populate the environment variables SPRING_DATASOURCE_URL, SPRING_DATASOURCE_USERNAME, and SPRING_DATASOURCE_PASSWORD. These environment variables allow the Course Tracker application to connect to the database. Refer to the application.properties file of the Course Tracker application. Next, we'll deploy the code by pushing the changes to the remote Heroku master branch, as shown in the following listing.

Listing 9.25 Deploying the Spring Boot application in Heroku

```
c:\sbip\repo\ch09\course-tracker-app-heroku>git push heroku master
Enumerating objects: 41, done.
Counting objects: 100% (41/41), done.
Delta compression using up to 8 threads
Compressing objects: 100% (30/30), done.
Writing objects: 100% (41/41), 64.32 KiB | 5.85 MiB/s, done.
Total 41 (delta 3), reused 0 (delta 0)
remote: Compressing source files... done.
remote: Building source:
remote:
remote: -----> Building on the Heroku-20 stack
remote: -----> Determining which buildpack to use for this app
remote: -----> Java app detected
remote: -----> Installing JDK 11... done
remote: -----> Executing Maven
remote:        $ ./mvnw -DskipTests clean dependency:list install
...
...
remote:        https://secure-journey-03985.herokuapp.com/ deployed to Heroku
remote:
remote: Verifying deploys... done.
To https://git.heroku.com/secure-journey-03985.git
 * [new branch]      master -> master
```

In listing 9.25, you may notice that Heroku uses the Maven wrapper (`.mvnw`) to deploy the application. Once the application is successfully built and deployed, it is accessible via https://secure-journey-03985.herokuapp.com. For you, this URL could be different, as Heroku uses a random name for the application. You can also run the `heroku open` command to automatically open the application URL in a browser window. You can check the Spring Boot startup logs by accessing the `heroku logs` command.

DISCUSSION

In this technique, you've deployed a Spring Boot application in the Heroku cloud platform. As you've noticed, it is extremely easy to build and deploy a Spring Boot application in Heroku. By using a few commands, you've got a running application with an HTTPS URL from your source code. The complexity of building, packaging, and deploying are taken care of by the platform. To make things further simplified, for Maven projects, Heroku provides the `heroku-maven-plugin` (https://github.com/heroku/heroku-maven-plugin). This plugin allows you to deploy the application without using a Git repository. You can find a detailed discussion on how to use the plugin at http://mng.bz/y47p. You can also refer to the Heroku documentation available at https://devcenter.heroku.com/ for a detailed discussion on various offerings and configurations.

9.5 Running Spring Boot applications as Docker containers

In previous sections, we learned a few deployment techniques. For example, the traditional deployments in which you package and deploy the application yourself into some server. The Cloud Foundry-based deployment is where you push the executable to the platform, and it takes care of the deployment. Lastly, we've seen the Heroku cloud platform in which you provide your source code to the platform, and it does the build, deployment, and execution.

In this section, we'll shift our attention to containers and use the most popular container implementation Docker to run the Course Tracker application as a containerized application. However, before we proceed to containerize the Course Tracker application, let's understand what a container is and why you should care about it.

A container image is a lightweight, standalone, executable software package that includes everything the application requires to run itself. These include application components, runtime, system tools, settings, and libraries. A container image turns into a container at its runtime, as shown in figure 9.6.

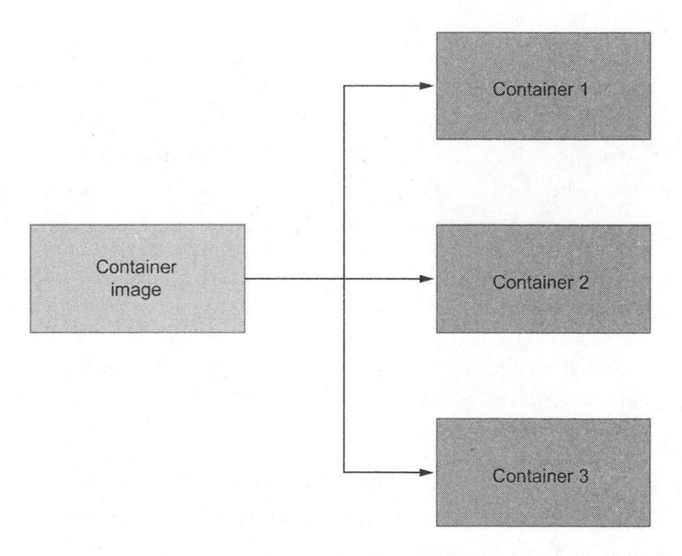

Figure 9.6 A container image can be used to create one or more containers.

The various components to run a container are shown in figure 9.7.

One of the most important reasons to use a container in the first place is due to its promise of reliable execution from one environment to another environment. It is a

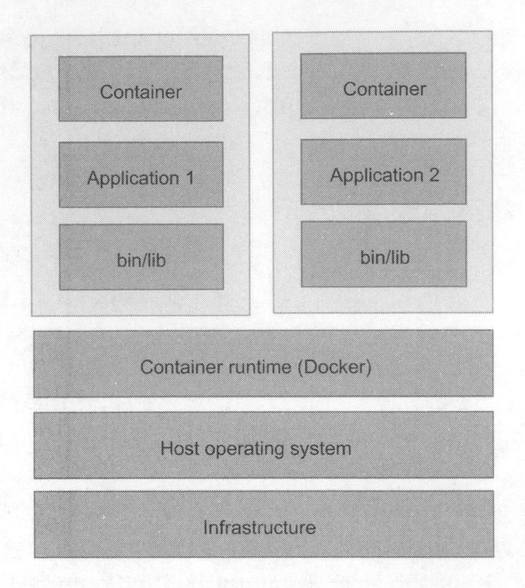

Figure 9.7 Various components to run a container. The infrastructure is at the bottom, and host operating systems run on top of it. A container runtime environment, such as Docker, runs on top of the host operating systems. The containers are run by the container runtime.

relatively common occurrence that in a typical infrastructure, applications may behave differently. For instance, we often found that applications working perfectly in the Dev environment may have some issues while running in UAT. Containers remove this problem, as it is a standalone package that contains everything the application requires to run. Thus, if the same image is used to run the application in Dev or UAT, it is expected to run uniformly.

Docker is the most popular and dominant container technology platform and can be used to deal with container and container images. Docker is so popular that it is almost synonymous with containers and container technology. However, there are other container platforms other than Docker, such as rkt (pronounced *rocket*) from Red Hat and LXD (pronounced *lexdi*). In this section, we'll focus on Docker, discuss creating a Docker image, and running the image as a container.

9.5.1 Technique: Creating a container image and running a Spring Boot application as a container

In this technique, we'll demonstrate how to generate a container image and run a Spring Boot application as a container.

Problem

You are running the Course Tracker application in your Unix server through the WildFly application server. However, you've heard a lot of good things about containers and want to run the application as a container.

Solution

To proceed with the next technique, you need to install and configure Docker. You can refer to Docker documentation available at https://www.docker.com/get-started for a detailed discussion on installing and configuring Docker. You can also refer to

Docker in Practice (http://mng.bz/M2aQ) by Ian Miell and Aidan Hobson Sayers from Manning Publications for an in-depth understanding of Docker.

In this section, we'll explore the following approaches to *Dockerize* the Course Tracker application:

1. Use `Dockerfile` to create the container image and then run the image to create the container.
2. Use Spring Boot built-in containerization (requires Spring Boot version >=2.3). This uses the Paketo buildpacks (https://paketo.io/) to build the image.

In these approaches, we'll use H2 in-memory database with the application to keep the examples simple.

Source code

The final version of the Spring Boot project is available at http://mng.bz/aDrj.

Let's begin with the first approach. We'll use a `Dockerfile` to create the Docker image for the Course Tracker application. Before we define the `Dockerfile`, let's execute the `mvn clean install` command to generate the JAR file of the Course Tracker application.

Let's now define the `Dockerfile` for the Course Tracker application. A `Dockerfile` is a text file that contains all the commands needed to assemble and create the image. You can refer to https://docs.docker.com/engine/reference/builder/ for further details on `Dockerfile`. The following listing shows the sample `Dockerfile` we've created for the Course Tracker application. This file is located under the root directory of the application.

Listing 9.26 Dockerfile to create the Docker image for Course Tracker

```
FROM adoptopenjdk:11-jre-hotspot
ADD target/*.jar application.jar
ENTRYPOINT ["java", "-jar","application.jar"]
EXPOSE 8080
```

In listing 9.26, the `Dockerfile` contains the following:

- `FROM`—We are using `adoptopenjdk:11-jre-hotspot` as the base image for our image. A base image is an image upon which your application Docker image is built.
- `ADD`—We then add the JARs from the target directory as application.jar in the image.
- `ENTRYPOINT`—This is the entry point where you run the image.
- `EXPOSE`—We expose HTTP port 8080 in the container.

We can now build an image for the Course Tracker application.

Next, let's execute the command, as shown in listing 9.27 to create the image. You need to execute the command from the location where the `Dockerfile` is located.

Listing 9.27 Building a Docker image for Course Tracker application

```
docker build --tag course-tracker:v1 .
```

In listing 9.27, note the period (.) at the end of the command. This indicates that the `Dockerfile` is available in the current directory. Besides, we tag the image with the name `course-tracker:v1` to refer to the image, while creating a container from the image. Once you execute the command, it will take a while to build the image. Once the image is successfully built, you can list the image using the command, as shown in the following listing.

Listing 9.28 Listing the Docker image

```
docker image ls
```

You can now run the image, and a Docker container will be created. The following listing shows the command to run the image.

Listing 9.29 Docker run command to run the course-tracker image

```
docker run -p 8080:8080 course-tracker:v1
```

We've used the `docker run` command to run the container image. We've also used a port mapping of local machine HTTP port 8080 to the container's HTTP port 8080. This ensures the HTTP request to the port 8080 in the local machine is forwarded to the container's port 8080.

Once the command runs successfully, you'll notice the console log of the Course Tracker application. Open a browser window, and access the http://localhost:8080 URL, then you'll be redirected to the Course Tracker index page.

Let's now briefly discuss the container image structure we've created in listing 9.26. Your Docker container image consists of multiple layers. If you recall, we started with the base image (adoptopenjdk:11-jre-hotspot). In our `Dockerfile`, we performed additional activities, such as adding the JAR file from the target location to the image. This has created an additional layer on top of the base image. Figure 9.8 shows the notion of layers in a Docker image.

If you are interested to see the various layers of the Docker image, you can use the dive tool (https://github.com/wagoodman/dive) to view the various layers of the created image. To view the layers, install Dive, and execute `dive course-tracker:latest`. Figure 9.9 shows the layers.

In the `Dockerfile`, we've added the fat JAR inside the image. However, we could write a better `Dockerfile` for Spring Boot applications. Instead of adding the complete JAR, we could add the layers from the generated JAR file. Recall from section 9.1 that Spring Boot provides a means to layer the JAR file through the layers.xml file. It

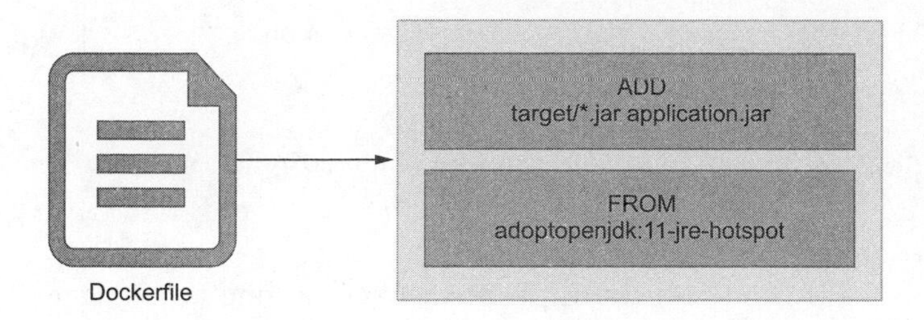

Figure 9.8 Various layers in a container image. These layers are added on top of the base image as per the instructions specified in the Dockerfile. In the example, the adoptopenjdk:11-jre-hotspot is the base image, and the Spring Boot application JAR is added on top of the base image as a new layer.

```
| ● Layers |
Cmp   Size  Command
     73 MB  FROM f532767635e7169
     43 MB  apt-get update     && apt-get install -y --no-install-recommends
    128 MB  set -eux;     ARCH="$(dpkg --print-architecture)";     case "${AR
     47 MB  ADD target/*.jar application.jar # buildkit

| Layer Details |

Tags:    (unavailable)
Id:      61c5b0c6b690ad276c73e83561ac49de3947c6777b0a225be83c168ddb5f2c35
Digest:  sha256:cb3e7ed8f94b3b2c23bbfd3d2b243f43ca8c09aed91cc59622e2ff35e71c03
77
Command:
ADD target/*.jar application.jar # buildkit

| Image Details |


Total Image size: 291 MB
Potential wasted space: 2.0 MB
Image efficiency score: 99 %

Count   Total Space  Path
    2        1.3 MB  /var/cache/debconf/templates.dat
    2        343 kB  /var/log/dpkg.log
    2        216 kB  /var/lib/dpkg/status
    2         37 kB  /var/log/apt/history.log
    2         28 kB  /var/cache/debconf/config.dat
    2         15 kB  /etc/ld.so.cache
    2         12 kB  /var/cache/ldconfig/aux-cache
    2         11 kB  /var/log/apt/eipp.log.xz
    2        2.1 kB  /var/lib/apt/extended_states
    2           0 B  /var/lib/dpkg/triggers/Unincorp
    2           0 B  /var/lib/apt/lists
    2           0 B  /var/lib/dpkg/lock
    2           0 B  /var/lib/dpkg/updates
    2           0 B  /var/cache/debconf/passwords.dat
    2           0 B  /var/lib/dpkg/lock-frontend
```

```
| Current Layer Contents |
Permission     UID:GID       Size  Filetree
-rwxr-xr-x         0:0      47 MB  ├── application.jar
-rwxrwxrwx         0:0        0 B  ├── bin → usr/bin
drwxr-xr-x         0:0        0 B  ├── boot
drwxr-xr-x         0:0        0 B  ├── dev
drwxr-xr-x         0:0     452 kB  ├── etc
-rw-------         0:0        0 B  │   ├── .pwd.lock
-rw-r--r--         0:0     3.0 kB  │   ├── adduser.conf
drwxr-xr-x         0:0      100 B  │   ├── alternatives
-rw-r--r--         0:0      100 B  │   │   ├── README
-rwxrwxrwx         0:0        0 B  │   │   ├── awk → /usr/bin/mawk
-rwxrwxrwx         0:0        0 B  │   │   ├── nawk → /usr/bin/mawk
-rwxrwxrwx         0:0        0 B  │   │   ├── pager → /bin/more
-rwxrwxrwx         0:0        0 B  │   │   ├── rmt → /usr/sbin/rmt-tar
-rwxrwxrwx         0:0        0 B  │   │   └── w → /usr/bin/w.procps
drwxr-xr-x         0:0      12 kB  │   ├── apt
drwxr-xr-x         0:0     2.0 kB  │   │   ├── apt.conf.d
-rw-r--r--         0:0       92 B  │   │   │   ├── 01-vendor-ubuntu
-rw-r--r--         0:0      630 B  │   │   │   ├── 01autoremove
-r--r--r--         0:0      623 B  │   │   │   ├── 01autoremove-kernels
-rw-r--r--         0:0      182 B  │   │   │   ├── 70debconf
-rw-r--r--         0:0       44 B  │   │   │   ├── docker-autoremove-suggests
-rw-r--r--         0:0      318 B  │   │   │   ├── docker-clean
-rw-r--r--         0:0       70 B  │   │   │   ├── docker-gzip-indexes
-rw-r--r--         0:0       27 B  │   │   │   └── docker-no-languages
drwxr-xr-x         0:0        0 B  │   │   ├── auth.conf.d
drwxr-xr-x         0:0        0 B  │   │   ├── preferences.d
-rw-r--r--         0:0     2.7 kB  │   │   ├── sources.list
drwxr-xr-x         0:0        0 B  │   │   ├── sources.list.d
drwxr-xr-x         0:0     7.3 kB  │   │   └── trusted.gpg.d
-rw-r--r--         0:0     2.8 kB  │   │       ├── ubuntu-keyring-2012-archiv
-rw-r--r--         0:0     2.8 kB  │   │       ├── ubuntu-keyring-2012-cdimag
-rw-r--r--         0:0     1.7 kB  │   │       └── ubuntu-keyring-2018-archiv
-rw-r--r--         0:0     2.3 kB  │   ├── bash.bashrc
-rw-r--r--         0:0      367 B  │   ├── bindresvport.blacklist
drwxr-xr-x         0:0        0 B  │   ├── ca-certificates
drwxr-xr-x         0:0        0 B  │   │   └── update.d
-rw-r--r--         0:0     5.7 kB  │   ├── ca-certificates.conf
```

Figure 9.9 Using dive tool to view the layers inside a Docker image. In the top-left corner is the list of layers. The first few layers are from the OpenJDK, and the last layer is formed by adding the jars from the target directory.

also provides the `jarmode` option to view and extract the layers. Let's add the JAR layers in the Docker image instead of adding the complete JAR file. The following listing shows the updated `Dockerfile`.

Listing 9.30 Dockerfile to create a better Docker image

```
FROM adoptopenjdk:11-jre-hotspot as builder
WORKDIR application
ARG JAR_FILE=target/*.jar
COPY ${JAR_FILE} application.jar
RUN java -Djarmode=layertools -jar application.jar extract

FROM adoptopenjdk:11-jre-hotspot
WORKDIR application
COPY --from=builder application/dependencies/ ./
COPY --from=builder application/spring-boot-loader/ ./
```

```
COPY --from=builder application/snapshot-dependencies/ ./
COPY --from=builder application/application/ ./
ENTRYPOINT ["java", "org.springframework.boot.loader.JarLauncher"]
```

Listing 9.30 contains a multi-stage `Dockerfile`. The builder stage (the first part of the Dockerfile) extracts the directories used later. Each of the `COPY` commands relates to the layers extracted by `jarmode`. Finally, we've used the `org.springframework.boot.loader.JarLauncher` as the entry point for the application. You can build the image using the same command shown in listing 9.27. Figure 9.10 shows the image layers.

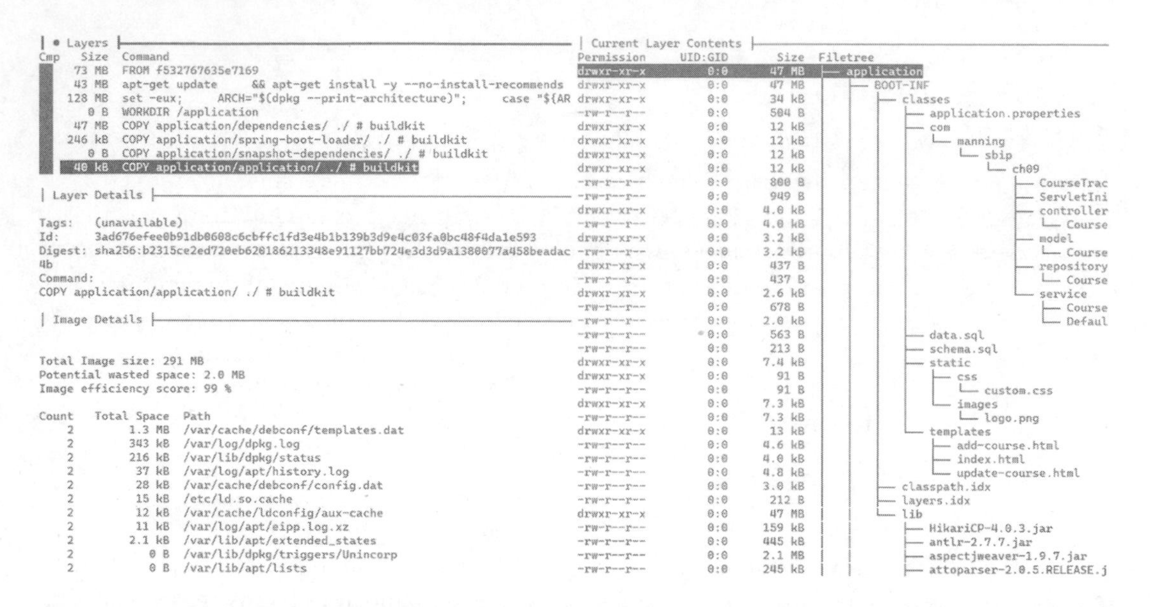

Figure 9.10 Layers of the course-tracker:v2 Docker image. Instead of the fat JAR, the directories are added as layers.

Now that you've seen how to create an image using `Dockerfile`, let's move on to building the Docker image, using Spring Boot's built-in approach. Previously, you noticed the deployment using Heroku or Cloud Foundry. With Heroku, you just provided the source code, and the platform does the rest to build the code, add a runtime, and make the application available for the end users. Similarly, Spring Boot provides support to directly build a Docker image from the source code through Spring Boot Maven (and also Gradle) plugins. Spring Boot uses Cloud Native buildpacks (https:// buildpacks.io/) to achieve this.

Buildpacks are the part of the platform (e.g., Cloud Foundry) that takes the application code and converts it into something that the platform can run. For instance, in the Cloud Foundry example, its Java buildpack noticed that you're pushing a JAR file, and it automatically adds a relevant JRE. The buildpacks allow us to build a Docker-compatible image we can run anywhere. Let's see this in action. You can run the command, as shown in the following listing, to generate the image.

Listing 9.31 Building a Docker image with Spring Boot Maven plugin

```
mvn spring-boot:build-image -Dspring-boot.build-image.imageName=course-
➥ tracker:v3
```

The command in listing 9.31 builds a Docker image with the name `course-tracker:v3`. By default, Spring Boot uses the `artifactId:version` to build the image. We've used the `-Dspring-boot.build-image.imageName=course-tracker:v3` to customize the image name to `course-tracker:v3`. You can run the image in the same manner you've executed the earlier images.

DISCUSSION

In this technique, we've learned how to build a Docker image from a Spring Boot application and run the image as a Docker container. Containers provide excellent portability support, as the container images can be run anywhere reliably. In this section, we've executed the Docker images manually using the `docker run` command. Although this approach works well, it does not scale. Imagine if you need to run hundreds of containers for your applications. It becomes quite tedious to run, update, and manage them. For instance, in a production system, if a container gets terminated for any reason, you need to ensure that you can bring up a new container. It will be excellent if there is a tool that could orchestrate the container management process. Thankfully, Kubernetes is there to address these concerns. Let's discuss Kubernetes in the next section.

9.6 Deploying Spring Boot applications in a Kubernetes cluster

These days there is a trend to use containers to package and deploy applications. Specifically, containers are an excellent choice to package microservices along with their dependencies and configurations. Based on the demand for microservices, you can increase the number of containers. However, as the applications grow into multiple containers and span across multiple servers, it becomes quite difficult to manage them.

Kubernetes provides an open source API to manage how and where to run the containers. It orchestrates a set of virtual machines, known as a Kubernetes cluster, in which it schedules and runs the containers. In Kubernetes, containers are packed inside a pod, which is the fundamental operational unit.

> **NOTE** In this section, we'll use a single-node Kubernetes cluster created in the local machine and focus on how to deploy a Spring Boot application into a Kubernetes cluster. If you are not familiar with Kubernetes, you can refer to Kubernetes documentation at https://kubernetes.io/ for an understanding and installation.

9.6.1 Technique: Deploying a Spring Boot application in a Kubernetes cluster

In this technique, we'll demonstrate how to deploy a Spring Boot application in a Kubernetes cluster.

PROBLEM

You've explored containerization and are fascinated by the way it works. However, you understand that manually managing containers for a large application is a tedious task, as there will be so many containers. You heard that Kubernetes is a container orchestration tool that can orchestrate the containers automatically and want to try it out.

SOLUTION

Using the previous technique, we created a Docker container image for the Spring Boot application. We'll use the same `course-tracker:v3` image in this technique. However, before proceeding with Kubernetes deployment let's tag the image. The following listing shows the command to tag the image.

Listing 9.32 Docker tag command to tag the image

```
docker tag course-tracker:v3 musibs/course-tracker
```

In listing 9.32, we used the `docker tag` command to tag the image. The first part of the Docker tag (`course-tracker:v3`) command specifies the existing image, and the later part (`musibs/course-tracker`) is the tagged image with the format `repository/image`. We haven't specified any version here, and the Docker takes the version as the default value `latest`.

> **Source code**
>
> The final version of the Spring Boot project is available at http://mng.bz/xvpW.

Once you are done with the tagging, you may push the image to the Docker registry. The Docker registry is a storage and distribution system for Docker images. You can pull images to your local machine from the Docker registry or push images from your local machine to it.

In this example, we'll use the Docker Hub (https://hub.docker.com/) as the Docker registry to store the image. Kubernetes pulls the Docker image from the Docker registry into the `kubelet` (the node where the image is run in a Kubernetes pod), which are not usually connected to the Docker daemon. In this example, though, as we are using the Kubernetes cluster in the local machine, you can skip this step. For completeness, be aware that you can use the `docker push` command (e.g., `docker push musibs/course-tracker`) to push the image to the Docker hub.

Now that we are ready with the docker image of the application, we are ready to run the application in Kubernetes. We need the following two things:

1. The Kubernetes CLI (kubectl)
2. A Kubernetes cluster to deploy the application

To interact with Kubernetes, you use the `kubectl` command to run commands against the Kubernetes cluster. Refer to https://kubernetes.io/docs/tasks/tools/ to install kubectl. For a Kubernetes cluster, we'll use Kind (https://kind.sigs.k8s.io/) to create a local Kubernetes cluster. Once Kind is installed, run the following command, as shown in the following listing, to create a Kubernetes cluster.

Listing 9.33 Create a local Kubernetes cluster with Kind

```
kind create cluster

Creating cluster "kind" ...
 ✓ Ensuring node image (kindest/node:v1.20.2) 🖼
 ✓ Preparing nodes 📦
 ✓ Writing configuration 📜
 ✓ Starting control-plane 🕹️
 ✓ Installing CNI 🔌
 ✓ Installing StorageClass 💾
Set kubectl context to "kind-kind"
You can now use your cluster with:

kubectl cluster-info --context kind-kind

Thanks for using kind! 😊
```

Once the cluster is successfully created, Kind automatically configures the Kubernetes CLI to point to the newly created cluster. To see that everything is set up as expected, execute the command, as shown in the following listing.

Listing 9.34 Kubernetes cluster information

```
kubectl cluster-info

Kubernetes control plane is running at https://127.0.0.1:49672
KubeDNS is running at https://127.0.0.1:49672/api/v1/namespaces/kube-
➥ system/services/kube-dns:dns/proxy

To further debug and diagnose cluster problems, use 'kubectl cluster-info
➥ dump'.
```

To deploy an application to Kubernetes, we specify the configurations in a YAML configuration file. However, instead of defining the configurations manually, let's use the kubectl command to generate them for us. Create a new directory called k8s anywhere in your machine and run the command, as shown in the following listing from the k8s directory.

Listing 9.35 Generate the deployment YAML file

```
kubectl create deployment course-tracker --image musibs/course-tracker -
➥ dry-run=client -o=YAML > deployment.yaml
```

The command in listing 9.35 creates the deployment.yaml configuration file in the k8s directory. The --dry-run=client option allows us to preview the deployment object that the kubectl create deployment command creates. The -o option specifies that the command output is to be written in YAML format. Listing 9.36 shows the contents of the generated file.

Listing 9.36 The generated deployment.yaml file

```
apiVersion: apps/v1
kind: Deployment
metadata:
  creationTimestamp: null
  labels:
    app: course-tracker
  name: course-tracker
spec:
  replicas: 1
  selector:
    matchLabels:
      app: course-tracker
  strategy: {}
  template:
    metadata:
      creationTimestamp: null
      labels:
        app: course-tracker
    spec:
      containers:
      - image: musibs/course-tracker
        name: course-tracker
        resources: {}
status: {}
```

The deployment.yaml file contains the specifications, such as the image to be used, how many containers to run, and more. Refer to the Kubernetes documentation for a detailed discussion on the purpose of various tags.

The deployment.yaml file specifies to Kubernetes how to deploy and manage the application, but it does not allow the application to be a network service to other applications. To do that, we need a Kubernetes `Service` resource. Execute the command, as shown in the following listing, in the k8s directory to generate the YAML for the service resource.

Listing 9.37 The Kubectl command to create a service

```
kubectl create service clusterip course-tracker-service --tcp 80:8080 -o
➥ yaml --dry-run=client > service.yaml
```

Listing 9.38 shows the generated YAML configuration for the service.

Listing 9.38 The generated service.yaml file

```
apiVersion: v1
kind: Service
metadata:
```

```
  creationTimestamp: null
  labels:
    app: course-tracker-service
  name: course-tracker-service
spec:
  ports:
  - name: 80-8080
    port: 80
    protocol: TCP
    targetPort: 8080
  selector:
    app: course-tracker-service
  type: ClusterIP
status:
  loadBalancer: {}
```

Let's now apply the YAML files (from the k8s directory) to Kubernetes, as shown in the following listing.

Listing 9.39 Apply the configuration in a Kubernetes cluster through kubectl

```
kubectl apply -f .
```

The command in listing 9.39 creates a new deployment and service. Execute the command in listing 9.40 to get a status of the created `Deployment` and `Service`.

Listing 9.40 Get the status of all Kubernetes components

```
kubectl get all
```

You'll notice an output similar to listing 9.41.

Listing 9.41 Status of all Kubernetes components

```
NAME                                READY   STATUS    RESTARTS   AGE
pod/course-tracker-84f4d94d5d-gbw99 1/1     Running   0          25m

NAME                             TYPE        CLUSTER-IP     EXTERNAL-IP   PORT(S)   AGE
service/course-tracker-service   ClusterIP   10.96.54.100   <none>        80/TCP    25m
service/kubernetes               ClusterIP   10.96.0.1      <none>        443/TCP   3h36m

NAME                             READY   UP-TO-DATE   AVAILABLE   AGE
deployment.apps/course-tracker   1/1     1            1           25m

NAME                                       DESIRED   CURRENT   READY   AGE
replicaset.apps/course-tracker-84f4d94d5d  1         1         1       25m
```

The last change we need to perform is to use port forward, so we can make an HTTP request to the application. This is needed, as the service we've defined is accessible in the Kubernetes cluster network and not accessible outside. Let's execute the following `port-forward` command, as shown in listing 9.42. Note that this command runs foreground, and the command does not return. Thus, you can open a new terminal window and execute the command.

Listing 9.42 Port forwarding to enable HTTP requests to the application

```
kubectl port-forward pod/course-tracker-84f4d94d5d-gbw99 8080:8080
```

In your case, the pod name could be different. You can find the pod name (highlighted in bold) in listing 9.41 Once the command runs successfully, you'll see the following output, as shown in listing 9.43.

Listing 9.43 Successful port forward output

```
Forwarding from 127.0.0.1:8080 -> 8080
Forwarding from [::1]:8080 -> 8080
```

That's all. You can now open a browser window and access the http://localhost:8080 URL. You'll notice that you are redirected to the application index page.

DISCUSSION

Using this technique, we've explored how to run a container image in a Kubernetes cluster. We created a local Kubernetes cluster with the use of Kind. We then defined a deployment and service using the `kubectl` command. After that, we applied the configurations, so the resources could be created by Kubernetes. Lastly, we applied port forwarding to the Kubernetes pod, so the application would be accessible outside of the Kubernetes cluster.

9.7 Deploying Spring Boot applications in Red Hat OpenShift

Red Hat OpenShift is an enterprise Kubernetes platform with support for several cloud providers. Previously, you've explored how to deploy a Docker container in a local Kubernetes cluster. Red Hat OpenShift provides the managed Kubernetes platform, on which you can deploy your application. You can find more details about various Red Hat OpenShift offerings at https://cloud.redhat.com/learn/what-is-openshift. In this section, we'll demonstrate how to deploy a Spring Boot application in the Red Hat OpenShift platform via the Red Hat OpenShift developer console.

9.7.1 Technique: Deploying a Spring Boot application in the Red Hat OpenShift platform

In this technique, we'll discuss how to deploy a Spring Boot application in the Red Hat OpenShift platform.

PROBLEM

OpenShift provides a self-service platform to create, modify, and deploy applications and provides faster development and release cycles. You need to deploy the Course Tracker application into the Red Hat OpenShift platform.

SOLUTION

In this technique, you'll learn how to deploy a Spring Boot application in the Red Hat OpenShift platform. There are several ways a Spring Boot application can be deployed in OpenShift, including `Dockerfile`, container image, Git, and others. In this section, we'll demonstrate how to deploy an application through GitHub.

> **Source code**
> The final version of the Spring Boot project is available at http://mng.bz/g42e.

To begin with, you need to create a Red Hat account to access the OpenShift platform. You can visit http://mng.bz/enZ9 for a developer sandbox account. If you don't have an existing Red Hat account, create a new one with the required details. If you already have an account, then log in with your credentials. Once successfully logged in, you can access the OpenShift Developer sandbox account. You'll find a page similar to that in figure 9.11.

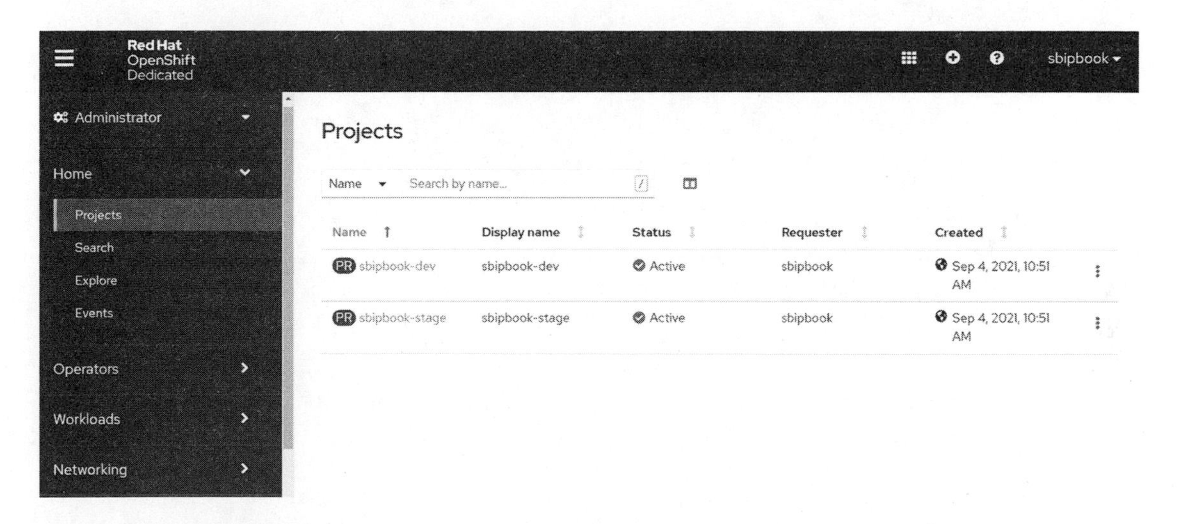

Figure 9.11 Red Hat Developer sandbox home page with administrator views. By default, Red Hat creates two projects, dev and stage, for us.

In the top left corner, switch to the Developer View from Administrator View, and you'll find a screen similar to that in figure 9.12.

Using this technique, we'll show you how to deploy a Spring Boot application using the From Git option. We've already created a GitHub repository for the Course Tracker application, and we'll use the same. You can access this repository at http://mng.bz/p275. Click on the From Git option in the Developer Sandbox page, and you'll be redirected to the next page, as shown in figure 9.13.

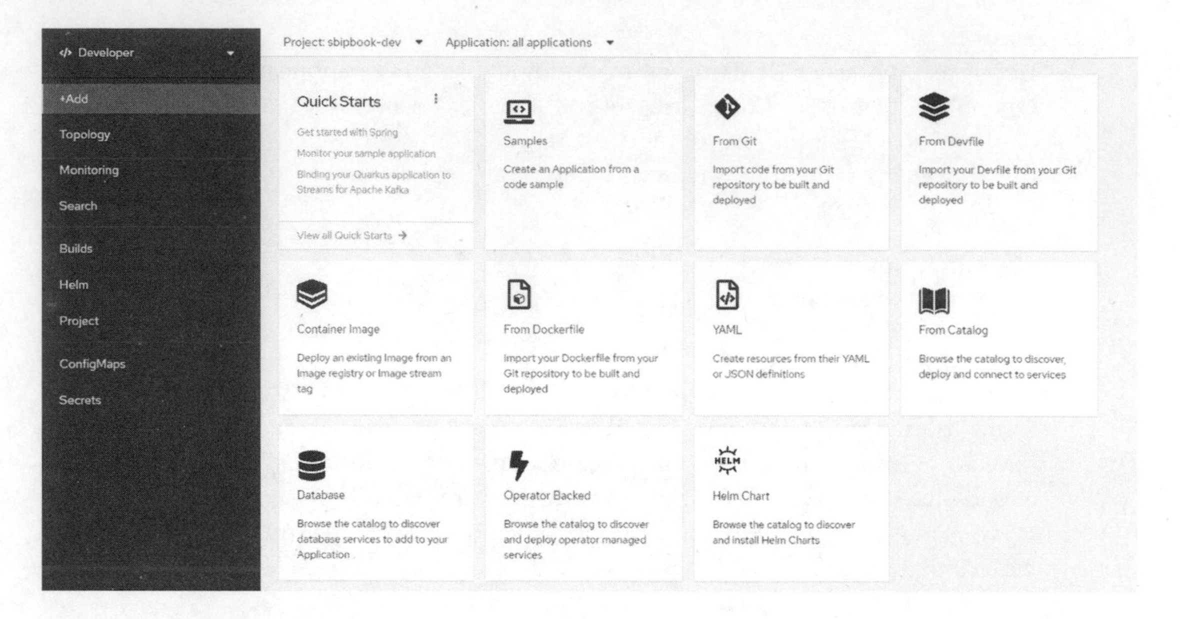

Figure 9.12 Red Hat sandbox Developer View. From this screen, you can select your application configuration for deployment. For instance, you can select the From Git option and provide your Git repository path.

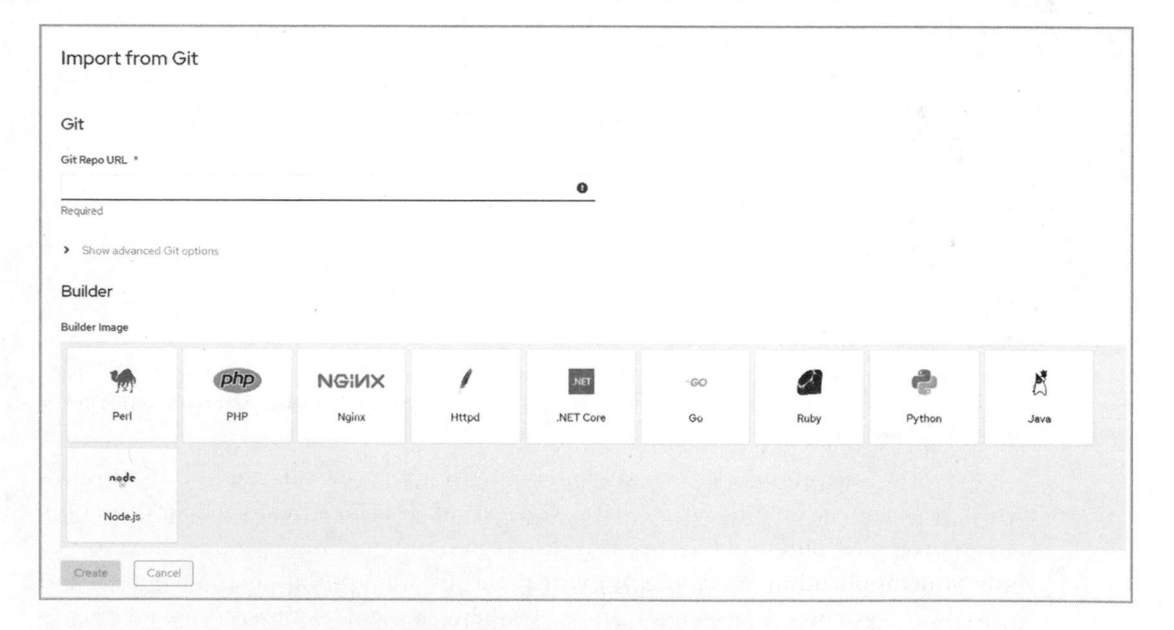

Figure 9.13 The Import from Git page to create a deployment from Git

Provide the GitHub repository URL for the Course Tracker application, and click Create. After successful deployment, you'll find a page similar to that in figure 9.14.

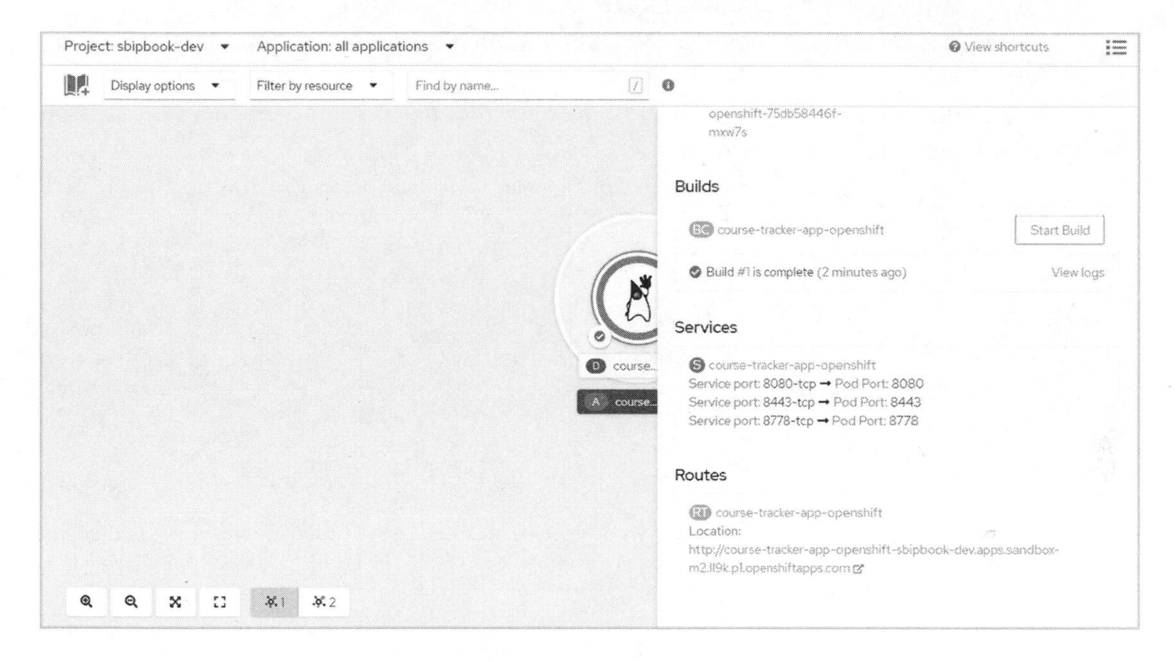

Figure 9.14 Course Tracker application deployed successfully

You can find the application URL in the bottom right corner in the Routes section. Click on the link, and you'll be redirected to the index page of the Course Tracker application.

DISCUSSION

With this technique, you've explored how to deploy a Spring Boot application in the Red Hat OpenShift platform. OpenShift supports a variety of approaches for deploying an application. For instance, in this example, you've provided the application source code from the GitHub repository, and OpenShift does the heavy lifting for us. It has taken the source code, built it, deployed it into a Kubernetes Pod, and made the application available to the external world.

OpenShift provides many features and configurations you can use in your application. For instance, in your application, you can add various health checks, such as startup probe, readiness probe, liveness probe, and others. These probes allow you to verify your application status. For instance, the liveness probe checks whether the application container is running. Failure of the liveness probe means the container is killed. To learn more about OpenShift, you can play around with the OpenShift Developer sandbox available at https://developers.redhat.com/developer-sandbox.

Summary

- We discussed deploying a Spring Boot application as an executable JAR file, and deployed it as a WAR file in the WildFly application server.
- We introduced deploying Spring Boot applications to Cloud Foundry and Heroku.
- We covered running Spring Boot applications as Docker containers and deploying them into Kubernetes clusters.
- We introduced deploying a Spring Boot application as a container in the Red Hat OpenShift platform.

Part 5

Part 5 of the book contains one chapter, which discusses Spring Boot with Kotlin, Native Image, and GraphQL. Chapter 10 starts with using Kotlin and Kotlin DSLs in the Spring Boot application. It then demonstrates how to use Spring Native in the Spring Boot application and generate a GraalVM native image. Finally, this chapter shows how to use GraphQL as an alternative to REST-style API development in a Spring Boot application.

10 Spring Boot with Kotlin, Native Image, and GraphQL

This chapter covers

- Using Spring Boot with Kotlin and Kotlin DSLs
- Using Spring Boot Native Image with GraalVM
- Using Spring Boot with GraphQL

In the previous chapter, you explored how to deploy Spring Boot applications on various platforms. In this final chapter of this book, we'll discuss Spring Boot with Kotlin, GraalVM Native Image, and GraphQL.

Spring Framework 5.0 provided extensive support for Kotlin programming language, and the nature of the support is such that you can develop Spring Boot applications with Kotlin without even writing a single line of Java code. Besides, Spring Boot provides several domain-specific languages (DSLs) to further simplify the code syntax.

GraalVM Native Image and GraphQL are two major technologies for which Spring Boot extends its support. Currently, these technologies have experimental support in Spring Boot, and features are under development. GraalVM Native Image turns the Spring Boot applications into an architecture-specific native executable, which has a faster start-up time and has a smaller memory footprint. GraphQL offers an alternative approach to REST APIs to develop efficient APIs. Let's see these in practice with Spring Boot.

Note

In this chapter, we will explore the use of Kotlin, GraalVM, and GraphQL along with Spring Boot. Note that all these topics are quite large, and there could be dedicated books on each of these subjects. Thus, in this book, we'll not deep dive into any of these technologies and just focus on introducing you to these technologies in the context of Spring Boot. Once you understand the basics, we recommend you read more of these subjects and explore more on your own or refer to dedicated texts on the topics. Following are a few useful documentation references:

- *Kotlin*—https://kotlinlang.org/docs/home.html
- *GraalVM*—https://www.graalvm.org/docs/introduction/
- *Spring Native*—http://mng.bz/Dx6n
- *GraphQL*—https://graphql.org/learn/
- *Spring GraphQL*—http://mng.bz/la76

10.1 Spring Boot with Kotlin

From its inception, Spring has been a Java-based framework and developers primarily use Java to develop Spring applications. Spring Framework 5.0 included dedicated support for the Kotlin programming language (http://mng.bz/Bxp0). With this, you can develop Spring applications with Kotlin without using Java. In this section, we'll introduce you to using Kotlin to develop Spring Boot applications.

Spring provides several Kotlin DSLs that makes code clean and concise. We'll explore some of the Kotlin DSLs in this section. However, before continuing with the Kotlin DSLs, let's explore how to develop a Spring Boot application with Kotlin. We'll rewrite the Course Tracker application with Kotlin.

Note

Kotlin is a full-fledged programming language with many excellent features, and it is beyond the scope of this text to provide in-depth coverage. In this chapter, we intend to show you how you can use Kotlin with Spring Boot and Spring Boot Kotlin DSLs. To keep the focus on Spring Boot, we won't dive into Kotlin and its features here. Thus, if you are not familiar with Kotlin, we recommend that you refer to Kotlin documentation.

For a better understanding of Kotlin, you can refer to the documentation available at https://kotlinlang.org/docs/home.html. Kotlin also provides a playground available at https://play.kotlinlang.org/, where you can try out various Kotlin features. The https://play.kotlinlang.org/byExample/overview provides a good starting point if you are completely new to Kotlin. You can also refer to Manning's *Functional Programming in Kotlin* by Marco Vermeulen, Rúnar Bjarnason, and Paul Chiusano (http://mng.bz/VlAP) to learn Kotlin.

10.1.1 Technique: Developing a Spring Boot application with Kotlin

In this technique, we'll demonstrate how to develop Spring Boot application with Kotlin.

PROBLEM

You have developed Spring Boot applications with Java. You recently learned Kotlin and were impressed with its conciseness, null safety, extensions, and many other powerful features. As Spring provides dedicated support for Kotlin, you can develop Spring Boot applications with Kotlin.

SOLUTION

In this section, we'll rewrite the Course Tracker Spring Boot application with Kotlin. We are using the same application, as we are already familiar with it, and we can keep ourselves focused on Kotlin-specific changes.

> **Source code**
>
> The final version of the Spring Boot project is available at http://mng.bz/Axez.

To start with, let's create a new Spring Boot application through Spring Initializr (https://start.spring.io/) with the language as Kotlin. Select Web, validation, JPA, h2, and Thymeleaf dependencies. You can refer to appendix A of this book for more information about using Spring Initializr. We'll also need the Web JAR dependencies for the UI. The following listing shows the final pom.xml file.

Listing 10.1 Maven pom.xml file

```
<?xml version="1.0" encoding="UTF-8"?>
<project xmlns="http://maven.apache.org/POM/4.0.0"
➥ xmlns:xsi="http://www.w3.org/2001/XMLSchema-instance"
➥ xsi:schemaLocation="http://maven.apache.org/POM/4.0.0
➥ https://maven.apache.org/xsd/maven-4.0.0.xsd">
    <modelVersion>4.0.0</modelVersion>
    <parent>
        <groupId>org.springframework.boot</groupId>
        <artifactId>spring-boot-starter-parent</artifactId>
        <version>2.6.3</version>
        <relativePath/> <!-- lookup parent from repository -->
    </parent>
    <groupId>com.manning.sbip.ch10</groupId>
    <artifactId>course-tracker-kotlin-app</artifactId>
    <version>0.0.1-SNAPSHOT</version>
    <name>course-tracker-kotlin-app</name>
    <description>Course Tracker Kotlin Application</description>
    <properties>
        <java.version>17</java.version>
        <kotlin.version>1.6.10</kotlin.version>
    </properties>
    <dependencies>
        <dependency>
```

```
            <groupId>org.springframework.boot</groupId>
            <artifactId>spring-boot-starter-thymeleaf</artifactId>
        </dependency>
        <dependency>
            <groupId>org.springframework.boot</groupId>
            <artifactId>spring-boot-starter-data-jpa</artifactId>
        </dependency>
        <dependency>
            <groupId>org.springframework.boot</groupId>
            <artifactId>spring-boot-starter-validation</artifactId>
        </dependency>
        <dependency>
            <groupId>org.springframework.boot</groupId>
            <artifactId>spring-boot-starter-web</artifactId>
        </dependency>
        <dependency>
            <groupId>com.fasterxml.jackson.module</groupId>
            <artifactId>jackson-module-kotlin</artifactId>
        </dependency>
        <dependency>
            <groupId>org.jetbrains.kotlin</groupId>
            <artifactId>kotlin-reflect</artifactId>
        </dependency>
        <dependency>
            <groupId>org.jetbrains.kotlin</groupId>
            <artifactId>kotlin-stdlib-jdk8</artifactId>
        </dependency>
        <dependency>
            <groupId>org.webjars</groupId>
            <artifactId>bootstrap</artifactId>
            <version>4.4.1</version>
        </dependency>
        <dependency>
            <groupId>org.webjars</groupId>
            <artifactId>jquery</artifactId>
            <version>3.4.1</version>
        </dependency>
        <dependency>
            <groupId>org.webjars</groupId>
            <artifactId>webjars-locator</artifactId>
            <version>0.38</version>
        </dependency>

        <dependency>
            <groupId>com.h2database</groupId>
            <artifactId>h2</artifactId>
            <scope>runtime</scope>
        </dependency>
        <dependency>
            <groupId>org.springframework.boot</groupId>
            <artifactId>spring-boot-starter-test</artifactId>
            <scope>test</scope>
        </dependency>
    </dependencies>
```

```
    <build>
        <sourceDirectory>${project.basedir}/src/main/kotlin</sourceDirectory>

<testSourceDirectory>${project.basedir}/src/test/kotlin</testSourceDirectory>
        <plugins>
            <plugin>
                <groupId>org.springframework.boot</groupId>
                <artifactId>spring-boot-maven-plugin</artifactId>
            </plugin>
            <plugin>
                <groupId>org.jetbrains.kotlin</groupId>
                <artifactId>kotlin-maven-plugin</artifactId>
                <configuration>
                    <args>
                        <arg>-Xjsr305=strict</arg>
                    </args>
                    <compilerPlugins>
                        <plugin>spring</plugin>
                    </compilerPlugins>
                </configuration>
                <dependencies>
                    <dependency>
                        <groupId>org.jetbrains.kotlin</groupId>
                        <artifactId>kotlin-maven-allopen</artifactId>
                        <version>${kotlin.version}</version>
                    </dependency>
                </dependencies>
            </plugin>
        </plugins>
    </build>

</project>
```

In listing 10.1, you may notice additional dependencies and plugins are configured, as we've selected the language type as Kotlin. Let's discuss each of these dependencies and plugins:

- `jackson-module-kotlin`—This dependency provides support serialization and deserialization for Kotlin classes and data classes (https://kotlinlang.org/docs/data-classes.html). As we have included the `spring-boot-starter-web` dependency in the application, this is included automatically. You can find more details about this dependency at https://github.com/FasterXML/jackson-module-kotlin.
- `kotlin-reflect`—This is the Kotlin reflection library. Like Java, Kotlin also provides support for reflection to allow introspecting the Kotlin program at runtime. To avoid unnecessary bloating of the runtime libraries, Kotlin distributes the reflection features separately with the `kotlin-reflect` dependency. You can find more details on this at https://kotlinlang.org/docs/reflection.html.
- `kotlin-stdlib-jdk8`—Kotlin provides its standard library through the `kotlin-stdlib` dependency. The `kotlin-stdlib-jdk8` is the Java 8 extension of the

kotlin-stdlib dependency. You can find more details about kotlin-stdlib at https://kotlinlang.org/api/latest/jvm/stdlib/.

- kotlin-maven-plugin—This plugin compiles Kotlin sources and modules. The -Xjsr305=strict enables strict support for JSR 305, which deals with null safety (https://kotlinlang.org/docs/null-safety.html) in the application.

Next, let's create the Course class, as shown in the following listing.

Listing 10.2 The Course JPA entity

```
package com.manning.sbip.ch10.model

import javax.persistence.*;
import javax.validation.constraints.*;

@Entity
@Table(name = "Courses")
class Course(

    @Id
    @GeneratedValue(strategy = GenerationType.IDENTITY)
    @Column(name = "ID")
    var id: Long? = 0,

    @Column(name = "NAME")
    @NotEmpty(message = "Course name field can't be empty")
    var name: String? = "",

    @Column(name = "CATEGORY")
    @NotEmpty(message = "Course category field can't be empty")
    var category: String? = "",

    @Column(name = "RATING")
    @Min(value = 1)
    @Max(value = 5)
    var rating : Int? = 0,

    @Column(name = "DESCRIPTION")
    @NotEmpty(message = "Course description field can't be empty")
    var description: String? = ""
)
```

- import javax.persistence.*: We are using the @Entity, @Table, @Id, @GeneratedValue, and @GeneratedType from this package.
- import javax.validation.constraints.*: We are using the @NotEmpty, @Min, and @Max annotations from this package.
- var id / var rating: We declare a variable with the var keyword in Kotlin. Also, the type of the variable is declared after the variable declaration. The ? along with the type indicates that the variable can contain a null value. By default, variables in Kotlin can't have null values.

Next, let's define the data access layer. We'll define the CourseRepository interface, as shown in the following listing.

Listing 10.3 The CourseRepository interface

```
package com.manning.sbip.ch10.repository

import com.manning.sbip.ch10.model.Course
import org.springframework.data.repository.CrudRepository
import org.springframework.stereotype.Repository
```

```
@Repository
interface CourseRepository : CrudRepository<Course, Long>
```

Next, let's define the service layer. First, we'll create an interface with a list of operations available in the service layer. The following listing shows the `CourseService` interface.

Listing 10.4 The CourseService interface

```
package com.manning.sbip.ch10.service

import com.manning.sbip.ch10.model.Course

interface CourseService {
    fun createCourse(course: Course): Course        <-- In Kotlin, we declare a function with the fun keyword.
    fun findCourseById(courseId: Long): Course
    fun findAllCourses(): Iterable<Course>
    fun updateCourse(courseId: Long, updatedCourse: Course): Course
    fun deleteCourseById(courseId: Long)
}
```

Next, let's provide an implementation of this interface. The following listing shows the `DefaultCourseService` class.

Listing 10.5 The DefaultCourseService class

```
package com.manning.sbip.ch10.service

import com.manning.sbip.ch10.exception.CourseNotFoundException
import com.manning.sbip.ch10.model.Course
import com.manning.sbip.ch10.repository.CourseRepository
import org.springframework.http.HttpStatus
import org.springframework.stereotype.Service

@Service
class DefaultCourseService (private val courseRepository: CourseRepository)
➥ : CourseService {

    override fun createCourse(course: Course): Course =
➥ courseRepository.save(course)

    override fun findCourseById(courseId: Long): Course =
➥ courseRepository.findById(courseId)
            .orElseThrow {
➥ CourseNotFoundException(HttpStatus.NOT_FOUND, "No course with supplied
➥ course id was found") }

    override fun findAllCourses(): Iterable<Course> =
➥ courseRepository.findAll()

    override fun updateCourse(courseId: Long, updatedCourse: Course):
➥ Course  {
        return if(courseRepository.existsById(courseId)) {
            courseRepository.save(
```

```
                    Course(
                            id = updatedCourse.id,
                            name = updatedCourse.name,
                            category = updatedCourse.category,
                            rating = updatedCourse.rating,
                            description = updatedCourse.description
                    )
            )
        }
        else throw CourseNotFoundException(HttpStatus.NOT_FOUND, "No course
➥ with supplied course id was found")
    }

    override fun deleteCourseById(courseId: Long) {
        return if (courseRepository.existsById(courseId)) {
            courseRepository.deleteById(courseId)
        }
       else throw CourseNotFoundException(HttpStatus.NOT_FOUND, "No course
➥ with supplied course id was found")
    }
}
```

Next, let's define the custom `CourseNotFoundException` class. We are throwing this exception if there is an attempt to delete or update a course that does not exist. The following listing shows this class.

Listing 10.6 The CourseNotFoundException class

```
package com.manning.sbip.ch10.exception

import org.springframework.http.HttpStatus

class CourseNotFoundException(status: HttpStatus, message: String) :
➥ RuntimeException()
```

You can find the Course Tracker HTML and CSS files in the project source code available on GitHub. These are the same files we've used previously in the application. Let's start the application using the `mvn spring-boot:run` command. You can access http://localhost:8080 from your browser to find the index page of the application.

DISCUSSION

In this section, you've explored the use of Kotlin in a Spring Boot application. We've shown you the previously developed Java-based Couse Tracker application with Kotlin. As you may have already noticed, there are not many differences in terms of the application design from the Java version. Thus, using Kotlin programming language in a Spring Boot application is a matter of preference of the user. The main benefit of using Kotlin over Java is that Kotlin provides several built-in features, such as null-safety, when expressions, and others, and its concise way of coding. There are several Kotlin DSLs that make the code less verbose and clean as you'll see in the upcoming technique. In the next technique, we'll discuss some of these DSLs.

10.1.2 Technique: Securing a Spring Boot Kotlin application with Spring Security

In this technique, we will discuss how to secure a Spring Boot Kotlin application using Spring Security.

PROBLEM

With the previous technique, you developed a Spring Boot application with Kotlin. You need to secure the application with Spring Security.

SOLUTION

The Spring Boot Kotlin application developed in the previous technique works well but has one issue: there is no security mechanism in place. Let's enable form-based login to secure the application access. Form-based login allows the user to log in to the application with a login form.

> **Source code**
> The final version of the Spring Boot project is available at http://mng.bz/Zz1P.

To continue with this technique, you can continue with the Spring Boot Kotlin application used in the previous technique. As we want to enable security through Spring Security, we need to introduce the `spring-boot-starter-security` in the pom.xml file. Include the following dependency in your Spring Boot application pom.xml, as shown in the following listing.

Listing 10.7 The Spring Boot starter dependency

```
<dependency>
    <groupId>org.springframework.boot</groupId>
    <artifactId>spring-boot-starter-security</artifactId>
</dependency>
```

Next, we'll enable the Spring Security configuration in the application. Listing 10.8 shows the `KotlinSecurityConfiguration` class that contains the necessary security configurations to enable form-based security in the Course Tracker application.

Listing 10.8 The KotlinSecurityConfiguration class

```
package com.manning.sbip.ch10.security

//imports

@EnableWebSecurity
class KotlinSecurityConfiguration : WebSecurityConfigurerAdapter(),
➥ ApplicationContextInitializer<GenericApplicationContext> {
```

The KotlinSecurityConfiguration class extends WebSecurityConfigurerAdapter and implements the ApplicationContextInitializer interface.

```
    val beans = beans {
        bean("passwordEncoder") {
            BCryptPasswordEncoder()
        }
        bean {
            fun user(user : String, password: String, vararg  roles :
➥ String) = User
                    .builder()
                    .username(user)
                    .password(ref<PasswordEncoder>().encode(password))
                    .roles(*roles)
                    .build()

      InMemoryUserDetailsManager(user("user", "password", "USER"),
➥ user("admin", "password", "ADMIN"))
        }
    }

override fun initialize(applicationContext: GenericApplicationContext){
        beans.initialize(applicationContext)
    }

    override fun configure(http: HttpSecurity?) {
        http {
            formLogin {
                loginPage = "/login"
                failureUrl = "/login-error"
            }
            authorizeRequests {
                authorize("/login", permitAll)
                authorize("/login-error", permitAll)
                authorize(anyRequest, authenticated)
            }
        }
    }

}
```

Defining the passwordEncoder, InMemoryUserDetailsManager beans, using the Spring Boot Kotlin Beans DSL. Note the concise nature of the code due to the use of beans DSL.

Overidden method of ApplicationContextInitializer. This is needed to initialize the beans defined previously.

Overidden method of WebSecurityConfigurerAdapter class. We are using the Spring Security Kotlin Beans DSL. Again, note the use of the DSL and how concisely the code is written.

If you've gone through the technique in section 5.3.2 in chapter 5, then the code snippet in listing 10.8 should look familiar to you. Nonetheless, it's the same Spring Security configuration that enables form-based, in-memory authentication in the Course Tracker application. However, the code in listing 10.8 is in Kotlin, and more precisely, we are using Kotlin's Spring Beans and Spring Security DSLs. The DSL provides syntactic sugar on top of existing APIs that make the code more expressive, concise, and readable.

In listing 10.8, we've defined `passwordEncoder` and the `InMemoryUserDetails-Manager` beans through the Beans DSL. The `passwordEncoder` bean definition is straightforward. We've created the `BCryptPasswordEncoder` bean. If you recall, a password encoder encodes a plain-text password to a scrambled text for security purposes. Next, we are defining the `InMemoryUserDetailsManager` bean, as shown in the following listing.

Listing 10.9 The InMemoryUserDetailsManager bean definition

```
bean {
            fun user(user : String, password: String, vararg  roles :
➥ String) =
➥ User.builder().username(user).password(ref<PasswordEncoder>().encode(pa
➥ ssword)).roles(*roles).build()
            InMemoryUserDetailsManager(user("user", "password", "USER"),
➥ user("admin", "password", "ADMIN"))
        }
```

To define the `InMemoryUserDetailsManager` bean, we've first created a function called user that allows us to define Spring Security `User` instances. Pay attention to how we are referencing the other `passwordEncoder` bean to encode the password. We've created two users, `user` and `admin`, in the `InMemoryUserDetailsManager` bean.

In the `KotlinSecurityConfiguration` class, we are extending the `WebSecurity-ConfigurerAdapter` class, so we can customize the `HttpSecurity` configuration. We've overridden the `configure()` method to configure the form-based login, as shown in the following listing.

Listing 10.10 Customizing HttpSecurity configuration

```
override fun configure(http: HttpSecurity?) {
    http {
        formLogin {
            loginPage = "/login"
            failureUrl = "/login-error"
        }
        authorizeRequests {
            authorize("/login", permitAll)
            authorize("/login-error", permitAll)
            authorize(anyRequest, authenticated)
        }
    }
}
```

In listing 10.10, we used the Spring Security Kotlin DSL to define the HTTP security configuration. We enabled form-based login with login URL as `/login` and failed login URL as `/login-error`. Also, we are allowing access to `/login` and `/login-error` endpoints to all users. Any other endpoints (`anyrequest`) requires users to be authenticated. Next, we'll configure the following property in the application.properties, as shown in the following listing.

Listing 10.11 The context.initializer.classes property

```
context.initializer.classes=com.manning.sbip.ch10.security.KotlinSecurityCo
➥ nfiguration
```

In listing 10.11, we are configuring the `context.initializer.classes` property for the `KotlinSecurityConfiguration` class, so the beans defined in the class are initialized. Next, let's define the `LoginController` class that defines the `/login` and `/login-error` endpoints. This Spring controller class is shown in the following listing.

Listing 10.12 The LoginController class

```
package com.manning.sbip.ch10.controller

import org.springframework.stereotype.Controller
import org.springframework.ui.Model
import org.springframework.ui.set
import org.springframework.web.bind.annotation.GetMapping

@Controller
class LoginController {

    @GetMapping("/login")
    fun login(): String {
        return "login"
    }

    @GetMapping("/login-error")
    fun loginError(model: Model): String {
        model["loginError"] = true
        return "login"
    }
}
```

The `/login` endpoint returns the user to `login.html` page. The `/login-error` endpoint redirects the user to the login page with the `loginError` flag set to `true`. This flag is used in the `login.html` page to display that the user login has failed.

Let's now start the application and access the http://localhost:8080 URL from the browser. You'll notice you are redirected to the application login page. Use any of the configured `username` and `password` to log in to the application. For instance, you can use the username as `user` and password as `password` to log in. For a successful login, you'll be redirected to the application index page.

DISCUSSION

In this technique, we have shown you how to secure a Spring Boot Kotlin application with Spring Security DSLs. We've also demonstrated how to use the Spring Beans Kotlin Beans DSL to define the bean definitions. These DSLs provide a very neat and clean approach to writing the code. There is the Spring Router Kotlin DSL that allows you to define the REST endpoints. You can find an example of the router DSL available at http://mng.bz/REdK.

10.2 Introducing Spring Native

Spring Native provides support to compiling Spring applications to architecture-specific native executables using the GraalVM native-image compiler. Native images offer several benefits compared to the traditional JVM-based approach in terms of a fast startup and a smaller memory footprint. A native image platform, such as GraalVM, statically analyzes the application source code and the classpath at compilation time. It considers only the codebase that will be used at runtime and discards everything else. This enables the native images to contain only the contents required at runtime.

In this section, we'll focus on Spring Native with GraalVM (https://www.graalvm.org/) and explore the approaches to using GraalVM with Spring Boot applications. However, before we dive into the use of it, let's understand GraalVM.

10.2.1 Introduction to GraalVM

GraalVM is a high-performance JDK distribution from Oracle that aims to accelerate the execution of Java and other JVM applications. It also supports non-JVM languages, such as JavaScript, Ruby, Python, and several others. This polyglot capability of GraalVM allows mixing multiple languages in an application. Before we explore some of these features, let's understand the high-level architecture of GraalVM, as shown in figure 10.1.

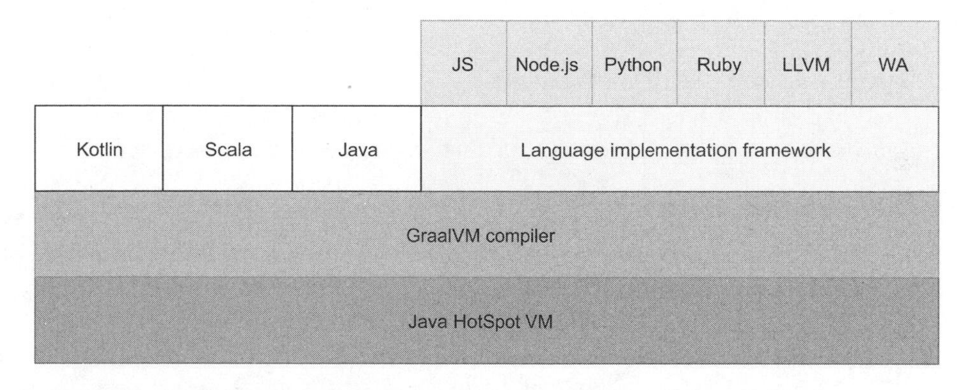

Figure 10.1 GraalVM architecture. The GraalVM just-in-time compiler is on top of the Java HotSpot compiler. The Truffle language implementation framework provides support for other non-JVM languages, such as JavaScript, Python, and others.

The GraalVM includes an advanced just-in-time (JIT) compiler on top of HotSpot Virtual Machine. It also includes the Truffle language implementation framework (http://mng.bz/2jP0) that allows GraalVM to run languages, such as NodeJs, Python, and others. Due to the GraalVM Truffle framework, it is possible for Java and other languages to directly interoperate with each other. The interpreters for the Truffle language that supports the other languages are Java programs running on the JVM. Thus, it is possible to define and invoke JavaScript code in your Java application. The following listing shows a sample.

Listing 10.13 Calling JavaScript code from Java

```
import org.graalvm.polyglot.*;
import java.io.PrintStream;
import java.util.Set;

public class Polyglot {

  public static void main(String[] args) {

    Context context = Context.newBuilder().allowAllAccess(true).build();
    Set<String> languages = context.getEngine().getLanguages().keySet();
    System.out.println("Languages available in GraalVM: " + languages);

    System.out.println("Java: Hello World");

    context.eval("js","console.log('JavaScript: Hello World')");
  }
}
```

Further, the GraalVM provides several runtime modes of operation: JVM runtime mode, Native Image, and Java on Truffle. While running applications on the HotSpot JVM, GraalVM uses the GraalVM compiler as the top-tier JIT compiler. At runtime, the application is executed normally on the JVM. The JVM passes the Java or JVM-native language to the compiler, which returns the machine code. In this book, we'll focus on GraalVM Native Image. You may refer to GraalVM documentation at https://www.graalvm.org/docs/introduction/ for further details on additional features.

10.2.2 GraalVM native image

GraalVM contains a native-image build tool. The native image is a new technology that compiles Java code directly into a standalone binary executable or a native shared library. The native image build includes application classes, dependencies, third-party libraries, and any JDK classes that are required in the application runtime. The generated native executables are specific to the operating system and machine architecture and do not require a JVM.

In a typical Java application compilation, first, the Java source code complies with the bytecode, and the bytecode is interpreted by the JVM. The JIT compiler identifies the frequently accessed bytecode and compiles it directly into native architecture-specific code for better performance.

The ahead-of-time (AOT) compiler in native-image builder takes the application components and statically analyzes them. It discards everything which is not relevant at runtime. This process takes a very long time, as the compiling process requires scanning all source files and the associated classpaths. The resulting native code after the compilation is relatively small, as it contains only the components needed at runtime.

It contains the minimum JRE and minimum types from all the libraries from the classpath that are required to support the application. You'll notice shortly that it is possible to generate the native image of a Spring Boot application that contains a Web server, data access support, and the minimum JRE.

> **GraalVM editions and installation**
> GraalVM is available in two editions: GraalVM Community and GraalVM Enterprise. It also has support for Java 8, Java 11, and Java 17. The community edition of GraalVM is based on OpenJDK, whereas the enterprise edition is based on Oracle JDK. You can download GraalVM from the https://www.graalvm.org/downloads/ URL. To configure it in your machine, you can refer to http://mng.bz/1j1j.

10.2.3 Spring Boot native image

Spring provides support to generate the native image of Spring applications through the Spring Native project. There are two approaches to building a native image of a Spring Boot application:

- *Spring Boot buildpacks support*—Generates a lightweight container containing a native executable
- *GraalVM native image Maven plugin*—Maven plugin that generates a native executable

Let's discuss these two approaches in the next two techniques.

10.2.4 Technique: Generating Spring Boot native image using buildpacks

In this technique, we'll demonstrate how to generate native image using buildpacks for a Spring Boot application.

Problem

So far, the Course Tracker application is built and executed using a traditional approach. You need to generate a native image of the Course Tracker application and run it.

Solution

Spring Native provides built-in support to generate the native image of a Spring Boot application through buildpacks. Buildpacks allow you to convert your source code to a container image. You can refer to https://buildpacks.io/docs/concepts/ for more details on buildpacks.

> **Source code**
> The final version of the Spring Boot project is available at http://mng.bz/PWln.

To continue with this project, you need to have Docker configured and running in your machine. The native image building process requires the Docker daemon to be available.

To start this technique, we'll use the same Course Tracker application we've used in the book so far. Let's create a new Spring Boot application with the following dependencies:

- Spring Native
- Spring Web
- Lombok

Listing 10.14 shows the final pom.xml file.

Listing 10.14 The pom.xml file for Spring Native application

```
<?xml version="1.0" encoding="UTF-8"?>
<project xmlns="http://maven.apache.org/POM/4.0.0"
➥ xmlns:xsi="http://www.w3.org/2001/XMLSchema-instance"
➥    xsi:schemaLocation="http://maven.apache.org/POM/4.0.0
➥ https://maven.apache.org/xsd/maven-4.0.0.xsd">
    <modelVersion>4.0.0</modelVersion>
    <parent>
        <groupId>org.springframework.boot</groupId>
        <artifactId>spring-boot-starter-parent</artifactId>
        <version>2.6.3</version>
        <relativePath/> <!-- lookup parent from repository -->
    </parent>
    <groupId>com.manning.sbip.ch10</groupId>
    <artifactId>course-tracker-native-app</artifactId>
    <version>0.0.1-SNAPSHOT</version>
    <name>native</name>
    <description>course-tracker-native-app</description>
    <properties>
        <java.version>17</java.version>
        <repackage.classifier/>
        <spring-native.version>0.11.2</spring-native.version>
    </properties>
    <dependencies>
        <dependency>
            <groupId>org.springframework.boot</groupId>
            <artifactId>spring-boot-starter-web</artifactId>
        </dependency>
        <dependency>
            <groupId>org.springframework.experimental</groupId>
            <artifactId>spring-native</artifactId>
            <version>${spring-native.version}</version>
        </dependency>
        <dependency>
            <groupId>org.projectlombok</groupId>
            <artifactId>lombok</artifactId>
        </dependency>

        <dependency>
            <groupId>org.springframework.boot</groupId>
```

```
        <artifactId>spring-boot-starter-test</artifactId>
        <scope>test</scope>
    </dependency>
</dependencies>

<build>
    <plugins>
        <plugin>
            <groupId>org.springframework.boot</groupId>
            <artifactId>spring-boot-maven-plugin</artifactId>
            <configuration>
                <classifier>${repackage.classifier}</classifier>
                <image>
                    <builder>paketobuildpacks/builder:tiny</builder>
                    <env>
                        <BP_NATIVE_IMAGE>true</BP_NATIVE_IMAGE>
                    </env>
                </image>
            </configuration>
        </plugin>

        <plugin>
            <groupId>org.springframework.experimental</groupId>
            <artifactId>spring-aot-maven-plugin</artifactId>
            <version>${spring-native.version}</version>
            <executions>
                <execution>
                    <id>test-generate</id>
                    <goals>
                        <goal>test-generate</goal>
                    </goals>
                </execution>
                <execution>
                    <id>generate</id>
                    <goals>
                        <goal>generate</goal>
                    </goals>
                </execution>
            </executions>
        </plugin>
    </plugins>
</build>
<repositories>
    <repository>
        <id>spring-releases</id>
        <name>Spring Releases</name>
        <url>https://repo.spring.io/release</url>
        <snapshots>
            <enabled>false</enabled>
        </snapshots>
    </repository>
</repositories>
<pluginRepositories>
    <pluginRepository>
```

```
            <id>spring-releases</id>
            <name>Spring Releases</name>
            <url>https://repo.spring.io/release</url>
            <snapshots>
                <enabled>false</enabled>
            </snapshots>
        </pluginRepository>
    </pluginRepositories>

    <profiles>
        <profile>
            <id>native</id>
            <properties>
                <repackage.classifier>exec</repackage.classifier>
                <native-buildtools.version>0.9.9</native-
➥ buildtools.version>
            </properties>
            <dependencies>
                <dependency>
                    <groupId>org.graalvm.buildtools</groupId>
                    <artifactId>junit-platform-native</artifactId>
                    <version>${native-buildtools.version}</version>
                    <scope>test</scope>
                </dependency>
            </dependencies>
            <build>
                <plugins>
                    <plugin>
                        <groupId>org.graalvm.buildtools</groupId>
                        <artifactId>native-maven-plugin</artifactId>
                        <version>${native-buildtools.version}</version>
                        <executions>
                            <execution>
                                <id>test-native</id>
                                <phase>test</phase>
                                <goals>
                                    <goal>test</goal>
                                </goals>
                            </execution>
                            <execution>
                                <id>build-native</id>
                                <phase>package</phase>
                                <goals>
                                    <goal>build</goal>
                                </goals>
                            </execution>
                        </executions>
                    </plugin>
                </plugins>
            </build>
        </profile>
    </profiles>

</project>
```

So far, Spring Native has experimental support, as this project is under development. In listing 10.14, let's focus on the `spring-boot-maven-plugin` and `spring-boot-aot-plugin` plugins configuration. In the `spring-boot-maven-plugin`, the Paketo buildpacks are used to generate the Docker Image. The `BP_NATIVE_IMAGE` argument is used to indicate a native image needs to be built. The `spring-aot-maven-plugin` provides the ahead-of-time compiler to compile the code. Note that this plugin is also in experimental mode. We'll deep dive into the role of this plugin and how it compiles the source later in this section.

We have also defined the `Course` domain object and created two courses. Refer to the application source code for further details. Let's start building the native image using the command, as shown in the following listing.

Listing 10.15 Generating native image

```
mvn clean package spring-boot:build-image
```

This command takes a while to generate the container image. After a successful build, you'll find output similar to what's shown in figure 10.2.

```
[INFO]     [creator]         web:          /workspace/com.manning.sbip.ch10.CourseTrackerNativeApplication (direct)
[INFO]     [creator]     ===> EXPORTING
[INFO]     [creator]     Adding layer 'paketo-buildpacks/ca-certificates:helper'
[INFO]     [creator]     Adding 1/1 app layer(s)
[INFO]     [creator]     Adding layer 'launcher'
[INFO]     [creator]     Adding layer 'config'
[INFO]     [creator]     Adding layer 'process-types'
[INFO]     [creator]     Adding label 'io.buildpacks.lifecycle.metadata'
[INFO]     [creator]     Adding label 'io.buildpacks.build.metadata'
[INFO]     [creator]     Adding label 'io.buildpacks.project.metadata'
[INFO]     [creator]     Adding label 'org.opencontainers.image.title'
[INFO]     [creator]     Adding label 'org.opencontainers.image.version'
[INFO]     [creator]     Adding label 'org.springframework.boot.version'
[INFO]     [creator]     Setting default process type 'web'
[INFO]     [creator]     Saving docker.io/library/course-tracker-native-app:0.0.1-SNAPSHOT...
[INFO]     [creator]     *** Images (e6ec00546e08):
[INFO]     [creator]           docker.io/library/course-tracker-native-app:0.0.1-SNAPSHOT
[INFO]     [creator]     Adding cache layer 'paketo-buildpacks/graalvm:jdk'
[INFO]     [creator]     Adding cache layer 'paketo-buildpacks/native-image:native-image'
[INFO]
[INFO] Successfully built image 'docker.io/library/course-tracker-native-app:0.0.1-SNAPSHOT'
[INFO]
[INFO] ------------------------------------------------------------------------
[INFO] BUILD SUCCESS
[INFO] ------------------------------------------------------------------------
[INFO] Total time:  29:51 min
[INFO] Finished at: 2021-10-30T15:25:46+05:30
[INFO] ------------------------------------------------------------------------
```

Figure 10.2 Building a native image of the Course Tracker application. Based on the CPU and RAM configuration, this process takes a little while to generate the image.

Once the image is built, you can start the application using the command, as shown in the following listing.

Listing 10.16 Docker command to run the generated image

```
docker run -p 8080:8080 course-tracker-native-app:0.0.1-SNAPSHOT
```

You'll find output similar to what's shown in figure 10.3.

```
  .   ____          _            __ _ _
 /\\ / ___'_ __ _ _(_)_ __  __ _ \ \ \ \
( ( )\___ | '_ | '_| | '_ \/ _` | \ \ \ \
 \\/  ___)| |_)| | | | | || (_| |  ) ) ) )
  '  |____| .__|_| |_|_| |_\__, | / / / /
 =========|_|==============|___/=/_/_/_/
 :: Spring Boot ::                (v2.5.6)

2021-10-30 10:08:16.986  INFO 1 --- [           main] c.m.s.c.CourseTrackerNativeApplication   : Starting CourseTrackerNativeApplicatio
n using Java 11.0.13 on 8122b2f6ee5f with PID 1 (/workspace/com.manning.sbip.ch10.CourseTrackerNativeApplication started by cnb in /wor
kspace)
2021-10-30 10:08:16.986  INFO 1 --- [           main] c.m.s.c.CourseTrackerNativeApplication   : No active profile set, falling back to
 default profiles: default
2021-10-30 10:08:17.019  INFO 1 --- [           main] o.s.b.w.embedded.tomcat.TomcatWebServer  : Tomcat initialized with port(s): 8080
(http)
2021-10-30 10:08:17.020  INFO 1 --- [           main] o.apache.catalina.core.StandardService   : Starting service [Tomcat]
2021-10-30 10:08:17.020  INFO 1 --- [           main] org.apache.catalina.core.StandardEngine  : Starting Servlet engine: [Apache Tomca
t/9.0.54]
2021-10-30 10:08:17.023  INFO 1 --- [           main] o.a.c.c.C.[Tomcat].[localhost].[/]       : Initializing Spring embedded WebApplic
ationContext
2021-10-30 10:08:17.023  INFO 1 --- [           main] w.s.c.ServletWebServerApplicationContext : Root WebApplicationContext: initializa
tion completed in 36 ms
2021-10-30 10:08:17.043  INFO 1 --- [           main] o.s.b.w.embedded.tomcat.TomcatWebServer  : Tomcat started on port(s): 8080 (http)
 with context path ''
2021-10-30 10:08:17.043  INFO 1 --- [           main] c.m.s.c.CourseTrackerNativeApplication   : Started CourseTrackerNativeApplication
 in 0.085 seconds (JVM running for 0.091)
```

Figure 10.3 Spring Boot Course Tracker native image startup logs. The application started in 85 milliseconds.

In figure 10.3, note the application start up time. In the example, the application started in 85 milliseconds. You can access the http://localhost:8080/courses endpoint and find the course details.

DISCUSSION

Using this technique, we've demonstrated how to generate a native image of a Spring Boot application. Spring Boot uses Paketo buildpacks (https://paketo.io/) to generate the image. First, the AOT compiler compiles the source code and identifies the smaller subset of code needed in the runtime. The `spring-boot-maven-plugin` uses this code to generate the Docker image. There is another approach to generate the native image without building a container image using the `native-maven-plugin`. Let's discuss that in the next technique.

10.2.5 *Technique: Generating Spring Boot native image using a Maven plugin*

In this technique, we'll demonstrate how to generate a native image using Maven for a Spring Boot application.

PROBLEM

In the previous technique, you explored the use of buildpacks to generate a native image. Spring Boot offers a Maven plugin-based approach to generate the native image. You need to explore this alternative approach.

SOLUTION

Spring Boot offers an alternative approach to building the native image of a Spring Boot application using the `native-maven-plugin`. This approach does not require you to have a Docker setup, and you can generate the native image via Maven build.

To continue with this approach, we'll continue with the Course Tracker application we've used in the previous technique. You'll notice in listing 10.14 that in the pom.xml there is a profile called `native`, and it contains the `native-maven-plugin` plugin among other details. Let's generate the native image using this plugin.

> **NOTE** On Windows, you need to use x64 Native Tools Command Prompt. It is recommended in the GraalVM native-image prerequisites.

The following listing shows the Maven build command. The `-Pnative` instructs Maven to use the native profile. The `-DskipTests` argument indicates Maven skipped executing the test cases.

Listing 10.17 Generating a native image using Maven plugin

```
mvn -Pnative -DskipTests package
```

Once the build succeeds, you'll notice an output similar to that shown in figure 10.4.

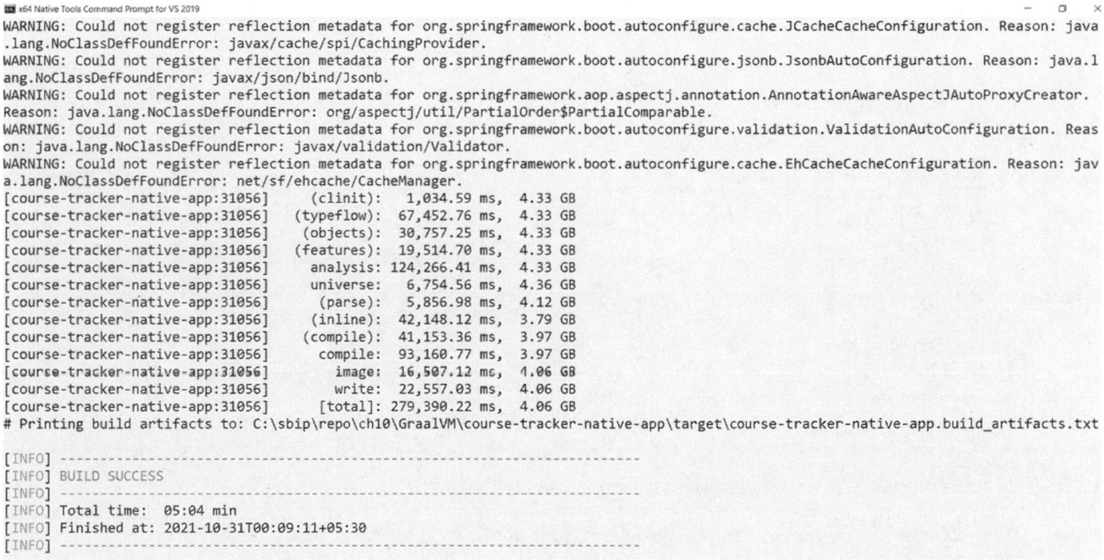

```
x64 Native Tools Command Prompt for VS 2019
WARNING: Could not register reflection metadata for org.springframework.boot.autoconfigure.cache.JCacheCacheConfiguration. Reason: java
.lang.NoClassDefFoundError: javax/cache/spi/CachingProvider.
WARNING: Could not register reflection metadata for org.springframework.boot.autoconfigure.jsonb.JsonbAutoConfiguration. Reason: java.l
ang.NoClassDefFoundError: javax/json/bind/Jsonb.
WARNING: Could not register reflection metadata for org.springframework.aop.aspectj.annotation.AnnotationAwareAspectJAutoProxyCreator.
Reason: java.lang.NoClassDefFoundError: org/aspectj/util/PartialOrder$PartialComparable.
WARNING: Could not register reflection metadata for org.springframework.boot.autoconfigure.validation.ValidationAutoConfiguration. Reas
on: java.lang.NoClassDefFoundError: javax/validation/Validator.
WARNING: Could not register reflection metadata for org.springframework.boot.autoconfigure.cache.EhCacheCacheConfiguration. Reason: jav
a.lang.NoClassDefFoundError: net/sf/ehcache/CacheManager.
[course-tracker-native-app:31056]     (clinit):   1,034.59 ms,  4.33 GB
[course-tracker-native-app:31056]   (typeflow):  67,452.76 ms,  4.33 GB
[course-tracker-native-app:31056]    (objects):  30,757.25 ms,  4.33 GB
[course-tracker-native-app:31056]   (features):  19,514.70 ms,  4.33 GB
[course-tracker-native-app:31056]     analysis: 124,266.41 ms,  4.33 GB
[course-tracker-native-app:31056]     universe:   6,754.56 ms,  4.36 GB
[course-tracker-native-app:31056]      (parse):   5,856.98 ms,  4.12 GB
[course-tracker-native-app:31056]     (inline):  42,148.12 ms,  3.79 GB
[course-tracker-native-app:31056]    (compile):  41,153.36 ms,  3.97 GB
[course-tracker-native-app:31056]      compile:  93,160.77 ms,  3.97 GB
[course-tracker-native-app:31056]        image:  16,507.12 ms,  4.06 GB
[course-tracker-native-app:31056]        write:  22,557.03 ms,  4.06 GB
[course-tracker-native-app:31056]      [total]: 279,390.22 ms,  4.06 GB
# Printing build artifacts to: C:\sbip\repo\ch10\GraalVM\course-tracker-native-app\target\course-tracker-native-app.build_artifacts.txt

[INFO] ------------------------------------------------------------------------
[INFO] BUILD SUCCESS
[INFO] ------------------------------------------------------------------------
[INFO] Total time:  05:04 min
[INFO] Finished at: 2021-10-31T00:09:11+05:30
[INFO] ------------------------------------------------------------------------
```

Figure 10.4 Native image generation through Maven Plugin

Once the image generation is successful, you can browse to the target of the application and find the generated native executable, as shown in figure 10.5.

Name	Date modified	Type	Size
classes	30/10/2021 2:56 PM	File folder	
generated-sources	31/10/2021 12:04 AM	File folder	
generated-test-sources	31/10/2021 12:04 AM	File folder	
maven-archiver	30/10/2021 2:56 PM	File folder	
maven-status	30/10/2021 2:56 PM	File folder	
surefire-reports	30/10/2021 2:56 PM	File folder	
test-classes	30/10/2021 2:56 PM	File folder	
course-tracker-native-app.build_artifacts	31/10/2021 12:09 AM	TXT File	1 KB
course-tracker-native-app	31/10/2021 12:09 AM	Application	68,649 KB
course-tracker-native-app-0.0.1-SNAPSHOT	31/10/2021 12:04 AM	Executable Jar File	48 KB
course-tracker-native-app-0.0.1-SNAPSHOT.jar.original	30/10/2021 2:57 PM	ORIGINAL File	48 KB
course-tracker-native-app-0.0.1-SNAPSHOT-exec	31/10/2021 12:04 AM	Executable Jar File	19,134 KB
sunmscapi.dll	20/07/2021 8:20 AM	Application extens...	43 KB

Figure 10.5 Generated native executable in the applications target folder.

To execute the native executable, you can either run it through the command line or double click on the executable file. In this example, the executable file is course-tracker-native-app.exe. Figure 10.6 shows the output.

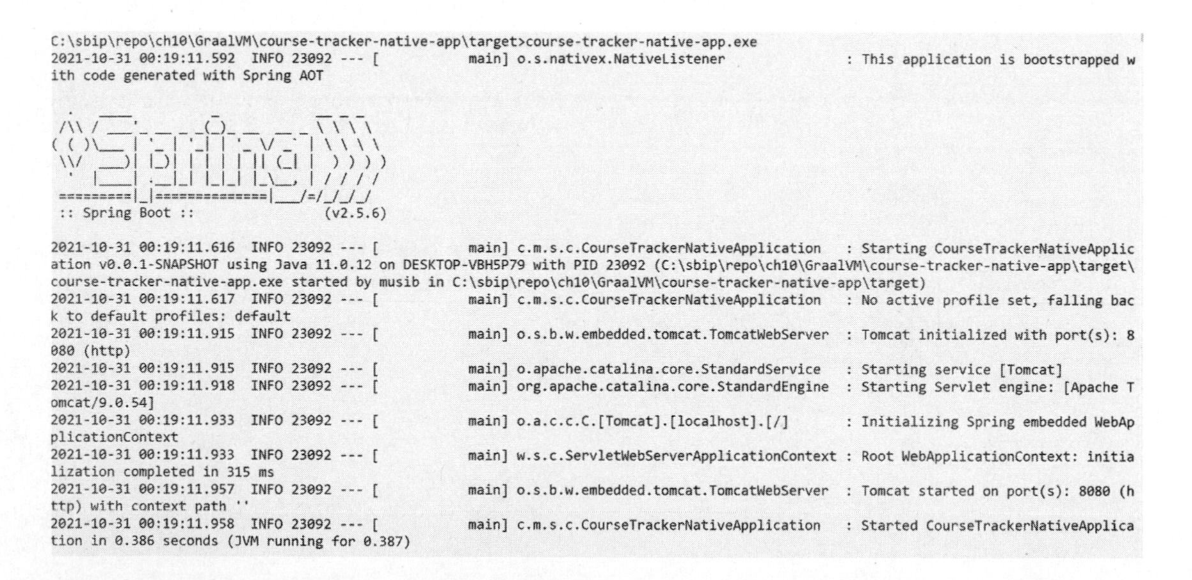

C:\sbip\repo\ch10\GraalVM\course-tracker-native-app\target>course-tracker-native-app.exe
2021-10-31 00:19:11.592 INFO 23092 --- [main] o.s.nativex.NativeListener : This application is bootstrapped with code generated with Spring AOT
:: Spring Boot :: (v2.5.6)
2021-10-31 00:19:11.616 INFO 23092 --- [main] c.m.s.c.CourseTrackerNativeApplication : Starting CourseTrackerNativeApplication v0.0.1-SNAPSHOT using Java 11.0.12 on DESKTOP-VBH5P79 with PID 23092 (C:\sbip\repo\ch10\GraalVM\course-tracker-native-app\target\course-tracker-native-app.exe started by musib in C:\sbip\repo\ch10\GraalVM\course-tracker-native-app\target)
2021-10-31 00:19:11.617 INFO 23092 --- [main] c.m.s.c.CourseTrackerNativeApplication : No active profile set, falling back to default profiles: default
2021-10-31 00:19:11.915 INFO 23092 --- [main] o.s.b.w.embedded.tomcat.TomcatWebServer : Tomcat initialized with port(s): 8080 (http)
2021-10-31 00:19:11.915 INFO 23092 --- [main] o.apache.catalina.core.StandardService : Starting service [Tomcat]
2021-10-31 00:19:11.918 INFO 23092 --- [main] org.apache.catalina.core.StandardEngine : Starting Servlet engine: [Apache Tomcat/9.0.54]
2021-10-31 00:19:11.933 INFO 23092 --- [main] o.a.c.c.C.[Tomcat].[localhost].[/] : Initializing Spring embedded WebApplicationContext
2021-10-31 00:19:11.933 INFO 23092 --- [main] w.s.c.ServletWebServerApplicationContext : Root WebApplicationContext: initialization completed in 315 ms
2021-10-31 00:19:11.957 INFO 23092 --- [main] o.s.b.w.embedded.tomcat.TomcatWebServer : Tomcat started on port(s): 8080 (http) with context path ''
2021-10-31 00:19:11.958 INFO 23092 --- [main] c.m.s.c.CourseTrackerNativeApplication : Started CourseTrackerNativeApplication in 0.386 seconds (JVM running for 0.387)

Figure 10.6 Executing the native image. The Spring Boot application starts in 387 milliseconds.

DISCUSSION

In this technique, we've explored the use of the `native-maven-plugin` to generate the native image of a Spring Boot application. The `native-maven-plugin` configuration is available through the native profile configuration in the pom.xml file. We've enabled this profile with `-Pnative` flag in the Maven package command, which generates the executable. In the next section, we'll learn the `spring-aot-maven-plugin` compilation process.

10.2.6 Understanding Spring AOT Maven Plugin

In the previous section, we discussed that the Spring AOT plugin provided ahead-of-time compilation support. The AOT compiler statically analyzes the application source code and the application classpath and determines the types needed at application runtime. Let's trigger the AOT compiler in the previously used Course Tracker application and explore its outcome. Listing 10.18 shows the Spring AOT command to trigger the spring AOT plugin's generate goal. Recall that in the pom.xml file we have the `spring-aot-maven-plugin` that allows us to execute this goal.

Listing 10.18 Invoking Spring AOT generate goal

```
mvn clean package spring-aot:generate
```

Once the command executes successfully, navigate to the target\generated-sources\spring-aot folder, and you'll notice an output similar to that shown in figure 10.7.

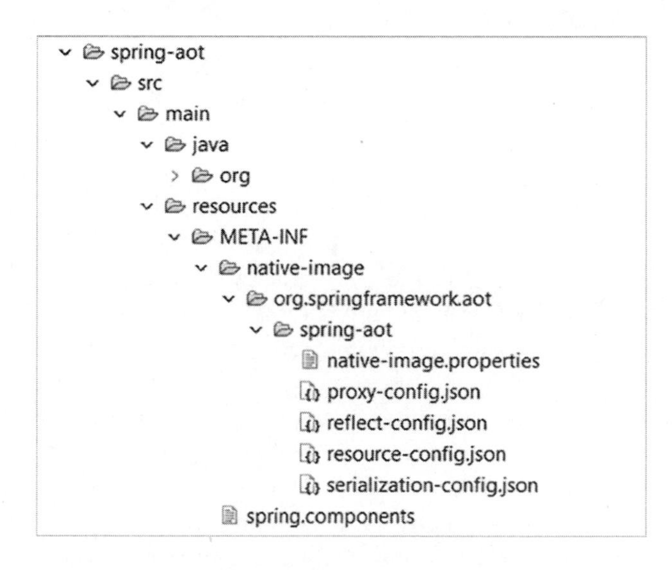

Figure 10.7 The Spring AOT-generated sources. The src\main\java folder contains the AOT generated source code, and the src\main\resources contains the generated configurations.

The src\main\java folder contains the minimal source code needed at application runtime. You can inspect the `StaticSpringFactories` class that contains Spring Boot Factory classes, interfaces, and more. The other packages (e.g., `boot` and `core.io.support`) contain various other Spring Boot and other additional configurations. The spring-aot folder inside the resources folder contains several important configurations used by the GraalVM native image builder. The following configuration files are provided:

- native-image.properties
- proxy-config.json

- reflect-config.json
- resource-config.json
- serialization-config.json

The native-image.properties files contain the arguments used by the native-image builder to generate the image. The other four configuration files provide details for the native-image builder related to the proxy, reflect, resource, and serialization configuration, respectively. All these features are related to application runtime behavior. For instance, by default the native image builder does not integrate to any resource (e.g., files, images, etc.) present in the classpath. Thus, if at runtime your code attempts to load these files, it won't be available. Therefore, you need to explicitly specify the AOT compiler about this.

Similarly, the Java reflection API allows inspecting classes, methods, and fields at runtime. The native-image builder needs to know about the reflectively accessed program elements ahead of time.

NOTE You can find further details about the native image and other configurations available at https://www.graalvm.org/reference-manual/native-image/.

10.3 Spring Boot with GraphQL

In this section, we'll discuss GraphQL and how to use GraphQL with a Spring Boot application.

10.3.1 Issues with REST

In chapter 8, you learned how to build REST APIs with Spring Boot. A REST API allows you to expose the application functionality through API endpoints. An API client can access the exposed API endpoints and interact with the application. For instance, in chapter 8, for our Course Tracker application, we developed a REST API that allows the API clients to interact with the application through the available endpoints. To get existing course details, a client can access the `GET /courses` endpoint and get all available courses. Similarly, to create a new course, a client can invoke `POST /courses` endpoint with a course request body, and the API creates a new course.

The above REST API-based approach works well, and REST has become the de facto standard to develop APIs. However, although REST is commonly adopted, it has some issues as well. One major issue with REST is it's overfetching of application data. The other issue is multiple API calls to retrieve the desired data. Let's explain these in detail.

In a REST API, you define endpoint per resource. A resource represents a specific part or feature of the application. For instance, in the Course Tracker application, the course is a resource we manage. For instance, if an API client requests details about course ID 123, all the details about the specific course ID are returned to the user. This includes course ID, name, category, rating, and description. This is where we have the problem of data overfetching. The API client doesn't have the flexibility to specify the set of fields they are interested in. It is always forced to consume the data the server provides. Thus, although the API client needs only a subset of the fields, it is overfetching the data. You'll notice how GraphQL solves this problem in the following sections.

Let's now talk about the multiple API invocation issues with REST API. As we've discussed in the previous paragraph, REST API endpoints are defined based on the application resource. The more application resources you have, the more endpoints you need to define in the REST API. Let's consider an example of a different scenario in the Course Tracker application. Imagine you are managing course details and the course reviews in the application, as shown in figure 10.8. Thus, you have two resources to manage: the course and its reviews. Hence, you need to define one set of endpoints related to the course and another set related to reviews.

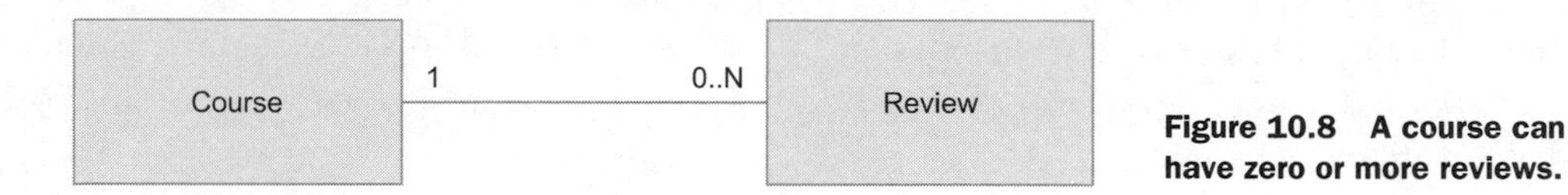

Figure 10.8 A course can have zero or more reviews.

Let's now imagine that an API client needs to access course details by a course name and reviews for the course. In a REST API, the client first needs to make an API call to obtain the course details and get the course ID. It then needs to make another API call to get all the reviews using the course ID obtained in the first API call. This is shown in figure 10.9.

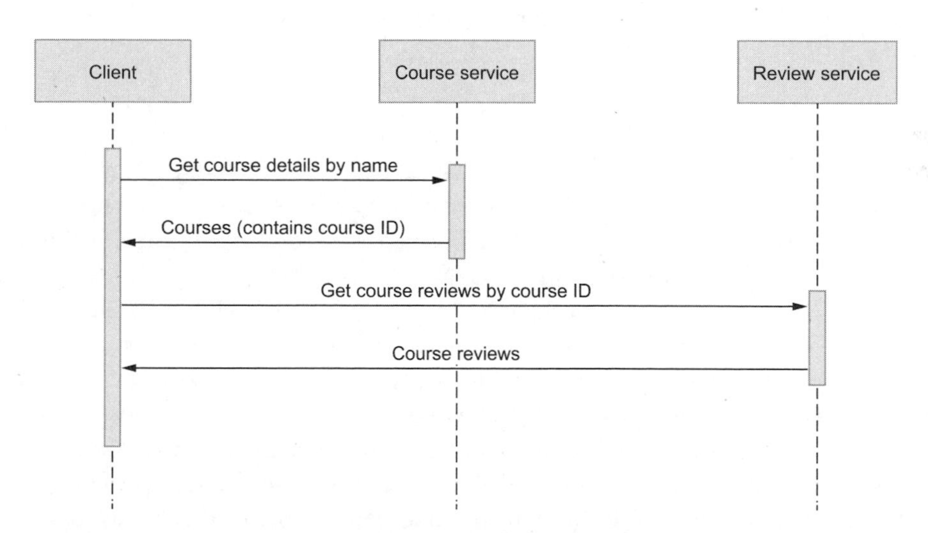

Figure 10.9 Multiple API calls to get the review details for a course

It will be better if the API client could access all these requested details in a single API call. In the next sections, you'll notice how GraphQL solves this problem of REST API.

10.3.2 Introduction to GraphQL

NOTE GraphQL is a large topic, and it is beyond the scope of this text to provide in-depth coverage. In this chapter, we intend to show you the use of GraphQL with Spring Boot and will focus on that. For a better understanding of GraphQL, you can refer to GraphQL documentation available at https://graphql.org/learn/.

GraphQL is a query language for API and a server-side runtime for executing queries. It uses a type system to define the application data model. We create a GraphQL service by defining types and the fields associated with those types. For instance, we can define a GraphQL service that returns all courses. We do this by defining a GraphQL Query type and a regular object type. Listing 10.19 shows this for the `Course` type. Create a folder called `ghraphql` inside the src\main\resources directory. Create a file called schema.graphqls inside the graphql folder, and insert the content from the following listing.

Listing 10.19 Defining a Query and a regular GraphQL type

```
type Query {
    courses : [Course]
}

type Course {
    id: ID
    name: String
    category: String
    description: String
    reviews: [Review]
}
```

We'll define the Review type shortly. To keep the example lean, we kept only the Course type.

In listing 10.19, we've defined a GraphQL type Query. A Query is a specialized GraphQL type that allows you to define query services to fetch data from a GraphQL server. Inside the `Query` type, we've defined a course service that returns an array of courses, which is represented with `[Course]`. Next, we've defined a regular GraphQL type that represents the type of data that is returned to the client. In the above example, we've defined the Course GraphQL type with the associated fields and their types.

The Query type allows a client to fetch data from a GraphQL server. GraphQL provides other specialized types: `Mutation` and `Subscription`. As the name suggests, the `Mutation` type allows you to define services to modify data in the GraphQL server. The `Subscription` type allows you to define `Subscription` to events in the GraphQL server. The following listing shows a sample of `Mutation` and `Subscription` type definitions in the previously defined schema.graphqls file.

Listing 10.20 GraphQL mutation type definition

```
type Mutation {
    addCourse(name: String, category: String, description: String) : Course
}
```

```
type Subscription {
    reviewEvents (courseId: Int) : Review
}
```

In listing 10.20, we defined a GraphQL `Mutation` type and defined a service that allows us to add a new course. Note that the service accepts several arguments and returns a `Course` type. Similarly, the `Subscription` type defines a subscription to review events and returns a stream of reviews.

10.3.3 Using GraphQL with Spring Boot

Now that we've introduced you to GraphQL, let's explore the use of it along with Spring Boot. We'll discuss two techniques: in the first one, we'll show you how to design an API with GraphQL that allows you to retrieve data, create new resources, or modify existing resources. In the second technique, we'll explore the notion of subscription over WebSocket in a GraphQL API. Let's start with the first technique.

10.3.4 Technique: Developing a GraphQL API with a Spring Boot application

In this technique, we'll discuss how to develop a GraphQL API with a Spring Boot application.

Problem

Previously, you developed REST APIs with Spring Boot. You recently explored GraphQL and need to redesign the Course Tracker REST API with GraphQL.

Solution

With this technique, we'll show you how to build a GraphQL API with a Spring Boot application. We'll use the previously used Course Tracker application with a few modifications to design the API.

> **Source code**
> The final version of the Spring Boot project is available at http://mng.bz/J1jV.

Let's begin by creating a new Spring Boot project through Spring Initializr with the following dependencies:

1. Spring Data R2DBC
2. Spring Reactive Web
3. Lombok
4. H2 Database

Note that the GraphQL support in Spring Boot is in experimental mode. This means GraphQL support is an experimental feature and under development. Thus, Spring

Boot GraphQL is not available in the Spring Initializr. We'll need to include this dependency manually in the pom.xml. Listing 10.21 shows the final pom.xml.

Listing 10.21 The pom.xml file for a Spring Boot GraphQL application

```
<?xml version="1.0" encoding="UTF-8"?>
<project xmlns="http://maven.apache.org/POM/4.0.0"
➥ xmlns:xsi="http://www.w3.org/2001/XMLSchema-instance"
➥ xsi:schemaLocation="http://maven.apache.org/POM/4.0.0
➥ https://maven.apache.org/xsd/maven-4.0.0.xsd">
  <modelVersion>4.0.0</modelVersion>
  <parent>
      <groupId>org.springframework.boot</groupId>
      <artifactId>spring-boot-starter-parent</artifactId>
      <version>2.6.0</version>
      <relativePath/> <!-- lookup parent from repository -->
  </parent>
  <groupId>com.manning.sbip.ch10</groupId>
  <artifactId>course-tracker-graphql-app</artifactId>
  <version>0.0.1-SNAPSHOT</version>
  <name>course-tracker-graphql-api</name>
  <description>Course Tracker GraphQL API</description>
  <properties>
      <java.version>17</java.version>
  </properties>
  <dependencies>

      <dependency>
          <groupId>org.springframework.experimental</groupId>
          <artifactId>graphql-spring-boot-starter</artifactId>
          <version>1.0.0-M2</version>
      </dependency>
      <dependency>
          <groupId>org.springframework.boot</groupId>
          <artifactId>spring-boot-starter-webflux</artifactId>
      </dependency>
      <dependency>
          <groupId>org.springframework.boot</groupId>
          <artifactId>spring-boot-starter-data-r2dbc</artifactId>
      </dependency>
      <dependency>
          <groupId>io.r2dbc</groupId>
          <artifactId>r2dbc-h2</artifactId>
          <scope>runtime</scope>
      </dependency>
      <dependency>
          <groupId>org.projectlombok</groupId>
          <artifactId>lombok</artifactId>
          <optional>true</optional>
      </dependency>
      <dependency>
          <groupId>org.springframework.boot</groupId>
          <artifactId>spring-boot-starter-test</artifactId>
          <scope>test</scope>
```

```
    </dependency>
</dependencies>

<build>
    <plugins>
        <plugin>
            <groupId>org.springframework.boot</groupId>
            <artifactId>spring-boot-maven-plugin</artifactId>
            <configuration>
                <excludes>
                    <exclude>
                        <groupId>org.projectlombok</groupId>
                        <artifactId>lombok</artifactId>
                    </exclude>
                </excludes>
            </configuration>
        </plugin>
    </plugins>
</build>

<repositories>
    <repository>
        <id>spring-milestones</id>
        <name>Spring Milestones</name>
        <url>https://repo.spring.io/milestone</url>
        <snapshots>
            <enabled>false</enabled>
        </snapshots>
    </repository>
    <repository>
        <id>spring-snapshots</id>
        <name>Spring Snapshots</name>
        <url>https://repo.spring.io/snapshot</url>
        <releases>
            <enabled>false</enabled>
        </releases>
    </repository>
</repositories>
<pluginRepositories>
    <pluginRepository>
        <id>spring-milestones</id>
        <name>Spring Milestones</name>
        <url>https://repo.spring.io/milestone</url>
        <snapshots>
            <enabled>false</enabled>
        </snapshots>
    </pluginRepository>
    <pluginRepository>
        <id>spring-snapshots</id>
        <name>Spring Snapshots</name>
        <url>https://repo.spring.io/snapshot</url>
        <releases>
            <enabled>false</enabled>
        </releases>
    </pluginRepository>
```

```
    </pluginRepositories>
</project>
```

We've included the `graphql-spring-boot-starter` dependency in the pom.xml file. Notice that the group ID of the dependency is `org.springframework.experimental`. Also, the artifact ID of the dependency is different than the other Spring Boot starter dependency. Lastly, the release version of the dependency indicates it is a milestone release. Due to this, we've included the `spring-milestones` and `spring-snapshots` repositories in the pom.xml, so Maven can download the required libraries.

Next, let's include the `Course` domain object, as shown in listing 10.22. Notice that we've removed the rating field, which we have used in the previous examples. As you'll notice shortly, we are using another domain object called `Review` to explain a GraphQL concept.

Listing 10.22 The Course domain object

```
package com.manning.sbip.ch10.model;

import lombok.AllArgsConstructor;
import lombok.Data;
import org.springframework.data.annotation.Id;

@Data
@AllArgsConstructor
public class Course {
    @Id
    private Integer id;
    private String name;
    private String category;
    private String description;
}
```

Each course can be reviewed by its users, and the review details are captured in the `Review` domain object, as shown in the following listing.

Listing 10.23 The Review domain object

```
package com.manning.sbip.ch10.model;

import lombok.AllArgsConstructor;
import lombok.Data;
import org.springframework.data.annotation.Id;

@Data
@AllArgsConstructor
public class Review {

    @Id
    private Integer id;
    private Integer courseId;
    private String reviewerName;
```

A review belongs to a course. Thus, the courseId is part of the review.

```
    private Integer rating;
    private String comment;
}
```

Let's create the repository interfaces to manage the `Course` and the `Review` details in the application. The following listing shows the `CourseRepository` interface.

Listing 10.24 The CourseRepository interface

```
package com.manning.sbip.ch10.repository;

import com.manning.sbip.ch10.model.Course;
import org.springframework.data.repository.reactive.ReactiveCrudRepository;
import org.springframework.stereotype.Repository;
import reactor.core.publisher.Flux;

@Repository
public interface CourseRepository extends ReactiveCrudRepository<Course,
     Integer>  {

    Flux<Course> findByCategory(String category);
}
```

Listing 10.24 contains a custom method called `findByCategory(..)` that returns a `Flux` of courses for a given course category. Also, the `CourseRepository` interface extends the `ReactiveCrudRepository` interface, which provides the CRUD operation support for the bounded domain object (e.g., `Course`). We've covered reactive Spring Boot application development in chapter 8. Let's now define the `ReviewRepository` interface, as shown in the following listing.

Listing 10.25 The ReviewRepository interface

```
package com.manning.sbip.ch10.repository;

import com.manning.sbip.ch10.model.Review;
import org.springframework.data.repository.reactive.ReactiveCrudRepository;
import org.springframework.stereotype.Repository;
import reactor.core.publisher.Flux;

@Repository
public interface ReviewRepository extends ReactiveCrudRepository<Review,
➥ Integer> {

    Flux<Review> findByCourseId(Integer courseId);
}
```

Listing 10.25 contains a custom method called `findByCourseId(..)` that returns a `Flux` of reviews for a given `courseId`.

Now that we've defined the domain objects and the associated repository interfaces, let's start building the GraphQL schema. Create a file called schema.graphqls in the src\main\resources\graphql folder. The following listing shows the contents of the schema.graphqls file.

Listing 10.26 The GraphQL schema file

```
type Query {
    courses : [Course]
    coursesByCategory (category: String) : [Course]!
    reviews (courseId: Int) : [Review]!
}

type Course {
    id: ID
    name: String
    category: String
    description: String
    reviews: [Review]!
}

type Review {
    id: ID,
    courseId: Int,
    reviewerName: String
    rating: Int,
    comment: String
}

type Mutation {
    addCourse(name: String, category: String, description: String) : Course
    addReview(courseId: Int, reviewerName: String, rating: Int, comment:
➥  String) : Review
}
```

In listing 10.26, we defined four GraphQL types: the `Query`, `Course`, `Review`, and `Mutation`. The query and mutation are special GraphQL types, whereas the course and the review are regular object types. The difference between special types and regular types is that special types provide an entry point to the GraphQL schema. For instance, the Query type allows us to fetch data from the server. The mutation type allows us to change data in the server.

In listing 10.26, in the `Query` type, we defined the following queries:

- `courses: [Course]`—Returns an array of courses, which is represented as `[Course]`.
- `coursesByCategory (category: String) : [Course]!`—It takes an argument of string type called `category` and returns an array of courses. The exclamation mark indicates the returned array can be empty.
- `reviews (courseId: Int) : [Review]!`—Takes an argument of integer type called `courseId` and returns an array of type `Review`.

Next, we defined the type of `Course`. It has the same fields specified in the `Course` domain object, as shown in listing 10.22. We've additionally included `reviews` that return the array of reviews for the `Course`. Note that the GraphQL types are slightly different than what has defined the `Course` Java types. The `id` field has a type of GraphQL type `ID`, the `reviews` field has an array type of `Review`, and all other fields are of GraphQL `String` type.

Next, we've defined the type of `Review`. It contains the same fields as specified in the `Review` domain object. Note that the `id` field has a GraphQL type `ID`, and the `rating` field has a GraphQL type `Int`. The other fields are of GraphQL `String` type.

Lastly, we defined the type `Mutation` and defined two different fields: `addCourse` and `addReview`. The `addCourse` field creates a new `Course` in the server and accepts `name`, `category`, and `description` as the arguments. It returns the created `Course` details. Similarly, the `addReview` field creates a new `Review` and accepts `courseId`, `reviewerName`, `rating`, and `comment` as the arguments. It returns the created `Review` details.

> **NOTE** You can find more information about GraphQL schema and types in the GraphQL documentation at https://graphql.org/learn/schema/.

Let's now define a Spring controller to define the GraphQL endpoints, as shown in the following listing.

Listing 10.27 The GraphQL Spring controller

```
package com.manning.sbip.ch10.controller;

import com.manning.sbip.ch10.model.Course;
import com.manning.sbip.ch10.model.Review;
import com.manning.sbip.ch10.repository.CourseRepository;
import com.manning.sbip.ch10.repository.ReviewRepository;
import lombok.RequiredArgsConstructor;
import org.springframework.graphql.data.method.annotation.*;
import org.springframework.stereotype.Controller;
import reactor.core.publisher.Flux;
import reactor.core.publisher.Mono;

import java.time.Duration;

@Controller
@RequiredArgsConstructor
public class GraphqlCourseController {

    private final CourseRepository courseRepository;
    private final ReviewRepository reviewRepository;

    @QueryMapping
    Flux<Course> courses() {
        return this.courseRepository.findAll();
    }
```

```
    @QueryMapping
    Flux<Review> reviews(@Argument Integer courseId) {
        return this.reviewRepository.findByCourseId(courseId);
    }

    @QueryMapping
    Flux<Course> coursesByCategory(@Argument String category) {
        return this.courseRepository.findByCategory(category);
    }

    @MutationMapping
    Mono<Course> addCourse(@Argument String name, @Argument String
➥ category, @Argument String description) {
        return this.courseRepository.save(new Course(null, name, category,
➥ description));
    }

    @MutationMapping
    Mono<Review> addReview(@Argument Integer courseId, @Argument String
➥ reviewerName, @Argument Integer rating, @Argument String comment) {
        return this.reviewRepository.save(new Review(null, courseId,
➥ reviewerName, rating, comment));
    }
}
```

Listing 10.27 is a Spring controller class consisting of three `QueryMapping` and two `MutationMapping` definitions. Recall from the GraphQL schema definition that we have three queries and two mutations defined in it. We've defined the GraphQL endpoints accordingly in the controller.

Let's now define the course and review table DDLs and add a few sample course and review details. Create a file named schema.sql in the src\main\resources folder. The following listing shows the contents of the schema.sql file.

Listing 10.28 The schema.sql file

```
CREATE TABLE COURSE (
  ID           INT auto_increment,
  NAME        VARCHAR(255),
  CATEGORY     VARCHAR(255),
  DESCRIPTION VARCHAR(255),
  PRIMARY KEY (id)
);

CREATE TABLE REVIEW
(
    ID        INT auto_increment,
    COURSE_ID INT,
    REVIEWER_NAME VARCHAR(100),
    RATING    INT,
    COMMENT   VARCHAR(2000)
)
```

Next, let's create a file called data.sql in the src\main\resources folder. The following listing shows the contents of this file.

Listing 10.29 The data.sql file

```
INSERT INTO COURSE(ID, NAME, CATEGORY, DESCRIPTION)  VALUES(1, 'Rapid
➥ Spring Boot Application Development', 'Spring', 'Learn Enterprise
➥ Application Development with Spring Boot');
INSERT INTO COURSE(ID, NAME, CATEGORY, DESCRIPTION)  VALUES(2, 'Getting
➥ Started with Spring Security DSL', 'Spring', 'Learn Spring Security DSL
➥ in Easy Steps');
INSERT INTO COURSE(ID, NAME, CATEGORY, DESCRIPTION)  VALUES(3, 'Getting
➥ Started with Spring Cloud Kubernetes', 'Spring', 'Master Spring Boot
➥ Application Deployment with Kubernetes');


INSERT INTO REVIEW(ID, COURSE_ID, REVIEWER_NAME, RATING, COMMENT)
➥ VALUES(1,1, 'John', 4, 'Excellent Course');
INSERT INTO REVIEW(ID, COURSE_ID, REVIEWER_NAME, RATING, COMMENT)
➥ VALUES(2,1, 'Jane', 5, 'Awesome Course');
INSERT INTO REVIEW(ID, COURSE_ID, REVIEWER_NAME, RATING, COMMENT)
➥ VALUES(1,2, 'Mark', 4, 'Useful');
INSERT INTO REVIEW(ID, COURSE_ID, REVIEWER_NAME, RATING, COMMENT)
➥ VALUES(2,2, 'Josh', 4, 'Recommended Course for all');
INSERT INTO REVIEW(ID, COURSE_ID, REVIEWER_NAME, RATING, COMMENT)
➥ VALUES(1,3, 'Stephen', 3, 'Good for beginners');
INSERT INTO REVIEW(ID, COURSE_ID, REVIEWER_NAME, RATING, COMMENT)
➥ VALUES(2,3, 'Laura', 4, 'Engaging Content');
```

That's it. Let's now start the application and test the GraphQL endpoints. There are several ways we can test the GraphQL endpoints. With this technique, we'll demonstrate three alternatives:

- GraphiQL
- Postman
- Httpie

GraphiQL (https://github.com/graphql/graphiql) is a browser-based IDE that allows you to explore GraphQL endpoints. It is an official project under the GraphQL Foundation. Let's demonstrate how to test the courses endpoint with GraphiQL. Open a browser window and navigate to http://localhost:8080/graphiql?path=/graphql. You'll find a screen similar to that shown in figure 10.10.

Let's now access the courses GraphQL endpoint. Figure 10.11 shows the output.

Notice that, unlike a REST API, in the GraphQL API, you have the flexibility to request the fields you are interested in. You are not forced to retrieve all fields of the domain object, as this happens with a REST API. For instance, we can request only course name and category, and the GraphQL will return only the requested fields. This is shown in figure 10.12.

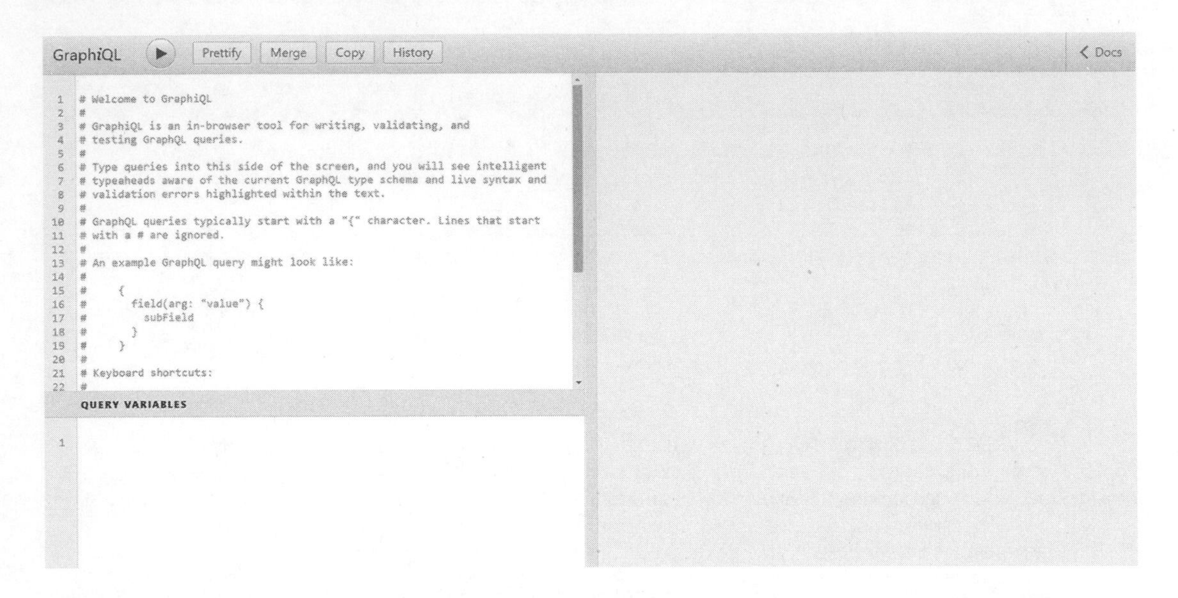

Figure 10.10 The GraphiQL in-browser IDE. The top-left window is the place we define the GraphQL queries and mutations. The bottom-left window is where we defined the query variables (if any) used in the GraphQL query. The right-side window is where the output is presented.

GraphiQL Prettify Merge Copy History Docs

```
query {
  courses {
    id,
    name,
    category,
    description,
  }
}
```

QUERY VARIABLES

```
{
  "data": {
    "courses": [
      {
        "id": "1",
        "name": "Rapid Spring Boot Application Development",
        "category": "Spring",
        "description": "Learn Enterprise Application Development with Spring Boot"
      },
      {
        "id": "2",
        "name": "Getting Started with Spring Security DSL",
        "category": "Spring",
        "description": "Learn Spring Security DSL in Easy Steps"
      },
      {
        "id": "3",
        "name": "Getting Started with Spring Cloud Kubernetes",
        "category": "Spring",
        "description": "Master Spring Boot Application Deployment with Kubernetes"
      }
    ]
  }
}
```

Figure 10.11 Accessing the courses endpoint in GraphiQL IDE. We've requested the ID, name, category, and description fields. On the right-hand side, the result is presented.

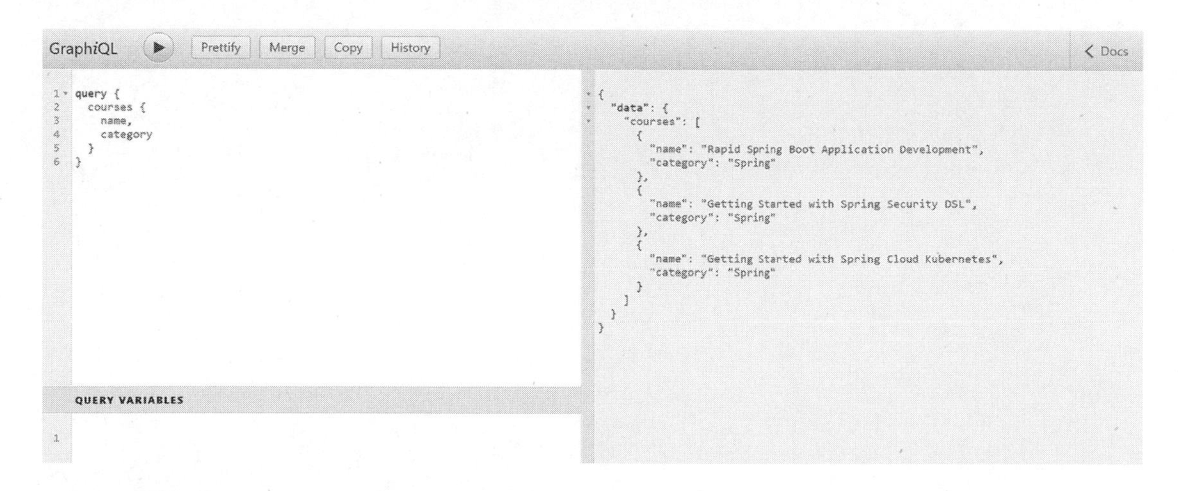

Figure 10.12 Accessing courses endpoint requesting only the name and category fields. The presented result provides names and categories for all available courses.

Let's now demonstrate how to use Postman to access the courses endpoint. Open Postman and create a new HTTP request. Create a POST request with the URL http://localhost:8080/graphql with the request body, as shown in the following listing.

Listing 10.30 The GraphQL query for the courses endpoint

```
query {
  courses {
    id,
    name,
    category,
    description,
  }
}
```

Note that you need to use the GraphQL radio button to indicate this is a GraphQL request. Figure 10.13 shows this. Click on the Send button, and you'll find the details of all courses.

Let's now demonstrate how to access GraphQL endpoint through HTTPie (https://httpie.io/). Open a command prompt or terminal window, and access the command, as shown in the following listing.

Listing 10.31 Httpie command to access the courses GraphQL endpoint

```
http POST :8080/graphql query="{courses{id,name,category,description}}"
```

You'll find the output as shown in listing 10.32.

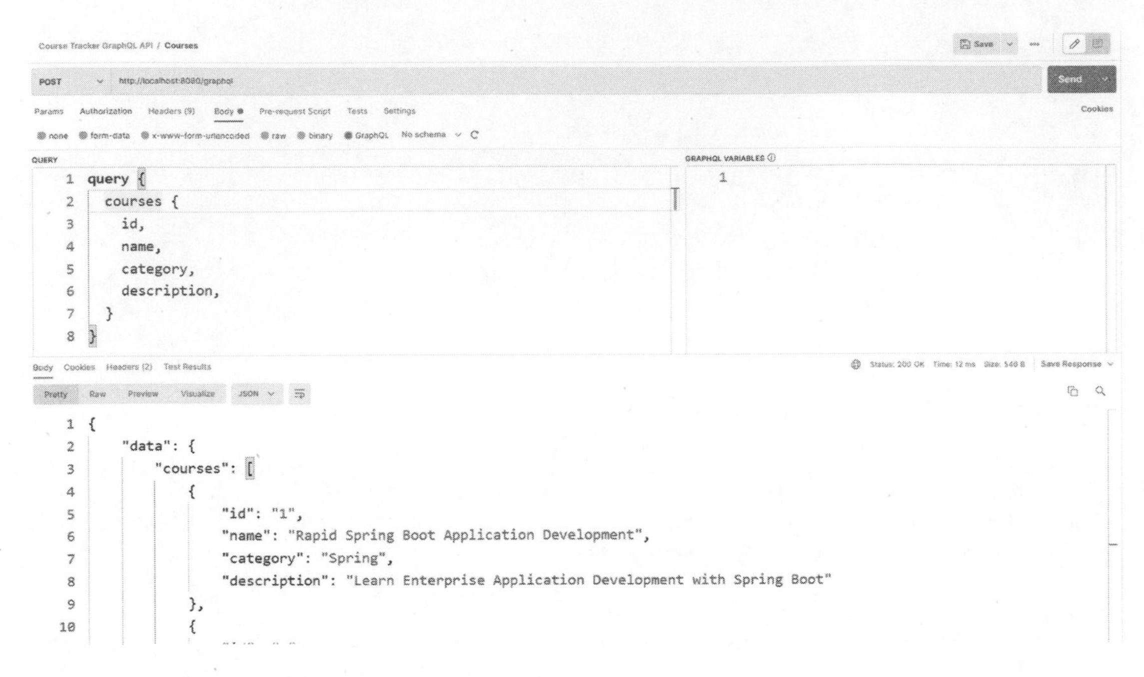

Figure 10.13 The GraphQL query request in Postman

Listing 10.32 Httpie command output of courses GraphQL endpoint

```
HTTP/1.1 200 OK
Content-Length: 474
Content-Type: application/json

{
    "data": {
        "courses": [
            {
                "category": "Spring",
                "description": "Learn Enterprise Application Development with
     Spring Boot",
                "id": "1",
                "name": "Rapid Spring Boot Application Development"
            },
            {
                "category": "Spring",
                "description": "Learn Spring Security DSL in Easy Steps",
                "id": "2",
                "name": "Getting Started with Spring Security DSL"
            },
            {
                "category": "Spring",
                "description": "Master Spring Boot Application Deployment
     with Kubernetes",
                "id": "3",
```

```
                    "name": "Getting Started with Spring Cloud Kubernetes"
                }
            ]
        }
    }
```

Let's now explore how to access the `reviews` GraphQL endpoint. Note that this endpoint accepts a `courseId` argument. Figure 10.14 shows how to supply the `courseId` argument in the request and the associated result.

Figure 10.14 Accessing reviews GraphQL endpoint for courseId 1 and the associated output

You have another query-based GraphQL endpoint `coursesByCategory`. We leave that as an exercise for you to try.

Let's now focus on the mutation types. We have defined two mutation types: `addCourse` and `addReview`. Let's add a new course using the `addCourse` mutation type. The following listing shows the request of the `addCourse` mutation type.

Listing 10.33 The addCourse GraphQL mutation request

```
mutation {
  addCourse(name: "GraphQL in Action", category: "GraphQL", description:
➥ "GraphQL in Action gives you a solid overview of GraphQL") {
    id,
    name,
    description
  }
}
```

In listing 10.33, the type is `mutation`, and the `addCourse` accepts the `name`, `category`, and `description` arguments. In the same definition, we also query for `id`, `name`, and `description` fields. Let's execute this request through GraphiQL IDE, as shown in figure 10.15.

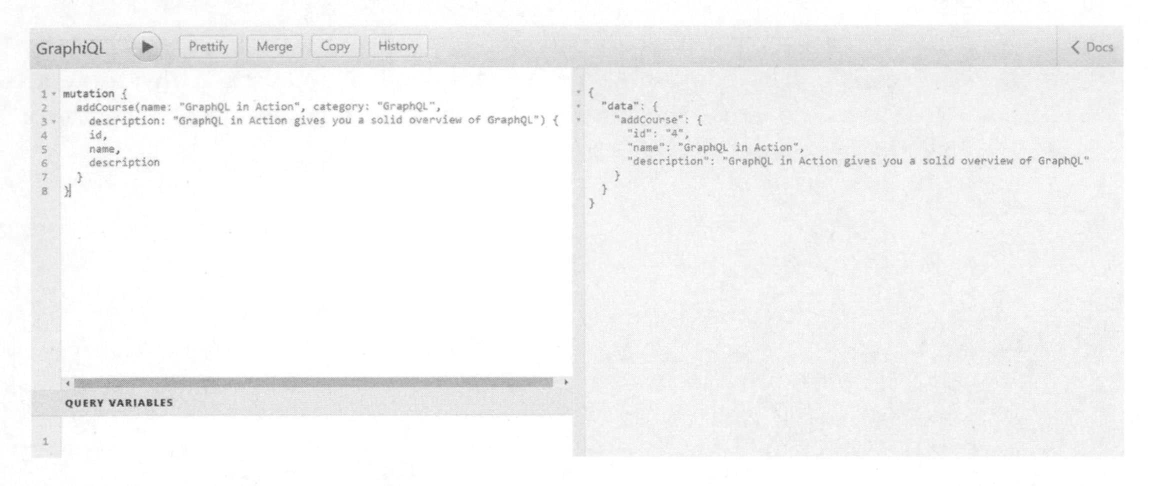

Figure 10.15 Accessing addCourse mutation endpoint to add a new Course. We are accessing the ID, name, and description fields of the newly created course. On the right-hand side, the server presents the requested course details.

We have another mutation type, `addReview`, which allows you to add a review for a given course. We leave that as an exercise for you to create a review for one of the existing courses.

Now that we are done with the basic endpoints, let's now understand another important concept. If you recall, the `Course` GraphQL type has the following definition, as shown in the following listing.

Listing 10.34 The GraphQL course type definition

```
type Course {
    id: ID
    name: String
    category: String
    description: String
    reviews: [Review]!
}
```

In listing 10.34, the `Course` GraphQL type has the `reviews` additional field along with the `id`, `name`, `category`, and `description` (which are also part of the equivalent Java `Course` type). Thus, in our GraphQL `courses` query, we can also access the reviews field. The following listing shows the modified courses GraphQL query request along with the review type.

Listing 10.35 The modified courses GraphQL query request

```
query {
  courses {
    id,
    name,
    category,
    description,
    reviews {
      id,
      courseId,
      rating,
      comment
    }
  }
}
```

However, if you try to access the `reviews` field, you'll find the `reviews` field for all courses are appearing as `null`. The output is shown in figure 10.16.

Figure 10.16 The courses GraphQL query output. The reviews fields in all courses are presented as null.

Although each course we've created in this application has reviews available, there is no mapping between a course and the associated review in the GraphQL schema. Let's do the schema mapping between the course and reviews. In the Spring Boot controller class, add the following `SchemaMapping` annotation, as shown in the following listing.

Listing 10.36 Schema mapping between course and review

```
@SchemaMapping(typeName = "Course")
Flux<Review> reviews(Course course) {
    return this.reviewRepository.findByCourseId(course.getId());
}
```

In listing 10.36, we provided the mapping through `@SchemaMapping` annotation for the `Course` type. The mapping is defined such that for a given course it returns all the reviews. Restart the application, and execute the GraphQL query, which is provided in listing 10.35. Figure 10.17 shows the query and the associated output.

Figure 10.17 The courses GraphQL endpoint output with the reviews mapping

DISCUSSION

With this technique, you've learned how to develop a GraphQL API with Spring Boot. Spring GraphQL is intended to provide GraphQL support on Spring Framework and is based on `graphql-java` (https://www.graphql-java.com/). The `graphql-java` project is the Java implementation of GraphQL.

Spring Boot provides support for GraphQL through the `graphql-spring-boot-starter` dependency. This dependency provides the necessary support for GraphQL autoconfiguration and brings necessary GraphQL libraries.

To define a GraphQL Spring Boot application, we've provided the GraphQL schema file inside the src\main\resources\graphql directory. You can customize this path by configuring the `spring.graphql.schema.locations` property in the application.properties file. Besides, in the Course Tracker example, we've placed all GraphQL type definitions in a single file. However, you can provide multiple graphqls files inside the graphql schema location if you need to segregate the type definitions. Further, by default, the Spring Boot GraphQL application runs on the /graphql path. You can customize the path to the `spring.graphql.path` property.

With this technique, we've used the Spring Boot GraphQL with the transport as HTTP. You can also use other protocols such as WebSocket as transport. Besides, with this technique, you've explored the `Query` and `Mutation` GraphQL types. We have another GraphQL type called `Subscription`. Let us explore these concepts in the next technique.

10.3.5 Technique: Developing a GraphQL API over WebSocket with a Spring Boot application

In this technique, we'll develop a GraphQL API over WebSocket protocol with a Spring Boot application.

Problem

In the previous technique, we saw the use of Spring Boot GraphQL over HTTP. We used the `Query` and `Mutation` GraphQL types. You want to explore the use of WebSocket as the transport. You also want to explore the use of the `Subscription` GraphQL type.

Solution

Previously, we used HTTP as the transport for the GraphQL Spring Boot application. Spring Boot GraphQL also allows you to use other protocols, such as WebSocket in place of HTTP. As we discussed in chapter 8, WebSocket is a different protocol that allows two-way communication between the client and server. With this technique, we'll explore using WebSocket protocol in the Course Tracker GraphQL Spring Boot application.

Source code

The final version of the Spring Boot project is available at http://mng.bz/wnNP.

To continue with this technique, we'll use the Spring Boot project used in the previous technique. The first change we'll introduce is adding the following properties to the application.properties file, as shown in the following listing.

Listing 10.37 Enable WebSocket support in the application

```
spring.graphql.websocket.connection-init-timeout=60
spring.graphql.websocket.path=/graphql
```

The first property defines the WebSocket connection initialization timeout to 60 seconds. It indicates the time within which a `CONNECTION_INIT` message must be received from the client. The second property enables WebSocket support in the application. Note that since we are using WebFlux in the current Course Tracker application, configuring the `spring.graphql.websocket.path` property is sufficient to enable the

WebFlux support. If you intend to use a Web MVC-based application, you need to include the `spring-boot-starter-websocket` dependency.

Next, let's define the `Subscription` type in the GraphQL schema. Open the schema.graphqls file available in the src\main\resources\graphql folder and include the following `Subscription` type definition, as shown in the following listing.

Listing 10.38 The subscription type definition

```
type Subscription {
    reviewEvents (courseId: Int) : Review
}
```

In listing 10.38, we defined a GraphQL subscription type called `reviewEvents`. It accepts an argument called `courseId` of GraphQL type `Int` and returns a `Review`.

Let's now define the associated subscription mapping in the Spring controller class. Open the `GraphqlCourseController` class, and include the following subscription mapping, as shown in the following listing.

Listing 10.39 The reviewEvents subscription mapping

```
@SubscriptionMapping
Flux<Review> reviewEvents(@Argument Integer courseId) {
    return this.courseRepository.findById(courseId)
            .flatMapMany(review ->
➥  this.reviewRepository.findByCourseId(review.getId()))
            .delayElements(Duration.ofSeconds(1))
            .take(5);
}
```

In listing 10.39, the `reviewEvents` mapping accepts the `courseId` argument and finds the available course. The `@Argument` annotation binds the `courseId` method parameter to the GraphQL input. Next, for the course, all available reviews are retrieved and sent back in one second. Note that, for simplicity reasons, we take a maximum of five reviews from the publisher.

The next step is to test the `Subscription` GraphQL endpoint. The tools, such as GraphiQL, Postman, and HTTPie, we've used to test the `Query` and `Mutation` endpoints are not suitable for `Subscription` type. Thus, we'll use a JavaScript-based HTML client to test the subscription mapping. The client is available at http://mng.bz/q2Kr. In this client, we are using a JavaScript library called `graphql-ws`, and this JavaScript file is intended for testing `Subscriptions`.

Start the application, and access the http://localhost:8080/index.html URL. Open the browser console, and you'll notice the following review details printed in the browser console, as shown in figure 10.18.

DISCUSSION

With this technique, you've explored the use of WebSocket in a Spring Boot GraphQL application. Also, we've demonstrated the use of GraphQL `Subscription` type with

Figure 10.18 Browser console output of the GraphQL subscription mapping. The reviews are printed in one second.

Spring Boot GraphQL subscription mapping. A subscription allows a client to subscribe to the events, and once the client accesses them, the events are streamed to the client. Like the other GraphQL types, Spring Boot provides the `@SubscriptionMapping` annotation to define a subscription mapping.

With the previous two techniques, we've covered how to define the `create` and `read` operations in a GraphQL API. You can also define the delete and update operations in a GraphQL API through the GraphQL `Mutation` type. We leave this as an exercise to you to develop the delete and update operations through the GraphQL mutation type.

Another important aspect is the GraphQL API security. Like you can secure REST API endpoints, you can also secure GraphQL API endpoints. Again, we are leaving using Spring Security to secure the endpoints as an exercise for the reader. You can find a sample application with HTTP Basic authentication available at http://mng.bz/7Wov.

Summary

- We introduced developing Spring Boot applications with Kotlin.
- We explored the use of Spring Boot with Kotlin DSLs.
- We covered generating Native Image of Spring Boot applications with GraalVM native image.
- We explored the use of buildpacks for building Spring Boot native image.
- We introduced generating a native image of Spring Boot application using GraalVM native build tools.
- We covered developing efficient APIs with Spring Boot GraphQL.
- We explored performing `Query`, `Mutation`, and `Subscription` with GraphQL.

appendix A Generating and building Spring Boot projects

In chapter 1, you learned the need for Spring Boot and its features and various components. In the next section, you'll learn the Spring Initializr tool and, subsequently, explore Spring Boot command-line interface (CLI).

A.1 Generating Spring Boot applications with Spring Initializr

In this section, we'll introduce the Spring Initializr tool and learn various techniques for generating a Spring Boot project through it.

A.1.1 Introducing Spring Initializr

Spring Initializr (https://start.spring.io/) is a project generation utility that allows you to generate Spring Boot projects. It also enables you to inspect the generated project structure before you download or share it. The generated project includes detail, such as the Spring Boot version; the project language, such as Java, Kotlin, or Groovy; the build framework, such as Maven or Gradle; and a few other configuration parameters.

Spring Initializr has an extensible API, which means you can customize it to suit your requirements. You can use the Web version of Spring Initializr API through a Web browser by visiting https://start.spring.io. You can also use the embedded version of this API integrated into popular IDEs, such as IntelliJ IDEA, Spring Tool Suite, and Microsoft Visual Studio Code.

Maven or Gradle?

Spring Initializr allows you to choose the build framework, while you generate a Spring Boot project. It supports two popular build frameworks: Apache Maven (https://maven.apache.org/) and Gradle (https://gradle.org/). Both frameworks have their merits and demerits. Many developers are comfortable with Maven, due to its widespread usage and familiar XML-based syntax; however, some developers prefer Gradle due to its conciseness, flexibility, and performance.

Either way, feel free to use your preferred build framework. In this book, our primary focus is on the Spring Boot features with minimal reference to the build tool. Thus, your selection of a build framework plays a small role in continuing with the techniques presented in this book.

We'll use Apache Maven as the default build tool in all techniques, as most readers are familiar with it. However, if you prefer Gradle over Maven, it should not be difficult to port the code snippets to Gradle-based project.

A.1.2 Technique: Generating a Spring Boot application with the Spring Initializr Web user interface

In this technique, we'll demonstrate how to generate a Spring Boot application with Spring Initializr Web user interface.

Problem

You want to generate a Spring Boot Project through Spring Initializr Web user interface.

Solution

Spring Boot provides a default instance of Spring Initializr at https://start.spring.io. This application has a Web-based user interface that allows you to choose various options to generate a Spring Boot project. These options include the project build tool (e.g., Maven or Gradle), language (e.g., Java, Kotlin, or Groovy), Spring Boot release version, and other options.

Spring Boot and Java version

Spring Boot and Java release new versions based on their release calendar. Thus, depending on when you access the Spring Initializr (website, IDE, or through other means), you'll find a different version than what is shown in this appendix. While you create Spring Boot projects, select the appropriate version available at the time you access the Spring Initializr.

Figure A.1 shows the https://start.spring.io Web page with the required details. Along with the basic details, such as the Spring Boot version and project metadata, you've also selected `Spring Web` dependency in this example. This dependency provides necessary supports for Web application development.

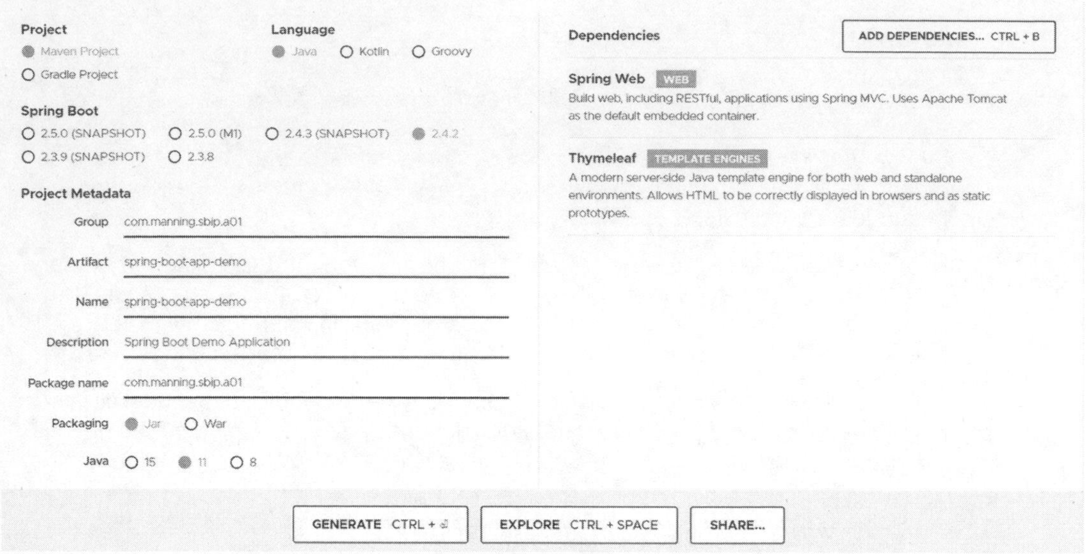

Figure A.1 Spring Initializr Web User Interface at https://start.spring.io

Spring Initializr changes its user interface periodically. Thus, you may find an altered user interface, depending on when you are reading this book. You may also find a different Spring Boot version if a new Spring Boot version is released.

Following are the list of supported Spring Initializr options for generating a Spring Boot project:

- *Spring Boot version*—This option allows you to select the Spring Boot version. Spring Initializr provides the current stable version, previous stable versions, and the snapshot versions. The default selected value is the current stable version.
- *Build system*—You can select the build framework for the generated project. The supported build systems are Apache Maven and Gradle. By default, Spring Initializr generates a Maven project.
- *JVM language*—You can choose the JVM language for the generated project. For instance, you can generate a Java, Kotlin, or Groovy-based project. The default language is Java.
- *Packaging*—A generated Spring Boot project can be packaged as a WAR or JAR file. You can select the packaging type as either JAR or WAR when generating the project. Based on the selection, Spring Initializr provides the packaging configuration in the generated project.
- *Java version*—Spring Initializr allows you to choose the Java version for the generated project. Supported versions are Java 15, 11, and 8, where Java 11 is the default Java version. Note that Spring Initializr updates the Java version with

newly released Java versions. Therefore, you'll find different values, depending on when you are accessing this content.

- *Dependencies*—Spring Initializr lists the frequently used Spring Boot starters and other required dependencies for you to choose from while generating the project. You can select one or more of these dependencies, depending on your requirement. For instance, if you are generating a Spring Boot Web project with Thymeleaf (https://www.thymeleaf.org), you can select the Spring Web and the Thymeleaf dependencies.

Specify all the parameters in the https://start.spring.io page, and select the required dependencies, as shown in figure A.1. You can then press the Generate button to generate and download the project to your machine. Spring Initializr provides a ZIP archive of the generated project. Figure A.2 shows the folder structure of the generated Spring Boot Maven project.

```
C:\sbip\repo\appendix01\spring-boot-app-demo>tree /f
Folder PATH listing for volume OS
Volume serial number is 8EF3-F5B9
C:.
│   .gitignore
│   HELP.md
│   mvnw
│   mvnw.cmd
│   pom.xml
│
├───.mvn
│   └───wrapper
│           maven-wrapper.jar
│           maven-wrapper.properties
│           MavenWrapperDownloader.java
│
└───src
    ├───main
    │   ├───java
    │   │   └───com
    │   │       └───manning
    │   │           └───sbip
    │   │               └───a01
    │   │                       SpringBootAppDemoApplication.java
    │   │
    │   └───resources
    │       │   application.properties
    │       │
    │       ├───static
    │       └───templates
    └───test
        └───java
            └───com
                └───manning
                    └───sbip
                        └───a01
                                SpringBootAppDemoApplicationTests.java
```

Figure A.2 Spring Boot Maven project structure

The generated project contains the following components:

- Maven wrapper
- Project source code
- Project test code
- Project resources

Spring Initializr provides a Maven wrapper to build the generated project. The purpose of it is that you can build the Spring Boot application with Maven without explicitly installing Maven on your machine. You can use the `mvnw install` command to build the application, as shown in figure A.3. Similarly, if you've generated a Gradle-based project, Spring Initializr provides a Gradle wrapper to build the application without explicitly installing Gradle in your machine.

```
C:\sbip\repo\appendix01\spring-boot-app-demo>mvnw install
[INFO] Scanning for projects...
[INFO]
[INFO] -------------< com.manning.sbip.a01:spring-boot-app-demo >-------------
[INFO] Building spring-boot-app-demo 0.0.1-SNAPSHOT
[INFO] --------------------------------[ jar ]---------------------------------
[INFO]
[INFO] --- maven-resources-plugin:3.2.0:resources (default-resources) @ spring-boot-app-demo ---
[INFO] Using 'UTF-8' encoding to copy filtered resources.
[INFO] Using 'UTF-8' encoding to copy filtered properties files.
[INFO] Copying 1 resource
[INFO] Copying 0 resource
[INFO]
[INFO] --- maven-compiler-plugin:3.8.1:compile (default-compile) @ spring-boot-app-demo ---
[INFO] Changes detected - recompiling the module!
[INFO] Compiling 1 source file to C:\sbip\repo\appendix01\spring-boot-app-demo\target\classes
[INFO]
[INFO] --- maven-resources-plugin:3.2.0:testResources (default-testResources) @ spring-boot-app-demo ---
[INFO] Using 'UTF-8' encoding to copy filtered resources.
[INFO] Using 'UTF-8' encoding to copy filtered properties files.
[INFO] skip non existing resourceDirectory C:\sbip\repo\appendix01\spring-boot-app-demo\src\test\resources
[INFO]
[INFO] --- maven-compiler-plugin:3.8.1:testCompile (default-testCompile) @ spring-boot-app-demo ---
[INFO] Changes detected - recompiling the module!
[INFO] Compiling 1 source file to C:\sbip\repo\appendix01\spring-boot-app-demo\target\test-classes
[INFO]
[INFO] --- maven-surefire-plugin:2.22.2:test (default-test) @ spring-boot-app-demo ---
[INFO]
```

Figure A.3 Building the generated application with Maven wrapper

In the project source code, Spring Initializr generates a Java class with the `main` method in the generated Spring Boot application (e.g., `SpringBootAppDemoApplication.java`). This class allows you to start the Spring Boot application. You can run this Java file using your IDE's application start option and see the generated Spring Boot project has started in the HTTP port 8080.

In the project test code, Spring Initializr provides an empty test class (e.g., `SpringBootAppDemoApplicationTests.java`) to write test cases for your project. Spring Boot automatically includes a few commonly used testing frameworks, such as

JUnit, Mockito (https://site.mockito.org/), and XMLUnit (https://www.xmlunit.org/) in your project.

In the resources folder, the generated Spring Boot project has an empty configuration file called application.properties. You can use this file to provide additional configuration to control the application's behavior. For instance, if you want to run the project in a different HTTP port other than the Spring Boot default port `8080`, you can configure it here by specifying the `server.port` property. Besides, since we've selected `Spring Web` dependency, Spring Initializr has also created the static and template folders for the static Web resources, such as CSS files, images, and HTML template files, respectively.

Spring Initializr also provides two additional features to view and share the generated project for convenience:

- You can explore the generated project structure on the user interface before downloading it to the local machine. This is a convenient feature that allows you to explore the project components before you download them. Figure A.4 shows the pom.xml file from the explored project components.

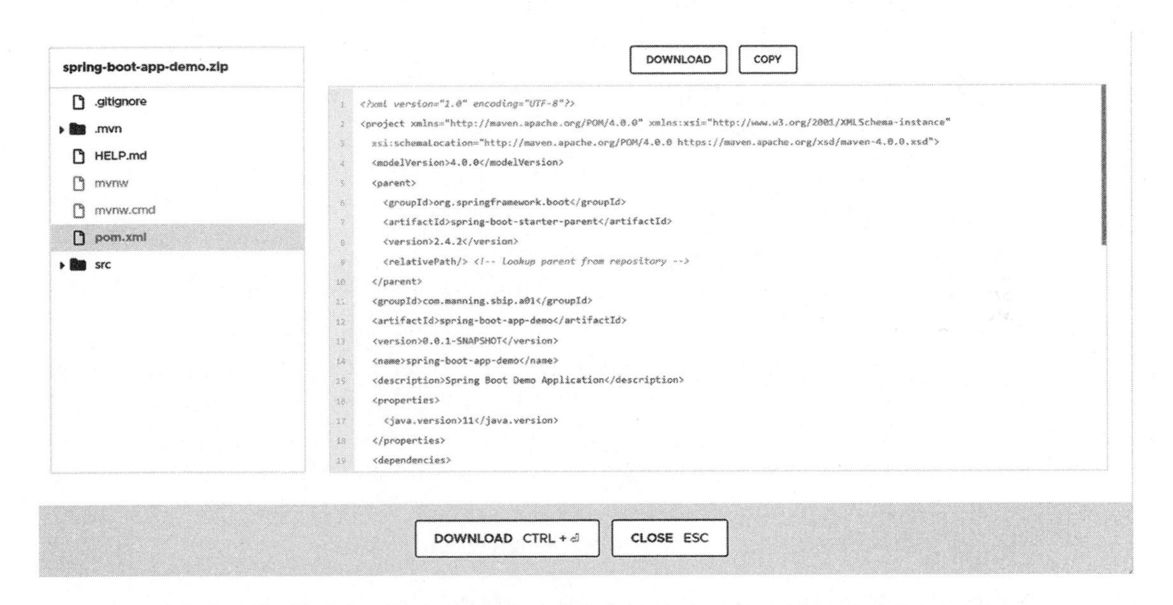

Figure A.4 Exploring the project structure of generated Spring Boot project in https://start.spring.io

- You can also generate a URL of the project that contains the configurations you've selected. This URL can be shared with anyone, and they can find the same selected details and dependencies once they access the shared URL. For example, in listing A.1, the following URL has configurations with Gradle build system, Kotlin language, Java 15, and WAR packaging.

Listing A.1 Sharable URL of the generated project

```
https://start.spring.io/#!type=gradle-
➥ project&language=kotlin&platformVersion=2.4.3.RELEASE&packaging=war&jvm
➥ Version=15&groupId=com.manning%2Csbip.a01&artifactId=spring-boot-
➥ app&name=spring-boot-
➥ app&description=Spring%20Boot%20project%20for%20Appendix%20A&packageNam
➥ e=com.manning%2Csbip.a01.spring-boot-app&dependencies=web
```

DISCUSSION

Spring Initializr is a fantastic tool that has made Spring Boot project generation an extremely easy task. The Web-based UI allows you to provide the configuration parameters needed to generate the project, and in a single click you have a workable project. It also allows you to inspect the generated project structure before you download it to your machine.

Although the Web-based version is useful, you'll eventually need to import the generated project into an IDE to continue with the application development. To make this process further simplified, Spring Initializr provides an extensible API that major IDE vendors embed, so you can generate the project in the IDE itself. Let's explore this, using the next technique.

A.1.3 *Technique: Generating a Spring Boot application with Spring Initializr in IntelliJ IDEA IDE*

In this technique, we'll show how to generate a Spring Boot application with Spring Initializr in Intellij IDEA IDE.

PROBLEM

You want to generate a Spring Boot project through Spring Initializr in IntelliJ IDEA IDE.

SOLUTION

Spring Initializr is a flexible API and is frequently used in standalone mode through the Web and the CLI. However, to further simplify the project generation, major IDE vendors have embedded Spring Initializr support into their IDEs. With this technique, you'll see how to generate a Spring Boot project in IntelliJ IDEA IDE using its built-in Spring Initializr support. You can find the generated project in the companion GitHub repository of this book at http://mng.bz/KByP.

> **IntelliJ IDEA editions**
>
> IntelliJ IDEA is available in two editions: Community and Ultimate (https://www.jetbrains.com/idea/download/). The Community edition does not have built-in support for Spring Initializr. However, the Ultimate edition, the paid version of the IDE, supports Spring Initializr. If you want to use the steps provided in this technique, you need to use the Ultimate edition. Although it is a paid version, the Ultimate edition is available for trial for 30 days, so you can try out the features it offers.

If you don't have access to the Ultimate edition, you can continue with the Community edition by generating the Spring Boot project through the https://start.spring.io, as shown in the previous technique and importing the extracted archive in the IDE.

To generate a Spring Boot project, browse to File > New > Project, and Select Spring Initializr, as shown in figure A.5. By default, the IDE selects https://start.spring.io as the Initializr service URL. Alternatively, you can provide your own Spring Initializr URL if you have customized the Initializr Service.

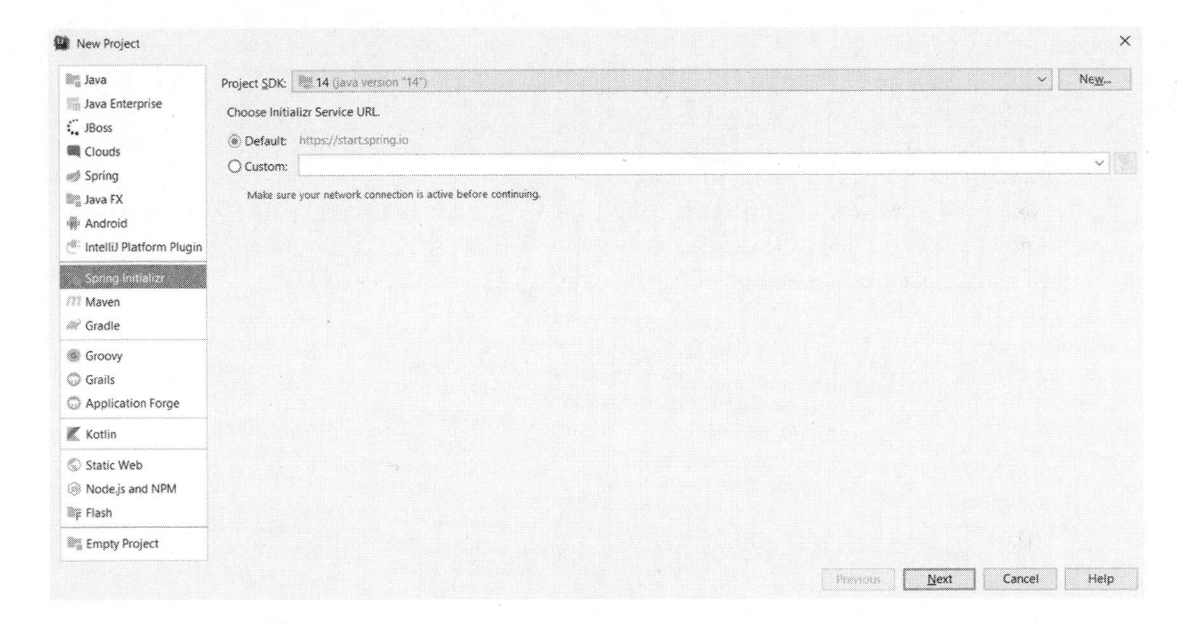

Figure A.5 Generating a Spring Boot Project in IntelliJ IDEA with built-in Spring Initializr support

On the subsequent page, you'll see the options to provide additional project metadata, such as project coordinates (e.g., group ID, artifact ID, and version), language, packaging type, and Java version, as shown in figure A.6. The group ID, artifact ID, and version allow you to uniquely identify your application. In general, the group ID represents the group or unit the application belongs to. The artifact ID is the application name, and the version is the application version. As you include new features to your application, you increase this version.

The type field indicates the build tool we'll use in our application. Supported types are Apache Maven and Gradle. Language represents the programming language you'll use to develop the application. Supported languages are Java, Kotlin, and Groovy. Packaging represents, once you build the application, how it should be packaged. JAR and WAR are supported types.

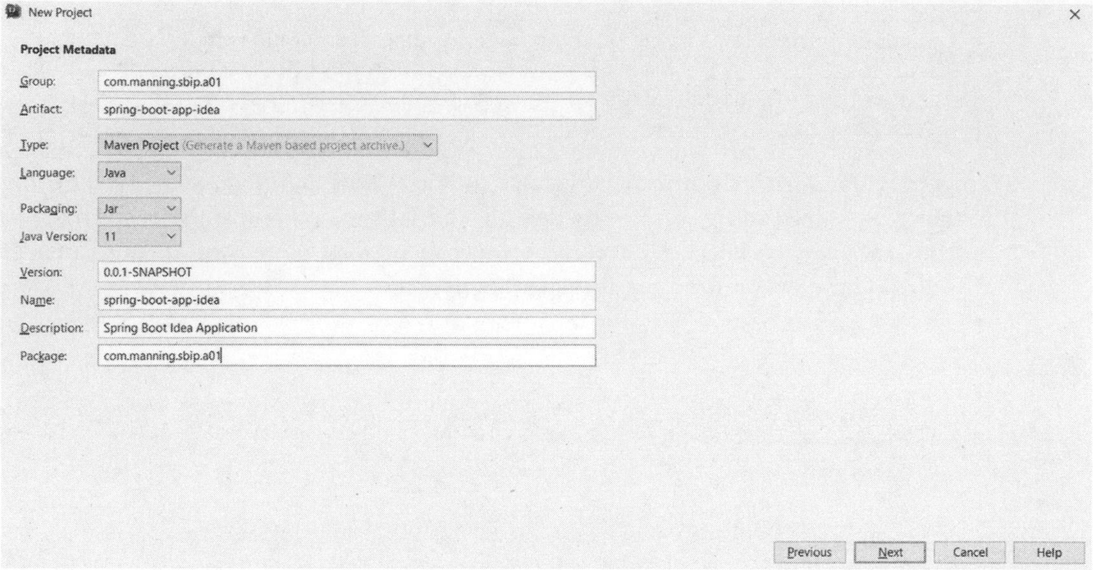

Figure A.6 Providing project metadata for the generated Spring Boot Project in IntelliJ IDEA

On the next page, you can choose the dependencies required for your project and the Spring Boot version, as shown in figure A.7.

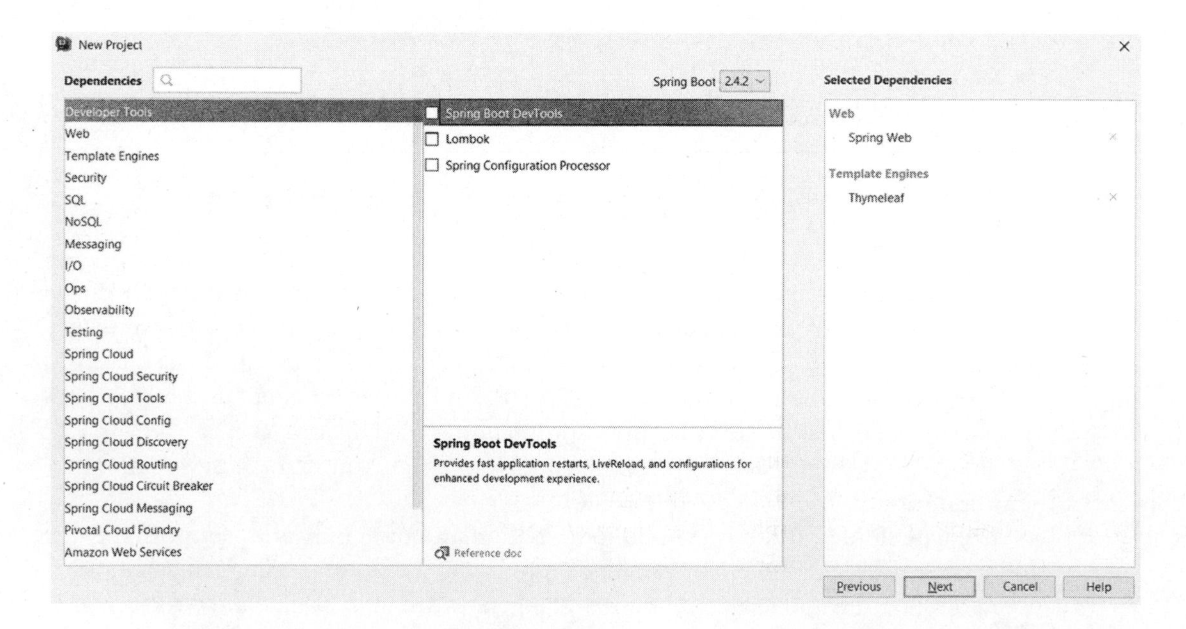

Figure A.7 Spring Boot dependencies list in IntelliJ IDEA

As shown in figure A.7, you can find the dependencies are categorized in the relevant headers, and all the related dependencies are listed under each category. After selecting the required dependencies, you can choose the project name and location and generate the project.

The IDE pulls the selected dependencies from the central repository and configures the project. Figure A.8 shows the final generated project in the IntelliJ IDEA. If you run the `SpringBootAppIdeaApplication` using the IDE's run option, you'll see the generated Spring Boot project starts in the default HTTP 8080 port.

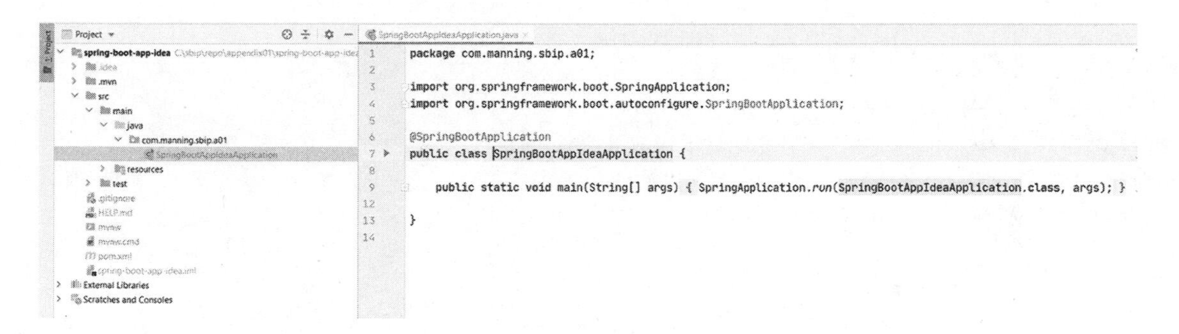

Figure A.8 Generated Spring Boot Project in IntelliJ IDEA

DISCUSSION

In this technique, you've seen how to generate a Spring Boot project in IntelliJ IDEA IDE. The IDE allows you to specify the Spring Initializr options to generate the project. Once you've provided all the required details, it generates the project and shows it in the project explorer. In the next technique, let's discuss generating a Spring Boot project in the Spring Tool Suite.

A.1.4 Technique: Generating a Spring Boot Application with Spring Initializr using the Spring Tool Suite

In this technique, we'll discuss how to generate a Spring Boot application with Spring Initializr in Spring Tool Suite (STS).

PROBLEM

You want to generate a Spring Boot application through the built-in Spring Initializr in Spring Tool Suite.

SOLUTION

Spring Tool Suite (https://spring.io/tools) is an eclipse-based IDE by the Spring team for Spring-based application development. Like the IntelliJ IDEA, STS also has built-in integration with Spring Initializr service and allows you to generate a Spring Boot project through the IDE.

To create a Spring Boot application in STS, click on File > New > Spring Starter Project, and you'll see the screen shown in figure A.9. You can find the generated project in the companion GitHub repository of this book at http://mng.bz/9Krx.

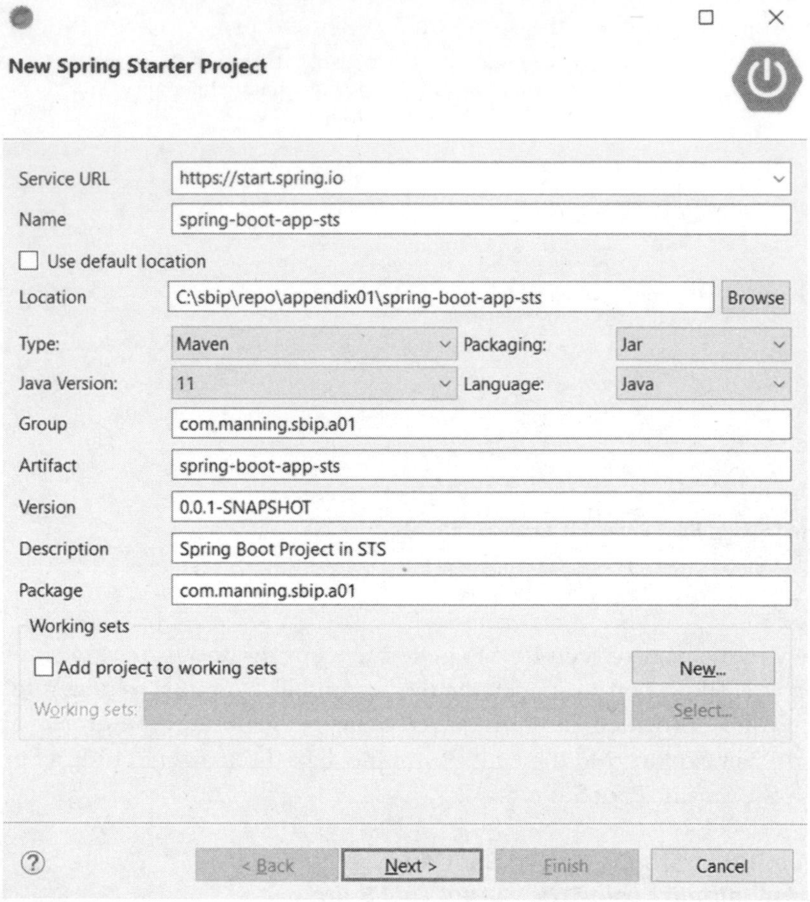

Figure A.9 Generating a Spring Boot project in Spring Tool Suite

STS loads these parameters and the default values from https://start.spring.io. On the next page, STS allows you to select the Spring Boot version and specify the required dependencies for your project, as shown in figure A.10.

After selecting the dependencies, STS generates the Spring Boot project and loads the selected dependencies, as shown in figure A.11.

STS provides a boot dashboard for developer convenience. It displays all Spring Boot projects available in the workspace and provides quick control, allowing you to perform several activities, such as restarting and debugging your application. You can

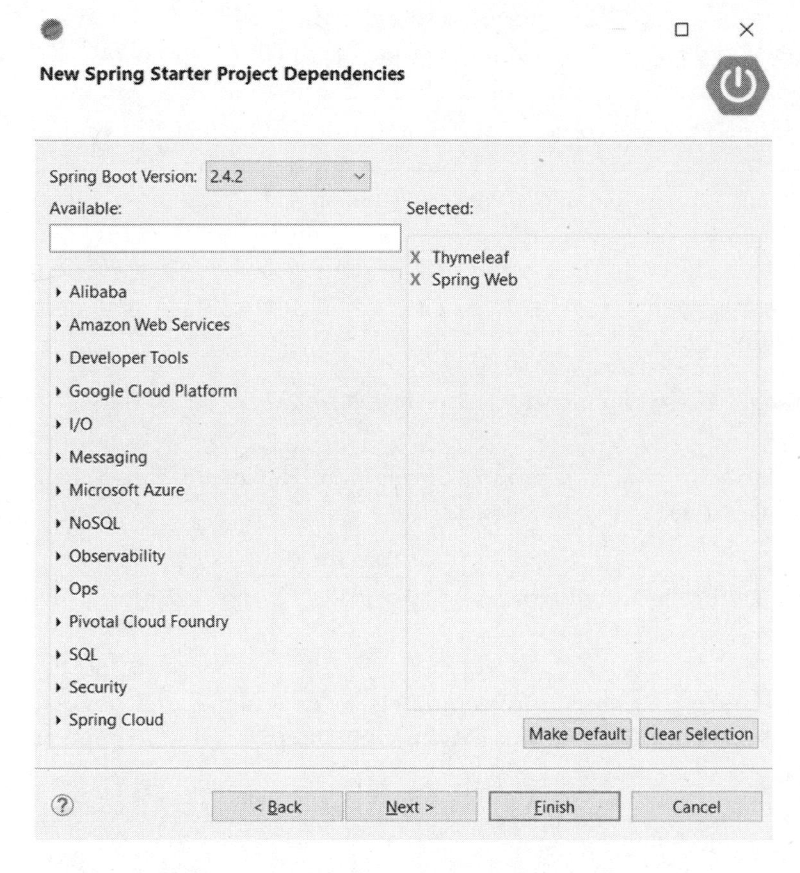

Figure A.10 Spring Boot Version and Dependencies list in Spring Tool Suite

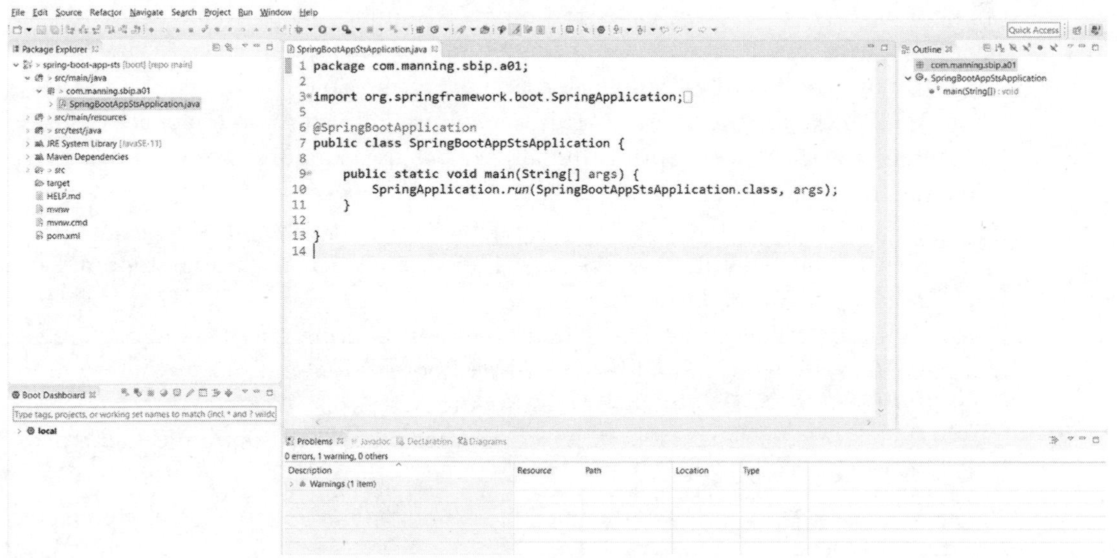

Figure A.11 Generated Spring Boot project and the Spring Boot dashboard in the Spring Tool Suite

run the `SpringBootAppStsApplication` Java file using the IDE's run option and see that STS starts the generated Spring Boot project in the default HTTP port 8080.

DISCUSSION

In this technique, you've learned how to generate a Spring Boot project in Spring Tool Suite. Spring Tool Suite, which is a customized version of eclipse for Spring application development, also implements Spring Initializr API and allows you to specify the required options to generate the project. The generated project is then displayed in the project explorer. In the next technique, let's learn how to generate a Spring Boot project in Microsoft Visual Studio Code—one of the most popular code editors across the technology spectrum.

A.1.5 Technique: Generating a Spring application with Spring Initializr in Visual Studio Code

In this technique, we'll discuss how to generate a Spring Boot application with Spring Initializr in Visual Studio Code.

PROBLEM

You want to generate a Spring Boot application with Spring Initializr in Visual Studio Code.

SOLUTION

Visual Studio Code (https://code.visualstudio.com/) is an extension-based popular text editor from Microsoft. This code editor is a lightweight alternative to the popular IDEs to develop Spring Boot applications.

To be able to generate a Spring Boot project in Visual Studio Code or VS Code in short, you need to install the following extensions:

- *Spring Boot tools*—This extension provides support for the validation and content assist for Spring Boot application.properties and application.yml properties files, and Spring Boot-specific support for Java files.
- *Spring Initializr Java support*—This is a lightweight extension to generate Spring Boot projects using Spring Initializr. This also supports Kotlin and Groovy-based project generation.
- *Spring Boot dashboard*—This extension allows you to view and manage all Spring Boot applications in the workspace with features, such as starting, stopping, and debugging the applications.

> **Configuring JAVA_HOME**
>
> You need to configure the Java home path for Visual Studio Code to use the appropriate Java version. You can do this by configuring `java.home` variable in Visual Studio Code. To set `java.home`, navigate to File > Preferences > Settings > Workspace, and search for `java.home`. You can find the option `Edit` in `settings.json` and provide the Java version of your choice.

> Note that Visual Studio Code does not let you select the Java version while you generate the Spring Boot Project with it. By default, it selects `Java 1.8`, while generating the project. You can edit the generated project's pom.xml (for Maven) or the build.gradle (for Gradle) file to provide the Java version you have configured in `java.home`.

Pivotal (the company behind Spring Framework) provides an extension pack to develop Spring Boot application applications in VS Code. This pack consists of several extensions, including the three mentioned earlier. You can install this Spring Boot Extension Pack to access the complete extension suite. To install the extension pack, browse to the extensions option in the editor, and search for Spring Boot, as shown in figure A.12.

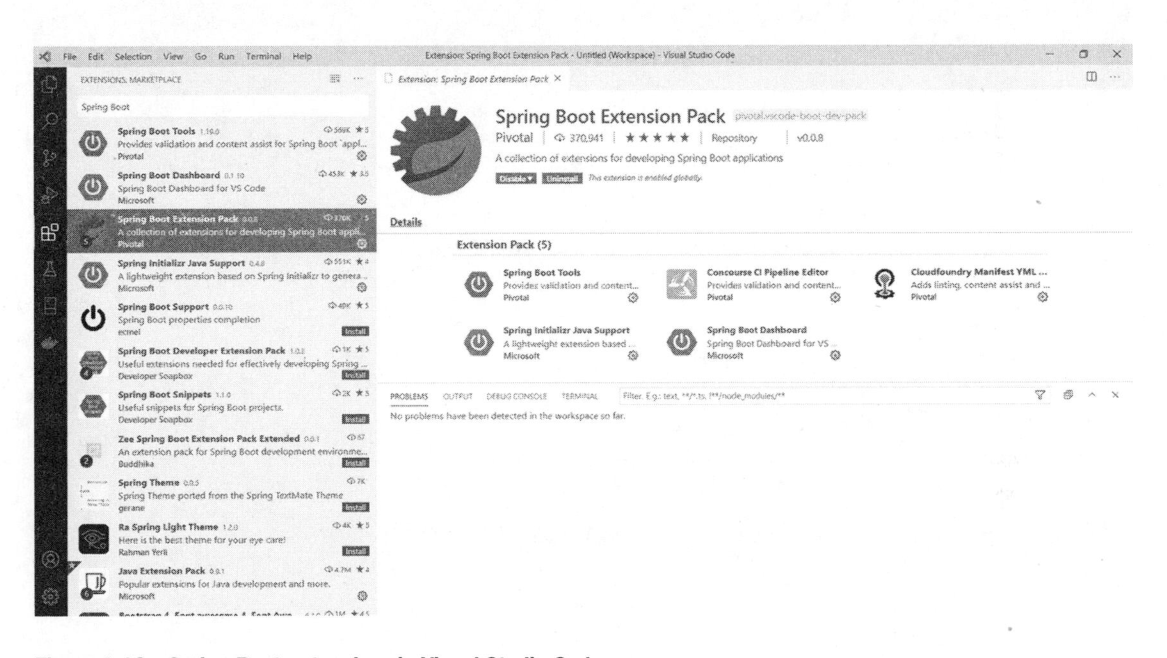

Figure A.12 Spring Boot extensions in Visual Studio Code

After successfully installing the extension pack, you can create Spring Boot projects in the editor. To start creating a Spring Boot project, open the Command Palette by browsing to View > Command Palette and searching for Spring Initializr. You'll find options to create a Maven- or Gradle-based Spring Boot application, as shown in figure A.13.

To create a project, select the required options, and follow along with the parameters. After the project is successfully generated, you will find the folder structure, as shown in figure A.14. On the left side, there is the generated project structure Spring Boot dashboard to start and stop the application, and in the editor, you can explore the project components.

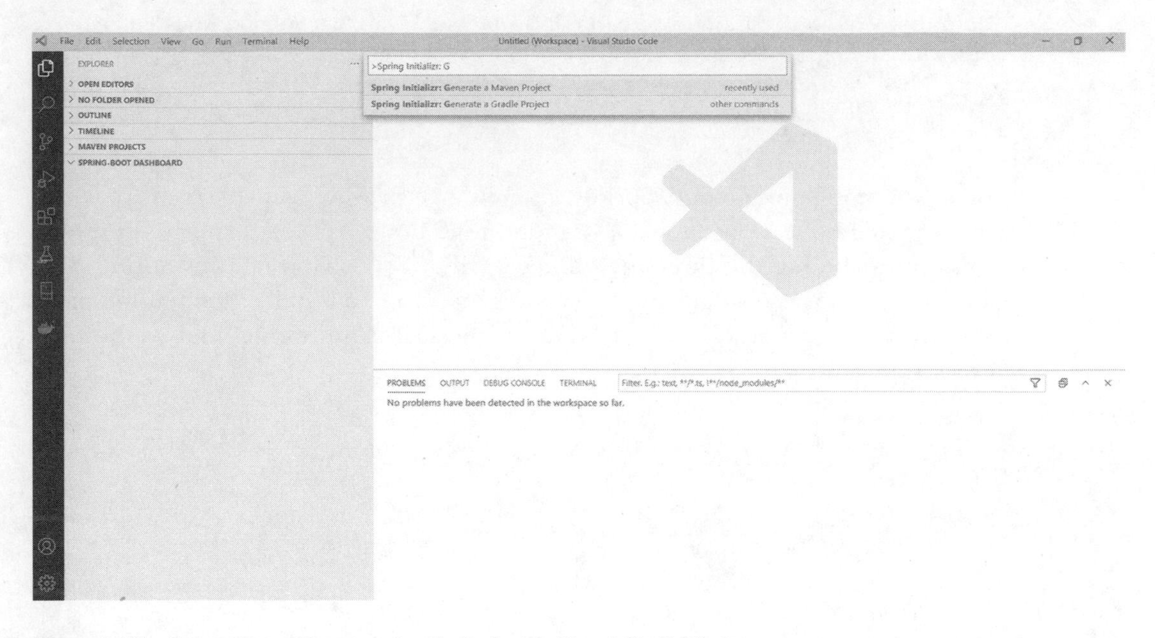

Figure A.13 Generating a Maven or Gradle Project in Visual Studio Code

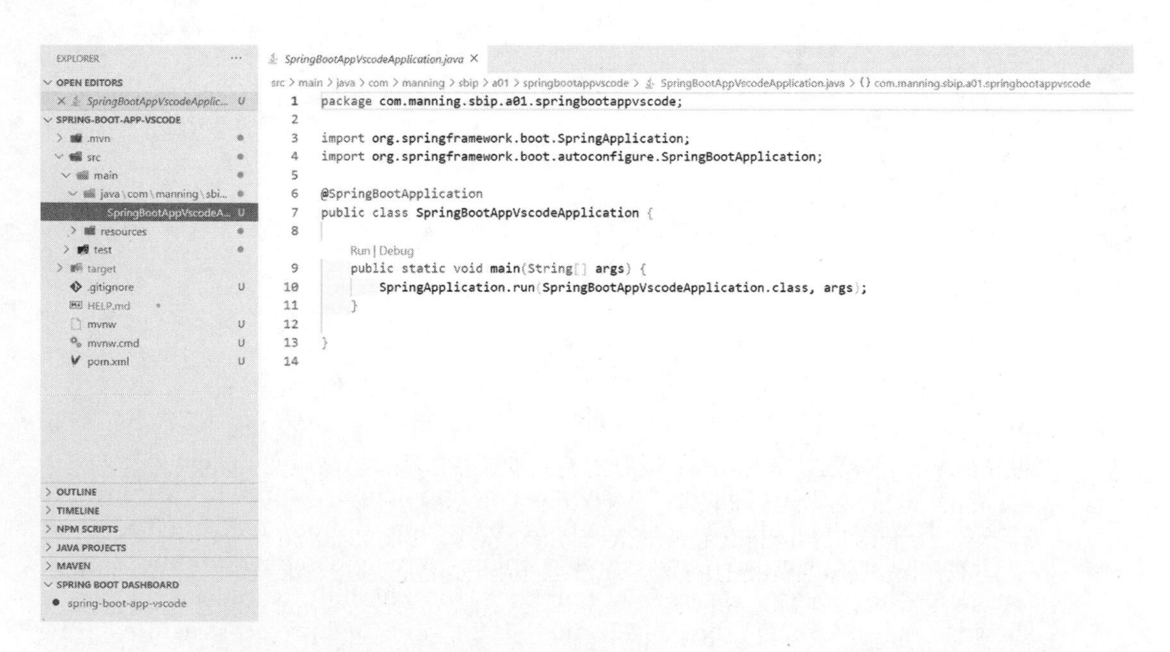

Figure A.14 Generated Spring Boot project in Visual Studio Code

You can find the generated project in the companion GitHub repository of this book at http://mng.bz/jyJz. After project generation, if you need to add additional dependencies, you can do it by using the Edit Starters option of the editor. You can navigate to the pom file and right-click to select the Edit Starters option. The editor will display the previously selected dependencies with the right tick symbol and allow you to specify additional dependencies, as shown in figure A.16.

In figure A.15, we have selected the Edit Starters option, and the Visual Studio Code shows us the previously selected dependencies with the right-tick symbol. We have also selected the Spring Boot DevTools Developer Tools dependency this time.

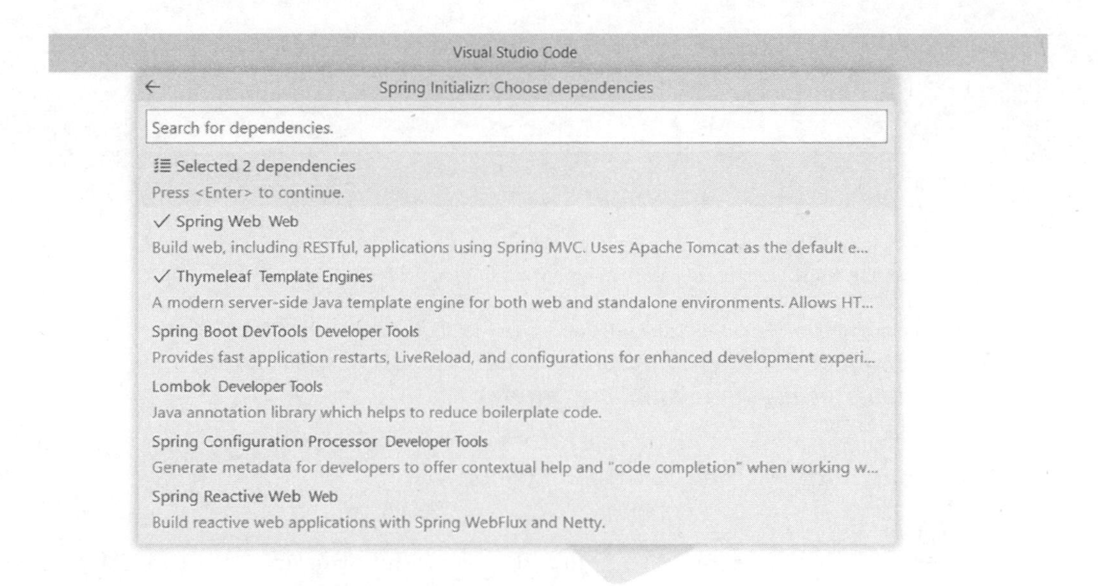

Figure A.15 Editing starter dependencies in Visual Studio Code

As shown in figure A.16, you can start the application from Spring-Boot Dashboard by clicking the start button and seeing the generated Spring project has started in default HTTP port 8080. Application startup logs are visible in the debug console.

DISCUSSION

With this technique, you've seen how to enable Spring Boot support in VS Code editor and generate a Spring Boot project. VS Code is a popular code editor, and many developers prefer this lightweight alternative for Spring Boot application development.

So far, you've seen the UI-based approaches to generate Spring Boot applications. However, there is a community of developers that prefers command-line utilities for their conciseness and simplicity. In the next technique, you'll see the use of Spring Boot CLI to generate a Spring Boot application.

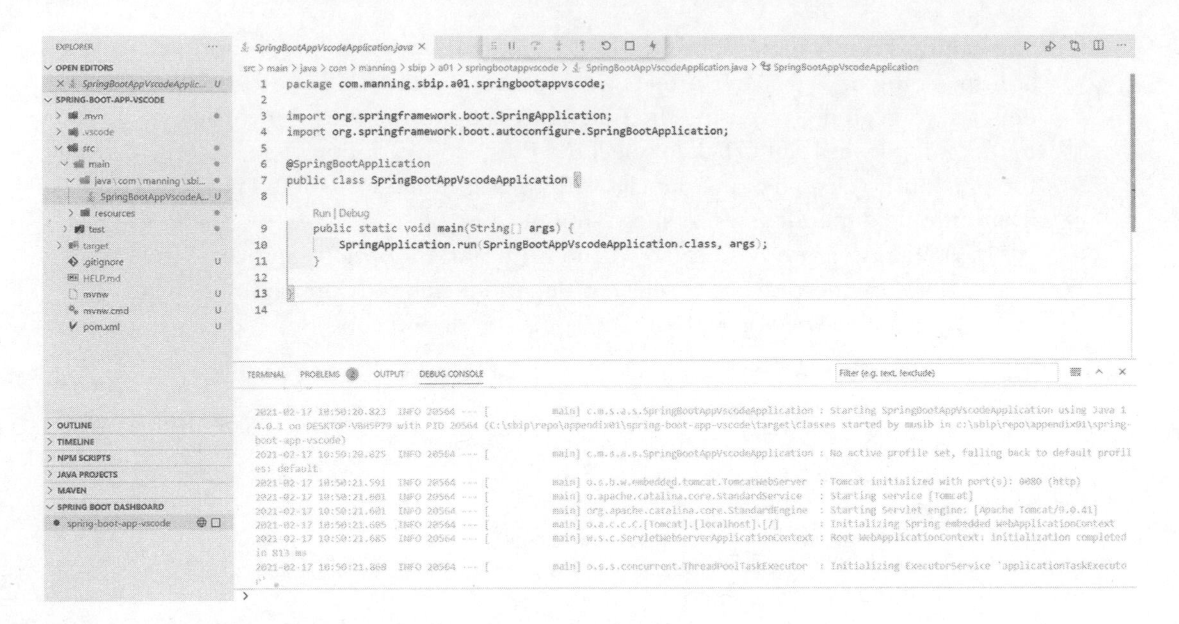

Figure A.16 Spring Boot dashboard and debug console in Visual Studio Code

A.1.6 Technique: Generating a Spring Boot application with Spring Initializr using Command Line Interface

In this technique, we'll demonstrate how to generate a Spring Boot application with Spring Initializr using Command Line Interface.

Problem

You want to generate a Spring Boot Project with Spring Initializr through CLI.

Solution

Spring Initializr has an extensible API and provides various ways to generate a Spring Boot project. The Spring Initializr Web interface is a popular option for Spring project generation. However, many developers prefer to use command-line tools to generate the project. Spring Initializr supports several popular third-party command-line tools, such as cURL, HTTPie (https://httpie.org/), and Spring's own CLI to create a Spring Boot project from the command line.

However, one of the drawbacks while using the CLI is that you need to be familiar with the parameter and dependency names beforehand to use those in the CLI command. To avoid this drawback, Spring provides nicely formatted tabular details of Spring Initializr options, which consist of the build framework, project parameters, and dependency names. This detail can be obtained by accessing the https://start.spring.io URL. Let's view these details from your command-line tool using the following command: `curl` https://start.spring.io.

Figure A.17 displays the options of Spring Initializr service in three different sections:

1. The first table provides the available project types. For instance, it lists four project types: `gradle-build`, `gradle-project`, `maven-build`, and `maven-project`.
2. The second table provides the set of available parameters, a brief description, and the default values. Most of these parameters are similar to what is available in the Web version with a difference in the `applicationName` and `baseDir`. The application name parameter can be used to define the application name instead of deducing it from the name parameter. The `baseDir` can be used to create a base directory in the generated archive, so you can extract the generated ZIP without creating a directory for it first.
3. The third table lists all the available dependencies you can use in your project.

```
C:\sbip\repo\appendix01>curl https://start.spring.io
  .   ____          _            __ _ _
 /\\ / ___'_ __ _ _(_)_ __  __ _ \ \ \ \
( ( )\___ | '_ | '_| | '_ \/ _` | \ \ \ \
 \\/  ___)| |_)| | | | | || (_| |  ) ) ) )
  '  |____| .__|_| |_|_| |_\__, | / / / /
 =========|_|==============|___/=/_/_/_/
:: Spring Initializr ::  https://start.spring.io

This service generates quickstart projects that can be easily customized.
Possible customizations include a project's dependencies, Java version, and
build system or build structure. See below for further details.

The services uses a HAL based hypermedia format to expose a set of resources
to interact with. If you access this root resource requesting application/json
as media type the response will contain the following links:
+-----------------+-----------------------------------------+
| Rel             | Description                             |
+-----------------+-----------------------------------------+
| gradle-build    | Generate a Gradle build file.           |
| gradle-project  | Generate a Gradle based project archive. |
| maven-build     | Generate a Maven pom.xml.               |
| maven-project * | Generate a Maven based project archive. |
+-----------------+-----------------------------------------+


The URI templates take a set of parameters to customize the result of a request
to the linked resource.
+-----------------+------------------------------------------+------------------------------+
| Parameter       | Description                              | Default value                |
+-----------------+------------------------------------------+------------------------------+
| applicationName | application name                         | DemoApplication              |
| artifactId      | project coordinates (infer archive name) | demo                         |
| baseDir         | base directory to create in the archive  | no base dir                  |
| bootVersion     | spring boot version                      | 2.4.2                        |
| dependencies    | dependency identifiers (comma-separated) | none                         |
| description     | project description                      | Demo project for Spring Boot |
| groupId         | project coordinates                      | com.example                  |
| javaVersion     | language level                           | 11                           |
| language        | programming language                     | java                         |
| name            | project name (infer application name)    | demo                         |
| packageName     | root package                             | com.example.demo             |
| packaging       | project packaging                        | jar                          |
| type            | project type                             | maven-project                |
| version         | project version                          | 0.0.1-SNAPSHOT               |
+-----------------+------------------------------------------+------------------------------+


The following section has a list of supported identifiers for the comma-separated
list of "dependencies".
+--------------------------------------+--------------------------------------------------------------+-------------------------------+
| Id                                   | Description                                                  | Required version              |
+--------------------------------------+--------------------------------------------------------------+-------------------------------+
| activemq                             | Spring JMS support with Apache ActiveMQ 'Classic'.           |                               |
```

Figure A.17 Accessing https://start.spring.io through cURL

You can generate a Spring Boot project with these parameters and the dependencies specified with the `-d` parameter. Table A.1 demonstrates the usage of Spring Boot project generation with `cURL` utility.

Table A.1 Using cURL to generate a Spring Boot project

Command	Remarks
`curl https://start.spring.io/starter.zip -o demo.zip`	This command generates a Spring Boot project with all default parameters. In the command, we download the generated project as demo.zip.
`curl https://start.spring.io/starter.zip -d dependencies=web,data-jpa -d type=gradle-project`	This command generates a Spring Boot Gradle project with Spring Web and Spring Data JPA dependencies.
`curl https://start.spring.io/build.gradle -d packaging=war -d javaVersion=15 -o build.gradle`	This command generates only a Gradle build file (build.gradle) with WAR packaging and Java version 15.

DISCUSSION

Using this technique, you've seen how to use the command-line utility `cURL` to generate a Spring Boot project. This CLI approach is flexible, and you can control the project generation using the appropriate parameters. Now that you've learned to generate a Spring Boot project, let's explore the various components of the generated project in the next section.

A.2 Bootstrapping and executing a Spring Boot application with Spring Boot CLI

The Spring Boot CLI is a command-line utility that allows you to create prototypes for Spring applications. It allows you to quickly bootstrap a Spring Boot application without the need for a dependency management tool, such as Maven or Gradle. Besides, Spring Boot CLI allows you to use Groovy (https://groovy-lang.org/) script, so you can use familiar, Java-like syntax but with less noisy syntax. For example, Groovy automatically includes several Java packages in your code, and you need not provide import statements for the members from these packages, as shown in listing A.2.

Listing A.2 Packages imported by Groovy by default

```
import java.lang.*
import java.util.*
import java.io.*
import java.net.*
```

You will also investigate a few other features of Groovy, where it is less noisy than Java. But before that, you'll install Spring Boot CLI and have some hands-on experience.

> **Spring Boot CLI and Groovy**
>
> Spring Boot CLI uses Groovy language. The primary agenda of the Spring Boot CLI tool is to quickly prototype a Spring Boot application and try out various features offered by Spring. Spring Boot CLI does not use a dependency management tool, such as Maven or Gradle, to keep things easy and straightforward. Groovy, being a less verbose language, is the choice while working with Spring Boot CLI. Furthermore, much of the Groovy syntax is similar to Java. Thus, to follow along with the code examples in this section, most of your Java knowledge will be sufficient. In the code examples, if we are using features specific to Groovy, we'll explain.

A.2.1 Installing the Spring Boot CLI

Installing the Spring Boot CLI is easy and can be done in several ways. You can follow any of the following approaches to install Spring Boot CLI:

1. *Manual installation through the Spring Boot CLI ZIP*

   Take the following steps to configure Spring Boot CLI manually:

   – Download the latest Spring Boot CLI archive from the Spring software repository (http://mng.bz/W794) to your machine.

   – Extract the ZIP to the development folder, and you'll find a folder structure, as shown in figure A.18.

bin	15/01/2021 2:55 AM	File folder	
legal	15/01/2021 2:55 AM	File folder	
lib	15/01/2021 2:57 AM	File folder	
shell-completion	15/01/2021 2:55 AM	File folder	
INSTALL.txt	15/01/2021 2:55 AM	TXT File	2 KB
LICENCE.txt	15/01/2021 2:55 AM	TXT File	1 KB

Figure A.18

   – Figure A.18 shows Spring Boot CLI components.

   – Inside the bin directory, you can find the Spring Boot CLI executables.

   – Set the bin directory path in your system's path environment variable, so you can access CLI's spring command from anywhere in the command prompt or terminal.

2. *Install through the package managers, such as Homebrew or Chocolatey*

   A *package manager* is software that automates the process of installing, upgrading, configuring, and removing software on your computer. You can use different package managers to install Spring Boot CLI, depending on the operating system you are using. For example, if you are using macOS, you can use Homebrew (https://brew.sh/) to install Spring Boot CLI, as shown in the following listing.

Listing A.3 Installing Spring Boot CLI in macOS using Homebrew

```
brew tap pivotal/tap
brew install springboot (for macOS)
```

If you are using Windows, you can use Chocolatey (https://chocolatey.org/) to install Spring Boot CLI using the command shown in the following listing.

Listing A.4 Installing Spring Boot CLI in Windows using Chocolatey

```
choco install spring-boot-cli
```

Note that you need to install the package manager before you use it to install Spring Boot CLI. You can refer to the links of the package managers for further information on the installation.

3 *Install through the Software Development Kit Manager (SDKMAN)*
SDKMAN! (https://sdkman.io/) is a software tool for managing Software Development Kits (SDK) in your machine, including Spring Boot CLI. You can download the SDKMAN from their website and install it on your machine. After that, you can use the command shown in the following listing to install Spring Boot CLI using SDKMAN.

Listing A.5 Installing Spring Boot CLI through SDKMAN

```
sdk install springboot
```

Once you have installed and configured Spring Boot CLI, you can verify the installation by accessing the CLI. To access Spring Boot CLI, open the command prompt (in Windows) or a terminal (in macOS/Linux) and type the command shown in the following listing. You can see the output as the installed CLI version.

Listing A.6 Spring Boot CLI version

```
$ spring --version
Spring CLI v2.3.0.RELEASE
```

You can now use the installed CLI to generate a Spring Boot project. Spring Boot CLI defines an `init` command that connects to https://start.spring.io and allows you to generate a project through Spring Initializr. Like the `cURL` command, you can obtain a textual representation of the Spring Initializr service by running the `spring init --list` command. You'll see a similar screen as that shown in figure A.19.

You can generate a Spring Boot project through the CLI by providing the project parameters and dependencies, as shown in the following listing.

Listing A.7 Spring Boot CLI to generate a Spring Boot project

```
spring init --dependencies=web,h2 --type=gradle-project --java-version=15 -
➥ -packaging=war spring-boot-gradle-app.zip
```

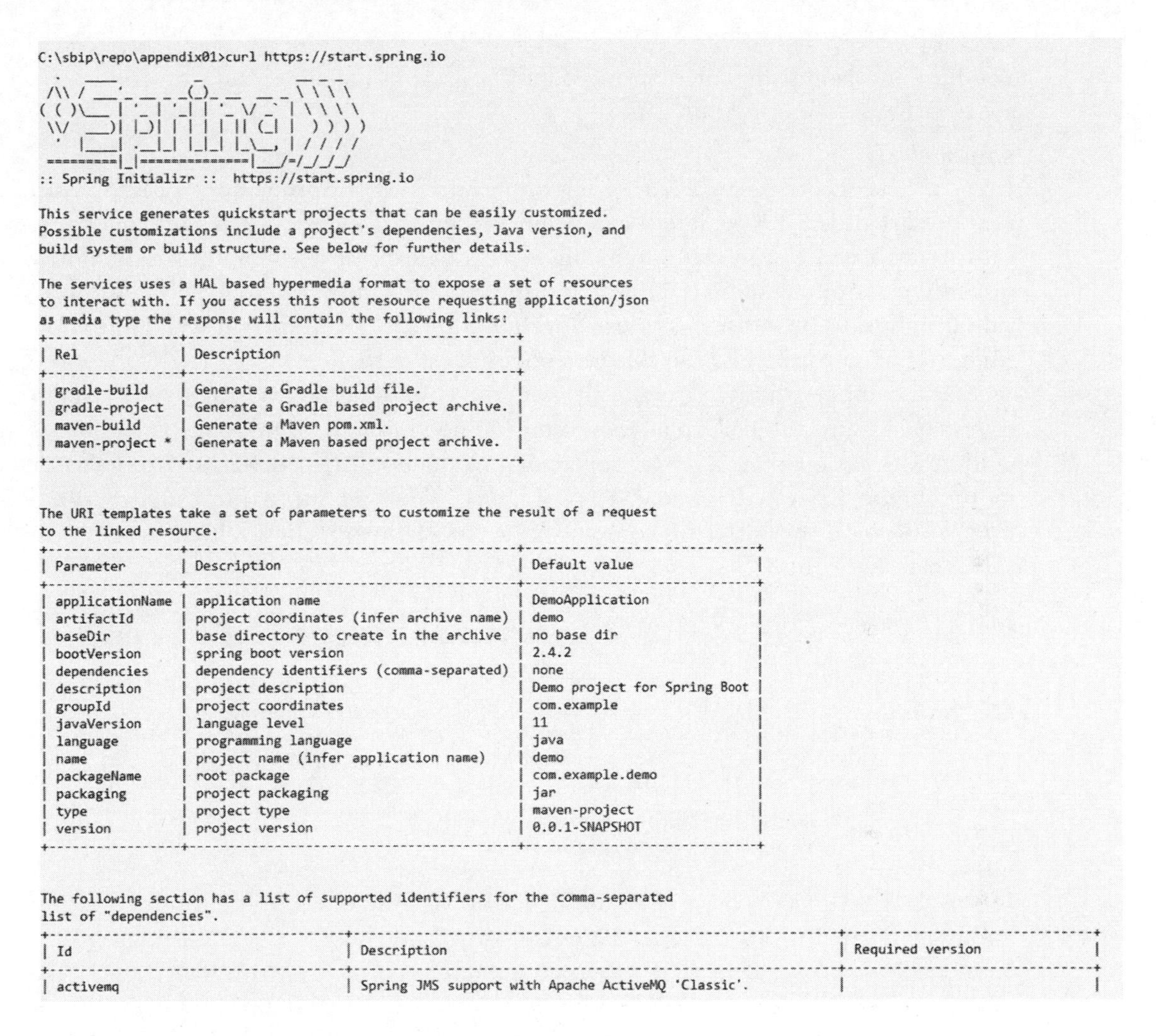

```
C:\sbip\repo\appendix01>curl https://start.spring.io

:: Spring Initializr ::  https://start.spring.io

This service generates quickstart projects that can be easily customized.
Possible customizations include a project's dependencies, Java version, and
build system or build structure. See below for further details.

The services uses a HAL based hypermedia format to expose a set of resources
to interact with. If you access this root resource requesting application/json
as media type the response will contain the following links:
+-----------------+------------------------------------------+
| Rel             | Description                              |
+-----------------+------------------------------------------+
| gradle-build    | Generate a Gradle build file.            |
| gradle-project  | Generate a Gradle based project archive. |
| maven-build     | Generate a Maven pom.xml.                |
| maven-project * | Generate a Maven based project archive.  |
+-----------------+------------------------------------------+

The URI templates take a set of parameters to customize the result of a request
to the linked resource.
+-----------------+------------------------------------------+------------------------------+
| Parameter       | Description                              | Default value                |
+-----------------+------------------------------------------+------------------------------+
| applicationName | application name                         | DemoApplication              |
| artifactId      | project coordinates (infer archive name) | demo                         |
| baseDir         | base directory to create in the archive  | no base dir                  |
| bootVersion     | spring boot version                      | 2.4.2                        |
| dependencies    | dependency identifiers (comma-separated) | none                         |
| description     | project description                      | Demo project for Spring Boot |
| groupId         | project coordinates                      | com.example                  |
| javaVersion     | language level                           | 11                           |
| language        | programming language                     | java                         |
| name            | project name (infer application name)    | demo                         |
| packageName     | root package                             | com.example.demo             |
| packaging       | project packaging                        | jar                          |
| type            | project type                             | maven-project                |
| version         | project version                          | 0.0.1-SNAPSHOT               |
+-----------------+------------------------------------------+------------------------------+

The following section has a list of supported identifiers for the comma-separated
list of "dependencies".
+-----------------------------------+--------------------------------------------------------+------------------+
| Id                                | Description                                            | Required version |
+-----------------------------------+--------------------------------------------------------+------------------+
| activemq                          | Spring JMS support with Apache ActiveMQ 'Classic'.     |                  |
```

Figure A.19 Accessing https://start.spring.io through cURL

The command in listing A.7 generates a Spring Boot Gradle project with the Spring Web and H2 in-memory database dependencies, Java version as Java 15, and project packaging types as WAR. It stores the generated project artifact with the name spring-boot-gradle-app.zip.

A.2.2 Technique: Developing a simple Spring Boot application with Spring Boot CLI

In this technique, we'll discuss how to develop a Spring Boot application with Spring Boot CLI.

PROBLEM

You have successfully installed Spring Boot CLI on your machine, and you want to create a Spring Boot application with it.

SOLUTION

It is straightforward to create a Spring application using Spring Boot CLI. You can simply start with a text editor. Let's begin by defining a basic REST controller that returns with a message. Although this is a straightforward example, you'll shortly notice the simplicity of the CLI tool and the concise nature of Groovy. It'll also provide insight into how easy it is to use Spring Boot CLI. Don't worry if you don't know what a REST controller is. You'll learn about it later in the book.

You'll compare this REST controller with the equivalent Java version to understand the verbosity and the boilerplate code you will need to write if the same controller is written with Java. Create a folder called cli-introduction in C:\ drive (in Windows) or in the home directory (in macOS or Linux). Then, create a file called application.groovy with the following content inside the cli-introduction folder, as shown in the following listing.

Listing A.8 Groovy REST Controller in Spring Boot CLI

```
@RestController
class DemoRestController {
    @GetMapping("/")
    def hello() {
        "Welcome to Spring Boot CLI"
    }
}
```

- `@RestController` — Spring Boot REST controller
- `@GetMapping("/")` — Maps all HTTP GET requests to this method
- `"Welcome to Spring Boot CLI"` — Response to all GET requests. The return keyword is optional and can be skipped.

In the above Groovy code, you've defined a REST controller, which returns a string Welcome to Spring Boot CLI as the output. You can execute this file using the `run` command of Spring Boot CLI. Open command prompt (in Windows) from C:\cli-introduction or a terminal (in macOS and Linux) and execute the command shown in the following listing.

Listing A.9 Executing application.groovy with Spring Boot CLI

```
$ spring run application.groovy
```

You can access this REST endpoint through the Web browser on http://localhost:8080 and notice the output, as shown in figure A.20.

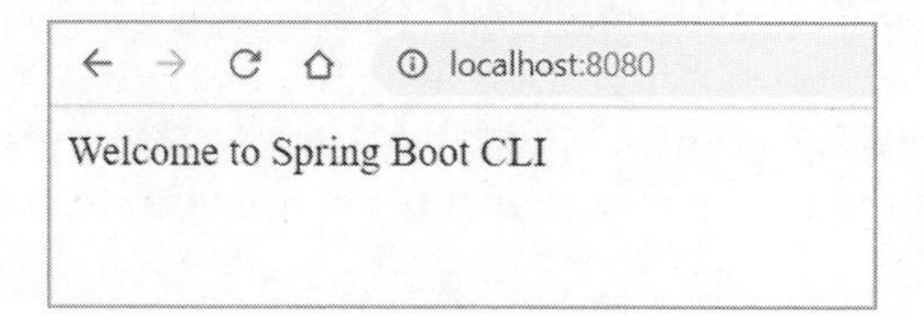

Figure A.20 Spring Boot REST endpoint output

Let's now see the Java equivalent of the Groovy code, as shown in the following listing.

Listing A.10 Java equivalent code of the Groovy REST controller

```
package com.manning.spring.boot;

import org.springframework.boot.SpringApplication;
import org.springframework.boot.autoconfigure.SpringBootApplication;
import org.springframework.web.bind.annotation.GetMapping;
import org.springframework.web.bind.annotation.RestController;    <-- Required import statements

@RestController                                                    <-- A Spring REST controller
@SpringBootApplication                          <-- Enables Spring Boot features
public class DemoSpringBootApplication {

    public static void main(String[] args) {
        SpringApplication.run(DemoSpringBootApplication.class, args);
    }
    @GetMapping                          <-- Maps all HTTP GET requests to this method
    public String hello() {
        return "Welcome to Spring Boot CLI";    <-- Response to all HTTP GET requests. The return keyword is optional.
    }
}
```

The Java version has several boilerplate codes compared to the CLI's Groovy version:

1. Import all the classes and annotations you are using in the Java file.
2. Specify the `@SpringBootApplication` annotation for Spring Boot to perform the autoconfiguration of the application.
3. Write a `main()` method to start the application and make this REST endpoint available to others.

Understanding the Spring Boot CLI commands

You've already seen how to compile and run the Groovy source code using the Spring Boot CLI run command. Following is the complete description of the `run` command: `$ spring run [options] <files> [--] [arguments]`. It takes one or more Groovy files with additional options and arguments. Note that `--` is used to separate the application options from the spring command line arguments. For example, to start the application in a port other than the default 8080, you can specify a different port using the `--server.port` argument: `$ spring run application.groovy -- --server.port=9090`. To find a full list of options supported by the Spring Boot CLI `run` command, you can use the `help` command of Spring Boot CLI. For example, if you execute `spring run help`, you can find the output, as shown in figure A.21.

So far, you are running the application through the Spring Boot CLI tool from the command line. However, this might be fine for quick prototyping and to try out Spring Boot features. But you might not always want to run the application from the command line. You may wish to create a runnable JAR file or create a WAR file to

```
C:\sbip\repo\appendix01\cli-introduction>spring help run
spring run - Run a spring groovy script

usage: spring run [options] <files> [--] [args]

Option                     Description
------                     -----------
--autoconfigure [Boolean]  Add autoconfigure compiler transformations
                             (default: true)
--classpath, -cp <String>  Additional classpath entries
--no-guess-dependencies    Do not attempt to guess dependencies
--no-guess-imports         Do not attempt to guess imports
-q, --quiet                Quiet logging
-v, --verbose              Verbose logging of dependency resolution
--watch                    Watch the specified file for changes
```

Figure A.21 Spring Boot CLI run command options

deploy the application in any of your environments. With the Spring Boot CLI, you can easily create a runnable JAR or a WAR file.

For example, you can create a runnable JAR file by using the following command: `$ spring jar app.jar application.groovy`. This command produces a runnable JAR file that can be executed using the `java -jar` command. Similarly, you can create a WAR file using the following command: `$ spring war app.war application.groovy`.

Grab Hints vs. @Grab annotation

Spring Boot CLI uses two techniques to download the dependencies needed for your application. The first and implicit technique is known as *grab hints*. These hints are mostly in form of Java classes and annotations. If these classes or annotations are present in your application code, Spring Boot CLI automatically detects the relevant dependencies and downloads them. You can refer to table A.2 for the list of grab hints.

However, as you might have already noticed, these grab hints are limited and might not suffice your needs. The second technique, `@Grab` annotation, resolves this limitation. The `@Grab` annotation allows you to explicitly specify the dependencies needed in your application. Spring Boot CLI pulls these dependencies, as specified in the `@Grab` annotation.

Groovy includes a `@Grab` annotation, which allows you to explicitly declare third-party dependencies in your application. This annotation allows you to download JAR files, such as a dependency management tool like Maven or Gradle. Spring Boot extends this grabbing technique and attempts to deduce the libraries based on the contents of your code as *grab hints*.

For instance, the presence of `@EnableJms` in your code hints Spring Boot CLI to download the necessary libraries required for a Java Messaging Service (http://mng.bz/8ldZ) application. Table A.2 shows the list of grab hints. Some of the grab hints are classes, and some are annotations. You'll see the use of `@Grab` annotation shortly in this section.

Table A.2 Groovy grab hints

Code item	Grabs
`JdbcTemplate, DataSource, NamedParameterJdbcTemplate`	Adds dependencies required for a JDBC application
`@EnableJms`	Provides dependencies required for a JMS application
`@EnableCaching`	Provides caching abstractions
`@EnableRabbit`	Adds dependencies required for a RabbitMQ
`@EnableWebSecurity`	Provides support for Spring Security
`@EnableTransactionManagement`	Spring transaction management
`@Controller, @RestController, @EnableWebMvc`	Provides support for a Spring MVC application with embedded Tomcat
`@EnableBatchProcessing`	Adds support required for a Spring Batch application
`@EnableIntegration @MessageEndpoint`	Provides support for Spring Integration

You've already seen the use of `@RestController` in the application.groovy file. The presence of this annotation allows Spring Boot to download necessary dependencies for a Spring MVC application and provides an embedded Tomcat server.

Let's now provide an additional grab hint in our application.groovy to demonstrate this feature further. Let's say you want to use Spring Security in the application and leverage the default security features provided by Spring Security. To do so, let's add `@EnableWebSecurity` in the application.groovy file, as shown in the following listing.

Listing A.11 A simple Spring Boot REST controller

```
@EnableWebSecurity
@RestController
class DemoRestController {

    @GetMapping("/")
    def hello() {
        "Spring Boot CLI"
    }
}
```

Run this application, and you can see that our application now has default Spring Security features enabled. Spring Boot now redirects us to a login page to access the endpoint. You can find the generated password from the console and log in with this and user as `user`.

Although grab hints seem to be a powerful feature, they are limited, as we have a limited number of such hints. You might need to use a third-party library outside of these hints. To remove this limitation, Spring Boot extends Groovy's standard `@Grab` annotation by allowing you to specify a dependency. Therefore, if there is a Groovy hint already in your application, the framework attempts to download it automatically. Later, when no hint is available, you can explicitly add dependencies using `@Grab` annotation.

For instance, we can tweak our previous example and use `@Grab` annotation to add the `spring-boot-starter-security` dependency, as shown in the following listing. Thus, by using `@Grab` annotation, you can explicitly specify the dependencies needed in your application.

Listing A.12 Using Groovy @Grab annotation to specify additional dependency

```
@Grab("spring-boot-starter-security")
@RestController
class DemoRestController {

    @GetMapping("/")
    def hello() {
        "Welcome to Spring Boot CLI"
    }
}
```

The code in listing A.12 downloads the `spring-boot-starter-security` dependencies. If you run this file with Spring Boot CLI, you can see the CLI is resolving the dependencies and asking you to log in to access the endpoint.

DISCUSSION

With this technique, you've seen the use of Spring Boot CLI by developing a tiny Spring REST Web service. The major takeaway in this technique is the use of Groovy language, which allows you to write concise code. You also don't need any build framework for dependency management and application packaging. With the next technique, we'll take this concept further by building a Web application consisting of UI and database.

A.2.3 Technique: Building a Web application using Spring Boot CLI

In this technique, we'll discuss how to build a Web application using Spring Boot CLI.

PROBLEM

You want to build a Web application with UI and database support using Spring Boot CLI.

SOLUTION

With the previous technique, you've explored Spring Boot CLI and learned the major commands to play with it. Using this technique, you'll extend that understanding further by developing a Web application with the Spring Boot CLI.

You'll build a UI-based application that keeps track of the courses in an e-learning platform. In this application, you will use Thymeleaf (https://www.thymeleaf.org/) to manage the UI components and H2 in-memory database (https://www.h2database.com/html/main.html) to persist the course data. Figure A.22 shows the outcome of the application you will build in this technique.

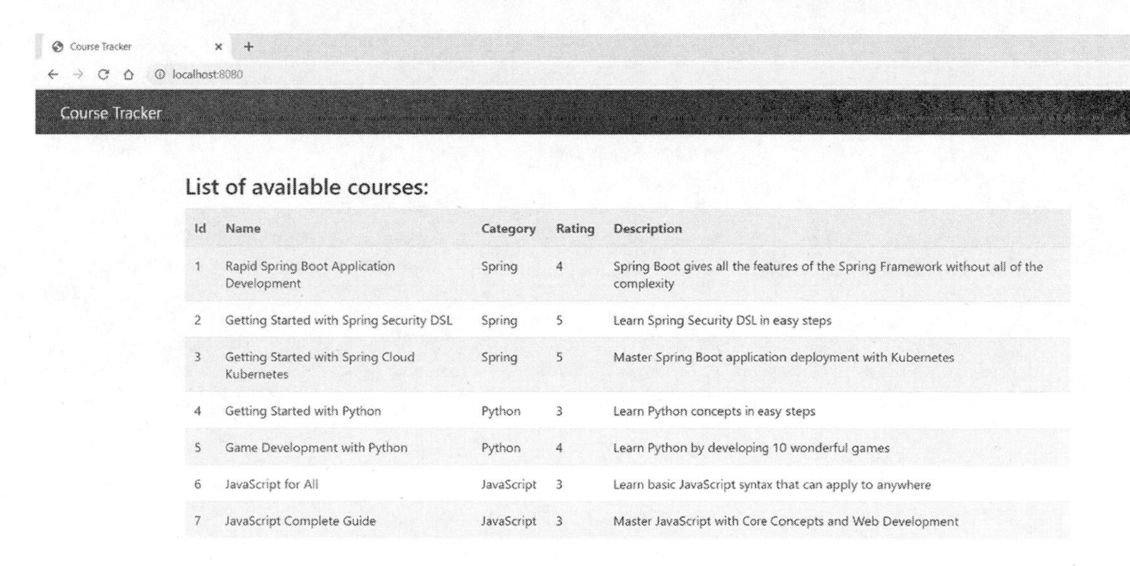

Figure A.22 Course Tracker application using Spring Boot CLI

In the development process, you will explore a few of the Spring Boot features, which will be useful in the chapters throughout the book. You can download the completed version of this application from this book's companion GitHub repository at http://mng.bz/NxgN.

To begin with, create a folder named $ mkdir course-tracker-cli. This folder acts as the root folder of the application. You'll create two more folders, config and templates, inside the root folder: $ mkdir config templates.

The config folder contains the application.properties file, and the templates folder contains HTML templates. The application.properties file contains optional Spring Boot configuration parameters. For instance, if you need to start the application on a different port than the default port 8080, you can configure the custom port in the application.properties. You can also specify your database or logging configurations in this file.

Figure A.23 shows the UML class diagram of the application you are going to build. You have a `Course` as the business domain class and a `CourseRepository` interface where you define the data access methods. The default implementation of this interface is represented by the `CourseRepositoryImpl` class. Lastly, you have a `CourseController` class that has an instance of the `CourseRepository`.

In this application, the `Course` is the domain class, which represents a course in the application. A course consists of a course ID, name, category, rating, and description. Following is the `course.groovy` class, as shown in listing A.13.

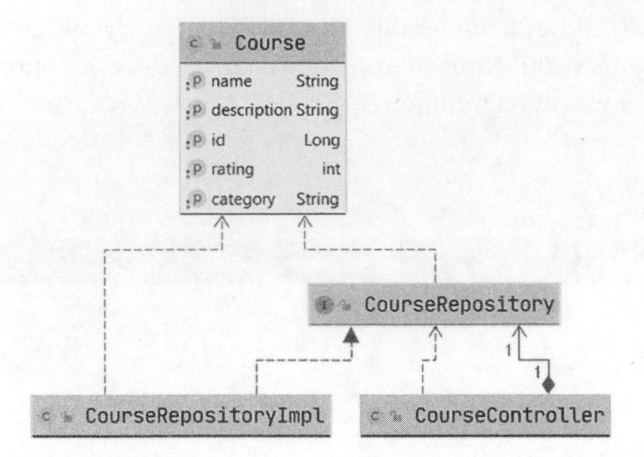

Figure A.23 Conference Tracker application using Spring Boot CLI

Listing A.13 Course POJO class

```
class Course {
    long id
    String name
    String category
    int rating
    String description
}
```

You will use Spring JDBC to communicate with the database. Thus, you will need to create the data access layer, using Spring `JdbcTemplate`. A `JdbcTemplate` is Spring's template-based approach that simplifies the use of JDBC and allows you to avoid common JDBC errors.

Let's define the `CourseRepository` interface inside the course-tracker-cli folder with the data access methods shown in listing A.14. In this interface, you declare different data access methods to find course details.

Listing A.14 Course repository interface to define data access methods

```
interface CourseRepository {
    Iterable<Course> findAll()
    Iterable<Course> findAllByCourseCategory(String category)
}
```

These data access methods perform the following activities and fetch information from the database:

1. `findAll`: Finds all courses available in the application
2. `findAllByCourseCategory`: Given a course category, it returns all courses that belong to the supplied category

You'll now define `CourseRepositoryImpl` class inside the course-tracker-cli folder. This class implements the `CourseRepository` interface and defines the behaviors of the interface methods.

Le's explain the actions you'll perform inside the `CourseRepositoryImpl` class:

- You need to annotate this class with `@Repository` annotation. `@Repository` annotation is a stereotype annotation that indicates that the annotated class is a Spring data repository. Spring Framework provides you a few special annotations that allow you to create an instance of the annotated class automatically. These annotations are known as *stereotype annotations*, and `@Repository` annotation is one of them. You'll find a detailed explanation of the `@Repository` interface in chapter 3.
- You'll need an instance of `JdbcTemplate` in the implemented class, so you can communicate to the database. You'll use `@autowire` annotation to do this. By providing this annotation, you ask Spring to provide an instance of `JdbcTemplate` when it creates an object of `CourseRepositoryImpl` class. Besides, declaring `JdbcTemplate` is a grab hint to the Spring Boot CLI to perform the necessary JDBC setup.
- Lastly, you'll provide an implementation for all methods defined in the `CourseRepository` interface. You've used Groovy closure to map the `Course` objects from the result set. If you are familiar with Java lambda expressions, then you can relate Groovy closures with them. You can refer to https://groovy-lang.org/closures.html to read more about Groovy closures.

Create a file called CourseRepositoryImpl inside the root folder of your application with the following content, as shown in the following listing.

Listing A.15 CourseRepositoryImpl class

```
@Repository
class CourseRepositoryImpl implements CourseRepository {

    @Autowired
    JdbcTemplate jdbcTemplate;

    Iterable<Course> findAll() {
        jdbcTemplate.query("""SELECT COURSE_ID, COURSE_NAME,
    COURSE_CATEGORY, COURSE_RATING, COURSE_DESCRIPTION FROM COURSES""", {
            resultSet, newRow -> new Course(
                id : resultSet.getLong(1),
                name : resultSet.getString(2),
                category : resultSet.getString(3),
                rating : resultSet.getInt(4),
                description : resultSet.getString(5))
        } as RowMapper)
    }

    Iterable<Course> findAllByCourseCategory(String category) {
        jdbcTemplate.query("""SELECT COURSE_ID, COURSE_NAME,
    COURSE_CATEGORY, COURSE_RATING, COURSE_DESCRIPTION FROM COURSES WHERE
    COURSE_CATEGORY=?""", {
```

Annotations:
- Spring stereotype annotation indicates that this class is a Spring Data repository.
- An instance of JdbcTemplate is autowired by Spring. This class lets you access the database easily.
- Implementation of findAll method to fetch all courses from the database
- Implementation of findAllByCourseCategory method that fetches all courses belongs to the supplied category from the database

```
            resultSet, newRow -> new Course(
                id : resultSet.getLong(1),
                name : resultSet.getString(2),
                category : resultSet.getString(3),
                rating : resultSet.getInt(4),
                description : resultSet.getString(5))
        } as RowMapper, category)
    }
}
```

Now that we are ready with the data access methods, let's define a Spring controller class to handle the incoming user requests. You'll create the `CourseController` class inside the course-tracker-cli folder of the application to do this task, as shown in listing A.15.

Apart from handling the incoming request, you are performing several additional activities in the controller. Let's explain these step by step:

- You have defined this class with `@controller` annotation. This indicates the class as a Spring controller to handle an incoming request.
- You have defined two endpoints to handle the incoming requests. To keep the application simple, you have defined HTTP GET endpoints only. Below are the endpoints:
  - /—Default endpoint, which returns all courses available in our application
  - /{category}—Provides all courses that belong to the supplied category
- As discussed previously, you are using the H2 in-memory database for the back-end database and Thymeleaf to manage the HTML templates for the UI. Thus, you have used `h2` and `spring-boot-starter-thymeleaf` dependencies.
- When you access any of the endpoints, the following activities are done:
  - The HTTP GET request is mapped to the appropriate controller method, as defined in the `CourseController` class.
  - The database repository class is invoked to fetch the data from the database.
  - This data with a view name is returned by the controller method. In listing A.16, you used a view named `Course`.
  - The view is then rendered with the fetched data and displayed on the screen.

Listing A.16 Course REST controller

```
@Grab("h2")
@Grab("spring-boot-starter-thymeleaf")

@Controller
@RequestMapping
class CourseController {

    @Autowired
    CourseRepository courseRepository;
```

Defines this class as a Spring controller, and HTTP requests can be mapped to this class

Using Groovy's @Grab annotation to tell Spring Boot to get the H2 database and spring-boot-starter dependencies

Autowiring the CourseRepository implementation. In this case, CourseRepositoryImpl will be injected by Spring here.

```
    @GetMapping
    def getAllCourses(Model model) {
        model.addAttribute("courses", courseRepository.findAll());
        "courses";
    }

    @GetMapping("{category}")
    def getAllCourses(@PathVariable("category") String category, Model
➥ model) {
        model.addAttribute("courses",
➥ courseRepository.findAllByCourseCategory(category));
        "courses";
    } }
```

HTTP GET request mapping endpoint to address all GET requests with endpoint /

HTTP GET request mapping endpoint to address GET requests with /{category}. The category is a PathVariable and is replaced with the actual course category.

You've defined the data access object and the controller class to handle the HTTP incoming requests. Let's now define the *view* of the application. Create a file named courses.html inside the templates folder of the course-tracker-cli, as shown in listing A.17.

In the view, you've done the following:

- Used Thymeleaf to iterate the courses and displayed the course details in a tabular format. You can refer to appendix B to learn Thymeleaf.
- You have used Bootstrap (https://getbootstrap.com/) to style the HTML page. If you haven't worked with Bootstrap before, it is a CSS library that allows you to design your HTML pages.

Listing A.17 Course Tracker HTML template

```
<html xmlns:th="http://www.thymeleaf.org">
<head>
    <title>Course Tracker</title>
    <meta charset="utf-8"/>
    <meta name="viewport" content="width=device-width, initial-scale=1"/>
    <link rel="stylesheet"
➥ href="https://maxcdn.bootstrapcdn.com/bootstrap/4.0.0/css/bootstrap.min
➥ .css"/>
    <script
➥ src="https://ajax.googleapis.com/ajax/libs/jquery/3.3.1/jquery.min.js">
➥ </script>
    <script
➥ src="https://cdnjs.cloudflare.com/ajax/libs/popper.js/1.12.9/umd/popper
➥ .min.js"></script>
    <script
➥ src="https://maxcdn.bootstrapcdn.com/bootstrap/4.0.0/js/bootstrap.min.j
➥ s"></script>
</head>
<body>
<nav class="navbar navbar-dark bg-dark">
  <div class="container-fluid">
```

```
        <div class="navbar-header">
          <a class="navbar-brand" href="#">Course Tracker</a>
        </div>
      </div>
    </nav>
    <div class="container h-100">
        <div class="row justify-content-left mt-5 mb-1">
            <h3 id="heading">List of available courses:</h3>
        </div>
        <div class="row table-responsive">
            <table class="table table-striped">
                <thead class="thead-light">
                <tr>
                    <th>Id</th>
                    <th>Name</th>
                    <th>Category</th>
                    <th>Rating</th>
                    <th>Description</th>
                </tr>
                </thead>
                <tbody>
                <tr th:each="course : ${courses}">
                    <td th:text="${course.id}">ID</td>
                    <td th:text="${course.name}">Name</td>
                    <td th:text="${course.category}">Category</td>
                    <td th:text="${course.rating}">Rating</td>
                    <td th:text="${course.description}">Description</td>
                </tr>
                </tbody>
            </table>
        </div>
    </div>
    </body>
    </html>
```

You are almost done with the application, except the database schema definition. If you recall, we are using the H2 in-memory database to persist the data. Spring Boot uses a convention to detect the schema definition files and the data files. It automatically loads the schema if it finds a file called schema.sql and loads the data if it detects a file called data.sql. For now, let's create both these files inside the course-tracker-cli folder of our application. The following listing shows the schema.sql file in which you are creating the COURSES table.

Listing A.18 The schema.sql file to create the COURSES database table

```
create table COURSES (
    COURSE_ID identity not null,
    COURSE_NAME varchar(100) not null,
    COURSE_CATEGORY varchar(10) not null,
    COURSE_RATING tinyint not null,
    COURSE_DESCRIPTION varchar(500) not null
);
```

We also want to load some course details to populate the table with data. The following listing shows the data.sql file containing a few SQL insert statements.

Listing A.19 The data.sql file to load the sample data by Spring Boot

```
INSERT INTO COURSES(COURSE_ID, COURSE_NAME, COURSE_CATEGORY, COURSE_RATING,
➥ COURSE_DESCRIPTION) VALUES(1, 'Rapid Spring Boot Application
➥ Development', 'Spring', 4, 'Spring Boot gives all the features of the
➥ Spring Framework without all of the complexity');
INSERT INTO COURSES(COURSE_ID, COURSE_NAME, COURSE_CATEGORY, COURSE_RATING,
➥ COURSE_DESCRIPTION) VALUES(2, 'Getting Started with Spring Security
➥ DSL', 'Spring', 5, 'Learn Spring Security DSL in easy steps');
INSERT INTO COURSES(COURSE_ID, COURSE_NAME, COURSE_CATEGORY, COURSE_RATING,
➥ COURSE_DESCRIPTION) VALUES(3, 'Getting Started with Spring Cloud
➥ Kubernetes', 'Spring', 5, 'Master Spring Boot application deployment
➥ with Kubernetes');
INSERT INTO COURSES(COURSE_ID, COURSE_NAME, COURSE_CATEGORY, COURSE_RATING,
➥ COURSE_DESCRIPTION) VALUES(4, 'Getting Started with Python', 'Python',
➥ 3, 'Learn Python concepts in easy steps');
INSERT INTO COURSES(COURSE_ID, COURSE_NAME, COURSE_CATEGORY, COURSE_RATING,
➥ COURSE_DESCRIPTION) VALUES(5, 'Game Development with Python', 'Python',
➥ 4, 'Learn Python by developing 10 wonderful games');
INSERT INTO COURSES(COURSE_ID, COURSE_NAME, COURSE_CATEGORY, COURSE_RATING,
➥ COURSE_DESCRIPTION) VALUES(6, 'JavaScript for All', 'JavaScript', 3,
➥ 'Learn basic JavaScript syntax that can apply to anywhere');
INSERT INTO COURSES(COURSE_ID, COURSE_NAME, COURSE_CATEGORY, COURSE_RATING,
➥ COURSE_DESCRIPTION) VALUES(7, 'JavaScript Complete Guide',
➥ 'JavaScript', 3, 'Master JavaScript with Core Concepts and Web
➥ Development');
```

The last change before you can execute the application is configuring the H2 database. So far, we've only provided the H2 database dependency in the Groovy file. But we also need to provide details, including database username, password, driver class, and URL.

Create a file called application.properties inside the config folder with the details shown in listing A.20. Spring Boot reads these details at the application startup and configures the H2 database automatically.

Listing A.20 H2 database configuration

```
spring.h2.console.enabled=true
spring.datasource.url=jdbc:h2:mem:testdb
spring.datasource.driverClassName=org.h2.Driver
spring.datasource.username=sa
spring.datasource.password=password
```

This ensures that you can access the H2 database console through http://localhost:8080/h2-console.

Adding the database configuration completes the application development, and you are ready to execute the application. You can run the application by executing the spring Boot CLI run command. Open your command prompt or the terminal window and run the following command from the course-tracker-cli folder: `$ spring run *`. You can see the application starts up and the startup logs in the console. By default,

HTTP port 8080 is used to run the application. If you access http://localhost:8080, you can see the output, as shown in figure A.24:

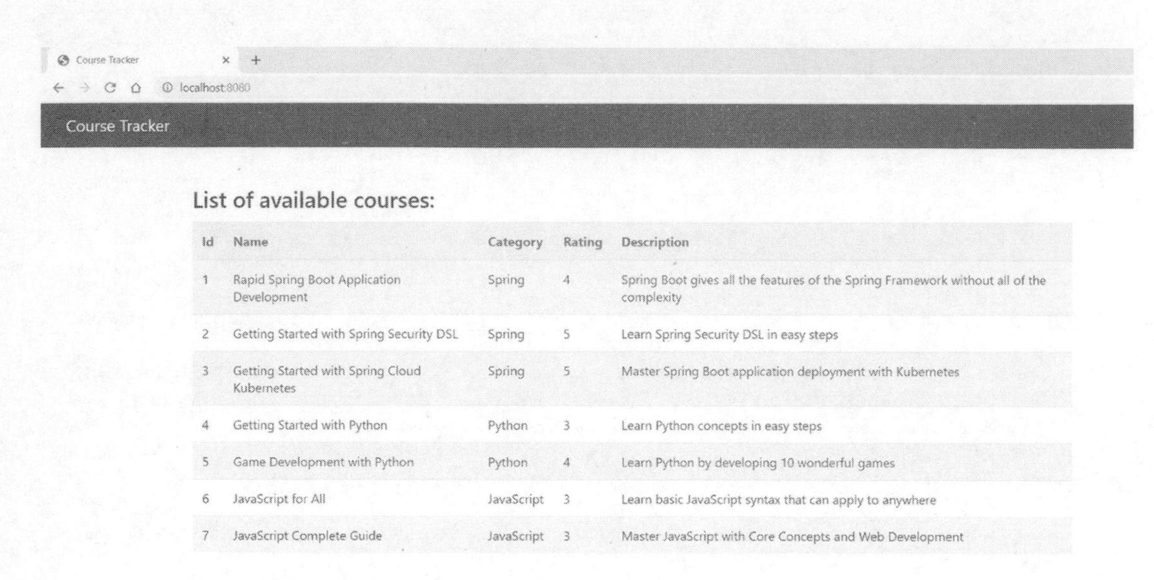

Figure A.24 Conference Tracker application displaying all conferences

You can also access other endpoints, such as finding all courses that belong to a category by navigating to http:/ /localhost:8080/{category}. For instance, if you visit http://localhost:8080/Spring, you can see all courses belonging to the `Spring` category. Figure A.25 shows the output. Nice! Thanks to the features of Spring Boot CLI we can track our favorite Spring courses!

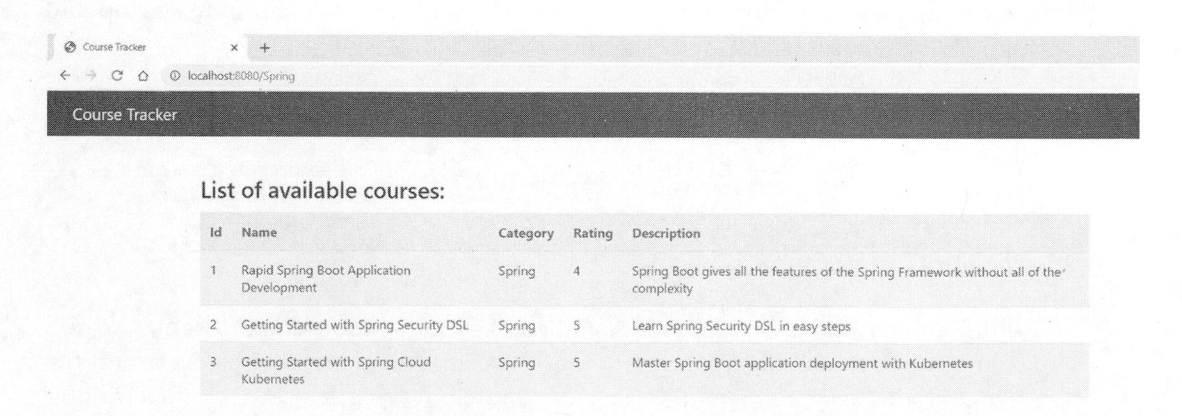

Figure A.25 List of courses belongs to the Spring category

DISCUSSION

Using this technique, you've seen the use of Spring Boot CLI for building a full-scale Web application with a frontend and a backend database. You haven't used any dependency management tool, such as Maven or Gradle; instead, Spring Boot CLI manages the dependencies for us.

appendix B Spring MVC and Thymeleaf Template Engine

In the next section, we'll revisit Spring MVC and provide an overview to Thymeleaf template engine.

B.1 Revisiting Spring MVC

Spring MVC is one of the important modules of the Spring Framework. The model–view–controller (MVC) is the popular design pattern to build UI-based Web applications. MVC allows you to decouple the application design in terms of model, view, and controller. A *model* encapsulates business data which is presented by a *view*. A *controller* is responsible for addressing the user requests and invoking back-end business services. After business service invocation, the controller prepares the model with the data for the views to render in the UI.

Spring MVC is the Spring Framework's implementation of the MVC design pattern. One of the powerful and key features of Spring MVC is that it is based on the Spring IoC container and tightly integrated with it to provide a simplistic configuration.

In this section, you'll revisit important Spring MVC concepts, such as the front controller design pattern and various other components Spring MVC uses heavily while processing the user requests. If you are not familiar with Spring MVC, refer to the Spring MVC documentation (http://mng.bz/YgWo) or introductory Spring MVC texts. Providing an in-depth guide to Spring MVC is beyond the scope of this text.

B.1.1 Front controller design pattern

Spring MVC is designed around a design pattern known as the *front controller pattern*. In this design, a central servlet is primarily responsible to handle all the requests. In Spring parlance, this central servlet is known as the *dispatcher servlet*. Although the dispatcher servlet handles all requests, it delegates the actual request processing task to several configurable delegated components.

In a typical Spring MVC application, you'll need to configure the `DispatcherServlet` in the application's deployment descriptor file (web.xml) or in a class that implements `ServletContainerInitializer` interface. Listing B.1 shows a sample configuration to configure a `DispatcherServlet` programmatically.

Listing B.1 Configure a dispatcher servlet programmatically

```
public class CourseCourtServletContainerInitializer implements
➥ ServletContainerInitializer {
    @Override
    public void onStartup(Set<Class<?>> set, ServletContext servletContext)
➥ throws ServletException {

        AnnotationConfigWebApplicationContext applicationContext = new
➥ AnnotationConfigWebApplicationContext();
        applicationContext.register(CourseConfiguration.class);
        DispatcherServlet dispatcherServlet = new
➥ DispatcherServlet(applicationContext);
        ServletRegistration.Dynamic servletRegistration =
➥ servletContext.addServlet("course", dispatcherServlet);
        servletRegistration.setLoadOnStartup(1);
        servletRegistration.addMapping("/");
    }
}
```

Create an instance of ApplicationContext

Create an instance of DispatcherServlet with the previously created application context

Dynamically register the DispatcherServlet with the ServletContext

B.1.2 Understanding request processing

Now that you've learned how to configure a dispatcher servlet, let's discuss how it processes an incoming request. In this section, you'll explore the steps a dispatcher servlet executes to process the incoming requests. Figure B.1 shows the sequence of steps.

Following is an overly simplified and high-level step of a request handling by the dispatcher servlet:

1. Any request to a Spring MVC-based application is initially addressed by the dispatcher servlet.
2. Once a request is received, the dispatcher servlet first delegates the incoming request to a `HandlerMapping`. A `HandlerMapping` finds a Spring controller configured to address the request.
3. Once a controller is found, the dispatcher servlet delegates the request to a `HandlerAdapter` that invokes the controller.
4. Generally, a controller invokes the business services and retrieves the application data.

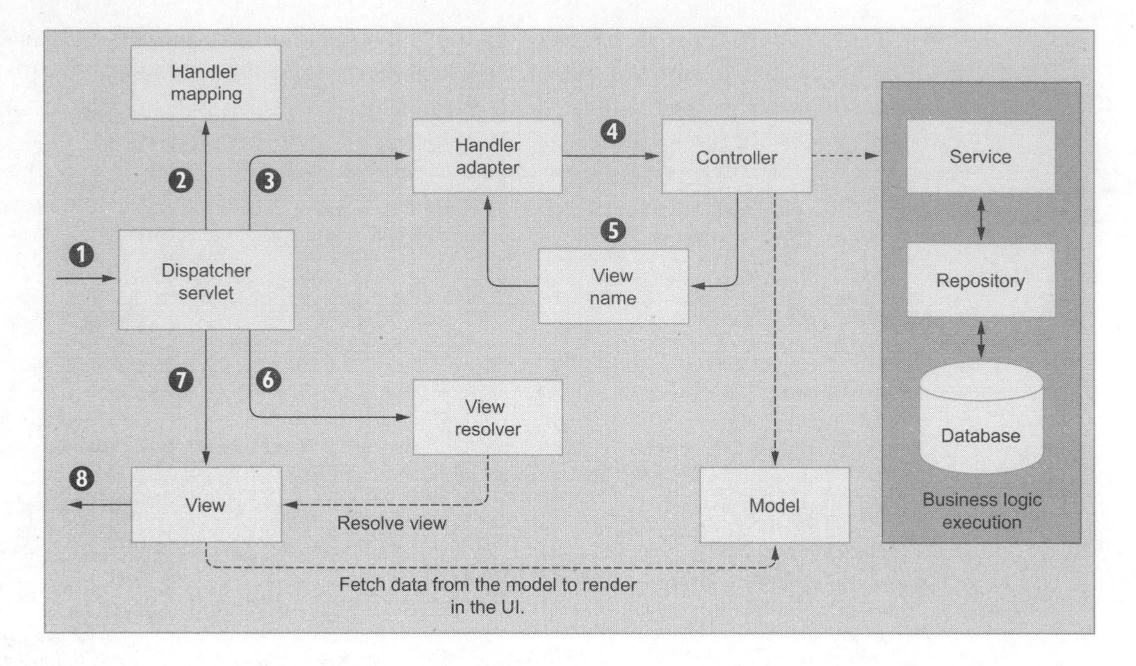

Figure B.1 Spring MVC components. The *DispatcherServlet* is the primary component, and it delegates the request to various other components.

5. After business invocation, a controller prepares a model that contains the returned business data. The controller also returns a logical view name to the dispatcher servlet.
6. The `DispatcherServlet` then invokes a `ViewResolver`, which maps the logical view name to the actual view.
7. The returned view uses the model data and renders it to the screen.
8. Once the view is rendered on the screen, the request is considered to be addressed.

Let's now briefly discuss a few of the Spring MVC components that dispatcher servlet uses for task delegation:

- `HandlerMapping`—This interface provides a mapping between the request URL and the handler objects. Spring MVC includes two major implementations of the `HandlerMapping` interface: `BeanNameUrlHandlerMapping` and `RequestMappingHandlerMapping`. The `BeanNameUrlHandlerMapping` implementation maps the request URL to the bean name of the same name. This is the default implementation used by Spring MVC. A `HandlerMapping` returns a `HandlerExecutionChain`, which contains the handler object and a list of interceptors. Depending on the configuration (i.e., pre/post), these interceptors are invoked while addressing the request.

- `HandlerAdapter`—This interface helps the dispatcher servlet to invoke a handler mapped to a request. The main benefit of this interface is that it shields the dispatcher servlet from the implementation details of the handler. Spring MVC provides four implementations of this interface: `RequestMappingHandlerAdapter`, `HttpRequestHandlerAdapter`, `SimpleControllerHandlerAdapter`, and `SimpleServletHandlerAdapter`.
- `ViewResolver`—Resolves the logical string-based view names to the actual view. Spring framework provides several `ViewResolver` and `View` implementations. Refer to http://mng.bz/GGvM for the list of `ViewResolver` implementations.
- `LocaleResolver`—This interface allows the dispatcher servlet to automatically resolve messages based on the client's locale configuration. For all the incoming requests, the dispatcher servlet asks the configured `LocaleResolver` implementation to resolve the locale and set it in the `HttpServletResponse`. Spring framework provides several `LocaleResolver` implementations. Figure B.2 shows the list of available `LocaleResolvers`. The default implementation used by the Spring MVC is `AcceptHeaderLocaleResolver`.

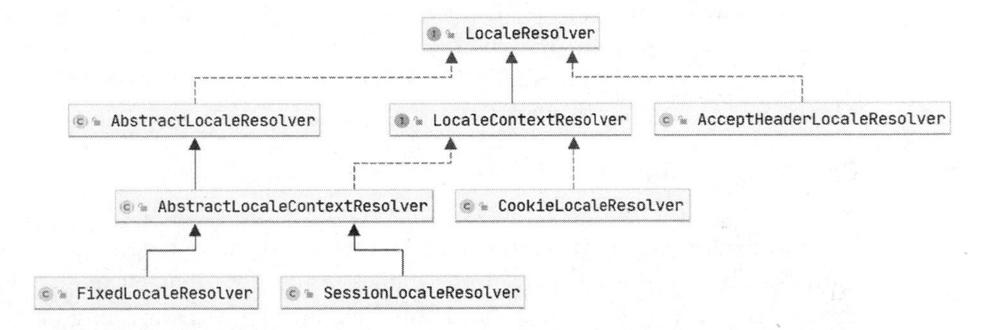

Figure B.2 Spring MVC LocaleResolver class hierarchy. The default implementation is AcceptHeaderLocaleResolver.

- `HandlerExceptionResolver`—This interface allows resolve exceptions to be thrown during handler mapping or execution. In case of an exception, the dispatcher servlet delegates to a chain of `HandlerExceptionResolver`. An exception resolver can either choose to handle the exception or delegate to another resolver implementation. A `HandlerExceptionResolver` can do any of the following:
  - Return a `ModelAndView` that points to an error view.
  - An empty `ModelAndView` if the exception is already handled in the `HandlerExceptionResolver`.
  - Return `null` if the exception is unresolved, and the subsequent resolvers should attempt to handle it. If the exception is unresolved till the end, it is finally addressed by the Servlet container.

The major `HandlerExceptionResolver` implementations are `SimpleMappingExceptionResolver`, `ExceptionHandlerExceptionResolver`, `ResponseStatusExceptionResolver`, and `DefaultHandlerExceptionResolver`. Now that you've refreshed the Spring MVC concepts and their various components, let's discuss the Thymeleaf template engine.

B.2 Understanding Thymeleaf

In this section, you'll learn the basics of Thymeleaf and its integration with Spring Boot. Thymeleaf is a server-side template engine that allows you to define several types of template. For instance, a Thymeleaf HTML template is an HTML page that contains HTML tags with special Thymeleaf tags. These Thymeleaf tags are processed at runtime by the Thymeleaf processing engine and replaced with the supplied data and plain HTML content is rendered on the browser.

Thymeleaf supports six types of templates: `HTML`, `XML`, `TEXT`, `JAVASCRIPT`, `CSS`, and `RAW`. Of these types, the `HTML`-based template is the most popular and frequently used for developing Java-based Web applications. In this section and the subsequent technique, you'll learn more about the usage of HTML-based Thymeleaf templates in the Spring Boot application.

A detailed explanation of Thymeleaf is beyond the scope of this book. You can refer to the Thymeleaf documentation (https://www.thymeleaf.org/documentation.html) for an in-depth understanding of Thymeleaf. Let's start with the necessary components of Thymeleaf.

B.2.1 Displaying attributes

Sometimes you send data from a Spring Boot controller through a model to the view layer to render the data in the UI. Along with the model, you typically send a view name in which the associated model data is rendered. The view name is mapped with the appropriate HTML page, and the Thymeleaf processing engine processes the Thymeleaf-specific tags to replace them with the supplied application data. Figure B.3 shows this process through a block diagram.

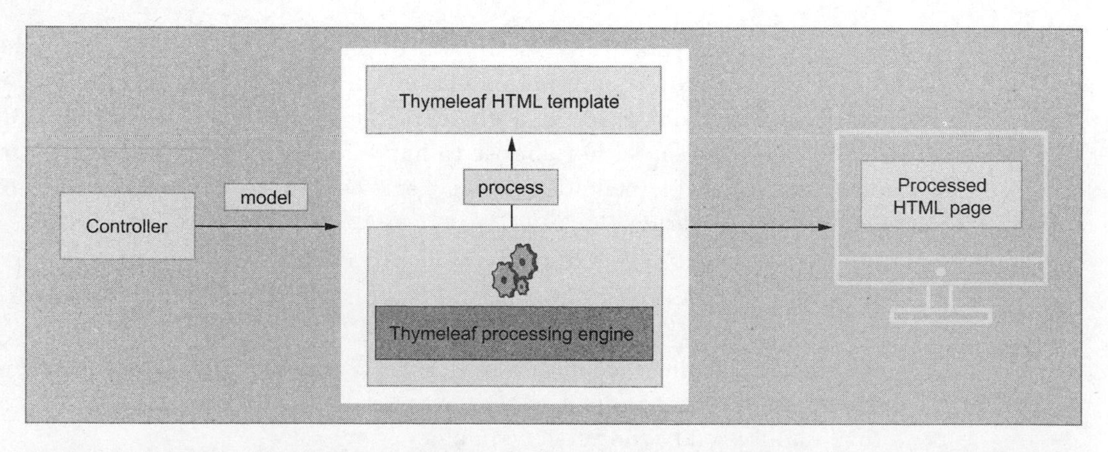

Figure B.3 Processing of Thymeleaf templates with Spring model by Thymeleaf template processing engine

In Spring MVC, a model typically stores the data in a `key-value` pair. If the value is a simple type, you can directly access it in the UI using the `key`. Listing B.2 shows how you can use the `key` provided in the model in the Thymeleaf template.

Listing B.2 Use of the th:text Thymeleaf tag

```
<span th:text="${key}" />
```

Let's understand the above syntax in detail:

- The `<span>` is an HTML tag that allows you to mark up a part of the text.
- The `th` specifies the Thymeleaf XML namespace in which all other Thymeleaf-specific tags (e.g., `text`) are defined. You can define the `th` tag in the HTML document, as shown in the following listing.

Listing B.3 The Thymeleaf namespace

```
<html xmlns:th="http://www.thymeleaf.org">
```

- The `${key}` replaces the value of the `key` with the appropriate value.

For example, let's say you need to render the logged-in user's name in the UI. So in your controller, you can add the `userName` as a key, and the user's name as the value. In the Spring controller, you define an HTTP endpoint (e.g., `@GetMapping`) and populate the model with the values, as shown in the following listing.

Listing B.4 Use of Spring model in a Spring controller

```
@GetMapping                                          // Defines an HTTP GET endpoint
public String getLoggedInUserName(Model model) {
    model.addAttribute("userName", user.getName());  // Adds the userName attribute with the username value to the model
    return "index";                                  // Returns a view named index
}
```

The associated HTML code to display the value of the `userName` attribute is the following: Logged In user: `<span th:text="${userName}" />`. The `userName` value from the model is rendered in the UI by the key name you have specified. Sometimes, you can have a collection of objects instead of a simple attribute type. For example, you can return a list of courses that should be rendered in the UI. So in the controller, you add the list of courses as follows:

```
List<Course> courseList = // Business service returns a list of course
model.addAttribute("courses", courseList);
```

You can use the Thymeleaf template code to iterate over the list to print the returned object details. For instance, you can display the course details in an HTML table, as shown in the following listing.

Listing B.5 Use of the Thymeleaf th:each tag

```
<tbody>                                          <-- HTML Table Body
    <tr th:each="course: ${courses}">             <-- The tr tag represents an HTML table row. The th:each tag represents a for loop here. You iterate the list of courses and for each course, and you access the associated properties.
        <td th:text="${course.id}" />             <-- The td tag represents the column data for the row. You access the individual property value from the course object and put into the column of the row. Recall that, for a single property, you can use the th:text tag to access the associated value.
        <td th:text="${course.name}" />
        <td th:text="${course.description}" />
    </tr>
</tbody>
```

B.2.2 Conditional evaluation

Sometimes you want to render texts in the UI based on some condition evaluation. The `th:if` tag allows you to display a section of the view if the condition is met. On the other hand, `th:unless` tag allows you to display a section of the view if the condition is not met. The following snippet shows the complete syntax:

```
th:if="${condition}"
th:unless="${condition}"
```

Imagine you have an entity called `Author` in your course-tracker application, and it has a property called `gender`, which can have two possible values (`M` or `F`) to indicate the author's gender. If you intend to display the words `Male` or `Female` instead of the single `M` or `F` character, we could accomplish this by using the following Thymeleaf code, as shown in the following listing.

Listing B.6 Use of th:if and th:unless Thymeleaf tags

```
<td>
    <span th:if="${author.gender} == 'M'" th:text="Male" />
    <span th:unless="${author.gender} == 'M'" th:text="Female" />
</td>
```

If you would like to use `switch` and `case`, you can do that as well. The `th:switch` and `th:case` tags are used to render content conditionally, using the switch statement structure. Imagine you want to render some information based on the course category. You can use the following `switch-case` code snippet to render different content based on the course content, as shown in the following listing.

Listing B.7 Use of Thymeleaf th:switch and th:case tags

```
<div th:switch="${course.category}">     <-- Using Thymeleaf switch-case statements to evaluate condition
    <div th:case="'Spring'">
        <h2>Spring Course</h2>
    </div>
```

```
    <div th:case="'Python'">
        <h2>Python Course</h2>
    </div>
    <div th:case="'JavScript'">
        <h2>JavaScript Course</h2>
    </div>
    <div th:case="*">
        <h2>Some other course:</h2>
    </div>
</div>
```

Notice that you've used the `th:case="*"` to handle the default case. If the value of the `course.category` is `Spring`, then it renders the message, Spring Course. If the course category is not Spring, Python, or JavaScript values, then the message Some Other Course is rendered.

B.2.3 Managing forms

HTML forms are an essential part of any Web application. You can use forms to collect and submit bulk data to the application backend. You also need to validate the form data to ensure appropriate value is keyed-in in the form fields.

You can manage the form data and validation errors easily with Thymeleaf. You can use the form action and input data with `th:action` and `th:object` attributes. The following listing shows this syntax.

Listing B.8 Thymeleaf th:action and th:object tag syntax

```
th:action="@{url}"
th:object="${object}"
```

The `th:action` tag allows you to specify the form action URL where the form data needs to be submitted. Notice the tag name is the same as the `action` attribute of an HTML form. The `th:object` tag allows you to specify an object in which the submitted form data is bounded.

The individual fields are mapped using the `th:field="*{name}"` attribute, where the `name` is the property defined in the Java object. For instance, if you are using the `th:object="${course}"`, then you can access all properties of the `Course` object in the `th:field`.

As discussed, you also need to show validation error messages to the user if there are any validation errors in the field. Thymeleaf provide few functions in the `#fields` object and the `th:errors` attribute for this purpose. The `hasErrors(..)` method of the `#field` object accepts a field expression as a parameter (e.g., name) and returns a `boolean` value specifying whether any validation errors exist for that field. The `th:errors` tag builds a list with all the available errors. The errors are separated by the `<br />` tag. The following listing shows an example of the usage of `hasErrors(..)` and `th:errors` tags.

Listing B.9 Thymeleaf #fields.hasErrors and th:errors tag syntax

```
<span th:if="${#fields.hasErrors('name')}" th:errors="*{name}" class="text-
➥ danger"></span>
```

Let's understand these concepts by defining a complete HTML form that allows you to create a course. The following listing shows the form snippet.

Listing B.10 The add course form with Thymeleaf tag

```
<form action="#" th:action="@{/addcourse}" th:object="${course}"
➥ method="post">
    <div class="row">
        <div class="form-group col-md-6">
            <label for="name" class="col-form-label">Name</label>
            <input type="text" th:field="*{name}" class="form-control"
➥ id="name" placeholder="Name">
            <span th:if="${#fields.hasErrors('name')}" th:errors="*{name}"
➥ class="text-danger"></span>
        </div>
        <div class="form-group col-md-6">
            <label for="email" class="col-form-label">Description</label>
            <input type="text" th:field="*{description}" class="form-
➥ control" id="email" placeholder="Description">
            <span th:if="${#fields.hasErrors('description')}"
➥ th:errors="*{description}" class="text-danger"></span>
        </div>
    </div>
    <div class="row">
        <div class="col-md-6 mt-5">
            <input type="submit" class="btn btn-primary" value="Add Course">
        </div>
    </div>
</form>
```

- Defines an HTML form. The th:action invokes the addcourse HTTP endpoint defined in the Spring controller. You have also defined the th:object that binds the provided form data into the course.
- You are using Bootstrap library to design the form.
- Checks if there are any errors for the name field. If there are any, then th:errors list them.

In the form specified in listing B.10, the /addcourse is the form action URL. The course object in the th:object holds the add course form data that is submitted. Let's show the addcourse HTTP endpoint, which is part of the controller to understand how the form and the controller interact. The following listing shows the associated HTTP POST endpoint from the Course example we are using in this chapter.

Listing B.11 The sample addCourse HTTP POST endpoint

```
@PostMapping("/addcourse")
public String addCourse(@Valid Course course, BindingResult result, Model
➥ model) {
    if (result.hasErrors()) {
        return "add-course";
    }
```

- Defines an HTTP POST endpoint with URL /addcourse
- The @Valid annotation evaluates all constraints defined in the Course class. BindingResult holds the validation errors.

```
    // Save the course details in database
    model.addAttribute("courses", //Get all courses from the database);
    return "redirect:/index";
}
```

Although the code snippet in the listing only contains a few lines, there are quite a few functionalities involved here:

- You've annotated the class with `@PostMapping` to ensure an HTTP POST request can be addressed by this endpoint. You've also declared the form with `method="post"` attribute. As an HTTP form contains bulk data, it is submitted through the HTTP POST method, so data can be part of the HTTP request body.
- The `@Valid` annotation ensures that all validations defined on the supplied object, and its properties, are performed. This annotation triggers Spring to invoke the validators associated with the object to be validated.
- The `BindingResult` is a Spring object that holds the result of validation and binding. It also contains the errors that it might have encountered in validation and binding. If `BindingResult` contains any error, you return to the HTML page showing the `add-course` form and the field errors.
- You've already seen the usage of the model in earlier discussions. In this example, Spring Boot autowires an instance of the model. You then load all course details into the model with key as courses and a list of courses as the value.
- You use the `redirect` prefix to redirect the flow to a view called `index`. This ensures a redirection happens to the index view, and it renders in the UI.

In this section, you learned the building blocks of Thymeleaf and saw the usage of a few tags you'll typically use frequently with a Spring Boot application. Let's apply this knowledge by building a complete Spring Boot application with Thymeleaf in the next technique.

B.3 Enabling a template engine in Spring Boot

Spring Boot applications are heavily used to develop Web-based applications. There are two major patterns for developing Web applications where Spring Boot suits well:

- In the first type, Spring Boot applications are used as the backend application in conjunction with single-page, application-based frontends, such as Angular (https://angular.io/), React (https://reactjs.org/), or Vue JS (https://vuejs.org/). In this pattern, the Spring Boot application is configured with the REST Web services, which provide data to the frontend for rendering.

  In figure B.4, the single-page application requests data through its HTTP library. This request is intercepted by the Spring Boot REST controller. The REST controller uses the underlying Spring Data (JPA) to communicate to the database. The returned result is then handed over to the HTTP library and subsequently rendered in the frontend application UI.

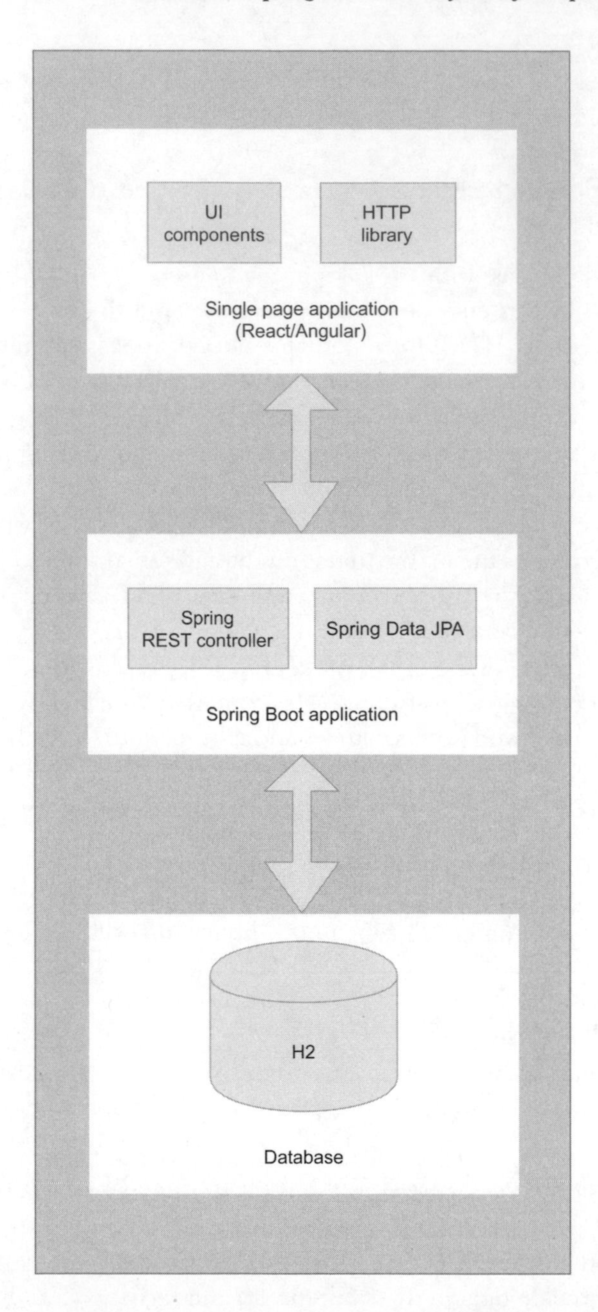

Figure B.4 Web application design pattern with SPA-based frontend and Spring Boot application

- In the second type, you use a complete Java-based technology stack and don't use JavaScript-based frontend frameworks. In this pattern, you use the traditional Spring MVC design pattern with frontend template engines, such as Thymeleaf (https://www.thymeleaf.org/), FreeMarker (https://freemarker.apache.org/), or Mustache (https://mustache.github.io/). Out of these template engines,

Thymeleaf is a popular and most widely used template engine used along with Spring Boot applications. Figure B.5 shows a sample of this pattern through a block diagram.

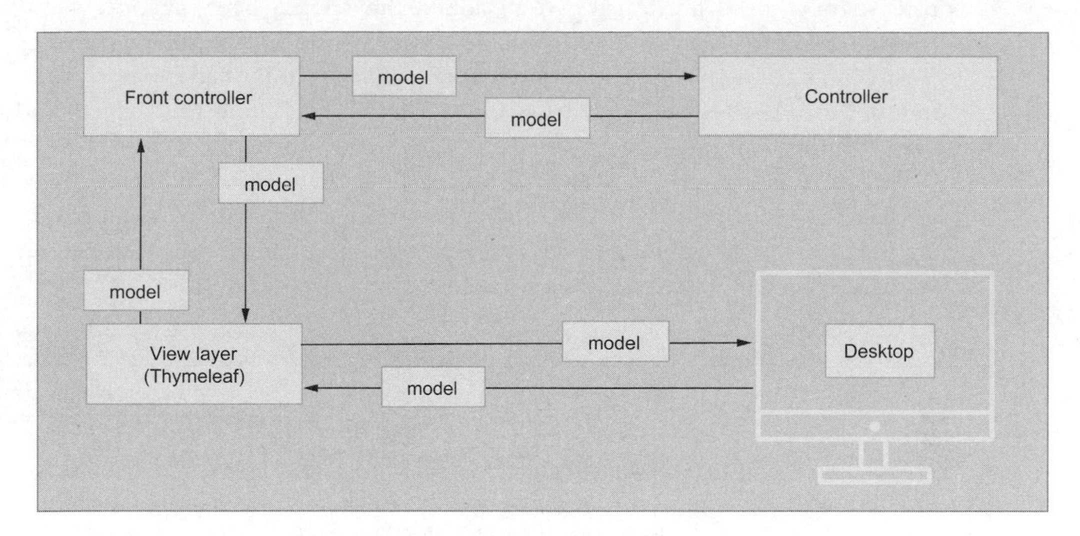

Figure B.5 Web application design pattern with Spring MVC and Thymeleaf

Figure B.5 shows a typical Spring MVC-based design, where both the frontend and backend components of the application are part of the same Spring Boot application. In this pattern, the view layer is represented by an HTML-based template engine, such as Thymeleaf. A *model* is a container that carries application data to or from the controller to or from the view layer. The data provided in the model is processed in the view layer by the template engines and rendered on the screen.

B.3.1 Technique: Building a Spring Boot Web application with Thymeleaf

In this technique, we'll demonstrate how to build a Spring Boot Web application with a Thymeleaf template engine.

Problem

You want to build a Web application with the Spring Boot and Thymeleaf template engine.

Solution

Thymeleaf is a popular and widely used server-side frontend template engine that is often used with Spring Boot to develop production-grade Web applications. Thymeleaf also provides excellent integration with the Spring framework, and in fact, there is a Spring Boot Thymeleaf starter that allows you to directly use Thymeleaf in Spring Boot applications.

To use Thymeleaf in a Spring Boot application, you create Thymeleaf HTML templates and place them into the src\main\resources\templates folder. From your Spring

Boot controller, you return the logical view name that gets mapped to the HTML pages. You use the Spring model to send the data that is used in the HTML page.

As usual, to proceed with this technique, you can continue with the Spring Boot project you've used previously. We've added the `spring-boot-starter-thymeleaf` dependency in the pom.xml file to enable Thymeleaf support in the application.

You can find the base Spring Boot project for this technique in the book's companion GitHub repository at http://mng.bz/zQ7w. You can clone this project and continue with this technique.

With this technique, you'll build a Spring Boot that uses a Thymeleaf-based user interface along with a service layer implementation. Before we proceed further, we'll add the `spring.mvc.hiddenmethod.filter.enabled=true` property to the application.properties file. Listing B.12 shows the modified application.properties.

Listing B.12 Application.properties file

```
spring.mvc.hiddenmethod.filter.enabled=true
```

Property that enables HiddenHttpMethodFilter in the application

This property enables `HiddenHttpMethodFilter` in your Spring Boot application. Sometimes in your application, you need to support HTTP methods, such as `PUT`, `PATCH`, and `DELETE`, which are not supported by the browser. To overcome this issue, you add a hidden form field (`_method`) in your HTML form that indicates the actual HTTP method. The `HiddenHttpMethodFilter` performs this conversion. You'll see the usage of this filter in the `Update` and `Delete` course operations. Figure B.6 shows the high-level block diagram of the application flow.

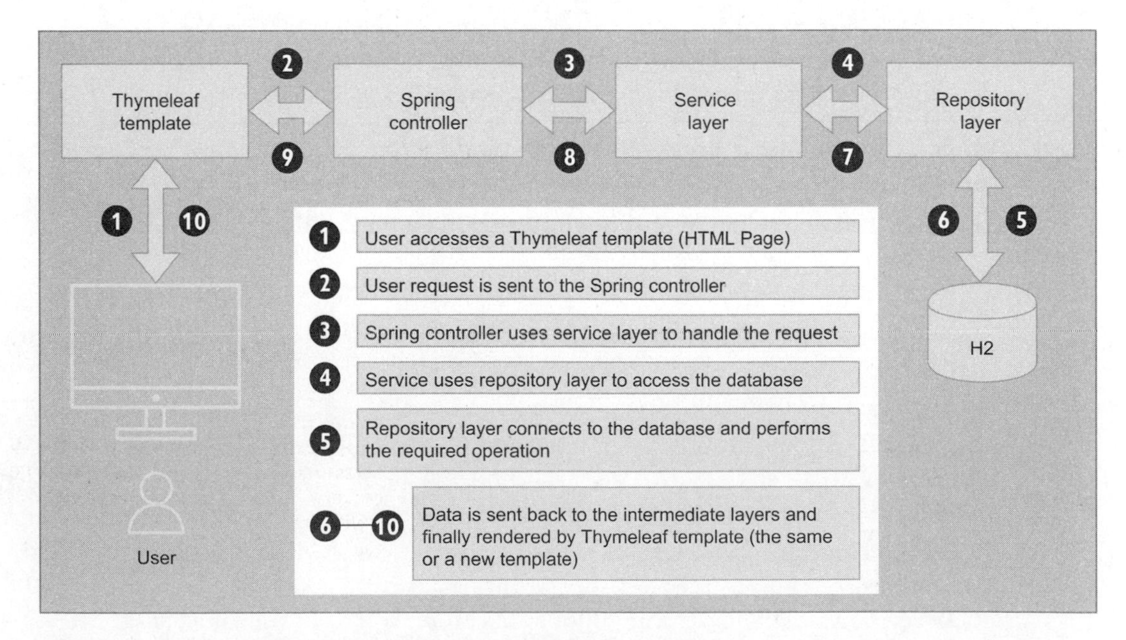

Figure B.6 Spring MVC-based Web application Thymeleaf flow diagram

In this technique, you are using the `Course` Java POJO as the business domain entity. We've added the `@NotEmpty` annotation to the `rating`, `category`, and `description` properties. This annotation is from `javax.validation.constraints` package that ensures that the supplied fields are not empty. We've added it here only to demonstrate how you can leverage this built-in annotation to perform field validation in the Thymeleaf UI. The following listing shows the updated content of the `Course` entity.

Listing B.13 The updated Course entity

```
package com.manning.sbip.a02.model;

import javax.validation.constraints.*;

public class Course {

    private int id;

    @NotEmpty(message = "Course name field can't be empty")
    private String name;

    @NotEmpty(message = "Course category field can't be empty")
    private String category;

    @Min(value = 1)
    @Max(value = 5)
    private int rating;

    @NotEmpty(message = "Course description field can't be empty")
    private String description;

    // Constructor, Getter, Setter
}
```

Let's first focus on the service layer of the application. As a practice, you first define an interface that represents the operations supported by the service layer. You can then provide an implementation of it by defining the operations. With this technique, you've defined the `CourseSevice` interface to manage the course CRUD operations. The following listing shows this interface.

Listing B.14 The CourseService interface

```
package com.manning.sbip.a02.service;

import com.manning.sbip.a02.model.Course;

import java.util.Optional;
public interface CourseService {
    Iterable<Course> createCourse(Course course);
    Optional<Course> findCourseById(int courseId);
    Iterable<Course> findAllCourses();
      Iterable<Course> updateCourse(Course course);
```

- **Defines the operations supported in the course-tracker application** (public interface CourseService)
- **Creates a new course** (createCourse)
- **Loads a course by the supplied courseID. The Optional return type indicates there might not be a course available with the supplied ID.** (findCourseById)
- **Loads all available courses** (findAllCourses)
- **Updates a course detail** (updateCourse)

```
    Iterable<Course> deleteCourseById(int courseId);
}
```

Deletes a course by the supplied courseId

You can refer to the inline code documentation to learn the purpose of the defined operations. The purpose of using an interface to define the services is that you can always provide a different implementation based on your requirement.

Let's now provide an implementation of these operations. In this example, we are not connecting to any database; instead using an in-memory map to store the course information. Listing B.15 shows the `DefaultCourseService` class.

Listing B.15 Default CourseService implementation

```
package com.manning.sbip.a02.service;

import com.manning.sbip.a02.model.Course;
import org.springframework.stereotype.Service;

import java.util.*;
import java.util.concurrent.atomic.AtomicInteger;
import java.util.stream.Collectors;


@Service
public class DefaultCourseService implements CourseService {
    private Map<Integer, Course> courses;
    private AtomicInteger courseIdGenerator;

    public DefaultCourseService() {
        this.courses = new HashMap<>();
        this.courseIdGenerator = new AtomicInteger(0);
        initializeCourses();
    }

    @Override
    public Iterable<Course> createCourse(Course course) {
        int courseId = course.getId();
        if(courseId == 0){
            courseId = getCourseId();
            course.setId(courseId);
        }else {
            courseId = course.getId();
        }
        courses.put(courseId, course);
        return findAllCourses();
    }

    @Override
    public Optional<Course> findCourseById(int courseId) {
        return Optional.of(courses.get(courseId));
    }
```

Provides an implementation of the CourseService interface

This map acts as the backing data store for the application, as we are not using any database.

Generates the course IDs

```
    @Override
    public List<Course> findAllCourses() {
        List<Course> courseList = new ArrayList<>();
        for(Map.Entry<Integer, Course> courseSet : courses.entrySet()) {
            courseList.add(courseSet.getValue());
        }
        return courseList;
    }

    @Override
    public Iterable<Course> updateCourse(Course course) {
        return createCourse(course);
    }

    @Override
    public Iterable<Course> deleteCourseById(int courseId) {
        courses.remove(courseId);
        return findAllCourses();
    }
    private void initializeCourses() {          // Creates a few sample courses and stores in the map
        Course rapidSpringBootCourse = new Course(getCourseId(), "Rapid
➥ Spring Boot Application Development", "Spring", 4, "Spring Boot gives
➥ all the power of the Spring Framework without all of the complexity");
        Course springSecurityDslCourse = new Course(getCourseId(), "Getting
➥ Started with Spring Security DSL", "Spring", 2, "Learn Spring Security
➥ DSL in easy steps");
        Course springCloudKubernetesCourse = new Course(getCourseId(),
➥ "Getting Started with Spring Cloud Kubernetes", "Spring", 4, "Master
➥ Spring Boot application deployment with Kubernetes");
        courses.put(rapidSpringBootCourse.getId(), rapidSpringBootCourse);
        courses.put(springSecurityDslCourse.getId(),
➥ springSecurityDslCourse);
        courses.put(springCloudKubernetesCourse.getId(),
➥ springCloudKubernetesCourse);
    }

    private int getCourseId() {
        return courseIdGenerator.incrementAndGet();
    }
}
```

You can refer to the inline code documentation of the listing to understand the implemented operations.

Let's define the `CourseController` that provides CRUD operations support to the application. You'll use these endpoints from the Thymeleaf templates. The following listing shows the `CourseController` class.

Listing B.16 The CourseController Spring controller

```
package com.manning.sbip.a02.controller;

import com.manning.sbip.a02.model.Course;
import com.manning.sbip.a02.service.CourseService;
```

An HTTP GET endpoint that returns all courses that need to be displayed on the index HTML page. If the course list is empty, then it returns an empty collection. Otherwise, all available courses are provided. You use a Spring model to add the courseList along with the key named courses. You also return a string called index, which is a logical view name. Spring Boot takes this view name and prepares the physical view named index.html. All views for Thymelaf are located inside the src\main\resources\templates folder.

An instance of the CourseService that is used by the controller to perform the CRUD operations. Notice that you've not used the actual implementation of DefaultCourseService. Coding to interfaces is always a best practice, as this approach lets you switch the implementation at your convenience. In this technique, you've only DefaultCourseService implementation. Thus, Spring can autowire this instance. If you have more than one service implementation, then you can use @Qualifier annotation to tell Spring which implementation qualifies for autowiring.

```
import org.springframework.beans.factory.annotation.Autowired;
import org.springframework.stereotype.Controller;
import org.springframework.ui.Model;
import org.springframework.validation.BindingResult;
import org.springframework.web.bind.annotation.*;

import javax.validation.Valid;
import java.util.Collections;
import java.util.List;

@Controller
public class CourseController {

    private final CourseService courseService;
    @Autowired
    public CourseController(CourseService courseService) {
        this.courseService = courseService;
    }

    @GetMapping("/")
    public String index() {
        return "redirect:/index";


    @GetMapping("/index")
    public String index(Model model) {
        List<Course> courseList = (List<Course>)
➥ courseService.findAllCourses();
        model.addAttribute("courses", courseList.isEmpty() ?
➥ Collections.EMPTY_LIST : courseList);
        return "index";
    }

    @GetMapping("/addcourse")
    public String showAddCourseForm(Course course) {
        return "add-course";
    }
```

An HTTP GET endpoint that returns the add-course view name. Based on this name, Spring Boot figures out the add-course.html page from the src\main\resources\templates directory and renders in the UI.

An HTTP POST endpoint that lets you create a course. The @Valid annotation enables Spring Boot to run all the validations associated with the Course class. If you recall, you've added the @NotEmpty annotation for a couple of the properties. Thus, if any of the annotated properties are empty, then the associated validation error will be recorded and stored inside the BindingResult. Also, notice how you've used the same endpoint name (/addcourse) in the previous @GetMapping as well. This is a general practice to drive the endpoints through the associated HTTP methods. You typically show an HTML page (e.g., a form) when the user accesses the endpoint over the HTTP GET method. Then, once the user submits the form, you invoke the HTTP POST endpoint. This enables you to accept the form data through the HTTP body and invoke the necessary CRUD operations.

```
    @PostMapping("/addcourse")
    public String addCourse(@Valid Course course, BindingResult result,
➥ Model model){
        if (result.hasErrors()) {
            return "add-course";
        }
        model.addAttribute("courses", courseService.createCourse(course));
        return "redirect:/index";
    }

    @GetMapping("/update/{id}")
    public String showUpdateCourseForm(@PathVariable("id") long id, Model
➥ model) {
        model.addAttribute("course", courseService.findCourseById(id).get());
        return "update-course";
    }

    @PutMapping("/update/{id}")
    public String updateCourse(@PathVariable("id") long id, @Valid Course
➥ course, BindingResult result, Model model) {
        if (result.hasErrors()) {
            course.setId(id);
            return "update-course";
        }
        model.addAttribute("courses", courseService.updateCourse(course));
        return "redirect:/index";
    }

    @DeleteMapping("/delete/{id}")
    public String deleteCourse(@PathVariable("id") long id, Model model) {
        model.addAttribute("courses", courseService.deleteCourseById(id));
        return "redirect:/index";
    }
}
```

An HTTP GET endpoint that returns the update-course view name. Based on this name, Spring Boot figures out the update-course.html page from the src\main\resources\templates directory and renders it in the UI. Notice that you've also supplied the course ID as the URL path variable. This ID is used to fetch the course details and attach them with the update-course view so that the same can be rendered in the UI. This ensures the user sees the current value in the UI and can make necessary modifications.

An HTTP PUT endpoint that lets you update a course. It first checks whether there are any validation errors, such as the fields being blank. It then saves the updated course details to the database and redirects the user to the index page with the course details. The HTTP PUT operation is used to update an existing entity. Also, notice that we've again used the HTTP method to drive the endpoint. The /update/{id} for GET returns the HTML page, whereas the PUT method for the same endpoint performs the actual update operation.

An HTTP DELETE endpoint that lets you delete a course by the courseId. It deletes the course if it exists and redirects the user to the index page. Notice that you are using the DELETE HTTP method to delete an entity, which is the designated HTTP method to perform a delete operation.

You've defined all Java components (class and interface) required in the application. Let's now focus to define the HTML-based Thymeleaf templates. There are three Thymeleaf templates:

- *index.html*—Defines the index page of the application. It shows the user all available courses with an option to edit or delete a course. It also provides an option to create a new course. If there are no courses previously created, it allows the user to create a new course.
- *add-course.html*—Allows you to add a new course. This contains an HTML that allows you to key in course properties.
- *update-course.html*—Displays existing course details and provides you an option to update the existing details.

Let's now start with the index page. Listing B.17 shows the created `index.html` page available at src\main\resources\templates folder.

Listing B.17 The index HTML page with Thymeleaf tags

```
<!DOCTYPE html>
<html xmlns:th="http://www.thymeleaf.org">
<head>
    <meta charset="utf-8">
    <meta http-equiv="x-ua-compatible" content="ie=edge">
    <title>Courses</title>
    <meta name="viewport" content="width=device-width, initial-scale=1">

    <link rel="stylesheet"
➥ href="https://stackpath.bootstrapcdn.com/bootstrap/4.5.2/css/bootstrap.
➥ min.css">
    <link rel="stylesheet"
➥ href="https://use.fontawesome.com/releases/v5.4.1/css/all.css">
</head>
<body>
<div th:switch="${#lists.size(courses)}" class="container my-5">
    <div class="row">
        <div class="col-md-2"></div>
        <div class="col-md-8">

            <div th:case="'0'">
                <h2>You haven't added any course yet!</h2>
                <p class="text-success">Add a course by clicking below!</p>
            </div>
            <div th:case="*">
                <h2 class="my-5">Courses</h2>
                <table class="table table-striped table-responsive-md">
                    <thead>
                    <tr>
```

Links the Bootstrap and Font Awesome libraries. Both the libraries are loaded from their respective Content Delivery Network (CDN). A CDN hosts the libraries, and the specified libraries are loaded when this page is rendered.

Uses Thymeleaf switch-case to determine whether the courses list is empty or contains course details. Recall that in the CourseController /index endpoint, you are returning an empty list or list of courses based on the course availability. Besides, #lists is a utility object from Thymeleaf that lets you perform useful operations on a list. In this example, you have used the size method to calculate the list size.

Thymeleaf switch-case if the courses list is empty

Thymeleaf switch-case if the courses list is not empty

```
                    <th>Course Name</th>
                    <th>Course Category</th>
                    <th>Course Rating</th>
                    <th>Course Description</th>
                    <th>Edit</th>
                    <th>Delete</th>
                </tr>
                </thead>
                <tbody>
                <tr th:each="course : ${courses}">
                    <td th:text="${course.name}"></td>
                    <td th:text="${course.category}"></td>
                    <td th:text="${course.rating}"></td>
                    <td th:text="${course.description}"></td>
                    <td><a th:href="@{/update/{id}(id=${course.id})}"
➥ class="btn btn-primary"><i class="fas fa-edit"></i></a></td>
                    <td>
                        <form action="#"
➥ th:action="@{/delete/{id}(id=${course.id})}" th:method="delete">
                            <button type="submit" class="btn btn-
➥ danger">
                                <i class="fas fa-trash"></i>
                            </button>
                        </form>
                    </td>
                </tr>
                </tbody>
            </table>
        </div>
        <p class="my-5"><a href="/addcourse" class="btn btn-primary"><i
➥ class="fas fa-plus-square"></i></a></p>
    </div>
    <div class="col-md-2"></div>
  </div>
</div>
</body>
</html>
```

An HTML anchor tag with Thymeleaf tags. The th:href tag lets you build the relative URL. The {id} represents the path variable in Spring controller. You set the course id to the path variable using (id=${course.id}) part of the URL.

Here you've used the th:action tag, as you are submitting a form. The th:method tag deserves special attention. Recall that this delete endpoint supports only the HTTP Delete method. But from a browser, you can only send HTTP or POST requests. The th:method instructs Thymeleaf to include a hidden input param <input type="hidden" name="_method" value="DELETE">. This hidden attribute is processed by Spring's HiddenHttpMethodFilter filter and changes the supplied HTTP POST method to the HTTP DELETE method.

Shows a link to add a new course. If you click this link, it invokes addcourse HTTP GET endpoint.

Figure B.7 shows the index page with the available courses.

Let's now add the add course page. Listing B.18 shows the created `add-course.html` page in the src\main\resources\templates folder. It allows you to add a new course. It has an HTML form that contains four fields: `course name`, `category`, `rating`, and `description`. The `th:object` binds this form data into the `course` object and is made available to the HTTP endpoint. Once you submit the form, the action (`th:action`) invokes the `/addcourse` HTTP POST endpoint provided in the controller. The `fields.hasErrors(..)` checks if there are any validation errors for any of the fields. The `th:errors` print the error messages if there are any.

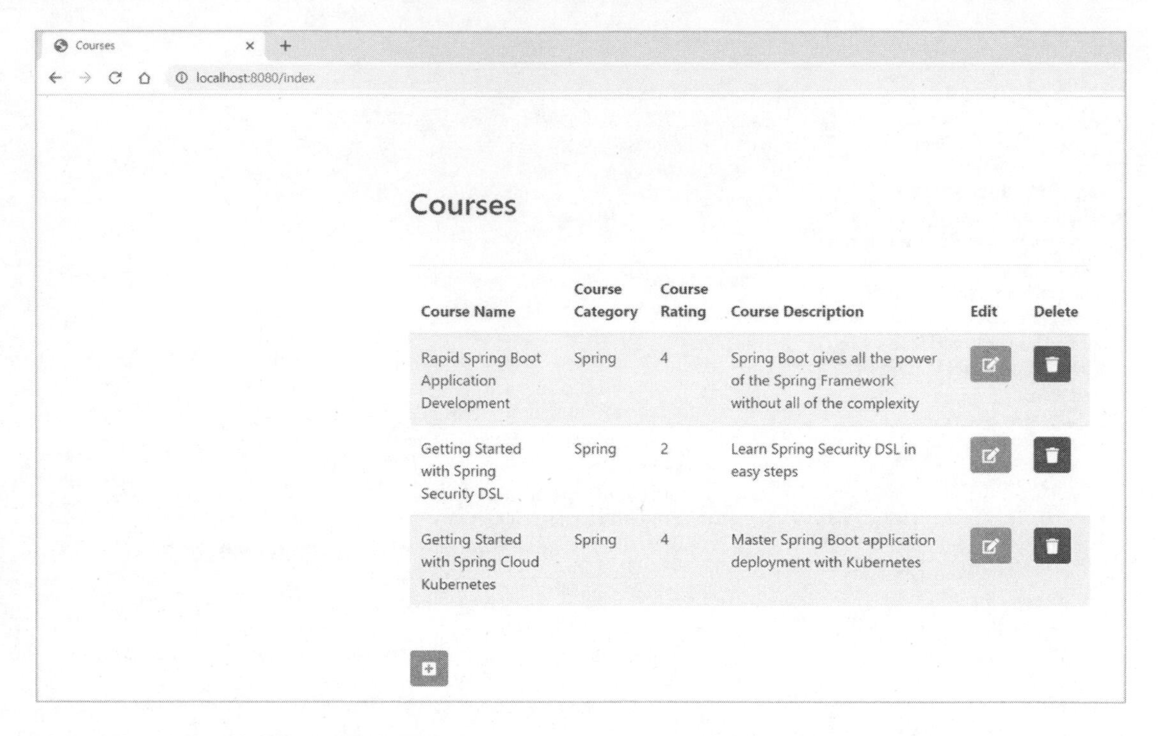

Courses
localhost:8080/index
Courses
Course Name
Course Category
Course Rating
Course Description
Edit
Delete
Rapid Spring Boot Application Development
Spring
4
Spring Boot gives all the power of the Spring Framework without all of the complexity
Getting Started with Spring Security DSL
Spring
2
Learn Spring Security DSL in easy steps
Getting Started with Spring Cloud Kubernetes
Spring
4
Master Spring Boot application deployment with Kubernetes

Figure B.7 Spring Boot Thymeleaf index page

Listing B.18 The Add Course HTML page with Thymeleaf tags

```
<!DOCTYPE html>
<html xmlns:th="http://www.thymeleaf.org">
<head>
    <meta charset="utf-8">
    <meta http-equiv="x-ua-compatible" content="ie=edge">
    <title>Add a Course</title>
    <meta name="viewport" content="width=device-width, initial-scale=1">
    <link rel="stylesheet"
➥ href="https://stackpath.bootstrapcdn.com/bootstrap/4.5.2/css/bootstrap.
➥ min.css">
    <link rel="stylesheet"
➥ href="https://use.fontawesome.com/releases/v5.4.1/css/all.css">
</head>
<body>
<div class="container my-5">
    <div class="row">
        <div class="col-md-3"></div>
        <div class="col-md-6">
            <h2 class="mb-5">Add a Course</h2>
        </div>
        <div class="col-md-3"></div>
    </div>
```

```
<div class="row">
    <div class="col-md-3"></div>
    <div class="col-md-9">
        <form action="#" th:action="@{/addcourse}"
➥ th:object="${course}" method="post">
            <div class="form-row">
                <div class="form-group col-md-9">
                    <label for="name" class="col-form-
➥ label">Name</label>
                    <input type="text" th:field="*{name}" class="form-
➥ control" id="name" placeholder="Course Name">
                    <span th:if="${#fields.hasErrors('name')}"
➥ th:errors="*{name}" class="text-danger"></span>
                </div>
                <div class="form-group col-md-9">
                    <label for="category" class="col-form-
➥ label">Category</label>
                    <input th:field="*{category}" class="form-control"
➥ id="category" placeholder="Course Category"></input>
                    <span th:if="${#fields.hasErrors('category')}"
➥ th:errors="*{category}" class="text-danger"></span>
                </div>
                <div class="form-group col-md-9">
                    <label for="rating" class="col-form-label">Course
➥ Rating</label>
                    <select th:field="*{rating}" class="form-control"
➥ id="rating">
                        <option th:value="1">1 (Lowest)</option>
                        <option th:value="2">2</option>
                        <option th:value="3">3</option>
                        <option th:value="4">4</option>
                        <option th:value="5">5 (Highest)</option>
                    </select>
                    <span th:if="${#fields.hasErrors('category')}"
➥ th:errors="*{rating}" class="text-danger"></span>
                </div>
                <div class="form-group col-md-9">
                    <label for="description" class="col-form-
➥ label">Description</label>
                    <textarea th:field="*{description}" class="form-
➥ control" id="description" placeholder="Course Description"></textarea>
                    <span th:if="${#fields.hasErrors('description')}"
➥ th:errors="*{description}" class="text-danger"></span>
                </div>
            </div>
            <div class="row">
                <div class="col-md-6 mt-5">
                    <input type="submit" class="btn btn-primary center"
➥ value="Add Course">
                </div>
            </div>
        </form>
    </div>
```

```
            <div class="col-md-3"></div>
        </div>
    </div>
    </body>
    </html>
```

Figure B.8 shows the Add a Course HTML page.

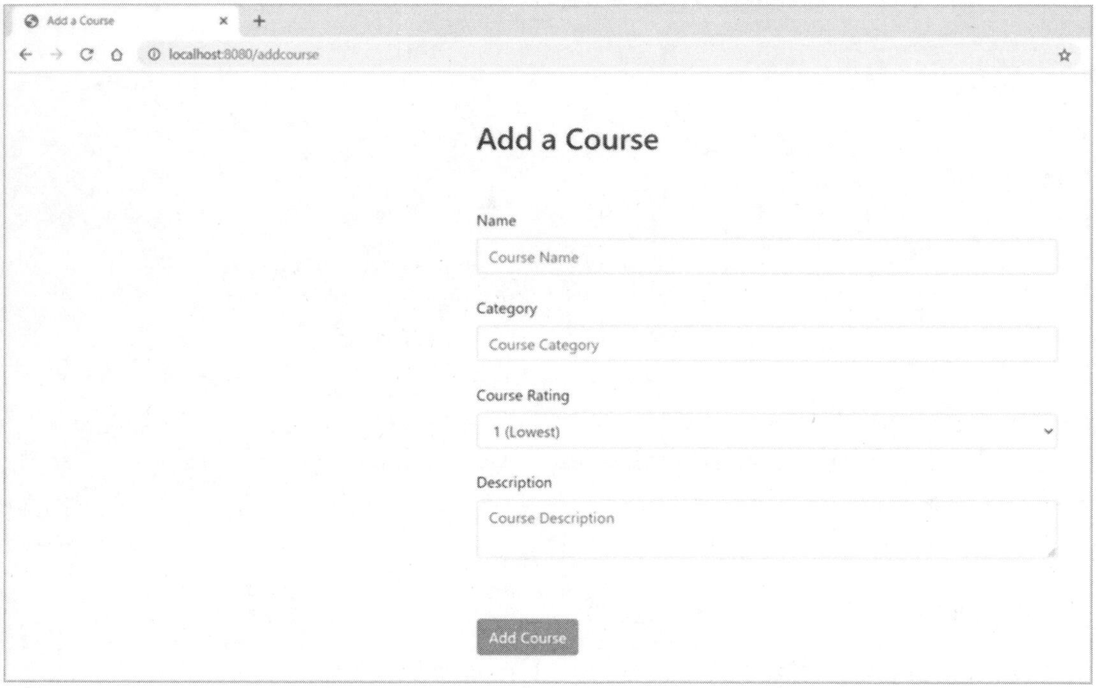

Figure B.8 Spring Boot Thymeleaf Add a Course page

You have added the `Name`, `Category`, and `Description` fields as mandatory. If you attempt to submit the page without these details, you can now see the inline error messages, as shown in figure B.9.

Once you add a course, the course details are stored in the in-memory map, and the user is redirected to the index page. This time the index page shows the course you've added. Figure B.10 shows the index page with the list of courses.

For each course, you have an option to edit the course details. You can also delete a course. For example, once you click on the Edit icon, you see the Update Course HTML page, as shown in Figure B.11.

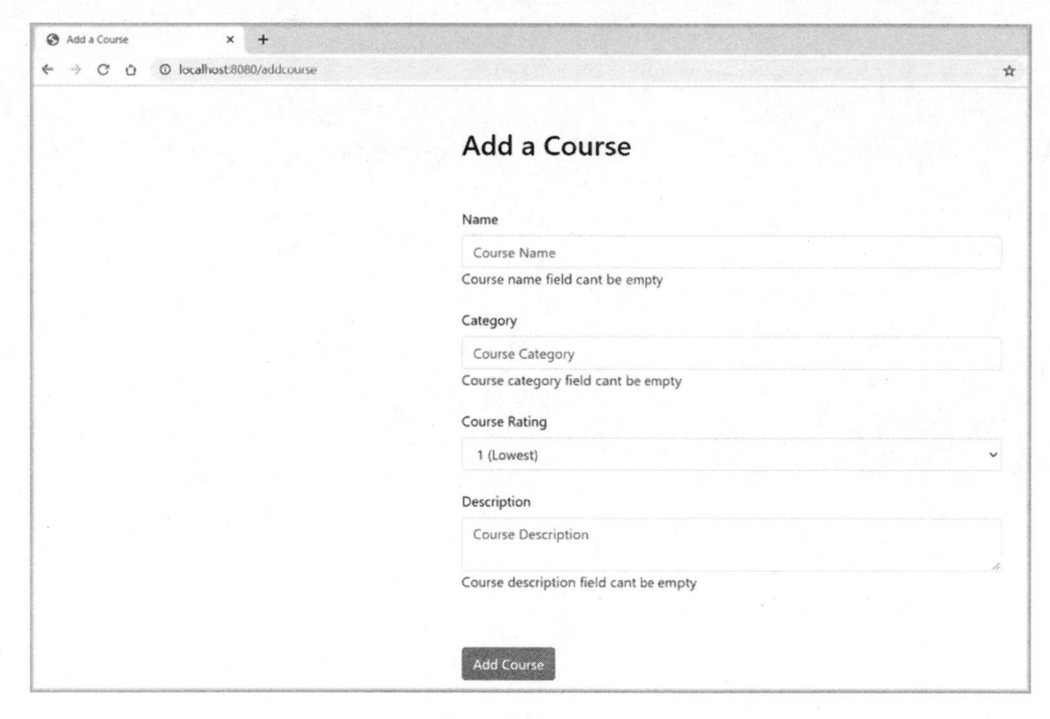

Figure B.9 Spring Boot Thymeleaf Add a Course page with the inline error messages

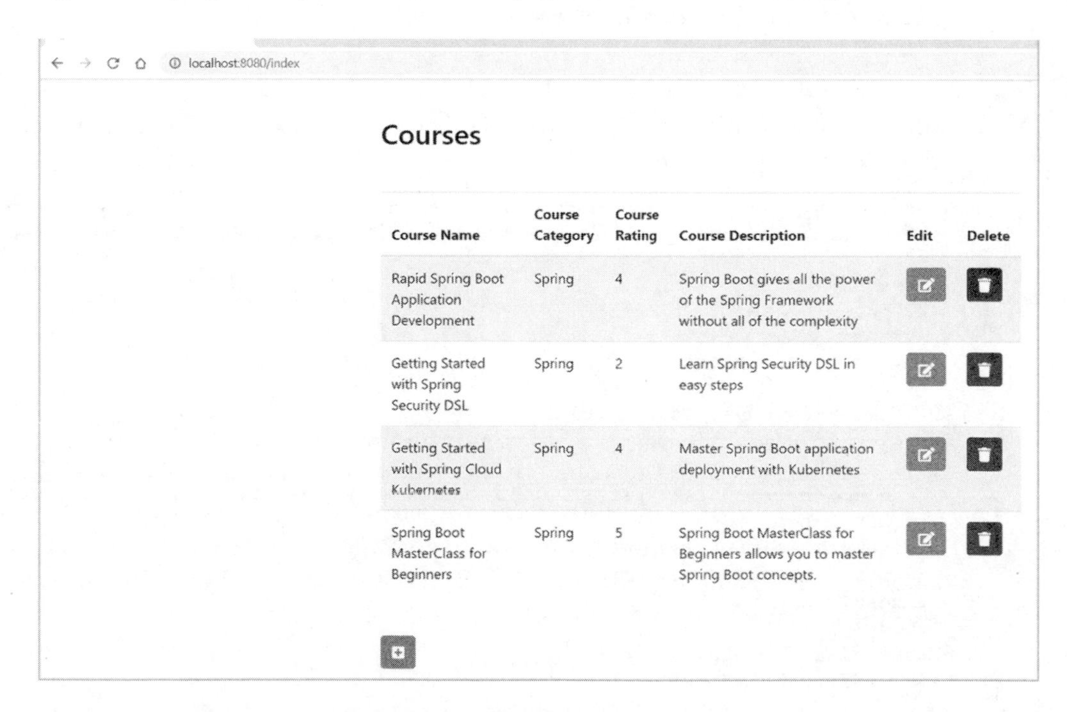

Figure B.10 Spring Boot Thymeleaf index page with courses

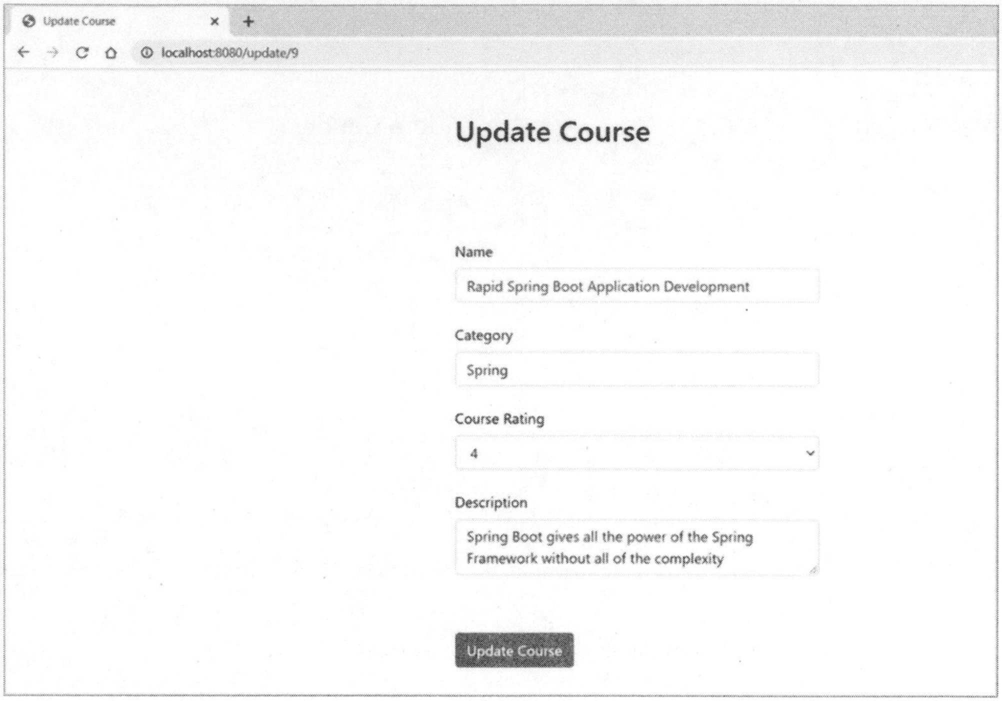

Figure B.11 Spring Boot Thymeleaf Update Course index page

If you update the course details, you'll be redirected to the index page with the updated course list. Listing B.19 shows the update course HTML page in the src\main\resources\template folder.

Listing B.19 The Update Course HTML page with Thymeleaf tags

```
<!DOCTYPE html>
<html xmlns:th="http://www.thymeleaf.org">
<head>
    <meta charset="utf-8">
    <meta http-equiv="x-ua-compatible" content="ie=edge">
    <title>Update Course</title>
    <meta name="viewport" content="width=device-width, initial-scale=1">
    <link rel="stylesheet"
➥ href="https://stackpath.bootstrapcdn.com/bootstrap/4.5.2/css/bootstrap.
➥ min.css">
    <link rel="stylesheet"
➥ href="https://use.fontawesome.com/releases/v5.4.1/css/all.css">
</head>
<body>
<div class="container my-5">
    <div class="row">
        <div class="col-md-3"></div>
        <div class="col-md-6">
```

```
            <h2 class="mb-5">Update Course</h2>
        </div>
    </div>
    <h2 class="mb-5"></h2>
    <div class="row">
        <div class="col-md-3"></div>
        <div class="col-md-6">
            <form action="#" th:action="@{/update/{id}(id=${course.id})}"
➥ th:object="${course}" method="post" th:method="put">
                <div class="form-row">
                    <div class="form-group col-md-9">
                        <label for="name" class="col-form-
➥ label">Name</label>
                        <input type="text" th:field="*{name}" class="form-
➥ control" id="name" placeholder="Course Name">
                        <span th:if="${#fields.hasErrors('name')}"
➥ th:errors="*{name}" class="text-danger"></span>
                    </div>
                    <div class="form-group col-md-9">
                        <label for="category" class="col-form-
➥ label">Category</label>
                        <input th:field="*{category}" class="form-control"
➥ id="category" placeholder="Course Category"></input>
                        <span th:if="${#fields.hasErrors('category')}"
➥ th:errors="*{category}" class="text-danger"></span>
                    </div>
                    <div class="form-group col-md-9">
                        <label for="rating" class="col-form-label">Course
➥ Rating</label>
                        <select th:field="*{rating}" class="form-control"
➥ id="rating">
                            <option th:value="1">1 (Lowest)</option>
                            <option th:value="2">2</option>
                            <option th:value="3">3</option>
                            <option th:value="4">4</option>
                            <option th:value="5">5 (Highest)</option>
                        </select>
                        <span th:if="${#fields.hasErrors('category')}"
➥ th:errors="*{rating}" class="text-danger"></span>
                    </div>
                    <div class="form-group col-md-9">
                        <label for="description" class="col-form-
➥ label">Description</label>
                        <textarea th:field="*{description}" class="form-
➥ control" id="description" placeholder="Course Description"></textarea>
                        <span th:if="${#fields.hasErrors('description')}"
➥ th:errors="*{description}" class="text-danger"></span>
                    </div>
                </div>
                <div class="row">
                    <div class="col-md-6 mt-5">
                        <input type="submit" class="btn btn-primary"
➥ value="Update Course">
                    </div>
                </div>
```

```
                </form>
            </div>
            <div class="col-md-3"></div>
        </div>
    </div>
</body>
</html>
```

The last operation is to delete the added course. In the index page course list, you have an option to delete a course. If you click on the Delete icon, the selected course will be deleted. You can download the completed version of the Spring Boot project used in this technique at http://mng.bz/0wjp.

DISCUSSION

With this technique, you built a complete CRUD application with Spring Boot and Thymeleaf. You've seen how seamless it is to integrate Thymeleaf with Spring Boot. You haven't added any special configuration other than adding the Spring Boot Thymeleaf starter dependency. You've also noticed the several powerful capabilities of Thymeleaf, such as conditional rendering, looping through the list, and handling validation with the `#field` utility class.

index

B

C

D

E

F

N

O

P

Q

R

S